Nary

K Y R G Y Z S T A N

Mijan +

Osh +

Kyzylsu

C H I N A

Kashgar

A N

P A K I S T A N

Murghab

TAJIKISTAN

0   50 km

0   60 miles

Authors

Dr. Robert Middleton worked for the Aga Khan Foundation as Legal Adviser and Co-ordinator of Tajikistan programmes from 1985 until his retirement in 2003. He initiated the Foundation's programmes in Tajikistan and Kyrgyzstan and has travelled extensively in Central Asia and throughout the Pamirs. His contribution to the historical section of this Guide is based on original source material in several languages, including Russian. Currently, he assists local and international non-profit organizations in promoting tourism in the region (see his website www.pamirs.org). He lives in Switzerland.

Huw Thomas graduated in history from Birmingham University in 1960, before joining the National Health Service. In the mid 1960s he worked for two years as provincial hospital secretary in Nyanza and Western provinces in western Kenya. He returned to the United Kingdom, but always nursed a wish to return to work in a less developed country. He retired as Chief Executive of Gwynedd Health Authority in North Wales, and became Programme Director of the Aga Khan Health Service, Tajikistan from 1999 to 2003, based in Khorog, capital of the Pamirs. He is a keen mountaineer and loved living amongst the great mountains of the Pamirs. He has returned frequently to Tajikistan from his home in Bangor, North Wales.

Cartographer

Markus Hauser works as a professional cartographer. Since 1989 he has travelled extensively in Tajikistan and the Pamirs. He is the founder of "The Pamir Archive", the world's largest book and map archive in private hands dealing with the Pamirs and Central Asia that has recently been acquired by the University of Central Asia. In 2004 he produced for the UNESCO project "Cultural and Eco-tourism in the Mountainous Regions of Central Asia and in the Himalaya" the first detailed, accurate map of the Pamirs. Currently, he is working on the second edition of the map "Pik Lenin" and on the map sheets "Khatlon" and "Sughd" to finish the mapping of Tajikistan in the same scale as the "Pamirs". He is based in Switzerland.

Traditional greeting to a visitor of bread and salt

ACKNOWLEDGEMENTS – ROBERT MIDDLETON

I would like to express my thanks to the following who provided historical and other information and made helpful comments on the text for the section on the Pamirs. If I have not followed any of the good advice given, it is my fault alone.

Sultonbek Aksokolov, Vatani Alidodov, Yorali Berdov, the late Paul Bergne, Mira Bubnova, Peter Burgess, Ergash Fayzullobekov, Svetlana Gorshenina, Jo-Ann Gross, John Hill, Nazardod Jonbabayev, Aiymgul Kalandarkhonova, Daulat Khudonazar, Hermann Kreutzmann, Rita Kurbonbekova, Boghshoh Lashkarbekov, Farangees Mamadshoyeva, Dima Melnichkov, Rahima Missidenti, Sarfaroz Niyozov, Nabot Qadamalieva, Claude Rapin, Gordon Read, Iqbol Shabosov, Surat Toimastov, Derek Waller, Daniel Waugh, Susan Whitfield and Mavzuna Yaminova.

A special word of thanks is needed for Markus Hauser who freely made available his Pamir Archive and made many valuable suggestions for the historical section, for Bijan Omrani who survived the task of editing this mass of heterogeneous material and for Helen Northey for her patience and equanimity in making the impossible possible.

ACKNOWLEDGEMENTS – HUW THOMAS

Foremost I must thank Monica Whitlock, who has contributed so much from her deep knowledge of the history, politics and culture of Tajikistan and Central Asia. She has also brought to bear her exceptional intellect and journalistic flair.

Of my many friends in Tajikistan I would particularly thank Ruslan Nuriloev, scholar and man of action, Sodatsho Sodatsairov guide, and ace photographer Mikhail Romanyuk, all who accompanied me on our adventures travelling around Tajikistan. Also thanks to Sherali Bakhtaliev, friend and former colleague, who has given me so much support and information, and to Manizha Rahmonova who gave logistical support when most needed. Sharofat Mamadhambarova gave me great insight into Tajik culture, and Sitora Shokamolova who provided much helpful information.

Thanks to Marydean Purves and William Lawrence for their advice, support and comments on innumerable drafts. Also thanks to Mary Helen Carruth and Katherine Lapham for useful information. Susan Whitfield and Ursula Sims-Williams of the British Library gave me invaluable advice and guidance, Norman Cameron and the staff of the Royal Society for Asian Affairs gave access to their excellent library.

Thanks to Dr T.I.Zeimal and Professor G.I. Semenov of the Central Asian section at the Hermitage Museum, St Petersburg, for allowing me a private viewing of the Sogdian frescoes and providing so much helpful background information. A special thanks to Helen Northey for her forbearance and unfailing help in guiding me through the complexities of producing the final version.

My daughters Nicola, Emma and Lucy all nursed their father through his computer traumas. Their chivvying kept me going. Finally thanks to so many Tajik people all over the country for their friendliness, humour and unfailing hospitality.

TAJIKISTAN

AND THE

HIGH PAMIRS

A COMPANION AND GUIDE

TAJIKISTAN

AND THE

HIGH PAMIRS

A COMPANION AND GUIDE

ROBERT MIDDLETON AND HUW THOMAS
WITH MONICA WHITLOCK AND MARKUS HAUSER

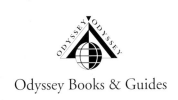

Odyssey Books & Guides

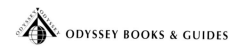

ODYSSEY BOOKS & GUIDES

Odyssey Books & Guides is a division of Airphoto International Ltd.
903 Seaview Commercial Building, 21–24 Connaught Road West, Sheung Wan, Hong Kong
Tel: (852) 2856-3896; Fax: (852) 2565-8 004
E-mail: magnus@odysseypublications.com; www.odysseypublications.com

Distribution in the USA by
W.W. Norton & Company, Inc.,
500 Fifth Avenue, New York, NY 10110, USA
Tel: 800-233-4830; Fax: 800-458-6515
www.wwnorton.com

Distribution in the UK and Europe by
Cordee Books and Maps,
3a De Montfort St., Leicester, LE1 7HD, United Kingdom
Tel: 0116-254-3579; Fax: 0116-247-1176
www.cordee.co.uk

Distribution in Australia by
Tower Books
Unit 2/17 Rodborough Road, Frenchs Forest, NSW 2086, Australia
Tel: 02-9975-5566; Fax: 02-9975-5599
www.towerbooks.com.au

Tajikistan and the High Pamirs: A Companion and Guide

Reading the safety information on these websites is advisable before travelling overseas:
US Department of State: www.travel.state.gov/travel/
UK Foreign and Commonwealth Office: www.fco.gov.uk/travel
Canadian Department of Foreign Affairs & International Trade: www.voyage.ge.ca/dest/sos/warnings-en.asp
Australian Department of Foreign Affairs & Trade: www.dfat.gov.au/travel/
http://www.sos.travel

In November, villagers near Anzob cover roofs preparing for winter (preceding page)

Front cover photography: Markus Hauser
Back cover photography: Mikhail Romanyuk

Grateful acknowledgment is made to the following authors and publishers for photography/illustrations courtesy of ISOGIS in *El Registan Tadshikische Sozialistische Sowjetrepublik Moskau*, 1937 (Serie: USSR im Bau, No 2, February) 212; George Allen & Unwin from *Ney Elias, Explorer and Envoy Extraordinary in High Asia* by Morgan, Gerald. 1971, London, 371; Planeta from *Pamir* by Gavriljuk, A., Jaroshenko, V; 1987, Moskva, 428, 429; V.A. Zhukov and V.A. Ranov, (Archaeological Discoveries in 1971), 1972, Academy of Sciences, Moscow, 635.

Other photography courtesy of :

Vatani Alidodov 228; Archive Daulat Khudonazar 435; Archive Pamir 45, 49, 197, 241, 244, 257, 297, 311, 327, 399, 411, 424, 425, 461, 481, 489, 621, 641, 651; Nabijan Baqi 126; The British Museum 222; Peter Burgess 547, 550, 551; Jean-Francois Charmeux 247, 542 (bottom); Peter Cunnington 251, 254, 255; Deutsches Alpines Museum (DAV) 261, 286, 366, 387, 439, 443, 469, 504, 505, 639; Markus Hauser 6–7, 11, 14, 48, 54, 65, 232, 236, 240, 242–3, 258, 267, 351, 359, 362, 366, 373, 377, 380–1, 384, 392–3, 397, 404, 408, 409, 412, 413, 416, 451, 463, 479, 491, 494, 510, 514, 519, 527, 530, 542 (top), 546, 555, 559, 561, 572, 573, 581, 584, 588, 589, 599, 603 (top), 606 (left), 607, 615, 618, 622, 625, 632, 633, 636, 644 (bottom), 701; Rodney Jackson 655; Khorog Museum of Regional History 466, 475; Bradley Mayhew 173, 233, 270, 343, 346, 355, 534 (right); Robert Middleton 68, 69, 266, 342, 367, 376, 396, 450, 455, 458, 459, 466, 467, 471, 486, 487, 498, 499, 502, 534 (left), 535, 538 (bottom), 539, 543, 554, 558, 564, 564-5, 576-7, 580 (bottom), 592, 593, 594, 595, 602-3, 606 (right), 614, 619, 623, 628, 629, 637, 640, 644 (top), 645 (bottom), 648; Museum of National Antiquities in Dushanbe 40, 184, 280; Mikhail Romanyuk 2, 33, 37, 50, 55, 58, 63, 76, 77 (top), 84, 85, 88, 89, 92, 96, 100, 101, 104, 105, 108, 109, 118, 119, 122, 123, 124, 127, 130-131, 134, 135, 138, 143, 145, 145, 148, 149, 169, 172, 176, 177, 210, 211, 218, 219, 225, 229, 237, 241, 246, 538 (top), 641, 656; Wolfgang Schatz 511; Huw Thomas 59, 77 (bottom), 97, 161; Rein van der Hoek 152, 153, 160; Beth Wald 652.

Managing Editor: Bijan Omrani
Associate Editor: Helen Northey
Design: Sarah Lock
Index: Don Brech
Cover design: Au Yeung Chui Kwai
Maps: Markus Hauser

Production and printing by
Twin Age Ltd, Hong Kong
E-mail: twinage@netvigator.com
Manufactured in China

Yurts in the Alichur Pamir (following pages)

CONTENTS

Drumkul Lake, Shakhdara

Editor's Note

The transliteration of modern Tajik words and names poses a set of peculiarly difficult challenges for an editor. Aside from the confusion in maps between Russian names left behind by the USSR and Tajik names (e.g. Nizhnii Pyanj and Panj-i Poyon), Tajik names have commonly been transliterated into English via the Russian; this leads to the distortion of names, e.g. "Hissar" becomes "Gissar" or "Khissar", on account of the absence of the "h" sound in Russian. An attempt has been made to return to the original Tajik in these and similar instances. However, beyond this there is a great variation in the pronunciation of vowels. A noticeable instance of this is the long Persian "a", which can be pronounced as anything between "ah" as in "par" and "oo" as in "poor". Thus, words which we are familiar with in English, such as "shah", which have been derived from Farsi (the Iranian branch of Persian/Tajik) are often written here as "shoh", especially in place names where a different pronunciation of the vowel locally might cause confusion. The Samanid Dynasty, familiar to students of Central Asian history, often appears here as "Somoni", and its most famous king, Ismail, as "Ismoil", especially given their frequent use in place names. Properly speaking, the familiar "Tajikistan" would by these terms be written as "Tojikiston" – a fact which shows that a consistent scheme of transliteration is not an easy thing to realise. I have tried to be as consistent and clear as possible, and have done my best to reconcile the ideas in this field between the various authors in this book. Any inconsistencies or errors are entirely of myself.

At the end of the day, Tajikistan is a wonderful country with wonderful people; however readers prefer to spell a term, this book is a paean to the rich history and extraordinary hospitality of the diverse people of this spectacular and, let it not be overlooked, strategically important part of the world.

Bijan Omrani, January 2008

Publisher's Note

The Publisher would like to thank the European Union (TACIS), the Aga Khan Foundation, the Mountain Societies Development Support Programme, the Open Society Institute, The Christensen Fund and the Swiss Agency for Development and Cooperation (SDC) without whose support this work would not have been possible.

The contents of this publication are the sole responsibility of *Odyssey Books and Guides* and do not necessarily reflect the views or opinions of the above sponsors.

Magnus Bartlett, Odyssey Books and Guides

Introduction

Why visit Tajikistan?

Many people know more about the surface of the moon than Tajikistan, a small jewel of a country perched between Afghanistan and China. This is mainly because it was part of the closed world of the Soviet Union, and one of the least known and remote destinations in that secretive place. Foreigners rarely visited, only on official invitation and under strict supervision. Even after the fall of the USSR in 1991, few outsiders visited beyond aid workers and journalists because of the civil war that made parts of the country insecure into the late 90s.

Now Tajikistan is independent and peace has returned, there is a chance for the traveller to visit and discover a country that, even now, few foreigners know. What they will discover is a land of huge and beautiful mountains, second only in height to the Himalaya/Karakoram range, with people whose hospitality is an integral and natural part of their way of life. The attraction of the country is enhanced by its ancient civilisation, stretching back well over 2,000 years, and a rich cultural history intertwined with its Persian inheritance. There are many small-scale places of wonder: shrines to Islamic saints on sites with much older traditions, stopping places on the Silk Road, old mosques and *medrassas*, and ancient fortresses in the Wakhan Corridor set against the backdrop of mountains and glaciers. All this in a country with 300 sunny days a year, and an abundance of delicious fruit and vegetables available in the colourful bazaars.

Tajikistan is a land of great diversity. Although it is almost completely mountainous, there is a great difference between the life of the pastoral farmers of the valleys of the Pamir and Fan mountains, and the semi nomadic Kyrgyz herders who tend their flocks and live in yurts on the high plains at 4,000 m around Murghab. There is another great contrast with the people who live in the hot and fertile Ferghana valley in the north, and those on the baking plains in the south stretching down to the Amu river, the border with Afghanistan.

Tajikistan is a country for the traveller rather than the tourist. It is a place for those ready to take the road less known, who want to discover a wild and beautiful landscape, meet warm, wonderfully hospitable people and walk in the steps of the giants of history from Alexander the Great to Tamberlane. Along the way, adventure will surely strike.

Apple harvest in the Khingob Valley

Highlights

The country is a paradise for walkers, trekkers, mountaineers, mountain bikers, cyclists, white water enthusiasts, photographers and people who just like to be in wild and beautiful places. The Pamirs, Fan mountains and the Zarafshan and Hissar mountain ranges give enormous scope for all these activities.

• The journey from Dushanbe via Khorog and Murghab and on to Osh in Kyrgyzstan must be one of the most dramatic and scenic in the world. It is even better if a detour is taken from Khorog to Ishkashim and then on to Murghab. This route goes along the Wakhan Corridor, with its fortresses, shrines, and Buddhist and Zoroastrian remains.

• The high plateau around Murghab in the far east of Tajikistan, with spectacular lakes and the semi nomadic Kyrgyz herders with their flocks and yurts.

• Exploring the dramatic Shakhdara and Bartang valleys in the Pamirs, with the hospitable villagers still practising traditional methods of agriculture, using oxen to plough and cutting wheat by hand.

• The journey north from Dushanbe to Khudjand, crossing two mountain ranges, taking a short detour to the mountain lake of Iskanderkul, with many legends about Alexander the Great, and on to the ancient city of Istaravshan with its superb mosques and *medrassas* and finally to Khudjand, the farthest place into Central Asia reached by Alexander.

• Combining a trek in the Fan Mountains with a visit to Penjikent, "The Pompeii of Central Asia" and possibly a visit to Samarqand, across the border in Uzbekistan.

• Visiting the ancient citadel of Hissar, with its fortress, *medrassas* and *caravanserai*, only 25 kms from Dushanbe.

• Enjoying a few days in the relaxed city of Dushanbe, with its fine neo-classical buildings, excellent Museum of National Antiquities and a developing café culture, and taking some day excursions to lovely scenery and interesting places in easy reach.

• Being able anywhere, apart from in the cities, to look up and see the wonder of the stars, with no light pollution.

• For something completely different, and if you are into post Soviet dereliction, there is plenty of that all over the country; and two mighty Soviet engineering projects which have survived, the great dam at Nurek and the enormous Aluminium works at Tursunzoda.

Facts for Travellers

Official title: Republic of Tajikistan
Population: 7,320,815 (July 2006 estimate)
Area: 143,100 sq kms
Ethnic division: Tajiks 79.9%, Uzbeks 15.3%, Russian 1.1%, Kyrgyz 1.1%, others 2.6 % (2000 census)
Religions: Sunni 85%, Ismaili 5%, others 10% (2003 estimate)
Languages: Tajik official, Russian widely used in government and business, also Uzbek and local languages.

President: Emomali Rahmon **Currency:** Somoni
Country phone code: 992 **Time difference:** GMT +5
(source: *CIA World Factbook*, March 2007)

SAFETY Tajikistan is a safe place, much more so than many European countries. However, because of the civil war of the 1990s, your embassy will have a website setting out their view of the latest assessment of the security situation. Register with your embassy on arrival, especially if you are going on remote treks. Bear in mind that your embassy is bound to be cautious in its assessment.

Photocopy your passport and Tajik visa and carry them with you as there are frequent document inspections by the police. Take your passport with you also – but keep it very safe.

There are some unexploded mines, particularly in off road areas immediately adjoining the Uzbek, Kyrgyz and Afghan borders, and a few places in the Rasht valley. UNDP have carried out an extensive clearance operation. Where there are unexploded mines, these areas are well marked and usually out of bounds. Independent travellers in the Tavildara area of the Rasht valley are advised to consult with officials of the local Hukumat (local government), and take a local guide.

THEFT Thefts do happen, especially as you may well carry large wads of cash. Do not leave valuables lying around hotel rooms. Lock away part of your money supply and keep the rest in a money belt.

HEALTH Health care is limited. Hygiene in hospitals is often poor and blood supplies unreliable. You are strongly advised to take out medical insurance, including emergency evacuation. Carry a first aid kit.

Have a dental check up beforehand – be very careful visiting dentists in Tajikistan because of blood contamination.

If you have a heart condition, check with your family doctor about going to relatively high altitudes.

Vaccinations Take advice from your family doctor. Consult TRAVAX. The vaccinations recommended for Tajikistan are: Diptheria, Hepatitis A, Tetanus and Typhoid. Additional vaccinations to be considered, particularly if staying for one month or more: Hepatitis B, Rabies, Tick-born encephalitis and Tuberculosis (BCG).

There is a risk of malaria (P *vivax* type) from June–October in the southern border areas (Khatlon). Prevention: take precautions to avoid mosquito bites. Prophylaxis: Chloroquine plus proguanil.

Vaccination certificates are not normally required for immigration requirements.

Drinking Water Do not drink tap water. Buy bottled water. In homes you will be offered tea – this is reasonably safe, as the water has been boiled.

Altitude Sickness 93% of Tajikistan is mountainous. It is quite normal to feel tired for the first few days in mountain areas. Drink plenty of water. Try and gain height slowly. On the Pamir Highway between Murghab and Osh, you cross two passes over 4,300 m, and some people suffer from altitude sickness. Drink plenty of water and take pain killers. Do not undertake strenuous physical activity. Also because of the altitude, you are exposed to high levels of ultra violet light. Wear a hat and use high-factor sun cream.

The commonest complaints are diarrhoea and throat infections. Bring anti-diarrhoea tablets and broad spectrum antibiotics. Also bring a supply of rehydration salts and strong throat sweets. There are plenty of pharmacies, but quality control of pharmaceutical products is uncertain.

If you become ill In Dushanbe, the Prospekt Medical Clinic, has English speaking doctors, and are used to arranging emergency evacuation. It also has links to the Russian Military Hospital which is the best local hospital.

There are two clinics, The Diagnostic Centre and Shifo Clinic. (See Dushanbe chapter.)

In the Pamirs, go to Khorog Oblast General Hospital, which has had support from Aga Khan Health Services, improving medical and nursing training. The medical staff worked with visiting Canadian doctors who assessed many of the local specialists as being very competent, particularly the surgeons. Some of them speak good English. Report to the admissions unit to the left as you enter the hospital grounds.

Essential kit Always take with you:
- Torch. Essential everywhere. Power cuts are frequent, holes in roads and pavements hazardous, toilets and stairwells to apartment blocks often have no lights.
- Swiss Army knife. Surprising how often they are useful.
- A universal sink plug. Often baths and wash hand basins do not have plugs.
- Bottle of water.
- Toilet roll. Often not provided in toilets.
- Hand washing gel/soap/shampoo
- Personal medicines, including anti-diarrhoea tablets.
- Hat and suncream.
- US Dollars (Euros are increasingly accepted too).
- Camera, plus supply of film and spare batteries.
- Adaptor (or voltage reducer) for electrical appliances.(European two-pin 220v)
- A couple of small padlocks to keep safe your money.
- For women, a small headscarf for visiting holy places.

Toilets Apart from in parts of Dushanbe, most toilets are the squat type. In homes in the country the toilet is usually in a separate place some way from the house with no light and often hens for company. Local people use stones, but toilet paper can be bought. The quality in country areas is poor, stock up in Dushanbe.

Public toilets, particularly on the main roads are awful. Usually just a low wall enclosing a small hole, surrounded by used paper and near misses. Do not drop your passport or spectacles down the hole or you will be in for an unforgettable experience retrieving them. Better go behind a rock.

CLOTHING Normal cool clothing is advised with sun hat and sunglasses. In the mountains bring a light sweater for the evenings. For walkers and trekkers bring normal walking gear, with stout walking boots. Paths are often steep and precipitous, and ski poles can aid balance and help take the strain. For trekking most companies ask you to bring a sleeping bag.

MONEY AND EXPENSES Credit cards are only accepted in a handful of hotels in Dushanbe, otherwise all payments are made in cash. There are ATMs (cash machines) in Dushanbe and Khudjand, but not elsewhere. All towns will have change kiosks to convert dollars, and sometimes euros, into the local currency, *somonis*. Take new, clean dollars no older than 1996. Worn notes are not accepted.

The national currency is the somoni, which has been slowly falling against the dollar. For rough calculations use three somonis to the US dollar.

A visit to Tajikistan is not cheap. Air fares are relatively high (in March 2007, return Istanbul-Dushanbe with Turkish Airlines US$825). Petrol is US$1 per litre making vehicle hire expensive, and unless you can find homestays, hotels are relatively dear for what they offer.

COMMUNICATIONS The coverage for mobile phones is improving all the time and it is easy to rent one (see page 104). There are no restrictions on bringing in satellite phones.

HOMESTAYS Tajiks are endlessly hospitable and generally in need of cash. Homestays therefore can be the perfect way to stay in Tajikistan. It is also enjoyable to stay with a family, learning something about Tajik culture and eating good food. Local travel agencies can organise a homestay, as can the Pamirs Eco-Cultural Tourism Association (PECTA) and the Murghab Ecotourism Association (META) – see pages 528–531. It is also highly likely that Tajik families will invite one to stay as a guest. But please remember that most people are very poor. Always insist on paying – call it a gift, and bring presents of food. A fair rate for overnight stay with breakfast would be US$10 per person. When invited for a meal, always bring gifts as Tajiks do themselves.

COURTESY AND ETIQUETTE

The people of Tajikistan are generally very courteous, friendly and hospitable. There are some basic rules of etiquette:

• Always take off your shoes when entering a house, apartment or yurt.

• The normal mode of greeting is the person puts their right hand across the heart, tilts the head forward and says "Assalom aleykum" (Peace be with you). This should be returned.

• It is very likely you will be invited into a home. The invitation is meant. Hospitality is a basic tenet of the people of Central Asia, particularly in the mountain areas. This is illustrated by the saying of the 14th century poet Hafez:

> *O brother respect the guest and look after him*
> *For the guest is the gift of God*
> *For the guest brings blessings and removes the sins of the host*
> *He who respects the guest, respects the Prophet and God*
> *He who insults and disgraces the guest, disgraces and insults*
>   *Allah and his Prophet*
> *He who serves the guest serves Allah and his Prophet Muhammed*

• If you have time take some chocolates or flowers. Even if you are invited for a cup of tea, it is always more than that. Be prepared for a meal with a cloth set out with fruit, nuts and sweets, followed by a full meal. Your hosts may even slaughter a sheep or goat in your honour. This whole process cannot be hurried, and it can be overwhelming. It is a special way of learning about your hosts and how they live, but if you do not have the time, refuse politely. If you stay, remember your hosts are likely to be poor. Offer some money or provisions as a gift. They will probably refuse to take money, so give it quietly to the eldest child.

• Avoid displaying the soles of your feet or shoes.

• Water will be normally be offered to wash your hands before the meal – always use it.

• Don't put your feet on the tablecloth – if necessary tuck them under it. Do not step across the tablecloth if you are seated on the floor, go round it.

• Even if food is unappetising, take at least a symbolic bite.

• A prayer will normally be spoken at the end of a meal, sometimes only a perfunctory 'Allah Akbar' (God is great) – during the prayer, cup your hands in front of you – when it is finished draw your hands downward over your chin as if you were stroking a beard.

• People will be very interested in your family and home. Take some pictures of your family and your home town to show them. (It is worth taking some postcards or calendars as small gifts.)
• It is offensive to blow your nose into your handkerchief.
• Do not wear shorts (including men), miniskirts or skimpy tops. Cotton shirts are better than T-shirts, especially to visit someone's home or a mosque.
• For women it is useful to carry a small headscarf for visiting holy places.

Alcohol Although Tajiks are Muslims, some men do drink vodka, often to please a guest. At a meal men may like to propose a toast to you and your family, swigging back a cup of vodka in the Russian style. You will be expected to respond by giving thanks to your host and his family, and also downing a cup of vodka. Beware, this can get out of hand, with more and more toasts. It is perfectly acceptable to refuse vodka (and have beer or tea), but difficult to stop once you have started the process.

SOCIETY AND RELIGION

Seventy years of the Soviet Union has led to a fairly secular society, in the main cities of Tajikistan. Many women are educated and some play a prominent role in society. In Dushanbe and Khudjand men and women often dress in western style clothing, though they may maintain a traditional lifestyle at home.

The small towns and villages have a much more conservative society. In country areas if male visitors have a meal with a family it is likely that the women will stay in the kitchen, although western women will sit with the men.

The vast majority of Tajiks are Sunni Muslims. There are wide differences in interpretation though, with some families extremely pious and others much more secular. In the Pamirs the majority of the population are Ismailis (followers of the Aga Khan). Ismailis are traditionally considered less conservative.

CLIMATE AND WHEN TO VISIT

Most of western Tajikistan has a continental climate, with hot summers and cold winters. In the mountains, summers are warm, but winters are very severe, with heavy snow falls. For 300 days in the year there are clear blue skies. In the Ferghana valley in the north and the plains of the south, summers are very hot, temperatures rising to 40 degrees plus. Tajikistan was subject to a very cold winter in 2007/8. In some areas electricity supplies were cut off and there were food shortages (see www.://news.bbc.co.uk/2/hi/asia-pacific/7250273.stm). Be aware that the country is subject to occasional earth tremors that can induce rockfalls, and mountain roads can be blocked by avalanches, especially in Spring. Always allow extra time when planning journeys. The best times to visit:

- The Pamirs and Fan mountains – end of May to end of September
- Ferghana valley and the south – mid March to mid May, and mid September to end of October
- The rest of the country – mid March to end of October
- Dushanbe from mid March to end of November

GETTING THERE

Please note the information in the following sections was correct at time of going to press, but situations change. Check with the airline or a local tour company about the latest situation before confirming travel plans. The best website to check all matters about travel, and entry regulations is www.pamirs.org (A well designed website with comprehensive information about the Pamirs, with superb pictures including some sensational aerial shots).

Other useful websites include:

> www.cia.gov/cia/publications/factbook/geos/ti.html
> http://newsvote.bbc.co.uk/mpapps/pagetools/print/news.bbc.co.uk/1/hi/
> world/asia-pacific/country_profiles/1296639.stm
> www.traveltajikistan.com
> www.fco.gov.uk/servlet
> http://travel.state.gov/travel/cis_pa_tw/cis/cis_1037.html
> www.voyage.gc.ca/dest/sos/warnings-en.asp
> www.wikitravel.com

BY AIR:

Turkish Airlines (www.thy.com)

Turkish Airlines operates flights from Istanbul (Ataturk) to Dushanbe. Turkish Airlines have an office at 18, Rudaki Avenue, Dushanbe at the south end of Rudaki Avenue on the left just before reaching Ayni Square. Tel: +992 372 214199.

Tajikistan Airlines (www.tajikair.tj)

Tajikistan Airlines operate a daily return service between Moscow and Dushanbe. This route gives greater flexibility over travel dates, but connecting flights from Europe with an overnight stay in Moscow will require a Russian visa. Flights leave from Domodedovo airport, Moscow. It is difficult to book Moscow-Dushanbe flights from Europe or the USA. A specialist firm that can do so is Great Game Travel (see below). In theory, tickets can also be booked on line. E-mail: mop_gart@tajnet.com In Dushanbe, Moscow flights can be booked at the Tajikistan Airlines office, 32/1 Titov Street. Tel: +992 372 211966.

Tajikistan Airlines also fly from Istanbul to Dushanbe. The US-based **Mircorp**, www.mircorp.com can also book with Tajikistan Airlines. See also **Hamsafar Travel**, www.hamsafartravel.com; **Steppes Travel**, www.steppestravel.co.uk; **Geographical Expeditions**, www.geoex.com and **Great Game Travel**, www.greatgame.travel who have an office in Ireland and Dushanbe. Another travel agent who specialises in arranging flights on this route is **Jubilee Travel**, 73 Great Titchfield Street, London, W1W 6RD, UK. Tel: +44(0) 20 7631 0224. Ask for Mr Moledina. E-mail: jubilee_travel@hotmail.com. Please note all tickets with Tajikistan Airlines are pre-paid tickets in advance – you collect your ticket at the airport. Schedules can be found on: www.domodedovo.ru/en/main/timetablenews and www.akdal.ru/eng/live/ timetable.asp

Other routes include from Dushanbe to Sharjah, United Arab Emirates; Bishkek, Kyrgyzstan; Almaty, Kazakhstan; Tehran; and other large cities in Russia, including weekly flights to St Petersburg. NOTE: Tajikistan Airlines is not a member of IATA, and only two of their current aircraft are allowed to fly into EU airspace.

Domodedovo Airlines (web site: www.akdal.ru/eng/live/default.asp)

Domodedovo Airlines operates flights daily from Moscow (Domodedovo) to Dushanbe. Please note all bookings are based on the issue and post of hard copy tickets. Allow at least two weeks to obtain tickets. There are complications about booking single tickets. Great Game Travel and possibly other local travel companies can book these flights. It is possible travel agents in Europe and North America may also be able to book with Domodedovo Airlines.

Samara Airlines (web site: www.samara-airlines.ru/english/index.php)

Samara Airlines operates twice-weekly services from Moscow to Dushanbe.

By Land

To Uzbekistan

Relations between Tajikistan and Uzbekistan vary from cool to hostile. It is important to check the situation with a local travel company, as there are constant changes in the situation. There is always the need for a double entry visa to both countries.

Vehicles cannot cross the frontier. It is necessary to arrange transport on the other side. The crossing points are:

- North at Oybek from the road from Bekabad to Khudjand.
- East at Isfara.
- West of Dushanbe on the road from Denau to Tursunzoda and Dushanbe.
- South at Termez – a beautiful drive along Alexander's route.

To Kyrgyzstan

Relations with Kyrgyzstan are cordial. Kyrgyz visas are easier to obtain, either from Kyrgyz embassies in USA and Europe, the Kygyz embassy in Dushanbe or through local travel companies in Tajikistan and Kyrgyzstan.

The main crossing points are: in the north east of Tajikistan at Sary Tash on the road from Murghab to Osh in Kyrgyzstan; at the time of going to press the Karamyk Pass at the top end of the Rasht valley at Jirgatal was not open to foreigners.

To China

At time of going to press the pass at Kulma, east of Murghab was not open to foreigners, although rumours are intensifying that this will change by the end of 2008. To reach China it is necessary to travel through Kyrgyzstan and cross at Irkeshtam (Taunmurun Pass) or further north via the Torugat Pass (but only as part of a private group booked through a tour agency). Currently, there are two flights per week between Osh and Urumqi with Altyn Air and China Southern Airlines.

To Afghanistan

Afghan visas can be obtained, either from embassies in the USA or Europe or from the Afghan consulates in Dushanbe and Khorog or by local travel companies. There are crossing points by bridge at Panj-i Poyon (Nijniy Panj), Ruzvay (Kala-i Khum), Tem (Khorog) and Ishkashim. A valid visa is necessary for entry to Afghanistan. There may be restrictions on foreigners crossing, check with a local travel company or a Tajik embassy (see page 30) on the latest situation.

AIRPORT PROCEDURES

You will need either to present your passport with a visa, or for those eligible, your passport with a Visa Support Letter/Letter of Invitation and appropriate fee (it helps to have the correct money). You must fill in an immigration form. One part is kept by the immigration officer and you retain the other half to hand in when you leave.

Customs You will be required to fill in a customs declaration form when you enter Tajikistan. Usually these forms are in Russian, but there may be some in English versions at the airport. Ask your local travel company if they have ones in English. You must declare all cash and valuables. Fill in two copies. Hand one in, ensure the customs official stamps the other copy and retain it. You will need to hand in on departure.

Luggage Collect your luggage from the carousel. You will be required to hand in your luggage tags as you leave the departure hall. Small boys will offer to carry your luggage. Normal fee US$1.

Transport from Airport There are buses from the airport. Taxis, expect to pay US$7 into Dushanbe. Agree the price before leaving.

VISAS

Regrettably we cannot be definitive about arrangements for obtaining visas. The regulations have been changed several times in the period leading up to the publication of this guidebook.

We would strongly advise all travellers who wish to travel to Tajikistan to check the situation about visas well in advance. The best sources of information are:
1. Embassies of the Republic of Tajikistan, listed on page 30
2. The appropriate overseas embassy covering your interests in Tajikistan, see list on pages 102–104
3. The foreign affairs department of your country
4. A local travel company, or one with significant business in Tajikistan, as listed on page 31.
5. Websites: www.pamirs.org and www.traveltajikistan.com

At the time of writing, the arrangements were as follows:
1. Nationals of countries where there is a Tajik embassy (see list page 30) are required to apply for a visa (tourist or multiple entry) to the relevant embassy. They cannot obtain a visa at Dushanbe airport.

2. Nationals of most other countries can apply for a tourist or multiple entry visa to one of the embassies listed on page 30. The procedure is you will need to send the following:

a) Your passport

b) One passport photograph

c) One visa application form. This can be downloaded from website:
   http://www.tajikembassy.org/consular.html

d) Fee (check with the embassy)

e) Stamped Addressed Envelope

For some nationals a Visa Support Letter/Letter of Invitation is also required. To save time and inconvenience, if you are intending to visit Gorno-Badakhshan Autonomous Oblast (the Pamirs), you can apply for the permit to visit the area at the same time as your visa application.

The staff at the European embassies are helpful.

In late 2007, in response to new UK visa requirements for Tajik nationals, Tajikistan introduced a regulation requiring UK nationals to go in person to a Tajik consulate to apply for a Tajik visa. At the time of going to press, however, the Vienna consulate was not implementing this requirement, although they now insist on a Visa Support Letter for UK nationals. It is worth checking with them on the current situation at tajikembassy@chello.at.

Visa Support Letter/Letter of Invitation

A Visa Support Letter/Letter of Invitation can be issued by any organisation registered in Tajikistan, and must be endorsed by the Ministry of Foreign Affairs in Dushanbe. Letters can be obtained from a local travel company or some hotels. Probable cost US$50. The Letter should provide the following information:

a) Name, nationality and passport number

b) Arrival and departure dates. (Be careful, your visa will not be valid outside these dates)

c) Name of the inviting organisation

Registration

You are required to register with OVIR (Department of Visas and Regulation of Foreign Citizens) within 72 hours of arriving in the country. If this is not done you could face a fine of US$300 on departure. There are OVIR offices in Dushanbe, Khudjand, Khorog and Murghab.

Dushanbe office is found at 67–69 Karabaev Street. Take Ismoil Somoni Street from the Presidential Palace, at two km turn left at the large roundabout by the Circus along Karabaev Street. The OVIR office is on the left, set back about 50 m at the junction with Shestapalova Street. Open Mon–Fri 0800–1200, 1300–1700, Sat 0900–1300.

Process: You need to provide your passport, a passport photograph, registration fee (US$22) and your address in Tajikistan. It is required that a local person or a representative of an organisation based in Tajikistan registers you at a specific address.

Go to kiosk 9. Receive form and take to another OVIR office; face out from the main door, turn left and immediately right, office on the right to pay fee. Return with receipt and passport. Collect your passport the next day from kiosk 3.

There are people milling around, staff are unhelpful and do not speak English. To avoid hassle you may find it helpful to arrange for a local travel company to undertake registration for you.

The OVIR office **Khudjand** is located in Room 104, 170, Kamol Khujandi Street, next to Bank of Tajikistan. Open: Mon–Fri 0800–1200, 1300–1700, Sat 0800–1200.

GORNO-BADAKHSHAN PERMITS

A permit is necessary to visit the Oblast (Province) of Gorno-Badakhshan, which covers the area of the Pamirs (see map on back inside cover). If you have not obtained it at the same time as your visa, you must get it from the OVIR office. It can be done at the same time as you register. In the application you must state where you will be going in Gorno-Badakhshan. It is important to list all the border areas in Gorno-Badakhshan. These are Khorog, Rushan, Kala-i-Khum, Ishkashim, and Murghab, to prevent any problems.

Travel to the following districts on the Afghan border in other parts of Tajikistan also requires permission – Shurobod, Farkhor, Hamadoni, Kumsangi, Kabodion, Shahr-i Tuz and Nosiri Khusrav.

Local travel companies and some hotels can expedite permission, and obtain in 3 to 5 days. They will require you to send a copy of the back page of your passport in advance. If you do it independently on arrival, expect to wait up to two weeks. Do not leave for the Pamirs without this permission. You will be required to produce it at police and military checkpoints.

Leaving the Country Confirm your flight at least three days before leaving. Arrive at the airport two and a half hours before departure, because the process of booking in is very slow. You will be required to hand in the other half of the immigration form. You will be required to hand in the declaration form you completed on entry and also fill in a new customs declaration form. Again note these forms are often only available in Russian. A local travel company may have an English version. You will be required to declare all valuables and cash. The upward limit for taking out cash is US$2,000.

PERMITS FOR LAKE SAREZ

If you wish to go to Lake Sarez, you will need a permit (propusk) from the Committee for Emergency Situations and Civil Defence of the Government of Tajikistan, Lakhuti Str. 26, 734013 Dushanbe, tel: + 992 37 221 1331. Your letter can be addressed to Mr. M. Zokirov, Chairman of this Committee, and should give full names and nationality of the persons and an explanation of the reasons for the visit. The application should be submitted at least ten days in advance of the date of intended travel. Expect the actual issuing procedure to take at least one full day. Without the propusk you will not be allowed to proceed beyond Barchadev, the last village before the lake on the approach from the Bartang Valley. Documents are checked in Barchadev village, and, for those trekking in from Murghab and Shughnan districts, at Usoi dam at the downstream end of the lake. A local tour agency may be able to help but will need considerable advance notice.

Combining a Visit to Tajikistan & Other Countries in Central Asia

A combined visit to Tajikistan and Kyrgyzstan would be the easiest to arrange. This would allow the traveller to undertake the whole length of the magnificent Pamir Highway, from Dushanbe to Osh. Local travel companies can arrange such tours—not cheaply—but one can also arrange independent travel.

A combined visit to Tajikistan and northern Afghanistan is feasible and extremely interesting. Northern Afghanistan is broadly Persian-speaking and there are endless cultural and social connections across the Amu Darya.

A combined visit to the Fan Mountains and Penjikent in Tajikistan combined with a visit to Samarqand in Uzbekistan can be arranged by travel companies.

TAJIKISTAN EMBASSIES

Visas for Tajikistan are available from these embassies:

[also refer www.tjus.org/embassies.htm].

Embassy to **Austria, Hungary and Switzerland**

Universitaetstr. 8/1a, 1090 Vienna, Austria. Tel: +43 (1) 4098266; Fax: +43 (1) 409826614/15; E-mail: tajikembassy@chello.at; Open: Mon–Wed, Fri 0900–1300, 1400–1800

N.B. The Vienna Embassy may also agree to process your visa application if you are not resident in Austria, Hungary or Switzerland. It is worth trying as they are friendly and efficient. Check by telephone.

Belgium

Avenue Louise 362-365, 1050 Brussels, Belgium. Tel: +32 (2) 6406933; Fax: +32 (2) 6490195; E-mail: tajemb-belgium@skynet.be

China

LA 01–04, Liangmaqiao Diplomatic Compound, Beijing, 100600, China. Tel: +86 (10) 65322598; Fax: +86 (10) 65323039; E-mail: tjkemb@public2.bta.net.cn

Germany

Otto Suho Allee 84, 10585 Berlin, Germany. Tel: + 49 (30) 3479300; Fax: +49 (30) 34793029; E-mail: info@botschaft-tadschikistan.de; www.botschaft-tadschikistan.de; Open: Mon–Fri 0900–1800, consular section Mon–Fri 0900–1300

United States of America

1005 New Hampshire Ave.

NW, Washington DC 20037, USA

Consular Department,

1725 K Street NW, Washington DC 20006

Tel: +1 (202) 223 6090   Fax: +1 (202) 223 6091

E-mail: tajik.embassy@verizon.net.

Opening hours: 0900–1600

Visa requirements and a downloadable visa form can be found on: http://www.tajikembassy.org/pages/4/index.htm.

United Kingdom

A London embassy was scheduled to open in April 2008, but at time of press no address or contact details were available. Check www.fco.gov.uk for current information.

TRAVEL COMPANIES IN TAJIKISTAN

It is perfectly possible to travel in Tajikistan independently but it is worth considering obtaining some assistance from local travel companies perhaps for the visa and registration formalities, initial accommodation and travel arrangements. The best local travel companies have had to be nimble in coping with the early stages of tourism in Tajikistan, and are very flexible. They will tailor a service to your needs from basic visa, registration and airport pickup, to a full-scale tour in a four-wheel drive vehicle. However, we must point out that companies are small undertakings and can struggle to provide services for larger groups. We recommend when negotiating, to obtain a clear schedule of what services will be provided, and by whom. This particularly applies to treks in the Pamirs and Fan mountains. (*Please note that inclusion on this list is not a guarantee of reliability. Tourism is only just beginning in Tajikistan and some companies are just getting going.*)

Hamsafar Travel and Guesthouse

Pulod Tolis 5/11 (formerly Proletarskaya), Dushanbe. Near Vodanasos Bazaar, north end of Rudaki Avenue.

Tel: +992 228 0093, +992 93 501 4593, +992 93 501 5431

www.hamsafartravel.com; E-mail: ruslan@hamsafartravel.com;

rick@hamsafartravel.com; hamsafarinfo@yahoo.com

Helpful staff at this eight-bed guesthouse can arrange tours and treks.

Aviatrans

71/46 Aini Street, Dushanbe 734024

Tel: +992 37 2262875; Fax: +992 37 22661038

E-mail: dmelnichkov@hotmail.com

Dmitry Melnichkov, the Manager, has considerable experience of travel in Tajikistan, being one of the first in the field. He is very helpful, speaks fluent English and Russian. He is also a scholar of distinction being the editor of the excellent local guidebook *Travel Through Tajikistan* and has many contacts in the museums and with academics.

His company can arrange visa support, trekking, jeep tours throughout the country and will tailor tours to suit the client.

Goulya's Outdoor Adventures

Marian's Guest House, House 67/1, Shotemur Street, Dushanbe

Tel: +992 93 5050567

E-mail: tajikoutdooradventures@gmail.com

Managed by Goulya Petrova, a fluent Russian/English and medium French speaker. Goulya is based at Marian's Guest House in Dushanbe. Goulya is supported by good local staff. The company provides:

    a) Visa support and permits for the Pamirs

    b) Regular Sunday hikes, day hikes and overnight hikes in the Dushanbe area

    c) Longer treks in the Fan mountains and Yagnob valley

    d) Jeep tours in the Pamirs

    e) Excursions to the museums and bazaars of Dushanbe

    f) Tours to suit the client's wishes

Pamir Adventure

43 Bukhoro Street, Dushanbe

Tel: +992 372 235424, 276524; mobile: +992 95 151 7567

E-mail: info@pamir-adventure.com and pamirad@gmail.com

www.pamir-adventure.com

Surat Toimatsov, the Manager, has been involved with tourism more than 20 years. He is a well known photographer. His company can provide visa support, trekking, and jeep tours. He has a very good knowledge of the Pamirs.

Pamir Intourservice

68 Jomi Street, Khorog

E-mail: pamirintourservice@gmail.ru

Run by two young Tajik men, Umed Bakhtaliev and his colleague, Nasim from the Pamirs. They are inexperienced, but have a determination to succeed. Would be strongest on basic services, such as obtaining visas, local tours around Dushanbe and possibly visits to the Pamirs.

State Utility Tourist Enterprise (SAYOH)

22 Shota Rustaveli Street, Dushanbe 734025

Tel: +992 372 278584; mobile: +992 93 55 5555; Fax: +992 372 219072

E-mail: pamir74@mail.ru

This company is the former government travel agency. It is trying hard to move away from the old image of the bureaucratic and "take or leave it" image. The staff are helpful, although most do not speak English. Will probably be strong on obtaining permissions. The Manager is Iqbal Shabozov.

INTERNATIONAL TOUR COMPANIES

In the USA, there are a small number of companies sufficiently enterprising to operate in Central Asia, and at this time, we would particularly like to recommend

MIR: 85 South Washington Street, Suite 210, Seattle, WA 98104, USA

Tel: +1-800-424 7289 or 206-624 7289

E-mail: info@mircorp.com; www.mircorp.com.

Other US-based companies include,

Abercrombie & Kent: Many offices, including USA, UK, Australia and Hong Kong. www.abercrombiekent.com

Distant Horizons: www.distant-horizons.com

Geographic Expeditions: www.geoex.com

A veteran UK-based business is **Great Game Travel Company Limited,** 112 High Street, Holywood, County Down, Northern Ireland, BT18 9HW

Tel: +44 (0) 28 9099 8325; Fax: +44 (0) 28 9099 8951

E-mail: info@greatgame.travel; www.greatgame.travel, www.traveltajikistan.com

Travel in the Upper Zarafshan Valley

Other international companies include, by region,

Audley Travel: New Mill, New Mill Lane, Witney, Oxfordshire, OX29 9SX, UK
Tel: 01993 838 000; www.audleytravel.com

Eastern Approaches: 5 Mill Road, Stowe, Galashiels, TD1 2SD, Scotland, UK
Email: info@easternapproaches.co.uk; www.easternapproaches.co.uk

Explore Worldwide: www.explore.co.uk

Steppes Travel: www.steppestravel.co.uk

Wild Frontiers Adventure Travel Limited: Unit 6, Hurlingham Business Park, 55
Sullivan Road, London, SW6 2DU, UK
Tel: +44 (0) 20 7736 3968; Fax: +44 (0) 20 7751 0710; www.wildfrontiers.co.uk

EUROPE & CENTRAL ASIA

Globotrek: www.globotrek.ch

Horizons Nouveaux: www.horizonsnouveax.com/esprits/central/asiecentrale.htm

Nomad Reisen: www.nomad-reisen.de/seit_reis/asien/Tadjikistan/tad574ein.html

Oriensce: www.oriensce.fr/tadjikis.html

Sairam Tourism: www.sairamtour.com

AUSTRALIA & UNITED KINGDOM

Sundowners Overland: www.sundownersoverland.com

TRAVEL WITHIN TAJIKISTAN

Road Travel Roads are hazardous. In the mountain areas the roads are always rough,
dusty and often with precipitous drops. Particularly in the spring, roads are subject
to avalanche and snowfall. Generally the standard of driving on the mountain roads
is good and courteous: this is not the case on the roads in towns and on the plains.
If roads are blocked they take time to clear, and vehicles often break down. It is
important to prepare for unexpected delays.

Minibuses (*Marshrutkas*) There is an excellent network of cheap minibus services
throughout the country.

Taxis There are taxis in most towns, usually elderly Jhigolis (Ladas), ideal for
Tajikistan, because they are simple to repair. Always agree a price before a journey. The
kilometre gauge is unlikely to work. Do not expect seat belts. In the main bus stations
it is possible to share taxis for longer journeys.

Types of vehicles

JHIGOLI ('LADA' in Europe), the basic car favoured by taxi drivers.

Russian UAZ Minibus. Sturdy, basic minibus.

Russian UAZ Jeep. Four-wheel drive, very sturdy, hot, dusty and uncomfortable.

Russian NIVA. Four-wheel drive car. Sturdy, reasonably comfortable.

Toyota Landcruiser. Four-wheel drive, sturdy, fast and comfortable. Expensive to hire. If you go to the expense, make sure the air conditioner works.

Self-drive We are not aware of any companies who provide self drive vehicles. If there are, think about the hassle of documentation, dealing with difficult traffic police, few signposts and frequent breakdowns.

Hitch-hiking There is nothing to prevent hitch-hiking. Visitors who have done so found most of their lifts were in Zil trucks. These are slow, very hot and subject to breakdowns. You will have plenty of time to enjoy the views. The drivers are a great bunch and you will meet local people.

Internal Flights

Khudjand: Tajikistan Airlines fly to Khudjand. Their office is at Nisor Muhamad Street (formerly Chekhov). Two flights per day or more. Flights are popular, so book well ahead. It is necessary to present your passport to obtain a ticket. This can create a problem, as obviously you require your passport to enter the country. Local travel companies can make a booking, using a copy of your passport, but obtaining the tickets must await your arrival.

Khorog: It is not possible to book flights to Khorog in advance. Flights are dependent on the weather and if there are sufficient passengers at both ends. The procedure is to turn up at Dushanbe airport at 8 am, inform the ticket office (usually upstairs) and wait to hear if there is a flight. When this is announced there is a scrum to get tickets. Be prepared for frustration; sometimes there can be no flights for days.

The flight itself is exciting. It is in a 16-seat Antonov 28 or Yak 40. Seat belts do not work. Flight time is one hour. There are wonderful views first over the foothills and Lake Norak, then into the Pamirs, with a panoramic view of many of the major peaks. There are mountains as far as the horizon in every direction you look. The plane skips over ridges with only 30 m to spare, and heart-stoppingly close to cliff faces. The pilots are very skilful. For a fee they may let you go into the cockpit and take a film. To make the return flight, try and book ahead with the airport staff at Khorog and turn up and wait. Be prepared for the wait to last several days.

SPECIAL INTERESTS

Tajikistan gives great scope for special interests.

Mountaineering – See the chapters on mountaineering in the Pamirs and Fan Mountains. Some local tour companies can give logistical support, and some have the expertise to lead expeditions.

White water rafting and canoeing – Bring your own equipment. The best time is September.

Mountain biking – Bring your own bike. N.B. Bikes can now be hired in Murghab (see p. 533)

Fishing – Bring your own fishing gear. You seem to be able to fish most places without permission. Consult with the local Hukumat (local government) officials. There is both river and lake fishing.

Photography – Best times to come are spring and autumn, when there is less glare. Taking photos of anything that could be perceived as being of military or security interest may result in problems with the authorities.

Archaeology – Enormous scope, there are many untouched sites. It would be necessary to join an established archaeological organisation undertaking excavations in Tajikistan, as unauthorised excavations are not permitted.

Hang gliding – Plenty of mountains to jump off. Bring your own gear.

RECOMMENDED MAPS

Central Asia, including Tajikistan

Central Asia – Cultural Travel Map of Central Asia   Scale 1: 1,500,00

Central Asia – Gizi Map   Scale 1: 1,750,000

Detailed Map of Tajikistan

The most detailed maps, with 109 separate sheets to cover the whole country is the Russian military map, that can be downloaded from http://www.topomaps.eu/asia/ tadj_100k.shtml. It is accurate, but the place names are in Russian and you would need to reproduce on large sheets to make the names readable.

Tajikistan

Practical Pilotage Charts   Scale 1:100,000

Most of Tajikistan, Series TPC, sheet G-6B

Northern Tajikistan, Series TPC, sheet F-6D

SDC Switzerland and Orell Füssli Kartographie AG will produce two 1:500,000 maps of Tajikistan in Spring 2008, distributed by Gecko maps.

The Fan Mountains

Fan Mountains – Map and guide, EWP   Scale: 1:100,000

The Pamirs

The Pamirs, Gecko Maps   Scale: 1: 500,000

A superb map of the Pamirs, including all sites of special interest, produced by Markus Hauser, the leading expert on the topography of the Pamirs. It is distributed by Gecko Maps (www.geckomaps.com) and is a must for all travel to the Pamirs. It is available through Stanfords (www.stanfords.co.uk).

Markus also maintains a 'Pamir Archive' of historical documents concerning the Pamirs. www.angelfire.com/sd/tajikistanupdate/historicalmaps.htm

Women and children, Penjikent

Pamirs – Trans-Alai Mountains, West Col Productions   Scale: 1: 200,000

Links to websites with fairly good overview maps are given below.

> http://www.lib.utexas.edu/maps/tajikistan.html
> http://www.un.org/Depts/Cartographic/map/profile/tajikist.pdf
> http://www.grida.no/db/maps/prod/level3/id_1281.htm

The following website is useful for finding some specific places in Tajikistan, and gives longitude and latitude references:

> http://www.multimap.com/index/TI1.htm

In 2002, with funding from the Swiss Agency for Development and Cooperation (SDC) for the International Year of Mountains, the University of Bern prepared a Geographic Information System for Gorno-Badakhshan. To make the database available to organisations and interested users, the Centre for Development and Environment (CDE) of the University Bern developed an internet-based interface for the visualization, query and download of spatial information.

It can be directly accessed at http://www.pamir-gis.info or through CDE's home page http://www.cde.unibe.ch.

PUBLIC HOLIDAYS

Take account of these in your itineraries, sometimes government offices are closed the day after.

January 1	New Year's Day
March 8	International Women's Day
March 20–22	Navruz
May 1	International Labour Day
May 9	Victory Day
June 27	Peace and National Accord
September 9	Independence Day
November 6	Constitution Day
November 9	National Reconciliation Day

There are also two Muslim holidays that have different days each year: Eid-i Ramadan, three days celebrating the end of the month long fast of Ramadan, and Eid-i Kurbon, the feast of sacrifice. There are additional festivals in Gorno-Badakshan.

A Short History of Tajikistan   Robert Middleton

The territory of what is today Tajikistan was a crossroads for the passage of the many different tribes and ethnic groups that ruled or inhabited Central Asia over the past 3,000 years: Scythians, Persian dynasties, Macedonian/Greek armies under Alexander the Great, Parthians, Kushans, Chinese, Huns, Hephtalites, Mongol hordes, Arabs, Russians, even Nestorian Christians, Jews and British – all left their mark on the region.

Any introduction to Tajikistan must first focus on the Tajiks. The name appears for the first time in the works of the 11th century Turkish historian Mahmud of Kashgar, who used it to describe all Persian-speaking peoples of the region who were of Iranian origin. It may have originated from the Chinese name for ancient Bactria: Daxia (or Ta-Haia). Until they were displaced by successive waves of Turkic invaders from the north and east, the Tajiks occupied a large part of Central Asia. Broadly speaking, the Tajiks were the sedentary inhabitants of the region as opposed to the Turkic peoples who were nomadic.

Tajiks are, of course, the main ethnic group in most of present-day Tajikistan (approximately 80%), but there is also a large Tajik population in northeastern Afghanistan and in Kabul, Mazar-i Sharif and Herat, making up more than a quarter of the population of Afghanistan. Tajiks are also in the majority in the Uzbek cities of Samarqand and Bukhara and along the Surkhandaria in eastern Uzbekistan: the official Uzbek statistics show only 5% of the population professing to be ethnic Tajiks, but under the present regime there are strong concerns about potential discrimination against non-Uzbeks and the figure is certainly much higher. A small Tajik community lives in Sarikol, Xinjiang Province, Western China, almost all of whom are Shia Ismailis, followers of the Aga Khan.

Substantial numbers of refugees fleeing the Tajik civil war and the more recent unrest in Afghanistan, as well as economic migrants, have found their way to Russia, Ukraine, Kyrgyzstan and Northern Pakistan.

Scythians

From as early as the second millennium BC, large areas of Siberia, Central Asia and Western China were inhabited by a group of peoples known collectively as Scythians,

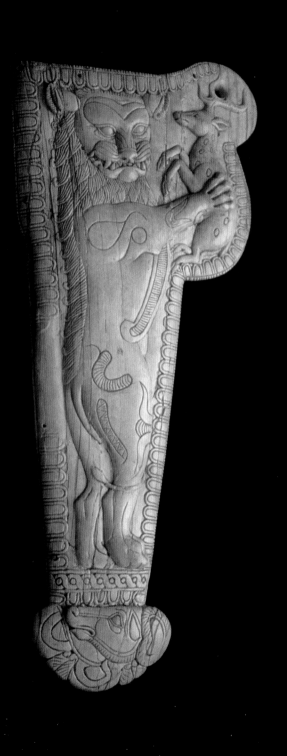

whose physical features were European and whose language belonged to the Indo-Iranian group of the Indo-European linguistic family. They may therefore be considered as the ancestors of the Tajiks.

Persian Empire

From about 500 BC until the Arab invasions in the 7th century AD, most of Central Asia was under Persian influence or control. Bactria (today the region around Balkh in Northern Afghanistan) on the banks of the Oxus (now called the Amu Darya) was the centre of Persian civilisation in Eastern Iran. The Persians displaced the Scythian nomadic tribes in the region. Afraysiab (now Samarqand) was the centre of the region known as Soghdiana that covered what is today Southern Uzbekistan and much of Tajikistan. The cities of Samarqand and Bukhara, although today in the territory of Uzbekistan, are centres of Tajik/Persian culture.

Alexander the Great, Kushans and Hephtalites or 'White Huns'

Alexander of Macedon defeated the armies of the Persian King Darius III between 336–330 BC and brought about the fall of the Achaemenid Empire. Alexander subjugated Sogdiana but, in order to promote the pacification of the conquered peoples, married Roxane, daughter of a local chieftain. When Alexander died in 323 BC, the Macedonian Empire broke up. After a long period during which Bactria was ruled by Graeco-Macedonian satraps and subjected to frequent invasions by nomadic Turkic hordes, the area fell under the control of the Yuechi (Kushans), from what is now the Gansu region in Western China, from the second century BC to the third century AD. The Persian Sasanids (224–642 AD) destroyed the Kushan Empire and the region reverted to Persian control.

In 400 AD a new wave of Central Asian nomads under the Hephthalites progressively took control of the region. The Hephthalites were defeated in 565 AD by a coalition of Sasanids and Western Turks. The Sasanids took Bactria and the Western Turks ruled over Soghdiana.

Arab Conquests

Soon after the death of the prophet Muhammed, Central Asia was invaded successively by the Arabs of the Umayyad and Abbasid dynasties. These conquests

Ivory scabbard from Takht-i Sangin, c. 6th century BC

brought a flowering of Islamic thought, philosophy and mysticism in Central Asia and stemmed Chinese expansion in the east. However, Persian influence remained strong, and new Islamic Persian dynasties sprang up, of which the most important was that of the Samanids (875–999). The Samanid period, marked by the scientific work of al-Khorezmi, al-Farabi, al-Razi (Razes), Ibn Sino (Avicenna), al-Biruni and the poetry of Rudaki and Firdowsi, made a major contribution to the development of the cultural identity of the peoples that were subsequently to call themselves Tajiks.

The defeat of the Samanids by the Turkic Ghaznavid dynasty in 999 marked the beginning of the decline in Persian influence in Central Asia. From the end of the first century AD, there had been sporadic westward movements of nomadic Turkic peoples from the area of what is now Mongolia: the massive military invasions under the leadership of Genghis Khan (Temujin 1167?–1227), Tamerlane (Timur-Lang 1336?–1405) and Babur (Zahir-ud-din Muhammed Babur, 1483–1530) ended Persian dominance in the region. Largely due to the protection provided by its mountainous terrain, the Tajiks in what is now Tajikistan and Afghanistan were better able to preserve their Persian culture. While the languages of Kazakhstan, Kyrgyzstan, Uzbekistan and Turkmenistan all have Turkic roots, Tajikistan and Afghanistan retained the Iranian language, and – not least in Tajikistan – music, dance and poetry in the Persian tradition play a major role in society.

From the 15th to the 19th century the area covered by present-day Tajikistan was under the nominal suzerainty of frequently competing Uzbek dynasties, albeit on the fringe of their territory. From the 1860s, Uzbek rule was progressively undermined by the Russian conquests in Central Asia. In 1865 Tashkent was taken, Bukhara fell to the Russians in 1867, and Samarqand in 1868. For tactical reasons, however, the Russians left the Uzbek power structures largely in place, and – in the 1868 treaty establishing a Russian protectorate over Bukhara – the Emirate of Bukhara gained territory including present-day Dushanbe in compensation for territory that had been conceded to Russia.

The Great Game

In the latter part of the 19th century, because of its geographical location at the confines of the Russian Empire and its proximity to China and British India, the territory of Tajikistan – especially the Pamirs – had considerable strategic importance.

The Great Game, between Russian and British adventurers, soldiers, spies and diplomats – staking the limits of the respective Empires – was largely played out in the mountains of the Pamirs and the Hindu Kush. Subsequently, at the time of the Soviet invasion and occupation of Afghanistan (1979–1989), the Pamir region again assumed strategic importance for the Soviet Union as one of the main supply routes for the logistic support of Soviet military operations in Afghanistan.

Soviet Union

After the 1917 Bolshevik *coup d'état*, communist power in Central Asia was challenged by the remnants of the White Army and a strong resistance movement organised by indigenous tribes (the so-called Basmachi revolt); moreover, the embryonic Soviet state was faced with vigorous opposition (including more or less covert support to the Basmachis) from Britain, with imperial interests to defend in the region. These concerns led to the determined military subjugation and forced sovietisation of the native peoples of "Turkestan" in the 1920s. Under Stalin, the region – in particular the Ferghana Valley, the most fertile area in Central Asia – was divided in 1924 between separate Soviet Republics in such a way as to maintain a mix of ethnic groups, the tensions between which could be exploited to justify the necessity of the strong centralising influence of the Soviet system. Tajikistan, initially an autonomous republic within Uzbekistan, became a federated Soviet Socialist Republic in 1929. Gorno-Badakhshan had already become an autonomous Oblast of Tajikistan in 1925.

The sovietisation of Central Asia, while imposing a degree of communist orthodoxy, did not lead to the total destruction of local culture and religion: the region was far from the centre, it comprised a large number of backward rural communities where traditions remained strong and, in addition, the government in Moscow found it politically advantageous to pay a certain amount of lip service to the concept of the 'multicultural identity' of the Soviet Union.

Soviet rule brought economic and social benefits for the Republics of Central Asia, especially for Tajikistan, the poorest among them. Universal education and health services achieved a level of literacy and public health far superior to that achieved in the former British Empire just across the Wakhan Corridor to the South. Subsidies from Moscow maintained a standard of living and social services in Tajikistan that bore little relationship to the actual economic development or potential of the region.

Independence and civil war

When the Soviet Union broke up in 1991, Tajikistan became an independent state but was immediately faced with the economic problems caused by the breakdown of the centrally planned Soviet economy: withdrawal of subsidies, disruption of former guaranteed markets, exchange instability, etc. Today Tajikistan ranks as one of the poorest countries of the world.

In 1992 civil war broke out (for further details see chapter Dushanbe: A Town Called Monday). Its causes are complex and relate to some extent to the previously mentioned ethnic and regional tensions that were the legacy of the boundaries attributed to the new Soviet Republics in 1924, but also to premature attempts – imitating the policies implemented under Gorbachev in Russia – to liberalise the Tajik political system. At the end of the Soviet period, power in Tajikistan was tightly guarded by representatives of the Leninabad district in the North. Gorbachev's perestroika and glasnost led to demands in Tajikistan that other regions of the country should also participate on equal terms in the political process and that the communist party should abandon its monopoly of political power in favour of a multiparty system.

1991 Presidential elections

In 1991, Tajikistan was the first ex-Soviet Republic to hold free elections: not totally free, of course, and probably subject to some manipulation, but, in comparison with experience under the Soviet regime, nevertheless free.

The new 'Democratic Party' had formed an alliance against the ruling Communists with the 'Popular Front' (Rastokhez) and the 'Islamic Renaissance Party', a moderate Islamic organisation that did not at the time agitate for Sharia law or the introduction of 'Islamic values' in society. The opposition presidential candidate – a popular film-maker with origins in Gorno-Badakhshan – was beaten by the communist candidate, but his score of some 30% of votes put pressure on the government to open the country to a multi-party system.

Refusal of power-sharing

Despite the moderating influence of Gorbachev, the Tajik regime was not ready to face up to the profound changes implicit in the fall of the Berlin wall in 1989 and

Early Soviet development in Tajikistan – the runway at Khorog [c.1930]

refused power-sharing. This inflexibility – and a lack of political maturity on the part of the opposition – led to civil war.

With support from the southern region of Kulob (and probably of the Russian military forces stationed in Tajikistan), the leaders of the government faction defeated the opposition coalition forces recruited essentially from fighters of Pamiri (Gorno-Badakhshan) and Garmi (Karategin/Rasht) origin. Large numbers of people from these mountainous regions had been relocated in the 1950s to the cotton-growing areas of the south-west (Kurgan-Tyube); in Dushanbe, the capital, many of the intellectual elite were of Pamiri origin.

Persecution of these ethnic groups in the aftermath of the civil war forced many to return to their traditional homeland. Opposition fighters fled to Afghanistan and subsequently returned with fundamentalist ideas gained in the refugee camps there, mainly to the Karategin valley but also to a few predominantly Sunni areas in the North of Gorno-Badakhshan. The result was a sharp polarisation of national politics and the radicalisation of the Islamic Renaissance Party.

Humanitarian crisis

The civil war compounded the economic disruption caused by the break-up of the Soviet system and the people of Gorno-Badakhshan and Karategin/Rasht found themselves virtually isolated. This national crisis was largely ignored by the international community: few had even heard of Tajikistan, fewer still knew where it was located, and most considered that it was a problem in Russia's backyard of little relevance to the West. Those few serious newspapers that reported a little of what was going on too easily adopted the cliché of a conflict between former hard-line communists and Islamic fundamentalists.

Peace agreement

The civil war continued at relatively low intensity – mainly through sporadic cross-border incursions from Afghanistan – until June 1997, when a peace agreement was signed between the government of Tajikistan and the United Tajik Opposition. This agreement opened the way for an interim 'power-sharing' government and Presidential and Parliamentary elections; it provided also for the integration of opposition forces into the regular armed forces of Tajikistan.

In November, President Emomali Rakhmon was re-elected for a seven-year term, and, in March 2000, elections were held for the upper and lower houses of parliament, in which the former opposition parties did not make a strong showing (around 10% of votes).

Although the speed in reaching agreement was undoubtedly influenced by the unstable situation in Afghanistan, the peace accord was nevertheless a remarkable achievement; its subsequent relatively problem-free implementation is even more remarkable. After a civil war characterised in its opening stages by extreme brutality (cf the Amnesty International report *Tadzhikistan – Hidden terror: political killings, 'disappearances' and torture since December 1992*, May 1993) the integration of former fighters in the national armed forces and in civil life has been exceptionally smooth: the process can indeed be held up as a model for other inter-community or ethnic conflicts in countries with considerably higher economic and social resources than Tajikistan.

Despite occasional "incidents", the peace process has so far been remarkably successful. Tajikistan today offers one of the few examples in the modern world of the full integration of opposition fighters into regular armed forces.

Pluralism

The Tajik civil war resulted directly from laudable efforts to promote pluralism and was not – as a reading of the contemporary Western press might have led readers to conclude – a conflict between neo-communists and Islamic fundamentalists. The eyes of Western journalists were turned towards other man-made tragedies closer to home in Bosnia and Somalia: Tajikistan was described in simplistic clichés for readers already saturated with disasters. Moreover, then as today, the cliché of the threat of Islamic fundamentalism served the interests of those major powers that wished to maintain or extend their power and influence in Central Asia.

Regrettably, much of the world press continues to be obsessed with fears of Islamic fundamentalism in the whole of Central Asia without distinguishing between the very different situations of each Republic. While the economic situation in Tajikistan remains probably more precarious than in any other former Soviet Republic, the exceptionally high level of literacy and secular education achieved under the Soviet Union and the political maturity shown by leaders of both government and

opposition in negotiating the peace agreement of 1997 give ground for some optimism that Tajikistan may ultimately prove more stable than its neighbours. If, on the other hand, the international community withdraws from engagement in the development of the country and its institutions from fear of Islamic fundamentalism, this fear may become a self-fulfilling prophecy.

Contrary to many people's expectations, President Rakhmon has brought a remarkable degree of stability to Tajikistan and has so far succeeded in balancing (and outmanoeuvring) the various factions and interest groups, although a number of recent monitoring reports point to signs that this balance may now be precarious and suggest that there is a danger of a return to factionalism.

As a tourist destination, however, given recent upheavals in its neighbours Uzbekistan and Kyrgyzstan, Tajikistan must be rated as safe and – especially in the Pamirs, that were virtually untouched by the civil war – does not deserve the poor security rating given it by the foreign ministries of many Western countries. Bear in mind that your embassy is bound to be cautious in its assessment.

(above) Paintings in red on the inner wall in a Pamiri house, Bartang valley [Zarubin, 1914]
(left) Civil War graveyard in Zhamag, last village in Yazgulem

(following page) Girl on the road to Khoit

TAJIKISTAN

THE NORTH AND WEST

HUW THOMAS

WITH CONTRIBUTIONS BY MONICA WHITLOCK

Dushanbe and Tajikistan

MONICA WHITLOCK

The Town Called Monday

A walk down Rudaki avenue, the spine of Dushanbe, is a walk into the story of the city and of Tajikistan too. The blasting Persian pop music, the money-changers with wads in half a dozen currencies, the plate-glass shops bursting with Chinese imports hauled across the Pamir mountains mark the economic vim that drives the city. It seems hard to believe that only a few years ago, Tajikistan was still in civil war (1992–97) and gunmen swaggered openly down Rudaki. Dushanbe – and the country – have moved on. What was a ghost-town after dusk, is now a lively thoroughfare where families stroll in the cool of the evening and the air is thick with the smell of shashlik.

Behind the glitz, look for the elegant and original buildings that give Dushanbe a special charm – the grand neo-classical ministries in their soft, paint-box colours and the curves of the Bauhaus pieces. From the 1920s come the now crumbling curlicues of the first Russian buildings – early ventures into what was then the southern tip of empire. Modern Dushanbe evolved through the Soviet century with all its triumphs and disasters. Set back from Rudaki are the 1950s apartment blocks, a legacy of massive urban expansion when all manner of peoples settled here from other parts of the USSR.

Under all this, though, lie far older stones. Dushanbe was a large, busy village centuries before the Soviet Union was ever thought of. The name – which means 'Monday' – stems from a weekly bazaar. The other cities of Tajikistan – like Qurghan Tappa, Hissar and Kabodion were important places in the medieval world and before. Alexander the Great fought at Khudjand. Babur stopped there, 1,800 years later, and noted the strong winds. (They still blow today, especially around the airport and landing at Khudjand can be exciting.) Babur then crossed the border at Auvaj into Afghanistan before heading south to conquer Kabul. Antiquity is never far away in Tajikistan. Even in modern Dushanbe, step off Rudaki into the lanes of traditional houses, each with its courtyard and fruit trees, and find lives changed only in the detail from those hundreds of years ago.

A New Country in an Old Land

Tajikistan as we know it was born out of the collapse of the Bukharan Emirate in the early 20th century. Up to then, it had been the eastern, mountainous edge of the state, run by lords or beks who answered to the Amir in Bukhara but governed with a large measure of autonomy.

When the imperial Russian army began its long march through central Asia in the 19th century, toppling local rulers and scattering their beks, Bukhara became a Russian protectorate, but nonetheless retained autonomy in its internal affairs. Yet, behind the ancient city walls, internal political collision split the Bukharans from one another. Some factions pressed for reform and others for the supreme rule of the Amir, Alim Khan, and the religious authorities of the madrassas, or universities. Caught in the cross currents, Alim Khan became more dependent on Russia, whose territories now surrounded the city-state. Isolated Bukhara grew weaker.

In 1920 the Red Army finally moved in. At dawn on the last day of August, aircraft began to bomb Bukhara. Residents rushed from their houses, amazed to see these flying machines for the first time, then horrified to see their dry, mud brick city burn. Troops moved in on the ground at the same time. It took three days for Bukhara to fall. By the time the old flag was struck, on September 2nd, Alim Khan was gone – fleeing though the mountains to the provincial outpost of Dushanbe. There the Amir held court until the spring of 1921 when he and his retainers floated across the river Amu on a raft into Afghanistan, where he lived for the rest of his days.

The New Order

After the dissolution of Bukhara and the other old states of Central Asia, the new Soviet authorities set to drawing up a new map. The 'Uzbek Soviet Socialist Republic', came into being in 1924, incorporating what we now call Uzbekistan with Tajikistan as an autonomous adjunct with its capital at Dushanbe.

A flurry of building began to turn a rural backwater, home to weavers, tanners and horse-traders, into a model Soviet city. Telegraph poles marched down the wide dirt road 'Prospekt Lenina' (now Rudaki) that formed the centre. The first electric lights blinked into action, powered by the new electricity plant. The effort and cost involved are hard to grasp nowadays. Local building materials (poplar wood, mud brick) did not fit the vision of the new Dushanbe, so each pane of glass, each timber, even each nail was procured elsewhere in the Union – mostly thousands of miles away in the forests of Siberia. Everything was then loaded into steam trains and freighted – a journey of weeks – down to the railhead at Termez, on the Afghan border. Then all was strapped to camels and hauled to Dushanbe along tracks so rough that each plank is said to have lost a metre in length and so dangerous that Red Army guards rode with each caravan to ward off bandit attacks. Food, tools and machine parts came the same way.

The coming of the new world swept away the old. The Arabic or Persian alphabet was banned, making outlaws of countless intellectuals, clerics, lawyers and other literate people. At a stroke, the Central Asians were severed from not only from the rest of the Muslim world but their entire literary canon. People who still used the 'old' script found themselves considered seditious. Some were sent to prison camps in the Russian Far East. Far more hid their literacy and their books. (When the Soviet Union eventually fell, thousands of Tajik families brought out treasured volumes of poetry and prayers they had kept secretly for seventy years.) In place of the Arabic script came the Latin alphabet, later replaced by Cyrillic – the Russian lettering that is still commonly in use in Tajikistan.

Dushanbe grew in leaps and bounds. In 1924 there were two cars in all Tajikistan – the year the first school primer in Tajik came out. In 1925 the first edition of the newspaper Eid-i Tajik (Tajik Holiday) rolled off the first printing press, and was

delivered on horseback along Lenin Prospekt. Two years later the first documentary film was shot in Dushanbe. It records some interesting details of life at this important turn of the story. The shaky scene is of an ordinary bazaar – men are selling grapes and melons, a farrier is shoeing a horse and a darvish or pious indigent, begs for alms. But there is already one figure dressed in the European-style short shirt and narrow trousers that gradually became standard wear for the modern young man.

In 1929 crowds lined the brand-new railway track (each sleeper tracked from a Siberian forest) to see the first train, driven by an Armenian, steam into Dushanbe station. That year Tajikistan was declared a Socialist Republic in its own right, separate from Uzbekistan and fully part of the Soviet Union. To mark the occasion, Dushanbe was renamed Stalinabad (it reverted in 1961). Khudjand became Leninabad, the name older people still often use.

The View from the Village

While this immense effort and expense was poured into Dushanbe, the view outside the new capital was very different. Just half an hour's ride from the city, were scenes of terrible destruction. As the Red Army moved through Tajikistan in the 1920s, securing the territory for the Union, often violently, it met both incomprehension and

Monument to the first car in Khorog (left)   *Road from Dushanbe to Khudjand (above)*

anger from villagers, many of whom lost their land and livelihoods. Very many families fled the country finding sanctuary mainly in Afghanistan.

Some young men took up arms. They became anti-Soviet partisans – known as basmachi – as did thousands of others in other parts of Central Asia. The long basmachi campaign followed tactics familiar to guerrilla groups all over the world. They ambushed Red Army horsemen and sabotaged their settlements, they scattered great quantities of leaflets to warn the local population against what they considered an alien, occupying force that would destroy their way of life and violate their religious beliefs. Many invoked the name of the name of the old king, Alim Khan, and promised his triumphal return from exile in Kabul. But Alim Khan was really more a figurehead than a leader for the basmachi and the movement thrived on powerful local figures (see page 125, Ibrahim Bek).

The Red Army took dreadful reprisals on the surrounding villages. 'Houses and other buildings are destroyed and ruined. Walls are levelled to the ground ... Fields, gardens and melon patches are full of weeds and fallow,' notes a Soviet committee sent to make an assessment in the Tajik countryside in the 1920s. Whole villages had been deserted in the highlands and on the plains between Dushanbe and the Amu. About one house in two stood empty in the old market town of Qurghan Tappa; fifty villages around it were abandoned. Little more than fourteen thousand people lived in the town of Fakhrabad – more than half the population there had been. Irrigation canals were destroyed and the amount of land under cultivation was halved. As much as a third of the population of the plains had disappeared; of these, Soviet accounts estimate, about half had gone to Afghanistan and half had been killed. Few places in Central Asia were hit so hard by the coming of communism as rural Tajikistan. Much of the countryside never caught up in the years that followed. Three generations later, in the 1990s, the gap between the Soviet city and the farming poor would re-emerge with terrible consequences.

To the Front

In the small hours of 22 June 1941, German forces launched a huge multiple assault on Minsk, Kiev and Sevastapol and so brought the Soviet Union into the Second World War. German troops advanced quickly through the western USSR during the freezing winter that followed. Far away in Central Asia, the war had long lasting repercussions.

Some Tajiks, and their cousins the Uzbeks, Turkmens and other Central Asians, fought in the elite corps of the Soviet army. Some were young men from the most remote villages who left their valleys for the first time to serve in the faraway western USSR. 'Salam from Grozny' begins one letter home from Rahmatullah Azimov, a farmboy from the Tajik-Afghan border, in 1942.

> To my brother, sisters and friends!
>
> I am in the North Caucasus, in Chechnya, at the flying school. I am learning a lot here and I'm fine. I miss you all so much. I miss my country, my son and the warm weather. Please say hello to all my friends.
>
> I don't know when my training will finish – perhaps I'll be away another six months or so. Then we must go to the war, to the front. But don't worry, everything will be all right.
>
> Your loving little brother.

Azimov was sent to fight soon afterwards. His plane was shot down over the Barents Sea and he never came home. Rahmatullah Azimov was hailed as a hero in his home town, Kulob, a symbol that Tajiks were now truly part of the Soviet Union.

The majority of Central Asians went to serve behind the lines, digging trenches, cooking and carrying supplies – at least in the early stages of the war. There was a reluctance to use many Uzbeks and Tajiks as combat troops, partly because many did not speak much Russian, and the officer corps was almost entirely Russian or otherwise Slav. As casualties mounted, though, between 1941 and 1943, far greater numbers were called up. Shepherds, farmers, and factory workers left for the front, even the mullas exiled in the gulags of Siberia. Most had very little training. Some blew themselves up with weapons they could barely use. Very many lost their hearing.

Such servicemen played an important role in the development of Tajikistan. They were among the first Central Asians, outside a tiny elite, to see anything of the wider USSR beyond their own countries. They fought alongside Russians and made friends with them. They became tremendous patriots and still stand in annual parade in Dushanbe, their chests filled with medals, on Victory Day each May 9th. Look out too for the huge metal V for Victory monument in south-central Dushanbe, erected some years after the war to mark the contribution of the village-turned-capital.

Tajiks played their own special role in the war, in addition to serving on the common fronts. As the only Persian speakers in the USSR, many were sent to Iran to help operate the trans-Iranian railway line from the Gulf to the Caucasus. This

Persian Corridor, built by British and Soviet troops was the only alternative to the perilous Arctic Convoys to Archangel. Vast amounts of supplies, trucks, uniforms, radio equipment and food passed along this lifeline to Soviet troops.

One fascinating but almost forgotten aspect of Central Asia in the war was the creation of the Turkestan Legion – a special Muslim unit of the German army. Founded by anti-Soviet nationalist intellectuals, it is said to have numbered about two hundred thousand men, recruited from the great many Central Asians taken prisoner by the Germans. For some, joining the Legion was a decision of principle. Most were probably simply trying to stay alive and out of German detention. The Legion fought in Italy, Greece and North Africa (as the Uzbek and Tajik graves there show) and its soldiers also served behind the lines as dog handlers, guards and cooks at detention centres.

Norman Lewis, a British officer who later went on to fame as a travel writer, crossed paths with the Legion when he was given the task of escorting 3,000 Tajik prisoners by ship to the Soviet base in Iran. These Tajiks had been wearing German uniform when they surrendered to the British, although at the last minute they had turned on the Germans and attacked them. During their ten-day voyage together, Lewis enjoyed the company of the Tajiks. 'Every day was a party,' he remembered. The Tajiks composed poetry, and turned zinc water bottles, mess cans, toothbrushes and combs into stringed instruments and drums. Gas capes and camouflage webbing became costumes for Tajik theatre, and so the prisoners played and sang their way to the Gulf. Lewis saw the Tajiks put into cattle trucks on a rainy day in the marshalling yard. He was sure that they were taken away to their deaths.

The Luckiest in the World

By the late 1950s Dushanbe bore little resemblance to its pre-war self, let alone the village it had been a generation before. It had quadrupled in size and had, in the centre, mains electricity, piped water, a 'modern restaurant' and (according to official

Veteran of World War II

data) 61 hospitals. The expansion had been brought about by the arrival of thousands of Slavs, Europeans and other Soviet nationalities who moved to the city before, during and after the war. Very many had been deported by Stalin from the Western Soviet Union, ostensibly for fear that they would collaborate with Nazi Germany. These groups included Pontic Greeks, Ingush, Chechens, Mesketian Turks and other. Other incomers, especially scholars and doctors, were banished individually to Central Asia. Still more chose to try their luck in the south, drawn by the prospect of a warm climate, jobs on building sites and bountiful fruit and vegetables.

Dushanbe benefited in particular from the enormous influx of Germans. The church in southern Dushanbe, with its narrow steeple and icing sugar plaster, is run now by the Seventh Day Adventists. But it was built as a Lutheran church, the heart of a German community that once numbered fifty thousand – almost a quarter of the city at one point – based in their own quarter, Sovietsky.

More than any other single group, it was the Germans who built modern Dushanbe. Some were prisoners of war who never returned home, as the lines of German graves in southern Tajikistan testify. The great majority, however, were among the half-million Soviet Germans deported from the Odessa and Volga regions of Russia in a single week of September 1941. Some were taken directly to Tajikistan, many arrived after years of exile in Siberia.

'We were given 24 hours to get out,' remembered Ella Ivanova, blue-eyed and fair haired, she still knows a few words of German even though she spent almost all her life in Dushanbe. 'We had to leave our cow, and everything but the clothes we wore. We were put under guard in a cattle wagon and sent to Siberia.'

Ella and her family endured more than ten years in exile, half-starved in a settlement so remote that wolves attacked and ate the school teacher. It was not until Stalin's death in 1953 that the political climate grew easier and they were allowed to leave Siberia. Like thousands of others, the family made its way south in search of work and ended up in Dushanbe.

Lutheran Church (now Seventh Day Adventist), Dushanbe

'We found a paradise on earth here,' said Ella, 'There was mud up to your knees on Prospekt Lenina then, but Father found work as a builder. We thought him the richest man in the world! In Siberia, children used to shout Fascist! Fascist! at us, but in Dushanbe all that stopped.'

The Germans were received warmly, by and large, and earned themselves a reputation for honesty and industry. But after forty years in Dushanbe, another twist of history moved them on. After the fall of the Soviet Union in 1991, the great majority moved to a Germany they knew only from grandparents' stories, or to Russia. Some came to regret the move, finding themselves foreigners once again. For older people, the isolation, especially in the freezing Russian winters, came as a horrible shock. But they had sold all they had and there was no way back to Dushanbe. The exodus has continued through the early years of the 21st century, but a scattering of German families still remains.

The coming of so many Slavs and Europeans changed Dushanbe profoundly. It became recognizably Soviet, part of the shared world that stretched from Vladivostok to Krasnovodsk. There was a botanical garden, cinemas and a zoo filled with animals supplied by Moscow. The mobile projector van brought films even to the villages, where the whole population would turn out on hot summer nights to watch Indian box office hits, whose mixture of romance, skulduggery and seductive song and dance routines was wildly popular, as they are today.

Many girls cut their hair, put on European dress and went to university. They loved their new freedoms and married at 21 instead of 17, often having some say in their choice of husband. 'I felt I was the luckiest girl in the whole world,' remembered one teacher. 'My great-grandmother was like a slave shut in the house. My mother was illiterate. She had 13 children and looked old all her life. For me the past was something dark and horrible, and whatever anyone says about the Soviet Union that is how I see it.'

The relationship between Moscow and this most southern republic, grounded in empire, flowered as such and remained entirely on Russian terms. The lingua franca of the city was Russian, and the new urban generation began to grow up knowing Russian better than Tajik. Those without Russian had no chance of a decent education or more than a manual job, so village Tajiks were often at a disadvantage, unable to better themselves. Politically, even educated, successful Tajiks were last among equals in Soviet-wide structures. They hardly ever took senior posts in other parts of the

Union, in the army or in the political apparatus around the Kremlin. Some prestigious occupations, like working for Aeroflot or Intourist, were also almost completely closed to Central Asians.

While the Union was in its heyday, however, most urban young Tajiks did not stop to question it. Cut off from the outside world, with nothing to compare their lives against but those of their parents, they felt themselves immensely privileged.

Another Country

Drive south out of Dushanbe along the Qurghan Tappa road, and the elegant stuccoed buildings and small apartment blocks soon give way to farms and roadside bazaars. As the road leaves the city limit it cuts through an outcrop of rock pitted with tiny holes, each one hiding a bird's nest. Beyond this twittering wall of song one can see green hills dotted with horses and brown fat-tailed sheep, sharp as cut outs in the clear light. This is the Fakhrabad pass, the gateway between Dushanbe and the settlements of Qurghan Tappa, Kabodian and Shahr-i Tuz that were old a thousand years before Dushanbe was any more than a village.

The villages of the south, built on ancient sites, look as though they have stood forever formed of the dust of the plains. Most, however, especially in the Vakhsh valley actually date from the 1950s when tens of thousands of Tajiks from the mountainous east were forcibly moved to the lowlands to work the cotton plantations. Compulsory migration had started as early as the 1920s, as a means of getting labour to where it was needed, but increased immensely after the war had beggared the Soviet Union. Cotton was in short supply and the hot, sunny Vakhsh valley seemed just the right place to break new ground.

The mahajarat-i ijbari or forced migration began in 1952 and lasted more than 20 years. It is remembered by many as the harshest time they ever endured.

The first to be evacuated were the very highest villages of the Pamir, which cling to the mountain walls at over 4,000 m. Then came the highland regions of Bartang, Darvaz and Gharm. Whole populations were ordered to collect their things and walk down to the road where they were put into trucks and driven to the plains. Livestock were herded down alongside.

In the lowlands, there were neither houses, nor food, nor clean water for the fifty thousand or so people who arrived in the initial migration. They scraped holes in the ground to shelter from the sun. More than a quarter, perhaps more, died in the first few months, mainly of dysentery and heatstroke. Children and elders could not breathe in the scorching dust and died in disproportionate numbers. People killed their animals and ate as much as they could before every single head of sheep and cattle perished in the heat. The wages the migrants had been promised did not come through, in many cases, until 1958 – six years after the deportations began.

Despite these catastrophic beginnings, the migration continued. Successive waves fared better as families moved in with relatives who had gone before them and there were fewer fatalities. The manner of deportation, however, changed very little. The last mountain people to be rounded up were the Yagnobis, a people living in a long, narrow fold of mountain above Dushanbe. From the main road it takes four days by donkey to reach the inner Yagnobi villages, which are built of the rock of the mountains and cut off for more than half the year. The deportation officers waited until deep winter, when the huts of the Yagnobis were banked in by snow, then they suddenly dropped military helicopters into the valley. The Yagnobis were given an hour to pack their quilts and pots, then put into the helicopters and flown to a kolkhoz on the banks of the Amu. They were set to work in the plantations in one of the hottest inhabited places on earth, and forbidden to return to their mountain homes for 15 years.

The Kaleidoscope Twists

Those who survived the deportations put down new roots. The villages they built were given patriotic, Soviet names, like Rah-i Lenin (Lenin's Path), Oktyabrsk, and Bolshevik. People of common origin stayed clustered together, village by village, yet outsiders often lumped them together, calling them all the mountain peoples 'Gharmi', after the town of Gharm, a trading centre of substance in ancient times.

The mountain people added new pieces to the old mosaic of the plains that run all the way to the border with Uzbekistan. One distinctive group in this mosaic is the local Arabs, who believe they arrived with the armies of Islam in the 7th century. There are also local Tajiks, Kirgiz, Turkmens and great numbers of Uzbeks, especially in the borderlands. Gradually, the incomers learnt new languages and married into other groups, whilst retaining their own identity. Having struggled to survive, the mountain people's perseverance paid off. They built up prosperous farms and fine homes. They began to buy cars and television sets.

Awake from this deepest sleep

In the 1980s changes began to stir in the deep heart of the Soviet Union. Far away in Russia, in Eastern Europe, intellectuals and others demanded reform. In Soviet Asia too, many young people wanted to take control of their lives, and nowhere more so than Tajikistan.

In Dushanbe, urban intellectuals wanted urgently to revive Tajik language and culture, eroded by the long Soviet years. They wanted too to mend their broken ties with Iran and Afghanistan, the other Persian-speaking countries. Young people were thrilled when Persian pop music arrived in Dushanbe – like that of the Afghan star Ahmad Zahir and the Iranian Gugush.

The proximity of Afghanistan gave an extra dimension to the unfolding of a new Tajikistan. From 1979 to 1986, Soviet troops had fought a disastrous war in Afghanistan and some Central Asian conscripts had been changed profoundly by the experience. They not only saw a world outside the Soviet one, but they met Afghans who spoke their own languages, shared their traditions and even, occasionally, were related to them through the generation that had crossed the Amu for fear of the Bolseviks in the 1920s and 1930s.

Village of Zumand in a side valley of the Varzob

From the villages of Tajikistan came yet another force for change – devout young men bent on reviving Islamic belief and learning. For generations, Tajiks had been saying their prayers and teaching their children the Qur'an in secret. Now, many had had enough. They wanted to express themselves openly as Muslims, travel on hajj and see the wonders of the Islamic world that were closed to them. So it was that the underground Islamic Revival Party was founded. Many of its members were the sons of the displaced mountain families, or 'Gharmis'. The movement attracted a new generation of young unemployed men who were tired of the narrow opportunities of village life.

On the snowy morning of 24 February 1989, hundreds of intellectuals and students met in Dushanbe to demand that Tajik replace Russian as the state language of Tajikistan. It was the first ever demonstration organized by the people, not by the government. It went peacefully and well and heralded a remarkable era. Tajikistan, the poorest republic in the Soviet Union, began to speak out.

Tajikistan began to produce probably more independent newspapers than any other republic, despite lack of paper and printing equipment. Some estimate that as many as 40 independent titles went into print in the late 1980s. Journalists discussed openly the issues of the day and printed poems and stories from Iran and Afghanistan. Political leaders sprang into being; new voices for a new time, like the articulate, charismatic Akbar Turajanzoda and the shrewd Davlat Usman. While other Central Asian capitals inched cautiously towards the future, a new energy raced through Dushanbe.

The Unravelling

On 19 August 1991, two thousand miles away from Dushanbe, Mikhail Gorbachev's rivals in Moscow staged the putsch that finally brought down both him and themselves. The USSR began to splinter, with republic after republic breaking away.

On 9 September, Tajikistan declared independence. Thousands of demonstrators arrived in Dushanbe from the villages, bussed in by the Islamic Revival Party. They settled at the Lenin statue on Lenin Prospekt. Country folk, they unrolled their quilts, lit fires and cooked rice in their pots, watched by the astonished Soviet city. Some read the Qur'an while others chanted the poem by Muhammed Iqbal that caught the mood of the time:

The East is no more than a trail of dust,
Nothing but a dying breath,
Awake! Awake from this deepest sleep.

In every corner of the earth, life stares without hope.
Awake! From India, to Samarkand, to Iraq and Hamadan.
Awake! Awake from this deepest sleep.

Men hoisted a rope around the Lenin statue tugged to and fro until – early the next morning – it came crashing down, the first Lenin monument in all Central Asia to fall.

The political leadership was nowhere near able to lead a brand new country. Almost all Tajiks were poor and impatient for change. More than half the population was under sixteen years old. President Nabiev was 59 and a man of his Soviet times. He smoked and drank to excess. He put in the briefest appearance in the office, turning up late and drifting home after lunch. He commanded no army or any of the usual state structures. When the new political forces began mass demonstrations at Shahidan Square on Lenin Prospekt (by now renamed Rudaki), Nabiev did nothing.

The demonstrations grew until, in the spring of 1992, fifteen thousand people gathered at Shahidan outside the Presidential Palace, camping by night, singing and

Demonstration in Dushanbe [4th September 1991]

chanting by day. Very many of the demonstrators were displaced mountain peoples, the 'Gharmis' and supporters of various opposition parties including the Islamic Revival Party. They shouted for Nabiev's resignation; some called for an Islamic state instead. Nabiev, drinking heavily, dropped out of sight all together. The crowds spilt out of the square and down Rudaki.

Nabiev's inner circle drew on an old Soviet-era strategy. They organized a counter-demonstration and bussed in hundreds of villagers from one of the poorest parts of the country, Kulob. They massed in Dusti Square on Rudaki (where the Foreign Ministry stands) less than a mile from the first demonstration.

Then Nabiev's people handed out guns to its own side.

In the early summer of 1992, people all across the plains of southern Tajikistan armed themselves in terrified self-defence as the centre collapsed, giving way to a coalition 'National Reconciliation Government'. Local militias formed. Trusting no one, they barricaded off their towns and villages with concrete slabs and old beds. Many crossed the border into Afghanistan to buy cheap guns. The complex mosaic of the population began to split, with village against village, local Uzbeks against local Tajiks, Kulobis against 'Gharmis', supporters of the old regime against the new Islamic Revival Party.

Fighting reached the main southern city of Qurghan Tappa in early September, when four or five thousand armed farmers and shepherds closed in. They divided the city district by district, dragging farm machinery and concrete blocks across the lanes. In Dushanbe, President Nabiev finally appeared, announced his resignation and slipped out of the city in the boot of a car, never to return.

Even now, it might have been possible to stop the tide of war, had there been enough outside support for a peaceful settlement. But the reverse happened. According to military commanders and politicians of every colour, weapons began to pour into southern Tajikistan as regional powers backed the groups they thought would further their advantage.

The forthright President of Uzbekistan, Islam Karimov, made no bones about his views. He had openly sneered at President Nabiev for his 'weakness' in allowing his people to demonstrate, and was terrified that political Islam might gain ground in his own country. Numerous witnesses testify that Uzbekistan supplied weapons by the planeload to ethnically Uzbek parts of southern Tajikistan. Later on in the war, soldiers in Uzbek army uniforms were operating openly even on the streets of

Dushanbe. Despite such testimony, the Uzbek government has repeatedly and angrily denied any part in the war.

Russia also sided with the fallen Nabiev and his kind against the new Islamic revivalists and their allies. All manner of supplies came via Russian troops who had served in Tajikistan as part of the Soviet army and were now left behind by the collapse of the USSR; the 201st Motorised Division (which still has a base in Tajikistan) and the Border Forces (withdrawn 2005). Many Tajik commanders report that the cash-strapped and hungry Russians never missed an opportunity, renting out their tanks and crews by the hour to one militia and then switching sides as the money ran out.

Some field commanders also report receiving weapons from the Afghan mujahedin group, Hezb-i Islami but not in great quantities. 'We had to pay for every bullet,' remembered one 'Gharmi' fighter. 'They got everything they needed. We did not stand a chance.'

War unrolled across southern Tajikistan through the autumn. Militias looted and burned their way through the southern farmlands, driving thousands of families from their homes. Those who could, fled to Dushanbe or to the mountains. Some escaped to relatives in Uzbekistan, Kyrgyzstan and Turkmenistan – where many still remain to this day. But thousands more – the 'Gharmis' – were trapped on the southern side, with nowhere to run except the river Amu.

By December 1992, 90,000 men, women and children were camped along the river, huddled against the winter cold. As the gunmen closed in, they jumped into the Amu. On planks lashed together on old tyres and tractor doors, they floated across to Afghanistan and safety.

Three days later, a column of troops marched into Dushanbe and captured the Presidential palace for a new man few had heard of. Emomali Rahmon, a farmer's son from the poor, remote region of Kulob suddenly found himself President of Tajikistan with the unspoken support of Russia and at least partial backing from Uzbekistan. Behind him came hundreds of village Kulobis, taking a share of the capital that many had never seen.

A guerrilla war continued mainly in the mountains, where forces of the new government shelled towns and villages it considered disloyal. Opposition forces, meanwhile, regrouped in Afghanistan where they found a natural affinity with the mujahedin of Ahmed Shah Mas'ud, the Afghan commander who had done so much to bring down the Soviet-backed government in Kabul. The Tajik opposition set up their headquarters in the little Afghan border town of Taloqan, led by a cleric Said Abdullah Nuri. From there, they slipped back across the Amu into the mountains, very much in the style of the mujahedin. What began as a fitful partisan campaign became, in time, a successful effort to bring the war to Rahmon. By the middle 1990s, the United Tajik Opposition had seasoned commanders based permanently on Tajik territory, the ear of the United Nations, an experienced team of peace negotiators and a lively radio station.

The UTO sustained its fight against the government for four years. For ordinary Tajiks, this unstable period was a miserably difficult time. Many had lost family members during the war, and the country was on its knees economically. Jobs were almost impossible to find. Public services, like schools and hospitals, were in a shocking state and business nearly non-existent. Worst of all was the feeling of unease. Gunmen openly walked the streets. Murder, robbery and kidnapping were rampant. Gas and electric and water were often cut and the winters were long, dark and frightening. No one knew what would come next.

Emomali Rahmon and Said Abdullah Nuri signed a UN-brokered peace deal in 1997. It was the formal end to the war, and much more. The accord gave the opposition a substantial slice of power and made legitimate the Islamic Revival Party. Tajikistan became the first Central Asian country with a legal, pluralist political system and the UTO finally came home.

The Peace

Considering the bloodletting and atrocities that had taken place, it says much for Tajikistan that reconciliation came about relatively fast. Of a population of five and a half million, about twenty thousand people had died, and around one-in-ten people had fled their homes. Yet by the end of the war,

Russian tank in the river, Kala-i Husein

almost everyone had returned. Numerous villages – some without a single house left standing – were rebuilt, and thousands of other properties that had been occupied by people other than their owners had been given back.

In mountain towns like Tavil Dara, where almost every building was razed, the sense of community is astonishing. Families are again living next door to families once their bitter enemies. Tajiks have no desire to dig up the mass graves that lie untouched. That is for religious and cultural reasons, but also perhaps for reasons of temperament. The war is over, and no one likes to look back.

Crossing New Frontiers

Tajikistan has had to re-invent itself yet again in the decade after the war. Economic desperation has forced thousands of young men off to Russia to find work, mainly in bazaars or on building sites. This mass migration has been exceedingly difficult. Tajiks, especially in Moscow and St Petersburg, have been attacked by racists, frequently murdered, and sometimes killed by the police. They are endlessly harassed, accused of smuggling opium, shaken down for bribes and forced to live rough in railway wagons.

Yet the money these workers have brought home has done wonders for the economy at home. Many families only survive on remittances from Moscow; but others have bought houses and land and set up businesses. The thousands every family spends on wedding parties and commemorations for the dead brings money into the bazaar through food, gifts, musicians and the like. Many who have spent time in Moscow come back with changed attitudes, a less traditional outlook, and greater confidence than their uncles and elders at home.

Kulma Pass – Chinese frontier with Muztaghata in the background

Tajiks strive too – with success – to make money through trade with their neighbours. The road to Kashgar, in western China, is now open allowing traders (Tajik and Chinese citizens only) to make the rough and vertiginous journey over the Pamirs through the Kulma pass – at 4,000 m, surely one of the highest bus stops in the world. Huge quantities of Chinese goods are available, especially in Dushanbe, at much cheaper prices than they are elsewhere in Central Asia.

Trade with Afghanistan is also developing. Tajiks import wheat, oil and tea from the Afghan side at the river crossing at Panj-i Poyon. Enterprising young Tajiks also make the short journey by barge to find work on Afghan building sites and otherwise do business. The common language and culture makes it easy for Tajiks to find their feet in Afghanistan and many Afghans too live on the Tajik side. The United States has put up the money for a road bridge to span the Amu at Panj-i Poyon – a project that will transform opportunities for both Afghans and Tajiks.

Relations with the Tajiks' western neighbour, Uzbekistan, however, are very poor. After helping President Rahmon to power, the Uzbek government has done nothing to support Tajikistan as it struggled through the post-war period. There is no air travel between the two countries – on Uzbek orders – and Tajiks are generally not granted Uzbek visas. Tajiks who do cross the border are often threatened by the police, bribed and sometimes arrested. Business, naturally, is almost non-existent. This sour relationship is extremely damaging to both countries. From the Uzbek government point of view, Tajikistan is still an undesirable country, even at peace, because of its freer atmosphere, relative political dynamism and more relaxed business climate.

The Bigger Picture

The terrorist attacks in New York and Washington on 11th September 2001 opened a new chapter in the story of Central Asia. Suddenly the outside world, politicians and journalists, came scrambling to the region because of its closeness to Afghanistan. For years, Tajikistan had been quietly supporting the anti-Taleban forces of Ahmed Shah Mas'ud in northern Afghanistan – now, suddenly, so was the United States.

President Karimov of Uzbekistan quickly made a deal with the Pentagon and handed over an airbase, Karshi-Khanabad, as the springboard for the US invasion of Afghanistan. 'K2' remained the main supply base for the US Afghan operation until 2005, when the Uzbek army shot dead large numbers of demonstrators in the Uzbek city of Andijan. Relations between Tashkent and Washington collapsed and Russia and China stepped quickly in as President Karimov's new friends.

Tajikistan has tried to keep its political footing in all this upheaval. It has kept decent relations with Russia, whilst welcoming US interest and financial help. Tajikistan is 'a key American partner' said US Assistant Secretary of State, Richard Boucher, in Dushanbe in October 2006.

The Opium Corridor

An important feature of contemporary Tajikistan is the rise of the drug trade, especially in heroin. Traditionally, Central Asians use a mild form of opium as a way to relax; but it is big business that drives the scene nowadays. Bordering the opium fields of Afghanistan, Tajikistan is the ideal corridor between the Afghan frontier and the northern markets of Russia and beyond.

In the mid 1990s, the confiscation of a kilo or two was significant. Now, seizures of 100 kg are commonplace. The UN estimates that perhaps fifty tons of heroin passed through Tajikistan in 2004 – about a third of the Afghan output – making Tajikistan one of the busiest heroin corridors in the world. Production in Afghanistan is still extremely high and growing. Turkmenistan and Uzbekistan, which also share borders with Afghanistan, have become lively opium routes too, but the state control on information in both these countries makes it harder to assess the extent.

Several factors have contributed to the growth of the heroin trade, beyond the geography of the region and the power of the market. Poverty means that some Tajiks cannot resist the opportunity of making a quick dollar. Often they have little idea what they are getting in to when asked to carry a 'package' to an airport or abroad. The deep corruption in official circles, as elsewhere in Central Asia, contributes to the trade. Add to all this the wild, remote terrain of the Tajik-Afghan border and it is not surprising that the heroin business is flourishing.

There is much discussion in Tajikistan about how the changing political scene may affect the narcotics business. Up until 2005, Russian border guards patrolled the Afghan-Tajik border, as they had since the coming of the Russian army to the region more than a hundred years ago. Now they have been replaced by Tajiks. Although few doubt that the Russians took their cut, many believe that the change of command will open up the frontier still further to drug couriers. The Tajik guards, though, say they will actually control the border more tightly as they know the terrain far better and speak a common language with the villagers in the borderlands.

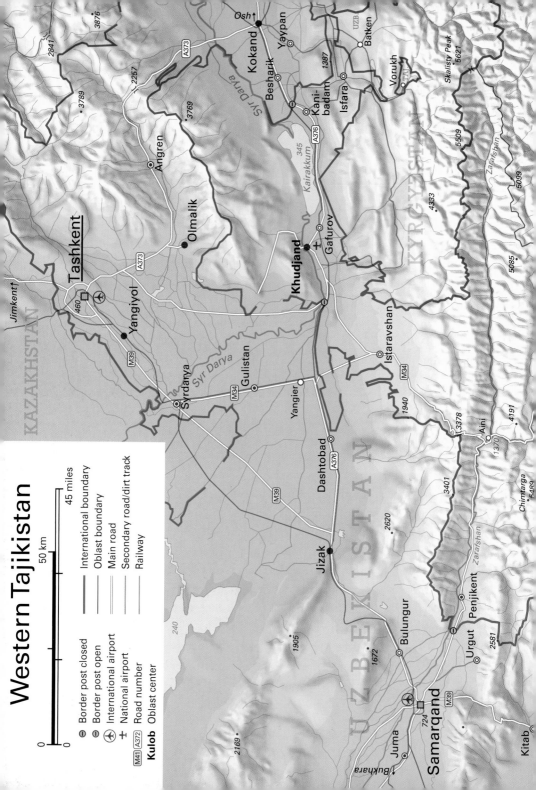

Western Tajikistan

0 | 50 km
0 | 45 miles

International boundary
Oblast boundary
Main road
Secondary road/dirt track
Railway

ⓘ Border post closed
ⓘ Border post open
✈ International airport
✦ National airport
M41 A372 Road number
Kulob Oblast center

KAZAKHSTAN

UZBEKISTAN

KYRGYZSTAN

Jimkent↑
• 2841
• 3876
• 3789
• 2257
Angren
• 3769
Olmalik
Tashkent
460
A373
Yangiyol
M39
Syrdarya
Syr Darya
Gulistan
M34
Yangier
A376
Dashtobad
M39
Jizak
• 2620
• 1905
• 2169
• 240
Bulungur
• 1672
Juma
↑Bukhara
Samarqand
724
M39
Urgut
Penjikent
• 2581
Kitab
Zarafshan
• 3401
Aini
• 1370
• 4191
• 1940
• 3378
Istaravshan
M34
• 4333
Skalisty Peak
• 5621
• 5509
• 5085
• 5099
Chimtarga
• 5489
Zarafshan
Khudjand
Gafurov
A376
345
Kairakkum
Syr Darya
Kokand
Osh↑
Besharik
Yaypan
• 1387
Kani-badam
Isfara
Vorukh
Batken
UZB
A373

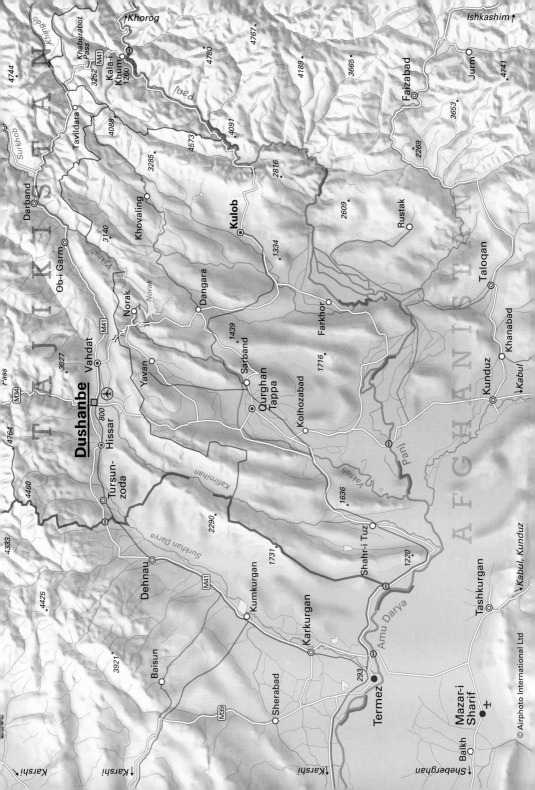

What now

Tajikistan has begun the 21st century with much more vigour and hope than one could have imagined. Dushanbe seems miraculously transformed from the city of the early 1990s when bread and even salt were hard to find and most residents went hungry and afraid. Tajikistan has a political opposition and many political personalities. The press is far freer than in many neighbouring states, and for all their isolation, Tajiks tend to be more switched on to the issues of the day than most other Central Asians.

That said, there are deep problems too. The Rahmon administration, in power for more than a decade, has moved from insecurity to confidence, slowly rolling back dissenting voices and making it almost impossible for other parties to climb the political ladder.

The presidential elections of November 2006 were uninspiring. Opposition parties, including the Islamic Revival Party, pulled out as they believed the process unfair. There was 'no genuine competition ...[and]... only nominal choice' reported the OSCE Election Observation Mission. 'The lack of any serious campaign and credible alternatives undermined this election to a degree that it did not provide an adequate test of Tajikistan's commitment for democratic elections.'

Schools and hospitals are in horrendously poor condition, outside the private facilities used by the elite. Many teachers are terrifyingly ignorant and children often sit through years of schooling learning very little. Many of the brightest and best Tajiks leave the country, to Russia but also to the US and elsewhere. The infrastructure of Dushanbe and elsewhere is crumbling. Even in the city centre, in the shadow of the Presidential palace, water supplies to ordinary homes are limited. The daughters of the house fetch filthy water from the river Vakhsh for cooking and washing. Typhoid recurs each year. There is no gas and many households keep a paraffin lamp against the frequent electricity cuts.

As I write, Dushanbe is yet again changing. The old central bazaar – Barakat – is being cut back and glassy new shop fronts are springing up. There are plans for a clutch of smart hotels, an aerial park and an immense new Presidential complex. Many residents are sceptical. They think the money could be better spent. But the government is determined to transform the city. Look around now at the older parts of the city, the parts that really tell the story, they may not be there on your next visit.

A Walking Tour of Dushanbe

Dushanbe is a little-known but attractive city in the heart of Central Asia. It is full of space, light and colour and has much old-world charm. Many local people have had little contact with foreigners and are extremely kind and hospitable, welcoming complete strangers to their homes. Dushanbe, backed by some of the highest mountain ranges on earth, is the ideal jumping off point for adventures around this beautiful country.

Dushanbe, at an elevation of 800 m above sea level, has a continental climate, extremely hot in summer, with a short, snowy winter. For most of the year there are clear blue skies and sunshine.

The city is set in a broad, fertile valley; the impressive Hissar range of mountains lies to the north, with saw-toothed peaks rising to 4,000 m that can be seen from the city. Fifty or so kilometres to the east are the foothills of the Pamirs. The city looks particularly beautiful in winter, when all the hills are snow covered. A fine view of the city and surrounding mountains can be had from Victory Park (Pobedy Park).

Traffic in Dushanbe is relatively light but fast-moving, and pedestrians should be careful. Streets are clean and main roads are generally lit at night, though there are occasional power cuts. Normal precautions should be taken, but Dushanbe is a safe city, with almost no street crime and attacks on foreigners are virtually unknown. It is perfectly normal to walk the main streets at night and feel unthreatened.

The buses are cheap and run very frequently between about seven in the morning until eight in the evening. Away from the main thoroughfare, Rudaki Avenue, there is a network of minibus (marshrutka) services that are efficient and cheap. There are plenty of taxis. In addition to the yellow official taxis, many private cars work as taxis. It is fine to use them, but check the price first. There are many restaurants of varying quality right across the city and more are opening all the time. It is possible to buy most items you might need in the markets and supermarkets, and there are plenty of small shops at street corners.

On the downside, the water supply is intermittent and can be polluted. Typhoid is a serious problem in the summer and tap water should be avoided. Hotels tend to be expensive, though several are currently undergoing renovation programmes.

Local police sometimes stop pedestrians and often stop cars and extort "fines" from motorists for supposed faults with their cars or driving errors. Occasionally, this happens to foreigners. If it does, stay calm and polite and show your documents. Do not hand over any money. Ask to see their senior officer and suggest they contact you through your embassy. If all fails call your embassy. It is a huge advantage to speak Tajik or Russian and to dress respectably. If the police can see you are confident and know what to do, they will probably back off. Keep the emergency telephone number of your appropriate embassy handy. Always carry your passport.

Highlights

• A stroll down Rudaki Avenue, admiring the neo-classical buildings, enjoying the flowers and trees, stopping off at a café, such as the Café Istanbul or Choikhona Rokhat to watch the world go by.

• Go on one of Goulya's Sunday walks, enjoy the fabulous places visited, and meet people who can give you the low-down on what is going on in the city.

• Walk in Central Park, have a shashlik, see local families enjoying a day out at the funfair and playing sports.

• Visit the superb Museum of National Antiquities, learn about the history and culture of Tajikistan, and view the magnificent reclining statue of Buddha, the largest in Central Asia. A new ethnographic museum is in an adjoining building.

• Visit the museums on Tolstoy Street, including the house of the celebrated writer Sadriddin Aini, and poet Mirza Tursunzoda and the musician Ziyadullah Shahidi.

• Go to hear Shashmaqam, the classical music of the Muslim world.

• Enjoy the scents and bustle of the bazaars at Shaikh Mansur (the 'Green' market) and the Barakat with the superb array of fresh and dried fruit, vegetables, and everything else imaginable.

• Go to Victory Park and look out over the city and the surrounding mountains.

• Visit the Bactria centre and buy some of the handicrafts made by women from high up in the Pamir region.

The Majlis or Parliament building

• Go to the Artists' Colony, view the paintings and carvings, meet the characters there, have a vodka with them, and perhaps buy a painting or a carving.
• Visit the Suhrob Art Gallery, and buy a present from the shop downstairs.
• Eat at La Grande Dame Brasserie (top end) or Oshi MChS Café (local café).
• Visit the Russian Orthodox Church, followed by the wonderful 15th century Yaqub-e Charki mosque and medrassa in the eastern suburbs.

City Layout

Rudaki Avenue runs north to south through Dushanbe for a little less than four kilometres, so all the main sights are within walking distance. A good starting point

for sight seeing is the Presidential Palace at the side of Shahidan Square, which stands on the junction with Ismoil Somoni Street. This large beige coloured building was originally the head quarters of the Tajik Communist Party, and its design is in the Soviet style, with a dash of the orient provided by decoration on the façade and fountains in the gardens to the front of the building. It is surrounded by high railings, and there are always armed guards outside.

Presidential Palace (top)   *Russian Orthodox Church*

President Emomali Rakhmon's motorcade sweeps through the gates each morning and evening, when as all other traffic is halted by the police to make way.

At the start of the disturbances that lead to the civil war in the 1990s, this square was the centre of demonstrations, with thousands of people camped out for fifty days.

Rudaki Avenue, North

From the Presidential Palace, go north up Rudaki Avenue. On the left is the Chinese embassy. The embassy is next to a road junction and a left turn leads towards the main entrance to the National Botanical Gardens, about 400 m from the intersection. The entrance fee is 1 Somoni. The gardens stretch for a kilometre, parallel to Rudaki Avenue. Although somewhat rundown and unkempt, they are pleasant and peaceful. There are many mature trees and walkways, and towards the back of the park there are excellent views over the Varzob river valley to the mountains and hills to the north and east of the city. On the riverside, there are four tree trunks carved into gnome-like personages. There is a large glasshouse conservatory, which houses the small national collection of exotic trees and bushes. The building is only opened for visitors by request. The gardens were founded by one of the many Germans who contributed to the development of Dushanbe; Konstantin Redlich, who imported plants from every continent. Some notable species include flowering magnolia trees, raspberry brambles and aloe vera patches.

Continuing north along Rudaki from the Chinese embassy, next on the left is the Orienbank. Opposite is the Vastan nightclub and restaurant, with Plazma the best internet café in town, up some outside stairs. Internet access is 4 Somonis per hour. Next on the right is the Lohuti Theatre, a grand theatre in the Russian style. The exterior is neo-classical and inside the impressive marble-floored auditorium are pictures of the great Tajik actors of the past. There is also a fine chandelier in the vestibule and inside the main theatre is plush, with a balcony and boxes, which overlook the stage, for the more important members of the audience to sit in. Upstairs great care has been taken to renovate the intricate woodcarving and painted ceiling. The theatre is now mainly used for sponsored concerts. However, there is a little cabaret restaurant on the second floor that often features live music quartets.

Further north up Rudaki on the right side is the large and popular Choikhona Rokhat Restaurant. The front part is on two storeys, open air, but under a very ornate ceiling painted in the Persian style. It is a good vantage point from which one can watch the world go by, especially in summer. Elderly men with Second World War medals pinned to their quilted coats sit for hours and talk with passers by. Waitresses wear national dress and serve moderately good and relatively cheap food.

After the Choikhona Rokhat, turn left for the Haji Yaqub mosque and medrassa, whose silver dome is clearly visible from Rudaki Avenue. It is named after Haji Yaqub, a Tajik religious leader, and this large mosque was built, mainly with Saudi money, starting in 1990, on the site of an earlier mosque. The driving force behind the construction was a famous and charismatic Tajik politician, Akbar Turajonzoda, who after studying abroad became a leading figure in the reform movement during the 1980s. He was appointed Qazi Kalan, the highest official religious authority in Tajikistan in 1989. The mosque became the informal head-quarters of the anti-communist alliance or opposition during the civil war. Visitors are welcome, and earnest young medrassa students will help people, while welcoming the opportunity to practice their English language skills on all who enter.

Further up on the same side of Rudaki is the Avesto Hotel. Set back amidst formal gardens it is a Soviet-era classic and there is some fine stained glass in the foyer. On the opposite side of the street is Café Merve, a popular café serving pizzas, burgers, cakes and good ice cream. Next door is the Orima Supermarket, which stocks a range of imported food, popular with expatriates. (There is another branch of Orima at the lower end of Rudaki Avenue.)

Slightly higher up Rudaki are the fine neo-classical facades of the main campus of Dushanbe University, and 500 m further on the right is the Presidential dacha set well back in wooded grounds, closely guarded by soldiers.

Opposite on the left is the Tojik Matlubot building, home to the Aga Khan Foundation, including the offices of its offshoot, the Mountain Societies Development Support Programme.

In a side street turning off Rudaki at 9, Firdousi Street is the NAVO Centre of Music and Poetry, the Academy of Shashmaqam, run by the respected Tajik musician Abduvali Abdurashidov. Shashmaqam is the classical music of the Muslim world. Abdulvali has given concerts of classical Tajik music internationally. He runs a school for young Tajik musicians, teaching them to play Shashmaqam on traditional instruments. The students also study poetry, history and Persian literature. Concerts are held occasionally. Visitors are welcome, but they should make an appointment first. The e-mail addresses are navo@mail.ru and navo@tajik.net.

City map of Dushanbe

Banks
Agroinvest	1 A5
Orienbank	2 B3

Cultural
Artists' colony	3 C2
Bactria Centre	4 D5
Modigliani Art Salon	5 C5
NAVO Musical Academy	6 C2
Salon Silk Road	7 C4
Suhrob Art Centre	8 B3
Ampitheatre	9 B3
Circus	10 A3
Zoo	11 B3

Embassies
Afghanistan	12 C4
China	13 C3
France	14 B1
Germany	15 B1
Great Britain	16 C3
India	17 C4
Iran	18 C4
Kyrgyzstan	19 B2
Japan	20 B5
Pakistan	21 C2
Russia	22 A3
Switzerland	23 B2
Turkey	24 C5
Uzbekistan	25 C3
USA	26 A4

Government Buildings
Majlis	27 C4
Ministry of Foreign Affairs	28 C4
OVIR	29 A6
Palace of Nations	30 B4
Post Office	31 B4
Presidential Dacha	32 C2
Presidential Palace	33 C3
Medical University	34 B2
State University	35 C5

Health
Diagnostic Centre	36 A6
Prospekt Clinic and Cardiology Hospital	37 B2
Russian Military Hospital	38 C2

Hotels
Avesto	39 B2
Dushanbe	40 C5
Tajikistan	41 B4

Markets
Barakat	42 B4
Green [Sheikh Mansur]	43 C5

Monuments
Aini	44 C5
Rudaki	45 C2
Somoni	46 B4

Museums
Aini	47 B3
Bekhzod	48 C5
Ethnography	49 B3
Firdausi Library	50 C4
Gurminj Musical Instruments	51 C4
National Antiquities	52 C5
Shahidi	53 C3
Tursunzade	54 C3
Writers' Building	55 B3

Religious
Haji Yaqub Mosque	56 B2
Jewish Synagogue	57 B4
Roman Catholic Church	58 C6
Russian Orthodox Church	59 D5
Seventh Day Adventist [formerly Lutheran]	60 A6
Yaqub-i Charki Mosque	61 D5

Theatres
Aini Opera and Ballet	62 C4
Jomi Theatre	63 B4
Lohuti	64 C3

Transport
Airport	65 D6
Bus stations Varzob	66 B1
Bus stations Nazarshoev	66 D6
Railway Station	67 C5
Tajikistan Airlines	68 C4
Turkish Airlines	69 C5

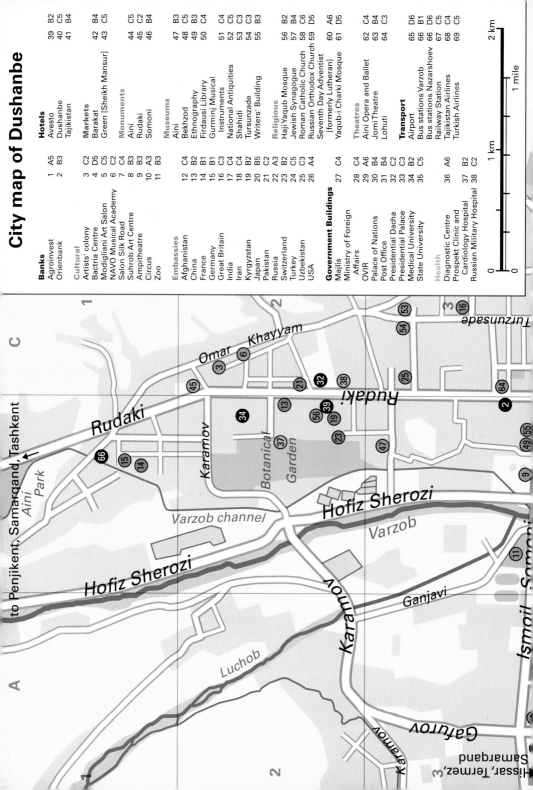

Running parallel to the east of Rudaki Avenue is Omar Khayyam Street. At this northern end, No. 13, is the Artists' Colony. The entrance is through a small gate to a garden with the studios in the houses on either side. Most of the studios are occupied by artists, who trained in Russia during the Soviet period and exhibited in the USSR. The artists are happy to sell direct – expect to pay US$400 – US$1,000. Even if you do not wish to buy, it is a refreshing experience to meet this group of bohemians. You will be made very welcome and certainly be offered a glass of vodka or two.

There are also studios with potters and traditional wood carvers. Expect to pay US$70 for a wooden casket. A purchase from here will be unique, will help artists who are struggling financially, and will help to sustain the renaissance of Tajik culture. A good idea of the range of art can be found on www.tajikart.com.

Further south Omar Khayyam merges into Mirzo Tursunzoda Street. At a crossroads with Loik Sherali Street, there is a short continuation to the east of Loik Sherali, leading after 50 m to a turn to the left. Immediately on the right is the Shahidi Museum. It is the former private house of Ziyadullo Shakidi, a distinguished Tajik composer, who lived here for 33 years, until his death in 1985. He wrote songs, operas and symphonies very much admired in Soviet times. His daughter Munira, who speaks good English, is pleased to talk about her father, his music and the historical context in which he worked.

Munira took part in the demonstrations in the area known as Shahidan Square, in front of the Presidential Palace, and is a passionate proponent of Tajik culture. Her grandfather was also a Persian intellectual, who died in Stalin's gulags. Munira arranges concerts in the delightful garden, and devotes herself to a foundation for music and art called "Peace Through Music".

Further down Tursunzoda Street to the south, at the junction with Loik Sherali Street is the Tursunzoda Museum, dedicated to Mirzo Tursunzoda, a distinguished poet and writer, and a prominent figure in the Soviet era. The museum includes his old house and a gallery next door, filled with memorabilia and his books. Open Tuesday to Saturday 10–4.

Also on Tolstoy Street is a museum dedicated to Sadriddin Aini (1878–1954), a celebrated poet and one of the central figures in modern Tajik history.

Aini was born in Bukhara in the 19th century and recorded the huge transitions of his land, from emirate to Soviet republic. Aini's account of his traditional Bukharan upbringing has been translated into English (*Sands of Oxus: Boyhood Reminiscences of Sadriddin Aini*, trans. John R. Perry and Rachel Lehr. Bibliotheca Iranica. Literature Series, No. 6, 1998). As the emirate began to collapse, and the floundering Amir threw scores of intellectuals into jail, Aini was arrested and lashed. A photograph of his mauled back became a symbol of the cruelties of old Bukhara for the generation to come. Aini wrote too of the iniquities of the new regime and remained a respected, independent-minded man of letters throughout his long life. He settled in Dushanbe, where he wrote quantities of fiction and became founder of the Tajik Academy of Sciences in 1950. The museum contains his furniture, library, pictures, and photographs.

Rudaki Avenue, South

Returning to the Presidential Palace, cross the road to the south west corner of the Ismoil Somoni Street junction with Rudaki on the south side, is the Suhrob Art Gallery, where paintings by local artists are for sale at reasonable prices. You may ask for a discount, but bartering is not generally encouraged here. The gallery has four floors of paintings, and the corridors and stairwells feature some outstanding examples of Soviet era "collectivist" art. At ground level, a separate entrance leads to a small state-run shop, which is a good place to buy souvenirs, including all kinds of craftwork, ceramics, wooden items and embroidery. Closed Sundays.

On the left side of Rudaki is the Mayakovsky Drama Theatre, currently closed for renovation.

On the right side of the street, just south down Rudaki from the Suhrob Gallery is a Soviet style, three-storey department store named TSUM. It is now privately let out to a variety of commercial shops selling household and electronic goods, furniture, photographic equipment, souvenirs and gifts. For those perhaps seeking an unusual gift there is a shop on the top floor, which sells fresh water pearls.

At the junction of TSUM, on Fateh Niyazi and Rudaki Avenue, there is a subway, which crosses beneath the street, and in the underpass the city centre's flower sellers ply their trade. The blooms are either imported from Iran or are locally grown. There is usually a wide range of flowers on offer, many arranged in a very ornate manner. Prices tend to be expensive and a bunch of a reasonable size might set you back US$30 or more, but the Tajiks love flowers and it is customary when visiting a Tajik home to bring flowers or chocolates as a gift to the host.

Continuing southwards there are a number of good shops and cafés in the next section of Rudaki Avenue, leading to the junction at Shotemur Street. The cafés include the Maxx, Eurasia Restaurant and the Istanbul Café. Turning right at the junction, the Tajikistan Hotel is reached after 100 m. Opposite the hotel, and occupying the corner with Rudaki Avenue is Lenin Park. This green and pleasant area is very popular for walks among mature trees, and there is also an amusement park with a ferris wheel and roundabouts, a basketball court for pick-up games, a football pitch, and numerous shashlik stalls. Overlooking all is a large statue of Lenin. The park is one of the places Tajiks congregate during national high days and holidays, when many people just take the air or promenade on sunny days.

Continuing west along Shotemur for another 500 m there is a good view on the left of the construction of the grandiose Palace of Nations. It is an enormous building, with Grecian pillars and an imposing appearance, being built on the site of the former Russian army barracks, which played a key role in the civil war.

Returning to the junction of Rudaki Avenue and Shotemur Street, and crossing over to the eastern side of Shotemur Street, the first turning right is Bokhtar Street. On the left by the law court is a fascinating private Museum of Musical Instruments. The museum was established by a famous Tajik actor, Guzming Zaukebekov and it is now run by his son Iqbol. It is small with four rooms, filled with an interesting array of musical instruments from the Pamirs, Afghanistan and China. Entrance fee is 5 somoni. The Silk Road souvenir/art gallery is nearby.

Firdousi Library

Shopping Centre

Continuing along Shotemur Street for 100 m, the children's park is reached on the left side of the junction with Avenue Turzunzade. Large cement gnomes and cartoon character statues for climbing are any mother's nightmare of broken teeth and bones. Opposite is the entrance to a small lane leading to Marian's Guest House. It is top of the range and at US$100 per night, it provides excellent accommodation. It is also a centre for information about activities in and around Dushanbe. It produces a weekly *What's On In Dushanbe*, distributed by e-mail. Linked to the guest house is Goulya's Outdoor Adventures which organises activities such as city tours, walking trips, skiing in winter and excursions to cultural events and buzkashi.

Continuing back to Rudaki Avenue, there are attractive stuccoed buildings on the left facing Lenin Park.

The avenue reaches Dusti (Friendship Square) formerly known as Azadi. Dominating all is the giant statue of Ismoil, often called 'Somoni', a cult hero of modern Tajikistan. Tajiks like to believe that his crown is solid gold. Ismoil was a great king of the Somonid dynasty (see page 91). His statue was erected in 1999, displacing a figure of the poet Firdousi, which had replaced one of Lenin in the early 90s. The ancient figure of Ismoil has been developed to be a symbol of modern Tajikistan as part of the government's efforts aimed at nation-building. On the curve of the Square is the Central Post Office. Some people have had their post box numbers since the early 30s, and there is a long waiting list to get a box.

Behind the statue of Ismoil is a garden with formal flowerbeds. Immediately behind the statue is a bronze map showing the spread of the family of Tajiks, including those in Afghanistan and Uzbekistan. Opposite the statue are the Ministry of Foreign Affairs and the Majlis, or Parliament, with fountains and flowerbeds in front. The Kino Theatre completes the square.

Statue of Ismoil (Somoni)

In 1992, during the demonstrations that heralded the civil war, Azadi (now Dusti) Square was where the supporters of the government congregated, in opposition to those in front of the Presidential Palace, the area formerly known as Shahidan Square, less than a kilometre away (see page 52).

Rudaki Avenue veers southeast at this point, continuing as a wide boulevard with a central area for pedestrians. There are further impressive buildings on both sides of the road, including the Firdousi Library on the left, just beyond the junction with Bukhara Street. If you use the entrance on Rudaki, you will find a small crafts shop that features woven crafts not usually found in other souvenir shops – baskets, wooden bowls, stands and wonderful outsized hats.

Three hundred metres further down on the left is a square dominated by the striking façade of the Aini Opera and Ballet Theatre. Inside is a very large auditorium with pictures of Aziza Azimova and other great Tajik ballerinas and actors. Inside is a wide marble staircase leads to the auditorium, with typical Russian plush décor. During Soviet times the theatre was a venue for touring companies from other parts of the Soviet Union, but these days is not so well frequented, although concerts are performed there for smaller audiences, sponsored by aid agencies.

On the south side of the square is the Vakhsh Hotel. During the Second World War, this was a hospital, and was briefly the headquarters of the United Tajik Opposition which fought against the government in the 1990s.

If you continue down the street of the Vakhsh Hotel, passing the opera on your left with the park behind it, you will come to Modigliani, an art gallery designed "Euro-style", and featuring some first class silver jewellery among other crafts. Their gallery space hosts international as well as Tajik exhibitors, and they regularly have Sunday afternoon receptions.

Continuing down to the intersection, you will come to the Green bazaar, properly known in Tajik as Shaikh Mansur bazaar. On that corner is the Tajik Stock Exchange, and just a few paces down the same side of the street, there are two excellent antique/vintage stores, selling jewellery, old Soviet memorabilia, Czech glassware, and Russian icons. The shops may be dusty and crowded, but the proprietors really know their stuff,

On the other side of the avenue is the turning into Rajabov Street. A hundred metres on the right is the excellent Museum of National Antiquities. This is a must for visitors to Dushanbe. Recently renovated, the centrepiece is an enormous reclining Buddha, excavated from a site near Qurghan Tappa in the south of the country.

Just beyond the DBD restaurant is a turning into Husravi Dekhlavi Street. Two hundred metres on the left is the Green Bazaar. It is bustling with stalls selling fresh fruit, vegetables, dried fruit and spices, even the occasional fish aquarium. A hazard in this area is the metal wheelbarrows pushed vigorously by small boys taking produce around the market.

On the outskirts of the city are much larger bazaars, selling everything from cars to gold. The largest is the Korbon bazaar in the southern suburbs.

Just behind the bazaar, at 22, Mirzo Rizo, is the Bactria Centre, run by ACTED, a French NGO, which has done much to encourage eco-tourism in the Pamirs. The Yakhouse, which is part of the Bactria Centre, sells Pamiri craftwork made by a woman's co-operative from Murghab in Badakhshan. Purchases are attractive and make excellent gifts, and also help some of the poorest people in the country. Art and photography exhibitions are also held here.

At the bottom end of Rudaki, on the left is the building site for the Serena Hotel, due to open in 2009. This will be a top of the range hotel, part of the chain built by the Aga Khan's organisation, with very high standards of service. Further down on the left is the office of Turkish Airways.

Rudaki Avenue ends at Maydon-i Aini (Aini Square). On the island is a statue of Aini, flanked by panels depicting a colossal Soviet-era monument showing various scenes – including a man breaking the chains of slavery, and a Bolshevik soldier shooting a basmachi rebel.

On the north side of the square is the rather quaint Bekhzod National Museum. It includes a fine mosque pulpit from Istaravshan, and a lot about the aluminium industry. Entrance 5 Somoni.

On the south side of the square is the enormous Hotel Dushanbe.

The main road to the left leaving Maydon-i Aini leads to Norak (70 kms), Gharm (190 kms) and Khorog (525 kms in summer). The first turn right goes to the airport (7 kms) (see separate section).

To the south from the square after 300 m is the Railway Station. Built in the grand Soviet manner, it has some fine bevelled and stained-glasswork in the main waiting area. Many Russians trying to escape from the civil war in the 1990s were stranded in coaches here.

Ismoil Somoni Street

Returning to the Presidential Palace, Ismoil Somoni Street leads westwards. The road is very wide for 500 m; there is an underpass to reach Barakat Market on the left. Like the Green Bazaar, it is busy, but less cramped. The large hall has stalls selling all kinds of fruit, honey, bread, meat, cheese and dried fruit. Around the south side there are stalls selling clothes, including traditional coats and hats, and wooden cribs.

Opposite, on the right hand side of the road going westwards, about 150 m from the Presidential Palace is the Writers' Union Building, with sculptures on the façade of great figures in Persian literature, Aini, Firdousi, Omar Khayyam and others.

After another 150 m on the right is the Ampitheatre and water park, still under construction. There is a very ornate arch for decoration. It will be a venue for meetings and concerts. There are fine views of the Jezira University and the mountains beyond.

Near Barakat Market at 26, Nozim Khikmat Street is the Jewish Synagogue. It can also be approached from the Tajikistan Hotel. Going westwards from the hotel, there is a turning to the right. After two hundred metres there is an opening on the left from

Writers' Union Building   *A Dushanbe street scene*

which the synagogue can be seen. This is one of the older buildings in Dushanbe. It is the last remaining synagogue in Tajikistan. It includes an impressive prayer hall, a separate one for the Ashkenazis, and a library with old texts in Hebrew and Persian. Most Jews have now left for Israel, but there is a small, poor, but active group who remain. They welcome visitors.

A further kilometre on the right is the Zoo. These were popular throughout the Soviet Union, and in its heyday had animals from every continent and all species from Central Asia. In the civil war, with acute food shortages, the animals were either eaten, or starved to death. It is now a sad, rather smelly place, with cramped cages of local animals, mainly bears.

Over the bridge that divides the "Center" of town from the other districts, you come to Komsomol, or "Friendship Park", which has a large lake with pedaloes, pleasant walks, and shashlik stalls.

A further five hundred on the left is the Circus, a permanent building that once housed a vibrant permanent local circus, and was a venue for touring circuses from other parts of the Soviet Union. It is now very run down, but the circus tradition is maintained by enthusiast, Asheer Rajabov, who runs a circus school there. The students give demonstrations on Monday and Tuesday afternoons, when visitors are welcome. The entrance is round the back.

On Sundays a Bird Market is held on a street, leading from Karamov Street, on the opposite side to the Diagnostic Clinic.

Victory Park (Pobedy Park)

One kilometre to the east is Victory Park. It is on a hill covered in pine trees, and celebrates victory in The Great Patriotic War (Second World War). There is a wide set of steps leading up to the wall with the victory citation. There are panoramic views over the city and surrounding mountains. Oddly, there is a Hare Krishna Temple in Victory Park, with one loyal devotee who will invite you in. The Hare Krishnas arrived in the early 1990s, along with other evangelising groups and stuck out the civil war in their temple.

The Suburbs

EASTERN SUBURBS

Continuing from the Shaikh Mansur Bazaar on Aini Road, east towards the Town of Vahdat (Kafirnihan), is the Russian Orthodox Church of St Nicholas, at 58 Drujba Narodov. It is now being renovated with the help of Russian troops. The main building is a good example of a traditional Russian Orthodox Church, set in pleasant gardens.

Nine kilometres further along Aini Road, continuing east is a turning to the right to the Guliston Jamoat (suburb) with the splendid Hazrati Mavlom Yaqubi Charki Mosque. It is a mosque, medrassa and mausoleum set in attractive gardens with mature trees, some six hundred years old. Most of the buildings are modern, but part of the mosque dates from the sixteenth century. The mausoleum is dedicated to the founder, a Sufi theologian, who translated the Qur'an into Persian. He came from Charkh near Ghazni in Afghanistan and died in Dushanbe in 1447. It was closed in Soviet times, but is now a centre for people who can profess their faith openly. Large numbers of people attend Friday prayers. It is a delightful place to visit and wander around the courtyards, the mosque and the gardens. The mullahs are welcoming.

SOUTHERN SUBURBS

Twelve kilometres along the main road south to Qurghan Tappa is the Seventh Day Adventist Church (formerly the Lutheran Church) at 117, Borbad Street. It is a typical German church with clean lines, an elegant spire and a sense of spaciousness inside. It was the centre of worship for the German community, who contributed so much to the building of Dushanbe and life in the country generally (see section on history). Nearly all the Germans have left now and the church is now run by the Seventh Day Adventists, who are very welcoming to visitors.

THE SAMANIDS

Huw Thomas

The Samanid dynasty were a line of Persian kings, spanning the ninth to the tenth centuries. The Tajik nation is considered to have emerged in this period, and President Rahmon has picked up the Samanids as a national motif. A huge statue of Ismoil, the most famous Samanid king, stands in Dushanbe opposite the parliament. The highest peak in the Pamirs is also called after Ismoil, and even the Tajik currency is called Samani (often pronounced 'Somon').

The Samanids are special because they invigorated the Persian world after a century of Arab domination. Their founder, Saman Khuda, was a local man – from Balkh in what is now northern Afghanistan. The dynasty was the first in Central Asia to create a strong, professional army rather than press-ganging local farmers at time of war. They governed competently from their seat at Bukhara, and their 100-year rule was a time of relative peace and commercial expansion. Trade in all sorts of goods flourished, with huge caravans travelling to and fro across the Muslim world and beyond. The slave trade in particular became immensely lucrative, with Turkic capitives taken off the steppes and sold as soldiers. The Samanid rulers controlled the business tightly, licensing slave dealers and collecting taxes on all sales.

With this new wealth came rapid urban growth. Villages became large merchant towns. Suburbs grew. Agriculture expanded to support the population, with new and better irrigation systems of pumps and canals.

During this prosperous time, the great houses of learning in Central Asia flourished, enriched by the exchange of ideas, books and scholars of the Arab world. With Europe in the dark ages, Biruni of Khorezm calculated longitude and latitude, recorded solar and lunar eclipses and mapped much of his world. He visited India and wrote a detailed study of his findings. He spoke Aramaic, Greek and Sanskrit and well as his native Persian and Arabic, the language of all educated people in the Muslim world. Avicenna (Ibn Sina)'s medical encyclopaedia became the standard textbook for European doctors for the next 500 years.

To Tajiks, and other Persian speakers, the most important figure of this time was Abduqasim Firdousi, the founder of Persian literature. Firdousi wrote the vast epic poem Shahnameh, that tells the tale of the heroic struggles between Iran and Turan (the lands north of the Amu). Many of the most common Tajik names (Rustam, Suhrab and many others) come from these legends.

Dushanbe Travel Advice

Accommodation

Many hotels and B&Bs are under construction in Dushanbe. Existing hotels are mainly from the Soviet era – often expensive and not very good, though there are exceptions (see below). Consider perhaps the following.

HOMESTAYS

This can easily be arranged privately, or though travel companies and some NGOs like ACTED. (See Introduction.)

RENTING APARTMENTS

This can be a cheaper and more flexible way of living in Dushanbe. Listings can be obtained from 'What's on in Dushanbe', an information pack for foreigners produced from Marian's Guest House. Contact marians@tajnet.com

HOTELS

If you do stay in a hotel, it is usually easy to find a room, but some fill up on public holidays or if there is a visiting head of state. At the time of writing all hotels with the exception of the Hotel Tajikistan and Hotel Mercury take cash only, in dollars or euros. Plumbing is sometimes poor – this is a city-wide problem.

Aini Opera and Ballet Theatre   *Soviet Tajik cinema poster*

Top of the Range

Dushanbe Serena Hotel

www.serenahotels.com

The Aga Khan Development Network is constructing a 5-star hotel with 95 rooms (suites and apartments), banquet hall and all conference and gym facilities, at the lower end of Rudaki Avenue; due to open March 2009. The Serena Hotels have an international reputation for excellence.

Hyatt Regency Dushanbe

E-mail: dushanbe.hr@hyatt.com; www.hyatt.com

Located in the city centre, on the grounds of City Park and adjacent to Lake Komsomol. Contemporary facilities. Spa and fitness centre. Opens July 2008.

Hotel Khayon One, 7, Boktar Street

Tel: +992 93 216229   E-mail: rayon@tajnet.com

New, clean, comfortable hotel. Pleasant staff. English spoken. Internet access, sauna. TV international channels. Bed and breakfast: Single US$50 per night, double US$70, luxe US$100–120.

Hotel Khayon Two, 1, Kuybeshov Street

Tel: +992 93 230761

Also new, clean and comfortable. Staff speak English. TV international channels. Internet access. Sauna. Water problems occasionally. Bed and breakfast: Single US$50 per night, double US$70, lux US$100.

Hotel Mercury, 9 Leo Tolstoy Street, 734003

Tel: +992 372 244491   Fax: +992 372 244137

E-mail; info@hotel-mercury.tj; www.hotel-mercury.tj

Luxurious. Credit and debit cards accepted. Recent reports are of good standards and service and value for money.

Marian's Guesthouse, House 67/1 Shotemur Street

Tel: +992 93 5050089   E-mail: marians@tajnet.com

Bed and breakfast US$100 per night. Australian Marian Sheridan, the owner, has developed a comfortable home from home, with seven ensuite air-conditioned bedrooms. Cats and guinea fowl wander around an attractive garden with water features. Swimming pool. International TV channels. Internet access. Sauna and laundry. Staff friendly and helpful. Driver service in the evenings. Marian can arrange letters of invitation and airport pickup. To find the guesthouse, go down Rudaki Avenue from the north, turn left into Shotemar Street, pass three right turns, the last being Tursunzoda Street, and take the next alleyway to the right, opposite the Children's Park. At the end of the short alleyway are black and white gates to the Guesthouse. Goulnora Razykova (Gulya), the very efficient administrator, speaks excellent English. She produces *What's on in Dushanbe*, a newsletter on social and cultural events, restaurants, schools, sport, apartments for rent, and items for sale; ask Gulya to e-mail you the latest edition before you arrive.

Tajikistan Hotel, 22, Shotemur Street
Tel: +992 93 270092   E-mail: hotel@tojkiston.com
Bed and breakfast: Single US$50 per night, double US$80, luxe US$130.
The former Intourist hotel has made strides in becoming a reasonable place to stay. It is a seven-storey block, with half the rooms having views over Central Park. The view is good, but it can be noisy at weekends. Helpful reception staff speak English. Russian *dezhurnayas* (floor managers) are obliging. Food reasonable. Business Centre with internet access. ATM 24 hours. TV international channels. Accepts debit and credit card payments. Rooms en suite adequate. It is to be hoped the plumbing will improve after renovations; it was dire.

This hotel was home from home for officers of the Russian 201st motorised rifle division in the 1990s. More recently it was popular with journalists covering the war in Afghanistan, post 9/11, and for many months was home to a French Army logistical corps.

OTHER HOTELS
Avesto, 7, Rudaki Avenue   Tel: +992 372 212357
Bed (breakfast not included) with ensuite bathrooms : Single US$55 per night, double US$68, luxe US$86–98. Set back amidst attractive formal gardens and fountains, this large hotel is from the Soviet era. Décor is dreary, apart from some fine stained glass windows in the foyer. Staff are undemonstrative. Hot water is a problem in winter, water in general a problem in summer. They will provide a bucket bath! TV international channels. ATM. Shop. Restaurant uninspiring.

It is popular with the new rich, who turn up in their Volgas with darkened windows, the men wearing full length leather coats. Usually dull, the hotel erupts into noisy life when this lot start partying.

Somoniyon Hotel, 2, Shesto Pavlova Street (near Circus)   Tel: +992 372 344878
Bed and breakfast: Single US$50 per night, apartments US$100. Very recently opened, looks good. Clean. Reasonable restaurant and bar. Internet. TV international channels. English spoken, polite staff.

Middle–low range

Hotel Dushanbe, 7, Rudaki Avenue   Tel: +992 372 212357
A large Soviet era hotel on Aini Square, at the bottom end of Rudaki Avenue. Spacious and clean. Rooms reasonable, but basic. TV international channels. ATM. Service expressionless. Fine stained glass windows on the stairway. Can be electricity and water problems.

Single/double US$25, luxe US$50–60, breakfast US$3.

If you really want to impress your friends, and you will need a lot of them, try the enormous Presidential Suite at US$250 per night.

Vakhsh Hotel, 24, Rudaki Avenue   Tel: +992 372 210510
A good site near the Aini Theatre. Recent renovations seem to be mainly a coat of thick paint everywhere. Was a hospital in the Second World War, and headquarters of the opposition at the end of the civil war. Rooms reasonable size. Service grim. In a part of Dushanbe subject to water shortages. Restaurant poor.

Bed and breakfast: Single US$25, lux US$45.

Museums

The Museum of National Antiquities, 7, Rajabov Street (off Rudaki Avenue)
Tel: +992 372 271350
Open: Mon–Fri 0900–1700, Sat 0900–1600   Admission 10 somonis.
This is a must for visitors to Dushanbe. Recently renovated with French sponsorship, exhibits are well set out, and some of the descriptions are in English. Staff are helpful. Excellent shop selling books, jewellery, pottery and gifts. Visitors required to wear over slippers (provided).

The highlight is the Sleeping Buddha in Nirvana, at 16 m long, the largest such figure in Central Asia. It dates from the Kushan period, around AD 500. It was excavated from Ajina-Tappa, near Qurghan Tappa, about 100 kms south of Dushanbe in 1966. Made of clay, it had to be removed in pieces, and reassembled in the museum.

The main entrance hall has two fine statues of mountain goats from the 5th–3rd century BC, and an altar from the Temple of Oxus, Takht-i Sangin, near the banks of the Amu Darya, in the far south of Tajikistan, from the 4th–3rd century BC. The coin collection features gold Alexander coins from Sughd region. According to the Greek historians, Alexander married a Sogdian princess, Roxanna.

Other highlights are frescoes from Penjikent and Bunjikat (Sogdian cities in the north of Tajikistan) and a miniature of Alexander the Great. There are artefacts from Hulbuk (now being rebuilt at Kurbonshaid in the east of the country), and from Murghab in the Pamirs.

Visitors intending to visit Penjikent and Bunjikat (now Shahristan), Hulbuk or travel in the Pamirs are advised that a visit to this museum will enhance their understanding of these places.

They have an excellent web site: www.afc.ryukoku.ac.jp/tj/

To the left of the main Museum of National Antiquities there is another building that houses the recently opened collection of national costumes and jewellery.

BEKHZOD

Tajik State Regional Museum, 31, Rudaki Avenue   Tel: +992 372 216036
Open: Mon–Fri, 0900–2100   Admission 3 somonis
Worth a visit. Still as it must have been in Soviet times. Descriptions in Russian and Tajik. The highlight is a superb minbar (pulpit) from Istaravshan in the north. There are some heroic pictures of Lenin talking to Tajik women and of Tajik nomenclatura. Plenty of natural history, agricultural artefacts and costumes. There is a good mock up of the interior of a Tajik house. Another exhibit is a model of a cell with hostages, illustrating the Soviet view of the horrors perpetrated by the previous regime. The top floor is given over to the achievements of the aluminium industry.

Fragment of fresco with heroic scene from Penjikent

Gurminj Museum of Musical Instruments, 23, Bokhtar Street
Tel: +992 372 233210
No set opening hours. Just go into the little courtyard, and somebody will come out
(Museum is near Argilys restaurant, and next to some law courts.)
Admission 5 somoni

Established by famous Tajik actor Guzming Zaubekov, it contains an array of
musical instruments from the Pamirs, Afghanistan, Turkey and China. Some are
extremely old, pre-Islamic. His son Iqbol now runs the museum. Tajik instruments
include the *tablak*, *buf* and *boira* (used only at weddings) The *tutuk* is played by
shepherds to the sheep at lambing time, and to their lovers at any season.

Iqbol does not speak English, but he can give a very knowledgable talk on the
instruments and their history. He has an ensemble called 'Shams', with four
instrumentalists and a singer. 'Shams' charge US$100 per hour for concerts. They
play Western rock as well as traditional music. Very popular with the ex-pat crowd,
they are a feature at UN parties, birthday celebrations and Aga Khan Foundation
events. They hail from the Pamir
region. Tel: +992 937 5052828 or
233210.

Museum of Ethnography, 14
Ismoil Somoni Street (opposite
Barakat market)
*(At the time of writing this museum
was closed for renovations.)*
Tel: +992 372 245759
Admission 50 dirhams
It contains exhibits of ceramics,
embroidery, woodwork, musical
instruments and jewellery.

Gurminj Museum of Musical Instruments

Ziyadullo Shahidi Museum of Musical Culture
108 Shahidi Street
Open: Tues–Sat, 1000–1600
Admission 40 dirhams
The former home of Ziyadullo Shahidi, a celebrated Tajik musician of the Soviet era who composed songs, operas and symphonies.
Tursunzoda Museum, 21, Loik Sherali Street
Open: Tues–Sat 1000–1700   Admission 20 dirhams
The museum is a celebration of the modern Tajik poet Tursunzoda, who is remembered for writing fine poetry celebrating the optimism of the Soviet era.

Aini Museum, 27 Sayid Nosir Street   Open: Mon–Fri 1000–1500
A museum devoted to the renowned Tajik poet and writer, Sadriddin Aini

Teahouses (choikhonas) and Cafés

The tea house is an ancient part of Tajik life. All towns have a central tea house, and it is more than just a restaurant. It is a meeting place, a messaging place, an informal court house, and a haven for elders who come daily for a free pot of tea.

Restaurants are opening (and closing) all the time, so no list is exhaustive. The best Tajik food is found at home – otherwise try:

Choikhona Rohat, 884 Rudaki Avenue
Tel: +992 372 217654   Open: 0700–2000
Very popular with locals and internationals alike. Serves Tajik food, such as kebab, grilled chicken, lagman and fresh tandoori bread (naan). The ceilings are all hand-painted in minute floral detail with a clear Persian influence, with fine wood carved doors and pillars. It is a large two-storey building, great for people watching from the first floor balcony. There is also a large indoor restaurant in the back courtyard, also decorated in the same style. An accomplished orchestra plays lunch and dinner hours. Cheerful waitresses wear national costume. The toilets are clean.

The food is not brilliant, but freshly cooked, best for shahliks and soups. Salads 3–5 somonis, soups 5–7, main 6–14. The menu is in Russian and English. There are some gems of translation. Try:
"Herring under fifty" at 5 somonis or
"Chicken loaf gentile from smoked bosom" at 9 somonis.

Merve Turkish Restaurant, 92, Rudaki Avenue (opposite Avesto Hotel)
Tel: +992 372 249409
Popular with locals, students, youth and the UNICEF crowd especially at lunch time.
Pizzas, snacks, Turkish kebabs, burgers, also good ice cream and cakes. No alcohol.
Good breakfasts. Clean, stainless steel tables and chairs. Snacks 2–5 somoni, main
7–10.

Morning Star, 47, Naberezhnaya Street (near Pedogogical University)
Tel: +992 372 95-111-1046   Open: Wed–Sat 0900–1600
E-mail: café@morningstarcafe.net   Web site: www.morningstarcafe.net
A little bit of America. Small café to sit in or for takeaway. Sandwiches, quiches, great
brownies, cookies, English scones and muffins. Good variety of coffees and teas. Run
by customer friendly Americans and local staff. Café is a faith based partnership
between local NGO El Shadi and an evangelical Christian NGO. Their stated aim
is to train impoverished young women to be financially independent. They have
Starbucks coffee.

Georgia Café, 29, Rudaki Avenue
Tel: +992 372 271526   Open: 1100–2300
A pleasant little café with only 5 booth tables. Georgian style food, good omelettes
2–6 somonis. Excellent mushroom julienne and passable cappuccino. Good Turkish
coffee. Full bar. Good ice cream.

Eurasia, Rudaki Avenue, next to TSUM
Charming interior, with extensive menu in English and Russian. Well trained
waitresses. A favourite with the French military contingent (so it must be passable!).
Very busy at lunch time.

Maxx Café, Rudaki Avenue, set back, almost across from TSUM
Fun "fast food" atmosphere with good hamburgers and cheese burgers.

Turkish Café, Across from TSUM.   Great fruit drinks, ice cream desserts.

Oshi MChS, 81, Popova Street
Near Ministry of Emergency. Also near petrol station in front of Tojiksodirotbonk,
Dehoti Street. Go down Popova Street 100 m on right through grey doors (not
obvious). Open: Mon–Sat, 1130–1400
Considered by some to serve the best plov, and mantou in Dushanbe. Cheap, 5
somonis per meal.

Top End Restaurants

Restaurant culture in summer goes outside, with pavement tables and beautiful fountains to cool the evening air. Some restaurants feature musicians and singers – often very loud so chose a table far away if you want to talk.

Salsa, 1, Karamov Street (corner with Omar Khayyam)
Tel: +992 372 248857   Open: Mon–Sat, 1200–2400
Carolina Torreano from Ecuador and her Tajik business partner runs this restaurant, specialising in Ecuadorian, South American and Italian food. Salads, soups, specialty dishes, good coffee, beer and spirits. Russian champagne at 25 somoni a bottle. Good ice cream, sundaes and banana splits. Clean, good service. English spoken. Mains 10–14 somonis. Alcohol expensive. Popular with expatriate community.

La Grande Dame, Corner of Bukhoro and Shevchenko Street
Tel: +992 93 5010089 or 93 5050089   www.lagrandedamecafe.com
Open: 10 till late
International cuisine, highest standard of cuisine and service in Dushanbe. Popular with the expatriate community. Starters 15–19 somoni, mains 20–37, sweets 11–15.

Argilis, 23/24 Bokhtar Street   Tel: +992 372 240541
Open: Mon–Sat, 1200–2400
Good choice of Middle Eastern, Turkish and Tajik food. Service reasonable. Energetic belly dancing on Friday nights, singers every evening from 1900. English spoken. Mains 5–12 somonis.

Choikhona Rohat

At the bakery

Kellers, 6, Ismoil Somoni Avenue
Tel: +992 372 240541
Open: Mon–Sat 1100–2300
Popular with locals. Tajik and European food, and German type beer, served by mini-skirted Russian waitresses. English spoken. Singers every evening. Mains 8–12 somonis.

Delhi Durbar, 88 Rudaki Avenue
Open: Mon–Sat, 1200–2400
Tel: +992 372 246611 / 273593
+992 917 700471
Passable Indian food. Popular buffets on Friday and Saturday nights. Part of a small chain with branches in Khudjand, Kabul and Mazar-i Sharif.

Other Restaurants

INDIAN
Ashoka, 4, Shotemur Street   Tel: +992 372 219534   Open: 1100–2300
Taj Mahal, 22, Rudaki Avenue   Open: 1200–2300

CHINESE
China Town, 30, Tursunzoda Street. Decent Chinese food.
Lunchen, Near the Opera House   Tel: +992 372 273701   Open: 1000–2200
Reasonable Chinese food in magnificent converted town house with high ceilings. Comfortable. Reasonable service. Huge TV set showing Chinese programmes. Chinese tea ceremony every day. Main 10–12 somonis.

DBD, 22 Rudaki Avenue   Tel: +992 372 278926
Iranian and local food. Music and dance in the evenings.

Sievish (Paparazzo), 70, Rudaki Avenue   Tel: +992 372 249221
Open: 1000–2400   Newly opened. Italian style.

Sorbon, 83/1 Tursunzoda Street   Tel: +992 372 249221   Open: 0800–2400
Reasonable Tajik food. Great setting in a garden with fountains.

Tea waitress

Night Clubs

(Note some local women in these clubs are commercial sex workers.)
Port Said, 114, Rudaki Avenue   Tel: +992 372 248802
Open: Mon, Wed, Fri 2100–0400   Admission 10 somonis.
Disco and restaurant. Main 15–30 somonis. Popular with expatriate community on Friday nights.

Vastan, 84 Rudaki Avenue   Tel: +992 372 240936.
Open: 2000–0400, every day except Mon.
Disco and restaurant. Tajik and international food.

Dior, 1, Ismoil Somoni Street   Open: Tues, Thurs, Fri, Sat, 2100–0400
Admission male 15 somoni, female 10 somoni

Triada, 7, Ismoil Somoni Street   Open: Tues–Sun, 1900–0300
Popular with expatriate community

CASINO, linked to **Farogat** (formerly Jomi Jomshad) restaurant. Lenin Park (opposite Tajikistan Hotel). Casino and restaurant.
Reasonable food. Entertainment. Once owned by the Head of the State Anti-Narcotics Agency, now in prison for possession of weapons.

Embassies

ALL VISITORS TO TAJIKISTAN ARE RECOMMENDED TO REGISTER WITH THEIR EMBASSY OR ONE PREPARED TO REPRESENT THEIR INTERESTS.

China, 143, Rudaki Avenue   Tel: +992 372 242188   Fax: +992 372 510024

France, 17, Varzob Street, 734017
Tel: +992 372 215037 / 217405 / 217855 / 246723   Fax: +992 372 510082
E-mail: cad.douchanbe-emba@diplomatie.gouv.fr

Germany, 16 Varzob Street, 734017
Tel: +992 372 212189 / 212198   Fax: +992 372 240390
Consular Section Tel: +992 372 212181   Fax: +992 372 212245
E-mail: info@dusc.diplo.de   Website: www.duschanbe.diplo.de

EMERGENCY: 917 727583 / 84
The German embassy provides information and assistance to German and Austrian citizens, and other EEC citizens, not represented by their country in Tajikistan.

Great Britain, 65, Mirzo Tursunzoda Street
Tel: +992 372 242221 / 241477   Fax: +992 372 271726
E-mail: dushanbe.reception@fco.gov.uk
Website: www.britishembassy.gov.uk/tajikistan
Opening hours: 0830–1300 and 1400–1700 Mon–Thurs, 0830–1330 Fri
EMERGENCY: Duty officer mobile (emergencies only) +992 917 708011
The British embassy provides information and assistance to British citizens, and Commonwealth and EEC citizens, not represented by their country in Tajikistan.

India, 43, Bukhoro Street   Tel: +992 372 217122 / 211803 / 213988
E-mail: eoi@netrt.org   hocdushanbe@tojkiston.com

Iran, 18, Bokhtar Street   Tel: +992 372 210072 /2 12059   Fax: +992 372 510089

Japan, 80, A. Khabibullo Nazarova Street, 734025
Tel: +992 372 213970 / 213724 / 235608 / 235609 / 212059
Fax: +992 372 235610 /+992 44 6005478   E-mail: embjpn@embjpn.tojikiston.com
Open: Mon–Fri, 0900–1300 and 1400–1800

Pakistan, 1-3 Dostoyevskiy St, Dushanbe
Tel: +992 37 2246839 / 2230177   E-mail: pareptaj@rs.tj

Russia, Abu Ali Ibn Sino 29/31
Tel: Embassy Reception +992 372 211005, Consular Dept +992 372 211015
Fax: Reception +992 372 211085, Consular +992 372 211165
E-mail: rambtadjikk@rambler.ru

Switzerland, 3, Tolstoy Street
Tel: +992 372 247316   Evenings/emergencies: +992 372 241950 / 247316
E-mail: duschanbe@sdc.net   www.swisscoop.tj
Sat phone: 00 873 761 846760, Sat fax: 00 873 761 243037

Turkey, 15 Rudaki Avenue   Tel: + 992 37 2210275 / 2210036 / 2211485
Fax: + 992 37 2510012   E-mail: turemdus@tajik.net

United States of America
109A Ismoil Somoni Street,
Main Tel: +992 37 2292000 (24 hours)
Fax: +992 37 2292050
Duty officer: +992 917 701032
E-mail: usembassydushanbe@state.gov.
http://dushanbe.usembassy.gov/
Consular Section: 109A Ismoil Somoni Street
Tel: +992 37 2292300 or through main
switchboard   Fax: +992 37 2292309
E-mail: DushanbeConsular@state.gov
Non-emergency service for American citizens:
Mon–Fri 1400–1600
EMERGENCY: Duty Officer 917 701032

The American embassy provides information and assistance to American citizens. Canadian citizens are entitled to register with the US embassy. This does not entitle them to routine consular services, but keeps registrants updated about the general situation in Tajikistan and neighbouring states, including emergency travel and health warnings

Internet Cafés

There are internet cafes all over Dushanbe. Normal charges are 4 somoni per hour. However, many do not have internet services, but just gaming computers.

The best is: PLAZMA, 84 Rudaki Avenue. 24 hour internet service, cheaper rates from 2200 to 0600.

Mobile Phones

These have become commonplace in Dushanbe. The coverage is limited to the main cities and towns, but the range is increasing all the time. Check the roaming facility of your mobile.

Sim cards can be purchased, or mobile phones hired. International calling facilities are available on local mobiles. Top up cards can be purchased in all main towns.

A few companies insist the phone is in the name of a local resident. If so you will need to arrange this with a local person.

Friendship House

Soviet Tajik cinema poster (right above)
Radio House (right below)

Companies are:

Indigo, 23, Tursunzoda Street. Tel: 232121, Fax: 232123
Web: www.indigo.tj   Costs vary from a wide variety of
tariffs, ranging from US$24–106 per month

MLT, 57, Rudaki Avenue. Tel: 700500, Fax: 214224
Web: www.mlt.tj

Babilon, 8, Somoni Street. Tel: 918 616161
E-mail: info @babilon-m.tj; www.babilon-m.tj

Todjphone, 89, Rudaki Avenue.
This is the cheapest, but reports of service are poor

Satellite Phones

Useful if you are planning long mountain trips where mobiles will not work. Probably
best to buy or hire in your home country, very expensive in Tajikistan. The system
used by most NGOs is Thuraya.

Places of Worship

Haji Yaqub Mosque This is the main Friday mosque, just off Rudaki Avenue, next
to the Avesto Hotel. Non-Muslim visitors welcome

Yaqub-i Charki Mosque A beautiful 15th century mosque in the eastern suburbs.

OTHER MOSQUES
There are many other Sunni mosques scattered around the city.
Roman Catholic Church, House 10, Proezd 21, Titova Street (near the airport).
Tel: 234269
Priest: Juan Carlos   E-mail: JuanCarlosSack@ive.org
Services: In Russian: Sundays 10am, weekdays (except Thursday) 8am
            In English: Saturdays 6pm
More information at www.Church.tj

International Church of Dushanbe [Protestant]
50, Gagarina Street (200 metres west of Varzob Bazaar). Tel: 931 5055414
Services Sundays in English at 4pm.
Sunday school classes for children 4–12. Tel: 93 500 5326

Russian Orthodox
Church of St Nicholas, 58, Druzhba Naradov Avenue. Tel: 251297

Seventh Day Adventists, 117, Borbad Street.

Cultural Centres

Bactria Centre, 22, Mirzo Rizo (near Green Bazaar)
Tel: 2370257, 2270369, 951314205
A cultural centre, including an art gallery, shop selling handicrafts made by a women's cooperative in Murghab in the Pamirs. An educational centre running courses in French, Russian, English, German and Italian. A good place to find out what cultural events are going on in the city.

Suhrob Art Centre On the corner of Rudaki Avenue and Ismail Somoni Street (opposite Presidential Palace). First floor collection of paintings by local artists. Can be purchased at reasonable prices

Shopping

The range of handicrafts is increasing, some produced by co-operatives. The items where designs are specific to the region are particularly knitwear (socks, skull caps, scarves), felt crafts (carpets, toys, slippers), embroidery (wall hangings, purses, bags), woven carpets, ceramics, wood carvings, traditional musical instruments and jewellery.

If you would like to buy an original painting or a unique piece of carving or pottery, it is fun to visit the Artists Colony at 13, Omar Khayyam Street. To see the range of paintings: www.tajikart.com

Suhrob Art Centre

At street level below the Suhrob Art Centre, is a shop, on the corner of Rudaki Avenue and Ismoil Somoni Street. It sells a large selection of local crafts, ceramics, pottery, wooden items and traditional clothing.

The Yak House at the Bactria Cultural Centre, 22, Mirzo Rizo   Tel: 248667
Shop next to the art gallery sells local craft work mainly made by a women's cooperative in Murghab in the Pamirs.

Modigliani Art Salon, 4a Chekhov Street (opposite LG shop, behind the Opera House)   Tel: +992 37 2270474   E-mail: art_modigliani@yahoo.com
Open: Mon–Fri 1000–1800, Sat 1000–1700
A good range of local souvenirs, handicrafts, painting and jewellry.

Sales Salon Silk Road, 32, Shotemur Street (150 m from Hotel Tajikistan)
Tel: 372 274305   E-mail: rukhom@tajnet.com   URL: www.rukhom.tajnet.com
A good range of folk art, wood and clay engravings, national clothing and traditional musical instruments.

There are many small shops selling most items that a traveller might need, but do bring your own medicines. The TSUM General store on Rudaki Avenue is a three-storey department store with a wide variety of goods. On the third floor, there are some specialty counters that sell rare antique clothing and jewellery.

There are a number of supermarkets selling imported foods. Probably the best is **Orima** on Rudaki Avenue, opposite the Avesto Hotel, with another branch on the south end of Rudaki. The same items are available at lower cost at the **Safar Centre**, at the lower end of Rudaki Avenue.

The **Sitora** department store (owned by the President's daughter) on Shotemur Street has a supermarket, casino, hairdresser, pharmacy and fast food café. For photographic items the best shop is **Radoga**, at the junction of Rudaki Avenue and Shotemur Street.

Health

See warnings and health services on page 18.

If you do become ill, try –

Dushanbe Prospekt Medical Clinic, 33, Sanoi Street, Dushanbe 734001 (in the grounds of the cardiology hospital)

This clinic provides a general practitioner service, including home visits, backed up by an X-ray, diagnostic laboratory and minor injuries service. The medical staff are English speaking, western-trained and provide a 24 hour service. The clinic is well equipped, with electricity on priority supply, and only uses filtered or bottled water.

If specialist medical or surgical care is required, the clinic has an arrangement to admit patients to the Russian Military Hospital, currently sited next to the Presidential Dacha on Rudaki Avenue. The hospital has 500 beds, and is of a higher standard than others.

Consultations, including follow up is US$40, with supply of pharmaceuticals and X-ray US$20. If emergency evacuation is necessary Prospekt can arrange it.

For appointments: +992 372 243062, +992 372 243092, and +992 935 019903

For emergencies: mobile phones +992 935 000447 and +992 935 019903

E-mail: prospect-clinic@tajnet.com; www.prospektclinic.org

National Diagnostic Clinic, 50 Dekhorti Street, 734055, off Karabaeva Street, 15 km from the city centre.

The clinic provides out patient clinics and a wide range of diagnostic services, including CT scanning, endoscopy and ultrasound. The Tajik staff are friendly, but do not speak English. Consultation fee US$2, tests 3–7 somoni, X-ray US$1–5. Patients requiring in-patient treatment are admitted to the local government run hospital.

Tel: +992 372 349204, 349206, 349202 (reception), 349206 (registration)

Fax: +992 372 349200

Snow on the streets of Dushanbe

Shifo Diagnostic Clinic, Near Green Bazaar. 3 Lakhuti Street, 734025
Outpatient clinic run by local doctors. Friendly, English not spoken. Range of
diagnostic tests. Patients requiring in-patient treatment are admitted to the local
government-run hospital.
Tel: +992 372 273459, (director) 233060   Fax: +992 372 270695
E-mail: farma_dushanbe@mail.ru   web site: www.shifo.tj

NEIGHBOURING COUNTRIES TO TAJIKISTAN
There is an excellent International clinic in Tashkent, Uzbekistan, which also provides
maternity care and has a small hospital. You need an Uzbek visa to get there.

Electricity
There is usually an electricity supply but there are power cuts. The plug points are
often loose and care is needed. Use standard European 2 point adaptors.

Bus stop

Money

Some places in Dushanbe will now accept credit cards, like the Hotel Tajikistan and Hotel Mercury. Otherwise use cash. Cash can be obtained using credit cards at major banks. ATMs at: Hotel Tajikistan (24 hours)
Agroinvest Bank, Head Office
TSUM Department Store
Airport (in arrival hall, and departure hall, 1st floor)
Computer café, opposite Choikhona Rohat

There are plenty of kiosks changing dollars and euros into somonis – bring your hard currency in new, clean notes.

Postal Services

To and from Dushanbe are very slow and mail often does not arrive at all.

DHL have an office at 105 Rudaki Avenue.   Tel: 2244768, 2210280, 2244720. Expensive, efficient

UPS, Dushanbe Center, 14a Aini Avenue, 734042 Dushanbe
Tel/Fax: +992 372 235 414   E-mail: webmaster@ups.com

Bus Travel

There are cheap and frequent bus services to all parts of the country.
– Buses going north leave from the Varzob Bazaar to the north of the city.
– Buses going south leave from Nazarshoev Street to the south of the city.
At both bus stations it is possible to share taxis.

Train Travel

All trains leave from the main station. Go to the bottom end of Rudaki Avenue to Maydoni Aini (Aini Square), the road veers south for 300 m to the Railway Station.

There is a train service to Khudjand in the north of Tajikistan. The journey takes 24 hours and involves going south to Termez, crossing into Uzbekistan and via Samarkand to Khudjand. An Uzbek visa would be required and a double entry Tajik visa. Bring food. The train is dirty and you should lock up valuables. This journey is only for real train buffs. There are shorter journeys within Tajikistan.

Trains to Kulob in the east leave on Thursdays and Saturdays, and trains to Qurghan Tappa on Thursdays. If you want just a taste of train travel an easier option is to combine a bus journey with the daily train to Hissar.

Activities

WHAT'S ON IN DUSHANBE

Marian Sheridan and her colleague Gulya Razykova at Marian's Guest House produce a newsletter for foreigners on activities; classes; religious services; jobs; souvenirs; accommodation; and so forth. marians@tajnet.com

WALKS & TOURS

Goulya Petrova – Goulya's Outdoor Adventures – arranges guided walks in the countryside within easy reach of Dushanbe. Transport is provided. Meet at the top end of Rudaki Avenue at the interchange with Karamova Street, (near the Agriculture University in front of the "Zvezdnaya noch" billiard club) at 9am on Sundays. Cost US$10 and US$10–15 for transport. Contact Goulya at Marian's Guest House or e-mail: tajikoutdooradventures@gmail.com or by phone at +992 93 5050567. Book no later than the Saturday evening.

Goulya also offers city tours and to nearby places of interest, such as Hissar Fortress and Norak Dam – car excursions with English/French speaking guides. E-mail tajikoutdooradventures@gmail.com or phone Goulya at +992 93 5050567.

INTERNATIONAL WOMEN'S CLUB/INTERNATIONAL CIRCLE

Meets second Wednesday of the month at 12.30 at 149, Rudaki Avenue, 1st Floor, above Sarvar Learning Center (across the street from the trolleybus terminal). Includes special interest groups, service projects, bridge, and cooking. Visitors welcome. Contact: dushanbeiwc@yahoo.com

RUNNING/JOGGING

The Dushanbe kennel of the Hash House Harriers is part of an international network (see www.gotothehash.net) that spans all continents. They offer a chance to discover charming parts of the city or area that you otherwise would never see, meet people, get some exercise, have a lot of fun and a laugh. Walkers and runners with a sense of humour are welcome.

LANGUAGE COURSES

A number of organisations run language courses, in Tajik, Russian and Uzbek. Try the university, your embassy, or consult the *What's on in Dushanbe* newsletter.

Day Journeys from Dushanbe

In easy reach of Dushanbe, there are a number of places of varied interest. These
include:
- Superb walks in the mountains, seeing how country people live and enjoying
  their hospitality.
- Opportunities to view wildlife.
- Visiting villages where the people speak a language Alexander the Great might
  have heard.
- Visiting the site of one of the ancient fortresses of Central Asia (Hissar).
- Seeing examples of impressive Soviet industrial achievements (and some of the
  failures).
- Just sitting in the shade at a choikhona (teahouse or restaurant by a river).
- Seeing buzkashi, the wildest game in the world.

Organised Trips

One of the best ways to see the countryside and sights around Dushanbe is to
join a Sunday guided walk with Goulya's Outdoor Adventures. These walks, which
are not very strenuous, are held every Sunday, lead by English-speaking guides.
Minibuses are provided to take walkers to the various destinations, and bring them
back. Meet at 9am at the top end of Rudaki Avenue, next to the Zvednaya noch
billiard club. It is necessary to book with Goulya Petrova by the night before, tel:
+992 93 5050567, e-mail: tajikoutdooradventures@gmail.com.

These walks are excellent value at US$10, with US$10–15 for transport. The
walks are very popular, giving the visitor an opportunity to learn about other
activities, places of interest and also about the country generally.

The Varzob Valley

The Varzob valley runs due north of Dushanbe, and is the route to the Zarafshan
valley and Khudjand. On leaving Dushanbe, the magnificent Hissar mountain range
is reached very soon with views of peaks of 4,000–5,000 metres. The excellent road
follows the left bank of the Varzob River.

Some of the highlights are:

– Simply being in the mountains, similar to the Pamirs, enjoying the fresh air, the stunning views and a chance to see some traditional villages, including some where the people speak the ancient Sogdian language.
– Following the course of a clean, fast flowing river, with many choikhona, restaurants and small parks along the banks.
– The chance to go on walks of anything from two hours to three days in dramatic scenery, and likely to be the only outsider there.

THE ROUTE NORTH TO THE VARZOB VALLEY

This route follows the main road, with some deviations, as far as the Presidential Dacha, at Poguz, 52 km from Dushanbe.

Taxis can be hired almost anywhere in the city. Minibuses leave from the Vodonasosnaya bus station near the Varzob bazaar and cement works, just to the north of the city. The road passes the cement factory with pictures of Tajik heroes on the walls, and then follows the canal to the arch marking the northern boundary of the city.

After 12 km the Varzob lakes are reached. These attractive, artificial lakes, surrounded by trees are very popular with local people in the summer. There are choikhona and shashlik stalls. It is possible to swim and hire small boats. The best restaurant is the Anzob, at the south end of the main Varzob Lake. There is a road all round this lake. Entrance fee is 1 somoni.

Apart from in spring time, the earth is parched, but there are irrigation canals and trees are being planted to prevent erosion. At 20 km the valley narrows and there are the first views of the high jagged peaks of the Hissar range.

The road follows the course of the river, which runs between the steep lower slopes of the mountains. At frequent intervals there are small parks with children's play areas, and restaurants and choikhona with awnings overlooking the river. There are many splendid new dachas built by the new rich. Some houses look like fairy tale fantasies, with pointed roofs, turrets, bright roof tiles and reflective glass windows – the status symbol of the wealthy Tajiks.

There are some places to stay in what were once camps for Pioneers (the youth section of the Communist Party). These are now private and some used for visitors.

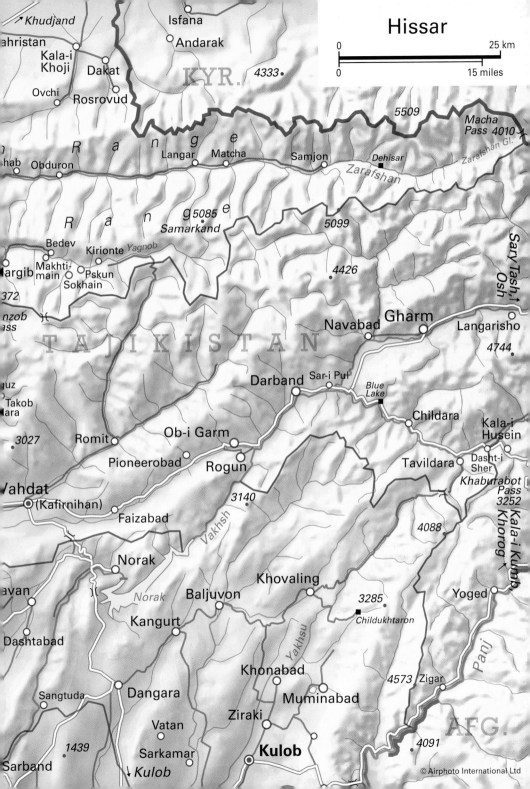

Hissar

0 ————————————— 25 km
0 ————————————— 15 miles

↗ Khudjand

Isfana
Andarak

ahristan
Kala-i
Khoji   Dakat

Ovchi
Rosrovud

KYR.

4333 •

5509

Macha
Pass 4010 ✝

Zarafshan Gl.

hab   Obduron

Langar   Matcha   Samjon

Dehisar

Zarafshan

R a n g e

Sary Tash ↑

Osh

R a n   g 5085 e
Samarkand

5099

4426 •

T A J I K I S T A N

Bedev
Makhti-   Kirionte   Yagnob
argib   main   Pskun
Sokhain

372

nzob
ass

Navabad   Gharm   Langarisho

4744 •

uz
Takob
ara

Darband   Sar-i Pul   Blue
Lake   Childara

Kala-i
Husein

3027 •

Romit   Ob-i Garm

Pioneerobad   Rogun

Tavildara   Dasht-i
Sher

Khaburabot
Pass
3252

Vahdat
(Kafirnihan)   Faizabad   3140

4088

Khorog

Kala-i Kumb ↗

Norak

Khovaling

avan

Norak   Baljuvon   3285 ■
Childukhtaron

Yoged

Dashtabad   Kangurt

Khonabad

4573   Zigar

Sangtuda   Dangara

Vatan
Sarkamar   Ziraki   Muminabad

Kulob
↓ Kulob

Sarband   1439 •   Kulob   4091 •

AFG.

© Airphoto International Ltd

GUZGARF FALLS

21 km from Dushanbe there is a path leading to the walk of 8 km (allow 5 hours there and back) to the magnificent Guzgarf Falls, which drop sheer for 30 m. It is a particularly beautiful spot in spring when the flowers are in bloom.

TAKOB VALLEY

At 33 km from Dushanbe there is a turn to the right, which leads to the village of Takob, which is 8 km after the turnoff. The road rises along a narrow valley, passing a derelict chemical plant built by German prisoners of war. The next village, after 10 km is Safidorak. Here, most of the 460 villagers speak Sogdian (see chapter on Anzob, Iskander kul and the Yagnob valley, page 127). Further on the road forks to the village of Zumand (a four-wheel drive is recommended for this 4 km section) with a population of 110 families, 960 people. This village is well worth a visit. Zumand is on a hill top at 2,000 m with views across the surrounding hills and mountains. The substantial two-storey houses are built of stone, with hay stored on the roofs. The people all speak Sogdian. They are subsistence farmers with cattle, sheep and goats, and they grow potatoes, cereals and vegetables. They are very hospitable and friendly, and there should be no problem in arranging a homestay.

The people moved voluntarily to the two villages at various times between 1870 and 1925, when conditions became too difficult in the Yagnob valley. They are proud to speak Sogdian, but the children are taught in Tajik at school. They retain some Zoroastrian traditions, particularly at weddings, when the bridal couple jump over a fire. They are very positive about their living conditions, which they consider are improving now they own their own land and the mosque has reopened. They are cut off from December to the end of May by snow. Their main concern is the lack of water, the poor road and the need for better education.

Zumand is a good example of a village with resourceful, proud, humorous and hospitable people existing on a subsistence economy. Despite living so near Dushanbe, they live in a different world, much more like that of the people of the Pamirs than the city folk.

The other fork in the road leads 2 km to the ski 'resort'. In Soviet times this was a popular place for skiers, with ski lifts and a large accommodation block. Now in winter, a few foreign skiers come up here with Goulya Petrova's staff, who bring up a generator, and the lifts clank back into action.

Judging by the gear lying around, there were plans for this to be a major resort. Now it is all a bit sad, with rusting machinery strewn about. The accommodation block is habitable in only a few rooms. There is no water, and the toilet is outside. Some metres below the main block is a sauna room, with tepid water and mice.

The slopes here are not as steep as those in some other valleys, and it is good walking country. It is a starting point for the attractive walk to the Ob-i Safed Gorge (allow 5 hours). From there it is a 2-day trek to the Romit valley.

BOTANICAL GARDENS, KONDARA

2 km beyond the turning to Takob, there is a turning to the left over a bridge at the village of Kondara to some botanical gardens. There was a proud tradition in Soviet times of botanical gardens that combined attractive gardens containing a wide range of flowers, plants, trees and bushes, with scientific research and the introduction of new species to Tajikistan. The best examples of these are the botanical gardens in Dushanbe and Khorog. These gardens at Kondara are somewhat rundown, but devoted staff try to maintain some of the standards of the past. There are attractive flowerbeds and a wide range of trees and bushes. It is a peaceful place to meander through the gardens and up the small valley beyond.

KHOJA OB-I GARM SPA

At 42 km from Dushanbe, there is a bridge across to the right bank and a good tarmac road winds 6 km up to Khoja Ob-i Garm, an enormous complex built for people to enjoy the delights of a spa. There is radon in the water, and it is claimed to have many beneficial properties. The complex is at 2,000 m, with great views over the mountains. Built in 1983, it has 700 rooms, mostly in a seven-storey block. There is a large central area, which has a pool, restaurant and massage treatment facilities. The whole place is now scruffy and rundown, but remains popular. The cost for the complete package is 250 somonis for 12 days (about US$70) or 250 somonis for 25 days. There is a charge of 3 somonis per vehicle at the entrance gate. Near the complex are some private facilities, which are upmarket with quite luxurious facilities, but charging much more.

It is worth sampling the facilities for a day, particularly to escape the heat of Dushanbe in summer. There are good walks to be had in the hills above the spa.

The site was once an important shrine. Soviet spa complexes often masked something more interesting. It was the Soviet way of de-spiritualising a place without closing it down.

PRESIDENTIAL DACHA, POGUZ

At Poguz, the President has a large modern complex as one of his dachas. Built on different levels along the bank of the river, it is surrounded by a wall, but a view can be obtained from the road. It is probably wise not to take photographs.

Up to this point the road is excellent, but it deteriorates beyond.

The Romit Valley

The Romit valley is a National Park, created in 1959, 70 km to the east of Dushanbe. It is largely an unspoilt valley with woodland, thermal springs, mountain streams and a good variety of birds and animals. It is reached by taking the main road east to Vahdat (Kafirnihan), a small post-industrial town. From Kafirnihan the road goes north through a broad fertile valley with peasant plots taking over from the abandoned factories, market gardens and trout farms. There are abandoned Pioneer camps and the Yavroz sanatorium, where it is possible to stay. In the west the word "sanatorium" denotes a place for sick patients, but in Soviet times the word was used more for a place where workers could relax.

At the village of Romit there is a turning to the left up a path through fields and homesteads to pastures beyond. The people practise subsistence farming. There is no rubbish, and nothing is wasted, e.g. brambles are not burned, but used to protect saplings and put on top of stonewalls to make them more stock proof. Cows eat vegetable peelings and cow dung becomes kitchen fuel.

The path follows the stream up a gently sloping valley through delightful woods and pastures. There is a good chance of seeing marmots and golden eagle. The walk is about two hours before the valley becomes very narrow, with the path crossing the fast flowing stream at frequent intervals. Further up the main valley there are excellent paths and better chances of seeing some wildlife.

Market at Norak

The Romit valley is a good place to come to experience being in the mountains, but without it being too testing on the legs and lungs.

Norak Dam and Resort

Norak is a popular destination for visitors from Dushanbe at the weekends in the summer. Minibuses run from Dushanbe. The road goes to Kafirnahan, and then on to the main road east to Kulob and the Pamirs. After 55 km from Dushanbe, there is a clearly marked road to the left to the town of Norak, which is 6 km from the junction. The road passes some attractive lakes before reaching Norak town, which has broad tree-lined streets and a pleasant square with *choikhonas*. The overall effect is rather spoiled by the large number of derelict factories that scatter the landscape.

Dominating all is the vast Norak dam, which rises in a series of giant walls, holding back the river Vakhsh to create Lake Norak. At 310 m it is one of the highest dams in the world. This huge lake, 70 km long and 5 wide is a reservoir for Dushanbe, and the associated hydro-electricity plant provides electricity for the city. The stored water is used for irrigating 700 square km of farmland.

This massive and uncompromising civil engineering scheme exudes the total confidence of the Soviets in the power of industry to transform society. The scheme took from 1961 to 1980 to complete. In Soviet times tourists were brought here to marvel at the scheme. The spectacle is enhanced by a number of waterfalls formed from an outflow. It is possible to go to a viewing area, just below the dam.

There is an excellent view of the lake to be had from the main road, turn left to Kulob and up the pass to a vantage point. The lake appears an impossible shade of turquoise. The view across the lake and to the far hills is impressive and worth the trip.

Timur Dara and Pairon Lakes

The road west to the Uzbek border passes through fertile land with orchards and vineyards. At 45 km from Dushanbe, at Shakrinam Settlement, is a turning to the right, leading to Timur Dara, a beautiful lake, reputedly a summer holiday destination for the emperor Tamerlane. The poor road rises for 18 km to the village of Hakimi. From there is a delightful walk of three hours to the lake, following the river through meadows and mixed deciduous and juniper woods. The aquamarine lake is surrounded by trees, with steep mountains slopes on three sides. There is a pebble beach at one end where the stream from the glacier enters the lake.

There is one steep section, but the path is generally good. Before the lake there is another path to Lake Pairon, also very beautiful, and the opportunity for a longer walk, possibly combined with some camping. There is a network of paths in these mountains, which provide some excellent treks.

Shirkent

In the Shirkent valley, north of the town of Tursunzoda, there is the chance to examine dinosaur footprints. These are fossilised footprints of Macrosaurus Gravis, a type of pangolin. The footprints are about 30 x 10 centimetres and when the eye becomes accustomed to their outline, are very impressive. There are two places where these can be seen. Both involve some steep scrambling, and the better example involves the need for a safety rope. Wise to go with a guide.

Hissar

The ancient fortress of Hissar is one of the most interesting places to visit in Tajikistan. The fortress is just outside the modern town of Hissar, 23 km from Dushanbe, just off the main road going east to the Uzbek border. The modern town has a fine new mosque, a bustling bazaar and a *hamam* (Turkish baths).

The fortress stands on a hill commanding the valley between two mountain ranges. There has been a settlement here since the Stone Age. The lines of the fortifications are clearly visible, and show the extent of a very large fortress. The gatehouse has been reconstructed, giving some idea of the scale of the walls. Outside the gates are two medrassas, the lower walls of a *caravanserai* and a sixteenth century shrine.

Due to its strategic position it had a violent history. It was destroyed twenty one times by invaders including Cyrus, Alexander, the Arabs, Genghis Khan, Tamerlane, and finally the Red Army. It was an important staging post on the branch of the Silk Road, which ran from Termez on the Amu Darya (Oxus), up the Rasht (Gharm) valley, through modern Kyrgyzstan to Kashgar and China.

Originally Hissar had been the capital of an independent khanate, but it was annexed by the Emirate of Bukhara and became the winter residence of the Kushbegi (Governor) of East Bukhara, a land stretching as far as the Chinese frontier i.e. modern Tajikistan. It retained a fair measure of independence and the local Kushbegi had high status as a key lieutenant of the Amir of Bukhara. Each summer the Kushbegi moved with his entire entourage to Karatagh in the mountains west of Dushanbe.

Visitors can explore the site for a small fee. The walls encompassed a large area, well defended at every point. There is a lake, and this with the wells, enabled defenders to hold out for considerable periods of time. On the site is a flat area now used at Navruz (the first day of spring, 21st March) for a great festival of *buzkashi*. Thousands come to watch the spectacle, and increasingly it is attracting foreign visitors. The game is more associated with northern Pakistan and Afghanistan, but the Tajiks play it enthusiastically and it is very popular in many parts of the country, as well as in Uzbekistan and other parts of Central Asia. The game involves an indeterminate number of men on horseback wrestling over a decapitated goat. It requires great skill and strength from the rider and great manoeuvrability from the horses. The winner is the rider who deposits the carcass between two posts. Before this

happens there is mayhem, with horses rearing and lurching, and whips cracking. Injuries to horses and riders are common.

Local champions also compete in gushtingiri (local wrestling) at holiday time.

In front of the gates to the fortress is a bent old mulberry tree, decorated with votive ribbons. For a small fee, the local mullah, Said Abrorkhon, will turn up on his motorcycle and recount a legend. Sometime a long time ago, perhaps in the eighth century, there was an evil magician in Hissar called Kahkahu Jodu, who took a dislike to some Arab missionaries from the holy land, and killed them all but one. The survivor was taken by an angel to Mecca, and informed Ali, son-in law of the Prophet. Ali flew straight away on his horse Hazrat-i Poyi Dul-dul and landed on a mountain near Hissar. He created a tightrope, and arrived outside the walls. There he lent on the mulberry tree, causing it to bend over. He then fought with the magician for three days before killing him. Subsequently Ali set off on his magic horse for Badakhshan, where he converted the population to Islam.

There is a holy well near the mulberry tree, dedicated to the Arab missionary who brought the news to Ali.

The excellent museum (entrance 3 somonis) is housed through the magnificent carved doors of the Medrassa Kuhna, the old medrassa, which faces the fortress. Each

Entrance to the museum at Hissar

Hissar – view of gateway,
old and new medrassas and caravanserai (right)

of the individual hujras, used by students for study and prayer, houses a different topic in the history of the area. In the former mosque are the main exhibits including a Bactrian column, catapult stones used by the Arabs, vast Ali Baba storage jars and a great range of pottery. There are short guidebooks in English.

The "new", nineteenth century, medrassa is no longer used, and is locked up, but a key can be obtained from the museum. It is worth a visit to clamber about on the walls and see the views.

The remains of a large *caravanserai* next to the museum are evidence of the importance of Hissar on the Silk Road. Within the old town walls, 200 m from the museum to the south is the sixteenth century Mahdumi Azam mausoleum, commemorating a Sufi saint. There is a lavishly decorated chaihkana near the museum. There are regular minibus services from Dushanbe. There is also a daily rail service. A combination of a minibus and train outing will give a flavour of the life of the market traders.

Tursunzoda Aluminium Works

Further along the main road at 53 km from Dushanbe is a giant Soviet industrial complex, the Tursunzoda aluminium works. This was the pride of the country, and is still making aluminium with 70s technology, reputedly consuming 40% of the electricity output of Tajikistan. The sheer scale of the enterprise is extraordinary. The site seems endless with many smoke stacks. The grounds are well kept, with lovely flower beds outside.

The town of Tursunzoda is named after Mirzo Tursunzoda, a national poet, prominent in Soviet times. He was born in the town. There is a china factory in the town and souvenirs can be purchased there.

In Tursunzoda there is the mausoleum of Khoja Nakhshoron (11th Century) built in an architectural style quite distinct from the Timurid style typical of cities such as Samarqand and Istaravshan. The building features intricate brickwork, carved terracotta inlays and calligraphic inscriptions.

Winter

Access can be had to many of the places mentioned in this section in winter. The snow adds another dimension to the scenery, and you can almost be certain you will be the only foreigner there.

IBRAHIM BEK
Monica Whitlock

Ibrahim Bek was by far the best-known basmachi commander in Tajikistan. A tall, long-eyed, black-haired man, he was born in the village of Koktash near Dushanbe in 1889, the twelfth and only surviving child of a smallholder who left him 'nothing but debts'.

When he took up arms against the Soviets in the early 1920s, Ibrahim Bek took the title Commander in Chief of the Armies of Islam. He commanded a large guerrilla force, especially among his fellow Lakai people (a tribe of Uzbeks still living south of Dushanbe.) Using the bluffs of the river Kafirnahan for cover, the basmachi harried and ambushed Red Army patrols already weak with malaria, disorientated and resented by local people. The reprisals taken by the military served only to broaden the ranks of the basmachi. Partisans were generally ordinary village folk – farmers by day and basmachi when called upon.

Each valley in Tajikistan soon had its own commander. Davlat Manbai led the basmachi in Kulob on the Afghan border, Fazel Maqsum those of the Gharm valley. By 1922, the basmachi could count on about twenty thousand men, according to Russian estimates. Even if there were, in reality, only half that number, they still constituted a very extensive fighting force.

The basmachi went from strength to strength. They drew in Bukharan officials disaffected by the regime, even Usman Khoja the first President of the Bukharan Republic. The Turkish adventurer Enver Pasha arrived to help after his fall from grace at home. On 14 February 1922 the basmachi even overpowered the weak Red Army garrison at Dushanbe and captured the city. A few weeks later, a separate group laid siege to Bukhara itself.

The basmachi did not build on their success, however. Proliferating commanders were divided among themselves: some supporting the fallen Amir Alim Khan, by now exiled in Afghanistan, some against; some Tajik, some Uzbek. Ibrahim Bek never trusted Enver Pasha; many trusted neither. Communication throughout the mountains was difficult, competition for scarce horses, money and ammunition was fierce.

The Red Army reclaimed Dushanbe in July and the basmachi fell back to the hills. Soldiers cut off supplies to the villages. Hungry basmachi extorted food from ordinary farmers with nothing to spare.

'When the basmachi were strong, we bowed before them and said they were right,' recalls one man, a bargee on the Amu at the time. 'When the Soviets were strong we bowed before them. All of them stole the grain of the poor for their fighters. What could we do?'

Once the Red Army had the upper hand, soldiers brought gifts to the villages – a little sugar, some oil, some bright satin – with the promise of more to come.

Ibrahim Bek and other commanders carried on their raids against Soviet enterprises, but the tide had turned. The Luddite nature of their campaign enabled the authorities to vilify them as simpletons, as well as religious fanatics. One successful piece of propaganda had it that Ibrahim Bek had conned the peasants into believing the imported tractors to be greased with pig fat, and this was why Muslim farmers stuck to their ox-ploughs. (In fact, these early tractors arrived with neither fuel nor spare parts.)

'It was senseless to remain on Soviet territory,' Ibrahim Bek dictated to his scribe. 'I had run out of money, men and ammunition. My problems were insurmountable.' On the night of 21 June 1926 Ibrahim Bek and fifty fighters crossed the Amu at Chubek into Afghanistan, just as amir Alim Khan had five years earlier.

Ibrahim Bek remained in Afghanistan for the next five years. But Afghanistan was in political turmoil and life for the émigré community ever more difficult (see special topic on the Great Migration, page 207). In 1931, life had become so perilous that about three thousand émigré families decided to chance it in the old country. On the morning of 30 March, they began to cross the Amu, under fire from the Afghan side. About a thousand made it to the north bank. Soviet troops interned them as they arrived. Ibrahim Bek and his men followed. They lasted two months at home before they were captured by local police who found only two rifles and two pistols on them. Ibrahim Bek was taken to Tashkent where he was charged with 'armed rebellion and invasion with counter-revolutionary purpose' and the following summer, executed.

Soviet history has it that the basmachi were nothing but thieves and liars. Many families, even those with basmachi roots, told their children likewise. To say or even think otherwise would have been dangerous – and even today, parents scold their noisy sons as 'basmachi'. Like so much in the Central Asian past, the story of the basmachi still lies largely undiscovered except by some notable scholars and, of course, the elders who knew everything but said nothing.

Ibrahim Bek, 1931 (above)   Anzob village and "minaret" in fact, a geological formation (right)

Anzob Pass, Iskander Kul and the Yagnob Valley

Journey North from Dushanbe

The road to the Zarafshan valley, and on to Khujund, the main city of the north, follows the Varzob valley north of Dushanbe. Allow 10 hours for the 340 km journey to Khudjand, but there can be hold-ups due to landslides and breakdowns. Consider making the journey in two days with a stopover, possibly at Aini. The road rises through two high passes, at Anzob (3,373 m) and Shahristan (3,378 m) and is open only when they are clear of snow (usually May to November). A long awaited 6 km tunnel at Anzob is scheduled to open in 2007, which should make the journey easier – though less spectacular. Get hold of a four-wheel drive if you can or pick up a driver who regularly makes the trip, and agree a price beforehand including petrol.

The first part of the journey from Dushanbe to the north of Tajikistan follows the Varzob valley. This section as far as the Presidential Residence at Poguz (60 km from Dushanbe) is covered in the chapter Day Journeys from Dushanbe.

Leaving the Presidential Residence, heading north, the road surface deteriorates into a mixture of tarmac and compressed dirt. The turn to the Anzob tunnel is clearly signposted. There will be a choice of going through the tunnel or driving over the Anzob Pass. The road rises to the foot of the pass and climbs in a series of zigzags to the top. There are stupendous views across to the north, and the Zarafshan range of mountains. The road can be busy with swaying Kamaz trucks crawling their way along the narrow and precipitous track and overtaking can be heart stopping. Trucks often break down, to be fixed by ever-resourceful drivers. There is no breakdown service in Tajikistan – do not even think of driving alone unless you are a decent mechanic.

The road now descends, with more zigzags. Three km before the village of Anzob, and 110 km from Dushanbe, there is a bridge from the left to right banks of the Fandarya river, marking a right-hand turn to the village of Margib and the Yagnob valley (See separate section). The main road then continues into Anzob, marked by a large boulder perched on top of a pillar of dried mud – the 'Anzob Minaret'. The houses of this pretty village are stone built with storage for dried dung and hay on the roofs.

After the hamlet of Zigarak, 7 km from Anzob there is an impressive waterfall, with a viewing platform at Taloqi Marzich. The river Fandarya now rushes through a steep gorge and disappears for 5 km. This phenomenon was caused by an earthquake and huge rock fall in 1903, which buried an entire village. Local folklore has it that the whole population was killed and only a cockerel survived.

The next village is Takfon, after 7 km. 4 km further is the village of Rabat, with a small café. On the left there is a subsidiary valley, where a landslide destroyed another village in the late 1980s. On the mountain slopes to the west, smoke, and flames at night, can be seen rising from vents. These are underground coal fires that have burned for thousands of years. Pliny the Elder wrote in the first century AD, "the tops of the mountains burn in Bactria at nights". Going back to the 7th century sulphur and ammonia were extracted using the following method: a windowless structure was built over the vents, so that smoke would settle on the walls. After a time, a person covered with wet blankets would enter the building, and collect the ammonia, by scraping it off the walls into sacks. Sulphur and ammonia were important ingredients in making jewellery and medicines.

At the foot of the Anzob pass is the village of Jizhdik, where in ancient times, merchants would buy the sulphur and ammonia, load up their animals to take along the Silk Routes.

The road then reaches Zarafshan 2, where gold and lead were mined in Soviet times and there are a number of derelict factories. Here there is a turn off to the left to one of the most attractive places in Tajikistan, Iskander Kul. Local legend weaves a wealth of stories around this lake and surrounding valley, where the armies of Alexander the Great (Iskander in Arabic) are said to have rested on their march to Samarqand.

The Cave Mummy

On the way to the lake, stop off at Khoja Ishaq to see a natural human mummy revered by pilgrims. Some believed it to be the remains of Spitamenes, the Sogdian general who fought against Alexander. Others hold it to be a cousin of the Prophet who came as a missionary to the area, fought and killed a devil, but died of his wounds.

The cave is high up above the village of Makshevat. Take the main road from Zarafshan 2 towards Iskander Kul. 8 km along the road is the village of Hayronbed. Take a left turn over the bridge to the south side of the river Iskander Darya. From there the track climbs 6 km to Makshevat. This is a delightful unspoilt village 750 m up in the mountains, with views across the valley to further ranges to the north. The houses are spread along river bluffs, interspersed with small fields and orchards. The local mullah can provide accommodation, with breakfast for 50 somonis.

The walk up to the cave must be one of the most attractive in the whole range, a mixture of woodland and bushes with superb views of the surrounding peaks. It takes 2 hours or more and a guide is recommended. The mullah will provide this service for 50 somonis. The path follows the stream. After 20 minutes the mullah will point out a mark on the cliffs on the other side of the stream. This is supposed to represent the devil and it is customary to throw stones at it.

The good path becomes steeper up the valley, which then opens out revealing more peaks and hanging glaciers. There is a guesthouse, furnished with blankets, cooking utensils and crockery and a stone hut with a spring, where visitors are expected to cleanse themselves by washing the face, hands and arms. They may then proceed to the cave. Local women are not allowed to go to the cave, but it is possible western women will be allowed. Ask the mullah.

While it is not necessary to be a rock climber, the route requires balance and a head for heights. Allow one to one and a half hours from the guest house to the cave and back. The path crosses some easy scree to a scrambling section. The subsequent traverse has two places where balance on small holds is required – though, like most mountain Tajiks, the mullah bounds across effortlessly. The path traverses under a cliff to a large ledge. From here there are fixed ropes to ease the ascent of the last 20 m to the cave entrance.

Iskander Kul (Lake Alexander)

It is forbidden to take photographs of the mummy as this is a holy shrine, but it is easily visible – a skull and torso with some mummified skin, set in a narrow, dusty cave which continues, we were told, deep into the mountain. As a spectacle it is low key perhaps – but as an excursion, this is hard to beat.

The walk back to the village takes between one and two hours.

Iskander Kul

It is 36 km from Zarafshan 2 to Iskander Kul. The road has a good surface and climbs between cliffs with a variety of geological features and colours, to the magnificent lake. The lake is surrounded by mountains, and is about four km across. Iskander Kul is a must, either as a detour travelling north or south, or as a starting point for treks in the Fan Mountains. It is a good centre for walking or mountain biking (bring your own bike). The views across the lake are impressive in all directions. At 2,000 m, it is pleasantly cool in summer.

"Iskander Kul or Lake Alexander is indeed a beautiful spot", wrote Mabel Rickmers in 1906, an English visitor and wife of Willi Rickmer Rickmers, the German explorer and mountaineer (see chapter on Rickmers).

"As it bursts on one's view the first impression is that of a Scottish loch in the wilder parts of the Highlands, but on a grander scale ... We found a secluded spot by the lake overgrown with tamarisk where we had a delightful dip. The water was delicious. The sky was flecked with fleecy clouds, the lake an exquisite shade of *eau de nil*, the silver grey of willow and tamarisk contrasted with the darker green of the mulberry, the westering sun brought out in all their fullness, the different tints – purple, red, green and grey of the mountains".

The scene has not changed.

Legends around the expeditions of Alexander the Great abound. Locals point out the saddle between two mountains that, the story goes, Alexander declared the summit of a race between his followers. Another story is that on moonlight nights, Alexander wearing gold armour and his famous two-horned helmet rises out of the lake on his black horse, Bucephalus. He remains with his sword raised until the morning, when he drops back below the waves. It is also believed that anyone who sees him will never leave Iskander Kul. Yet another tale tells of a lost city where the lake now lies. Alexander tried to besiege the city, but failed. He ordered his generals to build the embankment that stands at the entrance to the valley, and flooded the city.

At the far end of the lake are two grand buildings, one is the President's dacha, and the other his official residence. He is reported to have visited twice at time of writing. Less glamorous is the run-down and seedy Soviet-era holiday camp with 3 bedroom huts of a basic standard. There is an electricity supply, the bathrooms and toilets in separate blocks and a bar and restaurant. It is open from May to late October. From here it is possible to sail and canoe on the lake.

20 minutes walk from the camp, up a small hill to the north is Snakes' Lake. This is a reed-enclosed lake, with birch woods, leading up to a steep valley into the mountains. There are many waterfowl, and it is possible to fish in this tranquil and beautiful spot.

From the rock fall that formed Iskander Kul, the river flows east to impressive 40 m falls, nicknamed locally as "Niagara". There is a path from the camp going down the left bank, through ephedra bushes, to a somewhat rickety viewing platform, with good views of the falls. Nearby are trees with hundreds of votive ribbons hanging from the branches, a common practice at holy sites. On the return walk, investigate the Heath-Robinson raft – a platform that can be winched over the river to measure the flow. The mechanism is on the platform and it is very stiff, but with effort it is possible to reach the far bank.

From Iskander Kul, there is a road of 10 km to the village of Sarytag. It is dusty and steep and not worth walking. There are no buses, but taxis can be hired. The village is the starting point for delightful walks alongside the Kara Kul river, through meadows, birch and juniper woods. It can be the start of one of the most popular five-day treks in the Fan Mountains to Seven Lakes and Penjikent (see section on the Fan mountains).

The Yagnob Valley

From a turning to the right from the main road, 4 km before the village of Anzob is the entrance to one of the most attractive and interesting valleys in Tajikistan. Until a road was blasted out by the Russians it was almost inaccessible. The river Yagnob flows through a gorge, and the steep cliffs guarding access from the main valley ensured it was a place of refuge for people fleeing invasion. The valley is ideal trekking country, with good paths, mountains on either side, rising to the 5,000 m peak of Qullai Samarqand at the end of the valley. There are trekking routes across the ranges to valleys leading down to Dushanbe to the south, and to the upper Zarafshan valley to the north. There are a number of fascinating shrines in remote locations.

The local people are very hospitable, and will beggar themselves to accommodate a guest. Should you be invited home bear in mind that this region is extremely poor. Bring food, tea, sugar and other supplies as well as money, and do not take seriously attempts to refuse them.

HISTORY

The Yagnobis have a dramatic history. After the defeat of the Sogdians by the Arabs in 722 at Penjikent, their leader Dewashtich was finally captured and executed. The Arabs pushed up the Zarafshan valley. Some of the Sogdians fled to the Yagnob valley, where they were safe to practise their Zoroastrian religion. Here they continued undisturbed until long after the establishment of Islam in the rest of Tajikistan.

After the coming of the Soviet Union, the new authorities developed the cotton plantations in both the south of the country and also in the Ferghana valley to the north. Mountain people were forcibly moved from valleys in the Pamirs and other ranges to fill the labour shortages on the collective farms. The last to be moved were the Yagnobis, in late 1971. The whole population of the valley was transported north to Zafarabad near Istaravshan in the Ferghana valley. The Yagnobis were herdsman, used to the cold winters and cool summers of their mountain homes. Many died, unused to the searing summer heat.

When the heavy hand of the Soviet Union began to weaken in the 1980s, a trickle of people started returning to the valley, occupying their ruined homes and building them up again. Twenty years later, some of the villages are functioning again, but with a greatly reduced population. Some have only one or two families. It is the only place we witnessed in Tajikistan which is under-populated, that is where land cannot

be tilled because there are not enough people. There are a number of completely deserted villages.

SOGDIAN LANGUAGE

In spite of these upheavals, the Sogdian language survives. Not all the people speak it, but many do. It is estimated there are about 3,000 Yagnobi speakers (442 in Yagnob, 1500 in Zafarobad, 400 in Takob, and 500 in Dushanbe). Yagnobi is barely comprehensible to outsiders, even fellow Tajiks from neighbouring valleys and this almost private language creates a special bond through the ancient community. The government has been supportive, teaching material has been provided, and children are taught either in tiny schools, or by peripatetic teachers. There are academics at the Rudaki Institute of Languages and Literature Studies, Dushanbe, who provide written material, and encourage study of Sogdian literature and music.

In his book 'The Lost Heart of Asia', the author, Colin Thubron describes visiting these remote villages, and his amazement at hearing shepherds speaking in Sogdian.

"I listened almost in disbelief. This I told myself, was the last, distorted echo of the battle-cries shouted 2,500 years ago by the armies of the Great Kings at Marathon and Thermopylae, all that remained from the chants of Zoroastrian priests or the pleas of Persian satraps to Alexander the Great. Yet it was spoken by impoverished goatherds in the Pamirs".

TRAVELLING THROUGH THE VALLEY

Allow 4 days for a trek from Margib to the top end of the valley. Most walkers will be content to walk to the last village, Kirionte. For this allow 2 days, stopping overnight at Makhtimain or Bedev. Beyond Kirionte it would be necessary to take a tent and supplies.

There is rough track from the main road (four-wheel drive essential) of 5 km to the large pleasant village of Margib. The track has been blasted out of the cliffs along

Sogdian speaker, Takob

the river Yagnob. The village is dominated by rock faces. It is best to find a local official, who will be pleased to find accommodation and arrange a guide and donkey if required.

From the village there is a path over a small ridge behind the village. This joins the vehicle track, which is subject to rock fall, but is normally passable by four-wheel drive vehicles for 7 km. The road head is a small plain, with a deserted village. The track from here is usually opened in the summer for vehicles, after repairs have been undertaken to clear any obstructions caused by landslides, and goes for a further 16 km to the village of Bedev. However, this cannot be guaranteed, and visitors should allow for time to walk along the track.

From the road head there is a path up a subsidiary valley to the west, to the village of Khisortob. This is well worth a detour of 2 km. Like all houses in the valley, the ones here are made of stone with flat roofs. The people are Tajik speakers, and very hospitable. Accommodation will be found with no difficulty, but see advice on accepting hospitality above. The people grow wheat, potatoes and vegetables. There are apple, apricot and almond trees. The main source of income is the sheep, goats and upland cattle.

Village near Anzob Pass

There is a delightful Mazor or shrine here. The guardian, Kulmurod, who is very devout, will lead visitors to a nearby grove of mature trees on the banks of a river, between mountain slopes. The setting of Khoja Guliston must surely be on the site of an ancient shrine, the setting is so perfect. The shrine is a khomaka, a simple stone hut, inside which is a stone reputed to be that of Guliston. The legend is that she was being pursued by *nicholai* (Tsarist troops), and rather than let them capture her, she turned herself into the stone. Only women of good character are allowed to enter the shrine, men are forbidden. Nearby on a flat boulder is a square rock, shaped like a book. There are some marks on the stone. It is considered to be a copy of the Koran, turned to stone by Guliston. Visitors are expected to pray at the shrine.

From the road head if the road is not passable by vehicles, it is an easy walk along the valley. There is a near certainty of seeing marmots in the summer months. Birds are abundant, and eagles, Griffon vultures and lammergeier are very likely to be seen. The mountains along the route vary from 3,000 to 4,635 m, and there are hanging glaciers. Allow 6 to 7 hours walking to reach the villages of Bedev and Makhtimain. After about 3 hours the river can be crossed to the left bank, across a small bridge to another interesting shrine. This is Khoja Murodboukhsh, set in a copse with a huge fallen tree behind. It is a small stone building with a wooden screen and a hinged flap above. There is nothing inside, but outside is a star shaped stone wrapped in a cloth. The stone can only be lifted by a person with a pure heart. It is customary before entering a shrine to do a ritual cleansing or *tahorat*, involving washing the face and arms.

Look out for shepherds' tents, mainly in spring or autumn – though beware fierce dogs, kept for fear of wolves. The hospitable herdsmen will always call off their dogs and invite strangers for tea. Also on the route are the remains of a basmachi hideout, right next to the track. There was fighting here in 1937 against the Russians, when the story goes, 70 fighters under Juma Oskakol and his 7 brothers, took on 1,000 Russian troops. He was defeated, but not before inflicting heavy casualties.

The track reaches a wooden bridge over the river just before Makhtimain, a village on a bluff on the left bank. There is a room for guests at the main house of Niyazmamad, a Yagnobi speaker, who was deported with everyone else in 1971. Surprisingly there is satellite TV. Simple meals are served. Electricity is supplied from a mini hydroelectric plant. The path is still very good for a further 7 km. More small villages and shrines are passed on both banks of the river. The ruined settlement of Khisoki Darv marks the end of the former road, and it becomes a normal path.

A gorge is reached with 100 m cliffs. The road follows the right bank. On entering the gorge there is a perched stone in the river, reputedly put there by a holy man. Further along is a bush surrounded by a low wall, believed to have been the staff of a holy man. At the exit to the gorge is a traditional water mill. The valley opens up into some meadows. Ahead is the path to Pskun, one of the larger villages with a Sogdian-speaking population. Allow one and a half hours from the meadow. Pskun is probably the most interesting village as it is the home of some Yagnobi scholars. You will be asked to stay the night – bring useful or edible gifts. A further 2 hours walk of 8 km takes the visitor to Kirionte, the last habitation in the valley. It is a Tajik speaking village. Beyond Kirionte, the valley provides an excellent trek to the top end, or for the more adventurous, over the high passes to Romit to the south, and the upper Zarafshan valley to the north.

Instead of continuing along the main path, from the meadow before the final walk to Pskun, a turn can be taken to the right, up a subsidiary valley, the Tagobikl, with five Sogdian villages at high altitude. The narrow path follows the river for one and a half hours to the foot of the hill below the villages. Allow another half hour to reach Upper and Lower Garmen, and Sokhain, which has a comfortable guest room. At 3,000 m the houses have to be of sturdy construction, of stone with heavy beams. The local men are excellent horsemen and negotiate the steep slopes with great skill. They even have *buzkashi* competitions here in July and September. The local men and women are extraordinarily fit. Each day they take the animals from their stockades and drive them 1,000 m up the mountains in the early morning and back in the evening; all this on some very precipitous paths.

From the valley, the Akbakyl Pass leads to the village of Khoja Sanghok, a walk of about 4 hours. From there it is possible to reach Dushanbe. There is a rough road to Romit, which is deteriorating. It was built to take gold from the mine, closed in 1975.

The Yagnobi people retain some Zoroastrian traditions. At weddings there is emphasis on fire and light. The bride and groom jump over a fire, and candles surround the couple. Pottery is broken. Thursday is an auspicious day. There are similar traditions in the Pamirs and elsewhere in Central Asia. The traditional Pamiri

house with the 5 pillars, representing Mohammad, Fatima, Hussein, Hassan and Ali, are thought by some scholars to have their origins in five pillars used in houses from Zoroastrian traditions (see special topic on Pamiri Houses).

The Yagnob valley can be visited easily from early May to November. The best time to come is June, July and August. In May and September people are busy in the fields, and claim they cannot give visitors their full hospitality. I went in May and was overwhelmed, so the visitor is assured of a very warm welcome in the summer. Do bring gifts – no guest is expected to arrive empty-handed in Tajikistan and remember the extreme poverty of Yagnob.

Journey North Again

From the village of Zarafshan 2, the main road continues through a series of gorges to Zarafshan 1 (the Soviets had a way with words). From here the road winds over a pass to the town of Aini in the Zarafshan valley.

Baking bread in a tandoor oven, Takob

Zarafshan Valley

The Zarafshan is one of the great rivers of Central Asia. Its name translates as "The Strewer of Gold", and the name under which it was known to the Ancient Greeks – the Polytimetus, or "Abundant in Wealth" – reflects its nature throughout history. It has been the nourisher of the great cities of Samarqand and Bukhara, and the civilisations centred there. These cities and those all along the river have always relied on the *arriqs* (irrigation canals) to enable the production of a rich variety of crops. The regular flooding in the lower reaches provided the silt to form large areas of fertile fields. It has also been a gold bearing river – hence the name – and this has added to its economic importance. It flows in a remarkably straight line from its headwaters fed by the glaciers of both the Zarafshan and Turkestan ranges. Joined by numerous other tributaries, it flows to Bukhara and though it once joined the Oxus (Amu Darya), now it drains away into the deserts.

Aini
The main road north joins the Zarafshan Valley at the town of Aini (named after the renowned Bukharan intellectual, Sadriddin Aini, 1874–1954). It is the junction to go east up the valley to the river's source or west to Penjikent and Samarqand. The town has a main street with basic eateries, offices, the obligatory statue of Lenin and an internet café. The main point of interest is a 13 m tenth century minaret of mud brick, now protected by scaffolding. Next to it is the Jamaladin mosque, modern, but incorporating some tenth century pillars and beams. The new woodworking and painting is of a very high standard. Local fruit, especially apricots are exceptionally good, even by high Tajik standards.

Aini is a natural stopping off point for an overnight stay on the journey north. There are minibus services going north and south and very dilapidated taxis can be hired. There are two guest houses we recommend:

– At the roundabout where the road from Dushanbe meets the Zarafshan valley road, turn right and east towards the upper valley. After 1 km there is a large white house on the left, turn up a lane for 100 m. This is 1, Navobad Street, managed by Gulchera Hasanova, a charming and inspiring woman, who speaks some English. This clean guest house, within a large walled garden, has eight bedrooms and a spacious sitting room. There is a sauna and bathroom, and a clean squat toilet in a separate building. Hasanova works for a local NGO involved with women's rights and empowerment; a tough task in this very conservative area, but she is clearly making progress.

The charge is US$10 per night and US$15 with breakfast.

Tel: 93 501 32 53 and 83479 22445

– The NGO, German Agro Action, who are so prominent in this valley, have a guesthouse set in a walled garden at Tukkhtamurodov Street, just behind the War Memorial.

Tel: 83479 22644 and 92 77555669 (ask for Aziz Azizov)

The guardian does not live in the guesthouse, so he may take a bit of finding. There are four rooms, with high standards of cleanliness, a shower and a sit up toilet. US$10 per night, US$15 with breakfast (needs to be ordered the night before).

There is also the very basic Aini Hotel at 3, Lenin Street. 30 somoni per night.

Upper Zarafshan Valley

The upper Zarafshan Valley, runs due east of Aini for 200 km. The first half is less picturesque than other valleys, with long scree slopes leading down to the river gorge, interspersed with typical mountain villages surrounded by woods and fertile fields. In the second half, the valley broadens out with more variety of scenery, dominated by 5,000 m peaks on both sides. The valley is a dead end, finishing at the Zarafshan glacier. There are trekking routes following shepherds paths across to the north and south. The river would present a formidable challenge to canoeists and white water rafters. The people are conservative and hospitable. There should be no problems in finding accommodation for the night, but always give a gift and/or money. One of the attractions is that, apart from an occasional foreign aid worker from German Agro Action, the visitor is likely to be the only foreigner in the valley. The best time to visit is spring and autumn, summers being very hot. It would be wise to allow at least two days to reach the head of the valley, with an overnight stop at Obduron.

The road follows the course of the river, which runs much of its course in a gorge cut down through the centuries. The road from Aini is part tarmac and part dirt to start with, and after 50 km dirt, but passable, and trucks reach the top end of the valley. There are steep drops at many places on the road. Allow 25 km per hour in a car or jeep. There are no buses, but taxis can be shared.

At the village of Rarz (22 km) is an 8 m ruined tower from the tenth century, Hazrat-i Burq that was once part of a fortress. The first village of particular interest is Washab, after 30 km. On what is virtually a cliff face, are a succession of houses and cowsheds, each with the roof being the platform for the one above. The road follows a line roughly 300 m above the river, occasionally dropping down to the riverbank.

The next main village is Obduron, situated on a double bend in the river. The village has houses with walled gardens and orchards of apples, almonds, walnuts, apricots and mulberries, so creating a green patch in a rather arid area. There is an 18th century fortress, which has been renovated, providing precipitous views down to the river. It was one of the many forts built by local beks, who were continuously warring with each other. There was a tunnel, now blocked, which led down to the river, so that water could be obtained in case of siege, or for escape. Next to the fort is the residence of the local governor.

There is a guest house, Gozari Mir, near the mosque. Turn left by the school and continue for 400 m. It is free. It is basic but clean, with one room for sleeping and an outside toilet. Food can be provided. The guardian is very welcoming. This would be a natural place to break the journey both up and down the valley.

76 km from Aini is the curious settlement of Matcha. On a wind-swept pass, the Hukumat have built their headquarters. There are office blocks, but no sign of the life of a normal village. There is a guesthouse on the site.

Halfway up the valley is the village of Langar (106 km) with a good informal homestay run by the local head doctor, Mirzo Akbar. His house has a comfortable bedroom, with some fine carved beams. He provides the usual high standard of Tajik hospitality. He told us that in the 40s and 50s all the people, apart from a handful of shepherds were forcibly evicted and sent to the cotton fields of the north. People started returning in 1968 and the population is building up again, due mainly to the large size of families in this traditional, conservative community. In this area there are shepherd tracks over to the Yagnob valley to the south. We were told there were wolves, bears and occasional snow leopards in the mountains.

The last major settlement is Samjon (152 km). The houses and walls are constructed of stones in a herring-bone pattern, very typical of this part of the valley. As in every village, there is a *mazor* (shrine). The mountains now on the left are the border with Kyrgyzstan. 20 km further, the river rushes through a narrow gorge. Just below this gorge is the starting point for canoeists intending to reach Penjikent. This is a serious undertaking and only to be attempted by a very experienced and well-organised expedition. Local travel companies can arrange logistical support, but participants would need to bring their own canoes. Our understanding is that only one expedition, a Russian one, has reached Penjikent. A French one came to grief, fortunately with no casualties, near Khairobad.

The last village is Dehisar (175 km) The climate is much colder than further down the valley. The main crop is potatoes, which provide the main source of income. The local Mullah Abdullo is humorous and helpful. He has an informal homestay 2 km further up the valley. There is a bedroom and a separate living room with TV. He provides excellent food. There is a small grove of trees near the house where guests can lie on a tapchan and admire the wonderful view.

This top end of the valley would be excellent for mountaineering. There are some lower peaks in the 3,000 to 4,000 m range for acclimatisation, and 5,000 m ones are also accessible.

There is an army checkpoint just before Abdullo's house. To proceed to the glacier requires permission from the local military commander, but this was obtained with no problem. A vehicle can continue for a further 7 km to a small settlement. From there it is a 4 km walk to the flood plain and then another 15 km to the snout of the Zarafshan glacier. It is an easy walk on the stony flood plain, but it is necessary to cross the river to the left bank, and it would be advisable to hire a guide. Donkeys can also be hired in the village. Allow a day to reach the glacier snout and return. There is a difficult path across to the Rasht valley to the south.

It is a long journey up the valley and back down, but it is worth the journey to experience its remoteness, the constant sight of mountain peaks and the hospitality of the people living from their flocks and small fields in a harsh environment. The end of the valley is a particularly wild and dramatic place, yet full of peace.

Zarafshan Valley to Penjikent

From Aini the road to Penjikent goes west. Allow a day for the journey, but always be aware there could be hold ups due to landslips or breakdowns. The road surface is generally good and improves as you near Penjikent.

The traveller is now following along a section of one of the Silk roads, from Khujund to Bukhara. The road west follows the course of the river, which runs in a steep gorge. The fields are irrigated, with the sudden transition from fields and trees to arid mountainside. It is 13 km to the town of Dardar, which contains a 13th

century mosque, the only survivor of a string of seven ordered across the valley by Jalal-ud-din Khorezm-Shah. The inner area of the Dardar mosque has the original pillars. The outer area was built in 1890, by Murodboy, a local carpenter. It has a colourful decorated ceiling, with an unusual hue of red in the floral decoration. Local legend claims that this is because the paint included human blood. Like most mosques, it was closed in Soviet times.

The Fortresses of Dewashtich

Well worth a small detour are the villages and forts associated particularly with Dewashtich, the last leader of the Sogdians (see special topic). 20 km from Aini is a turning to the left, and the village of Khairobad is 2 km from the main road. Murali Lutfilo has a guest room and also a Russian Jeep, which he will hire out and drive for a reasonable fee. As always the people are very hospitable. Tohir, the head of the village, will be proud to welcome visitors, and show them around the village. The house in this and other villages in the area are substantial, and are evidence of some prosperity.

There is a reasonable road of 9 km up to the village of Kum. There are buses to Kum from Aini on Mondays, Wednesdays and Fridays. On a hill above the village is the Sogdian fortress of Kum. This was the scene of a battle between the Sogdians and the Arabs in AD 722 (see special topic on Dewashtich). It is on an outcrop, easily reached. There are substantial remains of the mud brick buildings, with barrel roofs. The views from the site down the Zarafshan valley are magnificent. In 2006 local people could only recall four visitors in the last five years.

Also near Khairobad is the fortress of Mount Mugh. This commands a view over a bend in the river, with steep hillsides right down to the riverbank. This was the scene of the last stand of the Sogdian king, Dewashtich, against the Arabs in the eighth century.

To reach the fort it is advisable to take a guide from the village; a scramble is required. Take the track from Khairobad going up from the village on the left. This runs above the river, and follow the path until it drops down to the riverbank. Move up rather indeterminate paths to a ridge, where an irrigation channel crosses it. Walk down the right of the ridge to the fortress. Once there you will understand why Dewashtich took his last stand here. An alternative route is to leave the road at a pylon, cross the hedge, and follow the course of the irrigation channel, which is now

dry, to the junction with the ridge. This is easier, but you need a head for heights, as there is a vertical drop below the channel. Local people believe Dewastich built this channel.

Little would have been known about Dewashtich, but for a chance find in 1932 by a shepherd at this site of a basket of 8th century documents on leather and bone of correspondence of Dewashtich. This has formed a very important understanding of his life and times.

Another link with Dewashtich, and one of the most attractive villages in the Zarafshan valley is Madm. Returning to the main road from Khairobad, there is a road to the left after 5 km. The road crosses a bridge and up a hill for 6 km to the village of Madm at 2,100 m. The village is built of substantial two storey mud brick buildings, surrounded by orchards and fields. Local historian and teacher, Jumaev Murod, lives in a delightful traditional house with painted ceilings and a walled garden. He can talk about Dewashtich and also the first arrival of the Russians in 1870.

The approach to the fortress would have been easily defended, and there are the remains of look out posts on the surrounding hills. To reach the fortress, there is a good track up from the village. After 500 m there is a memorial, with a *gumbaz*, to a local deputy in Parliament killed in the civil war of 1992–1997. There are lines

Penjikent old city

from the poet Rumi on a stone plaque. The fortress is a further 500 m along the track. There are the remains with some brickwork, and the foundations of houses excavated by Russian archaeologists. The houses were two storey buildings, with carved pillars. There are views of the mountains and the village below. It is more open than many sites, and the mountains feel less overpowering. The Sogdians chose a special site here. On the mountain sides high above the village can be signs of *lalmi*, fields with no irrigation, which relied on rainfall. These are now largely abandoned in Tajikistan, because there are alternative supplies of food, but in the past these fields would have provided vital extra crops. Such fields are still used in Afghanistan, and can be seen in the Pamirs from the road along the Pyanj riverbank going from Darvaz to Khorog.

There are two places worth a small detour from the main road:

MAUSOLEUM AT MAZOR-I SHARIF

After 30 km from the turning to Madm there is a left turn at Kolkhozchiyon to the shrine at Mazor-i Sharif. This is a jewel. From the turn off, it is 10 km on a good road to the shrine of Khoja Muhamad Majorah. He was a missionary, born in Basra in 743. The mausoleum has a fine dome, with exquisite blue tiling and woodwork on the exterior. It was built in the 8th and 9th centuries, with some additions in 1342–43. Inside is a high ceiling area, with the trunk of a tree used in the original construction as a centrepiece. There is superb woodcarving, including representations of fish. This is unusual, as images of living things are normally forbidden in Islamic art. The mausoleum contains the body of the saint, and his family in separate rooms. There are Kufic inscriptions on the walls, and a superbly carved *mihrab*. The guardian will take up the floorboards to show visitors the skulls of other good people buried here. There is a cell used by those wishing to withdraw from the world for 40 days to fast and pray.

It is a place of pilgrimage, and visitors come for cures of common ailments. It is particularly popular with women unable to conceive. It is customary for the supplicants to sacrifice a goat, which is then cooked and shared with other pilgrims.

THE TOMB OF RUDAKI, PANJRUD

The poet Rudaki is the founder of modern Persian. He is honoured throughout the Persian-speaking world, but especially in Tajikistan where he is one of the great figures of the past claimed by the modern state.

Rudaki was born at the village of Rudak ("Little Village") near Penjikent in the 9th century. He rose to fame as a great poet at the court of Amir Nasr of Bukhara, writing in clear simple language that became the standard of modern Persian. Legend has it that Rudaki was blind from birth (the Soviet version, of course, has him blinded by the cruel Amir). After a long career, Rudaki fell from favour. He died in poverty and was buried at Panjrud.

45 km before Penjikent there is a turning to the left, from where there is a good tarmac road for 17 km to Panjrud. Rudaki lies in a mausoleum built in 1956, surrounded by peaks of the Fan Mountains. The simple, but elegant mausoleum with superbly carved doors, is set in well kept formal gardens, with a small museum and superbly decorated choikhona. The poet lies under a simple marble slab, above him on the ceiling is written in Persian "Those who do not learn from experience will learn nothing from a teacher".

A guesthouse is being built nearby. There are minibuses from Penjikent (4 somonis). The road continues for a further 6 km to Artuch, a major base for climbing and trekking in the Fan mountains. It is a bad road and 4-wheel drive is essential.

Penjikent

The valley widens and there are vineyards, fields and orchards, leading to Penjikent, an important town on the Silk Road. It is known as the "Pompeii of Central Asia", because of the wonderful frescoes from the 8th century, which have survived. For visitors to Samarqand, it is an attractive addition to cross the border, visit Penjikent, and go on a trek in the Fan Mountains.

The modern town is on the banks of the Zarafshan River. It is a typical Soviet town with wide streets, some handsome civic buildings, and a dramatic statue of Dewashtich. There is a bustling bazaar and an 18th century medrassa. The old city, now abandoned, is on a hilltop to the east of the town. The excellent Rudaki museum in the town is a must for any visitor. Great pride is taken in the history of the town. There is a large bust to the great Tajik archaeologist Abdullo Isokov on the main road into the town.

The town grew up because it was strategically placed on trade routes. It is also the centre of a fertile agricultural area, and gold was panned here, using sheepskins.

The old city is on a hill top 4 km to the east of the town. It is helpful to have a guide, as apart from a few examples of ancient brickwork, the site is a series of mounds of earth, and it is not easy to disentangle the layout of the city. There is a general plan at the entrance. It should be possible to arrange to hire an English-speaking guide at the Rudaki Museum in the town.

The city was a sophisticated Sogdian one, on a major branch of the Silk Road, built in the 5th century, covering an area of 20 hectares, with a population of 5,000. At 1,000 m it is cooler than the new town in the river valley. The town had high defensive walls, with watchtowers on three sides, and was protected by a steep slope on the northern side. The walls were 12 m thick at the base and 5 m high at the top, with battlements and a wide pathway to allow rapid deployment of troops. It had two large Zoroastrian temples, with the holy fires burning continuously. There are traces of Buddhist, Nestorian and Manichean influence. There was a royal palace and a citadel. Perhaps the most impressive feature was the scale of the houses. These were 2 and 3 storey buildings of significant sophistication, with elaborate decoration.

The city was besieged by the Arabs for two years, but was eventually captured in AD 722. The Arabs set fire to the city, and this act meant that Penjikent became a repository for much of what is now known about the Sogdian civilisation. As at

Pompeii, the sudden destruction lead to preservation of magnificent frescoes, because in the fire some of the wall collapsed inwards, preserving the paintings under rubble for twelve centuries. Russian and Tajik archaeologists have excavated about half of the site, and painstakingly restored the frescoes to some of their former glory. The fact of the town being completely and finally abandoned in 770 has also helped its preservation.

Some of the frescoes are in the Rudaki Museum in Penjikent, and some others are in the Museum of National Antiquities in Dushanbe. There are also burnt altars and statues that were preserved by the fire. However, the finest examples were taken to St Petersburg, and can now be viewed in the Central Asian Section of the Hermitage Museum.

Mosque, Penjikent

The frescoes give a picture of life in a Sogdian town, much about their legends, and also proof that the Sogdians had links, possibly through their trading, with cultures as far away as India and Western Europe.

After the defeat, the Sogdian leader Dewashtich retreated and was finally defeated at Mount Mugh (see special topic on Dewashtich). He is now given the status of a local hero and there is a defiant statue of him in the main street.

There is a small museum on the site with an enthusiastic curator, and a number of artefacts.

The Rudaki Museum in the town is an essential visit in Penjikent. It helps to an understanding of the site of the fortress, and of the life of the people who lived there. The highlight is the Sogdian frescoes, showing the

(above) Fresco from Penjikent in Museum of National Antiquities, Dushanbe
(right) Rudaki Museum, Penjikent

hero Rustam fighting with devils, and also a three headed god, with similarities to the Indian god Shiva. There are other Sogdian relics such as statues, ossuaries (containers for bones from dead bodies after the birds had pecked away the flesh), jars and pipes. Other sections deal with local wildlife, the poet Rudaki, who was born near Penjikent, the Samanid dynasty, including Ismoil Somoni the national hero, and local costumes and furniture. There is also a section on the Russian legacy, with the first metal plough brought to the area, and the first diesel generator.

We recommend the homestay of Firdous Zainiev, Navbunod Street, behind a 12 storey apartment block, near the statue of Dewastich. Tel: 92 7701812. US$10 per night. The house has a walled garden, is clean, with an excellent shower and squat toilet.

The Hotel Penjikent (formerly Intourist) is at 12, Borbadi Marvazi Street. 100 large rooms with en suite facilities, but rather dilapidated. US$10 per night. Tel: 52270 / 92 7740737. There is an internet café on Rudaki Street, but no ATM in the town.

The DED Technical Advisor for ASDP NAU CBT in the Zarafshan valley may also offer travellers helpful information and guidance; located at 47, Khofizi Sherozi Street, Penjikent, Tel: +992-92 777 5357.

Sarazm

14 km from Penjikent and 10 km from the Uzbek border is the excavation of the ancient site of Sarazm, reputed at 5,500 years to be one of the earliest settlements in Central Asia. There are three sites all protected by metal roofs. The excavations show the layout of a sophisticated settlement. There is a museum on the site, but the more interesting items are in Dushanbe or St Petersburg. The most famous find is from about 3,000 BC, 'The Princess of Sarazm', a woman buried in clothes richly embroidered with turquoise, lapis lazuli, jasper and limestone beads. The beads and a bronze mirror are in the Museum of National Antiquities in Dushanbe.

The Airport

The airport is 4 km to the south of the town. It is only used in winter, when the passes are closed, and do not assume there are regular services. It is worth the short detour to see the heroic statue, in best Soviet style, of Oigul Muhamadjonova, the first pilot to land at the airport. She was a Tajik, but her likeness is very much of a standard Russian heroine. Above her is a representation of an aircraft.

DEWASHTICH, LAST RULER OF PENJIKENT   Huw Thomas

Dewashtich was a great hero to local Tajiks as the last ruler of the Sogdians, the ancient people of Tajikistan before they were conquered by the Arabs in the 8th century.

Little would be known about him, but for the chance find in 1932 of his correspondence at Mount Mugh in the Zarafshan valley. Written in Sogdian, this included secret letters between Dewashtich and his spies and allies, and also invading Arab commanders. There was also economic data about the area around Mount Mugh. Scholars have studied these documents and by comparing them with the main Arab sources, particularly the Annals of the Arab commentator al-Tabari, have been able to reconstruct the chronology of the last months of the rule of Dewashtich, lord of Penjikent and self proclaimed king of Sughd.

Dewashtich had a very brief reign. He was a Sogdian aristocrat who fought against the Arabs. He ousted Ghurak, king of Sughd, who appears to have wanted to appease the Arabs. Dewashtich won the recognition of the Sogdian aristocracy and was proclaimed king at the end of the summer of 721.

The Arabs began moving east from their heartlands after the founding of their religion in 622. By the middle of the century they had entered Central Asia and took Samarqand (a Sogdian city) in 712. Then, slowly, they began to make inroads into the Zarafshan valley leading to Penjikent. However, the Sogdians and their allies the Turks waged an effective guerrilla campaign against the Arabs. Dewashtich was master of the situation.

But in 722 a new and harsh Arab commander Said al-Harashi arrived in Samarqand. The Turks abandoned the Sogdians, who divided into two groups, one staying in the Zarafshan valley and the other moved up into the Ferghana valley, hoping to settle there. Al-Harashi first pursued the northern group of an estimated 14,000 Sogdians to Khujund, where, according to al-Tabari, they surrendered on the promise they would be allowed to return to Sughd. They were massacred.

In July 722 the Arabs moved south across the Shahristan Pass, along the Zarafshan River, and opposite Dardar turned up into the mountains. They surprised and defeated the Sogdians at Kum. Dewashtich retreated to Mount Mugh, was captured and according to al-Tabari crucified – in Islamic law the punishment inflicted on highwaymen. The Arabs moved down the valley and completed the siege of Penjikent.

Mountaineering and Trekking
in the Fan Mountains

RICK ALLEN

The border between Uzbekistan to the North and the Western part of Tajikistan is defined by a range of arid mountains called the Zarafshan Range. The Zarafshan River, originating in the Zaalaisky peaks flows to the south of this range past the ancient city of Penjikent before it enters Uzbekistan. From the border to Samarqand is just an hour's drive. South of the Zarafshan River the Hissar range of Mountains also runs roughly east-west and is clearly visible from Dushanbe. Between the Hissar and Zarafshan Ranges, west of the Anzob pass, lie the Fan Mountains or Fannsky Gori. This fabulous alpine area is one of the best kept secrets of Central Asia.

[Rick Allen has been mountaineering in the greater ranges of Asia for over 25 years – see page 566]

Geology

The geology of the area is immensely varied, although the main rock ridges are composed predominantly of metamorphosed limestone. Mountain ridges comprising shales have been more extensively eroded and tend to be lower and more rounded. There are granite intrusions, coal measures and some fine dark red sandstone exposures also. Semi-precious stones have been found, particularly around the area of the Seven Lakes.

Climate

The region has a semi-arid, continental climate, with an annual rainfall of about 25 cm (10"). Winter lasts from November to April during which time the road over the Anzob pass linking Dushanbe in the South with the Northern part of the country is permanently blocked. The wettest month is April. The months of June to September tend to be warm and dry and are the best time for visiting the area.

Landscape

Glacial activity has gouged out the principal valleys and the northern flanks of the high peaks and passes are still covered by numerous small glaciers. The area is dotted with spectacularly situated lakes, some left behind by retreating glaciers and others

Pristine lakes, Kul-i Kalon (left)   *Trekking (above)*

formed by major rock falls that have blocked the rivers. The largest, Iskander Kul, lies in the East of the mountain group and was formed by the partial blocking of the Iskander Darya. The lake is traditionally supposed to have been visited by Alexander the Great (Iskander is the Arabic rendering of "Alexander"). The western limits of the area are defined by the valley of the seven lakes feeding the Shing River which runs north to join the Zarafshan at Penjikent and the eastern limit is the Yagnob river or FanDarya, along which the road linking the two halves of the country passes.

The highest peak is Chimtarga at 5,489 m and Moskva, Energia, Chetny, Zamok, Linkor and Bolshoi Ganza all top 5,000 m.

Flora and Fauna

The lower reaches of the river valleys are forested with willow, walnut, apricot and maple but at altitudes above 2,000 m juniper is the predominant species with gnarled specimens surviving high amongst the mountain scree slopes. These trees are under pressure from the summer inhabitants of the mountain valleys who use them for fuel.

Excessive hunting has decimated the animal population of the region. Snow leopard and lynx are extremely rare, although occasional sightings of the magnificent horned sheep and wild goats can be had. Wild boar inhabit the lower reaches of wooded river valleys and wolves, foxes and marmots are still to be found. The only animal to be feared in the region is the shepherd's dog, trained to keep wolves and any other unknown visitors at bay.

Inhabitants

The mountains are inhabited from May to September by herdsmen and women from the valleys who bring their flocks and cattle to the high valleys for grazing. They are generally very hospitable and will usually press the passing traveller to sit down for tea, chunks of delicious, heavy wholemeal bread and yoghurt. No payment is expected. This can slow down progress on a trek considerably but is one of the highlights of travelling in the region. Some of these people will be fluent in several Central Asian languages and Russian. Most folk love to have their photographs taken but always ask first.

Police and army units also patrol the region to deter drug smuggling.

Exploration

Systematic exploration and mapping of the area began with officers and civil servants of the Russian government after the area was annexed for the Tsar in the nineteenth century. Fedchenko, of the eponymous glacier in the Pamir, visited the area. Exploration for fun, commonly known as mountaineering, began seriously in the 1930s when Soviet alpinists succeeded in making first ascents of Chimtarga and a number of the other prominent peaks. In the 1960s visitors from Eastern Europe as well as the Soviet Union began to discover the attractions of this alpine playground just half a day's travel from the bazaars of Samarqand. All of the passes were crossed and classified, the peaks climbed and a number of difficult routes were established from the 1970s onwards on the main peaks. Tourists and holidaymakers from the industrial centres of Dushanbe, the Ferghana valley and further afield were accommodated in purpose-build alpine holiday bases at Iskander Kul and Artuch.

With the collapse of the Soviet Union, visa barriers arose, money for travel evaporated and a civil war erupted in Tajikistan. Visitors to the region dwindled to a trickle, leaving the high mountain valleys once more to the summer flocks and their herdsmen. After peace had returned to Dushanbe in the late 1990s a few travellers and mountaineers began to rediscover the Fan Mountains but the area remains quiet and little visited, not much more than a record in the annals of Soviet alpinism.

Approaches and Accommodation

The mountains may be approached from Hissar to the South, from Dushanbe over the Anzob Pass or from Samarqand in Uzbekistan. Visa problems currently make the approach from Uzbekistan slightly more problematic, or at least requiring more planning in advance. The Anzob Pass closes in October and usually opens in mid-late May. Early in the summer season the road is usually in bad condition from mud slides and four-wheel drive vehicles are strongly recommended. A tunnel has been constructed through the Hissar range, bypassing the Anzob Pass and this was open, at least intermittently, in 2006. Once off the main road the tracks are potholed, steep and involve fording rivers. All wheel drive vehicles are essential. The southern approach is for trekking only, there is no accommodation.

Beginning in the West, from Penjikent it is possible to drive south to the Seven lakes from whence access to the high passes leading eastwards can be gained. An hour further east along the road towards Aini there is a turning South to the birthplace of

The Fan Mountains

the great Tajik scholar and poet Rudaki. Continuing on an increasingly rough road leads eventually to the mountain base of Artuch. Constructed for a trade union, this substantial establishment has a number of small chalets, long bunk houses and a large round central cooking and dining structure in natural stone and timber. It has a separate, dilapidated, shower and sauna block where, given enough notice, hot water can be delivered. Booking in advance is essential as all food is ordered specially from Penjikent. This base provides access to the northern part of the range over a number of high passes. There is a short, 50 m crag for rock climbing nearby but this base is not ideally suited for easy access to the main mountaineering areas.

The approach from Dushanbe over the Anzob pass leads in six or seven hours to a turning westwards at Zarafshan. This leads after 25 km to the lake shore of Iskander Kul where a Soviet-style holiday camp remains. Basic wood and stone chalets are scattered amongst the wooded lake shore and a there is a communal shower block, sauna and dining area. The toilets are fairly disgusting. Visiting parties need to bring all their own food. The lake is visually stunning and extremely refreshing for swimming on hot days. Mountains surround the lake on 3 sides and many treks through the range naturally lead to the valley at the far side of the lake where the president has a dacha. It is a great place to end a finish a trek with sizzling kebabs beside the lake shore as the sun sets on the tops.

Climbers do well to continue down the Fandarya a further 5 km before heading west up the Pasrud Darya for a bone shaking hour and a half. The reward at the end of this trail is a group of three relatively new (1993) chalets run by mountaineering enthusiasts from Moscow for three months each summer. Each chalet holds 10 people and there is a communal dining room where food is prepared daily. It has much more character and life than either Artuch or Iskander Kul. Each summer, climbers, mostly from Eastern Europe, are re-discovering the big walls and mixed climbs that the heart of the range has to offer. Each year a week long climbing competition, Russian style, is held. Chimtarga, Energia, Chapdara and Zamok are all accessible from the valley system leading South up the Chapdara, past the ravishing turquoise Lake Alaudin. The glacial streams feeding this lake make swimming here a very brief pleasure.

The shortest approach to the range from Dushanbe is to drive towards Hissar and head north to pick up the Karatag river valley. At some point, the most robust four-wheel drive will fail at one of the river crossings and from there the walking begins. There is no accommodation in this valley so this is for those who wish to spend four days trekking over Mura pass to Iskander Kul.

Passes are graded by the Russian numerical and adjectival system and a general definition is offered to help the traveller interpret the grading.

Not classified – easy walk.

1a – pleasant walking, passable by pack animals.

1b – tough walking, normally not passable by pack animals.

2a and **2b** – steep and requiring an ice axe, crampons and the experience to go with them.

3a and **3b** – very nasty. Not passes in most accepted senses of the word. Likely to require full mountaineering equipment and advisable only to approach neighbouring peaks as part of a climb.

Trekking

The Fan Mountains offer excellent treks of varying difficulty ranging from a few days to a week in length. The most obvious are described below but a number of other variations are possible.

The West-East Traverse

Described in this direction so that you have the accommodation at Iskander Kul to aim for. Allow five days. Road transport will take you as far as the sixth lake on the Shing River south of Penjikent. From there proceed up the valley of the Kiogli river to a level camping spot below the Tavasang pass. Cross the pass 3,300 m (not classified), from where the long haul up to the next pass is all too obvious and drop down to the valley of the Sarimal river. Cross the river and follow the Abusafedsol to another fine camping place. Cross the Munora pass in the morning 3,520 m (1a) and descend to the valley of the Archmaidon. Although a path is marked on the right (East) bank it is recommended to stay on the true left bank of the river all the way down and drop further down the Archmaidon to a bridge before beginning to travel up river again on the North bank of the Archmaidon. Cross this river after a couple of hours and continue up towards the Dukdon pass. Fine camping amongst trees can be found although some scrambling is required to reach the water. The Dukdon pass at 3,810 m (1a) is magnificently poised between the Dukdon range to the south and the end of the range leading up to Peak Moskva to the North. A variant over the Pushnovat pass 4,100 m (also 1a) is possible. The descent of the Dukdon is steep and without camping sites until a junction is reached with the Kara Kul River. It is advisable to cross to the West bank of the Dukdon and then re-cross to the East bank

on the way down the gorge. From the junction with the Kara Kul River continue along the North bank of the Sarytag until the dirt road from Iskander Kul to Kanchoch is reached. A hot and dusty descent of that road leads to the Western end of Iskander Kul from where an hour's walk leads to the chalets and a welcome beer.

After crossing the Tavasang pass on day two it is possible to branch up stream on the Sarimal River and head South East towards the Sarymat Pass 4,160 m (1a). This would lead the following day over a small glacier down into the upper reaches of the Kara Kul River. This can then be followed all the way to Iskander Kul. This route offers less variety than the one described above.

The South-North Traverse

Described in this direction because there is accommodation in the North but not in the South. This trek can be split at Iskander Kul or either half undertaken separately.

Drive up the Karatag river from Hissar until your vehicle cannot cope with the fording the boulder-strewn river beds. This leaves you stranded just off any published map. Keep walking North up the Karatag to a junction with a stream flowing in from the East where there is good camping. Continue next day up the Karatag and Zambar to the highest flat area conveniently to be found below the snow line. If you have any porters, they will need to collect firewood on the way up because the upper valley is barren of trees. Cross the Mura pass 3,790 m (1a) next day and descend the valley of the Zambar towards a wooded glade where there is good camping. From there it is possible to descend to Iskander Kul in an easy day.

Alternatively, cross the Kara Kul and head North up the Arkh for the second and more challenging section of this route. There is good camping along the river valley.

Tajik shepherd, Marguzor Lake, Fan Mountains   *Horse dealer, Fan Mountains*

Continue up the river, now called the Kaznok, and follow it as it turns west below steep peaks. Branch up northwards right towards Kaznok pass. Obvious dark red screes characterise the upper slopes. The scree is steep and loose and this ascent is hard work. The pass straight ahead is Kaznok West 4,000 m (2a) with a serious snow/ice climb awaiting on the other side. Instead, branch off right the top and go up the Col of Kaznok East 4,040 m (1b). A steep snow runnel leads down onto a glacier. An ice axe is a valuable asset at this point to avoid an uncontrolled glissade. Follow the glacier down heading slightly east of north towards a moraine slope that opens out between two rocky walls. Descend the snow and scree towards Mutny lake. Camping is possible here at a cave on the far side or continue down the valley, with Chimtarga looming above on the left to reach the glorious turquoise Alaudin lakes. Either branch up left to cross the Alaudin pass 3,860 m (1a) or continue down the Chapdara to meet the Pasrud Darya and climb more gently to the top of Laudan Pass 3,630 m (not classified). Either way leads to the high Kul-i Kalon lakes from where it is possible to descend in half a day to Artuch alpine base. Allow four days for each half of this trek, or a total of eight.

Chimtarga Circuit

This route circumnavigates the highest peak of the range and offers unsurpassed views. It can be done from Artuch or from the alpine base at Chapdara. It is described in a clockwise direction. Reverse the last day of the previous trek past Kul-i Kalon and over Alaudin or Laudan Passes to reach the Alaudin lakes. Ascend to Mutny Lake (half day). From there follow the glacial moraines coming down from Chimtarga pass. Turn up rightwards and ascend steep scree or snow as early as reasonably practical. Do not go to the end of the moraine and attempt to scale the steep scree gullies leading back right. They lead onto dangerously steep and loose shale ridges. Once at the top of the scree a path becomes quickly apparent and traverses the slopes of Chimtarga towards the pass 4,740 m (1b). There is snow all year round here and an ice axe is useful. The pass is flanked by the icy summit slopes of Energia on one side and the steep rocks of the South face of Chimtarga on the other. Once over the pass, descend the valley heading north-west to arrive eventually at Great Allo Lake, formed by a massive rock fall blocking the outlet from the glen. There are small level sites for tents above the lakeside in this remote and dramatic setting.

Descend next day down the Zindon gorge where the river is hidden under the rock fall and emerge in the valley of the Archmaidon where a motorable road follows the river.

From here it is possible to cut the trek short and be collected by a four-wheel drive vehicle. However, the more adventurous or goal orientated parties will stride manfully northwards up this hot valley for some 6 km past the village of Gazza until a tributary appears from the right. Strike off east up this river, where camping can be found after 2 km. Leave the stream and head south east from here through a narrow defile between rocky bluffs. Follow the trickling stream from the spring in the upper valley and keep heading up and eastwards towards Zurmech pass 3,260 m (1a). Descend from here to the small Chukurak Lake where two crags offer single pitch rock climbs on clean limestone. Descend to Artuch base in 30 minutes from here to complete the six day circuit and take a well earned sauna.

Climbing

Government charges are now levied for climbs: for peaks over 7000 m: $100; 4000–7000 m: $50. Russian climbing grades translate roughly as follows:

Russian	French	UIAA
1a,1b	F, PD inf	I – II
2a, 2b	PD	II – III
3a	PD – AD	III
3b	AD – D	III – IV
4a, 4b	D – TD	IV – V
5a, 5b	TD – ED inf	VI
6	ED	VI+

– Chimtarga South East ridge is a two day outing on very steep rock and easier snow with a further day to descend, VI or TD. The mountain has 4 other grade V routes.

– Energia offers two grade V routes, one of which is the short icy face directly above Chimtarga pass.

– Chapdara has twelve grade V routes and two at grade VI.

– Bodkhona has seven grade V routes and two at grade VI.

– Zamok has five V and three VI grade routes, and also an easy route.

Most of the routes on these peaks are big limestone walls and ridges.

Ferghana Valley and the North

The North of Tajikistan comprises part of the Ferghana valley, which is the very heart of Central Asia. The Tajik section is known as Sughd, replacing the old name of Khudjand that is still commonly in use. Sughd is separated physically from the rest of the country by the Zarafshan range of mountains. The passes are closed from the end of November to the end of May. The area was removed from Uzbekistan and tacked on to Tajikistan by Stalin in 1929, partly to ensure the criteria of a population of one million for a new Socialist Soviet Republic was fulfilled. It was also part of a general divide and rule policy, as the majority of the population in this northern enclave are Uzbeks, in a mainly Tajik state. In neighbouring Uzbekistan, great cities of Bukhara and Samarqand have large Tajik populations.

The story of this part of Tajikistan is much more closely linked with the other parts of the Ferghana valley in present day Uzbekistan and Kyrgyzstan, than to the country to the south. The area is the most productive in Tajikistan, providing two thirds of GDP, with a third of the population. It has 75% of the arable land.

Until Independence, this area was the powerhouse of the Communist Party in the Soviet Socialist Republic of Tajikistan. All the leaders of the country came from this area. It is only since the rise to power of President Rakhmon in the 1990s that this power structure has been turned upside down. Now the elite come from the southern province of Khatlon, centred on the town of Kulob.

During the civil war (1992–1997) there was no fighting in this area, although in 1998 an ex-civil war commander, Mahmud Khudoberdiev, led an uprising there. His three-day insurrection ended with a dramatic shoot-out at the medieval citadel in which about a hundred people were killed according to official figures. These days, Sugdh is again important politically. A strong Islamic tradition, coupled with a rising generation anxious for a better life, mean this is an area the Dushanbe government watches with care.

The Ferghana valley has been a centre of civilisation in Central Asia for centuries. It is very fertile and a famous trading post, sitting at the crossroads between China, India, Turkey and roads north. Babur, founder of the Mughal dynasty in India, was born at Andijan, one of the main cities of Ferghana. All his life he yearned for the delights of his home area, particularly the luscious melons. They are still luscious. The fields of wheat and orchards of the past have now largely given way to cotton, but the area still grows a rich variety of produce. The Tajik section includes the enormous Karakum Lake, 65 km long by 20–8 km wide, dug by the Soviets to provide irrigation, a reservoir and hydro-electricity. There are some tatty resorts at the western end of the lake.

It is uncomfortably hot in summer, and chilly in winter. Spring and autumn are the best times to visit.

Sughd can be reached from Dushanbe by way of the Anzob Pass (3,373 m) and the Shahristan Pass (3,378 m). The journeys are much easier from Uzbekistan, either from Tashkent along the M34 road, or from Samarqand along the M39 and A376 roads. An Uzbek visa is required. There is a good road from Andijan and Kokand in Kyrgyzstan, for visitors coming from the east. Again a visa is necessary. Travel companies should be able to obtain visas, but allow plenty of time.

Highlights

- Istaravshan, with its ancient citadel, old town and magnificent mosques and medrassas. All on a much smaller scale than Bukhara and Samarqand, but with no tourists.
- Khudjand, an ancient city with some relics of its past, overlaid with standard Soviet constructions. It is a bustling place with some fine buildings, and the extraordinary palace of the Arbob collective farm.
- A number of surprising gems in unlikely places, near Isfara and Kanibadam.

Journey

The first part of the journey north from Dushanbe is dealt with in the chapter on the Anzob Pass. From the town of Aini in the Zarafshan valley the roads rises over the Shahristan Pass in a series of steep Z bends. The road is busy and the surface uneven. There is a constant stream of trucks, which make you bite your lip as they sway towards your vehicle. There are regular minibus services from Aini to Istaravshan and on to Khujund.

Shahristan (Ancient Bunjikat)

The road descends from the Shahristan Pass through juniper woods, the valley broadens out and becomes arid. The first town is Shahristan, by a river with irrigated fields. The interest is the ruins of the ancient city of Bunjikat. Just across the bridge to the west of the town is a narrow road to the left after 100 m, leading to a flat area below the ramparts. Bunjikat was a major Sogdian city. The ramparts are very eroded, but it is easy to discern the citadel and the size of a fortified city, divided by a small valley. The scale takes some getting used to; this was far bigger than any city in Europe at the time of its heyday in the 7th century AD. The site has been extensively excavated, and there are several exhibits in the Museum of National Antiquities in Dushanbe, including burnt statues from a Zoroastrian temple and frescoes showing scenes from Aesop's Fables, similar to those at Penjikent. The most famous is of a she wolf suckling twins, probably showing that this town had some contact with Rome. (The mythical founders of Rome, Romulus and Remus, were said to have been suckled by a she-wolf.) There is a statue of the she wolf and the twins on the way south. This site is seldom visited, and you are almost certain to be the only visitor.

Just 3 km before Shahristan is the village of Jarqutan. Turn left, go across a causeway and follow a tarmac road for 1 km to where the road veers right up a small hill. A gate leads to a path through the cemetery for 200 m to Chehel Hujra, one of the best-preserved Sogdian buildings in the country. The castle stands on a bluff above the river and consists of two storeys with thick walls and a labyrinth of passages. The castle was continuously occupied from the 4th to 6th centuries AD, and intermittently to the 9th. Very seldom visited, it is worth the short detour.

Istaravshan (formerly Ora-tappa)
Population 52,000
Telephone prefix 3554
Istaravshan is one of the most interesting towns in the whole of Tajikistan, and is well worth a visit. It is claimed it was founded 2,500 years ago. In the first two centuries AD it was an important city with walls 6 km long. Later it became a staging point on the Silk Road.

The best place to start is the Mugh Tappa, the old citadel that dominates the town. A succession of sentries would have surveyed the countryside to the north.

In 329 BC a sentry might have heard some muffled footsteps below him in the gap between the next hill to the west, now occupied by the main road and a canal. These sounds would have been the commandos of Alexander the Great. He had failed to take the city by storm, but an informer had told him the water gate was left open. The commandos entered the city and opened the main gates. Because the population had resisted, all the males were executed and the women and children taken as slaves.

A sentry in 1220 would have scanned the horizon for a sight of the forces of Ghenghis Khan. In his turn, he would slaughter the people.

A sentry in 1866 would have watched as the Russians set up their artillery before shelling the town into submission.

There is a reconstruction of how one of the main gates would have looked in the 16th century. From the Mugh Tappa it is possible to see the line of some of the old city walls, and the old town. Like Bunjikat, this was a very large city, when some of the biggest in the world were in Central Asia. Now it is a modern bustling town.

The old town, Shahr-i Kohna, retains much of its character, with narrow streets between mud brick houses.

KOK GUMBAZ (BLUE DOME)

In the old town the most impressive building is the Kok Gumbaz, an impressive domed mosque and medrassa dating from the 15th century. It was built by Abdul Latif Sultan, son of Ulugh Bek, who built the Observatory at Samarqand. Ulugh Bek was a 'Renaissance' humanist, who has been compared to Galileo. His son was more conservative, and so enraged by his illustrious father's radical views is thought to have thrown him from the roof of the

Kok Gumbaz and Istaravshan minaret

Observatory. Whether or not he did commit parricide, Abdul Latif certainly left a beautiful memorial to himself in the Kuk Gumbaz. The building has turquoise tile work, and stands in an enclosed courtyard with the classrooms. The medrassa was closed in Soviet times but is now flourishing with 100 students undertaking a religious education, although not all go on to become mullahs. In addition to theology, the students study Arabic, Russian, English and computer studies. The teachers and students are welcoming.

SAR-I MAZOR

Sar-i Mazor has a special combination of a very peaceful setting, with three attractive buildings. There are two mausoleums from the 15th and 16th centuries. One is the Ajina Khona, which means the house of demons, which is an unusual name for a holy building. The mullah told us it was a Soviet era name, coined to scare away children from playing there. It is austere within, but the exterior has some intricate brickwork.

The other mausoleum is that of Hazraji Mekhdoni Azam and his family. He was a nephew of Mir Saheed Hamadoni, whose mausoleum is in Kulob (see chapter on Khatlon). Again it is plain within, although there are traces of Arabic and Farsi script on the walls. The exterior is ornate with fine stonework and tiling. His tomb is there, with those of his wife, son and a nephew. He was born in Khorezm, in modern Uzbekistan. He is reputed to have died while preaching, proving his closeness to God.

The third old building is the Sar-i Mazor mosque, built in the 16th and 17th century, and has had some recent renovations. It is built in the Central Asian style of intricately carved wooden ceilings and pillars, with brightly painted woodwork. A feature is the 18 chehelkhona (cells used by people who wish to withdraw from the world for 40 days; often they were studying to be mullahs). The room would be in darkness, apart from a small lamp, to enable the person to study the Qu'ran, read and meditate. Bodily needs were met by the person only leaving the cell at night, when they would not meet with anyone. In Soviet times the mosque was used as a wheat store.

There is also a modern mosque, which can accommodate over a thousand worshippers. The money for the construction was all raised locally.

The whole complex is set in beautifully maintained grounds, with some ancient trees considered to be 800 years old. This tranquil place, with courteous guardians, is a special place to visit. It is customary when visiting a mosque or medrassa to make a small donation in the box provided.

OTHER MOSQUES

There are other mosques worth visiting:

• Chahor Gumbaz or Four Domes, a small 19th century mosque set in a back street, with four domes and a central pillar. It is next to a holy pool, shaded by an ancient tree.

• Havzi Sangin, a beautifully constructed modern mosque, has a shrine with a holy pool. Near the Kuk Gumbaz.

• The main mosque, Hazrat-i Shoh is on the main road below Mugh Tappa. Great craftsmanship has gone into the impressive carving and painted ceilings. In the gardens are the likenesses of great Tajik figures on a wall, poets on the left, writers on the right.

Please note that Tajik women cannot usually enter mosques, though foreign women are generally welcomed, if suitably attired.

19TH CENTURY HOUSE

In the old town, with a prior appointment, it is possible to visit a rare example of a 19th century town house of Mirzo Bobojonov, 18 Rahmatov Street, Ghaffur district. In the guest room is a magnificent painted ceiling, and intricately designed wall cupboards. The house, built by Usto Karimfon, is in a courtyard. The lady of the house prefers her husband to be present, so it is better to arrange your visit in the late afternoon, when he has returned from work.

MUSEUM

Istaravshan has always been famous for its craftsmen. This is demonstrated in the exhibits in the museum, which is situated on the right of the main road leading up from the market. It may not be easy to find the curator, but it is worth the effort. Entrance 60 dirihms. The are sections for the various crafts, including leatherwork, wood carving, printing, copper work and knife manufacture. 10th and 11th century pottery is next to ancient ossuaries (where bones were kept of dead human bodies whose flesh had been eaten by birds, in the Zoroastrian tradition). There is a section on traditional dress and bridal wear, armour and a Russian canon ball from the siege of 1866.

CRAFTSMEN

Opposite the excellent bazaar are to be found a line of blacksmiths in small workshops, with traditional bellows, making and repairing all sorts of metal items. Some of them maintain the famous local tradition of knife making, which goes back

2,000 years. They will make presentational knives from a wide variety of designs to your choice.

The great wood carving tradition is maintained by Mira Hakim, with his father Miro Ali, and brother Histo Ali, at their workshop, Korkhoni Ustoi Ali Kandakori, at Stanzia Unitechnia. This is to the left, over the bridge from the bazaar. Hakim is a superb woodcarver, who creates ornate doors and screens in the traditional style for mosques and special events. He also makes beautifully crafted items such as backgammon sets, which make distinctive presents. There is also a typical busy bazaar selling wonderful fruit and vegetables and lots of everything else.

Accommodation

HOMESTAY

We recommend the homestay of Zafar Rajabov at 6 Kholiq, Rajabov Street. Tel: 24552. US$10 per night. A friendly family home within a courtyard, comfortable rooms and good food. Good indoor toilet. Water can be a problem (but this applies everywhere in Istaravshan). The clean public baths are nearby.

HOTELS

Presidential Hotel, Hayiot Mahal, 26, Dusti Street. Tel: 22911. Owner Abdullo Rajabov. 6 double rooms at US$50 per person per night. Within its own walls, good standard of accommodation with en suite facilities and a swimming pool. Has artesian well, so water not a problem.

Blacksmiths in Istaravshan

Hotel Istaravshan, Lenin Street near Firdousi cinema. Reasonable accommodation and clean. 25 somoni per night.

Hotel Guli Surkh, near main bazaar. 3 somonis per night. Noisy, dirty, but hot showers.

The road from Istaravshan to Khujund is 70 km, on a good surface. It passes a reservoir, with one of the ubiquitous busts of Lenin, and through a fertile area of fields of wheat, vegetables, vineyards and cotton. The produce from here is exported as far as Russia in refrigerated trucks.

Much of the land is planted with cotton. In the autumn large gangs of students are forced to spend a semester picking cotton, without pay, receiving just their very basic board and lodging. A student told me the only good thing was the discos in the evenings, but it was still "slavery" (see section Cotton – Blessing or Curse).

Small boys stand by the roadside holding up dead snakes, alleged to cure TB, and skins of hedgehogs, reputedly a cure for piles.

Painted wooden roof of the Chahor Gumbaz Mausoleum, Istaravshan

Khudjand

Population 166,000   Telephone prefix 3422

Khudjand, continuously occupied for 2,500 years, was founded – possibly on the site of an earlier settlement – by Alexander the Great. It is the furthest point he reached in Central Asia and the city was named Alexandria Eschate (Alexandria the Furthest). If you stand on the south bank of the Syr Darya (ancient Jaxartes), just to the west of the main bridge and look across at the large statue of Lenin on the north bank, you are standing near where Alexander stood watching his troops attacking the Scythians in 329 BC.

The Scythians were redoubtable warriors and formidable mounted archers. Alexander ordered an initial bombardment using catapults mounted on boats. His troops then crossed the river on inflatable ox skins stuffed with straw. His cavalry, supported by infantry and archers engaged the enemy and routed them. His scouts pursued the Scythians, but reported there was nothing beyond the river except desert hills. Alexander decided that was far enough.

The city became one of the most important places in Central Asia. It was a key junction on the Silk Road. The beautiful city was razed by Genghis Khan. Through history it remained a centre of considerable power. Prior to the Russian invasion in the nineteenth century it was one of the main emirates in Central Asia.

The modern city, the largest in the north, stretches along both banks of the Syr Darya. It has pleasant tree lined boulevards, and a number of impressive government and municipal buildings with carefully tended flowerbeds. There is a greater sense of prosperity than in the rest of Tajikistan. Most of the city population is Tajik, with the Uzbeks mainly living in the countryside around.

Pushkin Square has handsome neo-classical buildings. From the square, an attractive park, including a row of busts of the great men of Tajikistan, leads down to the banks of the Syr Darya. Along the riverbank is a tree-lined pathway, with a number of restaurants, cafes and *choikhonas*. Dominating Pushkin Square is the impressive Kamoli Khudjandi Theatre (named after the great 14th century writer born in Khudjand). It has an art nouveau feel about it, with an impressive vestibule and a large elegant auditorium. Definitely worth a look, though performances are limited.

There are ATMs at most banks, including an outside one at the Agrinovest Bank on Lenin Street. There are plenty of internet cafes.

For visitors needing to register, there is an OVIR office at 170, Kamoli Khujandi Street. Open Mon–Fri, 0800–1200 and 1300–1700, Sat 0800–1200.

The State University of Gafurov Bobojon is built in elegant neo-classical style.

The Somonyon Art Gallery at 69, Lenin Street houses a good collection of figurative, abstract and landscape paintings by local artists.

The main square is Registoni Panjshanbe. There is a particularly good bazaar, with a range of vegetables and fruit reflecting the fertile soil of the area. Part of it is housed in a very ornate pink and white building, in high confectionary style, with stalls spilling over to the surrounding streets. The bus station is near the bazaar with minibuses going to local towns in the Ferghana valley and to Dushanbe.

Across from the Panjshanbe bazaar is a new mosque, next to a 13th century mausoleum and shrine, dedicated to Shaikh Maslihaddin 1133–1223, with a gilded roof added. The craftsmen were the same Russians as those who gilded St Basil's cathedral in Moscow. There is a 21 m minaret of baked brick built in 1865 and renovated in 1902–3. In the square outside the mosque are people selling books, and beggars outside.

From the airport to the south of the city there are daily flights to Dushanbe.

There is a railway station with trains going to Dushanbe, taking 24 hours. This is because the train has to go via Uzbekistan. There is also a line to Kanibadam to the east.

Next to Victory Park are the remains of the old citadel rebuilt in the 13th century, and now being reconstructed. It is possible to see sections of the walls in the original brickwork. Excavations have revealed Greek and Bactrian coins. Inside the reconstructed main gate, with its impressive 19th century lamp, is a museum. There is a good range of exhibits of items found in the citadel, including a Colt pistol, apparently beloved of Russian officers.

A new museum, more like an "experience" has opened next to the fortress walls. It is far removed from the traditional Soviet museums. It is spacious, with exhibits shown imaginatively and explanations in Tajik, Russian and sometimes English. The museum is a celebration of Tajik history and culture. There are halls with separate themes, e.g. the Hellenistic Age. Archaeological exhibits are set out imaginatively, and good sections on Tajik/Persian writers, poets and politicians. There are rooms devoted to the Russian era and modern Tajikistan.

Dominating the large foyer is a statue of Timur Malik, another figure from the Tajik past, resurrected in the cause of encouraging a spirit of national identity. Timur was a local resistance leader against Genghis Khan in the thirteenth century. He

established a fortress on an island in the Syr Darya, from where his archers sallied forth against the Mongol positions, in boats covered in hides and dried clay soaked in vinegar, as a protection against fire arrows. The Mongols placed chains across the river, but Timur cut them with his sword. In the end Timur ran out of supplies and the Mongols cornered the Tajiks. The legend has it that Timur asked his troops to fight for their people, but any who wished could go now, as they faced certain death. None went and all were killed. In fact Timur escaped and fought one more successful battle against the Mongols.

There is an interesting small museum devoted to Rahimov Abduqoder at his former house at 7, Firdousi Street. Tel: 810 099 23422 / 63358. Rahimov was from Khudjand, served with the Red Army in World War Two, was wounded and captured at Smolensk. He refused to join the Turkestan Legion (see 'A Town Called Monday' page 58), was sent to a concentration camp in Poland, but escaped to France and joined the resistance in Normandy. He undertook sabotage prior to the Normandy landings. After the war he returned home, but as with many who had been prisoners of war, he was deemed a traitor and sent to the notorious Magadan gulag. He was released in 1949. He eventually contacted his French resistance friends, but was not allowed to visit France until 1987. He was decorated and given a pension by the French. He died in 2005.

His son Abdu Kahor will proudly show you the pictures of his father, his medals and letters from his French friends. The museum is in a room in the courtyard of a typical Khudjand town house, which adds to the attraction.

Lake Kairakkum

22 km from Khudjand is the enormous artificial lake of Kairakkum. It has a number of resorts along the northern shore with beaches, parks, playing areas and *choikhonas*. In the searing heat of the summer, these resorts are very popular with local people, particularly at weekends.

Leave Khudjand by the main road east and turn off after 11 km, past derelict factories to the dam over the outlet. Just beyond this is the popular beach resort of Bukhta Mirnaya. Nearby is the sanatorium 'Shifo' (Tel: 24387), with 150 rooms being renovated to a reasonable standard. A simple room with full board and massage treatment is 18 somonis per day. There are luxury rooms with en suite facilities with a separate sitting room for US$30 per day. The place gives the feel of the facilities provided for privileged workers in the Soviet Union, and the cuisine, atmosphere and loud-speaker-radio are of their era. It has attractive gardens, and although a bit run down now, and like all Soviet resorts a bit heavy on the concrete, it would be a reasonably pleasant place to spend a night or two.

Palace of Arbob

On the road east from Khudjand there is a turning to the left after 7 km, and then a further 3 km to the extraordinary Palace of Arbob. Definitely a place to visit. It was

Palace of Arbob (above left)   *Pushkin Square with Kamoli Khudjandi theatre (bottom left)*

the centre of the Voroshilov State Collective Farm, but rather than being a collection of huts, it is a recreation of the Winter Palace at St Petersburg! A series of water gardens lead up to the palace, with its two wings. From the complex there are views across to the hills to the north. Built between 1951 and 1956, it was the inspiration of the local head of the collective farm, O. Urunkojaev. From photographs of him, he was clearly a larger than life character, with a huge belly and a magnificent moustache. He was a man of importance: there are pictures of him with Krushchev and other Soviet dignitaries.

There is a splendid theatre that can hold 700 people, with a large vestibule, all now empty and echoing. It is essential to visit the museum on the first floor in one of the wings, (entrance 3 somoni). It consists of a corridor with several rooms off, all superbly decorated. The theme is the glorification of the achievements of the collective farm and its place within the Soviet system. There are exhibits about cotton production, a recreation of the boss' office, some evocative Soviet style paintings and propaganda posters. Amid the statistics of production figures there are pictures and posters of happy, productive workers. The reality would have been very different.

A plaque on the main building records an important occasion in the history of Tajikistan was held at this palace, "The 16th session of the Supreme Soviet of Tajikistan was held from 16th November to 2nd December 1992, when the new constitutional government has been established and the leadership of the Tajik state has been elected". It marked the political watershed of the civil war and the rise of an unknown young man from the south, Emomali Rakhmon.

Accommodation
Top of the range
Khudjand Hotel, 1, Rakhmovlon Beckova Street (just off Pushkin Square)
5 luxurious rooms with en suite facilities. 170 somonis per night. Tel: 3422 65994

Vahdat Hotel, 3, Rakhmovlon Beckova Street   Tel: 3422 651017
Luxurious rooms with en suite facilities. 160 somonis per night for standard, 200 for luxe

Tavhid, 117, Firdousi Street   Tel: 3422 67766
12 luxurious rooms with en suite facilities. 150 somonis per night semi luxe, 180 luxe

Middle Range
Ehson Hotel, 170 Lenin Street (2 km from city centre)   Tel: 3422 66984
66 rooms, some with en suite facilities and balcony. 60 somonis per night.
Popular with travellers.

Lower Range
Sharq, 1, Sharq Street (street off Registoni Panjshanbe Square)   Tel: 3422 60993
Entrance through neo-classical building with busts of Lenin and Stalin on the outside, on north side of street. Go up the wide stairs past shops to fourth floor.

Shared rooms. Toilet satisfactory. Owner Abdurakmon pleasant and speaks some English. For rooms with 5/6 beds 5 somonis per person, with 2 beds 7 somonis.

Hotel Leninabad Typical dreary former state hotel. Single 10 somoni, Luxe 60 somoni.

The **Intourist Hotel**, overlooking the river, is being renovated.

EATING
There are plenty of restaurants, cafes, bakeries and shashlik stalls. The local bread is excellent.
Pyramid Restaurant Popular with the small expatriate community, near the museum, serving international dishes. Main 9–12 somonis. Good food and ambience.

Uighur Restaurant, 63, Gagarin Street. Uighur and local dishes.

Rafshan By the river. Good shashlik, salads and fish dishes

Kanibadam
80 km from Khudjand on a good straight road east. The road follows the lakeshore, about 1 km inland. There are irrigated fields and orchards close to the lake, but the hills beyond the further shore and the countryside to the south are arid. There is a small oilfield, with the typical pumping "donkeys", used in oilfields worldwide.

Kanibadam is a modern city. In the northern suburbs at Saifuloev Street is the medrassa of Oym, built in the 16th and 17th centuries. It is only one of the few in Central Asia to have been founded by a woman (others include Bibi Fatima in Bukhara, and the Musalla of Gawhar Shad in Herat). It is not used as a medrassa, but it is well preserved after renovation in 1996. It consists of separate areas for boys and girls to study, with a number of individual cells. There is a well-kept garden.

In Soviet times it was first used as a prison in 1941, then as a store for a collective farm, and later a correction centre for boys. It is hoped to develop it as a museum of socialism. It is not easy to find. Ask for the Medrassa of Oym.

There is a mosque next door. The museum at Shokir Boirov Street nearby was closed when we visited.

Isfara

It is 30 km from Kanibadam to the modern town of Isfara, with its share of abandoned factories and an impressive golden Lenin. There are two interesting mosques and a craftsman using medieval techniques:

• The 200 year old Hodijon mosque (Mosque of the pilgrims) was closed under the Russians, but now we were told has 10,000 people attending on Fridays. Its ornate paintwork has been carefully restored, with a 30 m minaret built in 1993. To find it, cross the bridge, to Mirme Street, and turn right into Kalima Street.

• In the eastern suburb of Navigilem is a fine 16th century mosque, built by Abdullo Khan, Khan of Khudjand, an Uzbek and the last khan of the Shaibon dynasty. The entry is through gates on the main road into a large courtyard. The mosque has a plain exterior, and is austere within. The right hand side has been renovated, the left is in its original form. There is a 150 year old minaret, with an iconic stork's nest on the top.

• Dekonov Addusalom is a skilled woodcarver, who uses techniques from the 10th century. To find his workshop, leave the mosque at Navigilem (previous item) turn right and walk for 300 m to the office of a telephone company. On the opposite side of the road is a blue gate, leading to his workshop at 62, Dukchi Street. Tel: 2 61 36. Addusalom uses the ancient techniques. No power tools are used. His lathe is hand-held, rather like a bow from a bow and arrow. He works this backwards and forwards with his right hand, and carves with his left hand as the wood rotates.

Some of his other tools date from the 18th century. In spite of this primitive technique he produces delicate work, often incorporating snakes (guardians of gold) into his designs. He favours apricot wood, which is meant to have special qualities to bring luck. To have a walking stick of apricot wood will prolong life. He makes combs to a traditional design. If a woman has such a comb it will ensure she has the same number of suitors as there are teeth on the comb.

He is a friendly and welcomes visitors to his workshop, where it is possible to purchase a wide variety of item from the desirable combs to figures of animals.

His son is not interested, so this technique will probably die when he retires, although he is teaching some orphans, so there is a small possibility it might continue.

There is a museum, which is reached by crossing the bridge and turning right. There is likely to be the usual problem of finding someone to open up, but it is worth it. There are the usual sections on natural history, the Soviet revolution and local finds of pottery. There is also a mock up of the oubliette, the Zindan in Bukhara, beloved by the Soviets to illustrate the horrors of the regime they replaced. The gramophone is there which was played to announce victory in the Great Patriotic War in 1945.

Mosque of Hazrat-i Shoh

20 km south of Isfara in the village of Churku (or Surkh) is a mosque with some unusual and interesting woodcarving. It is worth the detour. The road passes along the fertile Isfara valley, with the remains of a castle on the right. In the village of Zulmrat there is a sanatorium, where it is possible to stay. It is reputed to be good.

On reaching Churku, turn left at the main square, and then left again to reach the mosque of Hazrat-i Shoh. Through the gates is a large courtyard. The 18th century mosque has ornate ceiling paintings of flowers. However, the most interesting feature is in the left corner of the courtyard: the ancient mausoleum of Kasim, a descendant of Ali. The woodwork dates from the 8th to 10th century. The heads of owls and other birds are depicted, which is unusual in Muslim art, which does not normally represent living things. There are Kufic inscriptions. (Eastern squarer Arabic script is different from Andalusian Kufi, derived from the Moors). In the darkened mausoleum, there is a feeling of being in a very ancient place, which has been revered for hundreds of years.

ALEXANDER THE GREAT
– ISKANDER'S TRAIL IN TAJIKISTAN   Huw Thomas

In the spring of 329 BC Alexander the Great's conquests brought him to the river Oxus (Amu Darya), which forms the boundary between Afghanistan and Tajikistan. After defeating Darius, the Persian king, Alexander pursued the royal pretender, Bessus who had murdered Darius, across the Hindu Kush mountains. His army moved north, crossing the 4,000 m Khawak pass in mid-winter and arrived at the banks of the Oxus to face a new challenge. Bessus had crossed to the far banks and had commandeered or burned all the river-boats. Crossing the wide and swift-flowing river seemed an impossible task. Alexander, always an original thinker, was undaunted. He gave instructions that his men should sew up the hides they used as tents, fill them with straw and use these to float across the river. Within five days his army had reached the north bank, probably at Kilif, about 30 km west of Termez on the Uzbek/Tajik border.

About 100 km east of where Alexander crossed is evidence of the Macedonian influence found at the temple of Takht-i Sangin. The temple architecture combines Persian and Greek styles. Many of the artefacts excavated from this site are now on display in Dushanbe's Museum of National Antiquities, including a perfectly preserved ivory head of Alexander. Found nearby is the magnificent collection of gold and silver objects dating from the Achaemenid Empire, known as the Oxus Treasure, now housed in the British Museum (see special topic).

Having crossed the Oxus, Alexander moved north. Bessus was betrayed to Alexander by his own troops. Alexander, viewing Bessus as a traitor to his former master, Darius, ordered him to be mutilated in the Persian fashion, his nose and ears cut off before being sent for trial and gruesome execution.

Alexander now became bogged down, fighting for two years against his most difficult adversary. He was faced with uprisings. Both in Bactria (now northern Afghanistan and southern Tajikistan) and Sogdia (now northern Tajikistan and eastern Uzbekistan) the ancient warrior classes were fiercely independent. They were excellent horsemen and archers, who lived in impregnable strongholds. Alexander fell back to Maracanda (present day Samarqand) and carried out a scorched earth policy against the surrounding region, inflaming the local opposition lead by Spitamenes, a high-ranking nobleman, who waged a guerrilla campaign against him.

Alexander moved north east for 250 km to the Jaxartes river (Syr Darya) and selected a site for his new city. Spitamenes was growing in strength. Alexander sent forces to blockade Cyropolis (Istaravshan), a city founded by Cyrus the Great around 530 BC, and attacked six other towns in the area. "No other town put up such a fierce resistance", reported the historian Curtius of the siege of Cyropolis. Alexander sustained a serious wound. His forces finally managed to enter the city through a water gate. In all seven towns the Macedonians executed all the males of military age and the women and children were enslaved.

Alexander returned to the Jaxartes to build his new town. In seventeen days a six kilometre wall of sun dried brick was built around his camp. This was to be among the thirty or more Alexandrias. This was Alexandria Eschate, or "Alexandria the Furthermost", which is now Khudjand. Greek coins and artefacts have been excavated from the foundations of the fortress and can be seen in Khudjand at the Museum of Archaeology and Fortifications in the reconstructed gateway.

Spitamenes' forces were encamped at Samarqand. Alexander sent an expeditionary force, but it was ambushed and two thousand infantry and 300 cavalry were lost. This was the first serious military defeat for Alexander for over twenty years.

To add to his troubles the nomadic Scythian warriors were gathering on the north bank of the Jaxartes. Curtius describes Alexander at Khudjand, "He had still not recovered from his wound; in particular he had difficulty in speaking, a condition stemming from malnutrition and the pain in his neck ... he could not stand in the ranks, ride a horse or give his men instructions or encouragement ... his voice was so quavering and feeble that it was difficult even for those next to hear him." But he had to act.

Alexander decided to tackle the Scythians first and attacked using catapults mounted on boats, driving the Scythians away from the riverbank. The infantry then crossed the river on ox skins stuffed with chaff. Once a bridgehead had been established the cavalry crossed and won a decisive victory (see chapter on The Ferghana Valley).

Still ill, Alexander marched back to Samarqand. The Sogdians continued their guerrilla war, but by the spring of 327 BC, Alexander had received reinforcements from Greece. 327 BC has been described as the missing year in the history of Alexander, because the sources are in disagreement. He marched south from Samarqand to the Oxus, following it for eleven days before crossing the river near the

Temple at Takht-i Sangin (see chapter on The South) to Ai Khanoum, at the junction of the Oxus and the Kunduz Darya flowing from Afghanistan. Here Alexander probably founded Alexandria–on–the–Oxus, the first Greek city ever to be discovered in Central Asia.

From this base, the army split up into five groups and crossed into present day Tajikistan, up the Vakhsh valley to Dushanbe and over the Anzob Pass, burning and killing all the way. Spitamenes was losing allies and after defeat in the deserts of Uzbekistan, his own associates murdered him and sent his head to the Macedonians.

The legend tells a different story, of how Spitamenes was pursued to Iskander Kul (Iskander is Alexander in Arabic), a beautiful lake in the Fan mountains (see page 131). Alexander ordered a dam to be built across the Iskander River, thus forming the lake. Spitamenes fled to Makshevat, a village in the Hissar mountain range, and hid in a cave high up on the cliffs. He refused to surrender and died of starvation. In the cave of Khoja Ishaq there is a mummy that can be visited, that some reckon is Spitamenes (see page 129).

Some of Spitamenes followers retreated to the Sogdian Rock, an impregnable natural fortress. Alexander called on the Sogdians to discuss surrender terms to allow them a safe passage home. The defenders laughed and told him to find soldiers with wings. Alexander hated to be mocked, and large bonuses were offered to mountaineer troops to scale

Figure of a zebu, fragment of a throne, Semiganch, 5th–3rd century BC

the cliffs. 300 ascended the cliff at night using tent pegs as pitons and flaxen ropes. 30 fell to their deaths, but the rest reached the summit. Next morning they looked down on the Sogdians. Alexander told the Sogdians to surrender as the soldiers with wings had flown to the summit. The Sogdians fearing they were facing many more troops than they could see, surrendered.

The final battle against the Sogdians was at another impregnable fortress, which was defended by Sisimithres (the locations of neither this fortress, nor the Sogdian Rock, are yet known). This time Alexander's tactic was to build a causeway across the abyss. Engineers climbed down the cliffs and drove stakes into the rock faces at the narrowest point in the ravine, then hurdles of willow were laid out in a network and surfaced with earth. The bridge was completed, and after a bombardment of arrows, probably from catapults, the Sogdians were persuaded to surrender. Sisimithres was spared.

It was here, according to some versions of the story, that Alexander set eyes on Roxanne (Rukshona meaning "Little Star" in Tajik), daughter of the Sogdian baron Oxyartes. Rukshona was "more beautiful than any woman except the wife of Darius". She had been captured at the Sogdian Rock and was dancing with other girls. Alexander fell in love. They were married at the fortress of Sismithres at a huge banquet, with Alexander and his Sogdian father in law cutting the bread with his sword.

It had taken two years of ferocious campaigning with heavy losses, but Alexander had pacified Sogdia and Bactria. He could now turn his attention to India.

Rukshona survived until after Alexander's death, but was murdered in 313. Their tale of love is still the subject of stories and legends throughout Central Asia.

Rukshona is still a popular name in Tajikistan, and you can still see beautiful girls of that name dancing as their namesake did 2,000 years ago.

Strabo and Pliny refer to Greek cities in Central Asia. There are likely to be the remains of more Greek cities buried along the banks of the Oxus and in the soil of the Vakhsh valley waiting to be excavated.

[**Acknowledgement:** I am indebted to Neville McBain for material in this article. I have also drawn heavily from *In the Footsteps of Alexander the Great* by Michael Wood (BBC Books, 2007), and *Alexander the Great* by Robin Lane Fox (Penguin, 2004).]

THE SOGDIANS, MASTERS OF THE SILK ROAD Huw Thomas

The phrase "Silk Road" conjures up visions of exotic cities, colourful bazaars and camel trains carrying precious goods over mountain ranges and across waterless deserts. This indeed was the reality. The traveller to Tajikistan can follow sections of the Road (or roads) that were once the greatest commercial highway in the world, linking China with the Mediterranean.

The people who played the key role on the Silk Road at its height were the Sogdians, the ancestors of the Tajiks.

The Silk Road

The term "Silk Road" or Seidenstrasse was coined in 1877 by German geographer Baron Ferdinand von Richthofen, great uncle of the Red Baron, the ace German fighter pilot in World War I. The Silk Road was not a single road – it was a vast network of land-based trade routes, and although silk was one of the main items of trade throughout, many other commodities were transported.

The trade was at its height from the 1st century BC to the 10th century AD. It continued in a diminished form, mainly because of political instability on the route, until the fifteenth century

Its origins are lost in the distant past, but evidence from burial mounds in Mongolia suggest there was already extensive contact between imperial China and the nomads of the northern steppes from the second millennium BC.

The Chinese had been concerned about the growing strength of the Xiongnu and other nomads, who controlled the grasslands in the curve of the Yellow River and parts of Central Asia. The Chinese strategy for countering the threat from the Xiongnu was a combination of bribery, strategic marriages and military action. To counter the military threat from the mounted nomads, the Chinese had first to take up horsemanship, and then they were hampered by the poor quality of the horses available to them.

In 138 BC, the Chinese Emperor Wudi dispatched an emissary, Zhang Qian in search of allies, particularly the Yuezhi, who controlled Bactria (present day northern Afghanistan). The Yuezhi were not interested, but Zhang Qian's discoveries were one of the factors which launched the greatest trade route in history. After many adventures he brought back the exciting news of the "heavenly horses" of the

Ferghana valley – horses that galloped so fast they sweated blood. Emperor Wudi sent further missions to acquire some of these horses for breeding stock, and territories to the west were gradually opened up for trade.

Long before the start of the Silk Road there had been trade on both sides of the Pamirs, jade within China and lapis lazuli from Badakhshan to Egypt, but it was not until the second century BC that there is evidence of sustained long-distance trade crossing the Pamirs.

It was silk that gave its name to the great east-west trade. It had enormous significance and was traded as far as Rome. It was the Chinese who cultivated silk. Wild silk had been harvested in the Middle East and India, but not on a significant scale.

According to Chinese legend the creation of silk is credited to Xi Ling, wife of the mythical Yellow Emperor, but it is probable that silk was made as far back as 4000 BC. Chinese silk is produced by unravelling and joining the strands of the cocoons made by caterpillars of the moth Bombyx mori. The caterpillars feed on mulberry leaves and produce a gum called sericin. To prevent breaking the silk thread, the majority of chrysalises are stifled in steam. The cocoons are placed in hot water, which softens it, making it possible to reel it.

Rome's first introduction to silk was in 53 BC at the Battle of Carrhae (modern-day Harran, on the boundary of modern Turkey and Syria) when the Roman army were resoundingly defeated by the Parthians. A possible factor in the defeat was the consternation caused in the Roman ranks by the unfurling of hundreds of silk banners – before that time generally unknown in Rome – by the Parthian troops. In spite of this first disastrous encounter with silk, it became a highly valued commodity in Greece and Rome. Chinese silk was the first significant commodity to be exported from east to west. In Greece and Rome it was associated with decadence. Grumpy old men like Seneca the Elder were particularly upset by the transparency of silk. "Wretched flocks of maids labour so that the adulteress may be visible through this dress, so that her husband has no more acquaintance than any outsider or foreigner with his wife's body" he bemoaned (The Elder Seneca, Declamation, translated by M. Winterbottom). Silk remained stubbornly popular.

The Chinese managed to keep the secret of silk production for many centuries, but eventually some silk worms were smuggled out, supposedly in the elaborate coiffure of a Chinese princess betrothed to a Khotanese king. In fact there was silk production in the kingdom of Khotan from the 4th century AD, possibly earlier.

Later it was developed in Sogdia, especially around Bukhara and then moved westwards following the Battle of Talas in 751, when the Arabs defeated a Chinese army. Chinese silk weavers were sent to Damascus. Even so silk continued to be exported from China.

The Routes and the Trade

There were many variations to the Silk Road. The main route east was from the Chinese cities of Luoyang and Xi'an (Chang'an), to Lanzhou. The main routes then diverged, one running north and the other south of the Taklamakan Desert to Kashgar. From there one route went along the Ferghana valley to Osh and Khudjand to Samarqand. Another went south to Tashkurgan and then to Balkh in northern Afghanistan. From these cities the main routes west were through northern Persia to Baghdad and the eastern Mediterranean or along a more northern route through modern Turkey to Byzantium. There were many variations, often depending on the political situation at the time.

Caravans headed west from China with silk, jade, porcelain, gunpowder, furs, paper, ceramics, dyes, spices and tea. The eastward flow carried wine, textiles, ivory, wool, gold, glass, gems, Baltic amber, Mediterranean coral, and even acrobats and entertainers for the Chinese court. From India came slaves, arena animals, sandalwood, palm oil, sugar, perfumes and precious stones.

Great cities such as Baghdad and Samarqand grew up as entrepôts, where goods were traded in both directions. These cities were far bigger than any in Europe. All along the routes settled agricultural towns grew up, alongside the nomadic livestock rearing people, who sold horses and camels to the traders. To provide food, fodder, sleeping accommodation, *caravanserai* were built at intervals of one day's journey. It must not be assumed a caravan went the whole distance from China to the Mediterranean; goods were exchanged all along the routes.

The Sogdians

In the heyday of the Silk Road, from the second century BC until the end of the tenth century, the eastern trade was dominated by the Sogdians, ancestors of the modern Tajiks. Little was known about these remarkable people until the twentieth century, when a series of discoveries helped to throw light on their civilisation.

More and more is coming to light about the Sogdians. The three main sources about them are the Dunhuang Sogdian letters, and two discoveries in Tajikistan in the Zarafshan valley: the Dewashtich documents and the excavations at Penjikent. Other sources are excavations at Afraysiab (near Samarqand), Chinese historical sources and discoveries of Sogdian funerary couches in the last two decades.

The Sogdians, an Aryan people, had settled in the lands between the Oxus (Amu Darya) and the Jaxartes (Syr Darya). Their capital was Maracanda (Samarqand), which is still a predominantly Tajik city in present day Uzbekistan. The name of the Sogdians is preserved in the name of the province in Tajikistan covering the Zarafshan valley – Sughd.

The Sogdians were formidable warriors, who could retreat to their mountain fortresses in time of war. The first written records about them are from the fourth century BC, when Alexander the Great invaded their land. He suffered his first major defeat at their hands at Samarqand, and it took him two years of hard campaigning to subdue them (see special topic On the Trail of Iskander).

The military power of the Sogdians did not recover, but they became merchants all over Central Asia and China. Their language (see page 133, Yagnob valley) became the language of trade along the Silk Road, and they were partly responsible for the movement of religions such as Zoroastrianism, Manichaeism and Buddhism eastwards along the Silk Road. Chinese stories of the Sogdians describe them as born to their trade, "at birth honey was put in their mouth and gum on their hands ... they learned the trade from the age of five ... on the age of twelve they were sent to do business in a neighbouring state". (Nicholas Sims-Williams, article on 'The Sogdian Merchants in India and China'.)

The Dunhuang Sogdian Letters

An important discovery that has lead to more knowledge about the Sogdians was that by the British explorer Sir Aurel Stein (1862–1943). He made eight major expeditions to Central Asia, investigating numerous ancient sites. The documents he discovered at Dunhuang Limes appear to have come from a postbag abandoned around AD 313–4, dated by mention of contemporary events in Luoyang. The letters were written by Sogdian merchants living in Dunhuang and other towns along the Silk Road to China, mainly about trading matters, such as commodities and weights. From these letters and other sources it appears that in the fourth century AD, the Sogdians had almost a monopoly of a triangular trade between India and Sogdiana, and India and China. Sogdian merchants settled in China, and became prominent in Chinese society.

The Sogdians organised the transport to China of grapevines and lucerne to feed the heavenly horses. They also carried the special mare's teat grapes from the oases of Kocho and Turfan, packed in lead containers. Luxury goods from the west included silverware from Persia which had an influence on Chinese silverwork, glass vessels and beads from Syria and Babylon, amber from the Baltic and purple woollen cloth from Rome. From China they brought silk, and used Chinese paper. In the eighth century they established paper manufacture in Samarqand, from where it spread to Europe.

Movement of Religions

The Sogdians did not just take goods to China. They were mainly responsible for the spread of their religion, Zoroastrianism, to China. Zoroaster or Zarathusra, lived in eastern Iran some time between the 10th and 6th century BC and preached a religion incorporating older Iranian beliefs. Zoroastrianism shared many ideas with Judaism – a belief in the Messiah, a resurrection, a last judgement and a heavenly paradise. The Supreme god of Zoroastrianism is the Ahura Mazda, the embodiment of light, life and truth. The incarnation of darkness, death and evil, Angra Mainyu, has always existed alongside him, and the two are engaged in a constant struggle. Although man was created by Ahura Mazda, he was given free will, and so can choose either good or evil: Zoroastrianism urges that man must resist evil in his thoughts, words and deeds, but that a saviour will come to the world and that good will triumph over evil. The symbol of Ahura Mazda is the eternal fire, and the Sogdians worshipped at fire altars in their temples, in which the fire was never allowed to die.

There were Zoroastrian temples in China, and much later in India where the successors of the Zoroastrians are the Parsees. In the Yagnob valley and in the Pamirs there are remnants of Zoroastrian practice and some shrines incorporate a few of their symbols. Recent archaeological reports report more finds identified as fire temples.

In the third century AD, Zoroastrianism was challenged by a prophet from Babylon called Mani, whose ideas offered a dualistic view of the universe, where good is balanced against evil and where esoteric interpretations lead to salvation through knowledge. Spirit was equated with light, matter with darkness, and good was seen as particles of light struggling to escape from the dark matter in which it was trapped. Mani declared himself a successor to Zoroaster, Buddha and Jesus Christ. He spoke of an "Elect" group, who would lead the faith wearing white, adhering to a vegetarian diet and refraining from reproduction. The ordinary followers – the Hearers – had a less onerous life style. Mani was crucified in AD 276.

Manichaeism was brought to Sogdiana in Mani's lifetime by Mar Ammo, the "Disciple of the East". Samarqand was a Manichean centre, and from there spread east, with monasteries all the way to China. The religion was adopted by the Uighurs in western China and survived until the rise of the Mongols. It appears to have survived in other parts of China until the fourteenth century.

Dewashtich Letters

A second discovery that throws light on the Sogdians was the chance find in 1932 of a cache of documents on Mount Mugh in the Zarafshan valley (see special topic on Dewashtich). These letters throw light on Sogdian politics and the economy in the Zarafshan valley in the eighth century, just before a series of defeats by the Arabs.

Excavations at Penjikent, the "Pompeii of Central Asia"

A third discovery is still continuing. Russian and Tajik archaeologists started excavations of ancient Penjikent in 1946. About half of the site has been excavated. (see chapter on Zarafshan Valley). The city was besieged by the Arabs in AD 722, and much of the city was set on fire. As at Pompeii, a record was preserved at a moment in time. Walls caved in preserving fragments of frescoes, which have been painstakingly restored. The fire also preserved some partly burned wooden statues and altars that would otherwise have rotted away.

It is possible to see a few of the frescoes in Dushanbe at the Museum of National Antiquities and some more at the Rudaki Museum in Penjikent. However, the majority and the finest examples are in the Hermitage in St Petersburg.

The frescoes help to illumine the legends and beliefs of the Sogdians, but also showed how they looked and dressed, and their way of life.

The frescoes show jousting and banqueting scenes. The Sogdians depicted themselves rather like modern Tajiks with Iranian type features, long thin faces, prominent noses and deep-set eyes. Nowadays most Tajik men sport moustaches, but the Sogdians had full-length beards. They wore a Phrygian hat, conical with the top turned forward; a knee-length jacket, with narrow trousers tucked into high leather boots, rather like the Kyrgyz wear today.

The 40 frescoes that have been discovered provide a rich repertory of legends, tales and myths of the Sogdians. Their art and literature included many motifs of

Greek, Persian and Indian origin. Among the pictorial narrative cycles are three epics: a local version of the Indian Mahabharata, the Roman story of Romulus and Remus and the Iranian legend of Rustam. There are also many pictures of parables, fables, fairy tales and anecdotes: scenes from Aesop's Fables, the Panchatantra and the Sinbadnameh

In Sogdiana, rulers were less despotic, the succession was not necessarily hereditary, and the noble and merchants held significant influence in the city. There appears to have been an element of social mobility and it was acceptable for the middle-class to aspire not only to economic and social advancement, but also to imitate the tastes of the ruler in decorating their houses.

The houses had two or three storeys, some with reception rooms. It was customary that there would be a symbol of protection against evil in the porch, but otherwise there was much variety of subject matter in the paintings. In the reception areas there were normally paintings at three levels. On top were religious paintings, connected with the family cult, in the middle heroic tales of warriors at the bottom parables and the life of Everyman.

The priming coats were of gypsum, the sky blue background was painted in lapis lazuli, the outlines in soot black or dark ochre red pigment. The main colours are in ochre paints. The paintings were fixed to the walls with vegetable glue.

The heroic panels were often about the struggles of Rustam, the great Iranian hero and his horse Rakhsh, against the divs (demons). At the lowest level there were scenes from Aesop's Fables, such as the Goose that Laid the Golden Egg or other parables such as the tale of the Stupid Sandalwood Seller, and the monkey who removes a flea from a man's head with a hammer.

The picture that emerges of the Sogdians is of an outward looking people, influenced by other cultures, thousands of miles away. Also of a resourceful and adventurous people, who admired courage, and did not have too much respect for authority. They also enjoyed a hedonistic life style with fondness for drinking and food.

The Silk Road in Tajikistan

For anyone wishing to follow the Silk Road in Tajikistan, the main route would be to start, if possible, at Samarqand in Uzbekistan. This was one of the main cities and mercantile centre of the Sogdians. From there thousands of caravans would have journeyed to Penjikent, and then up the Zarafshan valley to Aini, and across the Shahristan Pass. The route continued to Istaravshan and another important city on the Silk Road, Khudjand, and then on to Osh and Kashgar. The heavenly horses would have been driven from here all the way to China.

There are other routes that passed through Tajikistan. A route came from Termez on the Amu Darya to Hissar, which has the best-preserved caravanserai in the country, then on to Dushanbe, and up the Rasht valley, over the Karamyk Pass to Osh in Kyrgyzstan.

There were other even more difficult routes through the Pamirs, along the Wakhan corridor and over passes to Tashkurgan.

Further reading:
- *The Silk Road: Two Thousand Years in the Heart of Asia* by Frances Wood (University of California Press, 2003); a lucid and entertaining account of all aspects of the Silk Road.
- *Life Along the Silk Road* by Susan Whitfield (University of California Press, 2001); brilliantly brings to life how individuals actually lived and travelled on the Silk Road.
- *Legends, Tales and Fables in the Art of Sogdiana* by Boris Marshak (Bibliotheca Persica Press, December 2002); a scholarly and detailed account of the Sogdian frescoes.
- An excellent map is *The Ancient Silk Road: An illustrated map featuring the ancient network of routes between China and Europe*, published by Odyssey Maps (*refer* www.odysseypublications.com).

Rasht Valley

East of Dushanbe lies one of the most beautiful and interesting valleys in Tajikistan, seldom visited by foreigners. The official name is the Rasht valley, but it is often known as the Karategin or Gharm valley, from the name of the main town. It forms the upper reaches of the Vaksh River, flowing between the high peaks of the Pamirs to the east, and the Zarafshan range to the west. Many of the dramatic peaks are snow capped throughout the year, some over 5,000 m. The valley is broader than those in the Pamirs, and there is a great variety of scenery and vegetation. The river meanders through a mix of stony areas and fertile fields. There are a number of pleasant towns and villages. The people are very hospitable and give a genuine welcome to visitors. In the eighteenth century the population was mainly Kyrgyz, but there was an outbreak of a deadly epidemic and Tajik people moved up from Bukhara. The fertile fields provide excellent vegetables and fruit, some of which is sold in the markets in Dushanbe. There are some local dishes, mainly using bread, butter and yoghurt.

The climate is cool in spring and autumn, rising to 25 to 30 Centigrade in the summer. Winters are cold, but not as severe as in the Pamirs. The road from Dushanbe is open most of the year, but can be blocked by snow in mid-winter, and by mudslides in spring following rain. Visitors should be aware that in winter electricity supply is minimal.

The Rasht valley was the scene of some of the fiercest fighting in the civil war. It was not a safe place to visit until the end of the 90s. Visitors will see a few signs of the conflict, such as abandoned armoured personnel carriers. It is now safe to visit; the people have put past conflicts behind them and are concentrating on developing the economy.

Travellers will have the pleasure of knowing they are travelling along an important branch of the Silk Road, known as the Karategin route. Thousands of caravans would have passed this way making their journey from northern Persia on to Kashgar in China. The route followed the river to its headwaters, and then over the Karamuk Pass to what is now Kyrgyzstan. It would still be possible to travel this route, although the road can be blocked by snow in winter. From the pass it is 300 km to Osh in Kyrgyzstan. At the time of writing, the pass was not open to foreigners to cross into

Kyrgyzstan, but the situation may change. Check with your travel company. If opened it could lead to a superb circular tour from Dushanbe, up the Rasht valley to the Kyrgyz border, on to Osh, returning to Tajikistan, taking the Pamir Highway through Murghab and Khorog and back to Dushanbe. It would also be a good route from Dushanbe, through Kyrgyzstan and on – potentially – to China.

Travellers may also like to know that the valley is transit route for the transport of opium and heroin from Afghanistan to Russia.

It is a four to five hours drive from Dushanbe to the start of the valley, along a road, which is a mixture of tarmac in places or dirt surface. It is perfectly possible to do the journey in a Jhigoli (the Tajik Lada), but a four-wheel drive is preferable.

It is not necessary to obtain permission to come to the valley. There are good guesthouses in the main towns, and it is certain that accommodation could easily be found in any of the villages. There are plentiful supplies of reasonable meat and excellent vegetables and fruit. Although seldom seen, there is an abundance of wildlife including wild boar, bears, wolves and deer. There are a variety of birds. On one occasion I have watched Griffon vultures, lammergeier, and golden eagles circling over some carrion. The fishing is reported to be good, and no permits are required. It is a photographers' paradise. There is great scope for walking, trekking and mountain biking. There is a network of paths providing excellent day walks. There are also a number of passes over to neighbouring valleys that could be the basis for treks of 2 to 4 days. It would be advisable to hire a local person to act as guide.

Visitors should be aware that people do not speak English, and if you cannot speak Tajik or Russian, it might be wise to find an interpreter.

There should not be a problem in turning up at a guesthouse and finding a bed. However, our experience is that even if a guesthouse is full, somebody will appear who will sort out somewhere to stay the night.

Security

Be as sure as you can that you have a good driver who knows the roads and avoid mountain roads after dark. The road in parts is very narrow and prone to rockfall.

As elsewhere in Tajikistan, don't flash your cash.

The Journey

Leave Dushanbe by the main road east to the town of Kafirnihan (20 km). This is a typical Soviet style town with apartment blocks, wide streets and pleasant parks. There are many derelict factories.

It is not necessary to enter the town, cross the main bridge, take a fork left as the road enters the town, and then take the left turn at a roundabout with a statue of motherhood beyond it. This is the road to Faizabad and Ob-i Garm. The road passes through an increasingly hilly area, bypassing Faizabad. The road is mainly tarmac.

At 96 km Ob-i Garm is reached. It is a town with five spas. These are basic, with separate bathing for men and women. There is a recently renovated sanatorium at the start of the town, behind some blue gates. The charge is 10 somoni per night.

The road drops down to follow the river. Just beyond Ob-i Garm on the right across the valley is a multi-coloured housing complex, with high apartment blocks. This is Rogun, now in a sad state, established to provide housing for workers on a giant hydro-electric scheme in Soviet times. The scheme was abandoned and the area is littered with rusting machinery. There are plans to resurrect the project, involving flooding the valley many km upstream, and moving the local people to a new village.

The road follows along a bluff above the river, through pleasant villages. The last town before the road crosses the river is Nurobad. On most maps it will be marked as Darband. The authorities changed the name to Nurobad (Town of Light), when they had an electricity supply from a small hydro-electric plant. The town is just off the main road, but is worth a visit. On the main street is a fine choikhona with intricate woodcarving and painting. In front is a mulberry tree, reputed to be 1,000 years old. A local female saint, Hati Bibi is reputed to have sat under the tree and helped the poor. On the trunk of the tree is the likeness of a snake, which harmed no one as long as Hati Bibi was there. There are great views across the valley to the mountains.

Beyond Nurobad/Darband the road crosses the river on a massive iron bridge. The main road continues to Tavildara. Here is a turn up gorges and narrow valleys to the high pass to Kala-i Khum in the Panj valley. It is the main road to the Pamirs from end of May to end of October. In the mountains above Tavildara at the village of Sangor was the main hideout in the civil war for the opposition fighters in the area, particularly Juma Namangani (see special topic). If you are considering walking in this area, take a local guide; although there has been extensive mine clearance, it would be a wise precaution.

The junction is at the hamlet of Sarijar. Beyond the hamlet is a grass covered hill that appears to be part of the natural landscape. In fact, it is the fortress of Darband, with three separate, but interlinked forts covering many hectares. The outer walls are clearly visible. There are magnificent views of the Pamirs. The forts controlled the entrance to the Rasht valley. There is an easy route to the tops. About 2 km along the road to Gharm is a signpost to Gargana on the right. Follow the track for 300 m and there is a short, easy path to the forts. Just next to the forts are the derelict remains of a large industrial complex.

The sign showing the start of the Rasht valley is at 169 km from Dushanbe. The valley is wide, with a rich variety of vegetation, and good views of the meandering river, and the mountains. The road, which is mainly a dirt one, can be subject to occasional blocks due to mud slides, particularly in the spring. The road crosses back to the west bank to the town of Gharm, 190 km from Dushanbe.

Parade at Kala-i Khum [c. 1900]

Gharm

Gharm has one main street, with a reasonable bazaar and some smart looking *choikhonas*, particularly one with fine carving and paintwork that stands on a bridge across a small river. There is a new silver domed mosque. The town is showing signs of some prosperity after the ravages suffered in the civil war, with a number of new and renovated buildings. A large part of the male population is abroad, working in Russia and sending home remittances.

A popular place to stay is the MSDSP guesthouse at 52 Saimud in Burhon Street (the main street). Tel: 22289. The guesthouse is on the first floor above the MSDSP offices. It has 4 bedrooms, accommodating 9 people, bathroom, hot water, kitchen, 2 toilets, and a sitting room with satellite TV. The charge is US$12 per night, which includes breakfast. The guesthouse is popular with consultants inspecting NGO projects, and can be booked up in the summer. It is possible to book rooms ahead through the MSDSP office in Dushanbe.

A new hotel is due to open at time of writing. NGOs such as Mercy Corps and German Agro Action have hostels for their own staff, but could possibly accommodate visitors.

The Governor is keen to promote tourism. He emphasized the holiday of Navruz, 21/22nd March as being a highlight, with buzkashi and folk dancing.

Tajikabad

Tajikabad is 50 km from Gharm, on a reasonable road that follows the right bank of the Vakhsh. Here the views of the saw-toothed peaks are particularly fine. The town is the centre of a fertile agricultural area. There is an MSDSP office in the town with a small basic hostel of 4 beds. The Hukumat staff are especially helpful, including the deputy governor Zebo Humatova. The Hukumat have an excellent guesthouse, next to one reserved for the President. The bedrooms with 4 or 5 beds in each are clean, the staff are friendly and the outside bathroom and toilet reasonable. Meals can be provided. The charge is 15 somoni per night.

Near the town are two interesting shrines. The Mazor-i Fathabad is about 1 km from the centre. It commemorates a Sufi holy man, or Ishan, of the eighteenth century, famous for his good works. The shrine, which is surrounded by a graveyard, is not very impressive, but the views through trees to the high peaks are stunning. Women are not allowed beyond the gateway to the graveyard. There is a local curator.

The second shrine to Hazrat-i Bir Pustin is by the river, about 200 m from the Hukumat office. (Going west, take the first right, and then right again). This saint also lived in the eighteenth century. He began to live the good life, after being told to do so by his father's spirit. His name means "One Coat" in Kyrgyz. He gave away all his worldly goods, keeping only one leather coat. According to legend, this coat would grow wool in the winter, and shed it in the summer. The mausoleum is a small structure with a simple grave inside. There are guardians who will open the building, but women cannot enter. It is customary for the guardians to ask you to join them in prayer when visiting these places, and a donation is expected in return. You are bound to be offered tea.

There are a number of beauty spots around the town. Seven km away up a small valley is Dara-i Nushor. There is a guesthouse close to the village, where it is possible to stay, with permission from the Hukumat. The accommodation is basic, but there is electricity, and a pool with a fountain. If you would like to see wildlife, the local hunter Allaudin will welcome you to his house, provide a donkey, and take you on a search. He claims to be able to find wild boar, gazelle, bears, maybe wolves, and just possibly a snow leopard.

There is a local supply of good quality coal, which is mined at 4,000 m, but can only be mined and transported out in July and August, because this is the only time the road is open.

People will speak of the horrors of the civil war, when travel was very dangerous. Drivers were the unsung heroes, who put their lives at risk whenever they ventured on to the roads. Juma Namangani (see special topic) had a farm near the town. He and his followers travelled through the area, staying in *choikhonas* where people were sympathetic. The former manager of a collective farm told us how Namangani had demanded food for his followers, in spite of their being virtually none for the local people, a modern echo of the *basmachi*.

Khoit

Leaving Tajikabad there is a left turn after 3 km leading to the village of Khoit on the other side of the river. Turn left after the bridge, and continue for 9 km. The road has been washed away at one stretch, but a new track has been formed along the flood plain. The village of 5,000 people was the scene of a terrible earthquake in 1949, when we were told 20,000 people perished. Apart from being a pleasant village with orchards and carefully-tended fields, it is the home of a local writer, poet and historian, Hvrod Sharifhojaev. He is pleased to welcome visitors to his home and tell the history of the valley. On our visit he was away, but his charming daughter Musharafa Sharipova welcomed us to their traditional house, with a walled garden. We were, of course, offered lunch. To find his house, enter the village along the straight road from the riverbank, the road veers right and there is a small lane on the left. The house is 50 m on the right. Everybody in the village knows him, and can give directions.

Musharafa took us to a nearby cemetery to view a memorial to three women teachers who were killed in 1929 by Fugail Maksum, the local *basmachi* leader, supposedly because they were educated. It is a simple column, topped by a red star.

Jirgatal

The last town in the valley is Jirgatal, 38 km from Tajikabad, another pleasant town with bright roofed houses. It is 25 km to the Kyrgyz border, and a further 300 km to Osh, a major town in Kyrgyzstan. There are large fields, and many houses have gardens. The mountains are on three sides. We were told there are many tracks providing excellent walking and trekking. Again the Hukumat staff assured us that visitors will be given a warm welcome. There are two excellent guesthouses, next to each other, one a Hukumat one of 16 places, and a government one of 9 places. Both charge 15 somoni per night. The guesthouses are clean, the bedrooms well appointed. There is hot water, electricity and a sauna. Meals are provided from vegetables and fruit grown in the garden. The staff are very welcoming.

There is an airstrip from where helicopters can fly to the base camp on Peak Somoni. We were told mountain guides can be hired, but we would advise mountaineers to arrange guides through a reputable travel company in Dushanbe. Certainly guides could be found for walks and treks.

JUMA NAMANGANI AND THE ISLAMIC MOVEMENT OF UZBEKISTAN

Monica Whitlock

Jumabai Khujayev, called 'Namangani' after his birthplace in Uzbekistan was a Mujahed style commander operating in the Rasht Valley from 1993 to 1999. He was one of many young Uzbeks who challenged the authoritarian regime at home in the early 1990s during the collapse of the USSR.

Namangani joined a patchwork of groups that tried to introduce Islamic codes in the Ferghana Valley. They attracted crowds of supporters and the wrath of an alarmed President Karimov. Fleeing a ferocious crackdown, many escaped to Tajikistan. It was 1992. The Tajik civil war was at its height and the Ferghana Uzbeks joined in on the side of the Islamic Revival Party. Namangani is remembered for fighting bravely at Shahr-i Tuz where he lost many men and was forced across the Amu (Oxus) into Afghanistan along with many thousands of Tajiks. However, he was able to return there to become a field commander throughout the civil war (1992–7). He fought a long and often skilful campaign. Namangani was one of the few commanders able to put real pressure on the Rahmanov government, even though it was supported by the Russian army.

In 1997, the Tajiks signed their peace agreement. Namangani's fellow fighters started to disarm, some even accepting government jobs. There was no longer a role for Namangani, and he could not return to Uzbekistan, where a wave of new crackdowns was driving more and more Uzbeks into exile. Namangani crossed the border into Afghanistan, where he joined other Uzbeks in the Islamic Movement of Uzbekistan, the IMU, including its leader Taher Yuldash.

By 2001 the IMU was based in northern Afghanistan. Its strength perhaps numbered several hundred fighters. Its own agenda was to force out the Karimov regime – and staged several guerrilla raids on the Uzbek border. But as the Uzbeks inevitably became drawn into the web of Afghan politics, fighting alongside the Taleban as part of a multi-national, pan-Islamic force that increasingly used the language of jihad. When US forces flew into Afghanistan in 2001 to force out the Taleban, the IMU supported the Taleban to the last, especially in the northern Afghan town of Kunduz, close to the Tajik border.

It is considered that Namangani was killed at Kunduz along with many other Uzbek fighters, though some of his closest friends refuse to believe it, asserting that Namangani has – once again – given the authorities the slip.

Khatlon and the South East

The province of Khatlon, to the southeast of Dushanbe is rarely visited by foreigners, yet it has some unusual and interesting sites. The roads are good. The town of Norak, with its beautiful lake, is easily visited there and back in a day. Kulob town, and the surrounding area, has many places of interest, which can be visited with one overnight stop. Travellers going to the Pamirs tend to take the shorter route over the pass to Kala-i Khum (called the Khaburabot Pass, also the Saghirdasht or the Tavildara), which is open from late May to the end of October. The alternative route via Kulob is longer by about 4 hours, but it is open most of the year.

Khatlon was one of the more backward and poorest parts of Tajikistan in Soviet times. Mainly for this reason it saw much violence in the civil war. The region is the homeland of the winning side that fought its way to power in 1992–93, including President Rakhmon and his closest allies.

Norak

Leaving Norak, the road crosses over an undulating, treeless area of large wheat fields, with the headquarters of the collective farms in the distance. It is 55 km to the undistinguished town of Dangara, birthplace of President Rakhmon. There are some signs of prosperity, such as smart *choikhonas* and well stocked shops, but there is the overshadowing presence of derelict factories. There is an excellent tarmac road from Dangara to Qurghan Tappa, the main town in southern Tajikistan. (See also Day Journeys from Dushanbe p. 119).

Kurbonshaid

Travellers should continue on the main road to Kulob. At the village of Kurbonshaid, 35 km, prepare for a double take. The village is a rather dreary place, but in the midst is a pristine looking medieval fortress. As part of the 2,700th anniversary of the supposed founding of Kulob, a full-scale reconstruction of the citadel of the ancient city of Hulbuk is being built. From the 9th to 11th centuries it was the fourth largest city in Central Asia. It flourished under the Samanid dynasty. In the past Soviet archaeologists undertook extensive excavations on the site, and there are many exhibits in the Museum of National Antiquities in Dushanbe. So far the main gates and walls with 19 m watch towers on one side have been completed. Archaeologists might wince, but the architect in charge of the site claims every effort is being made to undertake a thorough archaeological excavation before each stage of the building. The design has been submitted to international experts, but nobody can be quite sure how Hulbuk looked.

Hulbuk flourished because of its strategic position, the fertile land surrounding it, and deposits of gold, copper and salt. The citadel of 2 square hectares is only the centre of a city, which had an inner wall and an outer one of 10 km. It suffered on account of various attacks in the 11th century, and was burned down in 1064. It was then abandoned, mainly it is thought because the waterways from the mountains became blocked.

The project staff are very helpful, and will show you around the site, and what remains of a very sophisticated city. The original ceramic brick streets survive in places. There is a stage, with a place for a prompter. The city had under floor heating systems, and an effective supply of clean water. Glass has been discovered, contemporaneously with the introduction in Europe. There is an unusual sundial and plenty of Aryan swastikas. Recent excavations exposed paintings of dancing girls, musicians and magic creatures. Such images would have been forbidden by Islam, but archaeologists consider Hulbuk shows a transition from Zoroastrianism to Islam, with the new religion adopting facets of the old one.

A museum next to the site is due to be opened, and should be worth visiting.

Khoja Mumin

8 km from Kurbonshaid is the town of Vose, named after a local hero who rose against the Amir of Bukhara in the nineteenth century. On the right is what looks like an average mountain, but with many white streaks on the hillsides. This is Khoja Mumin, a mountain made entirely of salt. It has been estimated that it contains 50–60 billion tons of salt. The salt is washed down in the streams, collected in settling ponds at a works, and distributed within Tajikistan and neighbouring Central Asian states.

To reach the salt works, and the paths up the mountain, follow the road to Kulob leaving the town, take a right turn by a garage with blue signs, opposite a cotton ginnery, and continue for 6 km to the salt works.

There is a network of paths on the mountain and there are good views over the surrounding plains. It is claimed there are 350 metre caves in the salt, which produce musical sounds generated by the wind passing salt stalactites hanging in the entrances to the caves. They may be there, but we cannot confirm.

The topography of the mountain is confusing, and it would be wise to take a guide. Namozi Morboz, who runs the shop at the salt works, knows the mountain well, and will take parties up for 10 somoni. The best time to visit is April or May, when the flowers are blooming, and it is not too hot, or in the autumn. It is essential to take plenty of water, as all the streams, as might be expected, are saltier than seawater.

Kulob

20 km from Vose is the large town of Kulob, another town with wide, tree-lined streets, but with some more substantial and handsome buildings.

The main point of interest in the town is the mausoleum of Khoja Mir Sayid Hamadani, a poet and scholar of the 14th century. Born in Hamadan, in Iran, he is famous for having spread the word of Islam in Kashmir. He died across the river in Afghanistan and was buried here – a reminder of Kulob's pre-Soviet significance as a corridor between India and the Arab world.

Hamadani's mausoleum is a splendid building renovated with Iranian money, of golden domes, and situated in pleasant gardens with some attractive *gumbaz*. Pilgrims come to the mausoleum to receive a blessing from the mullahs. The excavation of a house said to be almost 3,000 years is in one corner of the gardens. There is an excellent museum next to the mausoleum, with a very engaging curator. The museum is being renovated. It contains a number of books written by Hamadani, including one on guidelines for a wise ruler.

There are two guesthouses that give reasonable value:

– The United Nations guesthouse is on the edge of the town, heading east. Go down a lane on the left from the main road to Khorog and the Pamirs, some 500 m beyond the bazaar. It is signposted. It is popular with NGO staff. A shared room is US$25 for bed and breakfast. It is clean, the food is good and the gardens are pleasant. They prefer you to book ahead. It may be worth trying the UN office in Dushanbe.

– Guesthouse "Sano", Charmgaron Street. Tel: 23230, mobile 918 695350. It is 200 m down a lane that goes to the right, facing the Hotel Khatlon on Ismoil Somoni Street. It has 12 bedrooms and some are apartments, each with 2 rooms, toilet and bathroom. Clean, with well-kept grounds, the charge for a bed is US$10 per night, food is extra.

A new hotel, the Hamkoron has recently opened, with excellent facilities, at 21, Ismoil Somoni street, Tel: 22522, 23354. Four rooms with en suite facilities, sat TV, and bar. US$30 per night.

At the lower end is the Daler Hotel, on Tomain Street, just off Ismoil Somoni Street, opposite shop "Rafashan". It is at the crossroads near the edifice commemorating 2,700 years. 13 rooms, very basic. 10 somoni per night.

The large Khatlon Hotel at 4, Ismoil Somoni Street was closed for renovation on our visit.

Khovaling

45 km from Kulyab is the small town of Khovaling. It is in the Baljuvon district, which the government wants to develop for tourism. It is sparsely populated and hilly, green in spring, but arid for the rest of the year. There are fertile places in the valleys, with orchards and streams, and flocks graze on the hills.

Khovaling is a pleasant enough town, with a reasonable museum. There is an impressive waterfall nearby. The town is seldom visited by foreigners. A visit is worth though for those interested in the flamboyant figure of Enver Pasha (see page 209), who fled his native Turkey to fight alongside anti-Bolshevik partisans, the *basmachi*, in the 1920s.

Enver Pasha was killed by the Bolsheviks near the village of Ob-i Garm. According to local Hukumat officials Enver Pasha was fighting under the command of Davlat Mandbai, the local *basmachi* leader. A truce had been called for the holy day of Eid. Davlat Mandbai allowed his followers to return to their villages. A Bolshevik informer, 'Barfi Bolo' betrayed Enver Pasha's whereabouts, and he was cornered with only a handful of followers.

Russian troops advanced from Baljuvon and attacked. Enver Pasha fought them off with his English machine gun, but was eventually shot by a Russian soldier, Sverdilov. The story goes that Davlat Mandbai, who was immensely strong and a superb horseman, galloped to the Russian lines, grabbed Sverdilov, and threw him across the horse's neck in the style of a buzkachi player and rode off. But Sverdilov still had his pistol and he shot Davlat Mandbai, mortally wounding him.

Davlat Mandbai's dying words to his followers were not to allow the bodies of Enver Pasha and himself to be captured by the Russians and displayed in Tashkent.

So their remains were hidden in some rose bushes, and later taken and buried in the village of Chagan, 20 km away. The two were buried by the side of the road, so that people would remember them.

In 1995, the Turkish government sent a team to Tajikistan to recover the remains of Enver Pasha. They flew his body to Turkey for a grand state funeral in Istanbul. He is buried with other Turkish heroes on the Memorial Hill in Istanbul.

Davlat Mandbai remains in Chagan. The Hukumat staff arranged with us to meet the grandson of Davlat Mandbai, who took us to the village of Ob-i Garm. It is along rough tracks for 9 km. Four-wheel drive is essential. 1 km from the village is a ridge between Baljuvon and Khovaling, now covered in orchards. There are views to the Pamirs and the many ranges of hills in between. It is a very peaceful spot. Local villagers will show you the grove of trees where the bodies were hidden.

The grandson told us that even he was punished for being a grandson of a *basmachi*, and was not allowed membership of the Communist party, and therefore denied employment. He feels the *basmachi* do not deserve their name, which means "bandits". "They were just fighting against the infidels invading our land", he said.

Dasht-i Jum National Park

To the east of Kulob a road leads to Shurobod (25 km). To the north is a mountain area, hardly ever visited by foreigners. It is the Childukhtaron area, so called from the forty rocks, reputed to be forty virgins who fought valiantly against the troops of Genghis Khan, but realising defeat was inevitable, prayed that their virtue should be preserved and were transformed into the stones.

The area to the south as far as the Panj river is the 20,000 hectare National Park of Dasht-i Jum. The hills rise from 700 to 3,000 m. It is one of the last haunts of the very rare Markhor sheep, with their extraordinary curled horns. The best times to visit are spring and autumn. There are woods of juniper and pistachio. If you intend to visit it would be wise to visit of the offices in Dushanbe of the State Directorate of Protected Areas, National Parks to obtain a permit and obtain information about the Park.

THE GREAT MIGRATION
Monica Whitlock

Gul Muhammad sits drinking tea with a dozen friends, all Tajik elders in their eighties like himself. We could be in almost any Tajik village. But open the door – and we are in Karachi, Pakistan, at the settlement of Suhrab Godh. The mud houses are poor and dry. There are no trees and people have to buy their water in cans.

Suhrab Godh is home for some of the last Tajiks who survived the great exodus from Central Asia, when up to half a million people scrambled across the river Amu (Oxus) into Afghanistan to escape the wars, famine, and political oppression that convulsed their homeland from 1917 to the 1930s.

Gul Muhammad is from Kafirnihan, near Dushanbe. "The Russians stole our house and our land," he says. "We had to leave. I was six or seven. It was very late at night. We had some cow-skins and tied them together to make a raft. The women sat in the middle with us children. The men held on to the edges and once we were in we had to keep going, whether the horses rolled or not. Sometimes they rolled. I don't know how long it took, but when the morning star came up we were in Afghanistan. We had to give the horses back and we began to walk."

His dozen friends all have similar stories. One describes how his family left – eleven brothers together – because "my father could read" and was therefore seen as subversive. All made the crossing at Imam Sahib, south of Qurghan Tappa, and the route to the Afghan town of Kunduz. Once in Afghanistan, they build reed huts along the borderlands and waited for better times at home so they could return.

As the years went by, though, the migrants settled, cultivating the land and setting up the businesses they had left behind. They organised their own schools and built lasting villages. Gul Muhammad and his friends never saw Tajikistan again – except one man, Nurullah, from Hisar. He was three when he crossed the river and an old man when he at last paid a visit to Tajikistan after the fall of the Soviet Union. "It was marvellous," he says, "to me, even the hay looked like gold!"

The Tajiks made up only a small part of the great migration. Most of those who left were Turkmens mainly because, as herdsmen and shepherds, their lives were relatively simple to fold and reassemble. About a quarter of a million Turkmens drove their flocks into the plains of northern Afghanistan in the first wave of the migration. They brought with them their carpet-making skills, manufacturing carpets still known on the world market as 'Bukharan' rugs.

After them came migrants from every walk of life, from towns and villages all over Central Asia. Farmers and factory owners left, goldsmiths and paper-makers, saddlers and carpenters, weavers, dyers, tanners and tailors. Although many never saw a Soviet official, they were afraid that their workshops would be closed down and their houses seized. There were many well-grounded rumours too of village elders being shot and Muslim girls being made to 'dance for the communists'.

When official atheism began in the late 1920s, and with it religious persecution, many mullas left too. Richer people in the later waves of the migration sometimes managed to send ahead goods. But these were the minority. Most people took nothing but the clothes they wore and the little they could carry.

The border with Afghanistan was closed abruptly, without warning, one day in 1936. Those on the south bank of the Amu became Afghans while visitors on the north side became Soviet citizens. One Afghan draper and tailor from Balkh who happened to be on a business trip, never returned to Afghanistan. Fortunately, he had his wife and baby son with him. The boy grew up a Soviet Tajik, still living in Dushanbe in 2001.

Many of those who fled Central Asia moved on from their first place of sanctuary. Some went to British India and set themselves up especially in Peshawar, Lahore and Karachi. Others went to Istanbul; still more took ship for Jeddah where they settled in the cradle of Islam. The majority of migrants, that is, the poor, stayed on where they first landed in Afghanistan. They greatly increased the Turkmen, Uzbek and Tajik population of the north. As well as making carpets they worked as silk weavers, coppersmiths and farmers of sugarbeet. They became Afghans, while also remaining a distinctive, tightly-knit community, intermarrying and retaining the customs of the country they left behind. Two generations later, in 1979, the migrants were among the first to see Soviet tanks roll across the Amu into Afghanistan. It was time to move yet again. Great numbers fled south, through Soviet bombing raids, to Pakistan where they put up in refugee camps along with hundreds of thousands of other Afghans. Some have since returned to Afghanistan, only to flee for a third time, when the Taleban army marched across northern Afghanistan in 1997.

Gul Muhammad and his friends will most likely stay on in Suhrab Godh, too poor to move yet again to Afghanistan or to Tajikistan. Yet they and their families would never consider themselves Pakistanis. The elders speak together in the mountain accents of their villages and are Tajiks still, wherever they call home.

ENVER PASHA   Huw Thomas

The Turkish adventurer Enver "Pasha" was born in Istanbul in 1881, son of an official in the public works department. He attended military high school along with the boy who would become his great rival, Mustafa Kemal, (to become 'Ataturk', founder of modern Turkey) and graduated into the Turkish army where he won fame fighting Balkhan guerrillas. The Ottoman Empire was in decline, and Enver was drawn to the ideas of the revolutionary 'Young Turks'. In 1908 the Young Turks forced out the last Sultan and set up a junta, 'The Committee for Union and Progress' or CUP.

Like his fellow revolutionaries, Enver was filled with romantic notions of not just a great Turkey, but a union of all Turkic peoples from the Black Sea to China. "The country of the Turks is not Turkey, nor yet Turkistan. Their country is a vast and eternal land: Turan!" wrote the nationalist Ziya Gokalp in a poem that spoke for his generation. But Enver knew little about the wider world in reality, and his public life was filled with misjudgement.

In 1914 Enver became Minister for War and led his country into the Great War, having concluded a secret treaty with Germany. He led the catastrophic attack on the Russians in Sarikamis in the mid-winter of 1914–15 that left perhaps 100,000 Turkish dead. It was the single worst disaster the Turks suffered in the war. With the defeat of Germany, and the subsequent loss of the Ottoman Empire in the Middle East, Enver fled to Germany in 1918.

Enver's next move was to approach the Bolsheviks, offering to raise Muslims worldwide to revolution. Lenin went along with this plan, and despatched Enver to Bukhara in November 1921. But the Turk was a stranger caught up in violently changing times. Enver was out of his depth and ended up in Tajikistan, throwing in his lot with local anti-Bolshevik partisans, the *basmachi*, who had much support especially in highland areas (see special topic on Basmachi).

In February 1922, the *basmachi*, assisted by Enver Pasha, even captured the weak garrison town of Dushanbe. But the various bands of partisans failed to find a common purpose and build upon their strengths. Many mistrusted Enver – a foreigner and, to many, a Turk among Persians. The Red Army re-took Dushanbe in July 1922, and Enver Pasha was killed a month later.

[**Acknowledgment** is made for material in this section, including the quoted poem, to *Enver Pasha* by Andrew Mango.]

The South – Vakhsh and Kafirnihan Valleys

South Tajikistan does not have the dramatic splendours of the mountains. But what it does have, in abundance, is a rich sense of antiquity built in many layers. Alexander, Genghis Khan and Babur all passed this way. The most magnificent Buddhist findings in Central Asia come from southern Tajikistan, as does the Oxus Treasure now in the British Museum in London.

The south is dust dry for most of the year. But in spring the broad Vakhsh river valley is a delightful place, with its many channels interspersed with islands covered in mature trees, and with meadows of spring flowers. The traveller passes through irrigated fields of cotton, wheat and vegetables. Always there is the backdrop of the hills to the west bordering Uzbekistan. The friendly and hospitable villagers often wear traditional dress. Most of the houses and walls are built of local materials and blend with the landscape.

The south is accessible throughout the year. There is a good road south all the way to the Uzbek border. Virtually no foreigners come to the area. If you do come you are likely to be on your own when visiting any of the sites.

The best time to visit is the spring or autumn. Winters are mild, but it can be windy, and the there are frequent power cuts. The summer is unbearably hot with temperatures in June, July and August in the 40 to 50 degrees Centigrade range. Not for nothing are these months referred to as "Duzakh" or Hell.

Our highlights are the Tigrovaya Balka National Park, the springs at Chashma Chehel o Chahar, the ruined mosque of Khoja Mashad and the Temple of Oxus at Takht-i Sangin. All can be reached in a one-day journey from Dushanbe.

Girl with calf, Yavaj village, Shahr-I Tuz

The Journey

The main road leaves Dushanbe through the southern gates. There are regular bus services leaving from the bus station at Nazarshoev Street in the south of the city. It is possible to go by train from Dushanbe to Termez in Uzbekistan (see chapter on Dushanbe).

There is a good tarmac road over the two ranges of waterless hills to the large town of Qurghan Tappa, 87 km from Dushanbe. It is a pleasant town with wide tree lined streets and attractive parks, but the suburbs are full of derelict factories. On entering the town there is an interesting museum on a knoll on the right, opposite a dramatic statue of Somoni on horseback. The museum staff are friendly and the exhibits are well laid out. There are good views over the surrounding plains from the turret.

The main centre of the town is at the T-junction at the end of Somoni Street, where there is a statue of Bobojon Gafurov, eminent historian, General Secretary of the Communist Party 1946 – 1956, who wrote the seminal book 'The Tajiks', which traced the separate identity of the Tajik race. Turn right at the junction and 200 m on, facing, is the excellent bazaar with stalls and a mall.

As elsewhere in Tajikistan the best bet for accommodation may be a homestay. But there is also the Asia Hotel, with a red roof, 50 m from the bazaar on the road to the right facing the bazaar, providing luxurious accommodation. There are 5 rooms, all with en suite facilities at US$40 per night, and if you want your own dining room,

Sleeping Buddha from Ajina Tappa, Museum of National Antiquities, Dushanbe

US$50. We were assured there was no problem with water or electricity. Proprietor is Zina Petrovna. Tel: 27611. The Hotel Qurghan Tappa nearby is one of the former Soviet giant hotels. It is awful.

On the way into the town is the Maftuna Hotel, Vahdat Street, 27 beds. Tel: 918 895381. US$50 double room. Very spacious, water supply poor. You may not be the first to sleep in the sheets.

There are plenty of standard *choikhonas*. The small Russian Kitchen just before the T-junction provides good, cheap Russian food.

Of interest to visitors who have seen the magnificent Sleeping Buddha in the Museum of National Antiquities in Dushanbe, it is possible to see the site of the excavation. It is at the temple of Ajina Tappa. To find the site take the road to the airport, turn right after 6 km, and follow the small road for another 6 km to the site. The excavation was a major undertaking, and the statue had to be cut up and reassembled in Dushanbe. Unfortunately all that can be seen are mounds of earth and a few traces of mud brick walls. Disappointingly there is no plan of the site or even a notice to show it is the site. All other treasures uncovered here were taken to Russia in the Soviet era.

To travel south it is possible to avoid Qurghan Tappa by taking a turn to the right just before the large bridge over the Vakhsh, 10 km before reaching the town. This road follows the right bank, running along the edge of low foothills, giving good views across the plains. The road joins the main road at the bridge near Jilikul, at 167 km from Dushanbe.

The main road goes south from Qurghan Tappa, passing through cotton and wheat fields, small villages and isolated mud brick houses. Many southern villages have been rebuilt completely since the civil war of the 1990s. This was the area hardest hit in those bloody times, and it speaks much for the resilience and drive of the Tajiks that the south is now at peace.

Tiger near the Oxus River [1937]

Tigrovaya Balka

From the town of Jilikul (167 km from Dushanbe) there is a road that goes due south for 9 km to Tigrovaya Balka (Tiger Valley). This is a well-managed National Park of 50,000 hectares of riparian woodland with 10 lakes next to the river Vakhsh. In 1898 the geographer W. Rickmer Rickmers visited the area nearby on a hunting trip. He reported "I always had a man with a 577 express at my elbow, for tigers are very plentiful, as I plainly saw from their tracks". There are none now. The last one was seen by park staff in 1954. However, it is claimed there are 45 species of animal, 214 types of birds and 480 plants. There is a rich variety of animal life, including Bukhara and Saiga deer, hyenas, jackals, lynx, porcupine and wild boar. It is an excellent place for bird watching, particularly for hawks, falcons and waterfowl. There is a breed of flat fish unique to the area that grows to 100 kilograms. The habitat is a mixture of woodland, savannah, reed beds around the lakes and the great river Vakhsh is 400 m wide at this point.

There are 60 km of reasonable dirt roads within the park – a four wheel drive is to be preferred, particularly in the autumn wet season. There is a museum outside the gates containing tableaux of stuffed specimens of the species to be found in the park. The best time to visit is the spring and autumn.

It is not possible to gain entrance to the park without a permit. This can only be obtained from the office of The Protection of National Parks in Dushanbe at 64, Druzhba Narodov, near the Russian Orthodox Church, on Aini Road, the main road going east from Dushanbe to Kafirnihan. Tel: +992 372 262421 and +992 372 2261243. The cost of a permit is a steep 150 somonis (about US$40).

The park can done in a same day trip from Dushanbe, but to appreciate the park it would be worth travelling to Jilikul, staying a night at a homestay and visiting the park the following day.

Kabodion

The next main town south, 30 km from Jilikul, is Kabodion. The name comes from Kaboti Shahnor or Kabot the Builder, a mythological king in Firdousi's Shahnameh, who is claimed to have lived here. The town is well laid-out, surrounded by irrigated fields, with a range of hills to the east. The main place of interest is the Mir Kalai, a fortress with origins going back to Achaemenid times. It can be seen clearly from the main road coming into the town. There is no problem of access. One way in is to

scramble up the short slope behind the Café Takht-i Sangin, on the left from the road entering the town. The fortress covers several hectares and some of the walls and gatehouses remain. There are some holes leading down to dungeons. The fortress was the seat of the local *beks* for centuries. It was attacked by the Red army, and the last bek disappeared, probably in Afghanistan, in 1921. Russian archaeologists excavated the site in the 1950s, with most of the finds going to St Petersburg.

Opposite the Café Takht-i Sangin is a house with a small field, next to a garage. By the side of the house is a lane, with a blue door after 20 m leading to the house and field. This is a private house thought to be the birthplace of the great medieval poet, theologian and traveller, Nasir Khusraw. The owner is the elderly and courteous Nusratulo Khakimov, who will show you the ancient tree, supposedly there when Nasir Khusraw was born on this plot in 1004.

Nearby is a building used as a barn with thick walls. Soviet archaeologists thought it could have been part of a royal palace dating from Khusraw's time. Nuratullo's friend and neighbour Said Gholigov can show you the remains of what remains of a *gumbaz*, with some ancient plasterwork.

There is an interesting museum of four rooms, with exhibits from the Kala-i Mir, Takht-i Sangin, one devoted to Nasir Khusraw, and one to local daily life. The staff are helpful and pleased to see visitors.

Shahr-i Tuz

18 km south from Kabodian is the town of Shahr-i Tuz. Another pleasant town on standard Soviet lines; wide tree-lined streets and pretty parks. The Governor is keen to encourage tourism, and would provide guides if requested (they will not speak English). The Hukumat office is in the centre of the town. The former Soviet hotel is being renovated. We are not aware of any guesthouses, but a homestay would be easy to arrange. There is a delightful museum with enthusiastic staff. Alongside exhibits of artefacts excavated locally and agricultural implements are not only photos of local heroes of the Second World War, but also propaganda photographs of Russian heroes and heroines – the kind of exhibit that has been taken down in most Central Asian museums.

There are three places of special interest near the town:

1. TAKHT-I SANGIN

This is the Temple of Oxus on the banks of the Amu Darya. If intending to visit, it is well worth first going to the Museum of National Antiquities in Dushanbe. In the foyer is the altar from this site, and other artefacts excavated.

Between 1976 and 1991 Russian archaeologists excavated a temple on a citadel set within an enclosure of about 75 hectares. The central columned hall of the temple was surrounded by storerooms containing more than 5,000 objects, dating from between the sixth century BC and the third century AD. The temple was apparently built right at the end of the Achaemenid period, but some of the objects derive from an earlier date. The magnificent Oxus Treasure is thought to have been found nearby (see special topic on the Oxus Treasure). Local legend has it that Alexander worshipped at this temple.

The site is impressive, even though the artefacts have been removed and it is seldom visited. There are the excavation pits, with some dressed stone walls exposed, plinths of columns and a pit with the bones of animals sacrificed on the altar. The ancient writing on one of the stones turns out to be graffiti scratched by Russian soldiers. There is a range of hills behind, and across the reed beds of the Amu Darya lies an abandoned Afghan fort. The river cannot be reached because of a frontier fence. Just by the site is a watchtower, and a ruined gun emplacement, a reminder of the political sensitivities of this volatile region. Takht-i Sangin is 37 km from Shahr-i Tuz. From the town re-cross the Kafirnihan River to the north, and take a right turn after 200 m. It is 4 km to a cross roads, take the road to Chirik (6 km), bear right and at 7 km a T junction is reached. Turn left and left again after 2 km. The tarmac ends and there is a road leading over a pass in the hills, with fine views over the Amu Darya. On reaching the bank Takht-i Sangin is 2 km to the left, but visitors should turn right first to register at the military post at Takht-i Kulwad (2 km). The soldiers are courteous and pleased to see the occasional visitor. From the military post, drive along the track to Takht-i Sangin.

2. KHOJA MASHAD

Khoja Mashad is an abandoned mosque, mausoleum and medrassa, reputedly built by birds in 24 hours in the 9th century. It is one of those places in Tajikistan that surprise and delight. It is can be seen from the road and looks unimpressive, but when seen close up, it is marvellous. A twin-domed structure, which is much bigger than

when first seen from a distance, has superb brickwork, illuminated by the openings at the top of the two domes. The buildings are 30 m high, and would once have been adorned with writings from the Qur'an in gold. It is set in pleasant gardens, with some mature trees. The guardians are very welcoming and will show some of the objects excavated from the site, such as medieval oil lamps. You may be asked to join them in a short prayer. One of the buildings has been restored externally, the other still shows the damage supposedly done by the troops of Genghis Khan. Next to the buildings are the remains of a medrassa, where Nasir Khusraw is reputed to have studied from 1026–1033.

To reach Khoja Mashad, leave Shahr-i Tuz by the main road south to Termez. After 5 km there is a school on the right with a bust of Lenin in front, on the left is a building that looks like a mosque, turn left here. Go past another school on the right. Take the second left which takes you to the gates to Khoja Mashad.

3. CHASHMA CHEHEL O CHAHOR (44 SPRINGS)
In the baking summer heat, hundreds of local people come for relief to a remarkable oasis in the arid landscape. Chashma Chehel o Chahor is 8 km from Shahr-i Tuz on the road to Biskent. There is a bus service. The Chashma consists of 44 springs feeding running water to a number of pools. The water is a consistent 14 degrees throughout the year. Willow and mulberry trees shade the pools, each reputedly good for curing different ailments. Nearby is a wooded area with picnic tables.

Khoja Mashad (top) and Girls at Khoja Mashad (below)

There are a number of legends about the springs, but they all have a common theme. Hazrat Ali, son-in-law of the Prophet, was travelling through the desert with his army. They were very thirsty. Ali was particularly concerned about his wounded groom, Bobokamber. Ali prayed in the night, and the next day he bent down to touch the ground. He touched 44 times and everywhere his fingertips touched the ground a spring gushed forth. Bobokamber recovered.

The pools are full of harmless snakes and a type of fish, about trout size, which is reputed to be unique to the pools and poisonous to eat.

Local legend has it that Marco Polo visited in 1376 and noted that a large tree would still be there in 500 years time. It is still there.

The local mullah, who has helped to revive this chashma after the Soviet period, is pleased to

Khoja Mashad (top) and Chashma Chehel o Chahor (below)

recount the legends about Ali. He has built a comfortable guesthouse nearby with a number of rooms for two to four people sharing. He makes no charge, but welcomes donations. In the gardens are some rare deer from the mountains.

On a small hill by the chashma is a *gumbaz* and the mausoleum of Ali's groom Bobokamber. The tomb is very large, befitting a man reputed to have been 5 m tall.

In the spirit of local enterprise, water from the springs is being bottled and marketed as "Spring 44".

OTHER PLACES OF INTEREST
– **Utapur Fortress**   10 km from Shahr-i Tuz on the road to Vorohshiloh is the 15th century fortress of Utapur. It was not attacked by the Red Army and is in a reasonable state of preservation. It has impressive walls with some fine carved alcoves. There is a moat, which would have been supplied with water from Chashma Chehel o Chahor.

– **Khoja Sarboz**   This is the remains of a mausoleum to one of seven holy brothers. It is on the main road south, on the right, just before the turning to Khoja Mashad. Some walls remain.

Aywaj
The main road continues south to Aywaj, where it heads west to the Uzbek border. 18 km from Shahr-i Tuz there is reported to be the remains of a Nestorian church in the foothills, 3 km west of the main road.

Another 18 km is the small town of Aywaj, with a significant Arab population of Tajik Arabs – i.e. local people who trace their ancestry to the coming of Islam There is a mausoleum with walls standing and many votive offerings.

THE OXUS TREASURE

Huw Thomas

The magnificent Oxus Treasure is the most important surviving collection of Persian Achaemenid treasure. Housed in the British Museum, it consists of 180 exquisite objects in gold and silver. One of the earliest pieces in the Treasure is a gold scabbard, embossed with scenes showing a lion hunt. These hunting scenes are reminiscent of Assyrian reliefs from the mid 7th century BC. There are many magnificent objects in the Oxus Treasure, but among the best known are a pair of gold armlets, with the terminals in the form of winged griffins with horns, originally inlaid with glass and coloured stones. An outstanding piece is a model of a chariot pulled by four horses; in the chariot are a driver and a passenger wearing Median dress. Another much larger figure in silver is of a nude youth, wearing a Persian headdress, but his nudity indicates Greek influence. Other items include gold cups, a silver bowl with a rosette in the centre and radiating petals and a gold jug with a handle ending in a lion's mask. The largest single group of material is a collection of thin gold plaques ranging in height from 2 cm to 50 cm. Most have chased outlines of human figures, possibly of priests. The plaques are votive and they and the other objects in the Treasure have the appearance of material that was dedicated to a temple over a period of centuries

Originally associated with the Treasure were about 1,500 coins covering a span of about 300 years down to the early second century, which indicates that the treasure was buried about 200 BC. Local people found the treasure in the sands of the Oxus (Amu Darya) in the 1870s, probably at Takht-i Kuwat, which is close to Takht-i Sangin. "A large part of the treasure was nearly lost in 1880 and only recovered by chance in extraordinary, even bizarre circumstances. According to O.M. Dalton, whose 1905 catalogue of the Oxus Treasure remains the basic publication, in May of that year three merchants from Bokhara, who presumably bought the treasure from local villagers, were travelling with it from Kabul to Peshawar. East of Kabul they were attacked by local tribesmen, who seized them and the Treasure. However, their servant was able to escape and raised the alarm in the camp of Captain F. C. Burton, a political officer in Afghanistan. Burton set off with two orderlies and came across the robbers in a cave shortly before midnight. They were in the process of dividing up their spoil and were already quarrelling over it. Four were lying wounded. We are told that "a parley ensued", as a result of which much of the Treasure was given up to Burton. The next day he threatened to lead a force against the robbers, which persuaded them to bring in another large part of the Treasure. In this way about three quarters was restored to the merchants and, as a token of their gratitude, they allowed Burton to purchase the large gold armlet subsequently acquired by the Victoria and Albert Museum." (Quotation from *The Oxus Treasure* by John Curtis, published by the British Museum).

The merchants continued on their journey to Peshawar and eventually sold the treasure in Rawalpindi. Part of it was acquired from dealers there by Major General Sir Alexander Cunningham, Director General of the Archaeological Survey of India. Cunningham in turn sold the pieces to Sir Augustus Wollaston Franks, who on his death in 1897 bequeathed them to the British Museum.

Gold model four-horse chariot, Oxus Treasure
© The Trustees of the British Museum

COTTON: BLESSING OR CURSE?   Huw Thomas

Only 7% of Tajikistan is suitable for growing crops. This amounts to 720,000 hectares of arable land.

The cultivation of cotton is very significant both agriculturally and economically. Cotton covers more than 30% of irrigated land. It accounts for 30% of exports and 30% of all state revenue.

The government wishes to improve productivity and one aspect of that policy is to privatise the state collective farms. This policy appears to have stalled when it comes to the collective farms producing cotton. Given the economic importance of cotton, it is perhaps understandable the government wishes to continue to control all aspects of production and marketing. However, the reality of the situation about cotton is so serious, it needs a radical change of approach.

Travellers visiting the Vaksh and Kafirnihan valleys in southern Tajikistan and to Sughd province in the Ferghana valley in the north will pass by large fields of cotton. This crop and the way it has been exploited lies behind much human misery and environmental degradation. Journeying south there are many attractive mud brick villages. Monica Whitlock has explained that these are not ancient settlements going back to medieval times, but homes built by peasants forced out of their lands in the mountains to provide forced labour on the kolhoz (collective farms) to plant and harvest cotton. Many people died in the unaccustomed heat, the rest had had to survive on minimal wages. This forced migration of mountain people continued until the 1970s.

Although some land has been privatised, the government retains the cotton fields, paying derisory wages to the workers. Even where the farmers own their own plots they are required to produce a quota of cotton, and many complain they have to wait months for a price well below the market rate, or are not paid at all. Travellers in the autumn will see busloads of students in the Ferghana valley being sent to harvest the cotton, missing a whole semester of their studies. They are not paid, only receiving food and lodging.

In Soviet times the fields were sprayed with pesticides from the air. People reported to me that many died or were taken seriously ill and high numbers of babies were born with deformities after this spraying.

It is back breaking work. Go into a cotton field and pick a feather-light piece of cotton, and you will realise how much effort is required to fulfil a daily quota of 20 kilograms. Most of the picking is done by women.

Cotton is a thirsty crop and requires large amounts of water. Large irrigation systems have had to be developed. The result of this monoculture is the soil is degraded, due to excessive use of fertilisers and pesticides. The greatest example of the damage done to the environment by cotton is the Aral Sea. Once the fourth largest lake in the world, it is now a third of the size it was in 1970. This is due to the irrigation required to sustain the crop in Uzbekistan and Turkmenistan. Environmental degradation can be seen on a smaller scale in Tajikistan.

So who gains? It is certainly not the workers on the collective farms or the students. It is not the farmers who are required to plant a proportion of their land with cotton. The argument is that cotton is a commodity traded internationally and the government gains from the revenue generated. The argument is understandable, but there is the contrary view held in by some in Tajikistan that the main beneficiaries are a small elite group close to government.

The International Crisis Group consider that cotton monoculture is more destructive to Central Asia's future than the tons of heroin that regularly transit the region (ICG Asia Report No. 93, February 2005). The ICG consider there is urgent need to end government quotas, institute land reform, implement the International Labour Organisation conventions on enforced and child labour, and for international financial organisations and donors to put pressure for reform.

There is an urgent need to reform the whole system around cotton, but no pressure or incentive to do so. The best plan would probably be to reduce production, concentrating on more organic methods of cultivation, break up the cotton collective farms into private plots and let the farmers grow cotton, fruit, vegetables or whatever they want. The government should stop regulating the cotton market, and rely on taxing the farmers to finance public expenditure. There would be a gain in food security, farmers would receive a reasonable income, there could be an increase in government income, and the land could return to good health.

At least Tajikistan is spared the curse of oil.

Washing hands, Upper Zarafshan valley

Tajik-Persian Literature

Zarrina Muhammadieva

The Origin of the Tajik Language

The Tajiks are an Indo-European speaking people, whose forebears have inhabited Central Asia since the dawn of civilisation and are most closely related to the people of Iran. The majority of Tajiks live outside the borders of what is known today as Tajikistan (6.3 million). They also live in the cities of Samarkand and Bukhara of Uzbekistan, NW Kyrgyzstan, Southern Kazakhstan and Western China. The largest number of Tajiks lives in Afghanistan (10 million).

The Tajik language belongs to the sub-group of Persian languages of the south-western Iranian group of the Indo-European family of languages. The language had formed on the basis of Farsi and some of the eastern Iranian languages spoken in the 9th–10th centuries on the territory of Transoxiana and Khorasan. Early medieval manuscripts, especially of the 9th–10th centuries, refer to this language as "Farsi-Dari", "Farsi", or "Dari". This language is a common historical foundation of three contemporary literary languages: Tajik (in Tajikistan), Farsi (in Iran), and Dari (in Afghanistan). The history of the development of the Farsi-Dari language falls into the following stages:

1. Ancient Persian language (around 9th century BC – 3rd/4th centuries BC);
2. Middle Persian language (3rd/4th centuries BC – 7th/8th centuries AD);
3. New Persian language – Farsi-Dari (9th10th centuries AD – to the present day).

The first mention of the ancient Persian language refers to the 9th century BC. However, indigenous written manuscripts of the period are dated back to the 5th–6th century BC. The ancient Persian language which was the mother tongue of the Achaemenid kings – natives of Fars (Persia), had been used as a literary and official language of the Achaemenid Empire (6th–4th century BC). A few centuries after Alexander the Great's invasion and the subsequent collapse of the Achaemenid Empire, the Sasanid State, which played an enormous role in the development of the mid-Persian language, literature and culture, came into being on the territory of Persia. During the rule of the Sasanid dynasty, Middle Persian became the language of the government, literature and religion. Along with the now extinct Avestian language, Middle Persian was used as the second written language of Zoroastrism. The holy book of Zoroastrism, the Avesta, ultimately collected during this period and written in the Avestian language, survives to this day in two versions, and is still used by Zoroastrian priests living in some parts of modern Iran and India. Middle Persian manuscripts have also survived in the Pahlavi script, using characters created on the basis of Aramaic writing. However, after the Arab conquest and the expansion of Islam, a considerable part of the corpus of Middle Persian manuscripts was destroyed.

The "Farsi-Dari" language or "Farsi" was formed under the influence of eastern dialects of Transoxiana, including Sogdian dialects used at the outskirts and in the city of Bukhara – the capital of the Samanid State. It therefore reflects some features of eastern Iranian languages and dialects.

Literary Farsi was ultimately written using a modified version of the Arab script; this was developed in the 9th–10th century, and had four additional characters for sounds not used in the Arab alphabet. By that time, the people in Transoxiana had acquired a degree of political autonomy, and started using Farsi-Dari for official purposes and as a written literary language. The dialect of Bukhara played an important part in this process.

After the Persian territories had become part of the Arab Caliphate, Farsi developed under the influence of the Arabic. This influence continued through several centuries. This accounts for the presence of Arabic words in Farsi vocabulary and, later on, in the Tajik language. However, Arabic was not the only language that influenced Farsi. In AD 962 the Turkic Ghaznavid dynasty was established in Afghanistan. In 985 the Seljuk Turks moved to the vicinity of Bukhara and later in 999 the Ghaznavids defeated the Samanids in Khorasan, and the Qarakhanids captured Bukhara, the Samanid capital. The military conflicts between various Turkic tribes continued until the 13th century – Genghis Khan's invasion of Central Asia. Whilst, during this period of turmoil, Farsi remained the official language of state, it adopted numerous words from the Turkic invaders.

The second half of the 19th century witnessed the merger of the literary language with the speech of the Tajik dialect, yet these modifications did not make any considerable impact on the established literary norms. In the 20th century, the language of the Persian-speaking population of Central Asia acquired a new name – the Tajik language. This term is closely related to the political events that took place in Central Asian region in the first decade of the 20th century.

In 1924, following the national-territorial division of the USSR, the Tajik Autonomous Soviet Socialist Republic was formed. In 1929, it was transformed into the Tajik SSR, and Tajik was designated as the state language. Heated arguments around the further development of the Tajik language resulted in the main principles of the development of the literary language. The Tajik literary language developed on the basis of the living Tajik speech on the one hand, and on the classical Persian-Tajik literature on the other. Gradually, the Arab script was replaced by a new alphabet based on the Latin script, and in 1939, it was again replaced by the Cyrillic one.

Ancient Literature

The isolation of Eastern Persians (ancestors of the modern Tajiks) from Western Persians (ancestors of the modern Iranians) took place in high antiquity. The Eastern Persians inhabited, from time immemorial, the territory to the east and south-east of the Caspian Sea–Central Asia, including a significant part of modern-day Afghanistan and parts of the Hindu Kush. They had been in constant contact with the Eastern-European Plain, Turkic-speaking peoples, China and India. The centres of Eastern-Persian people were the Fergana region, Khorezm, Sogdiana, Bactria, the Pamirs and Khorasan.

The Western Persians lived to the west and south of the Caspian Sea, predominantly on the territory of modern Iran (excluding Khorasan), and had been in contact with the Mediterranean countries. Their centres were Media, Azerbaijan (Atropatena), and Fars. Despite this split, the close ties and relations between the Eastern and Western Persians had never been interrupted over the centuries.

The development of ancient Persian literature can be assessed on the basis of such literary works, as the Avesta, as well as fragments of Sogdian and Parthian literature. This development is often divided into two stages: early antiquity and late antiquity. Early antiquity is regarded as the period of transition from a primitive communal system to a class-based society, when the first written ancient Persian records emerged, containing significant elements of fiction, including poetry. The source of poetry was folklore, and its basis was Man's consciousness of his own progression from an early pristine bestial state of

Sufi poem inscribed on a stone, Yamg

nature to a higher level of sophistication, and civilised living. This self-awareness was reflected in mythology: the animal world – an image for that initial bestiality and chaos – was perceived as evil (dragons, genies, snakes), but Man in response was positive, kindly, and a bringer of order. Such was also echoed in the sphere of the gods; the 'good' gods, such as Mitra, Ardvisura, and Ahura Mazda, were seen as fighters against disorder. In essence, the leading idea is human heroism in struggle against the forces of evil.

The period of literary late antiquity is equated with early medieval times. Literature at this time, generally speaking, was semi-fictional and semi-religious by nature. It projected the image of man as friend of god, and dwells on the notion of the compassionate god, and the 'God-Man'. Consequently, the power of humanistic heroism was weakened by these religious concepts.

Literature of 9th–10th Centuries

The Arabs invaded Iran and Central Asia in the 8th century. Islam and the Arabic language were violently imposed on these countries; nonetheless, Persian-Tajik literature managed to preserve its traditions, distinct and characteristic features.

The 9th century saw the beginning of a new era in Persian-Tajik literature – the period of classical literature. The development of this literature was closely associated with the struggle of the Persian peoples against the Arab invaders and the Arab Caliphate during which the Tajik national ethos as well as the Tajik state and the language were formed – Dari (or Farsi-Dari).

The literary works of the 9th century were just the rudiments of the new Persian-Tajik classical literature which was to reach its zenith in the 10th century. Abu Abdulla Rudaki (858–941) is the founder of the Persian-Tajik classical literature. It was Rudaki who developed genres and forms of the Persian-Tajik literature, such as the *masnawi* (rhyming couplets of spiritual and educational meaning), *qasida* (panegyric), *qit'a* (literally 'fragment', a form of occasional verse usually four to eight lines in length),

Tomb of Rudaki, Panjrud

rubai (quatrains where the first, second and fourth lines rhyme), and romantic lyric. He laid the foundation of the ghazel genre which was perfected by Sa'adi and Hafiz of Shiraz and Kamal Khudjandi.

Rudaki's major themes include the power of human mind, wisdom of life, love, old age, the inevitability of death. His most cherished idols are knowledge and experience. The following *bayt* that appears at the bottom of his monument in Dushanbe describes his lasting dedication to knowledge and experience:

> *Har ki nomukht az guzashti ruzgor,*
> *Niz nomuzad zi hej omuzgor.*
>
> *[No ordinary teacher will ever reach,*
> *He whom the passage of Time failed to teach.]*

Epic forms of the Persian-Tajik classical literature were developed by Rudaki and Abdushukur Balkhi. A significant contribution to the genre of heroic epos was made by Dakiki (executed around 977) and Firdausi (934/41–1020/25) One of the most influential pieces of literary work in the history of the Persian-Tajik literature is the timeless epic of Abul Qasim Firdousi, the *Shahnameh* (Book of Kings). This heroic epic celebrated freedom, love, humanity, and the struggle against tyrants. The main character of the epic is Rustam, a courageous, powerful and magnanimous knight capable of self-sacrificing love and loyalty. The traditions established by Firdausi were continued in the following centuries, during which time the important emerging concept of Sufism was considerably reflected in the works of Abdul Madjud Sano'i (1070– c.1140) and further perfected by Fariddu-din Attar and Jalaluddin Balkhi (known in the West as Rumi).

Abu Ali ibn Sina (980–1037), born in Bukhara, often known by his Latin name of Avicenna was the most influential of all Islamic philosopher-scientists. He wrote on medicine as well as geometry, astronomy, arithmetic and music. Avicenna wrote about 450 works, of which around 240 have survived. Of the surviving works, 150 are on philosophy while 40 are devoted to medicine, the two fields in which he contributed most. His most important work, however, is his immense encyclopaedic work, the *Kitab al-Shifa* (The Book of Healing). It is known that he found cures for all the diseases of his time and was first to discover the use of snake venom in medicine. Avicenna also made a significant contribution to Persian literature. He wrote numerous *rubai* where he expressed his frustration with the ruling clergy, the unpredictability of life, and his sense of helplessness before the reality of death.

> *Az qa'ri gili siyoh to avji Zuhal*
> *Kardam hama mushkiloti getiro hal*
> *Berun jastam zi qaidi har makru hiyal*
> *Har band kushoda shud magar bandi ajal.*

> [*From the centre of the earth to Saturn's height,*
> *I have solved this world's enigmas and its plights.*
> *Rushed out to mark every little sight,*
> *All knots except the Human Fate I have untied.*]

Omar Khayyam (1048–1131) was one of the most well-known philosophers and mathematicians of that period; his timeless quatrains were popularised in the West by Edward Fitzgerald's translations in the 19th century. Omar Khayyam expressed his philosophical view on the mysteries of life and death, love, loyalty, betrayal, social injustice. He was sceptical about any type of prophesy and the afterlife. Atheism, and freedom from faith was his religion. Omar's Rubaiyat was heavily influenced Avicenna's work. In fact, Omar considered Avicenna as his Master, although they lived almost one hundred years apart.

The 12th century was the golden age of Sufism. The frustration and sufferings of the people caused by wars and disorder led to the flourishing of the Sufi movement which called for peace and unity of various religious movements. The most influential representative of this movement was Jalaluddin Rumi (born in 1207, Vakhsh, modern Tajikistan). He was one of the greatest spiritual masters and poetical geniuses and was the founder of the Mawlawi Sufi order, a leading mystical brotherhood of Islam. Escaping the Mongol invasion and destruction, Rumi and his family travelled extensively in the Muslim lands, performed pilgrimage to Mecca and finally settled in Konya, Anatolia, then part of the Seljuk Empire. If there is any general idea underlying Rumi's poetry, it is the absolute love of God. His influence on thought, literature and all forms of aesthetic expression in the world of Islam cannot be overrated. His Masnawi celebrated love as the principle of existence and nature as the embodiment of God.

The genre of the ghazel was successfully developed in the 13th and 14th centuries, and its contents changed dramatically with respect to the previous centuries. The new ghazel expressed the sufferings of people and criticised the prophets for the existence of an unjust social structure. The 'love ghazel,' celebrating the beauty of the human body and spiritual perfection of man, as well as his aspirations towards a free and happy life, was one of the leading genres used in the books of Sa'adi (around 1213-1219?–1292, Shiraz, Iran). He developed a distinct style in this genre. His best known works are *Gulistan* (The Flower Garden) and *Bustan* (The Tree Garden). Bustan is entirely in verse and consists of stories illustrating the standard virtues recommended to Muslims (justice, liberality, modesty, contentment). *Gulistan* is mainly in prose and consists of stories and personal anecdotes. It also has a variety of poems containing aphorisms, advice and humorous reflections.

The works of Hafiz (1324–1389) began a new era in the *ghazel* genre. His *ghazels* expressed love, worship of beauty and humanism. In the course of his life he wrote 500 *ghazels*, 42 *rubai*, and a few *qasida*. Hafiz only composed when he was divinely

Reading the Qur'an, Khovaling

inspired, and therefore he averaged only about 10 *ghazels* per year. His focus was to write poetry worthy of the Beloved.

Another greatest master of ghazel was Kamal Khudjandi (died in 1400). His *ghazels* were a flagellation of hypocritical worshippers, followers of the Shar'ia. He compared earthly love with the so-called pleasures of paradise.

The second half of the 15th century witnessed the growing public and social role of poetry and participation of representatives of all social groups in these processes. One of the most prominent figures of literature of this period was Abdu Rahman Jami (1414–1492, Jam, Iran) and the founder of Uzbek classical literature Alisher Navoi (1441–1501).

The Herat School of Literature headed by Jami and Navoi united the creative forces of Vasifi, Umedi, Hiloli, Binoi and many others. However, a significant part of poetry of this period was an imitation of the masters of the past.

The second half of the 15th century concluded the most significant, influential, expressive and rich in its form, style and contents of the Persian Tajik poetry. The golden age of the Persian-Tajik classical literature came to an end.

Dome of the Kok Gumbaz madrassah, Istaravshan

Literature of the 16th–19th Centuries

The cultural and literary life of Transoxiana and Khorasan in the 16th centuries experienced difficult times, which was due to the accession of the Shaibanid Dynasty to the throne. The invasion by the Uzbek leader Shaibani Khan (1451–1510) and his successors, attacks on the remnants of the Timurid Empire headed by Babur, constant conflicts between the Shaibanid Dynasty (1500–1598) and the Persian Safavid Dynasty (1502–1736), all caused immense suffering to the people. This was intensified by political intrigues within the ruling dynasty, and the irreconcilability of the Sunni and Shia groups. These events had a very negative impact on the spiritual life and the literature of the Central Asian peoples, including the Tajiks. The scientific and cultural centres of Samarkand and Herat, which were influential in the 16th century, fell apart. Some of the writers and poets moved to other countries, including India.

The distinguished Tajik poet and musician of that time Kamaliddin Binoi (1453–1512) who moved to Samarkand from Herat and subsequently started serving Shaibani Khan, was a master of ghazels. He continued the classical tradition of this poetic genre and slightly changed its contents by introducing biographical elements into his ghazels. Ghazels also played a considerable role in the poetry of Badriddin Hiloli (d. 1529). Perfect in their form, expressive emotions and feelings of man, musicality and simplicity made the love lyric of Hiloli particularly beautiful.

A progressive movement in Tajik literature developed over the 17th–18th centuries. This gave a new impetus to the development of the literary genres, widened the themes treated by Tajik literature, and strengthened its ideological and aesthetical contents, despite the historical conditions that hindered the development of secular culture and literature. The most significant representative of the progressive literature of the 17th and 18th centuries was Mirobid Sayidoi Nasafi (d. c.1710). In his works he protested against feudal subdivision and supported centralised power. Like some other Tajik poets Nasafi also wrote rubai – in total 32.

One of the most noticeable improvements in the progressive literature at the end of the 18th century and the first half of the 19th century was the development of social satire. Satire, particularly in the works of Gulkhani, Mahmur and Maadan, was at times ruthless in its contents and characters but closely reflected peoples' moods and hearts. The positive experience of the progressive poets and writers of this period defined the essence of the creative development of these literary traditions which had a major impact on the literature of the 19th century.

20th Century

Tajik literature in the 20th century was heavily influenced by the political developments in Central Asia. Soviet power was established throughout Central Asia and the Soviet Union was formed. Tajik literature lost its romanticism which was the essence of its Medieval period and mainly reflected Soviet realism particularly in the works of Sadriddin Aini (1878–1954) – the founder of modern Tajik literature of the Soviet period. Aini was one of the reformist intellectuals of Russian-ruled Central Asia (Jadids) who in the early 1920s joined the Bolsheviks to overthrow the Emir of Bukhara and propagate the revolution in Uzbekistan and Tajikistan. As the leading Tajik (Persian-speaker) among predominantly Uzbek (Turkish-speaking) colleagues, he was instrumental in establishing a distinctive Tajik Persian language and literature, written first in Latin characters and, from 1939, in Cyrillic. He helped to bind together a sense of Tajik nationalism that survived the collapse of the Soviet Union.

Aini attended a madrasa in Bukhara, where he learned how to write in Arabic. He attended the Soviet Congress of Writers in 1934 as the Tajik representative. By making a play of national identity in his writings, he was able to escape the Soviet censors who silenced many intellectuals in Central Asia. Aini survived the Soviet Purges, and even outlived Stalin by one year.

Many of Aini's contributions like *Ghulomon* (Slaves), *Odina* (Orphan) and *Marg-i Sudkhur* (Death of the Money Lender) have been subject of exciting movies, but his most remarkable work comes towards the end of his life when he writes, in the 1940s, an account of his life, especially the formative period. Called the *Yoddoshtho* (Reminiscences), this work details life in Bukhara of the turn of the century in a most vivid and informative way.

Other significant writers and poets of this period are Abulqasim Lahuti, Mirzo Tursunzoda, Abdusalom Dehoti and Mirsaid Mirshakar.

Zarrina Muhammadieva, originally from Tajikistan, is a linguist and a professional translator with a keen interest and passion for medieval Persian poetry. She spent many years studying this topic and translated some Persian verses into English.

GEOLOGY OF TAJIKISTAN

Dr Mike Searle

Tajikistan lies at the heart of Central Asia. More than half the country lies above 3,000 m altitude and the great Pamir mountain ranges, also called Bam-i Dunya or "Roof of the World", are aptly named. Tajikistan is a land of extreme climate, arid steppe plateau and massive mountains. It is a land rocked by some of the largest and most frequent earthquakes known on the continents, and has the deepest seismic zone known from any continental crust. It also has some of the most active faults in Central Asia. This mix of active tectonics, high plateau and thick crust results in a geologically extremely active terrane. The high peaks are heavily glaciated and arid climate has also resulted in a desert environment.

Five major mountain ranges fan out from the high Pamir. To the southeast the Himalaya stretch for 2,000 km along the northern borders of Pakistan, India, Nepal and Bhutan. The Karakoram range south of the Pamir has the highest concentration of large mountains, including five mountains over 8,000 m high, the steepest topography and the greatest erosion rates on Earth. Whereas the Karakoram includes many of the World's highest peaks and deepest valleys, the Pamir in Tajikistan is a high, desolate plateau with isolated large mountain massifs such as the two highest peaks, Peak Lenin (7,134 m) and Peak Communism (7,495 m). To the south, the

Hindu Kush ranges run along the border between Afghanistan and Pakistan and merge with the Pamir in the Wakhan corridor near the source of the Amu Darya (Oxus) River. To the east, the Kunlun and Altyn Tagh ranges run along the southern margin of the Taklamakan desert and Tarim basin, forming the northern boundary of the Tibetan Plateau. The northern border of Tajikistan is the Tien Shan Mountains, a 2,500 km long range that traverses Central Asia from Uzbekistan to the Altai range in southern Mongolia.

All of these great Central Asian mountain ranges owe their altitude to uplift following the collision of the Indian plate with Asia approximately 50 million years ago. Whereas some mountain ranges such as the Tien Shan, Altai, Kun Lun and Pamir were old mountain ranges, formed as a result of earlier plate collisions as continental fragments progressively accreted to the Siberian Shield, others such as the Himalaya were formed directly as a result of the Indian plate collision. This collision occurred roughly down at equatorial latitudes, and as India continued to move north, indenting into Asia as it went, the Asian crust was thickened and elevated. The Tajik continental crust has been above sea-level for at least 100 million years, but may have only reached its present high elevation during the last 10 or 20 million years.

Earthquakes result from stresses build up as a result of tectonic movement of the plates. Most earthquakes occur within the Earth's crust, which is normally between 30–35 km thick. In the Pamir of Tajikistan, the crust is double this thickness reaching 80–85 km thickness under the Karakoram and southern Pamir. The continental crust, dominantly composed of more buoyant granite and sedimentary rocks, lies above the denser mantle. The distribution of earthquakes shows the zones of active crustal deformation. Both the Tien Shan and Pamir ranges in Tajikistan have numerous earthquakes but the Tajik basin and the Tarim basin are seismically relatively inactive. They are strong blocks of old continental crust surrounded by active mountain belts that are both shortening internally and raising elevation. The Pamir knot of mountains is seismically active and contains two of the deepest known continental subduction zones, the Pamir and Hindu Kush seismic zones.

Box fold geological feature,
Lower Khingob Valley (left)

Aerial view north of Khovaling (above)

Earthquake epicentres of the south-dipping Pamir seismic zone curve around the Northern Pamir ranges south of the Tajik depression. They reflect southward subduction of the rigid Tajik-Tarim crust beneath the Pamir Mountains. Earthquakes extend to a depth of 180 km indicating subduction of cold continental crust to these depths within the hotter mantle. The north-dipping Hindu Kush seismic zone curves around the Southern Pamir and Hindu Kush mountains and reflects northerly subduction of thinned Indian crust from beneath the Himalaya. Earthquakes along the Hindu Kush seismic zone are the deepest known anywhere in the continents. They extend to depths of over 250 km along southern Tajikistan, the Wakhan corridor of Afghanistan and northernmost Pakistan. At these depths continental crustal rocks are subjected to pressures in excess of 25 kbar, and the rocks are metamorphosed to eclogites. The Pamir ranges are therefore supported by two continental crustal subduction zones converging at depth from both the north and south.

Global Positioning Satellite systems (GPS) are used to determine the present-day motion of the Earth's plates. Permanent GPS stations have now been installed across Asia for two decades enabling the active movements of the Earth's plate to be measured accurately. GPS data from Tajikistan indicates that the current crustal shortening rate across the Tien Shan is about 20 mm/year. This is a fraction of the total convergence between India and Asia (around 5–7 cm/year) most of which is accommodated in the Himalaya and Tibetan Plateau.

The crust of Tajikistan, like most of Central Asia, was amalgamated over several mountain-building (orogenic) cycles during the Palaeozoic and Mesozoic time. The geology of Tajikistan can be divided into three geographic regions, the northern Tien Shan Mountains, the Central Tajik basin, and the southern Pamir ranges which could also be described as a high-altitude plateau or steppe. The Tien Shan Mountains in Northern Tajikistan comprise mainly Mesozoic sedimentary rocks overlying older Palaeozoic basement crystalline rocks. The youngest rocks are thick piles of continental sedimentary rocks, frequently bright red and purple sandstones and shales. These rocks were deposited in inter-montane basins following uplift of the crust above sea-level. These Tertiary sedimentary rocks, together with their older basement, have been folded and faulted during recent geological history by renewed compression following the collision of the Indian plate.

The crest of the Tien Shan Mountains forms the southern border of Kyrgyzstan with Chinese Xinjiang and also with Tajikistan. The range separates the fertile Ferghana – Osh valley in Kyrgyzstan to the north with the Tajik basin to the south. Central and western Tajikistan is the high but relatively flat and fertile Tajik basin.

Although the surface is covered with Neogene sediments, the two deep seismic zones of the Pamir and Hindu Kush converge beneath this region, one that is constantly rocked by earthquakes.

At least three mountain ranges fan out across southern Tajikistan forming the Pamir Mountains. These ranges show a variety of old Palaeozoic and early Mesozoic sedimentary rocks intruded by several phases of granites. These granites are typical of active subduction zones above descending oceanic plates such as the present-day Andes. Geologists have interpreted these rocks to suggest that the southern margin of Asia, prior to the collision of India, was an Andean-type margin with thick crust, high elevation and characterised by intrusions of great granite batholiths and explosive volcanoes.

Since the end of the Cretaceous period about 65 million years ago tectonic activity changed abruptly. Oceanic subduction had ceased along the Tethys Ocean, the ocean that separated India from Asia and continent-continent collision began. The line of the collision stretches along the mountains of North Pakistan and Ladakh into southern Tibet. The crust thickened both to the south along the Indian plate Himalaya and to the north along the Karakoram and Pamir ranges. As the crust thickened by folding, thrusting and internal compression, rocks were progressively buried. The increase in pressure and temperature at depth resulted in old sedimentary and igneous rocks becoming metamorphosed to marbles, schists and gneisses. At the highest temperatures these rocks actually melted to form granite. The quartz and plagioclase rich granites are more buoyant than the surrounding rocks and the granite rose through the crust as intrusive plutons. The metamorphic rocks of the Karakoram and southern Pamir are a direct result of this Tertiary crustal thickening episode following the India-Asia collision.

Central Asia is transected by some of the World's longest strike-slip faults. These San Andreas-type faults move crustal blocks horizontally for hundreds of km. One theory suggests that as India collided into Asia, the thickened Tibetan crust was shunted sideways out of the way of the northward indenting Indian plate. Large-scale strike-slip faults such as the Altyn Tagh, Kunlun and Karakoram faults were responsible for the eastward motion of Tibet relative to stable Mongolia. In the west, the Chaman and Herat faults in Pakistan and Afghanistan were responsible for moving the Afghan-Tajik blocks westward away from the indenting Pamir knot. Although this theory is attractive, it is likely that the faults, although extremely impressive on the Earth's surface may not extend down to the hot, deep lower crust, where the rocks would deform by ductile flow, rather than brittle faulting.

The Karakoram fault is one of the most prominent such faults in Asia. It runs from the Kailas region of Southwest Tibet through Ladakh and the northern Karakoram into the southern Pamir. Two giant mountain massifs of Kongur (7,719 m) and Muztagh Ata (7,546 m) have been uplifted along the margin of the Karakoram fault in the northeastern Pamir. In Tajikistan the Karakoram fault terminates in the fold and thrust belt of the northern Pamir where the main fault splays into three branches, the Muji, Rankul and Karasu faults. Despite being such a prominent fault there has not been a major earthquake along it for over 100 years so there is every chance of a large rupture in the near future. In the northern Pamir the central steppe is cut by a series of north-south aligned normal faults indicating east-west extension. Lake Kara Kul (Uyghur for 'black lake') the largest lake in Tajikistan fills the rift valley.

The high altitude and the cold, arid conditions of the Pamir make for an extreme climate where average winter temperatures are around -20°C but can get down to -45°C. Coupled with strong winds and frequent dust storms it is hardly surprising that the geology and climate have conspired to make an inhospitable environment for human beings.

Dr. Mike Searle is a Lecturer in Geology at the Department of Earth Sciences, Oxford University, and a Fellow of Worcester College, Oxford. He has worked for 25 years along the Himalaya, Karakoram, Pamir and Tibetan regions.

River Muksu [Lipsky c.1899] (right)

Imprint of former glacier snout pushing on slope, Tanimas Valley (above)

Hot springs with mineral deposits at Garm Chashma (following pages)

BIRDING TAJIKISTAN

William Lawrence

Santa Barbara's *Bird Area* software programme lists 292 species of birds in Tajikistan; The *Fat Birder* website says there are 343 and the National Strategy on Conservation states that resident birds include 82 species, nesters – 150, migratory – 108, wintering – 80, birds of passage – 21, as well as over 20 species of ducks and sandpipers. 37 endangered species are listed in *The Red Data Book of Tajikistan*. Birdlife International mentions 8 globally red-listed species for Tajikistan. There are no endemics here, but quite a few uncommon birds and many raptors, including Lammergeier, Himalayan Griffon and Saker Falcon, as well as Short-toed Snake-Eagle, Bonelli's Eagle and Peregrine Falcon (in winter), which can all be seen in stunning circumstances within the mountains and valleys of the Pamirs and the mountain ranges of western Tajikistan, north of Dushanbe. In the summer one can even see such exotics as Paradise Flycatcher, Blue-cheeked Bee-Eater and Little Forktail. There are four species of Wagtail here, including the Yellow Wagtail, which I have read winters all the way down in Java. The delightful trilling of Red-headed Buntings often accompanies the lower elevations of mountain walks and they can be seen perched atop telegraph wires, small bushes and clumps of vegetation in many areas in spring and summer.

At the airport and into town one is bound to see flocks of noisy Mynahs, chattering and squawking in the trees on the capital city's main thoroughfare of Rudaki Avenue, or strutting along on the pavements. Laughing Doves are also common and plentiful, especially in towns and cities, where one sees singles, pairs and small flocks scavenging on the ground all over the place. Another species easily seen is the Tree Sparrow, replacing the House Sparrow as a town bird here. Good places for birds within Dushanbe are at the Botanical Gardens, between Karamova and Nosirov Streets, as well as within the city's other public parks. There are also some examples of large birds of prey at the Dushanbe city zoo – useful perhaps for pre-trip familiarisation, but their housing is not a pretty sight. Best time to be here for birding is during the Northern hemisphere late springtime and early summer, from about April to late June, or during late summer, from late August to late September – but any season including winter can be rewarding. Weather ranges from about minus 20°C in winter to more than +30°C in summer. During these periods migratory birds are on their way between the western Siberian breeding grounds and their wintering grounds, mainly in India, while local breeding species are singing and particularly easy to observe in springtime. The mountain passes are covered in snow far into June or even July.

South for the winter. Although many other birds choose longer migratory routes, the massive mountains of the Himalayas don't stop bar-headed geese, whose astonishing flight at 30,000ft takes them over the range, mostly to India.

Vultures in Tajikistan, from a 19th century engraving

Tajikistan is on a number of flight paths associated with bird migrations: Land birds, as well as various waterfowl (Ducks, Geese and Swans) migrate from India; birds of prey migrate from Africa, from as far south as Zambia, Tanzania and Zimbabwe. Shore and wading birds migrate from the Arctic Circle to India and back again, visiting Tajikistan on each leg of their journey.

During September to December each year, Barn Swallows and Northern Wheatears migrate over Tajikistan on their journey from Northern Russia to Africa.

All birding I have done in Tajikistan was at a very relaxed pace, often in tandem with other activities, such as work, sightseeing and mountain walking. Virtually every river valley in the mountains North of Dushanbe has its own resident populations of Blue Whistling-Thrush, Brown Dipper and White-capped Water Redstart and the further one drives away from civilisation, the more abundant and varied the birdlife becomes. A few days walk into the mountains in springtime or late summer can be rewarding, particularly at lower altitudes, Alpine Chough are easy to see and populate cliffs and mountain sides, often with Northern Ravens and flocks of Red-billed Chough in the same areas.

Birds of The USSR by V E Flint et al, and dated 1984 is a useful publication though the images in it are not great and it is intended to cover an enormous geographic range, including Tajikistan and the rest of Central Asia. I couldn't find one in Europe and finally bought my copy from a specialist bookseller in the USA for an outrageously expensive price. I also use my UK and Southern Africa bird books and CDs to help with identification and information about birds. Raffaël Ayé et al are currently compiling a book about the birds of Central Asia and this is due for publication around 2008. I have also found the following books useful; *Birds of the Middle East*, by Porter, Christensen and Schiermacker-Hansen; *Field Guide to the Birds of China*, by Mackinnon, Showler and Phillipps; *Raptors of the World – A Field Guide*, by Ferguson-Lees and Christie.

Few birders come to Tajikistan and there is little to no education about the

Istaravshan bird-sellers. The nightingales are kept either to sing in cages or for food.

environment here, so local attitudes to birds are coloured by the ignorance of an unenlightened population. During summer 2005 I saw at least one dead raptor almost every weekend, and sometimes saw two or three. All killed by farmers or homesteaders for reasons such as 'it was killing our chickens' or 'they are a nuisance' On one day I saw a dead Northern Eagle-Owl and a Black Kite within the space of a few minutes, the former shot by soldiers, presumably for sport and the latter killed by a local resident to protect his chickens. Little boys in rural areas carry catapults and some of them shoot at virtually any non-human creature they come across.

Low bird densities mean that birding in Tajikistan can be quite challenging, particularly so because, as related above, a fair proportion of the national population think that anything bigger than a blackbird is a menace to society, or fair game for food or sport. Chukar Partridges and other game birds are used like fighting cocks every weekend of the year at the bird market in Dushanbe.

Having said all that, birding here can be fantastic and there are regions which are virtually uninhabited that I have yet to explore. But I hope that the opportunity to add a few rarer or unusual species to a life-list or just to enjoy watching the birds within such spectacular scenery will increasingly attract pioneering birdwatchers and intrepid tourists in the future.

William Lawrence, has lived and worked in Tajikistan since 2005 and has an ongoing interest in the region's birds and mountains (email: willielawrence@hotmail.com).

Also see: www.osme.org/osmetrip/tajtrip1.html
www.bird-stamps.org/country/tajiki.htm (good images of Tajikistan birds)
www.bsc-eoc.org/links/links.jsp?page=l_asi_tj
www.birdlist.org/tajikistan.htm#BIRDING
www.asia-travel.uz (for regional birdwatching)
www.centralasiabirding.com (for birdwatching trips to Tajikistan, which will be
offered in the near future by Central Asia Birding Company)

Colias marcopolo; elevation: 4,200 m (left)

Parnassius charltonius deckerty (male); elevation: 4,100m (right)

BUTTERFLIES OF TAJIKISTAN

Jean-Francoise Charmeux and Jean-Marc Gayman

Since the first Russian scientific explorations of the 19th century, Tajikistan has been of particular interest to lepidopterists for its butterflies (*rhopalocerae*). In addition to the great variety of species and their beauty, some are native only to this region.

Most butterflies of Tajikistan belong to what is known as the palearctic fauna, comprising Asian species that live north of the 30th parallel. Some belong to the western palearctic group (N. Europe and Mediterranean) and others are found throughout the whole palearctic area, from France to Japan. Typically palaearctic, Tajik fauna has – contrary to the southern slopes of the Karakoram and Hindukush – no examples of tropical species.

The butterfly population varies according to altitude and in valleys at low altitudes almost all holarctic species are found. The situation is different on the high plateau in the eastern Pamirs and high mountain areas which are a sanctuary for species that have been isolated since the end of the glacial period and often cannot be found elsewhere (e.g. *Parnassius*). This rarity is the most remarkable feature of the butterflies of Tajikistan and Kyrgyzstan. The Pamirs, the Alai and the Tien Shan are indeed the refuge for species that have disappeared elsewhere and are an area permitting dispersion of these species and sub-species and even new species to the west (Iran, Turkey), e.g. *Colias thisoa, P. mnemosyne*; and to the east (Himalayas, Hindukush e.g. *Polyommatus devanica*. To the south, *Colias fieldii*, found in Ishkashim, is spreading throughout Northern Pakistan, Nepal, Bhutan and China.

The orographic and climatic variety within Tajikistan leads to a heterogeneity among biotopes and thus to a variety of species. The following major zones can be defined:

• North (Fergana): desert and sub-desert landscapes in which diversity is low; typical butterfly: *Polyommatus elvira*.

• Centre-west (Hissar–Darvaz): the mountains and forests lead to localisation of species ('endemism'): e.g. *Paralasa hades*. This is especially the case in the Peter the Great range, where there are numerous specific species: *Polyommatus kogistanus* (*lycænidæ* – blues), *Parnassius cardinal* (*papilionidæ* – swallowtails), *Pieris tadjika, Colias sieversi* (*pieridæ* – whites).

• South-west (Khatlon): steppes and savanes do not allow much diversification.

• Western Pamirs: the altitude favours a variety of species; the fact that the valleys are separated by mountain ranges (Vanch, Yazgulem, Rushan, Shughnan) leads to a multiplication of sub-species (*lycænidæ*).

• Eastern Pamirs : localized species are frequent on the high plateau (*Parnassius, Colias marcopolo*).

The fauna of Tajikistan and neighbouring regions were first discovered during the Great Game (see page 295) and is still relatively unknown. For example, the Pamirs are believed to be the home to *Parnassius tianshanicus griseldis* and *Parnassius simonius* and in July 2005, Sergey Churkin discovered in the centre of Kyrgyzstan, at 2,500 m, a new species that he named *Parnassius davydovi*. Tajikistan is also a terra incognita for fauna and the catalogue of species is not complete.

Among the butterflies in Tajikistan, the *Parnassius* (Apollos) and the *Colias* (Clouded yellows) are the most famous – as much for their beauty and rarity as for their endemism: for most lepidopterists they typify the Pamirs.

Sixteen of the forty species of the *Parnassius* butterfly distributed throughout the world are resident in the Tien Shan, the Altaï and the Pamirs, of which no less than fifteen are native to Tajikistan (*P. simo, P. simonius, P. delphius infernalis, P. staudingeri mamalevi et P. staudingeri staudingeri, P. cardinal, P. charltonius, P. autocrator, P. mnemosyne, P. apollo merzbacheri, P. tianshanicus, P. actius, P. epaphus, P. jacquemontii rubicundus, P. apollonius, P. honrathi*); nine of these are found in the Pamirs. The Pamirs, with the Alai and Kyrgyzstan, are the second richest area in the world for butterflies, after Tibet. Some fly around flowers at 2,000 m, (*P. Apollo, P. appollonius*), others are on the high pastures above the tree line at 3,000 m and higher (*P. Delphius, P. tianshanicus*), and some can even be found in the sub-glacial landscape between 4,000 and 5,000 m (*P. simo*).

The *Coliadinæ* (Clouded yellows) show the same diversity; the endemic species are: in the Alai and Transalai the magnificent *C. romanovi*, vermilion red; in the Pamirs, two of the largest, *C. marcopolo* and *C. cocandica*; in the Alai and Hissar, *C. christophi*; and, in the Peter the Great range, *C. sieversi*.

The *lycænidæ* (blues), *nymphalidæ* (fritillaries and vanessids) and *satyrinæ* (ringlets, graylings, browns), less famous, have also very specific taxa (groupings) such as: *Lycaena aeolus* (Ishkashim), *Iolana gigantea* (Ishkashim, Western Tajikistan), an exceptionally beautiful blue *Lycaena* type. Among the *Satyrinae* there are: *Erebia*, a typical mountain butterfly, the species of which differ according to the valleys in which they are found; and *Paralasa*, typical for Central Asia.

Several of these butterflies are today endangered species. After the collapse of the Soviet Union, commercial hunting became widespread. For example, in the eastern Tien Shan, there was a rush to collect *Parnassius loxias* that was selling at the time for several hundred dollars a specimen in the West and Japan. Fortunately for this butterfly the price has gone down since, but the same fate may await *P. davydovi*, since few collectors own this specimen, discovered only in 2005. In the Pamirs, commercial hunters are still trying to collect *P. autocrator* and *P. charltonius*.

Deforestation, erosion, pollution and reduction in pasture area are other factors threatening the survival of butterflies. For species endemic to the mountains, the main danger is global warming. From 1957 to 2000, the glaciers of the Pamirs and the Altai have lost 25 % of their volume of ice and the acceleration of this process is abundantly visible. In Western Europe, entire populations of Parnassius apollo are now extinct. Can the butterflies of Central Asia escape this fate?

Jean-François Charmeux is an amateur lepidopterist. As a specialist of the paleoarctics lycaenidae, he has many published papers and also conducted many expeditions in Central Asia (Iran, Pakistan, Kyrgyzstan, etc.).

Jean-Marc Gayman is professor of History at the Evry University, south of Paris. As an amateur entomologist, and member of the Lepidopterists of France Association (http://lepido.paris.free.fr/english), he organizes survey expeditions of the butterfly fauna in Central Asia and Papua (formerly Irian Jaya).

FLORA OF TAJIKISTAN
Peter Cunnington

The climate of Tajikistan, influenced by the weather systems of the oceans to the west, favours those plants adapted to the avoidance of summer drought, plants capable of lying dormant through the hottest part of the year by reliance on underground storage organs and spring flowering. Winters are long and cold with temperatures occasionally plunging to minus 20°C whilst summer may often produce maxima around 40°C.

Between Dushanbe and the high alps of the mountains are rolling hills of wind-blown loess, rusty brown earth covered by a cloth of bright green, pastures for the local breed of sheep herded by Tajik shepherds. Their outdoor life and familiarity with the country they love so much gives them first hand knowledge of the plants amongst which their flocks graze contentedly in early spring; knowledge, for instance of *Crocus*, *Iris* and *Corydalis* for which the area is renowned. Many will have come over the mountain passes, which are vital links between the various mountain communities and the major centres of population. The river Varzob, flowing south from the mountains towards Dushanbe, crashes its white waters through spectacular gorges just wide enough to allow a metalled road to follow the rocky banks north across the passes to Samarkand. Clinging to the cliffs above the foaming waters is a species of *Dionysia*, a primula relative that is more usually found in Iran and Afghanistan. Just at the entrance to Varzob Gorge grow tight cushions of *Dionysia involucrata* bearing tubular pink flowers in spring, each cushion pressed against the rock face to avoid excessive moisture falling onto its delicate leaves and to find protection from the winds that blow constantly from the snows above.

Leaving the cement works on the northern outskirts of the town the road heads north from the state capital to the small village of Takob from which a lateral valley may be seen to the east. Lined with Walnut, Almond and *Acer* the track winds upwards with slopes to left and right carpeted with yellow *Gagea* in such quantities as to create the illusion of an English Oil Seed Rape field. Several species of this bulbous genus are involved, all difficult, if not impossible, to identify, but one looking remarkably like *Gagea graeca* may be found in abundance These prove to be but an appetizer, a preliminary glimpse of better things to come.

As the valley narrows Juno Iris colonise the heavy soil, wet from snow melt, soil that will bake brick hard in the summer heat that will follow in eight weeks time. *Iris*

vicaria is a rather disappointing species, seen individually, with its greyish flowers, although some authorities would have them light blue, but in mass it redeems itself flowing down the hillside around and between the ice-strewn boulders to the streamside. Better by far, however, is *Iris bucharica*, its specific epithet taken and latinised from the town of Bukhara in the adjacent state of Uzbekistan further to the west. Rising above glossy, bright green leaves a flowering stem will hold six or more blossoms, white, flushed yellow with bright, butter yellow falls. Flower colour and quality varies and the two species may hybridise, but here and there a more fulsome specimen of *Iris bucharica* may be found with rich, golden yellow flowers, the falls marked with chocolate brown stripes, a garden worthy plant indeed.

Small copses of *Acer tataricum* with nectar-rich bunches of yellow flowers, Hawthorn scrub and *Exochorda korolokovii* provide a modicum of protection from the sun's glare and sanctuary from grazing animals for the scarlet tulip familiar in gardens, *Tulipa praestans*. Here too is blue *Scilla bucharica* and *Corydalis ledebouriana*, its spikes of burgundy and white-spurred flowers rising above the neat blue-grey foliage. Two other species of *Corydalis* flourish here one close to the margin of the well worn sheep tracks that allow trekkers easier passage than pushing through the shrubs, this is

Wild flowers and introduced South African Crocus in Savnob village, Bartang Valley

Corydalis popovii with large flowers held rigidly on the stems the white spur stretched horizontally behind the almost red, pouting tips The relatively coarse, glaucous foliage must be unpalatable for it is rarely grazed, just a little nibbled sometimes. Further up the valley in the litter of fallen *Juglans* leaves is *Corydalis nudicaule*, more curious than lovely, but definitely interesting. The flowers are in various shades of chocolate, milk chocolate for the spurs and dark chocolate for the swollen tips. Arranged in narrow, rather elegant erect spikes the impression created is of a spawn of newly emerged tadpoles reluctant to let go and venture alone into the world.

Emerging from the woods a series of sheer cliffs confronts the traveller who, if undaunted by the apparent cul-de-sac, may scale to the ridge. The effort is amply rewarded for the views alone but further benefits are in store as the eyes gradually pick out the colonies of *Iris rosenbachiana*, another Juno. Less than 15cms tall and flowering before the leaves which in April merely sheath the single flower, their colour varies from rich, imperial purple with white and yellow markings to rosy reds and pinks. Despite its lofty altitude this species is more at home in the bulb frame than the open garden situation where well-drained soil will suit its more robust cousins of the wetter, lower slopes.

Where the Varzob Gorge narrows between high cliffs which crowd and compress the available space so that road and river are almost as one, are a series of low, rock walls about 10 m high, orientated to the south west. Careful scrutiny through field glasses will reveal yet more cushions of *Dionysia involucrata* clinging limpet-like, but tantalizingly, beyond reach. A short detour may be taken, using as a starting point, a narrow, concrete bridge with considerately placed handrails, across a small tributary to the right of the gorge proper. The tributary seems to flow under its rocky bed rather than over it and by following its course northeast towards a low ridge one may gain easy access to *Corydalis macrocentra*. The land rises gently to the distant ridge and plants of blue *Gentiana olivieri* and *Ixiolirion tataricum* may take one's attention from the almost ubiquitous Juno Irises. Once on the ridge, carved and moulded by the erosive powers of storm water, the bright yellow flowers and grey-blue leaves of the rare fumitory reveal themselves on the gravelly screes. Gaining a foothold is difficult and it is not surprising to find oneself worrying about plunging into the valley below in a torrent of grit and boulders. However, with the reason for the effort now within reach it would be foolish to abandon the screes without first noting that the tubers are deep in their rocky substrate and that the stems arising from them twist and curl around the stones towards the light. So thankful are they, it seems, to reach the surface that here they stop, extending upwards no more, simply spreading out across the scree. How different in habit and intensity of colour from pot-grown specimens at home.

Returning to the main river and pushing northwards towards the snowfields is well worth the effort. Vehicles may pull off the road into a lay-by and by scrambling amongst the rocks plants of *Fritillaria bucharica* may be located. In this place, however, the specimens are poor, weak stemmed, small flowered and thin petalled, wretched forms when compared with the same, strong flowered species across the border in Uzbekistan where they may be found growing in the rocky chaos of the screes at the top of Nightingale Valley. No broad petals of purest white splashed with olive-green basal patches here below the snowline of Varzob, but a transparent, greyish flower the blotch being a drab-green, more like washing for the jumble sale than the 'bespoke tailoring' across the border. Compensation presents itself in the form of tall and elegant Umbellifers, *Prangos sp.* and stately Ferulas, pink almond blossoms and the yellow flowers of a plant, surprisingly related to the shrubby Berberis: *Bongardia chrysogonum.* The former spatter the hillsides with white or yellow on four foot high stems whilst the latter clings in pockets and cervices, packed with its own detritus, on the cliffs, its few flower stems gently blowing in the cool air rising from the river crashing below. The best forms in cultivation bear chocolate coloured markings in a rough horseshoe shape on each grey-green leaflet but this is a selected character, one not normally found in this area

Romit is a nature reserve where bears and snakes may be encountered but where protection of plants is not enforced. It is from here that the *Fritillaria eduardii* blooms were once plundered in abundance, to be handed out in a gesture of celebration to mark Lenin's birthday. The slopes are well endowed with this close relative of the crown imperial, bright brick red but only 75cms high, their whereabouts being given away by following the trail of broken stems, leaves and the odd bulb to their source. The easiest site is reached from the little village of Tany-Kha to the east of Dushanbe along the Kafimigan River. *Gagea*, Juno Iris, *Eremurus*, *Corydalis* and the little upright periwinkle *Vinca erecta* are abundant in Romit together with a scrubby member of the dock family, Polygonaceae, *Atraphaxis pyrolifolia*, more strange than beautiful. Deep pink *Prunus bucharica* forms isolated bushes a couple of metres high and spiny *Astragalus* clothe the hot slopes with impenetrable clumps of almost leafless stems. Sheltering in the lea of scrubby thorn bushes may be a large aroid. *Arum korolkowii*, its spathe the colour of congealed blood and fresh liver, a sort of reddish-brown. Little

wonder that it is fly-pollinated for it must seem to the fly too good an egg laying site to miss.

Other plants exist, curious *Solenanthus coronatus*, *Biebersteinia* a relative of *Geranium* with pinnate leaves and orange flowers, and yellow *Onosma* angling out from the exposed russet cliff faces of the loess. Attention however, is not drawn to these but to two species of *Anemone* occurring in such numbers as to be mind-blowing. *Anemone tschernjaewii* seeks a little shade running amongst the shrubs and small trees that form open woodland. Some 15cms high its foliage is vaguely reminiscent of our own Wood Anemone but with tougher, darker green leaves. Above the thin mat of foliage open white flowers tinged with mauve a colour that intensifies and spreads across the corollas as the blossoms age. The flowers are nutant at first exposing the purplish undersides of the perianth but they soon lift, opening their faces to the sun and revealing a strong contrast between the pale cups and burgundy anthers.

If it is possible, *Anemone petiolulosa* is more spectacular, stretching across the alps in a broad 'lake', like molten gold fingering between the rocks and clothing the high ledges. The undersides of the petals, more properly tepals, are, with age, tinted ruby red or burnished copper each tepal polished and shining. At first sight one almost rubs ones eyes with disbelief but so abundant, so widespread, are the populations that one may almost become dismissive of each successively encountered colony. Of course, growing in close proximity, hybrids are likely to occur and do, but these creamy flowered specimens will never outshine the glory of their parents. Thus, with no sense of reluctance, one turns ones attention elsewhere, perhaps to the Lion's Paw, *Gymnospermum albertii*. Thrusting through the wet earth recently vacated by the melting snow, maroon crosiers unfurl to reveal a spike of orange flowers sustained by

Fritillaria eduardii *in the Romit Reserve in April*

the irregularly shaped tuber below. Each petal has a central vein of red, echoing the stem, all five combining to create a star-shaped bloom. Nowhere are the leaves to be seen, they will come later unfolding to produce in outline a shape supposedly reminiscent of a lion's paw mark: imagination is a wonderful thing. As the season advances the foliage may become coarse, and with an eventual height of about 30cms, it is hard to believe that such fascinating flowers precede it. The best and earliest of these frequently encountered members of the Berberidaceae family are to be discovered in well drained gritty soil often on the margin of a melt-water stream particularly on south facing banks which warm rapidly in the brilliant April sunshine.

An unremarkable road runs south towards Norak and the Afghan border, unremarkable except that it is well tarmaced and provides a fast ride to the power station. Running through the eroded valleys one is conscious of the fact that this is earthquake country for past landslips scar the hillsides. The approach to Norak takes the traveller uphill initially through vineyards and orchards until the ridge is gained, a long string of wires strung beneath the pylons dominating its crest.

Turning towards the north a fine panorama of the Hissar Mountains, snow capped and rugged above their green skirts, is worth taking time to admire. In the

Corydalis nudicaule   *Gymnospermium albertii*

distance the roof tops of Dushanbe, red or burgundy coloured, but beyond the gash of Varzob and past remembered excursions. In summer the flowering of thousands of Foxtail lilies and herbaceous *Dictamnus albus*, the so-called Burning Bush, will enhance the view. Certainly not a bush in the woody sense of the word but burning, yes, for its essential oils sublime in the heat of summer and a match will set the vapours alight with a soft blue, short-lived flame and a gentle hiss as of exhaled breath, if applied on a windless day.

The brilliant scarlet flowers of *Anemone bucharica* are abundant, their petals paler, and almost buff coloured below, and with foliage reduced to such a deeply incised form as to be little more than a wing either side of the main veins – a method, no doubt, of avoiding excess water loss in high summer. Where the soil is thin on the ledges is Central Asia's version of England's Bird's Eye Primula. Growing either in shade or full sun, *Primula algida* is larger in all its parts than our native *Primula farinosa*. Yellow *Colchicum luteum* and yellow and brown *Crocus korolkowii* may cause a confusion of identification until it is pointed out that by counting the male sexual organs the difference becomes immediately obvious. *Colchicum* is a lily with six anthers whilst the *Crocus* belongs to the Iris family and has only three. Both flower in advance of foliage and, typically, at the edge of melting snowfields.

Iris stolonifera, with a strange mixture of purple, brown and white flowers, forms patches a metre or so in extent and associates well with a lilac flowered *Caragana* amongst the branches of which it seeks protection from the grazing herds. When the sun is warm a specimen of Hautlaub's Tortoise may be tempted into the open, awaking, gummy-eyed from winter's rest. Woe betide the tortoise which ventures out when Tajiks are about for it will most certainly be taken home as a pet.

As spring stretches into sizzling summer *Eremurus* will flower and fade and soon the landscape will become seared and brown. Plants will rest but not the people. There will be crops to gather, Tobacco, Grapes, the all-important cotton, and Mulberry leaves to feed the silkworms.

Formerly, Curator of the University of Liverpool Botanical Gardens at Ness, Cheshire, England, Peter Cunnington has travelled widely in search of plants and is well acquainted with the bulbous flora of the mountains of Central Asia.

Yulii Waterfall, Gulbas River [1890]

THE PAMIRS

EXPLORATION AND ADVENTURE

ON THE

ROOF OF THE WORLD

ROBERT MIDDLETON

Introduction

In approaching the story of the exploration of the Pamirs, three things must be borne in mind. Firstly, the Pamirs have never been a rich territory: the altitude and difficulty of the passes did not invite invasion for the promise of material gain. One of the first Europeans to cross the Pamirs in the nineteenth century, Guillaume Capus, commented:

> ... le Pamir, borne naturelle et forteresse bien défendue par la nature, n'a jamais été pris d'assaut par le conquérant ou l'envahisseur. Il n'en aurait pas été sans doute, si la possession de cette forteresse naturelle avait été très avantageuse. Deux causes, en effet, rendent cette possession, même de nos jours, illusoire et infructueuse: la première, c'est la facilité relative des autres voies de communication du Turkestan à l'Inde et en Kashgarie et de la Kashgarie à l'Inde; la seconde, l'habitabilité précaire du Pamir pendant la majeure partie de l'année. (The Pamirs, a natural frontier and fortress well defended by nature, have never been taken by storm by conqueror or invader. It would certainly not have been so if there had been some significant advantage in the possession of this fortress. There are two reasons why, even today, possession would be illusory and unprofitable: the first is the relative ease of access by other routes to India and Kashgar; the second the precarious living conditions in the Pamirs for most of the year.)[1]

Until the late nineteenth century, when the Pamirs became the scene of intense Anglo-Russian strategic rivalry, the region was marginal to the major military and political events affecting Central Asia. As a result, the population was largely spared the depredations inflicted on other regions of Central Asia during the conquests of Genghis Khan and Timur and it is plausible that the "gene pool" of the original inhabitants of Central Asia remains relatively intact in the Pamirs today (see page 264).

Secondly, until the mid-20th century, human settlement in the Pamirs was insignificant: indeed, on the high plateau of the Eastern Pamirs there were virtually no permanent human settlements. In 1880, Mukhtar Shah, a native explorer working on behalf of the British, (see page 364) estimated the total population of the Western Pamirs, including the left bank of the Panj, at some 30,000. In 1899, the Danish expedition led by Olufsen estimated the population of Khorog – now the capital of Gorno-Badakhshan – at only 33 houses and 120 persons. In 1908,

Cave at Savnob, Bartang Valley (previous pages)

A. Snessareff, Russian Academician and head of the Russian military administration in Khorog, estimated the total population of the Western Pamir (i.e. territory under Russian jurisdiction on the right bank of the Panj) at 17,000 and the Eastern Pamir only 2,000.

Thirdly, as is the case with any other area inhabited by nomadic peoples, the Pamirs were far from virgin unexplored territory. Long before the miners of spinel, lapis and silver, the silk road traders, the Chinese and Jesuit missionaries and the players of the 'Great Game' whom we shall meet in due course, the Pamirs had been criss-crossed by local nomadic herders since time immemorial. Exploration and discovery must be understood, therefore, in the sense of creating a scientific record of the region.

The expansion of empire in the 19th century – and also the insatiable curiosity of an age thirsty for knowledge of far-away places, combined with not a little sheer love of adventure – led to research according to modern scientific principles by Russian, British, French, German and Hungarian cartographers, ethnologists and others. The bulk of this section of the book concerns their adventures and achievements.

Russo-German Pamir Expedition, Farewell party in the Tanimas Valley 1928

The First Inhabitants of the Pamirs and Early Trade Routes

The Scythians

The physical features of most of the people living in the Pamirs today (and in adjacent parts of Western China, Northern Pakistan and Afghanistan) are markedly different from those of their neighbours in other regions of Central Asia. According to local legend, these are inherited from the remnants of the army of Alexander the Great who are supposed to have settled in the Pamirs. Others, not usually Pamiris, will tell you that they result from the Russian presence in the Pamirs since the beginning of the 20th century. In fact, their origin must be sought much further back in time.

The earliest evidence of human presence in the Pamirs was found in the cave of Darra-i Kur in what is today the Afghan province of Badakhshan, where a transitional Neanderthal skull fragment and contemporary tools were discovered, dated to around 120,000 years ago (Middle Paleolithic).[1] Excavations in Murghab district in 1960–61 uncovered evidence of permanent settlement on the high Pamir plateau dating from the 8th to the 5th millennium BC. The researchers noted that their work "was made difficult by strong cold winds at times developing into fierce sand storms" and had difficulty imagining how "people dressed in animal skins and equipped with primitive stone and wooden implements [could] live in this cold austere area." Noting, however that the fireplaces used had been open and that material excavated included ash of wood origin (whereas today not a single tree grows on the high plateau), they concluded that the climate must have been much milder at that time.[2] As late as the end of the 19th century, the climate in the Pamirs may have been less extreme than today: the Russian engineer Serebrennikov, who built the first Russian military base in Khorog in 1895, noted that "the climate is so mild that even vines grow here."[3]

The first written record of established human activity in the Pamirs is in historical accounts of the Scythians (frequently referred to in Central Asian ethnography by their Persian name 'Sakas'), a nomadic people who left no documentary and only fragmentary linguistic evidence of their existence, but about whom credible information is found in histories from the time of the Achaemenid dynasty in Persia (559–330 BC) and in the *Histories* of Herodotus (5th century BC).[4] According to the Greek historian, geographer and philosopher Strabo (approx. 63 BC–24 AD), the

Asii (Asiani), Tokhari, and Sakaraucae, the nomads who took Bactria from the Greeks, "migrated from beyond the Jaxartes, the territory occupied by the Sakas."

Much of our 'knowledge' of the Scythians is, however, speculative. We can safely put aside the many legends recounted by the early historians, that the Scythians were a one-eyed people, that they were constantly engaged in battle with the griffins who guarded the gold that they worked so skilfully or that the first Scythian was born from the union of Hercules and a snake-legged goddess. There is, however, general agreement among scholars that, from as early as the second millennium BC, large areas of Siberia, Central Asia and Western China were inhabited by a group of peoples known collectively as Scythians.

According to inscriptions left by the Achaemenid King Darius I (522–486 BC) in the city of Hamadan, one of the groups of Scythians was called *Sakâ tigrakhaudâ* ('Sacae with pointed hats').

Anthropological, archaeological and linguistic evidence indicates that the Scythians were Europoids[5], that they were fire and sun-worshippers and that their language belonged to the Indo-Iranian group of the Indo-European linguistic family. Among modern languages, Ossetian and some dialects still spoken in the Pamirs are probably the closest to the original Scythian language.

Ancient Chinese histories record that the *Wu-sun* (Asiani) who took Bactria from the Greeks were 'blue-eyed and fair' and that their allies, the *Ting-ling*, had blue eyes and red beards. Herodotus described them as having 'long chins' and Xuanzang (7th century AD – see Chapter 2) noted that the Kashgaris had green eyes and that one of the peoples living on the upper Oxus had eyes "of a bluish-green tint, different from all other people". The dictionary of Ashraf Ibn Sharaf Al-Muzakkir Al-Farruga, composed 1404–1405 in India (*Danish-nameyi Kadar-Khan* – 'Book of knowledge of Kadar-Khan'), notes that a group of peoples known as the *Sakaliba* live in Turkestan and are 'white' people.[6]

The presence in the Pamir region of people with fair complexions (and, in many cases, fair hair) is confirmed by later travellers long before the arrival of the Russians. In the early 17th century, the Portuguese Jesuit traveller, Benedict Goës (see page 292), noted a people called 'Calcia' (Galcha) on the Oxus who were distinguished by 'yellow hair and beard like the people of the Low Countries'[7]. A British officer, T.E. Gordon, on his visit to the Wakhan in 1874, noted that 'fair hair and blue eyes are not uncommon' and Ralph Cobbold, another British explorer, made a similar remark in 1897 in relation to Rushan.[8]

An anthropological survey was undertaken in 1877 by the Hungarian anthropologist and explorer, Charles de Ujfalvy, in regions adjoining the Pamirs (Karategin, Ferghana and Kohistan in Afghan Badakhshan). Although he himself did not travel to the Pamirs, he was told by local people that there was a strong presence of blond and blue-eyed people in the Pamirs.[9] A survey by the Anglo-Hungarian explorer Aurel Stein in Shughnan in 1908 recorded 37.7% with fair hair.[10] Stein commented on the appearance of a Sarikol Tajik: "With his tall figure, fair hair, and blue eyes he looked the very embodiment of that *Homo Alpinus* type which prevails in Sarikol. I thought of old Benedict Goëz, the lay Jesuit, who when passing in 1603 from the upper Oxus to 'Sarcil' or Sarikol, noted in the looks of the scanty inhabitants a resemblance to Flemings."[11] (See page 292 for an account of Benedict de Goës's travels.)

In 2001, researchers in the Institute of Ethnology and Anthropology of the Moscow Academy of Sciences reconstructed the physiognomy of skulls found in the Talgar archaeological site in the Semirechnye district of Kazakhstan, dated 11th to 12th century AD. The results indicated clearly that, immediately prior to the Mongol invasions, people with pronounced European (Caucasian) features inhabited large areas of Central Asia.[12]

Girl near Sezhd, Roshtkala

Girl, Zhamag

The most recent research in Tajikistan suggests that there were two separate groups in the Pamirs with distinctive features and culture: the "Markansu" group – associated with a late Mesolithic (approx. 8,000 BC) archaeological site known as 'Oshkhona' at 4,100 m in the north-eastern Pamirs, on the Markansu[13] river north-west of Kara Kul lake, and identified with the Sakas; and the "Istiksu" group, associated with another site to the north of what is now the village of Chechtebe on the Istyk river in the south-east. The latter group differed significantly from the former in the method of stone-working, in funeral traditions and in ethnic characteristics, corresponding more to a Mediterranean group than to the Sakas.[14]

The ehnonym 'Sak' has been linked to several place names in the Pamirs, e.g. Shughnan (ancient name 'Shakinan'), Ishkashim ('ancient name 'Sakasham').

Early Trade Routes

Ptolemy (approx. 87–150 AD), in his Geography, described a trade route across Central Asia drawn from the writings of his contemporary Marinus of Tyre. Marinus' work has been lost, but it was based on an account by the Macedonian Maës Titianus of his agents' travels to China. Ptolemy describes the route that took them from Bactria and Sogdiana through the Pamirs to Seres Metropolis, the Chinese capital, modern Xi'an[15] (present-day locations are shown in square brackets).

Ancient petroglyphs, Langar, Wakhan

Then the route runs on through Aria [Herat] to Margiana Antiochia [Merv], first declining to the south (for Aria lies in the same latitude as the Caspian Gates), and then to the north, Antiochia being somewhere near the parallel of the Hellespont. Thence the road proceeds eastward to Bactra [Balkh, near Mazar-i Sharif], and from that northward up the ascent of the hill country of the Comedi, and then inclining somewhat south through the hill country itself as far as the gorge in which the plains terminate. For the western end of the hill country is more to the north also, being (as Marinus puts it) under the latitude of Byzantium, the eastern end more to the south being under the latitude of Hellespont. Hence the road runs as he describes in the opposite direction, i.e. towards the east with an inclination south; and then a distance of fifty schoeni[16] extending to the Stone Tower would seem to tend northward.[17]

Beyond the Stone Tower, there was, according to Titianus, a trading station; the route then continued through the 'deserts of Scythia' before arriving in *Seres Metropolis* (Ptolemy, Book vi, Chapter 13). Another source[18] confirms that "in the ancient conduct of the silk trade the *Seres* deposited their bales of silk in the Stone Tower with the prices marked, and then retired, whilst the western merchants came forward to inspect."

The *Res Gestae*, a history of Rome by Ammianus Marcellinus, a Roman general and historian (AD 325–330 to 395), gives detailed descriptions of various 'barbarian' nations, including the Scythians and their successor tribes, and confirms Ptolemy's information about the route to China:

> Immediately after the Bactrians live the Sakas, a ferocious nation that inhabits marshy land suitable only for raising cattle. At the foot of their mountains there is a place called the 'Stone Tower' through which runs the road travelled by merchants after a long voyage on their way to the Seres.[19]

The actual location of these various places on the Silk Road through the Pamirs, to which Ptolemy and later historians refer, has given rise to lively scholarly debate over the years, as illustrated by the Proceedings of the Royal Geographical Society in January 1877: Colonel Henry Yule had just expressed the view that Ptolemy's Comedi must have been located in present Darvaz and Rushan, and that Titianus' route must have been close to there:

> *Sir H. Rawlinson* said that Ptolemy's line passed through Balkh. *Sir Douglas Forsyth* replied that it also went to Samarcand. *Colonel Yule*: Never.

Russian geographers, who were among the first to explore the Pamirs (see Chapter 6), concluded that the 'hill country of the Comedi' is the present day Karategin (valley of the Surkhob/Kyzylsu river), the 'Stone Tower' is Tashkurgan in Western China and the 'Place of Merchants' is Kashgar. Aurel Stein supported the conclusions reached by the Russians about the Comedi, but located the trading station at Irkeshtam, today the main border crossing from the Alai valley to China.[20]

The name Tashkurgan means literally 'stone tower', and there were, of course, many such towers built for defensive purposes throughout Central Asia, some of which gave rise to place names; until fairly recently, Khulm in Afghanistan and Savnob in the Bartang valley of the Pamirs, for example, were called Tashkurgan. However, the very persistence of the name of present-day Tashkurgan could be taken as circumstantial evidence that it was always the most important of these and therefore the place to which Ptolemy referred. As an example, we may note the persistence of the name Tashkent ('stone town') over the centuries, although at the beginning of our era there must certainly have been other towns in the region built with stone.[21]

Following from this, we may also suggest as another hypothesis that the route to Tashkurgan described by Titianus passed not through the Karategin but much further south in the Pamirs, up either

a) the Ghunt-Alichur valley, and thence across the high Pamir to Rangkul and one of the passes to the Karasu river on the other side of the Sarikol range,[22]

or

b) the Wakhan, and thence either to the Great Pamir and across the Nezatash or to the Little Pamir and across the Wakhjir, Beik or Nezatash pass.

These alternative identifications of Titianus's route are supported by archaeological evidence (including substantial Scythian burial sites) that these routes were frequently used in antiquity. The Wakhan route would also correspond to the approach to Tashkurgan in a northward direction, as described by Titianus. Moreover, if the trading station mentioned by Titianus was indeed Kashgar, as suggested by Russian scholars, it makes little sense for traders to travel from the Alai valley a long distance south to Tashkurgan only to retrace their steps north to Kashgar.

Chinese Travellers in the Pamirs

The teachings of Taoism and Buddhism locate Paradise in the far west of China. A Taoist legend describes this paradise in words that recall some features of the Pamirs:

> ... it does not breed any species of bird or beast, fish or insect, grass or tree. The country is flat in all directions, with high ranges all around it; and right in the middle is a mountain named Urn Peak, shaped like a pot with a bracelet, which is named the Cave of Plenty. Waters bubble out of it, named the Divine Spring, which smell sweeter than orchids and spices, taste sweeter than wine and musk. Four streams[1] divide from the one source, flow down the mountain and irrigate every corner of the country.[2]

Around 280 AD, several old texts were discovered in a grave in the district of Ji in the present-day province of Henan. Among them was an account of the legendary travels of King Mu, Son of Heaven (Mu Wang, c.985–c.907 BC). The *Mu tianzi zhuan*, written in the 5th–4th century BC[3], describes the journey of King Mu to Eastern Iran through the Tarim basin and the Kunlun and Pamir mountains, where he is reputed to have met the Queen Mother of the West (Xiwangmu) in her palace beside a Jasper lake (*Yaochi*), identified by some as the Heavenly Pool (Lake Tianchi) in Xinjiang.

Apart from legend, there are also reliable accounts of the Pamirs (described in the texts as the 'Tsung-ling' or 'Cong-ling') in the Chinese court histories from the beginning of our era. The court historians systematically collected information from travellers, visiting ambassadors and traders about the regions outside China's borders. Friedrich Hirth, one of the foremost authorities on early Chinese history, commented that

> Zhongguo [China] is fortunate enough to possess a series of historical works comparing most favorably, in some of its parts, with the historical literature of any nation in the West. Since the Han, each dynasty has had its own history, compiled from its court chronicles, or *Jih-li*, during the succeeding reigns. The *Jih-li*, literally 'Daily Chronicles', must be considered the prime source of all the information contained in these histories.[4]

Hirth added that the total collection of the Twenty-Four Dynastic Histories (*Ershihi Shi*) comprises over 3,000 books, the analysis of which would present the European scholar, interested in a specific aspect of Chinese dynastic history, with

Caravanserai 'Abdullah Khan' in Bash Gumbez, near Alichur

a Herculean labor were it not that the methodical mind of the Chinese writers had carefully put aside all he wants into special chapters regarding foreign countries. Thus we find chapters on the Hsiung-nu [Xiongnu] on the South-Western barbarians (Man); on the country of Ta-wan, generally identified with the present Ferghana, in the Shih-chi of Ssu-ma Ch'ien [Sima Qian – died about 85 BC], whose work opens the series …

Zhang Qian

In 138 BC, an envoy of the Han Emperor Wu, Zhang Qian, travelled west and brought back the first description of the Pamirs and the regions beyond. The Han at this time were engaged in a concerted effort to destroy the Hsiung-nu (in pinyin 'Xiongnu'), a group of nomadic tribes originating probably in Mongolia, that was continually attacking and plundering China's territories in the north and north-west. Zhang Qian, a palace attendant, accompanied by Ganfu, a Hsiung-nu slave, and a large caravan was sent as the emperor's envoy through Hsiung-nu territory to seek an alliance with the Yuezhi, a tribe living to the west of China[5]. Their dramatic journey was recounted by Zhang Qian's contemporary Sima Qian in the *Shiji* (Shih-chi), his official *Records of the Grand Historian*, as it is known in the West.[6]

Zhang Qian was captured by the Hsiung-nu and taken before their king, who refused to let him proceed. "The Yuezhi people live north of me," he said. "What does the Han mean by trying to send an envoy to them! Do you suppose the Han would let my men pass through China?"[8] Zhang Qian took a wife from the Hsiung-nu people, by whom he had a son and finally, after more than ten years, he escaped and continued his journey west across present-day Kyrgyzstan to the Yuezhi king in Bactria, whose father had been killed by the Hsiung-nu.

The Yuezhi, however, turned down the proposal of an alliance with the Han. Sima Qian notes that "the region he ruled was rich and fertile and seldom troubled by invaders, and the king thought only of his own enjoyment. He considered the Han too far away to bother with and had no particular intention of avenging his father's death by attacking the Hsiung-nu…"

His mission unsuccessful, Zhang Qian started on the journey back, but was again captured by the Hsiung-nu. In 126 BC, the Hsiung-nu king died and, in the turmoil that accompanied the fight over the succession, he was able to escape. Accompanied only by his wife, his son and Ganfu, he managed to return to China.

The emperor honored Zhang Qian with the post of palace counselor and awarded Ganfu the title of "Lord Who Carries Out His Mission." ... When Zhang Qian first set out on his mission, he was accompanied by over one hundred men, but after thirteen years abroad, only he and Ganfu managed to make their way back to China. Zhang Qian in person visited the lands of Dayuan [Ta-Yuan, Ferghana],[9] the Great Yuezhi [Bactria, north of the Oxus], Daxia [Ta.Hsia, Bactria], and Kangju [Sogdiana], and in addition he gathered reports on five or six other large states in the neighborhood. All of this information he related to the emperor on his return.[10]

In BC 119, Zhang Qian accepted a second mission from the emperor to seek an alliance with the Wu-sun, who were probably the Issedonian Scythians identified by Herodotus, living between the Tien-Shan and Lake Balkhash in present-day Kazakhstan.[11]

Zhang Qian set off again to the west with 300 men, 10,000 sheep, a large number of horses and much gold and silk. The Wu-sun, however, also refused alliance with the Han emperor. Zhang Qian then split up his delegation and sent several exploratory missions to other kingdoms, one of which travelled as far as Persia and was received with pomp by the Parthian king between BC 115 and 105 BC. The exchange of gifts led to silk becoming known in the West and this second mission can be said to have laid the basis for the development of the silk trade between China and Persia.

Histories of the Han and Wei dynasties

The "Description of the Western Regions" in the *History of the Han Dynasty* (209–220 AD)[12], contains a section on the Ta Yuezhi (Kushans) who also left traces of their presence in the Pamirs, mainly in the Wakhan.

The Ta Yue-she are a wandering nation, moving from place to place for the convenience of their flocks and herds, the same as the Hsiung-nu. They have more than a hundred thousand men skilled in the use of the bow; and in former times considered themselves strong enough to treat the Hsiung-nu with contempt. ... [They] established their metropolis on the north of the Wei (Oxus) river, where the King held his Court. A small section, who were unable to leave, fortified themselves at the southern mountains [probably the Pamirs], and were named ... the Seaou Yue-she.

Yu Huan (fl. 239–265 AD), in his account of the Wei dynasty (*Weilue*),[13] collected travellers' tales and provided a record of contemporary Chinese knowledge of the lands to the West. The original text of the *Weilue* has been lost but a key chapter on the 'Peoples of the West' was quoted in a footnote to a work by Pei Songzhi (420–479 AD). Much of Yu Huan's information had reached China well before his time and dates mostly from the late second and early third centuries AD; some can also be found in the sections dealing with the 'Western Regions' of the *Shiji* ('Records of the Grand Historian'), the *Hanshu* ('Book of Former Han'), and the *Hou Hanshu* ('Book of Later Han'). Yu Huan describes the three routes to the West known to the Chinese, two of which passed through the Pamirs.

Buddhist Pilgrims

With the growth of Buddhism in China and neighbouring regions, a new type of traveller emerged: the Buddhist pilgrim. According to legend, Ming Ti, the second emperor (ruled 57/58–75/76 AD) of the Eastern Han dynasty, had a dream which led him to send his agents to bring him information about regions to the west. They returned with a picture of the Buddha and a copy of the Sutra that was translated in 67 AD, thus becoming the first Buddhist text in Chinese.

Several Chinese Buddhist pilgrims are known to have travelled subsequently to western lands. Shi-tao-an (d. 385 AD) wrote a work on his travels to India, which is lost, and, in 399 AD, Faxian travelled to the edge of the Pamirs and then over the Hindu Kush to India. His account of his travels, the *Fo-kwô-ki*,[14] is short and he has only the following reference to the Pamirs.

> In Ts'ung-ling there is snow both in winter and summer. Moreover there are poison-dragons, who when evil-purposed spit poison, winds, rain, snow, drifting sand, and gravel stones; not one of ten thousand meeting these calamities, escapes. The people of that land are also called Snowy-mountain men.

In 518 AD, Huisheng (Hwai Seng, Hwei-Sang) and Sung Yun (Sung Yen) were sent by the Queen of the Wei country across the Pamirs to India to collect books and relics. The account of their travels[15] is also short but echoes the experience of the earlier Chinese travellers of the high mountain regions they crossed on their way.

> During the first decade of the 8th month we entered the limits of the country of the Han-Pan-to [Tashkurgan], and going west six days, we ascended the Tsung-ling

mountains; advancing yet three days to the west, we arrived at the city of Kiueh-Yu [the home of a Turkic tribe, probably the Huns]; and after three days more, to the Puh-ho-i mountains [Mustagh range?]. This spot is extremely cold. The snow accumulates both by winter and summer. In the midst of the mountain is a lake in which dwells a mischievous dragon. ... From this spot westward, the road is one continuous ascent of the most precipitous character; for a thousand li[16] there are overhanging crags, 10,000 fathoms high, towering up to the very heavens. ... After entering the Tsung-ling mountains, step by step, we crept upwards for four days, and then reached the highest part of the range. From this point as a centre, looking downwards, it seems just as though one was poised in mid-air. The kingdom of Han-Pan-to stretches as far as the crest of these mountains. Men say that this is the middle point of heaven and earth. The people of this region use the water of the rivers for irrigating their lands; and when they were told that in the middle country [China] the fields were watered by the rain, they laughed and said "How could heaven provide enough for all?"

At another point on their journey, Sung Yun gives what is probably the first description of snow-blindness:

A mischievous dragon took up his residence here and caused many calamities. In the summer he rejoiced to dry up the rain, and in the winter to pile up the snow. Travellers by his influence are subjected to all sorts of inconveniences. The snow is so brilliant that it dazzles the sight; men have to cover their eyes, or they would be blinded by it; but if they pay some religious service to the dragon, they find less difficulty afterwards.

After a journey lasting three years, Huisheng and Sung Yun returned with 175 holy texts.

The first account of the other major affliction of travellers at high altitudes, altitude sickness, was given by Too Kin, a Chinese official, in 37–32 BC, and also related to travel in the Pamirs. Chinese travellers on the Silk road were warned that there were certain passes designated as "big headache" and "little headache" and, in 1900, manuscripts were found by a Taoist monk in a cave in Dunhuang, in Chinese Central Asia, that included military reports about altitude sickness among soldiers fighting in the Pamirs.[17]

Xuanzang

Xuanzang[18] (?602–664 AD) is probably the best known of the Buddhist travellers. After many years of study, he concluded that there were major defects in the Chinese translations of the sacred books and decided in 629 AD to go to India in search of uncorrupted Buddhist texts in Sanskrit. His journey took him sixteen years and covered some 15,000 km. On return to Xian in 645 AD, Xuanzang wrote the *Record of the Western Regions*, a detailed description of his travels.[19]

Travel outside China was forbidden at the time and Xuanzang had to leave clandestinely on his mission. Reports differ on whether he disguised himself and joined a group of Central Asian merchants heading West along the Silk Road or moved west in search of food with groups of emigrants at a time of famine in China.

On the way to Samarqand, he crossed the Tian Shan range into the territory of modern-day Kyrgyzstan, near Lake Issyk-kul, where he met by chance the Great Khan of the Western Türks who received him royally. From Samarqand he travelled to India where he stayed more than 10 years. On his way back, he took the southern route through the Pamirs to Kashgar and noted the existence of a great Dragon Lake.

We have seen that Sung Yun also noted that "in the midst of a mountain is a lake, in which dwells a mischievous dragon" and his and Xuanzang's mention of a 'Dragon Lake' — has given rise to much speculation: the lake has been variously identified as Kara Kul, Rangkul, Chakmaktynkul or Zorkul.[20] As I noted in connection with the identification of Ptolemy's 'Stone Tower', I am a firm believer that names do not change much over time and that folk memory – in the form of names passed down from generation to generation – should have at least equal standing with scholarly speculation. There is indeed a 'Dragon Lake' (in Kyrgyz 'Ajdarkel') in the valley of the Aksu just north of the village of Shaimak, close to the cliff known as Aktash. At normal times, Ajdarkel is much smaller than the lake described by Xuanzang; it is, however – like Rangkul and several other lakes in the Pamirs – 'intermittent' and in the early summer, after the first major snow-melt, it increases in size. In years – such as 2005 – when much snow has fallen in the winter and there is a sudden rise in temperature in early summer (the time when Xuanzang passed there), the lake would appear to fill the whole valley of the Aksu. I admit that Ajdarkel would be longer in a north-south direction than east-west, but consider that it merits consideration in the list as a possible identification of the dragon lake of the Chinese pilgrims.

The Emperor Gaozong authorised a translation of the new Sanskrit texts brought back by Xuanzang and constructed the Big Goose Pagoda to store them, still standing in Xian. In China, Xuanzang is better known than Marco Polo and his travels have provided inspiration for much popular literature, including *The Monkey King* ('Sun Wukong'), the story of the eponymous monkey who travels west to retrieve Buddhist sutras from India.

In his preface to Xuanzang's account of his travels, written some fifty years later, Chuang Yueh (a court official) places the mountains through which Xuanzang travelled in a land of fable:

> In the middle of Jambudvipa there is a lake called Anavatapta, to the south of the Fragrant Mountains and north of the Snowy Mountains; it is 800 li and more in circuit; its sides are composed of gold, silver, lapis-lazuli and crystal; golden sands lie at the bottom, and its waters are clear as a mirror. … From the eastern side of the lake, through the mouth of a silver ox, flows the Ganges river; encircling the lake once, it enters the south-eastern sea. From the south of the lake, through a golden elephant's mouth, proceeds the Sindhu [Indus] river; encircling the lake once, it flows into the south-western sea. From the western side of the lake, from the mouth of a horse of lapis lazuli, flows the river Vakshu [Oxus], and encircling the lake once, it falls into the north-western sea. From the north side of the lake, through the mouth of a crystal lion, proceeds the river Sita, and encircling the lake once, it falls into the north-eastern sea.

Xuanzang himself gives the following more prosaic descriptions of the places he visited in and adjacent to the Pamirs (the modern place names in square brackets are those suggested by Samuel Beal, the translator, as corresponding to the names given by Xuanzang):

Ling-shan

This is, in fact, the northern plateau of the T'sung-ling range, and from this point the waters mostly have an eastern flow. Both hills and valleys are filled with snowpiles, and it freezes both in spring and summer; if it should thaw for a time, the ice soon forms again. The roads are steep and dangerous, the cold wind is extremely biting, and frequently fierce dragons impede and molest travellers with their inflictions. Those who travel this road should not wear red garments nor carry loud-sounding calabashes. The least forgetfulness of these precautions entails certain misfortune. A violent wind suddenly rises with storms of flying sand and gravel; those who encounter them, sinking through exhaustion, are almost sure to die.

Kiu-Mi-To (Kumidha, or Darvaz and Roshan)

This country extends 2000 li from east to west, and about 200 li from north to south. It is in the midst of the great T'sung-ling mountains. The capital of the country is about 20 li in circuit. On the south-west it borders on the river Oxus; on the south it touches the country of Shi-ki-ni (Shughnan). Passing the Oxus on the south, we come to the kingdom of Ta-mo-sih-teh-ti (Termez).

Po-to-chang-na (Badakhshan)

This kingdom is an old territory of the Tu-ho-lo country[21]; it is about 2000 li in circuit, and the capital, which is placed on the side of a mountain precipice, is some 6 or 7 li in circuit. It is intersected with mountains and valleys, a vast expanse of sand and stone stretches over it; the soil is fit for the growth of beans and wheat; it produces an abundance of grapes, the khamil peach, and plums, etc. The climate is very cold. The men are naturally fierce and hasty.

Shi-ki-ni (Shughnan)

This country is about 2000 li in circuit, the chief city is 5 or 6 li. Mountains and valleys follow each other in a connected succession; sand and stones lie scattered over the waste lands. Much wheat and beans are grown, but little rice. The trees are thin, flowers and fruits not abundant. The climate is icy-cold. …Their writing is the same as that of the Türks but the spoken language is different.

Tang Dynasty

In 618 AD, the Tang dynasty came to power and expanded China's territory to the west, incorporating almost all of what was known in the 19th century as East Turkestan. In the last quarter of the seventh century, however, the Tang empire started to clash in the west with the Tibetans, whose influence in the region was rapidly expanding. By the beginning of the eighth century, Tibetan power extended over large parts of eastern Central Asia, including the Pamirs, Gilgit and Baltistan: Tibet controlled access from Kashgar through the Mintaka pass to Kashmir and the Indus valley and established alliances with the Turkic tribes in the Tarim area and the Arabs in Central Asia.[22]

The Tibetans' route to their Arab allies passed through Baltistan to Gilgit and Yasin, and from there to the Wakhan across the Darkot and Baroghil passes. Baltistan fell to the Tibetans in 722 AD and in the years that followed they subjugated many kingdoms and petty principalities in the Hindu Kush and Upper Oxus. In 747 AD, faced with this threat, the Chinese Emperor entrusted Kao Hsien-chih, a general of Korean extraction commanding the military forces in the Tarim basin, with the difficult mission of dislodging the Tibetans and cutting their communications to the Arabs.

The Annals of the Tang Dynasty describe the Chinese military expedition into the Pamirs in 747 AD that is one of the most remarkable on record. In 1923, Aurel Stein published an analytical account of the campaign[23] based on a translation of the *Annals* by Edouard Chavannes,[24] and his own observations in the exact area.

After three months, Kao Hsien-chih reached Shughnan in the Pamirs with a force of some 10,000 horsemen and foot soldiers, facilitating their passage by dividing them into several groups so as not to exhaust the limited food and forage resources of the terrain with such large numbers of men and horses. As noted above, there are several alternative practicable routes from Kashgar into the Pamirs: a) across the Kulma pass and along the lower Aksu and Alichur rivers; b) across the Nezatash pass to Zorkul in the Great Pamir or along the upper Aksu to the Little Pamir; c) across the Wakhjir pass into the upper Wakhan; all of which offer grazing, limited in some parts, but in others excellent, at the time the Chinese passed (probably June–July). By August they were ready to attack the Tibetans at their base in Lien-yun (probably present Sarhad-i Wakhan).

In the early morning of the 7th of August, Kao Hsien-chih's forces converged from east, north-west and north, fording the 'P'o-le' (Wakhan) to the southern bank. The Tibetans were taken by surprise and thrown back across the Darkot pass into the Hindu Kush, losing three-quarters of their force and most of their horses.

The crossing of the Pamirs (and the Wakhan in flood) by a force of this size was, as Stein remarks, a "remarkable military achievement", and it was not repeated until the Soviet invasion of Afghanistan in 1979 with all the advantages of modern technology and logistic support.

Although remarkable, this military success was nevertheless short-lived. A few years later, in 751, the Tang dynasty suffered a major blow at the battle of Talas, when the Arab Muslims and the Türks combined forces and defeated General Kao Hsien-chih. In the same year, the new Kitai confederacy defeated the Chinese in their northeast and a Chinese expedition to the southwest into Yunnan failed. Then, in 755, the Tibetans instigated an eight-year insurrection against Tang rule, during which they invaded the Chinese heartland and occupied an area giving them complete control over the route through the Gansu corridor and the Tarim to Central Asia, Kashmir, India and, through what is now Afghanistan, to Transoxiana and Iran.[25]

The eighth century was a period of exceptional change in Central Asia, with the collapse of the Iranian Sasanid empire, the weakness of the Byzantine empire and the expansionary ambitions of China, the Turkic tribes, the Arabs and the Tibetans clashing almost simultaneously close to or in the Pamirs. The Pamirs became, then as later, an area of refuge, the inaccessibility of which gave some protection from pursuit: at the beginning of the eighth century, for example, the Türk ruler of Tokharistan removed his court to Badakhshan because most of his territory and his capital, Balkh, had been occupied by the Arabs.

By 907, China had lost all its western territories and Islam spread throughout Central Asia and into China.[26]

*Ritual vessel. Brass.
Murghab district,
10th–11th century.*

From the Arab Conquests to the 19th Century

Arab and Persian Geographers

Shortly after the death of Mohamed, Arab forces began conquests against the Persian Sasanian rulers in the East. Around 636 AD[1], at the battle of al-Qadisiyyah, they inflicted a decisive defeat on the Persian army, and, a few years later, crossed the Oxus to move against Sughd (eastern Iran). By the early 8th century, under the generalship of Qutaiba ibn Muslim, the Arabs were in control of Termez, Bukhara, Khorezm (Khiva) and Samarqand; raids extended as far east as Kashgar[2], although the Arabs did not occupy the city. There is no evidence that Arab forces penetrated into the Pamirs, but those areas that were inhabited at the time – in particular Badakhshan with its sources of spinel, lapis lazuli and silver – came formally under Arab rule and Islam spread progressively through the region.

During the Abbasid caliphate (749–1258), geographical and historical scholarship flourished and information on Central Asia was recorded in the works of, among others, Al-Istakhri, Ibn Hawkal, Al-Ta'Alibi, Ibn Al Balkhi, Ibn Khordadbeh, Ibn Yakub (Jakub), Al-Utbi, Al-Muqaddasi, Ibn Dasta (sometimes Dast, Rust, Rustah, Rustih or Rusteh), Al-Biruni, Al-Masudi, Ibn Fadlan, Yakut Al-Hamawi, Nasir Khusraw and in the anonymous *Hudud-al-Alam*, ("The Regions of the World"). In the fourteenth century, the remarkable travels of Ibn Battuta (1307–1377) included a journey from Bukhara and Samarqand through Afghanistan to India.

These authors were certainly aware of Badakhshan and the mountainous area to the east of it. Unfortunately, as Sir Henry Yule remarked in the prefatory essay to John Wood's account of his journey to the source of the Oxus (see Chapter 5) "not much information on Badakhshan and the adjoining valleys is to be got from the old Arab geographers." Al-Hamawi mentions Badakhshan and Ibn Dasta describes two regions called 'Famir' (or '*Qamir*')[3] and 'Rast', next to which lay the country of the 'Khomed' through which flowed the river Wakhsh, by which name the Panj/Amu Darya was known in the middle ages (and sometimes later)[4]. Ibn Yakub mentions Chumar-beg, ruler of Shughnan and Badakhshan; Al-Istakhri refers to three kingdoms in the Pamir: Wakhan, Shughnan and Kenan (according to the Russian scholar V.V. Barthold, Kenan was Rushan and Darvaz[5]), and both he and Ibn Hawkal speak of the chief town of Badakhshan as belonging to Abu l'Fatteh. Sir Henry Yule concluded from this that the region was at that time (10th century AD) already subject to Islamic rule, although Al-Istakhri states that the population had not yet been converted to Islam.[6]

Most frequently, Badakhshan is mentioned in these works in relation to the famous ruby mines; in a 12th century treatise on precious stones, for example, Muhammed Ben Mansur wrote that a hill at Khatlon had been broken open by an earthquake and within a white rock in the fracture was found the 'Lale-Bedaschan' (balas ruby). The women of the district tried unsuccessfully to use them to make dye, and then threw them away; it was not until later that their value was recognised.[7]

Only Nasir Khusraw left a record of having actually been there.

Nasir Khusraw and the growth of Ismailism in the Pamirs

It is perhaps ironic that one of the greatest travellers of the eleventh century, who left for posterity a fascinating and detailed account of his travels elsewhere, should have spent at least seven years in Badakhshan and yet left no personal observations of the geography and people there. His importance in the cultural and religious traditions of the Pamirs, however, justifies his inclusion among the early explorers.

Nasir Khusraw (approx. 1004–1077) is recognised as one of the great poets of the Persian language and as an important Muslim philosopher. For the Ismaili community in Central Asia, he is also revered as a saint and as the founder of Ismailism in the Pamirs, the only region of the world where Ismailis are a majority of the population. Sarfaroz Niyozov, a modern Ismaili scholar from Tajik Badakhshan, comments:

> Nasir Khusraw is a significant Ismaili historical figure and, therefore, is of profound importance to the Ismaili Community universally, and especially the Ismailis of the Persian-speaking diaspora. These communities have their roots in countries such as Tajikistan, Afghanistan, China, Iran and Northern Pakistan and are now migrating out of these areas in increasing numbers. .... Nasir Khusraw also offers a window into understanding the contextual traditions and rituals of the Persian speaking Ismailis, especially their philosophy, culture, and mythology. In other words, he offers an explanation to a deeper understanding of why and how the people of these areas (e.g. Tajikistan, Afghanistan) have preserved their faith, lived and survived despite various invasions and attempts at conversion.[8]

His *Safarnama* describes his travels from 1045 to 1052 from his native Balkh (Khorasan)[9] to the Fatimid court in Cairo – where he confirmed his conversion to the

Ismaili interpretation of Islam – and back through Mecca to Khorasan where he became head of the Ismaili missionary activity (*da'wa*) in eastern Iran. His poetry – mostly in the *qasida* form[10] – is known as the *Diwan*, totalling more than 15,000 lines.[11]

To hamchu Zaidu Amr maro kur bud dil
Aibam nakard hej kase har kujo shudam,
Gohe zi dardi isq pasi khub chehragon
Gohe zi hirsi mol pasi kimiyo shudam
Ne bok doshrtam ke hame umr shud ba bod,
Ne sharm doshtam ke zamire khato shudam
Waqti khazon ba bori razon shud dilam kharob
Waqti bahor shod ba obu giyo shudam
. . . . .

Bar joni man chu nuri Imomi zamon fitod
Lail un- nahor budamu shams uz- zuho shudam
Nomi buzurgi Imomi zamon-st az in qibal
Man az zamin chu zuhra badu bar samo shudam[12]

As long as my heart was blind like that of Zayd and Amr,
no one could find fault in me, wherever I went.
Sometimes burning with passion I followed beautiful maidens;
sometimes out of greed I sought the philosopher's stone,
I did not fear that my life was being wasted, nor was I
ashamed that I had vulgar or evil thoughts.
In autumn my heart was dissipated with wine;
*   in the springtime I happily looked for water and pasture.*
When the light of the Imam shone upon my soul, even though
I was black as night, I became the shining sun.
The Supreme Name is with the Imam of the time; I was like dust of the Earth
Yet through him, Venus-like[13], *I ascended to the heavens.*

Transliteration and translation by Sarfaroz Niyozov

In about 1057, under threat of death for his Ismaili missionary activities, Nasir Khusraw was forced to leave Khorasan and seek exile in Badakhshan under the patronage of a friendly prince, Ali ibn Asad, where he spent the remainder of his life in the small village of Yumgan, near Jarm to the south of Faizabad. There he continued his missionary activities, but his verses are tinged with a note of regret for his exile in a primitive environment:

> *Har sol yake kitobi Da'wat,*
> *Ba atrofi jahon hame firistam*[14]
>
> *Bigzar ai bodi dilafruzi Khurosoni*
> *Ba yake monad ba Yumgondara zindoni*[15]
>
> *Mol najustaast ba Yumgon kase,*
> *Zonki nabudast khud in joi mol*[16]

Each year I send a book on my faith
Out to the corners of the world.

O warm breeze of Khorasan, share your breath
with one exiled in the valley of Yumgan.

None has ever sought wealth in Yumgan
because wealth is unknown in that place.

Transliteration and translation by Sarfaroz Niyozov

The Ismailis of the Pamirs hold that they were converted by Nasir Khusraw and that he is responsible for the spread of their faith in the region.

The fall of the Ummayyad dynasty in 750 AD opened a period favourable to religious pluralism and open theological debate that was beneficial to the spread of Ismailism in Central Asia. Missionaries (*da'i*) succeeded in disseminating the Ismaili interpretation of Islam at the Samanid court and in converting Amir Nasr II bin Ahmed Samani (914–943). This was also a period of active intellectual exploration and many of the most famous Islamic scholars and poets of the period such as Rudaki (859–941), Abu Ali ibn Sina (Avicenna – 980–1037), Al-Biruni (973–1048) and Firdovsi (940–1020), worked under the protection of or with the encouragement of the Samanids. Their affiliation with Ismailism is a subject of speculation but they were certainly influenced by Ismaili thinking.

After their defeat of the Samanids in 999, however, the Ghaznavids – and subsequently the Seljuks (1034–1300) – forcibly imposed forms of Sunni orthodoxy across Central Asia. As a result, many Ismailis fled from Khorasan, Transoxiana and as far away as Sind to remote areas such as Badakhshan.

The grave of Nasir Khusraw still exists in the valley of Yumgan. A Russian scholar, W. Ivanow comments: "There is nothing remarkable, as I was told by many Ismailis who have visited the spot, and the grave is very modest. Local inhabitants ... by no means encourage Ismaili pilgrimages to the grave. They believe their ancestor, Nasir, was a Sufic pir, and, being a Sunni, had no connection whatsoever with Ismailism."[17]

In Tajik Badakhshan, there are several shrines to Nasir Khusraw, of which the most important is in the village of Porshinev, some ten kilometres north of Khorog on the Panj.

Marco Polo (1272–1273)

Marco Polo's famous journey to China was, of course, not the first by Europeans through Central Asia. There is a record of the journey, a century earler, of Benjamin of Tudela, a Spanish Rabbi, from Spain, through Syria, Baghdad, Persia and to the frontiers of China. We have also seen (refer page 267) that at least two branches of the Silk Road crossed the Pamirs and Marco's father and uncle had been to Bukhara and the court of Kublai Khan only a few years earlier. The account of Marco's journey is, however, the first written record of the trade route through the Pamirs since Ptolemy described the route of Maës Titianus in the 2nd century AD.

Marco Polo did not himself write the account of his journey. On his return from China, he served in the Venetian fleet and was captured by the Genoese during a major naval engagement in 1298 and sent as a prisoner to Genoa. During his imprisonment there he made the acquaintance of Rustacians (Rusticiano or Rustichello) of Pisa, a fellow prisoner, who took notes from his conversations with Marco. These notes form the basis of all subsequent accounts of 'The Travels of Marco Polo'.

The best known version in English is *The Travels of Marco Polo*, translated by Sir Henry Yule from several sources (principally a French version by Prof. G. Pauthier) and accompanied by comprehensive scholarly annotations. It was published in several editions, of which the third, in 1903, was revised by Henri Cordier, Professor at the Ecole des Langues Orientales Vivantes in Paris; Cordier subsequently added further notes and addenda in a 1920 edition that is still in print (and available as an 'e-book' on http://www.gutenberg.org/dirs/1/2/4/1/ 12410).

Nicolò, Marco Polo's father, and his uncle Maffeo had, on their earlier journey, been welcomed at the court of Kublai Khan, Great Khan of the Mongols, and had

been questioned in detail by him about the Christian religion. When they left the court, Kublai Khan had asked them to return with one hundred Christian scholars who could debate with him and convert his people and to bring him some "oil of the lamp which burns on the Sepulchre of our Lord at Jerusalem". On their way back, Pope Clement IV died and, until his successor was appointed, the brothers were unable to obtain a response to Kublai Khan's request and returned to Venice. Marco Polo was then fifteen years old.

When, after two years, a new Pope had still not been elected, the brothers decided that they could no longer delay the fulfilment of Kublai Khan's request and left Venice in early 1271, taking Marco with them. En route, they learned that a new Pope, Gregory X, had finally been appointed and travelled to Acre to seek an audience with him and pass on the request from Kublai Khan. Instead of the hundred theologians the latter had requested, Gregory appointed only two to accompany them, both of whom very soon abandoned their mission for fear of their lives.

Their journey back to the court of Kublai Khan lasted a good three years, and took them through Baghdad, to Hormuz at the mouth of the Persian Gulf, where they seem to have intended to go on by sea. Some unforeseen circumstance forced them to change their plans, and it is thanks to this that their route then took them overland

Inside a yurt, Russo-German Expedition 1928

through Persia to Badakhshan, "whence they ascended the Panja or upper Oxus to the Plateau of Pamir, a route not known to have been since followed by any European traveller except Benedict Goes, till the spirited expedition of Lieutenant John Wood of the Indian Navy in 1838."[18] Travel history is subject to such turns of fortune and we may also speculate that if the brothers had been able to return immediately to Kublai Khan's court, and had not been held up for two years in Venice awaiting the appointment of a new Pope, they might well have considered that Marco was too young to travel with them.

Marco Polo's description of the Pamirs follows.

Of the Province of Badashan (Chapter XXIX)

Badashan is a Province inhabited by people who worship Mahommet, and have a peculiar language. It forms a very great kingdom, and the royalty is hereditary. All those of the royal blood are descended from King Alexander and the daughter of King Darius, who was Lord of the vast Empire of Persia. And all these kings call themselves in the Saracen tongue ZULCARNIAIN, which is as much as to say 'Alexander'; and this out of regard for Alexander the Great.

It is in this province that those fine and valuable gems the Balas Rubies are found. They are got in certain rocks among the mountains, and in the search for them the people dig great caves underground, just as is done by miners for silver. There is but one special mountain that produces them, and it is called SYGHINAN. The stones are dug on the king's account, and no one else dares dig in that mountain on pain of forfeiture of life as well as goods; nor may any one carry the stones out of the kingdom. But the king amasses them all, and sends them to other kings when he has tribute to render, or when he desires to offer a friendly present; and such only as he pleases he causes to be sold. Thus he acts in order to keep the Balas at a high value; for if he were to allow everybody to dig, they would extract so many that the world would be glutted with them, and they would cease to bear any value. Hence it is that he allows so few to be taken out, and is so strict in the matter.

There is also in the same country another mountain, in which azure [lapis lazuli] is found; 'tis the finest in the world, and is got in a vein like silver. There are also other mountains which contain a great amount of silver ore, so that the country is a very rich one; but it is also (it must be said) a very cold one. It produces numbers of excellent horses, remarkable for their speed. They are not shod at all, although constantly used in mountainous country, and on very bad roads. They go at a great pace even down steep descents, where other horses neither would nor could do the like. And Messer Marco was told that not long ago they possessed in that province a breed of horses from the strain of Alexander's horse Bucephalus, all of which had from their birth a particular mark on the forehead. This breed was entirely in the hands of an uncle of the king's; and in consequence of his refusing to let the king have any of them, the latter put him to death. The widow then, in despite, destroyed the whole breed, and it is now extinct.

The mountains of this country also supply Saker falcons of excellent flight, and plenty of Lanners [another species of falcon] likewise. Beasts and birds for the chase there are in great abundance. Good wheat is grown, and also barley without husk. They have no olive oil, but make oil from sesame, and also from walnuts.

In the mountains there are vast numbers of sheep – 400, 500, or 600 in a single flock, and all of them wild; and though many of them are taken, they never seem to get aught the scarcer.

Those mountains are so lofty that 'tis a hard day's work, from morning till evening, to get to the top of them. On getting up, you find an extensive plain, with great abundance of grass and trees, and copious springs of pure water running down through rocks and ravines. In those brooks are found trout and many other fish of dainty kinds; and the air in those regions is so pure, and residence there so healthful, that when the men who dwell below in the towns, and in the valleys and plains, find themselves attacked by any kind of fever or other ailment that may hap, they lose no time in going to the hills; and after abiding there two or three days, they quite recover their health through the excellence of that air. And Messer Marco said he had proved this by experience: for when in those parts he had been ill for about a year, but as soon as he was advised to visit that mountain, he did so and got well at once.

In this kingdom there are many strait and perilous passes, so difficult to force that the people have no fear of invasion. Their towns and villages also are on lofty hills, and in very strong positions. They are excellent archers, and much given to the chase; indeed, most of them are dependent for clothing on the skins of beasts, for stuffs are very dear among them. The great ladies, however, are arrayed in stuffs, and I will tell you the style of their dress! They all wear drawers made of cotton cloth, and into the making of these some will put 60, 80, or even 100 ells of stuff. This they do to make themselves look large in the hips, for the men of those parts think that to be a great beauty in a woman.

Of the Great River of Badashan (Chapter XXXII)

In leaving Badashan you ride twelve days between east and north-east, ascending a river that runs through land belonging to a brother of the Prince of Badashan, and containing a good many towns and villages and scattered habitations. The people are Mahommetans, and valiant in war. At the end of those twelve days you come to a province of no great size, extending indeed no more than three days' journey in any direction, and this is called VOKHAN. The people worship Mahommet, and they have a peculiar language. They are gallant soldiers, and they have a chief whom they call NONE, which is as much as to say 'Count', and they are liegemen to the Prince of Badashan.

There are numbers of wild beasts of all sorts in this region. And when you leave this little country, and ride three days north-east, always among mountains, you get to such a height that 'tis said to be the highest place in the world! And when you have got to this height you find a great lake between two mountains, and out of it a fine river running through a plain clothed with the finest pasture in the world; insomuch that a lean beast there will fatten to your heart's content in ten days. There are great numbers of all kinds of wild beasts; among others, wild sheep of great size, whose horns are good six palms in length. From these horns the shepherds make great bowls to eat from, and they use the horns also to enclose folds for their cattle at night. Messer Marco was told also that the wolves were numerous, and killed many of those wild sheep. Hence quantities of their horns and bones were found, and these were made into great heaps by the way-side, in order to guide travellers when snow was on the ground.

The plain is called PAMIER, and you ride across it for twelve days together, finding nothing but a desert without habitations or any green thing, so that travellers are obliged to carry with them whatever they have need of. The region is so lofty and cold that you do not even see any birds flying. And I must notice also that because of this great cold, fire does not burn so brightly, nor give out so much heat as usual, nor does it cook food so effectually.

Now, if we go on with our journey towards the east-north-east, we travel a good forty days, continually passing over mountains and hills, or through valleys, and crossing many rivers and tracts of wilderness. And in all this way you find neither habitation of man, nor any green thing, but must carry with you whatever you require. The country is called BOLOR[19]. The people dwell high up in the mountains, and are savage Idolaters, living only by the chase, and clothing themselves in the skins of beasts. They are in truth an evil race.

There is no agreement among scholars on the exact route that Marco Polo took across the Pamir Plateau, nor on the identity of the 'great lake between two mountains' – to some extent almost all of the Pamir is 'between two mountains', dependent on where the observer is standing and what distance can be attributed to 'between'![20] Given Polo's comments on the pasture near the lake, however, it can hardly have been Kara Kul, nor is it likely to have been Rang Kul – and he cannot have travelled through the Taghdumbash Pamir, for there is no big lake on this route. The lake Polo describes may have been either Zorkul ('Wood's lake') or Yashil Kul, or even Shiva in Afghan Badakhshan above the left bank of the Panj (Oxus), and his route may have been either almost identical to Wood's (i.e. along the Wakhan, up the Pamir river and across the Great Pamir); or the equally plausible – if less widely recognised – route up the Ghunt valley to the Alichur Pamir and from there to what is now Murghab town and the Kulma pass (his remarks about the 'good many towns and villages and scattered habitations' en route could apply equally well to both).

Sir Henry Yule notes, in relation to the possible routes over the high table land of the Pamir between Badakhshan and Kashgar, that

> … the only notices accessible are those of the Chinese pilgrims of the early centuries, the brief but pregnant sketches of Marco Polo, so singularly corroborated even to minutiae in our own day by Captain Wood, and [the] fragmentary memoranda of Benedict Goës. It seems impossible absolutely to determine the route followed by Marco, but from his mentioning a twelve days' march along the lofty plain it seems probably that he followed, as certainly the ancient Chinese pilgrims did, a course running north from the head of the Oxus valley over the plateau to the latitude of Tashbaliq before descending into Eastern Turkestan.

The plain close to Zorkul (Wood's lake) does contain 'a fine river' (the Pamir), but it would be difficult to describe it as 'running through a plain clothed with the finest pasture in the world, although evidence of climate change suggests that the weather in some regions of the Pamirs that are today arid may once have been more temperate.

Sir Aurel Stein was more dogmatic, however.

> The elevated Pamir region stretching westwards can never, during historical times, have permitted of cultivation. The routes which, starting from Tagharma, connect Sarikol with Kashgar to the north-east and Yarkand to the east, lead by a succession of high passes over barren spurs of the great meridional range with narrow uninhabited gorges between them. It is true that the difficult and rarely frequented

tracts which cross the mountains between the Tash-kurghan and Yarkand rivers in the direction of Karghalik and Kök-yar, pass through some of the minor Sarikoli settlements. But the produce raised on their isolated plots of cultivable land does not suffice even for the maintenance of the small pastoral population scattered over this region. Finally, if the route be followed which leads northward past Muztagh-Ata and then descends along the Yaman-yar river into the Kashgar plain, as described in my Personal Narrative, an even greater distance has to be traversed before permanent habitations are reached.[21]

Other writers find it strange that Polo does not mention the difficulty of the route and that he did not observe the sheer cliffs or 'hanging passages' noted by earlier travellers[22]: from this they conclude that Polo may never have actually crossed the Pamirs but wrote about the region from hearsay and only got as far as Persia.[23] They point out also that much of his vocabulary is Persian rather than Chinese, and that he omits any description of the Great Wall and other highly visible aspects of Chinese life such as foot-binding which was well established by the 13th century.

Silver mining in the Middle Ages

It may at first sight be surprising that the Pamirs were once a centre of silver production for an international market. For some six hundred years prior to the twelfth century AD, Mawara'an-nahr (or Transoxiana, the civilized region in the basin of the Amu Darya and Syr Darya) dominated the world-wide production of gold and silver. There were three main production complexes: the valley of Angren and the mountains of Karamazar in present-day Uzbekistan; the upper reaches of the Talas river in Kyrgyzstan; and Bazar-Dara, Toguzbulak and Shughnan in the Pamirs.

The Pamir mines yielded silver from argentiferous lead and production there peaked between 850–960 AD before collapsing with the exhaustion of the deposits in around 1100 AD.[24] That there should be traces of human habitation in an area that is today uninhabited (and probably uninhabitable) suggests that the climate may then have been milder than today or that the rewards from silver mining at a time of world shortage in the very early middle ages may have been such as to justify seasonal settlement in this unhospitable region of the Pamirs.

Jesuit Travellers – Benedict Goës (1602–1603)

By the late sixteenth century, Jesuit missionaries were well established in Goa and other parts of Western India. In 1578, Father Antony Capral travelled from Goa to the Mogul court in Lahore at the request of the Emperor Akbar, who wished to learn about the Christian faith. He succeeded so well in his mission that, in the period up to 1594, three further Jesuit missions were sent to Lahore, of which the third, headed by Father Jerome Xavier of Navarre, reached Lahore in May 1595. It included a young Portuguese lay member of the order, Bento de Goës (better known today as Benedict Goës). He was born at Villa Franca do Campo in the Azores in about 1561 and, at the age of twenty-six, serving as a soldier with the Portuguese fleet, he appears to have experienced a form of spiritual revelation and became a lay brother with the Jesuits.

There were also Jesuits in China, one of whom, Father Matteo Ricci, had for some time been suggesting that the Chinese empire was identical with the fabled land of Cathay – 'il Gran Cataio' of which Marco Polo had written, and where, according to legend, Christians lived under the rule of 'Prester John'[25]. When, at the Moghul court, Father Xavier heard corroborative accounts by Muslim travellers of a land known as Cathay, in which there were reported to be Christian religious practices, he was sure that these Christians were descendants of Prester John.

> One day as Xavier was at the palace and engaged with the king, there presented himself a Mahomedan merchant of some sixty years of age. After he had made his salutations to the king, in answer to the question whence he was come, he said that he was lately arrived from the kingdom of XETAIA. This Xavier supposed to be the same as the Cathay spoken of by Marco Polo the Venetian in his Travels, and by Hayton the Armenian in his History, and which later writers have determined to be in Tartary, or not far from it. ... King Akbar asking how he had got admission into the empire, he replied that it was under the character of an ambassador from the king of *Caygar* [Kashgar]. ... When asked about the aspect of the natives, he said that they were the whitest people he had ever seen, whiter even than the *Rumis*, or Europeans. Most of the men cherished a long beard ... The greater number were *Isauites*, ie Christians.[26]

Concerned that their religious practices might have strayed from the orthodox faith, Father Xavier recommended to his Superior in Goa that an exploratory mission to 'Cathay' be undertaken. In 1601, approval was given by the authorities in Rome and Benedict Goës, who spoke Persian and had proven his courage, skill and judgement while at Akbar's court, was chosen to lead the mission.

In 1602, he set off disguised as a merchant, accompanied by Isaac 'the Armenian'. In Kabul, he joined a trading caravan and reached Yarkand in early 1604. He did not get much further and died close to the Chinese frontier at Suzhou, in Shanxi province, in April 1607. A Jesuit sent from Peking to assist him brought back his notebooks and an oral account by his companion Isaac; the narrative of his journey was put together by Matteo Ricci and published by another Jesuit, Peter du Jarric, in 1615.

The lapidary account by Ricci of Goës's itinerary in the Pamirs begins not far from Taloqan, in Afghanistan, where the caravan was delayed by civil disturbances and attacked by rebel bandits.

But just then a certain leading chief, by name Olobet Ebadascan of the Buchara country, sent his brother to the rebels, and he by threats induced them to let the merchants go free. Throughout the whole journey, however, robbers were constantly making snatches at the tail of the caravan. And once it befell our friend Benedict that he had dropped behind the party and was attacked by four brigands who had been lying perdus. The way he got off from them was this: he snatched off his Persian cap and flung it at the thieves, and whilst they were making a football of it our brother had time to spur his horse and get a bowshot clear of them, and so safely joined the rest of the company.

After eight days of the worst possible road, they reached the Tenghi Badascian. *Tengi* signifies a difficult road; and it is indeed fearfully narrow, giving passage to only one at a time, and running at a great height above the bed of a river. The townspeople here, aided by a band of soldiers, made an attack upon the merchants, and our brother lost three horses. These, however, also he was enabled to ransom with some small presents. They halted here ten days, and then in one day's march reached Ciarciunar, where they were detained five days in the open country by rain, and suffered not only from the inclemency of the weather, but also from another onslaught of robbers.

From this in ten days they reached Serpanil; but this was a place utterly desolate and without a symptom of human occupation; and then they came to the ascent of the steep mountain called Sacrithma. None but the stoutest of the horses could face this mountain; the rest had to pass by a roundabout but easier road. Here two of our brother's mules went lame, and the weary servants wanted to let them go, but after all they were got to follow the others. And so, after a journey of twenty days, they reached the province of Sarcil, where they found a number of hamlets near together. They halted there two days to rest the horses, and then in two days more reached the foot of the mountain called Ciecialith. It was covered deep with snow, and during the ascent many were frozen to death, and our brother himself barely escaped, for they were altogether six days in the snow here. At last they reached Tanghetar, a place belonging to the Kingdom of Cascar.[27]

Sir Henry Yule suggests that Olobet Ebadascan is Ala Beg of Badakhshan, and speculates that Goës and his caravan went from Kabul to Kulob via Kunduz and then followed Marco Polo's route up the Panj valley from about present-day Shurabad to the Wakhan (the narrow passage between high cliffs in present-day Darvaz and Vanch would correspond to what Goës calls the *Tenghi Badascian* – the 'Straits of Badakhshan'), then entering the Taghdumbash Pamir not by Polo's supposed route across the Great Pamir but through the Little Pamir and Pamir-i-Wakhan across the Wakhjir pass to Sarikol (Sarcil) and Yangihissar (Tanghetar).

Some correspondence to Agra from Goës in Yarkand survives, from which we learn that the men and horses in his caravan had difficulty breathing at high altitude in the Pamirs and that garlic, leeks and dried apples were used as a remedy for the men, while garlic was rubbed on the horses' gums. Regrettably, since Goës was the first European traveller to cross the Pamir since Marco Polo, that is all we have.

Yule, writing at the end of the 19th century, points out that the "chief obscurities attending the route of Goës, concern that section of his journey which lies between Kabul and Yarkand," and in particular "the ascent through Badakhshan to the Plateau of Pamir, and the descent to Yarkand."

> Altogether it is a miserably meagre record of a story so interesting and important; and had Benedict's diary, which he is stated to have kept in great detail, been spared, it would probably have been to this day by far the most valuable geographical record in any European language on the subject of the countries through which he travelled, still so imperfectly known.[28]

Other Jesuits travelled subsequently from India to Tibet: Antonio De Andrade and Manuel Marques set up the Tsaparang Mission in Tibet in 1624; Stephen Cacella and John Cabral Francisco De Azevedo were at the Tsaparang Mission a few years later; John Grueber and Albert d'Orville were the first Europeans to reach Lhasa in 1661; and Ippolito Desideri travelled to Tibet via Delhi, Kashmir, and Ladakh in 1712–1727.[29] Only Goës, however, was in the Pamirs. It is not until the 19th century that Europeans provide more substantiated accounts of their travels in the Pamirs.

The Great Game – Myth or Reality?

"Listen in the north, my boys, there's trouble on the wind;
Tramp o' Cossack hooves in front, gray great-coats behind,
Trouble on the Frontier of a most amazin' kind,
Trouble on the waters o' the Oxus!"
Rudyard Kipling, *Soldiers Three*

"More people debated the Great Game than ever played it."
John Keay, *When Men and Mountains Meet*, p. 140

The expression 'Great Game', describing the rivalry between the British and Russian Empires for influence, control and expansion of territory in Central Asia in the nineteenth century was coined by Lieutenant Arthur Conolly (1807–1842), a British Political Officer[1] of the 6th Bengal Native Light Cavalry, who initiated British reconnaissance and map making in the region and was executed along with fellow British officer Charles Stoddart by the Emir of Bukhara in 1842. In 1837, he wrote two letters to his fellow 'Political', Henry Rawlinson (one of the most distinguished 'players' in the Great Game as soldier, archaeologist, explorer and historian – at that time a Lieutenant, but later a Major-General, knight and President of the RGS), in which he wrote: "You've a great game, a noble one, before you"[2]; and, in another letter: "If only the British Government would play the grand game."

In 1837, Count Nesselrode, Russian Foreign Minister from 1822 to 1856, had created another highly appropriate term for this conflict, 'Tournament of Shadows', but it was the 'Great Game' that caught the popular imagination. The works of Rudyard Kipling, in particular *Kim*, published in 1901, revived enthusiasm for this period of empire and, almost a century later, the term took on a new life through the stirring tales recounted by, among others, John Keay in *The Gilgit Game*, published in 1979, Peter Hopkirk in *The Great Game: On Secret Service in High Asia* (1990), and Karl E. Meyer and Shareen Blair Brysac in *Tournament of Shadows: The Great Game and the Race for Empire in Asia* (1999).

If the object of the contest was hardly different from what was taking place simultaneously in the 'scramble for Africa' and elsewhere around the globe, attention was drawn to Central Asia by concerns in press and Parliament in Britain about threats to India, the jewel in the Crown of the British Empire, and by the publication of the adventures of many of the colourful characters involved. Central Asia was also associated with the Silk Road and with names and places redolent of romance and mystery. In one of his more poetic moments, on the Dorah Pass in the north-west of Chitral looking across the entrance to the Wakhan, Colonel Algernon Durand, British Agent in Gilgit from 1889–1894, described well the fascination that still attaches to Central Asia:

> We stayed a short time at the top, looking out over the Badakhshan mountains towards that mysterious Central Asia which attracts by the glamour of its past history, by the veil which shrouds its future. Balkh, Bokhara, Samarkhand, what visions come trooping as their names arise. The armies of Alexander, the hordes of Gengis Khan and Timur go glittering by; dynasties and civilisations rise and fall like the waves of the sea; peace and prosperity again and again go down under the iron hoof of the conqueror; for centuries past death and decay have ruled in the silent heart of Asia.[3]

The main theatre of Anglo-Russian rivalry was in and close to the Pamirs: the present-day frontiers in the region were determined as a result of the agreements reached by Russia and Britain during this crucial period in their relations.

Colonial policy

The extension by Russia and Britain of their zones of influence in Central Asia was bound to bring the two Empires into a conflict over their respective interests. For the British, the primary concern was to find a sound "scientific" defensive frontier for India, although the commercial consideration of finding markets to the north for the produce of India was also thrown into the equation. For the reformist Tsar Alexander II, after the Russian defeat in the Crimea War in 1854–56, the objective was to find new opportunities for territorial (and commercial) expansion in the only direction remaining, east.

> As at other times, failure of Russia on the side of Europe was followed by a great advance on the line of least resistance in Asia, with enormous accessions of territory. When this advance had been left to the Cossacks and peasants, the line which it followed had passed due eastward, north of the centres of Asiatic population, to the Pacific. …. But in this reign takes place a purely military advance in another quarter, central Asia, in character quite unlike the penetration of Siberia, except in

so far as the independent initiative of Russian generals might distantly recall the unfettered enterprise of the Cossacks. The way was cleared in 1859 by the surrender after a gallant resistance of the priest-prince Shamil, which brought to a close the long struggle against the gallant mountaineers of the Caucasus.[4]

Within ten years, Russia was well on the way to constituting a major empire in the east. Although the Russian move in this direction was certainly anticipated by British statesmen[5], it was nevertheless viewed with consternation by a significant section of the press and public and – more particularly – those in the field in India. The next forty years were marked by the manoeuvring, manipulation, duplicity, courage, posturing, self-delusion, chivalry, brutality and sometimes plain recklessness that now go under the name of 'Great Game'.

Rules of the Game

For most of the 19th century, the definition of the role and frontiers of Afghanistan as a territory lying between the two Empires was of central importance in Anglo-Russian relations. Since the Treaty of Paris in 1763, Britain was the undisputed major power in India and, already in 1809, recognising the strategic position of Afghanistan, concluded a treaty with the Afghan Amir, Shah Shuja'.

British policy towards Afghanistan suffered from lack of consistency. While on the Russian side, General Kaufmann was Governor-General of Turkestan from 1867 until his death in 1882, there were, during this period, no fewer than five Viceroys of India; similarly, while the Tsar exercised autocratic rule in Russia, the same period saw three changes of government in Britain. If Russophobia was generally a constant in Britain during this period, there were conflicting opinions about whether imperial interests would be best protected against supposed Russian ambitions by an Afghanistan that was: a) an independent and centralised state with institutions that could withstand encroachment (or blandishments)

General Kaufmann

from Russia; b) a weak client state, totally dependent on external military support and subsidy; c) a buffer whose territorial integrity was best protected by agreement between (and in the mutually acknowledged interests of) the two main protagonists; or d) totally dismembered and permanently weakened.

Inextricably linked to the imperial rivalry was the perception that most of Central Asia – and especially the Pamirs – was a 'blank spot' on the map: hence, as we shall see in later chapters, the central role of the explorer as a forerunner and agent of conquest and empire. This, combined with the declining ability of China to police its western frontiers and make good its territorial claims in Central Asia, gave urgency to laying down the markers of empire.

The Game was indeed one of high stakes: the players came into close territorial contact and friction was inevitable. The accounts of the main protagonists – and some histories of the period – suggest that this was a fraught and tense period in relations between the two Empires, during which, despite external courteous and 'gentlemanly' behaviour, ruthless intrigue was threatening peace and stability and that war was only narrowly avoided – the blame for which was generally attributed to the other side of the border from that on which the observer was standing.

A dispassionate look at the official record of diplomatic intercourse between the two Powers, however, shows that, during the whole period, each behaved according to fairly clear and consistent rules. Formal and informal contacts were intense and business-like and each was truly concerned to minimise flashpoints. As a consequence, there was never any real danger that their respective inroads in Central Asia would lead to armed conflict between them. The drama lay more in the contest between the 'peace' and 'war' factions within each country than in relations between the central governments themselves. In the British case, the determination of policy was complicated by differences of perception and judgement – sometimes extreme – between the government in London and the administration in Calcutta/Simla.

Certainly, if anyone was having fun during this time, it was the adventurers on the ill-defined frontiers who enjoyed the free run given to them by their chiefs in the military and intelligence services to hunt and play 'hide-and-seek' in the wide open spaces of Central Asia. As Hopkirk notes there was, however, a difference of approach between the two sides: "… in the coming years, 'scientific expeditions' were frequently to serve as covers for Russian Great Game activities, while the British preferred to send their officers, similarly engaged, on 'shooting leave', thus enabling them to be disowned if necessary."[6] Of course, the explorers on both sides made significant contributions to geographical knowledge, but both Russians and British saw success in Central Asia as a basis for building reputations and careers; in the case of the Russians – in the early years of Central Asian conquest, at least – by sometimes exceeding their orders; in the case of the British, self-promotion was achieved through the somewhat unseemly rush to publish personal accounts of adventure and survival in exotic places.[7]

The Pamir expeditions of the Russians almost always incorporated a serious scientific component and, whatever their other aims, brought back major contributions to cartography, botany, zoology, glaciology, ethnology and linguistics. Other travellers noted this also in their encounters with the Russians: Wilhelm Filchner, a Lieutenant in the Royal Bavarian Infantry, for example, noted on his way to the Pamirs in 1900[8] that the Russians had a highly professional cartographic department in Tashkent and a well-equipped astronomical observatory in Marghilan, where he was surprised to see that the main telescope had been made in Hamburg. Filchner further remarked that the Russian road from Osh was well-provided with regular distance (verst) markers and that the Pamirsky Post (the Russian military base at present-day Murghab) at the end of the road already had a meteorological station where readings were taken three times a day, even though the base had only been in existence since 1893 and the fort was not built there until 1895[9]. Moreover, when Filchner arrived at Pamirsky Post, a Polish professor, B. Stankewitsch, had just been assigned there to make scientific measurements.

The Great Game was a story of personalities, of whom the most visible were the men on the spot. Seen against the wider canvas of British-Russian relations in the latter part of the 19th century, however, their influence on events was marginal: their actions were the pin-pricks on the edge of empire, frequently provoking temporary flare-ups of tension but rarely achieving any fundamental change of direction. Several of the players were considered by their political superiors as loose cannons and were frequently the object of their wrath – and sometimes even disavowed publicly, as was the darling of the British public, Younghusband, for his appalling massacre of Tibetans in 1904. Their flamboyance and the daring of their adventures has tended to obscure the actions (often out of the public gaze) of their political and military masters at the centre of power, whose decisions determined the outcome of the Game.

Anglo-Russian flashpoints

Russian expansion in Central Asia was viewed from the outset with much suspicion by the British. In 1865, Rawlinson, always an advocate of a hard line towards Russia, nevertheless admitted:

> It is certain that the absorption of Georgia, the acquisition of the frontier provinces of Turkey and Persia, and the gradual subjugation of the Kirghiz Steppe, although cited by McNeill in his famous pamphlet 'On the progress of Russia in the East', as proofs of her insatiate thirst of conquest, were amply paralleled by our own annexations in India during the same period ... and excepting, therefore, that a certain mutual distrust was created between the two European powers, no great evil arose from their respective territorial extension.[10]

Later, in 1871, Rawlinson also conceded that

> although the question of the Russian approach to India was of great interest, it was one which we might look steadily in the face without any sense of danger... the nearer England and Russia approached each other in Central Asia, the more advantageous it would be in some respects for both nations, inasmuch as it would remove impediments to free communication, promote trade and put an end to the anarchy and disorder which were at present rampant ...[11]

At the time, not all in Britain saw it this way, however, and there were a number of major flashpoints in Anglo-Russian relations.

1837–41 – Persia and the first Afghan War

Anglo-Russian rivalry in Central Asia goes back at least as far as the Treaty of Turkomanchai in 1828, by which Russia obtained important concessions from Persia and significant influence at the Shah's court. The British feared that, from Persia, the Russians would attempt to extend their influence to Afghanistan and would thus obtain 'the key to India'.

At the time Afghanistan was, however, unstable and far from being a unitary state. Under the leadership of the first Pashtun ruler, Ahmad Shah (1722–1772), founder of the Durrani dynasty, Afghanistan began to take shape as a nation after centuries of foreign invasion and internal fragmentation. His death, however, was followed by a long period of unrest and Afghanistan disintegrated into a group of small units, each ruled by a different Durrani leader.

In 1826, Dost Mohammed took the throne in Kabul and began to consolidate his power. In 1834 he defeated an invasion by a former ruler, Shah Shuja, but, during the unrest, Ranjit Singh, the Sikh ruler, occupied Peshawar. In 1836 Dost Mohammed's forces defeated the Sikhs, but did not follow up by retaking Peshawar, and approached Lord Auckland, the new British governor general in India, seeking an alliance for dealing with the Sikhs. Auckland was unwilling to assist in the return of Peshawar to Afghan control but instead sent a mission led by Alexander Burnes, to Kabul: nominally to negotiate a commercial treaty but in reality to attempt by threats to persuade the Amir to have nothing to do with the Russians. The mission included John Wood, who left Kabul in November 1837 to make a brief detour to look for the source of the Oxus and discovered lake Zorkul in the Great Pamir (see page 337).

In 1837, Persia laid siege to Herat, over which Dost Mohammed's authority was at best fragile, if not non-existent. The British, with firm evidence of Russian complicity (in the machinations of the new Russian envoy to the Persian court, Count Ivan Simonich), protested vigorously to St. Petersburg, the first in a series of diplomatic exchanges between the two powers in relation to Central Asia. The Russians claimed, however, to have had no part in the Persian decision to attack Herat and to have advised the Shah against it. British pressure was so strong, however, that Simonich was recalled from Persia and his successor was instructed to limit his relations with Afghanistan to purely commercial matters. Russia also undertook not to interfere in Afghan affairs.

Dost Mohammed, understandably, considered that the British were demanding much and offering little. Thus began a period of deep distrust in Anglo-Afghan relations that resulted in the first Afghan war, much incompetent British meddling in Afghan affairs, a number of minor military operations, the deposition and subsequent reinstatement of Dost Mohammed and a further war (1878–1880), the consequences of which weakened rather than strengthened British influence in Afghanistan.

Alexander Burnes was recalled, his mission unaccomplished, and when Dost Mohammed agreed in April 1838 to receive a Russian envoy, Ivan Vitkevich, claiming to bear a message of goodwill from the Tsar, it was too much for Auckland.[12] In October, he issued the so-called 'Simla manifesto' in which he declared that

> The disloyalty of the present Emir of Afghanistan in treating with the Russians and failing to respect British interests makes it necessary to remove Dost Mohammed and restore Shah Shuja to the throne.

Hard on the heels of the manifesto, a British expeditionary force was dispatched and Kabul was taken. Dost Mohammed was deposed and replaced by the unpopular Shah Shuja. In 1841, an uprising forced the British out of Kabul and on its retreat the British force was almost annihilated at the Khurd Kabul pass. Shah Shuja was murdered in 1842, his son, Fateh Jung, fled Afghanistan and Dost Mohammed returned as ruler. British policy was in tatters.

Gerald Morgan, in one of the major recent studies of Anglo-Russian rivalry,[13] comments:

> The First Afghan War, besides being a military disaster, had settled nothing; indeed it delayed for many years to come any settlement of India's north-west frontier and in the long run added greatly to Anglo-Russian rivalry.

The judgement of Meyer and Brysac is even harsher:

> Only a willing suspension of disbelief can explain what came to be called the First Afghan War. As originally envisioned, the operation was based on four assumptions: that Ranjit Singh's Sikhs would do most of the fighting[14]; that Afghan Herat was about to fall to Persia; that Dost Mohammed was little more than a Russian vassal; and finally, that Afghans would tolerate, indeed even welcome, a British puppet in his place. Before a single soldier crossed the frontier, it was apparent that these assumptions were all mistaken or misguided.[15]

1859–1873 – Russian territorial expansion

As noted, Tsar Alexander II had approved early in his reign a strategy of military expansion in Central Asia. His advisers convinced him that as the British were sufficiently preoccupied elsewhere they would not seriously threaten force against Russian imperial ambitions. In addition,

> what finally persuaded the Tsar was something which had happened in America, whose Southern States had long been Russia's principal source of raw cotton. As a result of the civil war there, supplies of this vital commodity had been cut off, badly affecting the whole of Europe.[16]

The climate of Central Asia was ideal for cotton production. As is by now well known, this attraction was subsequently to prove disastrous: for the ecology of the region, by the diversion of water resources, and for the economy, by dependence on a monoculture. The problems of water allocation and management inherited by today's Central Asian Republics from Russian and Soviet obsession with cotton production are likely to be a serious future cause of friction between them.

In 1864 Prince Gorchakov, the Foreign Minister, had stated that Russian aims were not to extend Russian dominion beyond reasonable limits, but "to establish it on a firm basis, ensure its security and develop its commerce and civilisation"[17] – aims that should have struck a chord with British colonial administrators. He announced that Russian objectives were to: a) establish two fortified frontier lines, one from China to lake Issyk-Kul, the other from the Aral sea along the Syr Daria, with a series of forts offering each other mutual assistance against marauding tribes; b) situate these forts in fertile country; and c) base the frontier on "geographical, political and natural conditions" – while at the same time seeking the stability of a sedentary population. Gorchakov pointed out that "the United States in America, France in Algiers, Holland in her colonies – all have been drawn into a course where ambition plays a smaller role than imperious necessity" but was honest enough to conclude that "the greatest difficulty is knowing where to stop."

In 1865, the Russians took Tashkent and, in 1867, General Konstantin Kaufmann was instated there as Governor-General of a new province of Turkestan. By 1868, Bukhara, Khodjent and Samarqand were in the hands of the Russians. Kuldja (Yining), in Chinese territory, was occupied in 1871 (it was vacated in 1881, but the Russians obtained the right to establish a consulate there); Khiva fell to the Russians in May 1873 and Kokand was annexed in February 1876. Prince Gorchakov justified these annexations on the ground that constant raids by lawless tribes made advance unavoidable until order had been restored and the threat removed. The British ought not to have been surprised for, as Bernard Pares notes wryly in his *A History of Russia*, "the same plea has been made for the advance of other empires."[18] Another strong reason for Russian aggression was the large number of Russian slaves held in the Central Asian khanates.

For some vociferous – and sometimes influential – British circles, however, Russian expansion in Central Asia created an intolerable threat to India. The primary thrust of any Russian invasion was anticipated from the west through Afghanistan; later, a secondary threat was feared from the Pamirs. Progressive Russian territorial advance towards Afghanistan, coupled with uncertainty about the loyalty of successive Afghan Amirs, created an atmosphere close to paranoia in Indian political circles and the British press (the latter frequently drummed up by the former). In the late 1870s and early 1880s the 'Russian threat' was taken seriously as far away as South Africa and New Zealand, where coastal batteries were set up in Cape Town and Fort Kelburn in Wellington, respectively. How real was the threat?

Gerald Morgan concludes that

> There is no real evidence, except for Tsar Paul's aberration, of any serious plans to invade India – which is not to say that no plans were ever considered.[19]

Moreover, few political leaders in Britain (and certainly not all in India) really believed that Russia would be foolish enough to attempt an invasion of India, or that, if she did, she stood any chance of success. This judgement was based, in addition to political assessments, at least in part on the major logistical problems of such an invasion.

In 1836, the British Ambassador in St. Petersburg, Lord Durham, had written in a dispatch to Palmerston that the power of Russia had been greatly exaggerated: "There is not one element of strength which is not directly counterbalanced by a corresponding weakness." In 1840, Captain H. Garbett, stationed at Bamian during the Afghan war, had reconnoitred the passes of the Central Hindu Kush, mapped all the possible routes and concluded that any advance on India by the Russians in this region could only be accomplished by 'light' troops and that a large Russian army could not advance from Turkestan across the Hindu Kush into British India.[20]

In a famous 'Minute' written in 1867, the Viceroy, Sir John Lawrence, commented on the possibility that the Russians might occupy Afghanistan:

> I do not pretend to know what is the policy of Russia in Central Asia; what may be her views hereafter in India. But it seems to me that common sense suggests that her primary interest is to consolidate her hold on those vast regions now in her possession, in which there must be 'room and scope enough' for the exercise of all her energies and all her resources. Russia has indeed a task before her in which she may fail, and which must occupy her for generations. To attempt to advance before her power is firmly established, is to imperil all she has hitherto accomplished. ....
> I am not myself at all certain that Russia might not prove a safer ally – a better neighbour than the Mahomedan races of Central Asia and Cabul. She would introduce civilization; she would abate the fanaticism and ferocity of Mahomedanism, which still exercises so powerful an influence on India … But, supposing that Russia has the desire, and possesses the means of making a formidable attack on India … in that case let them undergo the long and tiresome

marches which lie between the Oxus and the Indus; let them wend their way through difficult and poor countries, among a fanatic and courageous population, where, in many places, every mile can be converted into a defensible position; then they will come to the conflict on which the fate of India will depend, toil-worn, with an exhausted infantry, a broken-down cavalry, and a defective artillery.[21]

In 1873, even the War Office conceded that "the Russians in any invasion of our dominions whether from the side of Chinese territory or Afghanistan, would have most formidable obstacles to encounter", pointing out that the distance from Samarqand to India via Bamian was about 900 miles, the number of men to be transported would certainly not be less than 30,000 and when and if they ever reached India, they would find a highly disciplined force under a British leader with good railway communications and fertile country in the rear.[22]

In November 1878, Prime Minister Disraeli declared that "it is not possible for any remote foe to threaten our Indian Empire from the side of the North-West Frontier, because the communications are so difficult and the geographical conditions adverse." Lord Salisbury, Prime Minister and Foreign Secretary, whatever his public posture, once advised an anxious contemporary to use large-scale maps: "A great deal of misapprehension arises from the popular use of maps on a small scale. If the noble lord would use a larger map, he would find that the distance between Russia and British India was not to be measured by the finger and thumb, but by a rule."[23]

George Nathaniel Curzon (who became subsequently Viceroy of India), argued in 1889:

> The overwhelming strategic importance of Merv in relation to India is a dictum which I have never been able to understand. I have seen it argued with irreproachable logic, in magazine articles, that Merv is the key to Herat, Herat the key to Kandahar, and Kandahar the key to India. But the most scientific demonstrations of *a priori* reasoning must after all yield place to experience and to fact. Russia holds Merv; and she could tomorrow, if she chose to bring about a war with England, seize Herat; not, however, because she holds Merv, but because she holds the far more advanced and important positions of Sarakhs and Penjdeh. But even if she held Herat she would not be much nearer the conquest of India. A great deal of nonsense has been talked in England about these so-called keys to India and Lord Beaconsfield [Disraeli] never said a truer thing, though at the time it was laughed at as a sounding platitude, than when he declared that the keys of India are to be found in London, and consist in the spirit and determination of the British people...

Curzon's conclusion was that not "a single man in Russia, with the exception of a few speculative theorists and here or there a giddy subaltern, ever dreams seriously of the conquest of India. To anyone, Russian or English, who has even superficially studied the question, the project is too preposterous to be entertained."[24]

As for the much feared 'Pamir gap', in any strategic sense it was largely a misnomer. If, as we shall see when we get to the 'Pamir incident' of 1891, the status of the territory in question was unclear, it was certainly not, in any logistical sense, a gap through which the Russians could come pouring into Chitral, Hunza or Kashmir. Colonel William Lockhart, who led the British military survey in Hunza and Chitral in 1885, argued on his return that

> earlier fears attached to the region, especially to the Baroghil Pass, were exaggerated, although a secondary Russian thrust might be directed across the Pamirs in support of a full-scale invasion via the Khyber and Bolan. But because the Pamir passes were closed every winter by snow, while in summer the numerous rivers became raging torrents, only during the short spring and autumn would the region be vulnerable.[25]

After his travels in the region a few months later, the British explorer Ney Elias concurred. Curzon considered that it might be used by the Russians as "a diversion, which might be troublesome but could not be really serious."[26] Even Colonel Algernon Durand, who, as British Agent in Gilgit from 1889–1894 was closer to the front line than any, considered that "no man in his senses ever believed that a Russian army would cross the Pamirs and attack India by the passes of Hunza and Chitral."[27] Lieutenant-General Sir Richard Strachey, a member of the Council of India during the critical period 1875–1889, and who spent most of his distinguished career in India, used even stronger language:

> It is a wonderful thing that rational people should talk about a region of this sort as something to be coveted and something even possibly to be fought over, and one might really almost as rationally talk of fighting for the possession of, shall I say, a square mile of the moon, or of Sirius. ... The possibility of anything like military operations being carried on over a country of that sort is so perfectly ridiculous that to my mind it is perfectly astounding that it should appear to be seriously discussed. The way in which the question of the occupation of this region, either by Russia, Afghanistan, China, or Britain, occupies some people's minds, I can only regard as an illustration of the folly of humanity.[28]

In 1887, the French adventurers Bonvalot, Capus and Pépin made the first north-south crossing of the Pamirs to India by Europeans; on arrival in Chitral they were arrested as suspected Russian spies and sent to Simla where, on discovery of their identity, they were debriefed by the British authorities. Their account of the extreme difficulty they had experienced on their three-month trek from Osh ought to have persuaded the British that the Russian presence in Kokand was neither close nor threatening.

Ralph Cobbold, the second Englishman to reach the Western Pamirs in 1898, agreed.

> Without wishing to pose as a strategist, I should say from some personal acquaintance with this part of the frontier that it would be an impossibility for any body of troops to force a passage to India by either of these [Chitral and Hunza-Nagar], and …. from information recently acquired during a journey on the Upper Oxus, it is evident that the Russians recognise the two routes I have commented on as presenting far greater difficulties of access to India than other roads through the Hindu Kush, respecting which the Russians are thoroughly well informed.[29]

1873 – the first Pamirs Border Agreement

During the period up to 1873, there were active negotiations between the British and Russians with a view to reducing tension in the region. In 1869, Britain suggested that both countries recognise some territory as neutral between their possessions. Agreement could not be reached at that time, supposedly because some of the territory in question was claimed by the Emir of Bukhara, although more likely because Russia saw further opportunities for territorial expansion. Russia agreed, however, to recognise as belonging to Afghanistan all the territory that the Afghan Amir then held and to exercise her influence to restrain Bukhara from aggression on Afghan territory.

In 1873, as a result of these negotiations, an exchange of letters took place between the Russian and British Foreign Ministers, Prince Gorchakov and Lord Granville, in which Russia reaffirmed that Afghanistan was beyond her sphere of influence and within that of Britain, while claiming similar freedom of action for Russia in Central Asia. Lord Granville stated that the British considered the following territories as belonging to the Amir of Kabul, but, by an unfortunate error, omitted the passage in square brackets in the communication to the Russians – a source of later confusion:

1. Badakhshan with its dependent District of Wakhan from the Sarikul (Wood's Lake) on the east to the junction of the Kokcha river with the Oxus [on the west, the line of the Oxus] or Penjah forming the northern boundary of this Afghan province throughout its entire extent.

2. Afghan Turkestan, comprising the districts of Kunduz, Khulm, and Balkh, the northern boundary of which would be the line of the Oxus from the junction of the Kokcha river to the post of the Khojah Saleh, inclusive, on the highroad from Bokhara to Balkh. Nothing to be claimed by the Afghan Ameer on the left bank of the Oxus below Khojah Saleh.

3. The internal districts of Aksha, Seripool, Maimanat, Shibberjan, and Andkoi, the latter of which would be the extreme Afghan frontier possession to the North-West, the desert beyond belonging to independent tribes of Turkomans.

4. The western Afghan frontier between dependencies of Herat and those of the Persian province of Khorassan is well known and need not be defined.

There was a degree of legal uncertainty (not to say wishful thinking) in the Amir's claim to some areas south of the Oxus: a contemporary British report stated that "it was only by the middle of 1870 that a semblance of Afghan sovereignty was extended to Andkoi, Siberghan, Siripul, Tashkurghan, Badakhshan and Kanduz when representatives of Siripul, Tashkurgan and other states attended a great entertainment" given by the Kabul government.[30]

It will be noted, in the light of subsequent events and accusations of Russian treachery, that the 1873 agreement makes no mention of any supposed Afghan claims to Merv (or Panjdeh), and that, at this time, the Russians limited themselves to expressing doubts about the Amir's claim to Badakhshan, suggesting that the "facts themselves seem to point rather to the real independence of Badakhshan than to its absolute subjection to the Ameer of Cabul," and proposed instead to "allow the present state of things to continue: Badakhshan and Wakhan would thus form a barrier between the Northern and Southern States of Central Asia ... strengthened by the combined actions [of] England and Russia."[31] This was what the British had suggested a few years earlier, but was now unacceptable to them.

The Russian response to the British refusal of their proposal was a model of moderation:

The divergence which existed in our views was with regard to the frontiers assigned to the dominion of Shere Ali. The English Government includes within them Badakhshan and Wakkan, which according to our views enjoyed a certain independence. Considering the difficulty experienced in establishing the facts in all their details in those distant parts, considering the greater facilities which the British Government possesses for collecting precise detail, and above all considering our wish not to give to this question of detail greater importance than is due to it, we do not refuse to accept the boundary line laid down by England. We are the more inclined to this act of courtesy as the English Government engages to use all its influence with Shere Ali in order to induce him to maintain a peaceful attitude, as well as to insist on his giving up all measures of aggression or further conquest. This influence is indisputable. It is based, not only on the material and moral ascendency of England, but also on the subsidies for which Shere Ali is indebted to her. Such being the case, we see in this assurance a real guarantee for the maintenance of peace.[32]

It was unfortunate that the British were not ready at this time to enter into a treaty with the Russians confirming this understanding – which was in essence the definitive frontier agreed just over twenty years later, including the notion of a neutral buffer zone (the Wakhan). Had they done so, a source of future tension might have been removed and the second Afghan war avoided.

The unwillingness of the British to guarantee Afghan territorial integrity continued to dog Anglo-Afghan relations. The Amir was not satisfied with the Anglo-Russian agreement, on which he had not been consulted, and tried to play on British fears of Russian intervention. His requests for money, arms, troops and a British commitment to protect his frontiers – although supported by the Viceroy of India – were turned down flat by London.

This refusal to entertain Sher Ali's request was most undiplomatic, even if a Russian invasion was not feared. Greatly disappointed, the Amir felt that he could no longer rely on British support or be sure of their professions. Had he been promised help in the event of foreign invasion, the history of Anglo-Afghan relations could have been different. Disillusioned in the British, on the arrival in Kabul of a Russian Muslim agent in the second quarter of 1875, he began exploring Russian intentions and gave him access.[33]

1876–1881: British 'forward policy' and the 2nd Afghan war

The response by the British Conservative government to the Amir's 'infidelity' in dealing with the Russians was to reverse the previous 'masterly inactivity' and initiate a more 'forward policy'.[34] Viceroy Northbrook (a Liberal), in disagreement with the change, resigned and was replaced in early 1876 by the inexperienced (but Conservative) Earl of Lytton.

As yet, however, there were no signs of renewed tension with Russia. In May 1876, Prime Minister Disraeli made the following declaration in Parliament:

> Russia knows full well there is no reason we should view the material development of her empire in Asia with jealousy, so long as it is clearly made aware by the Government of this country that we are resolved to maintain and strengthen, both materially and morally, our Indian empire… I believe, indeed, that at no time has there been a better understanding between the Courts of St. James and St. Petersburgh than at the present moment.[35]

The treaty of San Stefano in March 1878, following the Russian defeat of Turkey, significantly strengthened Russia's freedom of action in the east. In view, however, of the rising power of Germany, the Russians agreed to a significant withdrawal from these gains in the Treaty of Berlin that followed in July, as part of an effort to reduce tensions with the British.

Meanwhile, in June 1878, Kaufmann – contrary to stated Russian policy, and apparently on his own initiative – sent Major-General Stolietov from Samarqand to Kabul with proposals for an alliance, offering a guarantee of the Amir's borders that the British were still unwilling to contemplate, while not insisting on control of his foreign relations. The Amir – under extreme pressure from Kaufmann – received Stolietov with honours. This enraged Viceroy Lytton, who – without waiting for proper authority from London – immediately dispatched a British mission to Kabul preceded by an intemperate and threatening communication to the Amir, insisting that he receive the mission and accept British control over his foreign relations.

When the Amir temporised, Lytton – this time with reluctant approval from London – despatched an ultimatum requiring him to submit a written apology for his conduct, failing which he would be considered an enemy of the British government. In desperation, the Amir sought support from the Russians. In fact, Stolietov had already been recalled only shortly after his arrival[36] and Kaufmann, now aware of what he had set in motion, offered the Amir no support and advised him to make peace with the British.

It was too late: Lytton had already decided that the Amir must be deposed and had set in motion the events that led to the second Afghan war. The British were convinced that a secret agreement existed – Curzon claimed later (wrongly) that "General Stolietoff left Kabul at the end of September (1878) with a signed treaty in his pocket."[37] Although Disraeli and his Foreign Minister, Salisbury, hoping for a broader settlement with Russia, were furious at

Lytton's headstrong action and disobedience of instructions, they put a bold public face on it.[38] No answer to Lytton's ultimatum was received within the narrow time frame allowed and, on 21 November 1878, war was declared. "Sher Ali must have seen that the time allowed was farcical and, even if an apology were advanced, some other pretext would be found to subdue his independence."[39]

Lytton had greatly over-reacted to a non-existent threat.

> The fact that, during all the ten years Abdur Rahman had spent in Turkestan, von Kaufmann made no attempt to build him up as a potential Russian ally when the time was ripe, may be taken as one more sign that Russia had no intention of invading Afghanistan. The first chance had offered itself many years earlier when Russia withdrew and disowned the Vitkevich mission which had promised well. The second offered itself when Stoletov went to Kabul carrying a draft treaty with Sher Ali in his pocket. But again the mission was promptly recalled by von Kaufmann and although Stoletov did visit Kabul subsequently there were no offers of arms nor apparently any secret promises.[40]

The Indian Historian D.P. Singhal states definitively: "A close scrutiny of these letters [between the Amir and Kaufmann in 1878], which are now available for public inspection, does not reveal any secret alliance between the Amir and the Czar."[41]

In a study of the death toll from famine in India at this time[42] – for which the policies of Lytton bore a large measure of responsibility – Mike Davis points out that "it was widely suspected that the new viceroy's judgement was addled by opium and

Major-General Stolietov

incipient insanity. Since a nervous breakdown in 1868, Lytton had repeatedly exhibited wild swings between megalomania and self-lacerating despair."

Sher Ali fled to Mazar-i Sharif and died there in February 1879. He was replaced on the throne by his estranged son Yakub Khan. After a period of negotiations with the new Amir, the treaty of Gundamak was concluded in May 1879, ending the war but subjecting Afghanistan's foreign policy to British control accompanied by some territorial concessions to India on the north-west frontier. The status of the Amir became analogous to that of the Indian princes and he was promised aid against foreign aggression, but only at the discretion of the British. An army under General F. Roberts entered Kabul on 24 July 1879.

> The treaty involved the British in serious responsibilities for the sake of protecting the Indian Empire from imaginary attack, for no Indian or British authority – Lytton least of all – considered the danger of Russian invasion from that side a real one. If Russia had resources enough to undertake such an expedition, would she not have aided the Amir against English interference and won the sympathy of the Afghans by helping them in their hour of need? The facts indicate that Russia was not foolish enough to attack the strong Indian Empire from the side of the north-west frontier. All she wanted was to frighten the British in Asia by her diplomatic moves and thus lessen their grip in Europe. In this she was quite successful.[43]

The distractions of the war, the complications arising from the treaty of Gundamak, the problem of succession to the throne in Kabul and a change of government in London (brought about to a significant extent by popular dissatisfaction with the failure of the 'forward policy' in Afghanistan) enabled the Russians to consolidate their territorial expansion without threat from the British. The new British cabinet considered that there was no formidable danger to the security of India and decided on the withdrawal of British forces from Afghanistan. In 1881, the new Viceroy, the Marquis of Ripon, a cooler head than Lytton, recommended a treaty with Russia that, by giving legal recognition to the Russian presence in Central Asia, would give Britain a freer hand in Afghanistan without having constantly to look over her shoulder at Russian intentions. The cabinet had, however, an abiding distrust of Russia and London's attention was distracted by flashpoints elsewhere, in Egypt and the Sudan. Another opportunity was missed.

1882–1890: 'Scientific' Frontiers

After a brief pause, Russian territorial gains again became a major source of concern to Britain. In 1882, Merv capitulated to the Russians and, in Ashgabat in February 1884, the Turkoman tribes swore allegiance to the Tsar. The desirability of agreeing on "scientific frontiers" was now recognised by both sides, albeit with differing degrees of urgency. Negotiations began in mid-1884 on the formation of a joint Anglo-Russian boundary commission, but no agreement was reached on the starting point for their work or on the line on which the frontier was to be drawn

The Russians were now in no hurry and, indeed, were still advancing. In April 1885, they attacked a recently established Afghan post in Panjdeh: the absence of an agreed frontier line made the legal situation ambiguous, but the Afghans threatened to take action, and sought British support.

Russophobia, following reports of the bombardment and slaughter inflicted by the Russians at Geok-Tepe in 1881, was strong in Britain and by 1885 British public opinion had, once again, reached fever pitch, whipped up by the violently Russophobic press, that was aided and abetted by the supporters of the 'forward policy'. British troops were ordered into position near the Afghan border, the British fleet was placed on full alert and ships were moved to within striking distance of Vladivostok, where Russia was perceived to be most vulnerable.

None of the three governments, however, really wanted or was ready for war – despite public sabre rattling and manifestations of popular outrage. The Amir doubted the reliability of British promises of support and feared defeat by the Russians. The British were concerned about their long supply lines to one of the furthest points in Afghanistan from their base (and were doubtful about their welcome by the Afghan population en route); Sudan was the main theatre of British military activity at the time and military resources could not be spared for a further adventure in Afghanistan. While the Tsar was unwilling to disavow the actions of his senior officers, neither he nor his cabinet wanted war with Britain: they had other objectives. As Curzon observed at the time: "To keep England quiet in Europe by keeping her employed in Asia, that, briefly put, is sum and substance of Russian policy."[44]

A compromise was found that enabled the Russians to stay in Panjdeh while at the same time laying a solid base for the work of the boundary commission on the north-western frontier of Afghanistan, which commenced in November 1885, and, with the exception of the last few kilometres of the frontier up to the junction with the Oxus, was finished in nine months. The latter issue was finally settled in July 1887 by direct negotiations between the two governments.

This was a major achievement[45] and is proof that there was already a long-standing potential for agreement on essential questions. All that remained was to determine the extent of Afghan dominion over the Pamir region and the tribal areas contiguous with India in the west. While the latter were of exclusive concern to the British, the former required further negotiation with the Russians who objected (with British diplomatic support) to the Amir's claim to areas to the north (Darvaz) and east (Shughnan and Rushan) of the Oxus. Both parties considered the 1873 agreement between their respective Foreign Ministers as still valid: under this agreement, the Russians, while not refusing the claim of Afghan sovereignty over Badakhshan and Wakhan, had pointed out the need for a legally binding agreement and definition of frontier lines in the eastern confines of the Wakhan. They also wanted a reciprocal agreement from the British not to meddle in the affairs of Russia's new Central Asian territories.

The maps that had been used in drafting the 1873 agreement were vague and inaccurate. The Russians were using a map drawn up in 1759 on the basis of Chinese surveys that had been prepared in separate squares and compiled into a single map in Peking. By a perverse error, the square containing Wakhan and Badakhshan had been turned from east and west to north and south and the Russians, believing from this map that Wakhan was contiguous with Karategin, were therefore concerned about the concession to the Amir of territories so far to the north-east of the Oxus. Julius Klaproth (1783–1835), an oriental scholar, had made a copy of the Chinese map and sold it to both the Russian and British governments at the beginning of the century, providing at the same time a fraudulent account of the travels of an anonymous German horse-trader, Georg Ludwig von – , together with a fictitious earlier Chinese itinerary, that supposedly confirmed the map's authenticity and accuracy (see next chapter).

The Russians recognised that the British now had better maps, based on the reports of the pundits (Faiz Buksh, The Mirza and The Havildar – see the next Chapter) and of Forsyth's second mission to Yarkand in 1873, and future negotiations were easier as a result, although there remained a few blank spots on the map. In the introduction to the British report of the 1895 Pamir Boundary Commission (see below and Chapter 6.1). Major-General Gerard pointed out that

The frontier having been fixed diplomatically [in 1873], it remained for the two Boundary Commissions to trace its subsequent course eastward to the Chinese border. This apparently simple task might have been really so, had the agreement been based on a correct map, but a variety of conflicting views was possible when our surveys showed a wide discrepancy between the topography as it really is, and as it was supposed to be when the convention was drawn up.

The Pamir Incident

A few flashpoints remained. One lay in the eastern Wakhan, where a further crisis occurred in 1891. In 1888, a Russian officer had reached Hunza through the Pamirs and spent a month there: his warm reception by the Mir was a source of serious concern to the British. The officer, Colonel Bronislav Ludwigovich Grombchevsky, described his meeting with the Mir as follows:

> As I was leaving Kanjut, I found the Khan seriously ill. Nevertheless, he received me in his palace [Baltit Fort] in a solemn farewell audience: in the presence of dignitaries of the country and ambassadors from Gilgit, he charged me to inform the Sovereign Emperor, that he requested the grant of citizenship of Russia for himself and his country. Safdar Ali Khan, showing me casually the letter to him from Viceroy of India, told me: "Here is the letter in which he promises to make my country an arsenal and treasury of India (i.e. to overflow it with weapons and money). I hate Englishmen and have banished their envoys. I know that the English will punish me for this, but I am not afraid of them for I have leant against a rock on which the Great White Tsar stands firm." Further he asked for two mountain guns and a hundred shells, promising never to admit this to the English. The ruler of Kanjut finished his speech with the words: "I pray for health of the White Tsar, my great Patron" and, turning to the West, made a prayer together with all who were present.
>
> This request put me in extremely awkward circumstances. I had visited Kanjut for scientific purposes, not having any political mission and did not know what to answer the Khan, who was being courted by the English with generous offers. Therefore, having confirmed once again the absolutely private character of my visit, I advised the Khan to address his request to the Imperial Russian consul in Kashgar. Safdar Ali Khan prepared a mission to Kashgar, and supplied his envoy with letters in his own hand to the Consul, the Governor General of Turkestan and the Foreign Minister. The envoy was instructed to go as far as Tashkent and to hand over

personally the letters to the Governor General, but our consul in Kashgar detained him and confiscated the letters, and he himself did not get to Tashkent. I have no reliable information about the further progress of the petitions of Safdar Ali Khan. It seems the letters were sent to the Asian department of the Ministry for Foreign Affairs, and the ruler of Kanjut did not even receive an answer. Apparently, the letter from Safdar Ali Khan to me dated August, 30, 1888, met the same fate, in which he inquired about the person of the Sovereign Emperor, and asks me to pass on for the information of His Imperial Majesty his unlimited loyalty, of which he writes: "Having learned about the solemn day which is celebrated by all citizens of the Great White Tsar, I with my people put on a new dress and celebrate this day as solemnly as the means of my poor country allow. I have only one cannon and I have ordered that it be fired in honour of the Great Sovereign."[46]

Although the Mir was certainly trying to get the maximum advantage from putting the British in competition with the Russians for his favours, this was too much for the British, who resolved to try to motivate the Chinese to assert their supposed territorial rights in the eastern and southern Pamirs as a means of blocking the anticipated Russian territorial encroachment. Captain Francis Younghusband was sent by the Viceroy to explore the extent of Chinese authority in the region and the chances it might give to hold off the Russians.

In October 1889, Younghusband's path crossed fortuitously with that of Grombchevsky in the Yarkand valley: their meeting passed off cordially and without incident – indeed Grombchevsky seemed even to support the British thesis of Chinese sovereignty over the eastern and southern Pamirs. A second with Captain Ionov, however, in Boza-i Gumbaz in the Wakhan in August 1891, although also cordial, ended with Younghusband's ignominious departure under threat of arrest by Ionov, who claimed the territory as Russian. At almost the same time, Lieutenant Davison, an officer who had joined Younghusband in Kashgar after a nearly fatal attempt to explore the Mustagh range, was arrested by the Russians in the Alichur valley near Yashil Kul, and escorted to Marghilan where he was released to an official from the British Embassy in St. Petersburg, C.H.E. Eliot, who happened to be travelling in the region as a guest of the Governor-General of Turkestan, Vrevsky. There was a public outcry in Britain and India "and once again anti-Russian feelings hit fever pitch."[47]

In a letter to his father dated 4 August 1891,[48] Younghusband wrote that:

> [t]hings are looking a bit serious. I am on one side of a range of mountains and just over the other side in the Little Pamir is a Russian force which have just quietly

walked in and annexed the place in total disregard of the heathen Chinese general whom they met on the way and who tried to impress upon them the fact that the Pamirs belonged to China. The Russians have done a good many barefaced things in their time but by Jove this one takes the cake.

While, on the basis of the 1873 agreement, the Russians were arguably within their rights in arresting Davison, the situation of Boza-i Gumbaz was ambiguous. The area was inhabited mainly by nomads, it was unmapped, there were no effective signs of external authority and the legitimacy of claims to it were uncertain (indeed, the Amir had made it clear to the British that he felt unable to hold the territory militarily). The 1873 agreement had not covered any territory to the east of Zorkul (then known also as Sarikul, Lake Victoria, or Wood's lake).

The British were aware that the Russians were on strong ground. The Ambassador in St. Petersburg wrote to the Foreign Secretary in January 1892:

> I perceive from the correspondence that the Indian government seems desirous to induce the Chinese and Afghans to meet north of Lake Victoria on the Alichur Pamir, and that it would appear that Captain Younghusband actually invited the Afghans to occupy Yashil Kul. Now, it appears to me that this would be a most dangerous policy to follow. It would be acting in flagrant disregard of the engagement of 1872–73; it would give a most legitimate "casus belli" to the Russians against Afghanistan, and we could not honourably encourage the Afghans to carry out such a plan unless we were ready to give them physical support. It seems to me absolutely necessary, if we are to enter upon these negotiations, that we should rigidly adhere to the binding character of the Agreement of 1872–73.[49]

In correspondence with the Foreign Secretary a month earlier, the Ambassador had also confirmed that the Russians were aware that Younghusband and Davison were fishing in troubled waters:

> I ought to say that in the course of conversation M. de Giers [the Russian Foreign Minister] mentioned in explanation of Colonel Yonow's [Ionov's] high-handed treatment of Captain Younghusband, that he had come across, almost everywhere he went, the traces of that officer's handiwork in exciting the Chinese against Russia. A statement made by Mr. Davison to Mr. Eliot at Margilan would seem to a certain extent to corroborate this assertion. Mr. Davison said that Captain Younghusband had in the first instance invited the Afghans to take possession of the Alichur Pamir, but on meeting with no response to his overtures had urged the Chinese to strengthen themselves there in view of a possible invasion by the Afghans.[50]

Of course, the British must have believed that Grombchevsky – and possibly also Ionov, who, at the time he met Younghusband, had just returned from a short excursion over the Baroghil pass – were probably doing something very similar in Hunza immediately prior to this incident.

Although he had invaded and subjugated trans-Oxus Shughnan and Rushan in 1883 "with characteristic brutality"[51], even the new Afghan Amir, Abdul Rahman Khan, was uncertain about the actual limits of his territory. To the embarrassment of the Indian and British authorities, Younghusband had exceeded his instructions in the Pamirs: in addition to attempting to mobilise a Chinese presence in the Pamirs, he had written to the Afghan governor in Shughnan saying that the Chinese had heard he had occupied Sumantash and wished him to withdraw. As a result, in October 1891, the Amir requested "the exalted Government of India to send me a correct map, which may have been prepared with the inquiries and surveys of the English Surveyors made in those regions, showing how far the limits of the Afghan territory extend and how far those of the Chinese and Russians, so that I might be able to know about it, and with due knowledge, be able to send instructions to the Sarhaddar (governor) of Shighnan."[52] Again, the question was whether the Amir's territories included Shughnan and Rushan on the right bank of the Oxus, as well as Badakhshan on the left bank, and Wakhan.

A contemporary British memorandum commented that

> In 1877, Bokhara assumed the direct administration of Darvaz; in 1884, Afghanistan assumed the direct administration of Shignan-Roshan. Against this action of the Amir, the Government of India remonstrated.[53]

As noted, C.H.E. Eliot, from the St. Petersburg Embassy happened to be in Osh as guest of the Governor-General of Turkestan at the time of the incident: he recounts an amusing exchange on the vexed subject of Boza-i Gumbaz with the Governor of Ferghana and Colonel Galkin, chief of the Governor-General's chancery. They had backed up the Russian position, and pointed out that

> Boza-i Gumbaz formed part of the Khanate of Kokan, which had been annexed 'ipso facto' by Russia when Kokan itself was captured. That it did form part of the said Khanate was proved by the existence there of a tomb of a Kokan tax-collector Boza by name (whence the name of the place Boza-i Gumbaz, or rather Gumbez-i-Bozas, "the tomb of Boza"), with an inscription saying that he had met his death

in the discharge of his official duties …The next day the Governor-General spoke to me at considerable length on the same subject… The Governor-General said I must see that both the Yashil Kul and Boza-i Gumbaz were in Russian territory. The former was well to the north of the line claimed by Her Majesty's Government in 1873, and that the latter was part of the Khanate of Kokan was proved by the tomb of the tax-collector; I said I did not presume to discuss the question of boundaries with his Excellency, but that the murder of the tax-collector appeared to me to indicate that the local population did not admit the claims of the Khan of Kokan. His Excellency said that tax collectors were always killed in the east and that this proved nothing.[54]

Again, however, the Russians were not anxious to pick a quarrel. As Grombchevsky complained, the Mir of Hunza never got a reply to his overtures to the Russians: the Russian Consul-General in Kashgar, Petrovsky, was far too shrewd to risk a major diplomatic incident by being perceived by the British to be encouraging the Mir and had suppressed his letter. The Russian Foreign Minister had even confided to the British Ambassador that "Grombchevsky was dangerous, mischievous and quite untrustworthy" – an undeservedly harsh comment, in the light of Grombchevsky's own description of his caution in dealing with the Mir. Finally, in February 1892, the Ambassador was informed that an apology had been made by the Foreign Minister: "I have been informed by M. de Giers that he has addressed a despatch to M. de Staal (the Russian Ambassador in London) in which admission is made of the illegality of the acts of Colonel Yonow, and regret expressed at the expulsion of the two British officers. His Excellency has obtained the sanction of the Emperor to this."[55]

1892–1907: Crisis management and the settlement of frontiers

The outcome of the incidents described above shows that, despite public protest and the clamour of many of the players of the 'Great Game', cooler heads in both Britain and Russia were at pains to avoid war and to settle their differences by agreement. Both governments appreciated the contribution made by the other to the pacification of their respective frontier regions and recognised what they considered to be the "civilising" influence each brought to bear in regions inhabited mainly by nomads and 'unruly tribes'. Towards the end of the century, both were concerned by the rise of Germany and foresaw a need to settle their differences with a view to a future alliance.

In fact, both empires had held closely to the 1873 agreement. As far as the Pamirs were concerned, the British had more than once reminded the Afghan Amir that he had no rights on the right bank of the Oxus, and, with the exception of the Ionov-Younghusband incident, the Russians had not over-reached themselves by any incursions across the Wakhan or to the left bank of the Oxus. In March 1895, Britain and Russia agreed on the basis for a final boundary settlement and a new commission was formed to draw the exact line and place the marking pillars. The "Agreement on the Sphere of Influence between Russia and Great Britain", in addition to the technical boundary issues, contained the following political provisions:

• The Commission shall also be charged to report any facts which can be ascertained on the spot bearing on the situation of the Chinese frontier, with a view to enable the two Governments to come to an agreement with the Chinese Government as to the limits of Chinese territory in the vicinity of the line, in such manner as may be found most convenient.

• Her Britannic Majesty's Government and the Government of his Majesty the Emperor of Russia engage to abstain from exercising any political influence or control, the former to the north, the latter to the south, of the above line of demarcation.

• Her Britannic Majesty's Government engage that the territory lying within the British sphere of influence between the Hindu Kush, and the line running from the east end of Lake Victoria to the Chinese frontier, shall form part of the territory of the Amir of Afghanistan, that it shall not be annexed to Great Britain, and that no military posts or forts shall be established in it.

• The execution of this agreement is contingent upon the evacuation by the Amir of Afghanistan of all the territories now occupied by His Highness on the right bank of the Panja, and on the evacuation by the Amir of Bokhara of the portion of Darvaz which lies to the south of the Oxus, in regard to which her Britannic Majesty's Government and the Government of His Majesty the Emperor of Russia, have agreed to use their influence respectively with the two Amirs.

By the end of July, the work was complete and in September final protocols were signed. Starting from the eastern end of Lake Zorkul, the agreed frontier line followed the crests of the mountain range south and then east to the junction with the Aksu river; then along the Aksu river until the river turns north and from there directly to the Chinese frontier.

As Singhal comments,

> The territory in question was important only from a strategic point of view, for at one point it was only eight miles wide. The Amir himself was not interested in this piece of land, for it was too distant and difficult a country for him to hold. But the India authorities did not care about the Amir's desires; they wanted to secure their own safety. The work which in prospect had seemed difficult in the event proved quite straightforward.[56]

Thus, after several abortive attempts over the previous quarter of a century, the frontiers that hold today in the Pamirs were fixed: with the exception of a minor (but bloody) extension in Tibet a few years later in which Younghusband was involved, the Great Game was over.

A few practical matters remained to be settled between Britain and Russia. In a diplomatic note dated 25 January 1900, the Russian government notified the British of their intention to establish direct relations with the government of Afghanistan on some outstanding frontier and other non-political issues.

> *Les rapports de la Russie avec l'Afghanistan ont été définis par les arrangements intervenus en 1872 et 1873 entre les Cabinets de Saint-Pétersbourg et de Londres. En vertu de ces arrangements qui sont encore en vigueur, la Russie reconnaît que l'Afghanistan est entièrement en dehors de sa sphère d'action. ... Bien qu'elle n'eût renoncé qu'à l'exercice d'une action politique dans l'Afghanistan, elle a consenti, guidée par un sentiment d'intérêt amical à l'égard de la Grande-Bretagne, à s'abstenir, dans des circonstances données, même de rapports non-politiques ainsi que de l'échange des manifestations de courtoisie qui sont généralement d'usage dans ces contrées.* [The relations of Russia with Afghanistan are defined by the arrangements of 1873 and 1874 reached between the cabinets of St. Petersburg and London. By virtue of these arrangements, which are still in force, Russia recognises that Afghanistan is wholly outside its sphere of action .... Although she has only renounced the exercise of political activity in Afghanistan, she has, guided by a spirit of friendship towards Great Britain, agreed to abstain under the circumstances even from non-political relations and from the exchange of acts of courtesy such as are usual in these regions.][57]

In view of the independent action undertaken by Kaufmann and others a few years earlier, it is significant that Russia here reaffirmed her recognition of the exclusive British sphere of influence in Afghanistan. At the same time, however, it was a warning to the British that the Russians did not interpret their obligations as requiring them to request British approval for direct relations with Afghanistan on non-political questions. The British, still distrustful of the intentions of both the Russians and the Amir, expressed displeasure at the proposal. The Russians did not force the issue and it was only settled to Russian satisfaction in the Anglo-Russian Convention of 1907.

There was still some unfinished business. Although the frontiers between Afghanistan and Russia now appeared clear, as a result of an oversight no agreement was reached on exactly where on the Oxus (Panj) the border was to be fixed. The issue was finally resolved in 1946, when the border was fixed at the 'thalweg' line (the mid-point of the channel of the river). China did not formally accept the new boundary with Pakistan until 1963 and it was not until 17 May 2002 that agreement was reached between China and Tajikistan on the Pamir boundary – and even then, ominously, the Chinese inserted in the agreement the words 'for the time being'.

Conclusion

As abundantly noted, both Empires exercised considerable restraint in their relations during the period 1828–1907, when their rivalry was at its height. In the end, "the claims of Afghanistan and Badakhshan ... reflected, in reality, the interests of Calcutta and Tashkent, tempered only by the expediency of getting their respective protégés reconciled to the bargain that would be struck."[58] Both managed generally to keep their primary objectives clearly in view, although, on balance, the Russians were more consistent in their policies. That the results of their joint negotiations, the Pamir frontiers, stand today is a tribute to the wise counsels that prevailed in their mutual relations.

If there was a 'game', it is hard to avoid the conclusion that the Russians played it rather better than their competitor. In logistics they were far ahead of the British: by 1889, the Russians had already completed a railway line from the Caspian to Tashkent (at the rate of "a mile to a mile and a half a day"[59]), while the India Council was still arguing about an extension of the railway to the Afghan frontier; it was not until the British realised that Hunza and Chitral were threatened that they started planning improved communications with these distant regions.

The Russians were more successful (and ruthless) in subduing the native population and better able to consolidate their territorial gains than the British with their hybrid system of alliances, financial inducements, threats, arms supply and shows of pageantry. Despite the ruthlessness with which the peoples of Central Asia were subdued by the Russians, even Rawlinson had to admit that

> the extension of Russian arms to the east of the Caspian has been of immense benefit to the country. The substitution, indeed, of Russian rule for that of the Kirghiz, Uzbegs and Turkomans throughout a large portion of Central Asia has been an unmixed blessing to humanity. The execrable slave trade, with its concomitant horrors, has been abolished, brigandage has been suppressed, and Mahommedan fanaticism and cruelty have been generally mitigated and controlled. Commerce at the same time has been rendered more secure, local arts and manufactures have been encouraged, and the wants of the inhabitants have been everywhere more seriously regarded than is usual under Asiatic rulers.

In 1892, W. Barnes Steveni, a correspondent for the London Daily Chronicle quoted approvingly the opinion of a German newspaper article:

> It is not by might alone that Russia impresses the peoples of the East. Remembering the wise maxim of Skobeleff, she takes care to 'smooth over, with love and attention, the sharp strokes of the sword' – a policy somewhat more effective than the wavering and partisan policy of the rulers of the British Empire.[60]

In the account of his ride across the Pamirs in 1900, Filchner made a similar comment:

> In these regions, as well as in Chinese Turkestan, the Afghans show more respect for the Russians than the English. I attribute this to the deliberate and firm policy of Russia in Central Asia. ... And yet the Russians manage, in their dealings with Asiatic peoples, to reach out to their hearts, whereas the English, in their relations with natives, make a show of their cultural superiority. And it is this ability of the Russians to recognise even the wildest native as a fellow human being that gives them their strength in Asia ....[61]

Curzon too pointed out that

> Russia unquestionably possess a remarkable gift for enlisting the allegiance and attracting even the friendship of those whom she has subdued by force of arms ... The Russian fraternises in the true sense of the word ... and he does not shrink from entering into social and domestic relations with alien or inferior races. ... A remarkable feature of the Russification of Central Asia is the employment given by the conqueror to her former opponents on the field of battle. ... I was a witness at Baku, where the four Khans of Merv were assembled in Russian uniform to greet the Czar.[62]

It is hard to imagine that a British general would have dreamt of calling on a local religious leader to pay his respects just after conquering his country, yet this is what Cherniaev did after taking Tashkent in 1865. Indeed, in many of the pronouncements by the British on relations with the Afghans, perceived insults to Britain and affronts to the dignity of her representatives are often mentioned as justification for military retribution. We may also note Curzon's slighting reference to 'inferior races' and similar remarks by others such as Francis Younghusband (see page 484), suggesting that several of the British in India found it difficult to accept the native peoples as equals – a latent racism on the part of some of the British in Central Asia that must have made it hard for the British to gain the full confidence of the peoples with whom they came into contact.

The Russians' policy was opportunistic, pushing their advantage as far as it would go without actually becoming embroiled in major military confrontation and knowing just when to hold back. Accusations of bad faith have to be measured against the fact that Russia honoured her undertaking to return Dzungaria (in 1877) and Kuldja (in 1881) to the Chinese once the latter had shown that they were able to maintain order in these regions after the death of Yakub Khan.

Russia played the game of bluff with great skill, leaving the British continually guessing what her real intentions were. As Hopkirk suggests:

> One cannot but be struck by the number of these [Russian] invasion plans which somehow reached British ears over the years. It could well have occurred to the Russian military that there was profit to be gained from such leaks, since they obliged the British to garrison more troops in India than would otherwise have been necessary. After all, it was not only the British who were playing the Bolshaya Igra, the Great Game.

Moreover, as Hopkirk concludes, "Russian officers serving on the frontier had long been given to such bellicose talk … Its encouragement was one way of keeping up morale …"[63]

Despite the courage and daring of the individuals involved, as Hopkirk points out, British military intelligence "had been extremely haphazard, and compared badly with the well-organised and efficient Russian system … Contrary to the impression given by Rudyard Kipling in Kim, there was no overall intelligence-gathering or co-ordinating body in India at that time."[64] Moreover, there was at least one extraordinary breach of security. Petrovsky, the Russian Consul-General in Kashgar expressed to one British visitor his astonishment at the "shortsightedness of the British Government in permitting the publication of MacGregor's book on the Russian advance towards India (*The Defence of India*, Simla, 1884), and asked me how it was that a staff officer had been permitted to make public the secret dispositions of the British forces in case of war. The book, he added, had been read by the Russian officials, and had created a great sensation."[65]

After the Russians had consolidated their gains, they facilitated travel by distinguished British visitors, such as Curzon and Dunmore, whom they certainly knew to be spies but ostentatiously feted: they had everything to gain by exhibiting the extent of their control over the conquered territory. The British were not so imaginative – and were perhaps less confident of what they had to show.

The Marquis of Ripon, probably the wisest of the Viceroys of the period, whose cool political judgement was the opposite of Lytton's rashness, expressed well the realities of territorial expansion in Central Asia in 1881:

> I have always thought that it was altogether unnecessary to seek for an explanation of Russia's advance in Central Asia in any far-reaching scheme of India conquest; the circumstances in which she has been placed seem to me quite sufficient to account for that advance without supposing her to be animated by any special hostility to England, or by any deep designs against our power in the East. I can scarcely conceive it possible that any Russian Government can seriously desire to acquire the possession of a vast territory like India lying at an enormous distance from their own country[66], and I have the fullest confidence that England could successfully defend herself against any attack which Russia could make against her Indian dominions. But I hold that Russian interference in Afghanistan is to be deprecated in the interest of England and Russia alike.[67]

The Russians had the advantage of an autocratic centralised administration and a clear military policy of subjugation. Officers, if not encouraged to take rash initiatives, were at least rewarded for success – and they achieved it. The British were handicapped by a lack of consistency in their strategy in Afghanistan and were constrained by public opinion from exercising the ruthlessness shown by Kaufmann in suppressing local dissension. Lord Salisbury, who served in or led several administrations during the period, was well aware of the limits of action in a Parliamentary democracy: "You would not venture to ask Parliament for two extra regiments on account of a movement in some unknown sandhills which is supposed to be a menace to Merv. That being the case, no despatches from this office ... would in the least degree disturb P. Gortchakoff or provoke a single telegraphic order to Turkistan."[68] As Hopkirk points out, in commenting on Cherniaev's disobedience that led to the capture of Tashkent by the Russians: "Such an action by a British general would have brought the wrath of Parliament and press down upon his head, not to mention that of the cabinet and his own superiors. In Russia there was only one man ultimately to please or displease – the Tsar himself."[69]

Skobelev described his military policy as follows:

> I hold it as a principle that in Asia the duration of peace is in direct proportion to the slaughter you inflict upon the enemy. The harder you hit them the longer they will be quiet afterwards. My system is this: To strike hard, and keep on hitting till resistance is completely over; then at once to form ranks, cease slaughter and be kind and humane to the prostrate enemy.[70]

Curzon commented approvingly:

> A greater contrast than this can scarcely be imagined to the British method, which is to strike gingerly a series of taps, rather than a downright blow; rigidly to prohibit all pillage or slaughter, and to abstain not less wholly from subsequent fraternisation. But there can be no doubt that the Russian tactics, however deficient they may be from the moral, are exceedingly effective from the practical point of view ...

In 1894 an "Indian Officer" published anonymously in London an extraordinarily well-informed book entitled *Russia's March Towards India* that describes the manner in which, under the leadership of Skobelev, the Russians established their authority in Kokand and found themselves at the foot of the Pamirs.

> By these movements the rising in the Namangan district was effectually suppressed; but the disorders in other parts of the Khanate still continued, and Kaufmann therefore ordered Skobeleff to march through the country between the Naryn and Kara Daria, which was considered to be the centre from which the Kipchak malcontents carried out their hostile demonstrations, It was thought that this movement could be made with the most telling effect if it was carried out in the early winter, when the nomads had moved, with their families, into their winter settlements, as they could then be more easily got at, and their escape would be rendered difficult, if not altogether impossible, on account of the deep snow with which the surrounding mountains would then be covered.

Skobeleff therefore left Namangan on January 6, 1876, with a force of 2,800 men, and, crossing the Naryn river, moved along the right bank of the Kara Daria, while a detachment was sent, under Baron Meller-Zakomelsky, to reconnoitre the country to the south of the river. The cold at this time was intense; but, in spite of the severe frost (15° B.), the force marched eastwards, ravaging the country, and burning all the settlements which were passed through. The important village of Paitok was completely destroyed, and, while a force was detached to operate against the Kipchak villages in the mountains, the main body continued its advance along the northern bank of the river to Yani-Sarkarba.

As the Kipchaks saw that their settlements were threatened with complete destruction they sent envoys asking for mercy; and these men were informed by the Russian general that the tribes would be spared if they proved their sincerity and complete submission by delivering up the heads of the rebellion and the parties who had incited the people to enter upon the Holy War against the Russians. As these terms were not complied with the advance was continued, and after some skirmishes on January 12 and 13 the Russians crossed the Kara Daria at Yani-Sarkarba on the following day, and established a fortified camp on the left bank of the stream. A halt was then made for several days while reconnaissances were pushed forward towards the city of Andijan, where Abdul Rahman was reported to have collected a force of 10,000 horsemen and 5,000 foot soldiers, independent of some 15,000 armed inhabitants who had expressed their determination to oppose the Russians to the death.

Two messages were then sent demanding the surrender of the city; but as these were not answered Skobeleff determined to assault the place; and, advancing on January 20, he stormed the village of Iskylik, and then commenced the bombardment of Andijan. After the artillery had fired some 500 rounds, two storming columns advanced to the attack and soon penetrated to the centre of the

General Skobelev

town, where another battery was brought into action and continued the destruction of the place. By the next day all resistance had ceased: Andijan, which had inflicted such a serious reverse on Trotzky's column, was now subdued by the ever-victorious Skobeleff; and the Russian troops occupied the remains of the sorely-punished city, Skobeleff himself taking up his quarters in the Bek's palace, which Trotzky – in his anxiety to minimise his defeat – had reported to have been destroyed.

On January 30 news was received that the Khokandians who had fled from Andijan were again assembling near Asaki, and Skobeleff therefore marched out and captured that town after severe fighting. This battle, following closely after the capture of Andijan, completely broke the power of the Khokandians. Margelan and Shahr-i-Khana tendered their submission once more; and on February 5 Abdur Rahman, Batyr Tiura, Isfend Yar, and other leaders of the insurrection surrendered themselves unconditionally to Skobeleff and threw themselves on the mercy of the Emperor.

By this time also the inhabitants of the city of Khokand found that they were no better off under the leadership of Fulad Bek and Abdul Gaffar Bek than they had been under Khudayar's son, for these two chiefs, taking advantage of their accession to power, appeared determined to enrich themselves as much as possible at the expense of their adherents, while the former also committed the greatest atrocities and seemed to revel in bloodshed. The people, therefore, sent to Nasr-Eddin and begged him to return. The Khan was then at Makhram, and after some hesitation he set out for the Khokandian capital; but before he arrived there the Kipchak and Kirghiz adherents of Fulad Bek attacked him and forced him to return precipitately to the Russian frontier. Skobeleff was then ordered to occupy the capital; and this he did on February 20, when sixty-two guns and a large supply of ammunition and provisions were captured. Fulad Bek in the meanwhile had taken refuge in the mountains to the north of Karategin, and when captured a short time afterwards he was justly hanged for his barbarous actions.

By this time it had been decided that the whole of the Khanate should be annexed. General Kaufmann had left Tashkent in the previous December for the Russian capital, and on his arrival there had persuaded the Czar's Government that such a step was necessary for the security of the south-eastern frontier of the Turkestan province; and on March 2, 1876, the Emperor signed an order by which it was decreed that the whole of Khokand was incorporated in the Russian Empire under the name of the Province of Ferghana, and that this new province was to be under the direction of the Governor-General of Turkestan, who was to reorganise its administration by means of a provisional arrangement such as had been introduced in the Amu-Daria and Zarafshan districts. Immediately on receipt of this order General Kolpakoffsky, who had temporary command during Kaufmann's absence, set out for the city of Khokand, and there proclaimed to the still disquieted inhabitants that the White Czar had 'approved of their submission' and had decided to take them under his protection. Nasr-Eddin, Abdur Rahman, and other leaders of the insurrection were then deported to Tashkent, and General Skobeleff was placed in command of the new province.[71]

The Russians were, indeed, fully occupied consolidating their territorial gains in Central Asia and it would have been folly for them to invade India. Their expansion into Central Asia was inevitable and foreseeable. Had there been less Russophobia among the British, it might have been possible to reach a final settlement with the Russians long before 1895 that would have given the British a completely free hand in northern India and Afghanistan. Salisbury had suggested in September 1878 that it might be more convenient simply to "seize the provinces which are financially and strategically the most desirable"[72] and Kaufmann never understood why the British had not simply taken over Afghanistan and applied tactics similar to his own to ensure their authority. In 1897, Petrovsky had expressed similar views to Ralph Cobbold.

> The Tirah Expedition [against a Pathan uprising on the North-West Frontier in 1897] also afforded us much food for conversation. Petrovsky told me that he had taken in an English paper throughout the campaign in order to get full details, and adverted strongly on some of the action taken by the British Government in dealing with the Pathan. In his opinion the only satisfactory method to have adopted would have been to say to the general selected to command the expedition: "Take what troops you require, settle these troublesome people in the quickest manner possible. You have *carte blanche*, now go and do it." Instead of which the officer in charge was hampered in every way by orders from London and from Simla emanating from people, the majority of whom had never been near the scene of operations, and who possessed no personal knowledge of the *status quo*. It was a first principle of the Russian administrative method to trust the general in command of an expedition implicitly. He would not be hampered in any way. If he succeeded, he would be rewarded; if he failed, his career would be closed. In the result a successful issue was assured from the outset; the desired end was attained in the shortest possible time. The loss of life involved was greatly lessened by the brevity of the campaign, and the cost would probably be one-half that involved by the British method.[73]

The British never defined a consistent policy towards Afghanistan. Curzon commented mercilessly:

> We owe our record of Afghan failure and disaster, mingled indeed with some brilliant feats and redeemed by a few noble names, to the amazing political incompetence that has with fine continuity been brought to bear upon our relations with successive Afghan rulers. For fifty years there has not been an Afghan Amir whom we have not alternately fought against and caressed, now repudiating and now recognising his sovereignty, now appealing to his subjects as their saviours, now slaughtering them as our foes. It was so with Dost Mohammed, with Shir Ali, with Yakub, and it has been so with Abdurrahman Khan. Each one of these men has known the British both as enemies and as patrons, and has commonly only won the patronage by the demonstration of his power to command it. Small wonder that we have never been trusted by the Afghan rulers, or liked by the Afghan people! In the history of most conquering races is found some spot that has invariably exposed their weakness like the joints in armour of steel. Afghanistan has long been the Achilles' heel of Great Britain in the East. Impregnable elsewhere, she has shown herself uniformly vulnerable here.[74]

The legacy of this inconsistency was a weak and divided country, and the Afghans were never encouraged to develop strong native institutions or given the support or external stimulus that would have enabled them to do so. It is clear from the contemporary accounts of Wolff, Vambéry, and others – especially MacGahan – who travelled among them[75], that the Turkomans and other tribes subdued by the Russians were just as fierce, belligerent and unruly as the Afghans and it is arguable, although perhaps politically incorrect, that, had Afghanistan been subdued in the same way by the British in the 19th century, it might have emerged as a stronger state in the 20th and avoided the destiny with which we are today all too familiar in the 21st.[76]

Scientific Exploration in the 19th Century

The 19th century was the golden age of world exploration. Ethnography and evolution were also enjoying notoriety with the rise of popular science, and contemporary theories identified the Pamirs as the cradle of the European race. In April 1873, for example, the London Quarterly Review commented at the time of the first Pamirs border agreement between Russia and Britain (see page 307):

> Yet this barren and inaccessible upland, with its scanty handful of wild people, finds a place in Eastern history and geography from an early period, and has now become the subject of serious correspondence between two great European Governments, and its name, for a few weeks at least, a household word in London. Indeed, this is a striking accident of the course of modern history. We see the Slav and the Englishman – representatives of two great branches of the Aryan race, but divided by such vast intervals of space and time from the original common starting-point of their migration – thus brought back to the lap of Pamir to which so many quivering lines point as the centre of their earliest seats, there by common consent to lay down limits to mutual encroachment.[1]

The French explorer, J.B. Paquier, wrote in 1896: *"C'est sur les contreforts occidentaux du Pamir que commence véritablement pour nous la première histoire des races européennes."* (It is really on the western slopes of the Pamirs that the first history of the European races begins.)

It is difficult for us today to appreciate the fascination of Central Asia for educated people of the 19th century. The Oxus, in particular, seems to have been endowed with almost mystical qualities: Captain Henry Trotter, the third European to visit its upper reaches since Marco Polo and Benedict Goës, wrote of an "almost sacred interest" attached to it.[2] G.E. Wheeler, in the introduction to the 1976 edition of John Wood's account of his famous *Journey to the Source of the Oxus* (see page 337), comments that "throughout the nineteenth century the pin-pointing of a great river's source was regarded as a matter of much greater importance than it is today, especially when the river was the Oxus, to which a romantic aura had long been attached. The reason for this aura is far from clear."

This aura was well reflected in Matthew Arnold's poem *Sohrab and Rustum*:
... But the majestic river floated on,
Out of the mist and hum of that low land,
Into the frosty starlight, and there moved,
Rejoicing, through the hush'd Chorasmian waste,
Under the solitary moon; – he flow'd
Right for the polar star, past Orgunjè,
Brimming, and bright, and large; then sands begin
To hem his watery march, and dam his streams,
And split his currents; that for many a league
The shorn and parcell'd Oxus strains along
Through beds of sand and matted rushy isles –
Oxus, forgetting the bright speed he had
In his high mountain-cradle in Pamere,
A foil'd circuitous wanderer – till at last
The long'd-for dash of waves is heard, and wide
His luminous home of waters opens, bright
And tranquil, from whose floor the new-bathed stars
Emerge, and shine upon the Aral Sea.

Matthew Arnold (1822–1828)

Curzon was also typical of his generation:

Descending from the hidden "Roof of the World", its waters tell of forgotten peoples and whisper secrets of unknown lands. They are believed to have rocked the cradle of our race. Long the legendary watermark between Iran and Turan, they have worn a channel deep into the fate of humanity. World-wide conquerors, and Alexander and a Tamerlane, slaked their horses' thirst in the Oxus stream; Eastern poets drank inspiration from its fountains; Arab geographers boasted of it as 'superior in volume, in depth, and in breadth to all the rivers of the earth'.[3]

Another intrepid traveller, Ralph Cobbold, waxed equally lyrical:

The scenes that have been enacted on the banks of the mighty Oxus are multifarious; indeed, one conjures up visions of mighty conquerors who have founded dynasties, which in turn have been vanquished by mightier men; of Alexander and his conquering Greeks; of the Chinese, the Arabs, the Mongols, and now the Muscovite. What tales of bloody wars and countless battles could not the Oxus unfold had it the gift of speech.[4]

In this review of European exploration of the Pamirs, we shall encounter mainly travellers and explorers who went and wrote an account of their travels; there were also some, such as Mr. and Mrs. Leslie Renton, who were definitely in the Pamirs but who left no written record of their travel (the Rentons at least left photographs) and some – such as George Hayward, who made four unsuccessful attempts to reach the Pamirs – who set out but never completed the journey.

There were also others who, on the contrary, invented reports of fictitious travels in the Pamirs: for example, the fascinating but totally bogus journey of the mysterious German, Georg Ludwig von – , a product of the fertile mind (and greedy hands) of the orientalist Julius Klaproth. The circumstances surrounding the itinerary of Klaproth's fictitious German are sufficiently curious to justify including an account in this narrative.

Heinrich Julius Klaproth

Klaproth, born in Berlin in 1783, devoted his life from an early age to the study of Asiatic languages. In 1802 the first edition of his *Asiatisches Magazin* was published in Weimar, as a result of which he was invited to take a post at the Academy of Sciences in St Petersburg, set up in 1724 by Peter the Great. In 1805 he travelled to China as a member of a delegation led by Count Golovkin and, on his return, was sent to the Caucasus from 1807–1808 to undertake ethnographic and linguistic research. He is best known for his *Asia polyglotta*, published in Paris in 1823 and 1831, that summarised the current state of knowledge of the Eastern languages, especially those of the Russian Empire.

We have seen briefly, in 'The Great Game' (see page 295), that, in the course of Anglo-Russian negotiations on issues relating to the Afghan frontier prior to the 1873 Agreement, it became apparent that the Russian maps were wildly inaccurate. As a result of the incorrect piecing together of a Chinese map from 1759, the Russians were under the impression that the Wakhan lay adjacent to Karategin and were therefore opposed to recognition of the Wakhan as belonging to Afghanistan, since this would mean that Afghan territory would have been extended far to the north. The British knew from the travels of Wood and the Pundits (see below) that Wakhan is, in reality, nowhere near Karategin. In 1872, Sir Henry Yule cleverly deduced how the Chinese map came to be wrongly pieced together[5] and, a year later, Sir Henry Rawlinson, President of the Society, explained to the RGS how the Russians had been misled.[6]

About ten years ago, then, it was announced to the Imperial Geographical Society of St. Petersburg, by one of its most distinguished members, the late Mons. Veniukoff, that a manuscript had been discovered at the archive of the 'Etat Major,' which professed to give a minute account of all the country intervening between Cashmere and the Kirghiz Steppes. The author was said to be a German (George Ludwig von –), an agent of the East India Company, who was despatched at the beginning of this, or the end of the last, century, to purchase horses in Central Asia, and who, having on his return from his mission, quarrelled with the Calcutta Government on the subject of his accounts, transferred his MSS. to St. Petersburg, where they had remained for over fifty years unnoticed in deposit. The chapters which Mons. Veniukoff published from this work, and which were certainly very curious, were received at St. Petersburg with the most absolute confidence, as extracts from official documents, and were cordially welcomed even in Paris; but in England they were viewed with suspicion from the commencement; and no sooner were the details brought forward than they were pronounced impossible, and the whole story of the horse-agent and his journal were accordingly declared to be an impudent fiction.

It was thus pretended that a doctor had travelled up from Cashmere to the Oxus with a guard of Sepoys, having penetrated through the mountains accompanied by camels in an incredibly short space of time. When he had reached the middle of the Pamir Steppe, it was further stated that he found horses in abundance, and had sent back 160 to Calcutta under charge of half-a-dozen Sepoys. The whole story was so absurd that it could not be believed for an instant, but at the same time some curious geographical features were correctly described: the names of places, indeed, were apparently genuine, and even specimens of the Kafir language were accurately given, so that a great deal of mystery was admitted to attach to the story. Thereupon arose a controversy of some warmth, which was not yet finished.

The most plausible solution was somewhat to the following effect: The great Oriental scholar Klaproth, it seemed, must have determined to mystify the world, whilst at the same time he replenished his own pockets. He took the trouble accordingly, in the first place, to invent a journey from the plains of India to the Russian frontier through a country which was at that time entirely unknown to the majority of geographers. To illustrate these travels, he compiled very elaborate maps, the sketch-route of the journey, indeed, being contained in twenty sheets, and the MSS. thus illustrated was sold to the Russian Government. Next he invented a Russian mission to the frontiers of India, also through an unknown country, and this he illustrated in a similar manner, selling the MSS. to our Foreign Office for 1000 guineas. Then, in order to confirm the accuracy of both these journeys from what might be supposed to be an independent source, he invented a Chinese itinerary, passing through the same regions and corroborating their geography. The whole three accounts were purely fictitious, but they were for a long time accepted as genuine both by the Russian and English Governments, and Mr. Arrowsmith was allowed to consult the Foreign Office manuscript in order to incorporate some of the details in the map which he constructed in 1834 for the illustration of Burnes's travels. The Russian cartographers, in the same way, followed the authority of their MS. and delineated the country accordingly, but the position of Wakhan was entirely wrong, and thus the Russians were misled.

In his Introduction to Wood's Journey to the Source of the Oxus, Yule's judgement was equally harsh:

> … there can be little doubt, it is to be feared, that the acute and brilliant linguist and geographer was himself the author of all three sets of papers; nor was there any contemporary capable of accomplishing a fraud of this kind so successfully.

Despite a spirited defence by a member of the Geographical Society of St. Petersburg, Nicolas de Khanikoff,[7] of the authenticity of the itinerary of Georg Ludwig von – , the careful research by Yule and Rawlinson was undoubtedly the reason why, in the 1873 Agreement, the Russians gracefully acknowledged the "greater facilities which the British Government possesses for collecting precise detail" of the geography of the Pamirs at that time.

Alexander Gardner (1831)

In addition to the above curious story, there are also some 19th century travellers who may have been to the Pamirs but whose reports are not sufficiently clear and specific to enable us to say with certainty that they were really there. One of these was Alexander Gardner.

His purported travels remain an enigma, and opinions differ on their authenticity ever since his first claims were made. His strange story is well told by John Keay in *When Men and Mountains Meet* (OUP, 1977) and it will be sufficient for the present account only to note that Gardner claimed to have crossed the Oxus from Afghan Badakhshan to Shughnan some time between 1826 and 1830, and to have gone from there perhaps to the Alai Valley and/or across the Pamirs to Yarkand.

Henry Yule thought he was an impostor and ridiculed him in his introduction to Wood's *Journey to the Source of the Oxus*:

> But amid the phantasmagoria of antres vast and deserts idle, of weird scenery and uncouth nomenclature, which flashes past us in the diary till our heads go round, we alight upon those familiar names as if from the clouds; they link to nothing before or behind; and the traveller's tracks remind us of that uncanny creature which is said to haunt the eternal snows of the Sikkim Himalya, and whose footsteps are found at intervals of forty or fifty yards!

Ney Elias (see page 371), however, was inclined to believe him; and Henry Rawlinson was prepared to give him the benefit of the doubt for some parts of his journey. If indeed he was in the Pamirs as early as 1826, the first European after Benedict Goës, he made no contribution to our knowledge of the region or its peoples. As Keay remarks, he may have crossed every one of the six great mountain systems long before modern maps acknowledged their existence,

> But to win acclaim as an explorer, to enjoy the publisher's royalties, the medals and the honours, it is not enough just to have travelled. The successful explorer must interrupt his movements to take measurements and observations. He must carefully identify physical features and place names and, at the end, he must write a convincing, coherent and consistent report. On all these counts Gardner failed.

It is a pity that Keay, in making his very balanced judgement of Gardner,[8] perpetuates one of the myths of the Pamirs that may discourage all but the most hardy and adventurous of modern travellers from attempting to follow in the early explorers' footsteps. The Pamirs are not, as he describes them, "a polar wilderness combining the bleakness of Tibet with the ruggedness of the Karakorams." It is indeed true that many of the early travellers chose to visit the Pamirs in the winter or early Spring – in some cases for the practical reason that the water courses could then easily be crossed because they are frozen, and in some cases from sheer ignorance about the climate in the Pamirs – and that their accounts therefore emphasise the wind, snow, ice and cold. At that time of year the Pamirs are indeed formidable but, at least from May to November, almost all of the region is accessible and hospitable and there are now roads and bridges leading to the top of the furthest valleys which, during these months, are anything but bleak.

He is also incorrect in saying that "no one actually lives there" – today even on the high plateau there are permanent settlements – and unfair to suggest that the main features of the Pamirs are only "two or three crumbling tombs and a dreary muddle of lakes and rivers." At the time Keay wrote, it would have been difficult to visit the Pamirs and he cannot have been aware of the spectacular unspoilt scenery and archaeological treasures of the Pamirs.

Wood's Journey to the 'Source of the Oxus' (1837–38)

As we have seen in the 'The Great Game' (p 295), 1837 was a year of crisis in Britain's relations with Dost Mohamed and Afghanistan. At the beginning of the year, Alexander Burnes – who had distinguished himself already in 1832 on a famous journey to Bukhara in native dress – was despatched on an 'extraordinary mission' to negotiate with Dost Mohammad and seek to pre-empt the establishment of friendly relations with the Russians. This mission – the failure of which led directly to the first Afghan war and the subsequent murder of Burnes in Kabul – was passed off as commercial in nature and included a survey of the upper reaches of the Indus to assess its potential as a trading thoroughfare. For the latter purpose, it included a young lieutenant from the Indian Navy, John Wood.

John Wood was born in 1812 in Perth in Scotland and, after attending school at the Perth Academy, joined the Indian Navy. His abilities in surveying were soon noticed and several of the surveys he made remained for some time the standard authority on the geography of these regions.

Wood left the port of Karachi on 17 December 1836 for the Indus delta and transferred to a native riverboat from which, for the next three months, he recorded in remarkable detail his observations of all that he saw. On 25 March 1837 he was joined by Burnes and a medical doctor, Percival Lord. Concluding that the river was impracticable for navigation beyond Kalabagh, they continued overland through Peshawar to Kabul where they arrived on 20 September.

Towards the end of October, an envoy sent by Murad Ali Beg of Kunduz arrived in Kabul with gifts for the Emir. The British had so far been unsuccessful in establishing friendly relations with the ruler of Kunduz and, learning that Murad Beg's brother was going blind, Burnes decided to despatch Lord and Wood on a goodwill mission to Kunduz with the offer of whatever treatment Lord could provide. After one false start, having been forced by early snow to turn back from the Parwan pass, they left Kabul on 15 November for the longer but lower route to Kunduz via Bamiyan, arriving at Murad Beg's court on 4 December 1837.

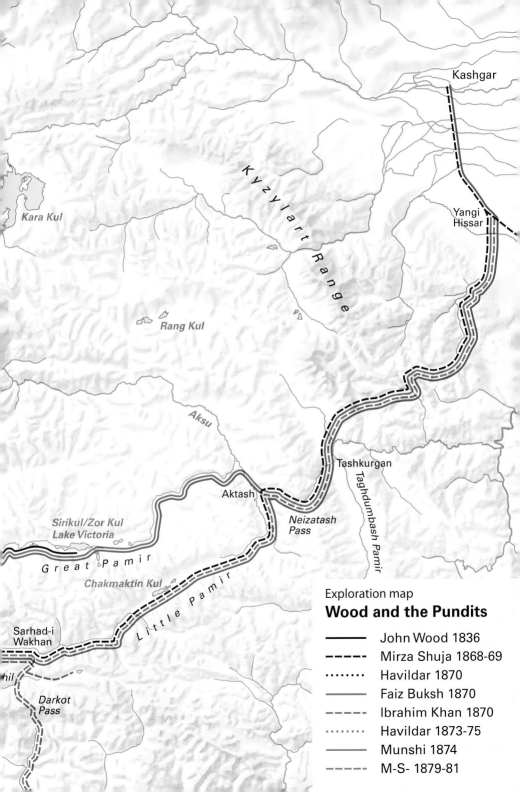

Kashgar

Kara Kul

Kyzylart Range

Rang Kul

Yangi
Hissar

Aksu

Tashkurgan

Aktash

Taghdumbash Pamir

*Sirikul/Zor Kul
Lake Victoria*

Neizatash
Pass

G r e a t   P a m i r

Chakmaktin Kul

L i t t l e   P a m i r

Sarhad-i
Wakhan

hil

Darkot
Pass

Exploration map
Wood and the Pundits

————— John Wood 1836

– – – – – Mirza Shuja 1868-69

· · · · · · · · Havildar 1870

————— Faiz Buksh 1870

– – – – – Ibrahim Khan 1870

· · · · · · · · Havildar 1873-75

————— Munshi 1874

– – – – – M-S- 1879-81

Lord was not optimistic about the possibility of treating the eye condition of Murad Beg's brother and, with winter setting in, Wood was concerned about

> how we could most profitably employ this sojourn in Turkistan. The great object of my thought by day and dreams by night had for some time past been the discovery of the source of the Oxus, and …. Murad Beg on the 10th of December conceded his permission to me to trace the Jihun, an appellation by which this river is better known among the Usbeks.

In his book *Travels into Bokhara*, published in 1834, Burnes had already expressed his great interest in tales of the Pamir and in Marco Polo's report of a large lake there; from native travellers' tales he received confirmation of the existence of this lake, that it was called 'Surikol' and that it was reputed to be the source of the Oxus, the Jaxartes (Syrdaria) and a branch of the Indus. There is no evidence that Wood's excursion was officially mandated by the Indian government, but it is safe to assume that it had been encouraged, if not actually put in his mind, by Burnes.

Deciding to travel as light as possible, Wood "adopted the costume of the country, as a measure calculated to smooth our intercourse with a strange people," and was accompanied only by "natives": three Indians, a Tajik Mullah in the service of Murad Beg and five Afghans. Like some, but by no means all, of his contemporary colonial officers, Wood never had any difficulty in establishing easy relations with 'natives'.[9] His comment on his companions reveals much about his innermost sentiments:

> More intimate acquaintance with the Eastern countries has considerably modified my unfavourable opinion of their inhabitants, and taught me to dissent from those wholesale terms of abuse which Europeans too often lavish on the native population. It will generally be found that our opinions of a people rise as our acquaintance with them increases. Vice in every community is sufficiently prominent to be seen without being sought after; but the wise and good shun notoriety, and it is only when we probe society deep that they are discovered.

Wood developed a special affection for the Tajiks of Badakhshan and felt strongly for the sufferings inflicted on them by their Uzbek rulers.

> The Tajiks make good companions, particularly the Mullahs, who have far more liberality of sentiment than their untravelled disciples. They were always pleased to be visited by us, and used to say that we were no Uzbeks but like themselves in features and complexion. Though their own temperament is grave, they delight in

a lively associate. Keep talking to them, and no European, with such an audience, can ever want subjects of conversation – and you are sure of their good-will. ... Nowhere is the difference between European and Mohamedan society more strongly marked than in the lower walks of life. The broad line that separates the rich and poor in civilised society is as yet but faintly drawn in central Asia. Here unreserved intercourse with their superiors has polished the manners of the lower classes; and instead of this familiarity breeding contempt, it begets self-respect in the dependant. ... Indeed all the inferior classes possess an innate self-respect, and a natural gravity of deportment.

Wood left Kunduz on 11 December and his spirits were high, despite extreme weather and a difficult route: he was, by nature, undemanding for his personal comfort. In Khanabad, their first overnight stop,

> It was late when we entered the village, and to the hospitality of some of the students in its Madrasa, or colleges, we were indebted for shelter and for firing. Our horses were soon stabled in a corner of the court-yard and, having seen that their provender bags were not empty, we entered as snug a berth as the most fastidious traveller could desire. A march of seventeen miles through a thick grass jungle often knee deep in water, performed on a keen winter's evening, had prepared us to welcome rest and shelter wherever found; and as we stretched ourselves on the comfortable warm felts, and sipped our tea, I felt a glow at my heart which cannot be described. A calmness of spirit, a willingness to be satisfied and pleased with everything around me, and a desire that others should be as happy as myself.

Wood's prose is functional – although he has moments of good description verging on the poetic – and he is not as eloquent as Cobbold or as entertaining as Dunmore and Littledale, whom we shall meet later. Few 19th century explorers, however, express so succinctly a joy in simple creature comforts and the company of other human beings 'wherever found'.

Murad Beg considered the Ismaili beliefs held by a substantial number of the local inhabitants as heretical and persecuted them savagely. On reaching Faizabad, Wood learned that Murad Beg had recently destroyed the town, "once celebrated throughout the East," and had taken its inhabitants as slaves to Kunduz, "a place only fit to be the residence of aquatic birds."[10]

> It was impossible to behold the desolation of so fair a scene, without commiserating the unfortunate exiles and execrating their tyrant, or without shuddering to think,

that one man, as ill-advised as cruel, should have the power to work so much mischief and to make so many of his species miserable!

As his hosts described the iron rule of Murad Beg "they all but shed tears." As we shall see later, the unmitigated brutality of the rulers of Badakhshan was one of the main reasons for the welcome given by the local population to the Russians when they entered the Western Pamirs at the end of the century: indeed, one of the most important benefits of Russian occupation was to put an end to the incursions from across the Oxus to capture slaves. Wood gives a graphic example of the rampant slave trade from the experience of his Tajik companion:

> I found Abdul Ghuni in earnest conversation with a stranger on horseback, behind whom was sitting a very handsome female slave, and it was evident from his manner that the Mullah was waxing wroth. ... sighing most piteously, he said, "Alas, alas, my lord! When I left my house in Talikhan, the very last order I gave was, that she whom you have just seen should not be sold. My other slaves were all for sale: but this one! This favourite one! I had thoughts of taking to wife!" and here the sighs began again. It appeared that in the Mullah's absence at Kunduz, a Khurm slave-dealer had visited Talikhan, and made a tempting offer for the favourite. The sum was large, and Abdul Ghuni's brother at once concluded a bargain. ... Among the slaves of Abdul Ghuni ... were two Kirgis from Pamir. Although their features were Chinese, their complexions were fair, and even rosy. One, a good looking young

Assembly of Kyrgyz at Alichur

woman, had a child at her breast, and cried bitterly when detailing the circumstances attending her capture… For my own part I can perceive one and only one mode, by which the traffic in human beings may be done away with. It is in the general diffusion of knowledge. The time will come, though it may be still far distant, when the printing press shall perform as great wonders through the whole of Asia as it has done, and is still doing, in Europe.

In his response to what he saw of the slave trade in Central Asia in 1838, Wood was well in tune with the most liberal opinion in his home country: the Slavery Abolition Act, that gave all slaves in the British Empire their freedom, had been passed by the British Parliament only five years previously and, in North America, John Brown's raid on Harpers Ferry was still over twenty years off and Abraham Lincoln had only just got his lawyer's licence.

Interestingly, one of the native explorers who followed Wood's itinerary many years later (the 'Munshi' – see page 360) relates that, while he was in Ishkashim in 1874, a present of slaves from the headman of Yasin (Mir Wali, who, as we shall see, was responsible for the murder of a British explorer) for the Governor of Balkh was refused because the latter had prohibited slave-trading. Henry Trotter, in his account of the Havildar's second journey to Badakhshan (see page 358), noted that he "speaks

Yurt in the Gumbezkol Valley, Murghab

very highly of the moderation exercised by officials throughout the whole of the Bokhara dominions – a striking contrast to what goes on south of the Oxus," (by the Afghans) and that "no oppression is committed by the local Governments."

Passing through Jerm, then the capital of Badakhshan, to visit the legendary lapis lazuli mines they spent the night at the shrine of Nasir Khusraw, and, continuing the next day in a blustery storm, Wood thought nostalgically of "Scotland and the social gaieties of winter."

On return to Jerm, they were held up for over a month by the unexpected severity of the weather, giving Wood the opportunity to record the local habits and make many friends. He noted in particular that

> In former times, Badakhshan was noted for the social qualities of its inhabitants, and we could still discern indications of this generous spirit, but few have the means of being hospitable; and poverty under a task-master has produced a selfishness that exists not among Tajiks who are free.

Visitors to the Pamirs today can confirm that this tradition of generosity and hospitality is alive and well again.

Wood also noted that the women "are fair, tolerably good-looking, and do not veil themselves as is customary in most Mohamedan countries" and that the children were brought up to be part of adult society.

> Frequently have I seen the children of chiefs approach their father's durbar, and stopping short at the threshold of the door, utter the shout of "Salam Ali-kum," so as to draw all eyes upon them; but nothing daunted, they marched boldly into the room, and sliding down upon their knees, folded their arms and took their seats upon the musnud, with all the gravity of grown-up persons.

Zoroastrian traditions had survived and "I remarked a great disinclination to extinguish a light by blowing on it with the breath."

On 30 January, a group from Shughnan arrived in the village and informed Wood that the Oxus was frozen. This was good news, since it would facilitate crossing the river and enable him to visit the famous ruby mines in Gharan on the other side. They left the next day and crossed the Oxus at Ishkashim, only to be prevented by ice and snow from getting to the mines. Wood learned, however, that

> The mines have not been worked since Badakhshan fell into the hands of the Kunduz chief, who, irritated, it is supposed, at the small profit they yielded,

marched the inhabitants of the district, then numbering about five hundred families, to Kunduz, and disposed of them in the slave market. The inhabitants of Gharan were Rafizies, or Shiah Mohamedans [Ismailis], and so are the few families which still remain there.

Crossing the Oxus again, they proceeded up the left bank and spent the night in a traditional house built with an open skylight in the roof and heavy with Zoroastrian and Ismaili symbolism, observed by Wood with his usual acuity.

We discovered that the holes in the their roofs, besides giving vent to the smoke, perform the office of sun-dials, and when the sun is shining indicate the hour of the day. Before the housewife begins to prepare the family meal, she looks not up at a clock, but round the walls or upon the floor for the spot on which his golden light is streaming. The seasons are also marked by the same means; for when the sun's rays, through this aperture, reach one particular point, it is seed time.

The next night was spent further up the valley in a Kyrgyz encampment, where the hospitable and curious villagers prepared their best yurt for Wood's comfort.

Its outside covering was formed of coarse dun-coloured white belts about five feet above the ground. To these the dome or roof was secured by diagonal bands, while the felts which formed the walls were strengthened by other bands, which descended in a zig-zag direction between those first mentioned and the ground. Close to the door lay a bag filled with ice – the water of the family. On drawing aside the felt which screened the entrance, the air of tidiness and comfort that met our eyes was a most agreeable surprise. In the middle of the floor, upon a light iron tripod, stood a huge Russian cauldron, beneath which glowed a cheerful fire, which a ruddy-cheeked, spruce damsel kept feeding with fuel, and occasionally throwing a lump of ice into her cookery. She modestly beckoned us to be seated, and continued her household duties, unembarrassed by the presence of strangers. If unable to praise the men of the Kirghiz for their good looks, I may, without flattery, pronounce the young women pretty.

Arriving in Hissar, where the Pamir and Wakhan rivers join to become the Panj (Oxus), he now had to make his best guess which valley to follow to identify the main stream and source of the Oxus.

The Kirghiz had unhesitatingly told us that the object of our search was to be found in a lake upon the 'Bam-i-duniah,' or 'Roof of the World', in Pamir, and that the road to it was up the durah [narrow mountain valley] or Sir-i-Kol; but though the

northerly direction of that valley and of the countries to which it led was, when compared with the Mastuch [Mastuj], as the Chitral durah is sometimes called, almost sufficient evidence in favour of Sir-i-Kol, I thought it prudent to visit the junction of the respective waters.

Finding the temperature lower and the velocity greater in the stream coming from the north (the Pamir river), Wood decided to follow it. At this point the officer in Murad Beg's service announced that he would go no further and Wood could not persuade enough of the local Wakhis to accompany him up the Pamir river. In desperation he turned to the hospitable Kyrgyz with whom he had spent the previous night, and was rewarded by the arrival the next day of a party of men with five horses.

The first night was spent in a howling wind at a temperature lower than could be recorded on Wood's thermometer (it must have been at least -20°C) and the only respite came from the tea that the Kyrgyz managed to prepare.

> … before long the tea cup had gone its rounds, infusing a warmth into our frames, and a glow into our hearts, that made us, I dare say, happier than many a party who were at that moment quaffing their claret, and surrounded with all the luxuries of civilised life.

Three men had suffered so much from the cold in the night that they had to be sent back down the valley. Some of the Kyrgyz defected over the next two days, leaving only five in the party. They had been following an existing track in the snow, but from now on, as Wood remarks ironically, "we had no occasion to remark the absence of snow," and at one point it took them two hours to cover five hundred yards. They could only make progress on the frozen surface of the river. Finally,

> at five o'clock in the afternoon of the 19th of February, 1838, we stood, to use a native expression, upon the Bam-i-Duniah, or 'Roof of the World,' while before us stretched a noble but frozen sheet of water, from whose western end emerged the infant river of the Oxus.

Contrary to the legend that persists in some histories, Wood did not actually name the lake 'Victoria'.

> As I had the good fortune to be the first European who in later times had succeeded in reaching the source of this river, and as, shortly before setting out on my journey, we had received the news of her gracious Majesty's accession to the throne, I was much tempted to apply the name of Victoria to this, if I may so term it, newly re-

Inside a traditional Kyrgyz felt yurt, Jalang Valley

discovered lake; but on considering that by thus introducing a new name, however honoured, into our maps, great confusion in geography might arise, I deemed it better to retain the name of Sir-i-kol, the appellation given to it by our guides.[11]

If, as suggested in an earlier chapter, Marco Polo did not actually visit the Great Pamir, then Wood is too modest: he was indeed the first non-indigenous visitor to the famous lake.

His first reflection on his achievement was typical of the man.

> How strange and how interesting a group would be formed if an individual from each nation whose rivers have their first source in the Pamir were to meet upon its summit; what varieties would there be in person, language and manners; what contrasts between the rough, untamed, and fierce mountaineer and the more civilized and effeminate dweller upon the plain …

Since he was clearly talking about the native population, these views are indeed far ahead of his time.

That Wood's identification of Zorkul as the source of the Oxus was later refuted by Curzon and others and that the Pamirs are not actually the source of the four great rivers of antiquity, does nothing to diminish the extraordinary achievement of his journey: no European followed in his footsteps for another thirty-two years.

The Pundits

Travel in Central Asia had always been dangerous and with the exception of Russian merchants, only a few other Europeans had ventured there since Marco Polo. This small and somewhat improbable group included: an Embassy to Tamerlane from the Spanish court in 1403–1406, led by Ruy Gonzalez de Clavijo[12]; a Turkish Admiral of the Egyptian fleet, Sidi Ali Reis (also known as Katib-i-Rumi), in 1553–56[13]; an intrepid English trader, Anthony Jenkinson, who got as far as Bukhara in 1558[14]; and several Jesuit missionaries in the 17th and early 18th centuries who travelled to Tibet, including Benedict Goës, whom we have already met.[15]

In the 19th century, with the exception of Wood's remarkable journey, there was much to discourage the European adventurer. William Moorcroft, the army veterinary doctor and horse purchaser, had died near Bukhara in 1825 under what were thought at the time to have been suspicious circumstances (the cause was determined later to have been a fever); Adolph Schlagintweit, the German explorer and scientist, had been put to death as a spy in Kashgar in 1857[16]; and George Hayward had been murdered in Gilgit in 1870 on his attempt to reach the upper Oxus and explore the Pamirs – a crime that generated outrage in the British press and a famous poem by Henry Newbolt (1862–1938).

He Fell Among Thieves

'Ye have robb'd,' said he, 'ye have slaughter'd and made end,
Take your ill-got plunder, and bury the dead:
What will ye more of your guest and sometime friend?'
'Blood for our blood,' they said.

He laugh'd: 'If one may settle the score for five,
I am ready; but let the reckoning stand till day:
I have loved the sunlight as dearly as any alive.'
'You shall die at dawn,' said they.

He flung his empty revolver down the slope,
He climb'd alone to the Eastward edge of the trees;
All night long in a dream untroubled of hope
He brooded, clasping his knees.

He did not hear the monotonous roar that fills
The ravine where the Yassîn river sullenly flows;
He did not see the starlight on the Laspur hills,
Or the far Afghan snows.

He saw the April noon on his books aglow,
The wistaria trailing in at the window wide;
He heard his father's voice from the terrace below
Calling him down to ride.

He saw the gray little church across the park,
The mounds that hid the loved and honour'd dead;
The Norman arch, the chancel softly dark,
The brasses black and red.

He saw the School Close, sunny and green,

The runner beside him, the stand by the parapet wall,
The distant tape, and the crowd roaring between,
His own name over all.

He saw the dark wainscot and timber'd roof,
The long tables, and the faces merry and keen;
The College Eight and their trainer dining aloof,
The Dons on the daïs serene.

He watch'd the liner's stem ploughing the foam,
He felt her trembling speed and the thrash of her screw;
He heard the passengers' voices talking of home,
He saw the flag she flew.

And now it was dawn. He rose strong on his feet,
And strode to his ruin'd camp below the wood;
He drank the breath of the morning cool and sweet:
His murderers round him stood.

Light on the Laspur hills was broadening fast,
The blood-red snow-peaks chill'd to a dazzling white;
He turn'd, and saw the golden circle at last,
Cut by the Eastern height.

'O glorious Life, Who dwellest in earth and sun,
I have lived, I praise and adore Thee.'
A sword swept.
Over the pass the voices one by one
Faded, and the hill slept.

The self-proclaimed 'civilising mission' of the Europeans was – at least at the outset – not much appreciated by the local population and, in the general absence of law and order, travellers were fair game for bandits. Even the French explorer Bonvalot, at the end of the century, was reduced to banditry in the Wakhan for survival. In addition, the British government discouraged travel in frontier areas of India where it was as yet unable to take retaliatory action against the local perpetrators of crimes against its citizens. At the same time, however, the authorities wanted to extend their knowledge of the adjacent territories – and assess the risks of invasion – by undertaking geographical surveys.

The 'Great Trigonometrical Survey' (GTS) of India was begun early in the 19th century and concluded in 1883, when the triangulation of most of the sub-continent had been completed. Already in 1774, a native officer had collected data on the territory between Bengal and the Deccan and, in 1812, the ill-fated Moorcroft was using Indians to measure distance through use of a measured pace.[17] By the 1830s – despite some official disapproval of the use of natives for such skilled work – Indians were being employed for surveying. One, Mahommed Ali, travelled with Alexander Burnes to Bukhara in 1832.

As British distrust of Russian intentions grew, so did the need for more accurate information about those same frontier areas that were dangerous for Europeans to enter. In November 1852, Thomas George Montgomerie was appointed to the GTS, and, in 1856, was put in charge of the Kashmir surveys. Under his leadership, there came into being a new class of native Indian surveyors, the "Pundits", immortalised in Rudyard Kipling's *Kim*. The failure of two British expeditions to Tibet in 1861 and 1862 overcame official scepticism and Montgomerie's proposals for training Indian surveyors were approved in 1863.

Langar, junction of Pamir and Wakhan rivers

In 1871, the President of the Royal Society, Sir Henry Rawlinson, described the thinking on the issue:

> It was quite impossible to employ European surveyors to explore these countries, though one – Mr. Johnson – had successfully gone to Ilchi and come back, to the astonishment of everybody, with his head upon his shoulders. The difficulties were so great that even the Pundits of the survey could only go into a Buddhist country, while for Mahommedan countries it was necessary to employ Mahommedans, generally Pathans.[18]

In 1863, Montgomerie

> at length succeeded in finding an intelligent Moonshee[19], named Mahomed-i-Hameed [also known as Abdul Hamid], willing to run the risk of carrying instruments to Yarkund, in Eastern Turkestan, to fix its position, besides surveying the route thither from the trigonometrical station in Ladakh. He was trained by Captain Montgomerie to take observations for latitude with a small sextant, to record the temperature of the air, and of boiling water, and to make a rough skeleton route-survey from point to point.[20]

For this purpose, he practised the "measured step" and was given a specially made set of 100 – as opposed the normal 108 – prayer beads, every tenth one of which was larger than the others. By counting one bead for 100 paces, with each larger bead corresponding to 1,000, he could thus keep a mental note of the distances covered. He had, in addition, a pocket sextant, compasses, thermometers and watches. Subsequent pundits were given a Tibetan prayer-wheel, the interior of which could contain, instead of prayers, written notes and observations.

Regrettably, Mahomed-i-Hameed died on his return journey in 1864, but his papers were recovered and a detailed report was prepared by Montgomerie and submitted to the Royal Geographical Society (RGS). When the Society met in May 1866 to hear the report of the Munshi's work, Sir Henry Rawlinson, the President, described it as "a magnificent feat" and commented that "if Captain Montgomerie's Moonshee had lived he would have been a very deserving object for a similar recognition" to the award of "a watch of the value of 25 guineas" made by the Society that day to another native explorer for his journey across the Pamirs in 1860.

Abdul Mejid

Abdul Mejid, the recipient of the watch, was the first native explorer to provide a written account of a journey across the Pamirs from south to north.[21] Prior to Abdul

Mejid's mission, another native, Mahomed Amin, who had served as the guide of Adolph Schlagintweit, also claimed to have direct knowledge of several routes across the Pamir, but his credibility was in doubt and he left no substantiated written record.[22]

Montgomerie reported the pundits' explorations to the RGS – often, for reasons of secrecy, without revealing their real names – and received the Society's gold medal in 1865 for his (and their) work. Abdul Mejid's mission, however, was a diplomatic one, on the instructions of the authorities in Punjab and not as part of Montgomerie's survey. It was undertaken in great secrecy and his award from the RGS neither cited him by name nor mentioned the purpose of his mission or his itinerary. The British had been trying for some time to establish friendly relations with the Khan of Kokand in the hope that he might request assistance against anticipated Russian encroachment. An envoy from Kokand had delivered a letter of goodwill from the Khan to the British authorities in Peshawar and Abdul Mejid was instructed to accompany the envoy on his return journey with presents for the Khan and with the aim of assessing the degree of Russian influence in Kokand.

Abdul Mejid was related by marriage to the Amir Dost Mohamed[23] and although the British were accordingly somewhat concerned at the possibility of intrigue, he had several advantages for his mission: his father had been a distinguished religious leader in Kabul, and his Islamic credentials were therefore impeccable; and he was actively engaged in trading and had experience of travel in difficult conditions.

He left Peshawar for Kabul on 28 September 1860 and reached Kokand via Kunduz, Badakhshan and the Pamirs on 17 December. After first following Wood's itinerary along the Wakhan ("nine difficult marches"), he struck north across the Khargush pass and travelled past Sasik Kul, Chatyr Tash, Kara Su, Murghab, Ak Baital, Kara Kul and Kyzyl Art to the Alai valley (from Sasik Kul, almost the exact route of the present Pamir Highway). This was quite a physical achievement, since his itinerary in the Pamirs to the Alai valley must have covered nearly 500 kilometres:

> From Lungur Wakhan [Langar], fourteen weary days were occupied in crossing the steppe. The marches were long, depending on uncertain supplies of grain and water, which sometimes wholly failed. Food for man and beast had to be carried with the party, for not a trace of human habitation is to be met within these inhospitable wilds.[24]

He observed the incidence of altitude sickness in his party, which was thought by the locals to be caused by a noxious wind which prevails at certain seasons called *Dummuk* and he was warned never to sleep lying down.

Mulla Khan, the ruler of Kokand, was far too canny to enter into formal relations with the British without any guarantee of support against the Russians – and the British were, of course, unwilling (and probably unable) to make any such commitments. Indeed, Abdul Mejid had strict instructions not to say or do anything that might give the impression that his mission was anything other than one of courtesy.[25] The arrival of an envoy from the British, however, "strengthened Mulla Khan materially, bringing neutral tribes to his standard", and enabled him to recover territory seized by the Bukharans.

Abdul Mejid left Kokand on 31 January 1861 and reached Peshawar on 26 June via Kulob and Kabul. Despite the historic nature of his journey, he had not been trained as a surveyor and the information he brought back was more anecdotal than scientific. He was followed by pundits who made more substantial contributions to geographical knowledge of the Pamirs.

The Mirza

In 1867 Mirza Shuja (sometimes Sudja or Sajjad), known as 'the Mirza', was sent to survey the route from Peshawar to Badakhshan through Chitral, the shortest way to the Pamirs, and the upper Oxus route to Kashgar and Yarkand; it was also intended that he should travel from there to Kokand, but he was unable to fulfil this part of his mission.[26] Although he left Peshawar in the autumn, early snow prevented him from taking the Chitral route and, after four unsuccessful attempts to cross the Hindu Kush, he was forced to travel via Kandahar and Kabul, where he arrived at the end of June 1868. Further delayed by unrest in Kabul, he was only able to start for Badakhshan in October.

He left Faizabad, the capital of Badakhshan, on 24 December 1868, reached Ishkashim, where the Panj (Oxus) makes a right-angle turn north, in the first week of January 1869, and continued east up the Wakhan to Kala-i Panj and "twelve miserable days" from there through the Little Pamir to Tashkurgan, noting that the inhabitants of the Wakhan, then as now, are Ismailis. His party also suffered from altitude sickness and he suggests a remedy that is valid for today's travellers in the Pamirs:

View of the Wakhan Valley with Afghanistan in the background

Some of the men became nearly insensible, but soon got over it when they had eaten a little dried fruit and sugar, which the Mirza served out as soon as he saw the state of affairs.[27]

Stopping near Chakmaktynkul in the Little Pamir, the Mirza commented, in words curiously reminiscent of the Taoist legend (see page 271) that the scene "was the most desolate he ever saw – not a sign of man, beast or bird, the whole country being covered with a mantle of snow." In Sarikol, he noted that the Tajiks had been driven from the region by the Atalik Ghazi, Yakub Khan, because of their presumed allegiance to his predecessor, and their place taken by Kyrgyz "who seemed to like the change", probably because the climate was better than on the steppe.

Although he did not cross the Pamir steppe, the Mirza brought back the first detailed reports, including a route survey, of the area to the south (Ishkashim, Sarikol and Taghdumbash) through which he travelled, corroborating the data collected earlier by Wood.[28] The following year, T. Douglas Forsyth, Robert Shaw, George Hayward and the pundits in their mission provided further information on the route through Tashkurgan to Kashgar.

Faiz Buksh

Faiz Buksh (sometimes Baksh, also known as Ghulam Rabbani) was assigned to the 1870 Forsyth mission to Yarkand.[29] He had already travelled extensively in Central Asia and had been in Badakhshan in 1867, although apparently he was not trained as a surveyor until just before the mission. On his way to join it, he undertook surveys in Badakhshan, the Wakhan and Sarikol and described the two alternative routes (Little Pamir and Great Pamir) from the Wakhan to Aktash and Tashkurgan. Taking the latter route, he passed Zorkul and noted that the whole area from the Wakhan to Sarikol was uninhabited, although the evidence of place names and graveyards indicated that the Kyrgyz were once there in significant numbers.

He gave a detailed account of altitude sickness, and noted that it was called 'tunk' by the people of Badakhshan, and 'ais' by the Turkic speakers.

> The liver and stomach become irritated. The travellers get headache and blood flows from the nose. In the face of men of weak constitutions, the face as well as the hands and feet become swollen. The greater the cold, the more marked are those affections. The people of Badakhshan and Wakhan use acid, dry apricots, and plums to check those affections. At night, if the head of a man should not be two feet higher than the ground inclining towards his feet, respiration is checked in sleep.

The Havildar

Hyder Shah, known by his code name 'the Havildar' was sent on two surveying missions to the Pamirs, to complete the unexplored part of the Mirza's planned route, namely the approach to the Pamirs through Chitral, and to continue further down the Oxus and explore the territory to the east and north of the river. In order to have the time and freedom to make his observations, the Havildar was to pretend to be illiterate and poorly educated, and a corporal from the Indian Sappers was to behave as though he were the head of the caravan.

Leaving Peshawar in August 1870, earlier in the year than the Mirza, the Havildar reached Chitral on 31 August, where, on 4 September, he had a "very remarkable interview" with Mir Wali, the headman of Yasin (west of Gilgit, close to the Darkot pass) who was responsible for the murder of George Hayward. Mir Wali gave the Havildar the following account:

> I was in no way inclined to quarrel with Hayward sahib, for I had seen him on a former occasion while he was travelling through our country, when we interchanged civilities and presents, and parted good friends; but on this latter occasion of his travelling through the country he was forcibly pressing coolies and other people to carry his baggage from stage to stage on his way to Badakhshan, besides taking supplies of food for his followers from the villagers by force, and several complaints from the zemindars [local leaders and tax collectors] reached me to this effect. On Hayward sahib coming up to the village where I was, I remonstrated with him and advised him not to act as he was acting towards the people, whereupon the sahib turned round on me and abused me, telling me that this country did not belong to us, but to the English, and altogether his attitude on the occasion was very violent, so much so that I feared his using personal violence to myself, and in consequence I kept quiet. The sahib encamped for that night near the place I was, but, towards morning, I sent some sixty men to a place a little distance ahead, called Oshgoom, with orders to wait in ambush for the sahib and his party, and on their way thence to fall upon them and kill them – which they did, killing Hayward sahib and seven of his servants.[30]

The Havildar further notes that the people of Chitral were convinced that Hayward was murdered on the orders of Aman-ul-Mulk, the chief of Chitral. Although obviously self-serving, Mir Wali's explanations, if taken at face value, while not in any way excusing the crime, put it in a very different light from that of

Newbolt's poem quoted above, which contrasts English 'heroism' with native 'barbarism'.

The Havildar reached Badakhshan but was unable to continue to the Oxus. In 1869, the Amir of Afghanistan, Sher Ali, had deposed the Mir of Badakhshan, Jehander Shah, an ally of the future Amir of Afghanistan, Abdul Rahman, then in Bukhara under the protection of Russia. The new Mir, Mahmood Shah, had forbidden travellers to go beyond Faizabad in order to prevent communication between Abdul Rahman and his supporters in Kabul. Mahmood Shah was not popular and the Havildar noted that that his predecessor had maintained the independence of Badakhshan and had not paid tribute to Kabul – a fact of some significance for later disputes about whether Badakhshan recognised the suzerainty of the Amir of Afghanistan or was an independent territory.

The Havildar was obliged to return and reached Peshawar on 13 December, bringing with him, however, a survey of a hitherto unmapped route covering 286 miles through Chitral, accounting for "the geography of about 13,000 square miles of this *terra incognita.*" There were now "but two gaps – the first between Chitral and the Mirza's bearing from the edge of the Pamir steppe … ; and the 2nd gap between Chitral and Chigur Serai [Asadabad, Kunar province, Afghanistan] …".[31]

Despite doubts about his honesty and accuracy arising from a mission he claimed to have made through Balkh to Bukhara shortly after his return, Montgomerie sent the Havildar on another survey to the Pamirs in 1873.[32] After reaching Faizabad in November, he delayed the start of his survey of the Oxus north of Ishkashim until April of the following year, claiming plausibly that the roads to the Oxus were blocked by snow (although Trotter, Montgomerie's successor, was sceptical about this excuse). He crossed the Oxus at Samti (due south of the town of Kulob), followed the Yakhsu river north and crossed the mountains to enter Darvaz at Saghirdasht. He reached the Oxus again at Kala-i Khum in July and was able to survey upstream as far as the entrance to the Yazgulem valley, before being turned back by the local authorities.[33]

In Darvaz, he noted that the women go about unveiled and that the inhabitants,

> Sunni Mahomedans, are religious, and very regular in their devotions. They are a quiet hospitable race. They are, most of them, able to read and recite the Koran, and there are a great many Mullahs or religious instructors.

The Mirza had already provided detailed survey information from Ishkashim up to Lake Zorkul and the Havildar had been instructed to fill the gap downstream

between Ishkashim and Yazgulem, the point where he had been forced to turn back. He determined to make one more attempt to visit Shughnan, this time by returning to Faizabad and travelling from there to Ishkashim. Although he reached Ishkashim in mid-October 1874 without incident, he was able to survey only thirty-five miles downstream before he was stopped and turned back by the guards of the King of Shughnan. There were civil disturbances on the Badakhshan side and the King, probably fearing for the stability of his own territory, allowed no one to enter Shughnan without a letter from the Governor of Turkestan. Giving up in despair, the Havildar returned to Kabul via Kulob and Balkh.

Unknown to him, however, another pundit had arrived in Ishkashim in April on the exact day when he had crossed from Samti to the right bank of the Oxus en route for Kala-i Khum; this pundit had already almost completed a survey of the unexplored 'gap' downstream.

Yakhsu valley, Childukhtaron in background

The Munshi

In 1873, the Superintendent of the GTS, Colonel Walker, learned by chance that Forsyth was planning a second mission to Kashgar, and suggested that Trotter (who had just succeeded Montgomerie as head of the Kashmir survey) should join it. Abdul Subhan, known as 'the Munshi', a pundit in the Gwalior survey team, was attached to the mission as Trotter's assistant. Recognising his abilities, Trotter detached him at several points on the mission to undertake independent surveys.

On 21 March 1874, on the return journey from Kashgar, Forsyth sent a team from Yangi Hissar to undertake exploration of the Pamirs.[34] This team, under the leadership of Colonel T.E. Gordon, included, in addition to Trotter, Captain John Biddulph, Dr. Ferdinand Stoliczka, the Munshi and Kishen Singh, another pundit. At Kala-i Panj – the name of which, according to Trotter, comes from the presence of a stone there bearing the imprint of the hand ("panjah") of Hazrat Ali, sacred to the Ismailis – they learned that the Afghan Amir had refused them permission to continue down the Wakhan to Badakhshan and Kabul. The Munshi was instructed to continue alone to Ishkashim and to survey the Oxus down river from there. With the exception of Biddulph, who continued to explore the Little Pamir up to the Baroghil Pass, the rest of the team headed for Lake Zorkul and the Great Pamir. Biddulph rejoined the team in Aktash.[35] Trotter was able to determine definitively, with the help of the observations of Kishen Singh who made a detour to the lake on the return journey to Zorkul, that the Little Pamir lake (Chakmaktynkul) flows east into the Aksu and is not a (or the) source of the Oxus.

Trotter equipped the Munshi with the usual instruments and impressed on him the special importance of getting a survey – "however rough" – of the Oxus below Ishkashim.[36] The Munshi set off on 29 April, and made a first stop in Khandut, on the left bank, where he noticed, on the other side of the river,

> a fort called 'Maichun' [Yamchun], which I visited. Facing the river are stone walls rising successively one above the other, there being a distance of about 200 paces between each pair of walls. These were made of rough stone and lime. A stone road still in preservation leads to the upper fort from the bank of the river. The lower wall was entirely in ruins, but all the others are in good preservation. Within the fort is a large piece of level ground about 75 paces wide by 150 long, and oval-shaped, originally containing houses of which no vestige remains. … I made enquiries and was told that this fort belonged to the *Zardushtis* or *Atash-parast* (fire-worshippers)

or *Parsees* (Farsi) who were said to have ruled the country eight hundred years previously. There exist two other sets of remains of their people. One is a zanguebar or temple near Hissar, and the other at Kahkaha in the Sad Ishtrak …. the residence of the ruler of the Zardushtis, and bears signs of having been better built than the other remains I saw. It consisted of a single stone building of stone and lime, and is close to the river on its right bank.[37]

The ruins of several other spectacularly located forts that were not noted by the Munshi can still be seen in the Wakhan today.

In Gharan, downstream from Ishkashim, where the famous ruby (spinel) mines are located, the Munshi noted that several villages were deserted and that most inhabitants had migrated to escape the oppression of successive Governors of Badakhshan. The mines were still a substantial source of income for the Mir of Badakhshan and people were panning for gold in the Garm Chashma stream that joins the Oxus at Anderob.

A little way north from there the path went along a precipice and then into the State of Shughnan through a narrow tunnel supposedly built 300 years previously, called Kuguz Parin, that the Shughnis described as the most effective safeguard of their territory. He estimated that the chief town, Kala-i Bar Panj – the name of which is also related to the presence of a stone similar to that at Kala-i Panj – had some 1500 houses and that Shughnan was sometimes called 'Zuján', or two-lived, because the climate was reputedly so good that people had two lives. The Munshi reported that the road to Kashgar up the Ghunt valley "is said to be a much easier road than that by Tashkurgan."[38]

The Munshi reached Vomar on 11 May. He was received cordially by the King of Shughnan, who was on a visit there, at a private dinner where he was offered local wine[39], and allowed to visit the *Fatila Sang* (wick-stone) that was known to him from a book on the region[40] as one of "the two sights of Badakhshan." It was "a sort of fibrous stone which can be twisted into the shape of a wick, and when saturated with oil will burn almost forever." He also witnessed a game of polo – locally known as 'Chaugan-Bazi' – that was similar to that played in Ladakh.

The Munshi noted that the King "only keeps one wife, and no mistresses, and is very much loved by his people," adding almost as an afterthought that "the women of Shighnan are very beautiful." The King refused to sell any of his subjects as slaves or to give any as tribute to Badakhshan, paying with horses instead. He confided in

the Munshi that he was concerned about the security of his kingdom now that the Anglo-Russian frontier agreement had allocated the left bank to Afghanistan and expected no help from Kabul if he ever had conflict with his neighbours in Darvaz or Kulob.

> He thought his best policy under those circumstances would be to surrender to Kabul those few villages he possessed on the left bank of the river, and then throw himself into the arms of Russia and Bokhara, by which means he would hope to secure himself in possession of his present territories on the right bank of the river.

His ancestor, 'Shah-i-Khamosh' was reputed to have come originally from Persia some 500–700 years earlier, when he converted the people to Ismailism and conquered Kahkaha, Governor of Shughnan and Rushan, under the Zoroastrians whose seat was then in Balkh. He is interred in Kala-i Bar Panj.

Laden with presents from the king for his British employers, the Munshi prepared to return to Wakhan on 15 May without filling the gap in knowledge of the Oxus. Since his declared mission was to bring presents and letters to the King, we have to assume that he did not feel it would be appropriate to request permission to travel further downstream, as this might have raised suspicions about his real intentions.

He provided, however, much new information about the course of the river as well as confirmation that Gharan, Shughnan and Rushan extended to both sides of the river and were direct or indirect tributaries of the Mir of Badakhshan who, at that time professed allegiance to the Amir of Afghanistan – as we have seen, this was an important issue in determining the extent of Afghan territory when final borders were fixed a few years later. He was offered an opportunity to travel up the Bartang to Kashgar but concluded that his orders did not permit this. He would have liked to reach the Wakhan through the Shakhdara and Jawshangoz, but it was already too late in the year and the road was closed by snow.

The Munshi is an informative and engaging narrator, not as dry and matter-of-fact as most of his fellow pundits and it is a pity that he was unable to pursue either of these alternatives as we would otherwise have had an additional lively narrative. The combined work of the Havildar and the Munshi completed the survey of the course of the Oxus with the exception of the section between Vomar and Yazgulem, corresponding to about 70km of its course. It was not until 1881 that this gap was filled.

Yamchun fortress, Wakhan

M-S-

Mukhtar Shah – known only as M-S- in the official documents – was a holy man from Kashmir. In 1878, as he was about to start on a journey to Kulob, his friend Abdul Subhan, "the Munshi", put him in touch with the Superintendent of the GTS, James Walker (recently promoted to General) who arranged for his training as a surveyor. After spending the winter of 1878 in Yasin, Mukhtar Shah finally set off for Badakhshan in September 1879 on a journey that was to last for two and a half years and completed the mapping of the course of the Oxus.

Colonel H.C.B. Tanner, Deputy Superintendent of the GTS, who wrote up his report[41], noted that during the period of his explorations the countries along the Panj were

> a hotbed of intrigue and rebellion. Armies were on the move the whole time; battles were fought at many places; rulers were deposed and countries changed hands frequently. In those days all travellers were looked on with suspicion as being possible spies.

However, in Kulob and Darvaz

> the Tajik inhabitants had quite settled down under the rule of Bokhara, which had been established some two years prior to his visit. The rule of the king of Bokhara, though severe and strict to the last degree, was still carried out on principles that saved the newly conquered people from any great oppression, and roads that for a long time had become impassable from complete neglect were now being put into a state of repair, and traffic was to a certain degree encouraged … The country is in a prosperous condition owing to the sensible rule of the King of Bokhara, who sees wisdom in allowing the inhabitants to till the soil and take from them his share rather than depopulate the country by acts of exacting oppression, such as are now inflicted on the people of Badakhshan by the Afghans, and such as were formerly inflicted on Kolab and the adjacent countries by the tyrant king Murad Beg of Kataghan.

From Faizabad, (where, interestingly, he noted that there were schools for girls run by women) Mukhtar Shah followed the route taken by the Havildar to Kulob, and then surveyed a slightly different route to Sagridasht. Snow prevented him from travelling on the Havildar's route from there to Kala-i Khum, and he was obliged to retrace his steps, finally reaching the Panj at Zigar, today the first village in Gorno-

Badakhshan on the road from Kulob. From there he surveyed almost up to Voznavd before being turned back by Shughnan guards.

Mukhtar Shah was, however, obstinate. There now remained a gap in the survey of only about 50km upstream to Vomar, where the Munshi, coming from the opposite direction, had been unable to continue his work. Returning the way he had come, he crossed again to the left bank of the Panj and made his way across the mountains back to the Shiva lake, down to Kala-i Bar Panj and on to Vomar, where he finally completed the survey as far as Voznavd.[42]

Surprisingly, however, his survey work was not over, and a new opportunity arose.

> Having now connected my work, I returned to Barzud village on 27th September [1880]. Being known as a great physician, I was requested by a man from the Bartang valley ... to accompany him to Sarez and attend a sick person who was seriously ill.

The Bartang survey – up to Pasor and Sarez[43] – was completed on 23 October 1880 but, on his return to Kala-i Bar Panj, he fell ill and it was not until the following Spring that he could envisage returning home. The route upstream through Gharan to the Wakhan was closed because of political disturbances and, on 1 April 1881, he set off up the Shakhdara valley in the hope of reaching the Wakhan by this route, allowing him to make another unplanned survey.

He reached Jawshangoz a few days later, but the road beyond was blocked by snow and he was forced, yet again, to retrace his steps back to Kala-i Bar Panj. He confirmed, however, that "a road leads southward to the Panjah fort in Wakhan ... [the Mats pass], and another eastward to Sar-i-Kul ... [over the Koitezek pass to Murghab and Rangkul – or to Khargush and the Great Pamir]." He also reported that the castle at Jawshangoz "was once, according to my guide, a very flourishing town and the capital of Shakh Dara when Wakhan is said to have been subject to it." Finally, on 23 April, he was allowed to leave Kala-i Bar Panj and reached Gilgit on 8 July.

Mukhtar Shah provided not only the missing information on the Panj, but, by good fortune, surveys of the Bartang and Shakhdara valleys as well. The former confirmed Trotter's conclusion – based on local anecdotal evidence – that the Aksu, originating in the Chakmaktyn Lake in the Little Pamir became later in its course the Murghab and Bartang rivers, and was thus "the longest branch of the Oxus".[44]

The pundits did their work conscientiously under dangerous and difficult circumstances. While they certainly added to the sum of scientific knowledge of the Pamirs in the short period during which they were active, it may legitimately be asked whether this contribution was worth the physical and political risks involved. The pundits received very little for their labours, several of them fell seriously ill as a result of the hardships suffered and a few died. Saluting the achievement of the pundit Chandra Das, who provided the first surveys of Tibet, the American explorer and diplomat William Woodville Rockhill (1854–1914) commented that, had he been a European, "medals and decorations, lucrative offices and professional promotion, freedom of the cities and every form of lionisation would have been his; but as for these native explorers a small pecuniary reward and obscurity are all to which they can look forward."[45]

While the Anglo-Russian frontier understanding of 1873 was certainly facilitated by the existence of the pundits' surveys, both sides wanted an agreement and, despite the work of the first pundits, there was still considerable uncertainty at that time – not to say confusion – about the key strategic area of the upper Wakhan and the source and course of the Oxus. The pundits revealed nothing about Russian intentions nor about the feasibility of Russian incursions into British India and, within a few years, their work was superseded by the results of scientific explorations by British, Russian and other missions. The reports by the pundits are, for the most part dry catalogues of what they saw; while they provide some interesting historical and political information, they give little feeling for the adventure of travel in uncharted territory and spectacular natural scenery.

Their masters were aware of this and sometimes complained about the lack of imagination of the 'natives'. In his summary of Mukhtar Shah's travels, for example, Colonel Tanner, gave full vent to his frustration.

M-S- says that there are lions also, and *babars*, an indefinite animal always played by the Asiatic on the European, and which is intended to represent a kind of condensed epitome of all

Marco Polo horns

unknown members of the cat tribe. The pacing of M-S- is not always strictly accurate; his historical facts can often be questioned: but his ignorance of the animal kingdom is beyond belief. To him there are *hiran*, which include all kinds of antelope, deer, stags, and the like; *shers* and *babars*,[46] by which he means tigers, lions, panthers and wild-cats. The mountain-goat, '*buz kohi*', comprises every other wild animal that exists on the face of the globe which is '*halal*' or eaten by Muhammadans. His ignorance of the vegetable kingdom is equally profound. I can only get out of him: 1. 'The black tree of Kashmir'; 2. 'The *safeda*', or poplar; 3. 'Thorns' or *khar*. The latter means ordinary vegetation, of whatever kind or sort, and which is beneath notice altogether. ...

Most natives ... pass by the mightiest works of nature without lifting up their eyes to regard them, even for a moment. Our explorers have now traversed Upper Chitral, Yasin and the Oxus valley in many directions, and not one of them has ever given a hint of the existence of the immense mountain chains that wall in nearly every valley between Gilgit and Badakhshan. Not one of them has mentioned the lofty Tirach Mir or any of its huge snow-clad companions. The 'Havildar' gives a vivid description of his miseries when crossing the Nuksan

Aksu river with Aktash

pass and tells how he fell about amongst the blocks of ice at its base; but there is no mention of the peak of the great mountain between 25 and 26 thousand feet high that rears up its summit almost over head, and which actually gives origin to the ice masses over which he had to scramble and to the crevasses which he had to avoid. The 'Mullah,' who surveyed along the Kho and Mastauj valleys, makes no mention of the great expanse of snow which covers the lofty heights of the Tirach Mir, situated only a few miles distant, which, as Major Biddulph writes, 'fills the entire view'. The Mullah, the Havildar, Abdul Subhan, and lastly M-S-, who one after the other travelled along the valley of the Oxus, made no mention of the immense snow needles which rise up south of Zebak and Ishkashim, and which many centuries previously had attracted the attention of the Chinese explorers when passing down that way. A native cannot give the slightest description of any country, however well he may be acquainted with it. Into trivial particulars he will minutely enter, and while he will tell you how at such and such a camp, which was 267 yards from the stream, there were only three mulberry trees, and one of them was broken off at the top, the great works of nature take no hold on his imagination, or if they do, the recollection of them is quickly effaced from memory.[47]

While this is unfair – not to say racist – given the bravery and devotion to duty of these early explorers, we turn nevertheless with some relief to the more colourful accounts of the European explorers.

In 1870, at the end of his report, Faiz Buksh noted that

During the period of the mission to Yarkand, a European traveller, who possessed maps, instruments and medicines, and professed himself to be a Greek, and called himself Peters or Petros, arrived at Kashgar, having travelled from Kabul through Kunduz, Badakhshan, Wakhan, Pamir and Yang Hisar.

His name was actually Potagos and if it was odd that Wood, the first European in the Pamirs since Marco Polo, an Italian merchant, and Benedict Goës, a Portuguese Jesuit, should have been a naval officer, it was perhaps even odder that the next should have been a Greek doctor.

Papagiotis Potagos

In July 1866, a young doctor returned from Paris, where he had just finished his medical studies, to his home in the Peloponnese. He found the political situation unstable and his own family and friends divided by violent political disputes. The ill-fated struggle in Crete for independence from the Ottoman empire was under way and there was much pressure on young Greeks to join the insurrection. Cynical about the likelihood that the European powers would support the Cretans, Papagiotis Potagos felt that this was a lost cause.

> I decided therefore to travel with a view to promoting the progress of science, saying to myself that if I came back safe and sound, I would have been useful to my country and that, if I did not, at least I would have died with honour.[48]

As we shall see, he did indeed come back safe and sound, still echoing the self-importance of this statement, but his contribution to science was more than a little questionable.

In October 1867, he set off from the Peloponnese for Central Asia "with the aim of verifying the information given by the classical geographers about the location of these regions." Travelling through Syria and Persia, he reached Kabul in May 1870, where, if we are to believe his narrative, he was received like a brother by the Amir, Sher Ali. The Amir was concerned about Potagos' safety on the route he was planning to take to Badakhshan and Kashgar and gave him a letter of recommendation to the ruler of Badakhshan, suggesting he should disguise himself as a Persian, since he was likely to be taken for a Russian or Englishman and killed. Potagos replied that he would "rather die a Greek than to even think of taking another nationality" but compromised by disguising himself as a Greek priest. It is a pity there are no illustrations in his book as his improvised costume was, to say the least, colourful – and certainly not designed to pass unnoticed.

> I chose Bukhara silk for my cassock, green with yellow stripes as if of gold, and for my jacket a good English broadcloth, that I also used for the hood; I chose a magnificently embroidered Kashmir scarf as a belt, with the embroidery hanging down at the left; my overcoat was of fine camel hair from Turkmenia.

On 16 June he reached Faizabad, where, according to his account, he was warmly received by the Amir of Badakhshan, Mahmoud Shah. From here, unfortunately, his account of his travel up the Wakhan through Kala-i Panj, Sarhad and Tashkurgan to

Kashgar is a muddle of reminiscences combining high cliffs, difficult river crossings, unfriendly natives and ill-defined lakes.

Potagos has a penchant for hyperbole and melodrama and often stretches the reader's credulity: for example, after going to great lengths to describe his disguise as a Greek priest for his journey to Badakhshan (see previous page), when he gets there he has suddenly changed into robes of Azeri cloth and a turban. He also asks the reader to believe that after nearly drowning during a river crossing, he was brought back to life by swallowing gold nuggets – a fairy tale hardly worthy of a medical doctor. He is invariably welcomed with honours by the local rulers, who share many confidences with him – all somewhat improbable given the information we have from the pundits of the deep suspicion with which foreigners were regarded at that time.

Like Alexander Gardner, his geography is more than a little shaky and it is not easy to put together his route with any conviction. As we have seen in the previous chapter, his presence in Kashgar was corroborated by a report from one of the pundits, and there is no reason to doubt that he did actually travel up the Wakhan. The place names he gives appear to be authentic but could very well have resulted from an attempt to piece together his itinerary from memory with the help of one of the fairly accurate contemporary maps published in later years by the Geographical Societies in London and Paris. Overall, he is more interested in tall tales than in scientific observation and we learn very little from his account, beyond a few snippets of local information and cross-references to the texts of the Greek and Roman geographers that relate to the different stages of his journey. Despite the lack of precision in his own geography, he has no hesitation in questioning whether John Wood was actually in the Pamirs and dismisses totally the possibility that Marco Polo was there. Claiming for himself the honour of being the first European to identify them, Potagos tells us that the lakes in the Little Pamir (or perhaps in the Great Pamir, depending on where he really was) should appear on the maps as Castor and Pollux, since these were the names he gave them.

In 1885, when his book had been translated into French and published, Ney Elias, one of the most serious and reliable explorers of the 19th century was in the Pamirs verifying and confirming the findings of the pundits.

Ney Elias

For the public of his day, Ney Elias (1844–1897) was as famous an explorer as Stanley and Livingstone. In 1873, when Elias received the coveted Founder's Medal of the Royal Geographical Society, Stanley received the slightly less prestigious Patron's Medal. Elias's surveys and reports on the Pamirs are still among the most reliable historical sources of information we have on the region, yet he has since, undeservedly, sunk into almost total oblivion. One of the reasons is his own modesty: unlike most of his contemporary British explorers, Elias never published a full

account of his adventures, and information on his exploits must be sought painstakingly in the Indian Archives in Delhi, the records of the India Office Library and the Royal Geographical Society in London, the few scientific papers he wrote for the RGS and other learned societies, and in the many articles written by him but published anonymously in British newspapers.

The only biography of Elias ever written[49] comments that

> Presenting a picture of the man he was, as opposed merely to describing his career, has proved singularly difficult. Elias so totally screened himself from scrutiny by revealing nothing of himself unconnected with his work that it must have been deliberate. … He was only in his early fifties when he died, leaving his work unfinished and without leaving a single personal reminiscence of thirty years of risk and adventure.

By 1885, when he visited the Pamirs, Elias had already made his scientific reputation with his survey of the new course of the Yellow River in 1867-8 and had established his credentials as a serious and determined explorer with his journey from Peking through Western Mongolia in 1872 – both of which were cited in connection with the award of the RGS Founder's Medal.[50]

These journeys were essentially private. In 1874, however, on the recommendation of Sir Henry Rawlinson, President of the RGS, Elias was appointed as 'Extra Attaché' in the Foreign Department of the government of India and, in 1877, the Viceroy, Lord Lytton, who had quickly recognised his talents, sent him to Leh (Ladakh) as 'Joint Commissioner' to watch events across the border in Kashgar, where Yakub Beg's power was waning, the Chinese were beginning to reassert their sovereignty and the British feared Russian meddling. In 1879, he was promoted by Lytton to the Political Department, a pensionable and permanent posting. Elias was now an official player in the Great Game.

As noted above, Merv capitulated to the Russians in 1882; in February 1884, the Turkoman tribes swore allegiance to the Tsar in Ashgabat; and in April 1885 the Russians created the famous border incident in Panjdeh. Russophobia was at its height in Calcutta and London, it was feared that Russia would not abide by the terms of the 1873 Pamir boundary understanding, there were rumours that Russian spies were skulking on the boundaries of the British Empire and reports of invasion plans abounded. No Briton had been in the Pamirs since Wood travelled to Zorkul in 1838, whereas the Russians had recently been highly active (see next Chapter). In 1878, a Russian expedition had travelled to Afghan Badakhshan; in 1882, a Russian botanist, Alfred Regel, had explored the Panj as far south as the ruby mines in Shughnan[51]; and, in 1883, a military expedition (comprising Putyata, Ivanov and Bendersky) completed the most extensive exploration of the Pamirs hitherto undertaken: moreover, their itinerary was public knowledge as it had been published – together with Regel's – in the Proceedings of the RGS in 1884 with the explicit support of the Imperial Russian Geographical Society.

The first British response to this revived Russian activism was, as we have seen, to agree to the formation of a Boundary Commission that began its work on the lower Oxus in November 1885. The Viceroy also saw that there was a need for closer observation of the Russians than was possible from Ladakh and approved a major reconnaissance mission to Kashgar and the Pamirs, including the territories along the upper Oxus. Elias had been on sick leave in Britain but returned to India just in time to be put in charge. The mission was, of course, secret, and Elias published no account of his adventures in the Pamirs: information must be sought in the confidential report submitted to his superiors on his return and in his handwritten diary.[52]

On 26 May 1885, Elias officially received in Simla the documents confirming his appointment and noted in his diary: "Thus mission begins today." He reached Leh six weeks later and, anxious to reach the Pamirs before the onset of winter, spent

a frustrating month waiting for his passport from Peking and, not least, his final instructions. Inexplicably, the former did not grant him official status as a representative of the British government in India; his instructions, however, gave him – in addition to the authority to conduct negotiations in Kashgar on trade, political and consular issues – what he probably wanted most, a mandate to "explore the Afghan districts of the Upper Oxus" and attempt to determine the extent of Afghan sovereignty there, as well as the boundaries of territory claimed by China and Russia.

Leaving Leh on 15 August, he arrived in Yarkand a month later. Only a few days there were enough to tell him that any hopes of establishing a British representation in Kashgar and improving trade were unrealistic. The Chinese had accepted a Russian consulate in Kashgar and – prompted almost certainly by the Russian Consul, Petrovsky – were unwilling to accept any other diplomatic representation there or to facilitate British or Indian trade. The Pamir winter would soon set in and Elias decided to set out on the second part of his mission immediately.

Leaving Yarkand on 28 September, he travelled down the Tashkurgan river to the little Kara Kul, where he observed, as the first European since the time of Marco Polo, that where there had previously been thought to be a single high peak,

Shakhdara, Dasht village completely destroyed after landslide

Tagharma, there were in fact two: today known as Kongur (7,719 m) and Mustagh Ata (7,546 m).

He reached Rangkul on 11 October – probably over the Ak-Bhirdi and Kok Beless passes – and recruited two men "as guides to the first Shighnan villages, either on the Ghunt or Shakhdara route, whichever I please." He would certainly have preferred to follow the Aksu/Murghab/Bartang river as far as the junction with the Oxus/Panj but had been informed that "a loaded pony can go no further down the stream than Sarez and that the main route from Rang Kul lies past Ak Baital, across the Murghabi to Nezatash or Chadir Tash, then past Yashil Kul and down the Ghunt."

On 14 October, Elias left Rangkul and reached a caravanserai at Bash Gumbez on the 17th where Elias noted that "up this ravine there lies a pass into the Great Pamir – I went up the ravine for some distance over some of the spurs (after *Ovis Poli*) and could see the pass." His route then took him past Sasik Kul and Tuz Kul to Yashil Kul and he remarked that the map of the Russian 1883 expedition "appears to be very accurate." Continuing down the Ghunt to Sardem – then the highest inhabited village in Shughnan, "two or three miserable huts and a few scratchy fields of barley" – Charthem, Wer and "the Shakhdara confluence at Kharok. ... a long and well cultivated village, with good orchards etc.; by far the best village we have seen," he reached the Afghan fort at Kala-i Bar Panj on the left bank of the Panj on 29 October.

On his way down the Ghunt, Elias saw several deserted villages and, where there were inhabitants, they were "poverty-stricken, half-clad wretches living in as many dilapidated huts ... which at a glance told a tale of tyranny and bad government." Shughnan was "a broken people and a half-ruined country." In Ishkashim "the inhabitants look even more miserable than in Shughnan."

Although "wretched inhabitants in a well-favoured country means bad government," Elias did not attribute the misery of the local population to Afghan oppression but to the slave trade carried on by the local Shughni Mirs; frequent raids had been undertaken among the Kyrgyz and in the upper Ghunt, in Khuf near Vomar and in the first villages in the Bartang valley. According to Elias, the Afghans had ordered the abolition of the slave trade, although he heard that "secretly some buying and selling of domestic slaves – probably women mostly – still goes on."[53] At the time, several families, who had run away from their homes to escape the slave-dealing activities of the previous Shughni ruler, Yusuf Ali, were reported to be returning from Kokand and Elias notes that "this tells a tale in favour of Afghan rule." Of the

Afghans, he wrote that they were "a rough and ready set of wild Irishmen but somehow I take to them more than to the sneaky Chinese and Kashmiris."

As we shall see, the Russians saw the situation in a different light. From their accounts – of which the first was from Dmitri Lvovich Ivanov, who visited Sarez in 1883 – it would appear that the local population was seeking relief from Afghan oppression and slave raids. That the Russians would emphasise this was, of course, in part self-serving, but perhaps even Elias was telling his government what they wanted to hear, for, in his diary, he admitted that

> These provinces are inhabited by people who have little or nothing in common with the Afghans and who hate them with the kinds of hatred which taken together make up the most intense form of enmity. … the people are not only disaffected as regards the Afghans; it is not only that they have hankerings after their former Mirs, but in the chief provinces of Badakhshan they have distinct leanings towards the Russians. … It might be asked whether English influence could effect nothing towards creating a better feeling and bringing the Badakhshi population to a more loyal frame of mind towards their rulers and our allies. My impression is that little or nothing could be done short of direct interference with Afghan rule, promises of protection against Russian invasion backed by the presence of a British force on the frontier of the country as a visible guarantee that we intended to carry out our engagements in these respects.

After a very short stay in Kala-i Bar Panj, under the watchful but friendly eye of the Hakim of the Ghunt valley, Gulzar Khan, an Afghan from Kandahar, Elias set off to survey the Bartang valley, arriving in the first village, Shujand, on 5 November and continuing as far as Savnob at the confluence of the Murghab and Ghudara rivers. His aims were to determine

> (1) whether its stream might prove to be of greater volume than the Panjah, and, therefore, the main feeder of the Oxus, as reported (I believe) by one of the native explorers, and (2) how far certain passes leading over from the Darvaz valley of Yaz Gulam might be considered practicable roads into Roshan.

On the first issue,

> From the inspections of the confluence of the Panj and Bartang which I was able to make on the upward and the return journeys, from careful enquiries made from the people of Wamar regarding the fluctuations of the two rivers, during the course of the year, and from estimates made by fording both (on horseback) at short

distances above the confluence, I was able to satisfy myself that the Panjah is a very much more voluminous stream than the Murghabi.

He identified six passes from the Yazgulem valley into the Bartang:

"(1) Behind the village of Yemts. Footpath closed from about October to July.

(2) Behind Bhagu. Footpath closed from about October to July.

(3) Behind Sipunj. Footpath closed from about October to July.

(4) Baju ravine, between Sipunj and Darjomj. Footpath closed from about October to July.

(5) Behind Upper Bijravd village. Practicable for led ponies for two months of most favourable season, by crossing a snow top, closed even for men on foot early in November 1885.

(6) Behind Rah Sharv, a pass called 'Khurjin'. Practicable for led ponies for two months of most favourable season by crossing a snow top, closed even for men on foot early in November 1885."

and concluded that

not one of them can be a source of danger to the Afghan provinces, as affording a road to an invader. All of them were closed by the autumn snow at the time of my visit, so that I was unable actually to examine any of them, but from what I could

Man with donkey, Vanch

see, from a distance, and learn from the inhabitants in their neighbourhood, I do not think the above opinion is likely to prove incorrect. It will be seen ... that none of them are practicable for baggage at any time of the year; only two of them are passable for led ponies during the period of highest snow line (say part July, August and September), and the rest can be used only by men on foot during the two or three most favourable months in the year. Moreover, as regards the four upper passes, the road along the Murghabi valley is so bad that supposing an enemy to have crossed from Yaz Gulam during the summer, it would only be necessary to destroy the ladders of twigs and basket-work which form the "road" along the face of the cliffs, at some places, to prevent him from descending the valley. And further, there is a spot – a "rafak" or spur – below the lowest pass, and only some six miles from Wamar, where the exit from the valley could be defended by a mere handful of men at the high-water season. Lastly, there are no fords during the season that these passes are open, so that, supposing one of them to have been crossed, boats or rafts would be necessary in descending the valley, for the only practicable track crosses and re-crosses the river at intervals of every few miles, from about six miles above Wamar, upwards.

Like his fellow-countryman, Ralph Cobbold, a few years later, he found the 'road' hair-raising.[54]

"Road along the face of the cliffs" – Ovring between Vanch and Yazgulem on the Afghan side

The "road," as it is called by the natives – whether by way of pleasantry or for want of a more expressive word, I know not – is quite impracticable for baggage animals, and riding ponies can only be used at intervals, though it is possible, by leading and swimming them, in certain places, to take them up as high as the Kudara during the low-water season. At the high-water season the road must be considered closed to ponies altogether. In some places ledges of rock, slightly improved, serve as a footpath; in others, a path has been made of poles twigs, stones, & c., bound together in a very rough way, or of twig ladders suspended against the face of the cliff, by means of sticks or pegs let into holes and crevices of the rocks. They ascend, descend, or are carried along at a level, according to the facilities offered by the natural configuration of the cliff. Pathways of this kind are required in order to pass round points, or spurs, jutting out into the river, or along steep cliffs, where the water is deep up to the foot. They are called "rafak," and it is not always easy for a nervous traveller to pass over them, and to keep up a show of indifference which he does not feel. The natives of the country not only cross them as a matter of course, but carry loads over them. They, however, look to the foot-hold only, for, like other Asiatics, they have no nerves to speak of. In some places the "rafak" is to be outflanked by climbing a high and difficult pass over the ridge above; at some others a ford, always deep and always in icy cold water, is the only alternative.

Elias was back in Vomar on 15 November and went down the Panj as far as Voznavd to determine the frontier line between Darvaz and Rushan. He returned to Kala-i Bar Panj on 21 November and, after a few days' rest, set off up the Panj to Ishkashim, making a short excursion to the Shiva lake before finally leaving the Panj on 7 December. He travelled through Faizabad, Taloqan and Balkh to Maimana, where he linked up with the Boundary Commission on 24 February.

Elias was in the Pamirs for less than two months, but brought back much valuable information – gathered largely due to his exceptional ability to establish a warm relationship with the local people he encountered. It is a tribute to these qualities that people in the Bartang still remembered Elias many years later. In 1898 Ralph Cobbold was told in Savnob that

thirteen years before a white man had come from Badakhshan with an Afghan escort and paid them a visit; he had treated them liberally, asked them many questions, and they had the pleasantest recollections of him. … I subsequently ascertained that the person described was Mr. Ney Elias, and I found that throughout Roshan the people had always tales to tell of his kindness and liberality.[55]

He also gained the confidence of the Kyrgyz on the high plateau, who told him of the hardships they suffered as a result of Chinese attempts to confine them in the territory east of the Murghab and Akbaital rivers and prevent them trading with Shughnan but confided that they sent secret expeditions to buy grain.

> The strange part of this is that these people seem to have little hesitation in trusting me and my followers with these secrets on the simple premise that we will say nothing about them in Chinese territory.

From his own observations and many conversations with local people, Elias confirmed (and made a few corrections to) previous surveys and provided vital intelligence about the frontiers recognised (but unmarked) in the Pamirs, as well as offering sensible advice to the Indian government on the policies to be followed to protect British interests – as well as some personal opinions expressed in the pages of his diary.

On frontiers in general, his view was that

> In settled countries, rivers that are easily crossed form bad boundaries, but in nomadic countries one line is nearly as good as another, and, in the absence of an inaccessible range of hills, even a small stream like the Upper Murghabi would serve as an indication as well as anything else, either natural or artificial.

In the case of the Pamirs, he thought it

> most desirable to leave no strip of unowned land between Afghan and Chinese territory; any such strip would lead directly from Russian territory towards passes leading into Chitral, and might be occupied at any time by Russia or by Russian partisans.

Elias's determination that the main feeder of the Oxus was the Panj and not the Aksu/Murghab/Bartang was of considerable strategic significance in relation to the 1873 Anglo-Russian border agreement. This had stated that Afghan territory included

> Badakhshan with its dependent District of Wakhan from the Sarikul (Wood's Lake) on the east to the junction of the Kokcha river with the Oxus [on the west, the line of the Oxus] or Penjah forming the northern boundary of this Afghan province throughout its entire extent.

The words in square brackets had, however, been erroneously omitted from the version communicated to the Russians. The Kokcha joins the Amu Darya between

Afghan side of Panj, opposite Vanch valley (following pages)

Kunduz and Kulob, far to the west of the Pamirs and, without the missing words, this section of the agreement was incomprehensible. Elias was aware that the Panj was not only a "northern boundary" for Afghan Badakhshan but could be taken (once the Russians had fully comprehended the implications of their new maps) as an eastern one as well, and that taking the Panj (and not the Aksu/Murghab/Bartang) as the boundary would effectively place all territory on the right bank of the Panj outside the sovereignty of Afghanistan and leave the Pamirs open to contest.

He noted that

> the Russian flag was, I believe, 'planted' on the Kara Kul-Rang Kul water-parting about nine or ten years ago by Prince Wittgenstein's expedition [see page 395] and it is just possible that the Russian government may have recognised the acquisition by marking it on their maps, but may never have assumed jurisdiction over it.

Moreover, Bukhara had valid claims to Darvaz, which it had ruled since 1877,

> though previous to that date the Mirs, no doubt, sent tribute to Bokhara as well as to other neighbouring states. The last Mir of Darvaz was one Mahomad Suraj, who in 1877 (it is said) was called upon to carry his tribute personally to the Amir of Bokhara. On arrival, he was seized and imprisoned on a charge of meditated treason, and a hakim was appointed to administer Darvaz. The present hakim is one Yusuf Diwan Begi, whose seat of government is at Wanj.

It was therefore in the interest of Afghanistan

> to avoid making a claim to any part of Darvaz, and on the other hand to stick to her claim to all the possessions of the late Shughni Mirs as far east as where she comes in contact with Chinese territory. In this way she would gain the maximum of hill frontier and be burdened with the minimum of river frontier. No doubt this would necessitate a revision, or the total abrogation of the agreement of 1873 but as that document is based on a misconception of the boundaries as they stood at the time it was made and on a general ignorance on the part of the contracting parties of the geography of the country, there ought to be little difficulty in coming to an arrangement on the subject.

He concluded by formulating the following warning to the British and Indian governments.

> If, next summer, a similar expedition to that of Prince Wittgenstein were to hoist the Russian flag on the Alichur and Great Pamirs, my impression is that the Afghans

would find a difficulty in proving that these regions belonged to them. About eight or nine years ago a Russian officer, who knew these parts (Colonel Kostenko), wrote: "The extent of country between the most southern portion of the province of Farghana and the pass mentioned above (the Baroghil) lies in the Pamirs and belongs to no one. ... This belt of no-man's land must probably, sooner or later, be included in Russian dominions, which will then be in immediate contact with the range forming the water-parting from the Indus." It is precisely this fulfilment of a Russian desire that I believe can be frustrated (as long as Afghanistan and China remain outwardly friendly to England) by closing up Afghan and Chinese territory to a common frontier line across the belt in question, and leaving to Russia only the possibility of violating it by an open act of aggression or war. I am well aware of the political obstacles which stand in the way, at present, of adopting any course which would have the effect of causing the Afghans to advance their position. If, however, existing engagements with Russia, regarding the Oxus frontier, should be modified, an opportunity will be afforded to the Afghans to occupy a common frontier line with China, so as to leave no unclaimed territory between two states.

It was too late. The Russians were moving fast and, as Elias feared, were finding little resistance.

It is puzzling that Elias never received the official recognition he so amply deserved. In addition to the suspicion – mentioned in passing by his biographer Morgan – that his Jewish origins may have had something to do with it, Elias was certainly not helped by the fact that he gave his superiors advice they did not want to hear and information they did not want to know. His natural modesty, compared with the self-aggrandisement of many of his contemporaries, was certainly a handicap. He was also exceptionally competent, a quality that does not always ensure friendship and support.

• • • • •

The last blank spot on the map was now beginning to take on the contours with which we are familiar today. Although the British were the first to produce accurate maps, it was the Russians who began multi-disciplinary scientific exploration of the Pamirs: the name of the first Russian explorer in the region, Alexei Pavlovich Fedchenko, is now forever linked to the great glacier system at the heart of the Pamirs.

The Last Blank Space

> Now when I was a little chap I had a passion for maps. I would look for hours at South America, or Africa, or Australia and lose myself in all the glories of exploration. At that time there were many blank spaces on the earth and when I saw one that looked particularly inviting on a map (but they all look that) I would put my finger on it and say: When I grow up I will go there.
>
> Joseph Conrad, *Heart of Darkness*

This chapter tells the tales of the explorers and adventurers from many countries who contributed to the definitive mapping and scientific exploration of the Pamirs – thus filling in the last blank space on the map of Central Asia. In addition to being a chronology of Pamirs exploration, it aims also to delineate some of the remarkable personalities who engaged in this ambitious and often dangerous enterprise. Courage – sometimes bordering on foolhardiness – and an obsessive curiosity were the key characteristics of those who embarked on this journey in the 19th century. A sense of humour was useful in confronting setbacks and a natural modesty was essential in establishing friendly relations with those encountered en route (whether indigenous inhabitants of the Pamirs or foreign soldiers and adventurers), and may be considered as an insurance policy, today as then, for survival in the Pamirs. The most interesting, informative and engaging travellers had these latter qualities and the space devoted to them is proportionately greater than that given to others, for which no apology is made.

This history of the exploration of the Pamirs ends in 1935. By this time the age of pioneers had past; even the remotest mountains had by now been conquered and mapped. The Russians and Soviets had firmly established their control over the territory that was by now the Autonomous Oblast of Gorno-Badakhshan and there remained only unimportant details to settle in terms of definitive boundaries.

The natural environment of the Pamirs is inhospitable for long periods of the year and, even today, travel is physically demanding. However, many of the 19th century explorers noted that the people of the Pamirs more than compensate by the warmth and enthusiasm of the welcome given to visitors from the outside world.

Kyrgyz couple, Kyzylrabot, Eastern Pamir

Russian Expeditions

Although Wood and the pundits were the pioneers of exploration of the Pamirs, the annexation of the Khanate of Kokand in 1876 made it possible for the Russians to extend their knowledge of the heart of the Pamirs in a systematic manner, in many cases with direct military support. It is striking that while contemporary British explorers of the Pamirs in most cases travelled alone and frequently revelled in highly personal accounts of their exploits, almost all Russian expeditions were organised for specific scientific purposes and concentrated on the collection of data.

In 1896 George Nathaniel Curzon paid tribute to the scientific rigour of the Russian explorers,

> who, though appearing on the field much later than their British or Anglo-Indian rivals, have yet during the last twenty years, owing to the superior proximity of their base, and to the consistent patronage of the Imperial Government, made a more thorough and detailed survey of the northern and central Pamirs, with occasional rushes and excursions to the southern or more British zone, than British officers have ever been able to do of the regions lying beyond the recognised frontier of Hindostan. In the majority of places the Russians have not been the first in point of time to arrive; but, having arrived, they have commonly effected more.[1]

In 1887, Francis Younghusband noted on his first visit to the home of Nikolai Fedorovich Petrovsky, Russian Consul in Kashgar, that he had

> many volumes by the best English writers on Indian subjects … But comprehensive as was M. Petrovsky's knowledge of India and Central Asian affairs, I am not sure they were what chiefly attracted him; and I am inclined to think that his heart really lay in scientific pursuits. In his library were large numbers of books of science, and his room was full of instruments of various descriptions – an astronomical telescope, barometers, thermometers of all kinds, an apparatus for measuring the movements of earthquakes, and various other instruments.

The scientific exploration of Russia's newly acquired territories in Central Asia received official encouragement from an early stage and most military missions were accompanied by a broad range of experts: cartographers and surveyors, of course, but also zoologists, botanists, entomologists, anthropologists and others. The result was not only a major improvement in Russian maps and in assessments of geological

resources, but also a surge of Russian official and academic interest in Central Asia. A methodical and broad-based approach to the integration of the new territories into the Russian Empire was adopted, leading to the development of an extensive scientific literature on the region that was pursued until the break-up of the Soviet Union in 1991, when state funding for such activities virtually ceased.[2]

Alexei Pavlovich and Olga Alexandrovna Fedchenko (1871)

Born in Irkutsk in 1844, Alexey Pavlovich Fedchenko entered the faculty of physics and mathematics of Moscow university at the age of only 16 (as did his fellow explorer Severtsov – see page 405). Specialising in anthropology, zoology and entomology, he was a founder member of the 'Association of Friends of the Natural Sciences' at the university – where students could debate the latest scientific theories, including the work of Darwin, and challenge conventional wisdom. He became secretary of the committee on anthropology and chairman of the committee on entomology.

Russo-German Expedition [1928]

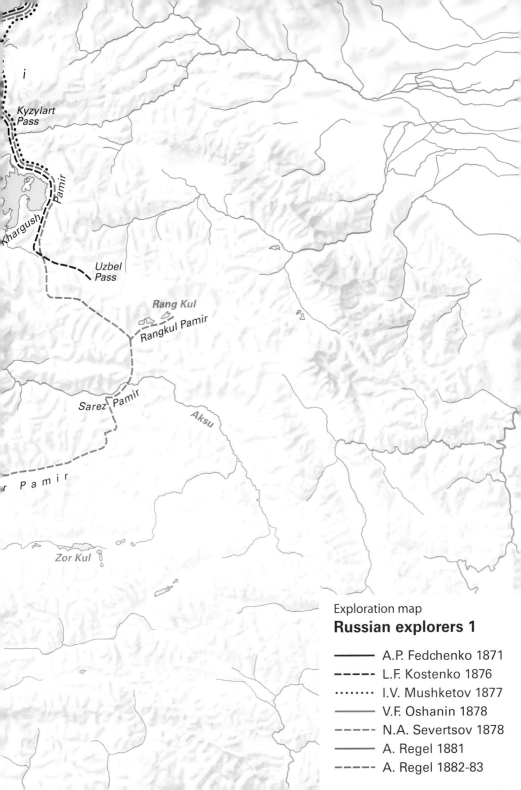

Exploration map
Russian explorers 1

——————— A.P. Fedchenko 1871
------- L.F. Kostenko 1876
············ I.V. Mushketov 1877
——————— V.F. Oshanin 1878
- - - - - N.A. Severtsov 1878
——————— A. Regel 1881
- - - - - A. Regel 1882-83

Fedchenko graduated in 1864 and took up a teaching post at the university's Nikolaev Institute. In 1866, he married Olga Alexandrovna Armfeldt, also a founder member of the Association, whose father was a professor at the university. They travelled on their honeymoon to visit museums in Finland and Sweden and began one of the most remarkable husband and wife partnerships in science.

Tashkent, Bukhara, Samarqand and Khudjand had recently come under Russian control and Kaufmann had been installed as Commander-in-chief and Governor-General of Turkestan. The Russian authorities had decided to undertake scientific studies of these newly acquired regions of Central Asia and, in 1868, the Fedchenkos travelled to Tashkent – a coach journey of 53 days – and began the first of their expeditions to Turkestan with the exploration of Samarqand, Penjikent and the Zarafshan valley, bringing back, among other things, 791 plant specimens. Another expedition in 1870 took them to Zarafshan and Hissar, including the Fan Mountains and Iskanderkul Lake; and, in 1871, they were in the Kyzyl Kum Desert, the Ferghana valley and the foothills of the Pamirs. Their discoveries brought enormous advances in contemporary knowledge of the mountain chains of Central Asia.

On 1 June 1871 the couple left for Kokand to obtain permission from the Khan, Khudoyar, to visit the Alai valley. Their previous missions had been undertaken in the company of Russian troops who were engaged in cartographic studies, but in Kokand they were on their own, with only a letter of recommendation from Kaufmann. The Khan of Kokand did not submit to Russian arms until 1876 and they were entirely dependent on his goodwill.

Fortunately, Kaufmann's letter had the desired effect and, after dressing Fedchenko in a multi-coloured gold-embroidered robe and picturesque hat, the Khan gave them a small lightly armed escort to pursue their journey. Fedchenko had difficulty keeping a straight face as he rode out of Kokand in his new dress, on top of his formal dress coat, but wisely recognised the value of making a public show of their acceptance by the Khan. For their protection they had between them two shotguns, two pistols and a bow and arrow.

The Fedchenkos knew that the nearest and easiest route to the Alai valley was to the east of Kokand through Osh, but the Khan – probably suspicious of their real intentions – insisted that they travel back to Isfara and cross into the Alai from there. Despite obstruction from their escort, they were able to survey the Isfara and Sokh rivers and reached the Zarafshan glacier, the source of the river of that name, and named it after their teacher, Shurovsky.

Finally, travelling from Shakhimardan up the valley of the Isfairam-sai, they reached the Tengiz-bai Pass on the crest of the Alai range and were dazzled by the spectacular peaks opposite them on the other side of the Alai Valley – the northern edge of the Pamirs. Fedchenko called this range the Trans-Alai and identified what was for some time believed to be the highest peak in the Pamirs and named it after the Governor-General of Turkestan; this name remained until it became Pik Lenin in the 1920s.

> To the north too there were the mountains close to us, clearly visible, but my eyes seldom looked in that direction, they were fixed on the view to the south, spellbound by the grandeur of the virgin panorama in front of me. The massive snow ridge was like a wall, stretched before me at a distance of some 30 versts.[3] I had not yet the feeling that these mountains would become for me a real wall, behind which I shall see nothing. I hastened downwards to penetrate into these mountains, and dreamed of going up to those places where the imagination of the natives places the 'roof of the world.'[4]

They camped on the banks of the Kyzylsu, near what is today the town of Daroot Qurghan. On the other side of the river they observed a stream – the Altyn dara – coming down from the opposite side and recognised that it was the route to the 'roof of the world.' This stream leads directly up to the glacier that was later named in honour of Fedchenko. Excited about their first view of the 'roof of the world' in 1871, they decided to explore it more thoroughly.

> My deepest desire was to be in the Pamirs and I had cherished dreams of this since the time of my departure in 1868 to Turkestan – I did not achieve it, and managed to reach only the northern fringe. It remains my principal objective to discover the river systems feeding into the Pamirs from the north. If now, after compiling the data that I have collected on this journey, it would be possible to enter the Pamirs I would abandon everything, not asking anybody's permission...
> The Pamirs and the region of the upper Oxus have been unexplored for a long time: whether by Russians or Englishmen, their secrets will soon be opened ... I hope and believe, however, that it will be Russians who will get there and once again enter their name in the annals of geography which, we know, already owe them so much.

It could not be done on this trip, however. Their escort from Kokand was becoming worried and refused to let them go further: there were marauding Kyrgyz tribes in the Alai and there was unrest in the Ili valley near Kashgar. Kokand was not

Tanimas Pass to Fedchenko Glacier (following pages)

yet under Russian control and it was dangerous to travel in the region – more preparation would be necessary before attempting to explore the Pamirs and they would need to be accompanied by experienced mountaineers. They returned to St. Petersburg and prepared reports on their travels. In addition to their cartographic work, they had also collected specimens of the local flora and fauna, and identified 110 species of birds in the Alai as well as the parasite *dracunculus medinensis* (guinea worm) that was a widespread source of illness in Central Asia at the time.

From local informants in Kokand, Fedchenko gleaned information about the hitherto unexplored region of Darvaz and its chief settlement, Kala-i Khum, also known as Iskander Zindona ("Alexander's prison"). He also learned that Darvaz included a territory beyond Karategin known as "Wachia" by ancient geographers that had sometimes been confused with the Wakhan in the south.[5]

Fedchenko's report to the Imperial Russian Geographical Society (IRGS) in December 1871[6] caused a sensation, as it was the first report by a Russian on the

Pamirs and was considered as equivalent in importance to the discovery of the sources of the Nile. Having seen the chain of high mountains running along the south of the Alai valley, Fedchenko felt confident in confirming the hypothesis of a vast plateau behind them. He reported the information given him by the local inhabitants that there were two Pamirs: the "little" Pamir ("Pamir-Khurd") that he supposed to be the area around Wood's lake; he suggested that the "great" Pamir ("Pamir-Kalyan") was to be found directly behind the Transalai range.

After a short period of European travel, including visits to Paris, Leipzig (where their son Boris was born), Heidelberg and Lucerne, the Fedchenkos were finally able to plan their return trip to the Pamirs. Fedchenko travelled to Mont Blanc in the French Alps in the hope of finding guides who could accompany him. At the end of August 1873, he arrived in Chamonix and took on two local guides, Joseph and Prosper. On 14 September they left Montenvers for the Mer de Glace. Caught in a sudden storm, the group attempted to return but Fedchenko was weak and, after carrying him for a few hours, the guides decided they would have to spend the night on the mountain. At 2 o'clock in the morning, it was clear that Fedchenko was suffering badly from exposure and, fearing the same fate, his guides abandoned him. When they returned with help in daylight he was dead.

Fedchenko was buried in Chamonix and his gravestone was engraved with the inscription "You sleep but your work will not be forgotten."

One of the reasons it was not forgotten was the untiring pursuit of Fedchenko's research by his widow Olga, a remarkable woman who overcame many male prejudices against her participation in her husband's expeditions by her professionalism and scientific competence. It was Olga who prepared for publication all the materials collected during their travels in Central Asia (Путешествие в Туркестан – *Travel to Turkestan* – published in several volumes in 1875: their journey to the Alai is described in Part II of the first volume), together with several articles describing in detail their discoveries. She also translated the reports of Yule, Trotter, Gordon and other British explorers for the Journal of the IRGS.

In 1900, together with their son Boris, she finally fulfilled her husband's ambition to travel to the Pamirs. Their stay in Shughnan led to the publication by the Academy of Sciences of extensive studies on the flora of the Pamirs in 1901, 1905 and 1906. She died in 1921, leaving more than sixty scientific publications under her name and with the distinctions of correspondent member of the Russian Academy of Sciences and honorary member of the French Société de Géographie, the Boston Academy of Science and the International Academy of Botanical Geography – truly one of the foremost women scientists of the nineteenth and early twentieth century. Her name lives on in the designation by the Leningrad Botanical Garden of the Central Asian plant *Olgaea Iljin*.

A map showing the route taken by the Fedchenkos was published in *Petermann's Geographische Mittheilungen* in 1874.

Captain Lev Feofanovich Kostenko (1876)

In 1873, an insurrection broke out in Kokand against the Khan, Khudoyar, with whom Fedchenko had negotiated his passage to the Alai valley. Khudoyar was deposed in favour of his eldest son, Nasir al-Din and sought Russian protection in Tashkent. Nasir al-Din signed a peace treaty with the Russians, but was unable to control the other rebel factions and was in turn deposed by his relative Pulat Bey who started attacking Russian outposts. In October 1875, the Russian forces under Skobelev began counter offensives and, in February 1876, annexed the Khanate of Kokand to the Russian Empire.

In July, Skobelev sent a military expedition to subdue the marauding Kyrgyz tribes under the leadership of Abdul Beg, on their summer pastures in the Alai. The expedition included Captain Lev Feofanovich Kostenko (1841–1891) – for geographical and statistical studies; Vasily Fedorovich Oshanin – as the mission's naturalist – see below; A. R. Bonsdorf – as surveyor; and eight topographers under Lebedev (among them Korostovstsev and Zhilin). Three columns were formed to travel to the Alai by different routes. Kostenko, Oshanin and Bonsdorf were sent to Gulcha to catch up with the column led by Prince Wittgenstein, a colonel on the Turkestan General Staff. They crossed the Archat pass into the Alai, and, at the top of the pass, even Kostenko is forced to pause in his normally factual and unemotional narrative to remark on the breathtaking view that confronted him.

> A magnificent panorama opens to the view from the top of the pass. In the foreground is the Alai plateau, beyond it rises the Trans-Alai mountain range, screening from sight the least known portion of the Pamir.
>
> The valley, or rather high tableland of the Kyzylsu river, which stretched out before us, was skirted on the south by a grand mountain-chain, snow-capped throughout its entire extent. Almost immediately opposite the pass rose the peak

which the late Mr. Fedchenko called Kaufmann Peak, in honour of the Governor-General of Turkestan.[7]

At the end of July, news arrived that Abdul Beg had killed a Russian messenger and Skobelev sent Wittgenstein in hot pursuit over the Kyzylart pass to Kara Kul – Wittgenstein was thus the first European in modern times to see the lake. Some of his officers returned to camp shortly afterwards and reported that the Kara Kul was so high that "many of the men bled from the nose, while several of them fainted away." Skobelev, who had just received the submission of the Kyrgyz in the Russian camp, despatched another group to assist Wittgenstein at Kara Kul and ordered Kostenko to accompany it.

Crossing the Kyzyl Art pass on 14 August, Kostenko noted that

> From the summit of the pass a view is obtained of the Pamir generally, and in particular of the Pamir Khargoshi (of the hare), in the southern portion of which lies the Kara Kul lake. A mass of bare mountains, snow-capped and otherwise, stretching in various directions, also open to the view, and these seem to be intersected by more or less wide valleys and gorges as denuded of vegetation as the mountains themselves. … the descent is into the hollow of the Kara Kul Lake, and

Caravanserai, Daroot Qurghan

the eye takes in the wide basin of the lake encircled by mountains. These mountains are mostly snow-capped, especially those on the east, and it is only on the west and north sides that a break in the snow-line is observable. The aspect of the hollow, with the large azure lake and its elevated islands, is very grand.

The next day, Kostenko explored the island off the north shore (actually then a peninsula, since Kostenko crossed on a narrow bridge of sand that no longer exists) and took measurements. He noted that

A rude piercing wind blows daily from the north, beginning at 2 or 3 p.m. I never experienced more violent gusts. The hard sandstone exposed to the wind is strongly affected by it. Some of the rocks are perfectly drilled. In spite of the violent gusts of wind, I ascended to the top of the highest elevation, and was well rewarded for my pains. A magnificent scene opened to the view. The mountain circle seemed to spring directly from out of the water, proudly looking at its own reflection in the glassy lake whose blue waters lave the feet of the heights.

The next three days were taken up with further exploration round the shores of the lake and Lebedev made a sketch map of it.

Kara Kul Lake

A scout had been sent on to seek information on the whereabouts of Abdul Beg and returned with a report that he had already escaped to Afghanistan. Since no order had yet been received to return to the Alai, Wittgenstein authorised Kostenko to undertake an exploratory expedition to the regions of Rangkul and Sarikol.

The expedition, comprising Kostenko, Lebedev, Bonsdorf and fifteen horsemen, left Kara Kul on 18 August. From the Uzbel pass (4,651m) they were able to confirm Humboldt's hypothesis of the existence of a north-south range of mountains bordering the Pamirs on the east (the Kongur and Mustagh Ata massif), that Hayward had seen from Kashgar in 1869 – Kostenko estimated their height more correctly than Hayward, at 25,000 feet. They had underestimated the distances to be covered, however, and shortage of food forced the expedition to return before being able to explore Rangkul.

A further expedition with Prince Wittgenstein took him to Daroot Qurghan, where there was a fort established by the Khan of Kokand to keep a watchful eye on the nomadic Kyrgyz in the valley. Wittgenstein sent him on a reconnaissance across the Kyzylsu and up the Min Teke river to the Ters Agar pass where they discovered an ancient shrine (Altyn Mazar), identified the three confluents of the Muksu (Sauksai, Kaindy and Selsu) and saw glaciers and high peaks beyond.

The expedition moved on to Karamyk to discuss the delimitation of frontiers with an envoy of the Shah of Karategin, and returned through Shakhimardan to Kokand at the end of September 1876. They had mapped, at a scale of 2 versts to the inch, 3,700 square versts of what Kostenko describes as "the most interesting and least known portion of the Pamir upland." In 1880 Kostenko's account of his work was published in St. Petersburg under the title Туркестанский край. Опыт военно-статистического обозрения Туркестанского военного округа (*The Turkestan frontier: Report on the military-statistical overview of the Turkestan military district*).

Kostenko comments, correctly, that "I am the first European who has obtained a sight of the headwaters of the Muksu river." What he did not know was that the glacier arms he saw from there were part of the glacier system later named after Fedchenko. No European would actually set foot on the glacier for another two years and it would not be fully explored until 1928.

Ivan Vasilievitch Mushketov (1877)

Ivan Vasilievitch Mushketov was born in Alekseyevskoi on the Don on 21 January 1850. In 1866, the Russian College of Mining began research into the coal resources of the Donetsk basin and began recruiting promising students from the area for training as geologists. After starting his studies in the faculty of history and letters at St. Petersburg, Mushketov was selected for an army scholarship and transferred to the College of Mining under Professor Romanovsky, and graduated in 1872 with a first class degree. Geology was to become his consuming passion.

In 1873, on Romanovsky's recommendation, he was attached to the Russian General Staff in Turkestan, where other famous names had preceded him: Semyonov Tienshansky, Severtsov (see below) and Fedchenko. None before him, however, had specific responsibility for geological and geographical surveying. Expeditions to the western Tian Shan, the Syr-Darya, the Zarafshan valley and western Ferghana led him to the conclusion that the proper study of the geology of Central Asia necessitated an understanding of its mountain systems and, in particular, the Pamirs.

In 1875, he explored the Tien Shan and, for his work there, was elected a full member of the IRGS and was awarded its silver medal.

Mushketov's diary reveals his disgust with Russian Tashkent society, "these thieves, swindlers and debauchees," and this may have been one of the reasons he left his service in 1875 and returned to the university – it may also explain why he elected to undertake research on the far edge of Russian territory. Over the next five years, he returned each summer for an expedition in the region, hurrying back to St. Petersburg for his courses in the autumn.

In 1877 he travelled from the Alai to explore the Muksu valley and got a glimpse of the glacier above it:

> Huge bluish formations rise in strips on the steep slope, with a backdrop of silvery summits: an impressive picture. Together with this, the wild valley with snow and rough streams makes a very strong impression.

Ivan Vasilievitch Mushketov

Exploration map
Russian explorers 2

— D.V. Putyata, N.A. Bendersky and
     D.L. Ivanov 1883

- - - G.E. Groum-Grshimailo 1883-87

····· B.L. Grombchevsky 1885, 1888-90

— M.E. Ionov 1891

- - - M.E. Ionov and
     A. Serebrennikov 1892

— Vannovsky 1893

© Airphoto International Ltd

0   30 km

0   30

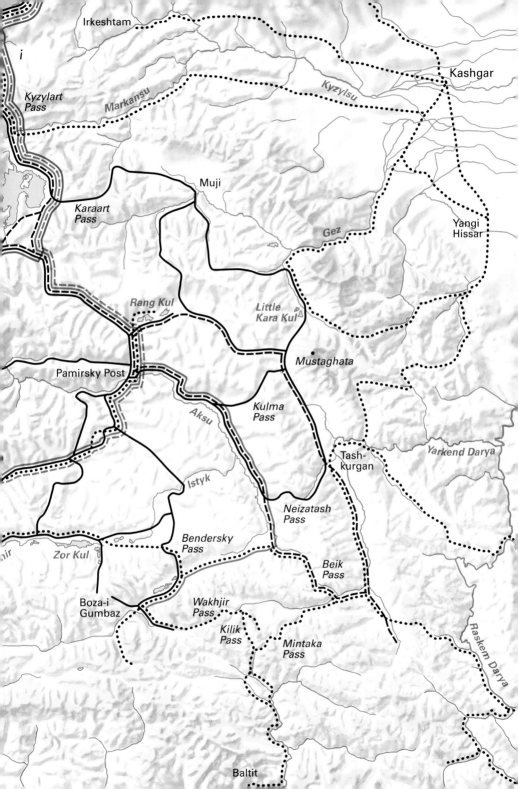

Returning to the Alai valley, he went into the Pamirs as far as Kara Kul, but had to cut short his explorations because of the unsettled situation in Kashgar. In 1878, he explored the upper Alai valley, the Kyzylsu and the geology of the central Tien shan range up to Chatyrkul.

Mushketov concluded, from their geology, that the Pamirs were once on the seabed.

> If we could go back in time to the period of the tertiary deposits, we would see instead of the present mountains an entirely different picture. Where there are now the massifs of the Pamirs there was then a stormy sea which extended far to the West, probably as far as the Caspian, and, to the east, covered all of East Turkestan and the deserts of Gobi and Mongolia, the Hanhai of the Chinese. In this sea only here and there would we be able to see some island formations... At the end of the tertiary period, these island masses were mainly to be found where are now the Pamirs: they increased in volume and began to stand apart as mountain ridges. In the process of drainage the sea receded, and the Pamirs area became more and more prominent and formed a land mass protruding from the sea; its height increased, but not so high that life was extinguished, for we must suppose that at that time the climate on the Pamirs was more temperate than now, and plant and animal life incomparably richer.

> ... Finally the sea gradually recedes, and as the land is drained and raised, the upper parts of the Pamirs become less accessible, less suitable for life and more deserted: the fauna moves to more hospitable ground and humans gradually descend in search of better refuge, following the path of the waters, so to say, and are spread across the continent in proportion to the retreat of the sea.[8]

Mushketov and Romanovsky produced the first geological map of Turkestan (30 versts to the inch) in 1881. The first volume of Mushketov's Туркестан. Геологическое и орографическое описание по данным собранным во время путешествий с 1874 по 1880 гг. (*Turkestan: Description of Geology and Relief on the Basis of Data Collected during Travels in 1874–80*) was published in 1886 and led to a much better understanding of the mountain system of the Pamirs. For this work, he received the Makarev prize of the Academy of Sciences and an award from the Russian Mineralogical Society. In 1887 he studied the causes and effects of the great earthquake that devastated Verny (Almaty) and, shortly before his death, was involved in the extension of the Trans-Siberian railway.

He died of pneumonia in 1902, and the second volume of *Turkestan* was published posthumously in 1906. It was republished in 1915 with additions and notes from subsequent scientific explorations and was a major work of reference for the next generation of researchers of Central Asia. He was also the author of a work in French, *Les Richesses Minérales du Turkestan Russe* (*The mineral wealth of Russian Turkestan*), published in Paris in 1878. He received the highest award of the IRGS – the Konstantinov medal – and was made an honorary member of the Vienna Geographical Society. A glacier in the Tien Shan range in Kyrgyzstan is named after him.

In his obituary, V.F. Oshanin wrote:

> The seven best and most productive years of the scientist's life were devoted to geological research of our outer regions, and these works gave him widespread and well-deserved fame... People possessing such abilities, with such energy and love of their work, are not frequently encountered in the scientific community: the death of such an outstanding scientist, at the age of only 52, is a heavy and irreplaceable loss for science and for all humanity.

Vasily Fedorovich Oshanin (1878)

Vasily Fedorovich Oshanin (1844–1917) was born in Lipetsk Oblast south of Moscow. He entered the faculty of physics and mathematics at the university of Moscow at the age of seventeen and graduated in natural history in 1865. After beginning his career as a teacher, he was sent to Turkestan in 1872 by the Ministry of State Properties to study silk-making and took up a teaching position at the Tashkent school of silk manufacture and later became the secretary of the Turkestan section of the IRGS.

As we have seen, Oshanin was in the Alai in 1876 as part of Skobelev's mission and in 1878 he returned as the head of a scientific expedition put together by the Moscow 'Association of Friends of the Natural Sciences', that – in addition to Oshanin as entomologist – included the topographer G.E. Rodionov and the botanist M.J. Nevessky. Leaving Samarqand in July 1877, the expedition reached the Karategin in April 1878. In Jayilgan, just above the junction of the Muksu with the Kyzylsu ('red river' in Kyrgyz; further downstream it is known by the Tajik equivalent 'Surkhob'), where Oshanin noted some very high peaks to the south-east to which he gave numbers, leaving it to others to give them names. The easternmost and highest

(to which he gave the number 1) he estimated at about 25,000 feet. Not long afterwards, the Russians named several of Oshanin's numbered peaks in honour of contemporary explorers and scientists: Severtsov (see below); Jean Louis Rodolphe Agassiz, US naturalist born in Switzerland (1807–1873); and John Tyndall, Irish physicist, naturalist and educator (1820–1893) – evidence of a world where the scientific community was still truly global and not divided by ideology.

Unable to travel with loaded animals up the valley of the Muksu, the expedition continued up the Kyzylsu as far as the Min Teke river and followed it to Altyn Mazar. From there they were able to ascend to the tongue of the great glacier at about 3,000 m, which they named after Oshanin's friend Fedchenko, and explored the Seldara river and the little Tanimas glacier. In his report, Oshanin estimated the length of the Fedchenko glacier at some twenty versts (the 1928 Russo-German scientific expedition measured it more accurately at 77 km, confirming it as the longest mountain glacier in the world).

It was originally intended that the expedition would attempt to travel from the upper Muksu to look for a way into Shughnan and explore Yashil Kul. The narrow rock-strewn valley of the Belandkiik was impossible to pass on horseback, however,

Altyn Mazar

and, after only 15 km, with several of his party suffering from illness, the expedition was forced to turn back. From local Kyrgyz, Oshanin learned that their preferred route to Murghab was up the Kaindy river and over the pass of the same name (4,822 m). It was, however, still covered in deep snow from the preceding heavy winter and an attempt to cross it was out of the question. The expedition came down to the Alai and returned to Tashkent via Gulcha and Osh.

A map showing their route was prepared by Rodionov and published in *Petermann's Geographische Mittheilungen* in 1882.

Colonel P. G. Matveyev (1878)

The map showing Oshanin's route also showed part of the route of a Russian expedition later the same year to Badakhshan under the leadership of Colonel P.G. Matveyev. This expedition included the German director of the Tashkent observatory, Schwartz, and a surveyor, Lieutenant Trotsky. After crossing the Oxus near Kulob, they were first stopped in Rostak on orders of the Afghan government and then taken over a very difficult mountain route to Faizabad where the late season forced them to abandon their intention of visiting Kafiristan and return to Samarqand through Taloqan, Kunduz and Mazar-i Sharif. The unusual route forced on them by their Afghan 'hosts' across the central mountains of Badakhshan enabled them, however, to map hitherto unexplored territory and add considerably to the data on the region collected by Wood and the pundits.[9]

Nicolai Severtsov (1878)

By the time he undertook his exploration of the Pamirs, Nikolai Severtsov (1827–1885) was already a seasoned and famous traveller. Privately educated, he entered the faculty of physics and mathematics of Moscow university at the age of only 16 and began zoological research in his home province of Voronezh, completing his Master's degree in 1855. Shortly afterwards he was sent on a scientific expedition to the lower reaches of the Syr Darya. This work was not without danger, as he was attacked and badly wounded early in the mission by marauding bands from Kokand, who carried him off to Turkestan. Freed after a month in captivity, he took up his research work in the field almost immediately.

In 1864 he was attached to the staff of general Chernyaev and in the period 1865–68 made expeditions to the Syr-Daria region, the Tien Shan, lake Issyk Kul and

Khodjent. The results of these expeditions were published in 1873 (Путешествия по Туркестанскому краю и исследования горной страны Тянь-Шаня – *Travels on the border of Turkestan and research in the high Tien Shan*) for which he was awarded an honorary degree of doctor of zoology at Moscow university, the Litke gold medal of the IRGS and the gold medal of the Paris International Geographical Congress.

On Kaufmann's instructions, a first attempt was made to reach the Pamirs at the end of 1877, hard on the heels of Mushketov's expedition to the Alai. The expedition, under the command of Captain Skorniakov, included – in addition to Severtsov – Schwarz, head of the Tashkent observatory, the cartographer Skassi and the botanist and entomologist Captain Kushakievich.[10] They left Tashkent on 30 September and, travelling via Osh and Gulcha, reached the Alai on 26 October. At the Kyzylart Pass they encountered severe weather conditions, and were forced to return to Osh, not entirely without results since Severtsov had collected many specimens, Skassi had been able to measure fifteen mountain peaks and Schwarz had made several measurements of terrestrial coordinates.

The next year, Severtsov put together another expedition, that started research in the Ferghana Valley and reached the Alai on 27 July. After a few days' independent research, the scientists met up at Kara Kul on 12 August and continued together beyond Kara Kul into unexplored territory in the eastern Pamirs: Rangkul, Murghab, Alichur and Yashil Kul – and, as Severtsov put it in the report of the expedition, "made the first comprehensive, multi-disciplinary and thorough research of the Pamir and finally determined its orography and scientific geography in relation to the Tian-Shen."

Unfortunately, a caravan bringing food was plundered en route by local Kyrgyz and the team had to cut short its work before reaching the Great Pamir and Zorkul. They returned to Ferghana on 26 September, bringing back specimens of 20,000 plants (representing some 1,000 different species), 60 mammals, 350 birds and 20 fish. Their work filled in many blanks in knowledge of the Pamirs and permitted major improvements in the maps produced by the Russian General Staff. In 1880, Severtsov published a map (Карта Памира и сопредельных стран, дополненной по съемкам монографа Скасси и сведениям доктора зоологии Северцова – *Map of the Pamir and adjacent countries, supplemented by the surveys of the topographer Skassi*" – 30 versts to the inch) that showed the main mountain ranges and valleys of the Pamirs and the subdivision between the different principalities of the Pamirs (Karategin, Darvaz, Rushan, Badakhshan, Shughnan) and the historico-geographical provinces of the Pamirs (Alichur, Khargush, Great, Little, Rangkul, Sarikol, Sarez). A map showing Severtsov's route was also published in *Petermann's Geographische Mittheilungen* in 1880.

Like his contemporary Pyotr Semyonov – who explored the Tien Shan and was later permitted by Imperial decree to add the word Tienshansky to his name – Severtsov enjoyed a high reputation during his lifetime and he had hardly returned from the Pamirs in 1878 when he was awarded the Imperial gold medal for his work there. It was, however, his last expedition. He was still cataloguing and writing up his collections of specimens and giving lectures at the Moscow university and the IRGS when, in 1885, he was the victim of an accident in which his carriage broke through thin ice on a river near his home. The complete results of his work were published posthumously in 1886 by the IRGS.

As we have seen, at the time of Severtsov's Pamir expeditions the Russians knew little about the western and southern parts of the Pamirs – Shughnan, Wakhan, Rushan and Darvaz – and were dependent on the British for their maps. The exact status of these districts was moreover uncertain and would not be clarified until 1895 (and not finally settled until 1907). The next Russian expeditions brought back more knowledge on these regions.

Dr. Albert E. Regel (1881–1883)

The Russian botanist and explorer, Dr. Albert Regel, son of the director and founder of the St. Petersburg botanical garden, was the first European in the Western Pamirs (with the military topographer Kossiakov) and made a total of 3 expeditions to Shughnan, Rushan and Darvaz between 1881 and 1883. The king of Shughnan, Yusuf Alikhan, offered him generous assistance and encouraged his work – hospitality that cost the king his life, for when the news of Regel's mission reached the Amir of Afghanistan Yusuf Alikhan was arrested and executed. The Russians concluded that the British had instigated the execution as a warning to the local leaders not to encourage Russian exploration of Shughnan.

Regel had already travelled to the Tien Shan and Turfan in western China. In 1881 he travelled from Samarqand to the region of the Zarafshan glacier and entered the Pamirs through Gharm and Saghirdasht to Kala-i Khum. The Afghans had just occupied Shughnan and the uncertain political situation prevented him from travelling beyond Vanch. He returned to Samarqand on 12 December through Kulob.

A report of his journey was published in the Bulletin of the IRGS in 1882 (Vol. XVIII, pp. 127–141: "Путешествие в Дарваз" – "Travel to Darvaz").[11]

In June 1882, Regel set off again from Samarqand to Saghirdasht and travelled up the Panj from Kala-i Khum as far as the ruby mines in Shughnan, which he reached at the end of the year. En route he made detours to the Shiva lake on the left side of the Panj, the hot springs in Garm Chashma on the other side, Yemts on the Bartang, Durumkul in the Shakhdara valley and the Ghunt as far as Yashil Kul. After more than twelve months' pioneering research, he returned to his base in Baljuvon (north of Kulob, near what is now the Nurek lake). In November and December, despite illness, he returned to the Pamirs and travelled up the valley of the Khingob river, almost as far as the Garmo glacier.[12]

Captain D.V. Putyata (1883)

The materials from Russian surveying activity up to 1880 were recorded on a new map: Рекогносцировка путей, ведущих с урочища Сары-Таш к озеру Кара-Куль и на перевалы Кальта-даван и Кокуй-бель, произведенная инструментально с 11 по 23-е июля 1880 г. классными топографами Шемановским и Данковым – *Reconnaissance of routes leading from the fixed point Sary Tash to Kara Kul and to the Kalta Dawan and Kokuibel passes, measured with instruments from 11 to 23 July 1880 by the senior topographers Shemanovskiy and Dankov – 5 versts to the inch.*

In the summer of 1883, the new Governor-General of Turkestan, Chernyaev, sent another military expedition to the Pamirs, under the leadership of an officer of the General Staff, Captain D.V. Putyata, to complete Severtsov's work. The mission included the geologist D.L. Ivanov (1846–1924) and the military topographer Bendersky (formerly attached to Stolietov's mission to Kabul in 1878 and subsequently member of the 1895 Anglo-Russian Boundary Commission).

Harvest in upper Khingob Valley (right)
Woman digging, Arzing (left)

The group travelled together as far as Kara Kul. From there, Putyata and Bendersky travelled through Bulunkul and Little Kara Kul (in Western China, today Xinjiang) to Tashkurgan, Ivanov taking the route through Rangkul before joining them in Tashkurgan. The group returned to the Pamirs across the Neizatash pass and down the Aksu to the junction with the Akbaital. Splitting up again, Putyata went to Alichur and Yashil Kul and then made a circuit across the Koitezek pass and back up the Toguzbulak confluent of the Ghunt. Meanwhile, Ivanov and Bendersky travelled through Chechtebe to Chakmaktynkul in the Little Pamir and went down the Wakhan as far as the Urta Bel pass and from there to Zorkul, and through Bash Gumbaz to Alichur where they met up with Putyata. Returning by the Khargosh pass to the Great Pamir, Putyata and Bendersky discovered the Andamin pass (later named after Bendersky). Ivanov travelled to Yashil Kul across the Mats and Koitezek passes and then went down the Ghunt as far as Sardem, which was at that time the highest inhabited village of Shughnan. The group reunited and went up the Ghudara river to the foot of the Fedchenko glacier and returned to Marghilan in December.[13]

Putyata, Bendersky and Ivanov covered more territory and provided more detailed and accurate information than any previous or subsequent expedition and completed the work reflected in the 1880 map. In his report, Putyata summed up the outcome as follows:

1. The drawing up of a map of all places visited on a scale of five versts. The topographic work achieved in the Pamirs was joined in the north and west to previous Russian and English surveys. In the Khanate of Bukhara it covered a few unexplored routes.

2. Achieved 17 astronomical observations with the aim of defining longitudinal and latitudinal points. The observations resulted from application of basic measuring points of the Russians and English intermediate on the route followed by the expedition.

3. Plot of the locality around the points to a size of 1 square verst taken at 250 sazhen scale [a sazhen corresponds to 7 feet].

4. Collected herbarium of Pamir flora.

5. The geological member, mining engineer Ivanov, put together a rich mineralogical collection and made a great quantity of pencil sketches.

6. Made observations with thermometer, barometer and aneroid for determining heights.

Putyata was also an accomplished artist and in 1895 published in St. Petersburg a handbook on military drawing: Принципы военного искусства в толковании китайских полководцев – *Principles of Military Drawing in the Representation of Chinese Military Leaders*. Ivanov's diary and sketch map of the expedition are kept in the Russian State History Archive in St. Petersburg.

Dmitri Lvovich Ivanov (1883)

Ivanov had a somewhat unusual military and academic career. While studying at Moscow University, he was convicted as an accomplice in the April 1866 assassination attempt on Tsar Alexander II, had to abandon his studies and – in lieu of banishment – was compulsorily drafted to the front line battalion in Orenburg as a foot soldier, and later transferred to Tashkent. He participated in the campaigns in Samarqand and Khiva and was rewarded for his bravery by being made an officer. His military experience made him a convinced pacifist, and he left the army as soon as he could to resume his studies. After graduation as a mining engineer, he returned to Turkestan and, in 1880, travelled with Mushketov on an expedition to the Zarafshan glacier, and, as we have seen, was attached to Putyata's 1883 Pamirs expedition.

In August 1883, Ivanov left Putyata's camp near Kara Kul and set off on his own down the Akbaital river to Murghab and Sarez in search of provisions for the detachment. *Shughnan*, the account of his journey was published in 1885. His encounter with the mountain Tajiks has a certain poignancy: less than thirty years later a major earth slide blocked the Murghab river just downstream from their meeting-place and the village of Sarez was fated to disappear under the waters of the lake that built up behind this enormous natural dam – and that bears today the name of what was once a village.

Dmitri Lvovich Ivanov

The fields are scattered around Sarez, rising in fine terraces, one above the other. The grain has already been harvested and the sheaves are stacked upright near the threshing floor, in a long pile, around which a group of bulls and donkeys moves stupidly round and round, a square wicker basket in the centre.

They stopped me 3/4 versts before Sarez, under big poplars with grassy knolls. The fresh wind was unpleasantly sharp despite the fact that it was about 11 o'clock and the sun shone in a clear sky.

Soon a group of some twenty five mountain men came from the settlement to the poplars. In front were the old men, the 'white beards' (Aksakals), in new light-coloured cloaks and with fresh turbans on their heads. At their sides they carried huge wooden cups. The deputation moved without haste, with eastern dignity. On a meadow they spread two long felt carpets: one for me, one for the deputation.

The meeting began in a most friendly way.

"You will not believe how glad we are at your arrival," the headman started saying. "Such a visitor we never thought to see in Sarez."

I answered with an appropriate greeting. We were content. Opposite me they set out some flat plates about three feet wide. In each of them there was local mountain food. Among the most typical I will mention the thin (2 mm.) flat cakes covering the whole plate, easily rolled in a tube; like big flat cakes, but magnificent, reminding me of our rural "pancakes" with a filling of oil and sour cream; rich pasta in thin quadrangular slices with the same filling; clearly, moreover, such hospitality had to include curdled milk.

"Now that you are among us, we count ourselves already as Russian citizens," the old men pressed forward with their political conclusions, "already we are no longer afraid of the Afghans! Give us only a note in your hand and nobody will dare touch us."

I did not really expect such a resolute move from secular delicacies directly to the question of citizenship and, I must admit, rather hesitated in the presence of such a large group of people who were clearly used to plain speaking. To be a diplomat with simple people is indeed a most difficult thing, and it seemed to me that I was now in a delicate diplomatic situation.

Sarez Lake

"My dear friends!" I began my diplomatic reply, "I must thank you for your hearty welcome and I hope I shall manage to repay you for your kind attentions. But I came here as a simple scientist who is interested in stones, mountains, rivers and glaciers: it is not my business to interfere in your people's lives."

"We understand," they answered, "that you have many occupations! But we ask you, we beg you, please to take us under the protection of Russia."

"You live here far from the world outside," I continued, "but you know that such things cannot be done as simply as you would wish them to be. Only the will of the Great White Tsar can decide on your naturalization."

In this way I tried to hint delicately that it was not appropriate to conduct such conversations in public.

"Ah! In this respect we are not afraid," the old men quickly replied, "there are no traitors among us! Here we are one family, with one soul. Each of us thinks the same: all, as one, and one, as all. For us there is only one enemy: the Afghan!"

In face of such sincerity, I immediately decided to abandon diplomacy and to use simple language with these simple people. I tried to give them the best advice, since I had no clear orders. I told them that the best action for them was to approach the Russian leadership (the Governor of Ferghana) though I did not hide the fact that their isolated position in the mountains far from Ferghana, Alai and Pamir, would make it very difficult to fulfill their wishes in relation to citizenship of Russia.

Pilgrim on the way to the shrine of Hazret-i Burkh, one of the holiest sites in Tajikistan

It would be easier to address themselves to the Emir of Bukhara.

"We already tried it," they answered. "The Bukharans have tightened their rule, and we no longer trust them. We are reluctant to pass under their authority." (This last comment hinted at a difference in Moslem doctrines.)

"Well, and how about the Afghans?" I asked.

"The Afghans cannot reach us here, and we shall not go to them. There are only three roads from here to Shughnan: this one here, the Marjanai, the one through Langar and the one down the Murghab river. To get here is difficult, and Bartang cannot be passed at all. You know now the road here along the Murghab from above; downstream the road is ten times more difficult. Here you may walk, but there even on foot you will not get through." "No, they will not pass!" someone added confidently.

After further discussion about my mission, I asked to visit Sarez.

"For you there is nothing forbidden. You, as our chief, may see everything," the foreman answered kindly. "We doubt though that you will find anything interesting – we are so poor."

The villagers gave Ivanov a letter for the Russian authorities, which had been sent up the Bartang from Shughnan, confirming the request of the local population for Russian citizenship and for help against the Afghans.

Leaving Sarez, I again complained about fate, that she yet again did not give me an opportunity to peer closely and at length into the life of a people interesting in every respect. I needed to hurry to join Putyata's detachment in order to deliver the urgent provisions I had obtained.

The Journal of the IRGS published the following notice shortly after the return of Putyata, Bendersky and Ivanov:[14]

1883 will remain forever engraved in the history of the exploration of the Pamirs. All the scientific expeditions and travellers that have been recently to the Pamirs – whether from our country or from India – described relatively unimportant territory, between which there remained many unseen and disconnected areas. What Pamir travellers brought us was each time only a small part of what was hoped from them.

Already for some time there was a feeling that a larger and properly equipped expedition would be necessary, one that could at once settle the array of unanswered geographical questions in relation to the Pamirs. The Pamir expedition that was organised last year meets this criterion exactly, at least for the eastern Pamir. ...

Thanks to the energy of these persons, the eastern part of the Pamir highland has now been covered in all possible directions.

A map showing the routes taken by the individual members of the expedition was also published by the Society.[15]

In May 1885, Ivanov spoke to the IRGS about his travels and experiences in the Pamirs:[16]

> Agriculture is characterised by ... back-breaking and difficult work – for meagre results. To prepare the fields, they must begin by removing the vast deposits of stones. It is not enough to move aside just the large stones – the main task is to collect the mass of small stones that cover the earth. If you see the land of these mountain people, you would not believe that they are fields and not stone-paved roads. But when you catch sight of the stone walls that surround every little parcel of land, and when you understand that these walls are built with the millions of stones collected in their fields, you begin to appreciate the work put in by these mountain people to obtain some kind of a living from this land. And then you understand their great need to settle and cultivate and live on their own land, however tiny in size. ... If a mountain dweller saw a narrow stream and a piece of land next to it, he would go there, even if he had to travel 20 versts to get there and his harvest were only a few handfuls of barley. Admit that one must have a very great love of the land!

Ivanov was deeply impressed by his encounter with the remarkable people of the Western Pamirs and started to put together a glossary of local words. Published in 1895,[17] it awakened enormous interest in the academic community, and led to the systematic study of the Pamir languages, for here was living proof that the inhabitants of the Pamirs were the direct descendants of the peoples who had created the Avesta and Zoroastrianism – and theories emerged that the Pamirs were the cradle of Aryan civilisation and that their languages might be older even than the Avesta.

Grigorii Efimovich Grumm-Grshimailo (1884)

Grigorii Efimovich Grumm-Grshimailo was born in St. Petersburg in 1860. Entering the faculty of physics and mathematics at the university of St. Petersburg in 1880, he quickly developed an interest in entomology and, after publishing a scientific work on the butterflies of the Crimea in 1881, was elected a member of the Russian Entomological Society.

On vacation in Saratov in 1883, he met the German collector G. Rückbeil who had made collections in Turkestan and probably awakened his interest in exploring the butterflies of Central Asia. Shortly after his return to St. Petersburg, he was introduced to the Grand Duke Nikolai Mikhailovich Romanov – also a keen lepidopterist – who expressed interest in publishing an article by him in his *Mémoires sur les Lépidoptères* (St. Petersburg, 1884–1901).

This meeting had a major influence on the course of Grumm-Grshimailo's subsequent work. The Grand Duke offered to finance an expedition to the unknown regions of the Pamirs on condition that part of his collections should be placed at the Grand Duke's disposal. Excited at the prospect, Grumm-Grshimailo obtained permission to bring forward his final examinations – refusing the offer of a faculty post at the university – and, with the help of Mushketov, Oshanin and Ivanov, put together an itinerary for his journey in the Pamirs.

In early 1884, he left St. Petersburg and arrived in Osh two months later. Accompanied by an escort of Cossacks, he left for the Pamirs on 20 May. Reaching the Alai a few days later over the Vuadil pass, he started up the Altyn Dara to the Ters Agar pass, with the aim of exploring the upper Muk Su and getting on to the

Grumm-Grshimailo glacier

glacier. However, bad weather forced him to return to the Alai valley and he travelled from there over the Kyzylart pass as far as Kara Kul, completing his collections along the way.

The expedition returned to Osh on 20 August with 12,000 specimens of 146 different species – of which 30 were hitherto unknown. Excited by the wealth of information assembled, he decided not to return to St. Petersburg, but to stay in Turkestan to assess his collections and write a report for Romanov's *Mémoires* (published in the 1885 volume). In agreement with Romanov, he put together the itinerary for a new expedition for the summer of 1885.

This time, in addition to Romanov's financial support, the IRGS gave him a grant and the Governor-General of Turkestan, Rosenbach, provided an escort of Cossacks and two laboratory assistants. Rosenbach also arranged for the topographer Rodionov to accompany the expedition. They left Samarqand on 29 March and travelled to the Khingob river and Tavildara before exploring Karategin, Darvaz and much of Kulob.

The expedition returned to Samarqand on 9 August, bringing with it more than 20,000 entomological specimens and many animals and birds, a large number of which had never been seen before. Grumm-Grshimailo worked on classifying the collections during the following year: his report was published in the *Mémoires* in 1887 and the collection of animals and birds was transferred to the Zoological Museum of the Academy of Sciences.

Grumm-Grshimailo was elected as a full member of the IRGS and was awarded the Society's silver medal for his work on these two expeditions. After an expedition to the Tien Shan in 1886, he was again in the Pamirs in 1887, travelling from Kara Kul to the Tanimas and Ghudara rivers (the easternmost glacier in the Fedchenko system, close to this route, was subsequently named after Grumm-Grshimailo). He also explored the Ak Baital river, the Great Pamir (Zorkul) and Sarikol. On their way from there to the Wakhan, Petrovsky, the Russian Consul-General sent them orders to return. Travelling down the Ak Su to Murghab, they reached Osh on 17 August and brought with them a large collection of specimens from the eastern Pamirs.

In 1889–1890, he travelled on an expedition to Western China and, in 1890, his monumental work on the butterflies, flora and fauna of the Pamirs: 'Le Pamir et la faune lépidoptérologique', was published in four volumes in Romanov's *Mémoires*. In the last years of his life, Grumm-Grshimailo served as Vice-President of the IRGS. He died in 1936.

The legacy of his published works is more than enough to confirm Grumm-Grshimailo's scientific reputation, although many are now out of print and only available through antiquarian booksellers. Several of his writings are as yet unpublished and remain in the scientific archive of the IRGS: diaries of expeditions to the Pamir (1885–1886), to Western China and Mongolia, reports on expeditions and texts of lectures on the geography of China and Mongolia. Many butterflies are named after him.

Colonel Bronislav Ludwigovich Grombchevsky (1888–1892)

Bronislav Ludwigovich Grombchevsky (Grabczewski) was born into a Polish noble family in 1855 and, like many young men of his class at that time, joined a Russian infantry regiment. As soon as he became an officer, he was sent to Turkestan where he served as an aide-de-camp successively to General Skobelev and Prince Wittgenstein: in 1875–6, he participated in Skobelev's campaigns in Kokand and the Alai and, in 1878, in Samarqand. In 1880, he was appointed to the military staff as deputy head of the Marghilan district. In addition to his military duties, he rapidly developed an interest in surveying, entomology, botany and ethnography, that he was able to put to good use on his travels, of which he also kept a hitherto unpublished photographic record. He had a gift for languages and spoke fluent Tajik and Uzbek.

In 1885 he was sent to Kashgar as a member of the Russo-Chinese border commission and took the opportunity to explore large parts of the frontier regions and survey some 1,000 kilometres of routes. For this work he was awarded the silver medal of the IRGS.

We briefly encountered Grombchevsky (see page 315) when he travelled from Kara Kul through Sarikol to Hunza in 1888. Just after leaving Hunza, Grombchevsky received an invitation from the ruler of Wakhan, Ali Mordan Shah, to visit his territory, offering him a safe passage to Shughnan because (according to him) the Afghans had now withdrawn. Reluctantly, however, he was forced to abandon this idea.

> … my remaining financial resources consisted of 37 roubles. Moreover, I no longer had any gifts and almost all my horses, and those of my Cossacks, had died. To travel on foot in Wakhan and further through Shughnan and Badakhshan to Bukhara on foot, without money and the gifts required in Central Asia was not appropriate for my national pride. I changed direction to Kashgar, hoping to borrow

money in the consulate to get horses and gifts and, then, freshly equipped, to travel through the Pamirs to Wakhan. In Kashgar I received the most hospitable and a cordial welcome in the family of the consul N.F. Petrovsky who, having supplied me all my needs for my return travel in winter through the Tian-Shen to Ferghana, categorically rejected my plans for a journey to Wakhan, on the grounds that he did not have the approval of the Ministry for Foreign Affairs for such a venture.[18]

On this journey Grombchevsky travelled some 2,800 kilometres through the Pamirs, much of it in hitherto unexplored territory, described twelve high passes and made a detailed survey of a large part of this route. He also established 14 astronomical positions and measured 158 heights, as well as bringing back entomological and geological collections. For this expedition he was awarded the gold medal of the IRGS.

In 1889, Grombchevsky was sent by the IRGS to explore Kafiristan, Chitral and neighbouring regions, accompanied by the botanist Conrad. Leaving Marghilan on 12 June, he travelled through the Alai and Karategin and reached Darvaz and Vanch in July, but was prevented from going further south.

When we came to the borders of Roshan the ruler, Said Akbar Shah, had sent me a letter containing the following: "To the Conqueror of the world who resembles an eagle, the Great Lord. I pledge to you, to the possessor of the universe, that up to the present time I counted my country as part of the possessions of the Great White Tsar – and then thieves and bandits were here and have seized half my possessions. I have previously sent a report about my situation to the servants of the Great Sovereign, but have not yet received an answer. As far as my affairs are concerned, I express my hope that my country will be accepted under the protection of the Great White Tsar, that the thieves will depart and will cease to ruin my native land. I shall inform you in due time about subsequent events. While Roshan is in my hands, count this province as your possession. What can I say more?" The letter was signed: Said-Mahomed-Akbar-Khan, son of Said-Emir-Khan.

After this came a second letter from the ruler of Shughnan, who writes: "Having inquired about your desire to pass to Kafiristan, I must report, that the roads through Shughnan are held in an iron ring by the Afghans and everyone is at their mercy. The road to get out through Bartang to the Pamir is blocked by the collapse of the cliff-ledges and by the flooding of the river – this is a serious danger and it is hardly passable even for pedestrians. Do not think that I want to prohibit you from passing by the river Bartang! In response to your request, I only report on the difficulties awaiting you.[19]

As a result, he was obliged to adopt the alternative plan given him by the IRGS to explore the upper Yarkand valley. He went back through Karategin to the Alai, and made his way to the Taghdumbash Pamir through Ghudara, Sarez, Murghab and Yashil Kul.[20]

In 1889, being unable to get into Kafiristan from the Badakhshan side, I decided to try to get there through Chitral and, for this purpose, I sent a courier with a letter to Aman-ul-Mulk in which I asked him to help me reach Kafiristan, only accompanied by one of my servants, and that I would recompense him with whatever he wished to take from the property of my expedition. Having sent the letter, I went to explore the upper Aksu and, accompanied by 3 Cossacks, reached the sources of the river Wakhan-darya with the purpose of reaching the Hudargurt (Sukhsu-rabot) pass, the entrance to Chitral and Yasin. This excursion was very risky, as it was necessary to pass over a kind of natural boundary at Langar, where there was an Afghan post. Due to strong winds we were able to get past Langar unnoticed, but the same winds wiped out the traces of the path and heaped up such huge snowdrifts that we could go no further. Nevertheless we were able to determine precisely the position of the Hudargurt and Kelenj (Irshud) passes into Hunza. On our return we had to stop in a lodging for the night so close to the Afghan post that we clearly heard the neighing of the horses and the calls of the night-watch.

We passed the post before daylight and left on the main route to Boza-i-Gumbez and on the fourth day returned to camp. Shortly afterwards, my courier returned from Chitral and brought a letter from Sarvar-ul-Mulk, the ruler of Mastuj who wrote: "In the name of my father I inform you that my country is overflowing with Englishmen who watch my every step and it is therefore impossible to help you to pass in any way. You wrote: 'Let me pass with one or two servants; what harm I can cause your native land, having come alone?' You do not know what that means. As a herd of sheep runs in panic in front of one wolf so the Ferenghis are afraid of one Russian. How can I protect you from your most malicious enemies who, I tell you, are all over my country? And if anything should happen to you, what can I tell the White Sovereign?"

The letter it is interesting in that it is written by the ruler of a country that has no relations with Russia and, on the contrary, has for many years been receiving a grant from the Indian government.[21]

Changing his plans yet again, he travelled to the Yarkand valley where, as we have also seen, his path crossed with that of Francis Younghusband, who described their meeting as follows:

> At the camping-ground near the junction of the Ilisu with the Yarkand River, I received a letter from Captain Grombtchevsky, written in Turki, saying that he had halted at Khaian-aksai and was anxious to meet me. I answered, in Persian and English, that I was very glad to have the opportunity of meeting so distinguished a traveller, and would arrange to encamp with him the next day.
>
> On October 23 we marched to Khaian-aksai, leaving the valley of the Yarkand River and ascending a narrow valley whose bottom was almost choked up with the thick growth of willow trees. Rounding a spur, we saw ahead of us the little Russian camp, and on riding up to it a fine-looking man dressed in the Russian uniform came out of one of the tents and introduced himself as Captain Grombtchevsky. He was about thirty-six years of age, tall, and well built, and with a pleasant, genial manner. He greeted me most cordially, and introduced me to a travelling naturalist. We had a short talk, and he then asked me to have dinner with him, and we sat down to a very substantial repast of soup and stews, washed down with a plentiful supply of vodka.
>
> This was the first meeting of Russian and English exploring parties upon the borderlands of India, and there was much in each of us to interest the other. Captain Grombtchevsky had already been to Hunza, having made a venturesome journey across the Pamirs into that country in 1888, that is, the year before we met. It had on the present occasion been his intention, he informed me, to penetrate to the Punjab through Chitral or Kafiristan, but the Amir of Afghanistan had refused him permission to enter Afghan territory on his way there. He had accordingly come across the Pamirs, and was now hoping to enter Ladak and Kashmir, for a permission to do which he was writing to the British Resident in Kashmir.[22]

Grombchevsky nearly met his death on attempting to reach Tibet after their meeting: Younghusband had – probably with malicious intent – recommended a wholly impracticable itinerary across the Karakoram pass to the edge of the high Tibetan plateau in the middle of December that led to the death of twenty-five of his thirty-three horses and to severe frostbite for his cossack escort.[23] He was understandably aggrieved at the British refusal to allow him to pass the winter in Kashmir since:

> .... at the very time when he was thus treated, the Russian government had given permission to (1) Major Cumberland to travel all over the Russian strategical frontier, viz., through Cashgar, Fergana (Fergistan), Samarqand, Bokhara, and to proceed to Europe by way of the Trans-Caspian Railway; and (2) Lieutenant Littledale to travel in a contrary direction to India, viz., through Turkistan, the Pamir region, Tchatra, etc. and to enter Cashmere by the same route of which Colonel Grambcheffsky desired to make use.[24]

Not long afterwards, similar permission (and VIP treatment) was accorded by the Russians to Lord Dunmore. Grombchevsky commented ironically: "My expedition comprised only 13 persons, the majority of whom were ignorant Asiatics. Surely, British rule in India is not in such a precarious condition that it has cause to fear such a formidable expedition?"[25]

He deserved better in his relationship with Younghusband. He had shared with him (and the Chinese) the latest Russian cartographic information as well as his honest perception of the vexed issue of legal sovereignty over the Pamirs: he was well aware of the signal importance of the stone with Chinese inscriptions at Sumantash (see pages 466 and 608) and hoped sincerely that the assertion of Chinese sovereignty might put an end to Afghan atrocities against the population of the Pamirs. His openness caused him some problems at home, but was typical of the approach taken by most Russian explorers – even if they were officers – that scientific research came before military ambition and he could be forgiven for assuming that Younghusband was playing the 'game' by similar rules. Moreover, it was not at all clear at the time of his meeting with Younghusband that the Russians would adopt a 'forward policy' and if he caused political problems for his masters, he at least had the merit – by pushing into the outer edges of the Pamirs and by his unprecedented visit to Hunza – of provoking them to define and implement a policy for the territory of the Pamirs.

In February 1890, he started again for Tibet, reaching the Tibetan plateau in May. In September, he was in the lower Yarkand, where he again met Younghusband (and shared several cordial dinners in his company). In October he returned along the upper Kyzylsu to the Alai.

On his 1889–90 expedition, Grombchevsky covered 7,680 km (of which 5,300 in unexplored territory), fixed 73 astronomical points, measured 351 heights and brought back some 32,000 zoological and botanical specimens together with geological samples and many photographs.[26] On return to St. Petersburg, he suffered a physical and mental collapse and was reportedly on crutches for some time.[27] He was placed on leave for two months to convalesce abroad but was unable to leave immediately as the Tsar had requested that he present to him personally his collection of photographs. In 1891, he accompanied Vrevsky, the Governor-General of Turkestan, to the Pamirs, and in 1892, was part of Ionov's 'flying detachment' (see below).

Grombchevsky drew particular attention to the sufferings of the local population, of which he had direct evidence.

> The Pamir is far from being a wilderness. It contains a permanent population, residing in it both summer and winter. ... The population is increasing to a marked extent. ... Slavery on the Pamir is flourishing; moreover, the principal contingents of slaves are obtained from Chatrar [Chitral], Yasin, and Kanjut [Hunza], Khanates under the protectorate of England. ... On descending into Pamir we found ourselves between the cordons of the Chinese and Afghan armies. ... The population of Shignan, numbering 2000 families, had fled to Pamir hoping to find a refuge in the Russian provinces from 'the untold atrocities which the Afghans were committing in the conquered provinces of Shignan, &c.'[28]

In 1892 he was promoted to lieutenant-colonel and appointed head of the military district of Osh; in 1903, he became governor of Astrakhan. His three-volume account of his travels was published (in Polish) in Warsaw in 1924–5; his Memoirs were published the following year, also in Warsaw.[29]

Grombchevsky made a major contribution to knowledge of the Pamirs and enjoyed a high reputation both inside and outside Russia. His social origins, his fame, as well as his friendly relations with the Tsar, however, did not serve him well under the Bolsheviks and he died in poverty in 1926.

Pamirsky Post:
Establishment of a permanent Russian presence in the Pamirs

In 1876, after the annexation of the Khanate of Kokand, a young captain, Mikhail Efremovich Ionov, was appointed head of the new military administration in Osh. His post required unusual talents: strong military qualifications, a cool head at a time when Russian power was constantly under threat from local leaders – frequently with

the encouragement of the British – and an ability to understand and negotiate with the local population, jealous of their freedom and nomadic traditions. It was under his supervision that the contours of modern Osh were developed: roads, bridges, canals, bazaars and public buildings.

In 1891, Ionov was put in charge of a 'flying' Pamir detachment that was sent in July to report on the security situation throughout the Pamirs and make a demonstration of Russian sovereignty. They left their camp in Bordaba (now the site of a customs post at the Kyrgyz frontier) on the north side of the Kyzylart pass on 21 July.

One of Ionov's first acts was to appoint a Kyrgyz, Kurumchi-Bek, as headman of the local communities in Rangkul, Murghab and Alichur. This provoked, naturally, the hostility of the Chinese and it did not take long before the Kyrgyz elders wrote formally to Ionov requesting Russian protection. Captain Vasili Nikolaevich Zaitsev – who succeeded Ionov as civil and military administrator of Osh and then of the Pamirs – in his book Памирская страна (*The Pamirs*), published in New Marghilan in 1903, quotes Kurumchi-Bek's reaction to the arrival of the Russians in the Pamirs.

Pamirsky Post [1900]

In the Spring of 1891 the Chinese fetched me to their leader and handed over an order from the Kashgar governor that the Englishman Younghusband was to be received with honours, and shortly afterwards he arrived with 10 armed riders and 20 horses in train. At our first meeting he gave me a double-barrelled breech-loading shotgun, a big Yamba [piece of silver] worth 110 roubles and tried to persuade me to be his faithful servant, promising me the highest position after their occupation of the Pamirs. He said that

the English would first send the Afghans, and then occupy the Pamirs themselves – according to him there may be many Russians here but they are a bad people and their soldiers are undisciplined thieves; his, however, are restrained and honest. For myself, I never saw any English soldiers, and I don't know how they are, but from the Russians we get now only help, without insults and are surprised that we don't hear any bad words from their officers about the English, while they are always swearing about the Russians. Why is this? The Chinese and the Afghans have put a price on my head and now the English are probably angry with me because I took their presents but have not yet provided them with any information.[30]

By early August Ionov reached Boza-i Gumbaz in the Wakhan, and was surprised to find Francis Younghusband camped there. This is how Younghusband described the encounter.

On August 13 the [Russian] reconnoitring party returned [from the Baroghil pass]. As I looked out of the door of my tent, I saw some twenty Cossacks with six officers riding by, and the Russian flag carried in front. I sent out a servant with my card and invitation to the officers to come in and have some refreshments. Some of them came in, and the chief officer was introduced to me as Colonel Yonoff [Ionov]. He and all of them were dressed in loose 'khaki' blouses, with baggy pantaloons and high boots, and they wore the ordinary peaked Russian cap, covered with white cloth. Colonel Yonoff also wore on his breast a white enamel Maltese cross, which I recognised as the Cross of St. George, the most coveted Russian decoration, and I at once congratulated him upon holding so distinguished an order. Colonel Yonoff

Captain Mikhail Efremovich Ionov

was a modest, quiet-mannered man, of a totally different stamp from Captain Grombchevsky. He had less of the bonhomie of the latter, and talked little; but he was evidently respected by his officers, and they told me he had distinguished himself in the Khivan campaign. I gave the Russian officers some tea and Russian wine, which M. Lutsch, the consul's secretary had very kindly procured for me from Marghilan; and then I told Colonel Yonoff that reports had reached me that he was proclaiming to the Kirghiz that the Pamirs were Russian territory, and asked him if this was the case. He said it was so, and he showed me the map with the boundary claimed by the Russians coloured on it. This boundary included the whole of the Pamirs except the Tag-dum-bash, and extended as far down as the watershed of the Hindu-Kush by the Khora Bhort pass.[31]

Ionov invited Younghusband courteously but firmly to leave what he considered to be Russian territory: the famous 'Pamir incident' described in Chapter 4. Ionov's group then travelled to Zorkul over the Bendersky pass and on to Alichur, where – in the second 'Pamir incident' – they met Lieutenant Davison at Sumantash and obliged him to return with them to Marghilan. Ionov also encountered a Chinese armed group in the Alichur Pamir, the leader of which obeyed without demur his request to leave – an act that convinced the Russians that the Chinese had effectively conceded the territory to them. The detachment returned to winter quarters in Marghilan on 13 September, having covered some 1,800 km and asserted *de facto* Russian sovereignty over almost all of the eastern Pamirs.

A much larger Pamir detachment was formed under Ionov in 1892, comprising three cossack squadrons and a battalion with 4 artillery pieces – a total of 3 officers, an engineer, administration officials, 906 lower ranks and 508 horses. The detachment left Marghilan for Osh on 2 June and, on 15 June, set off for the Pamirs with orders to "maintain calm and protect the local population from violence and plunder."

One of Ionov's officers, B.L. Tageyev, wrote a memoir of the expedition, extracts of which were published in the journal Нива (*Field*)[32] the following year, in which he described the suffering of the soldiers unused to marching at altitudes, as they crossed the Taldyk pass ('only' 3,615 m).

> With every hundred steps, the air got thinner and at last got to the point where it was almost beyond human strength to climb higher than we had ever been before. A rifle was no longer an ordinary weight and pressed hard on their shoulders. The

soldiers crept along – some took ten steps and had to sit down, equipment was dragged along, horses fell, the group had to stop and wait and meanwhile all felt the penetrating cold from the snow that covered the pass. And so it was with our transport – I cannot describe the chaos, in which it was impossible to disentangle anything.

And then our eyes took in the majestic and awe-inspiring view of the wide Alai valley, with the Kyzylsu running through it and the white peaks of the Trans Alai beyond. Our attention was involuntarily fixed on this mass of snow reaching up to the clouds and disappearing behind them and we could not escape the thought that in two days we would have to cross it.

In July, Ionov's detachment went on a reconnaissance to Yashil Kul, where they skirmished with a small group of Afghans and effectively ended the Afghan presence in the eastern Pamirs – the British explorer Lord Dunmore (see page 460) arrived very shortly afterwards at the place where the Russians had camped.

.... the marks of their encampment were perfectly fresh; broken bottles, cigarette ends, etc., were all lying about , amongst other camp débris. But the most gruesome sight was that of the Afghan great-coats, which had been taken off the bodies of the dead by the Kirghiz, and had been left lying on the ground as useless, between the scene of the engagement and the camp. These coats were all blood-stained, and on examining them closely, we could guess pretty clearly how each of their ill-fated owners had met his death.

.... I was told afterwards by the Russian officers that Colonel Yonoff had only an escort of nineteen Cossacks, and the officers who were present with him were Colonel Grombtchevsky, Captains Sheremetieff (son of the Governor-General of the Caucasus) Gourko (son of the famous General), and a young officer of Cossacks who commanded the escort. .... the Afghans were well-nigh wiped out, as out of fifteen, fourteen were killed including their captain, Golam Haider Khan.

The Russians were convinced that the British had encouraged the Afghans to attempt to extend their control over the territory on the right bank of the Panj and had armed them specifically for this purpose.[33] Tageyev, in another part of his memoirs,[34] describes the British uniforms of the Afghans they met.[35]

They were dressed in uniforms of red cloth with a white collar and cuffs, and white shoulder flashes and side packs. Their buttons were of copper, with the English royal arms, and they had narrow red shoulder straps with an embroidered inscription 'S. Stafford' – it was obvious that their uniforms were English.

The detachment spent the winter in yurts on the Murghab river, near the ancient cemetery of Schajan at 3,500m. In his memoirs Tageyev described the conditions there.[36]

The first garrison under the command of Captain Kuznetsov of the Joint Staff spent the winter in this fort, living in yurts adapted for the winter conditions. Despite the terrible winds and frosts, all ranks courageously overcame all disasters and deprivations under the leadership of their beloved first officer, and, having safely wintered, returned and were replaced by Captain Zaitsev and his group. In 1893 Major General Povalo-Shveikovsky of the Joint Staff was again appointed as commander of the armies of the Ferghana area, and, on arrival in Marghelan, left directly for the Pamirs, where he made an inspection of the group that had wintered there and, finding all in good condition, expressed his gratitude to the chief of the group, Captain Kuznetsov.

In April 1893, Vasily Nikolaevich Zaitsev was appointed as head of the military and civil administration in the Pamirs and, at the end of July, the military engineer Captain A. Serebrennikov began construction of the Pamirsky Post at the junction of the Akbaital and Murghab rivers – the site of modern Murghab town. By November, they had completed the defensive earthworks, a reception area with a small pharmacy, an officers' wing with offices and a common canteen, together with huts for half a company, a kitchen, a bakery and a sauna. In August 1894, the new construction was inspected by the head of the Turkestan military engineering division, Major-General Klimenko, and Serebrennikov received a high commendation.[37]

Zaitsev was a cultured and well-educated officer, who used his time in the Pamirs to further knowledge of the region by studying its people and their environment. He participated actively in the work of the IRGS, the Asian Society, the Association of Friends of the Natural Sciences and subsequently rose to the rank of Major General. Coming from a humble background, he survived the Bolshevik revolution better than many officers and served in the Red Army. He was highly respected by the local people and, at the age of 75, was invited back in 1926 as an honoured guest to Osh.

Captain Serebrennikov

After spending the winter safely in the Pamirs, Zaitsev's detachment, was replaced in 1894 by a group under Captain Alexander Genrikhovich Skersky – who was the first Russian officer to be accompanied to the Pamirsky Post by his wife.

In August 1894, Sven Hedin was the first non-Russian traveller to visit the new post and described it as follows[38]:

> The Pamirsky Post makes a quite pleasant impression on a foreign traveller. After a long and tiring road through uninhabited and wild mountain regions, he suddenly arrives at this little piece of Great Russia, where a group of the kindest and most hospitable officers receive you like a fellow countryman, like an old acquaintance.
>
> In general the Pamirsky Post reminds one of a naval ship, the walls are the hull, the Murghab river – visible everywhere – is the sea, the courtyard is the deck on which we often strolled and from which we observed with our telescopes the farthest boundaries of vision, where on Tuesday a single rider appeared. It was the Djigit-Courier, who brought the longed-for mail from Russia. His arrival was a real event.
>
> After receiving the mail, the whole day is spent reading it. News from the Fatherland is consumed eagerly and at lunch the officers exchange their impressions about important items of information and events outside in the maelstrom of the western ocean of life.
>
> Everyone shows an exemplary manly bearing, displaying no sign of the long cold Pamir winter that they spend in this desert, in almost the same conditions as polar navigators on their ships frozen in the ice – not a trace of sluggishness, apathy or passivity. Now, when the sun is getting warmer and the snow in the mountains and the ice on rivers and lakes is melting, and new life is awakening, the inhabitants of the fort are especially lively and happy – a new interest in life and nature is awakening. The relations between officers and men are optimal. At the end of their period of service thirty soldiers will return to Osh and it was touching to see how, according to Russian custom, the officers kissed three times each departing member of the lower ranks.

Captain Skersky

Skersky was assailed with reports from the local population of atrocities committed by the Afghans. He reported to his chiefs in Fergana:

> I have received sixteen letters from the local population in Rushan and Shughnan in which they complain of the continuous taxation and oppression of the Afghans. According to the letters, ten of the most typical of which I attach for Your Excellencies, the population is driven to despair.[39]

The following from the headman of the population of Yazgulem, is typical.

> I must tell you that Ibadullah Khan [ruler of Badakhshan] has called us to him. If we do not come he threatens to plunder our homes. We are now poor and in difficulty. We beg you to think of our poor people and trust in your goodness. Ibadullah Khan says the Russians will not defend us.[40]

On 9 July 1894, Ionov arrived with his staff, with orders to mount an extensive reconnoitring expedition to the Shakhdara and Ghunt valleys and to the small settlement of Khorog at the junction of the latter with the Panj, in order to forestall a strengthening of the Afghan positions on the right bank of the Panj. Although the Russian forces had extensive survey knowledge of the Pamirs, they had not yet penetrated this far into Shughnan: in 1883, Ivanov was in Sarez and the Ghunt valley as far as Sardem, in 1886 Captains Pokotilo, Trussov and the surveyor Glagoliev had travelled in Darvaz along the right bank of the Panj – followed in 1891 by Komarovsky and, a year later, by Kuznetsov. In August 1893, a small survey group under captain Vannovsky had travelled from Pamirsky Post to Savnob and then almost all the way down the Bartang. They had engaged the Afghans at Yemts and escaped into the Yazgulem valley at Andarbak, returning from there to Ferghana through Vanch and Kala-i Khum.[41] In October-November of the same year, another Russian officer, Captain Bedryag, had made a reconnaissance tour from Savnob through Sarez and then to Kara Kul and along the Markansu to Kashgar, returning to Pamirsky Post via Rang Kul. Regel, as noted above, had been to Shughnan for purely scientific purposes in 1882.[42]

Captain A. Serebrennikov kept an account of life in Pamirsky Post in his diary.[43] After a long winter there, the Russians were suffering from the "monotonous run of garrison life" and Ionov's orders provided welcome relief.

> ... we were all heartily sick of the great 'monotonous Pamir,' which should furnish an ideal country for the pessimist if he is ever in want of such. Indeed, for an image to express downright, utter melancholy, in the abstract, I cannot think of anything

more apt than the picture of a pessimist reading Schopenhauer in the Pamirs. It is the 'land of no hope.'

On 19 July,

> Our two parties, each consisting of three officers, twelve infantry, twenty cossacks, and some guides, set out at eight o'clock this morning in a drizzling mist. We forded the river Murghab after parting from and receiving the good wishes of all our brother-officers remaining behind, and also—last but not least—those of the only lady on the Pamirs, Madame S.G. Skerskaya, who had, in spite of the weather, made one of our honorary escort up to this point.

The group reconnoitring the Ghunt valley was led by Lieutenant-Colonel Judenich; that in the Shakhdara valley – in which Serebrennikov participated – was led by Skersky.[44] On 22 July they camped at Tuz Kul.

> Here we received a deputation of a hundred Shughnanis, who petitioned us on behalf of the inhabitants of the Shakh-Dara for protection against the Afghans. They were a poor, dispirited looking body of men, and must have stood to the Afghans as sheep to wolves. Their dress, made from the coarsest stuffs, led us to think that they were all simple peasants; but in this we were mistaken, as we soon perceived, for no less a personage than Azis-Khan, nephew of the last independent ruler of Shakh-Dara, was amongst them. This was the ruler who had been executed in Rosh-kala by order of the Shughnan ruler (Shah-Abduraim-Khan).

Serebrennikov's group crossed the Koitezek pass and travelled down the Shakhdara from Jawshangoz 'accompanied by an enthusiastic and increasing crowd of Tajiks and Kirghiz' as far as Roshtkala, where they encountered the first Afghan troops. After a short skirmish, Russian reinforcements arrived and the Afghans retreated to their base at Kala-i Bar Panj, enabling the Russians to continue their explorations as far as Khorog, where they were joined by the group that had descended the Ghunt valley. Undisturbed by the Afghans, the Russians completed a survey of the Panj between the ruby mines and Vomar.[45]

> On the right (Russian) side of the Panj are about fourteen kishlags. The whole country is rather densely populated, and the inhabitants are fairly well-to-do. The climate is so mild that even vines grow here, and are cultivated by the Tajiks. A nearer acquaintance with the Tajiks, and the study of their customs and manners, forces us to sympathize with this persecuted nation, which has gone through so many trials. Indeed, it is a wonder how it is they have not disappeared from the face

of the earth. In far-off times this nation turned their eyes towards the north, to the Russians, and waited patiently for the occasion when they might become subjects of the great white Tsar, and thus free themselves from the persecution of the Afghans. This desire to be under Russian government, which was one of the principal reasons why the Afghans persecuted them, did not weaken as time went on, notwithstanding that their hopes were not soon realized. With the appearance of the Russians on the borders of Shughnan in 1894, it seemed that the end of their miseries had come, but fate has once more mocked their hopes, for, as we could not gain permission to leave even a small garrison to winter in Shughnan, we had to return. This we did *via* the Gund valley on September 15, followed by a great number of Tajiks and their families. The latter were forced to migrate in anticipation of revengeful reprisals from the Afghans, which would undoubtedly follow their having extended such a friendly welcome to us.

Serebrennikov estimated the inhabitants of Shughnan (right bank) at 3,779 in 1894 and the 1896 census carried out by the Russians recorded a total of 2,221 Kirgyz in the eastern Pamirs. Serebrennikov also noted that

The position we occupied in the valley of the Kharokh offered many conveniences, and if at some future time we should have to maintain a garrison in Shughnan, and to erect a fortified position there, this place should undoubtedly be chosen.

This was to be realised only a year later.

Russo-British Border Agreement
and Transfer of the Russian Base to Khorog (1895)

In March 1895 – as we have seen in Chapter 4 – agreement was reached between the Russians and the British on the need to reach a final settlement of the boundaries and respective spheres of influence in the Pamirs. A Boundary Commission was set up and both parties gathered on the banks of Lake Zorkul in June: the Russian mission, under General Povalo-Shveikovsky, included Colonels Galkin and Zaleski, Lieutenant Orakolov, Captains Krutorogin and Alexandrovich, Mr. Bendersky (the two last-named acting as surveyors), Dr. Welman and Mr. Panafidine (a Frenchman who acted as Secretary); and the British, under Major General M.G. Gerard, included Colonel T.H. Holdich, Captain E.F.H. McSwiney, Major Wahab and Dr. Alcock).

The work of the 1885 Afghan Boundary Commission had been hampered by the absence of comprehensive topographical knowledge of the area and the Russians had bowed to the better survey data possessed by the British; in the case of the Pamir boundary, the situation was reversed as the Russians by now possessed more accurate information extending as far north as Osh that was recognised by their British colleagues as "of the first rank." At their first meeting each side compared the other's data on the frontier region with its own and Holdich commented:

> We found ourselves standing on the roof of the world, with practically no differences between us to eliminate and disperse as far as our mapping was concerned.[46]

On 28 July the first two pillars were placed; a third – on the pass subsequently named after the Russian surveyor Bendersky – on 5 August; the fourth and fifth at the Urta Bel pass on 14 August; and the last ones on 8 September just before the advent of snow. The final protocols were concluded shortly after. A delegation from Afghan Badakhshan arrived on 27 July and set their seals to the protocol and other official documents, and the British representative in Kashgar, George Macartney, arrived on 7 August with some Chinese representatives from Kashgar to witness the work. It is perhaps amusing to note that, since the Secretary of the Commission was French, that language was used for all documents, correspondence and discussions.

The English version of the Commission's report was withheld from publication until 1899 for reasons that are not fully apparent. Gerard contributed an account of the arrangements preliminary to delimitation (and of his journey through Russian Turkestan after the completion of its work); Holdich gave a report of the proceedings – together with historical and geographical notes on the Pamir region; Wahab wrote the detailed technical report *per se*; and Alcock added a section on natural history.[47] Holdich gives a vivid description of the ceremonies at the farewell dinner organised by the British:

> The scene of the dinner was one which will be long remembered in the Pamirs. With considerable difficulty and delay a supply of wood had been collected from valleys south of the Hindu Kush as a provision against a winter sojourn on the Pamirs.[48] All this wood was now stacked into such a bonfire as the Pamirs will never see again, and round about it various dances were performed with much spirit and energy. The night was still, and as cold as 25 degrees of frost could make it, and the moonlight glinted on the freezing surface of marsh and river, adding not a little to the fantastic effect of the scene. Men of Hunza and Nagar, Khataks and Cossacks, Kirghiz and Wakhis, all danced to the inspiriting strains produced from two

kerosene tins and a reed pipe, with a Cossack concertina accompaniment. The dances were led by a most able master of ceremonies in the person of Lieutenant Miles, who had joined the Commission party for a few days from a political tour in Hunza. The proceedings closed with the old-world chorus of 'Auld Lang Syne.'[49]

Following the border settlement, Captain Sulitsko replaced Skersky as head of the Pamir forces and, in early 1896, when the transfer of territory between Afghanistan and Bokhara was complete, the Russians began construction of a base in Khorog. The main Russian garrison was moved from Murghab to Khorog in the following year. Sulitsko reported that more than a hundred Pamiri families then returned from Ferghana to Shughnan, where they were resettled without incident. He added that he was able to free some of the last slaves on the Pamirs and help them establish an independent existence by a gift of cattle.[50]

Sulitsko was replaced by Captain Eggert and, in August 1897, Captain Edward Karlovich Kivekes, a Russian of Finnish origin took over the command in Khorog. The following year, the British explorer Ralph Cobbold (see page 491), having been arrested by the Bukharan rulers in Vomar, became an involuntary "guest" of the garrison in Khorog (although with all courtesy and actually in Kivekes's residence) and noted that the Russian fort was

> strongly built of clay, wood and stones, and the earthworks are of great thickness. The fort was laid out under the direction of Kevekiss [Kivekes], who certainly deserved great credit for his work, considering the means at his disposal and the lack of skilled labour. The garrison consisted of four officers and about fifty Cossacks, and there were two Maxim guns mounted on the earthworks facing the river, as a warning to the Afghans of what might be expected if trouble arose.

Kivekes – who is still held in great esteem in the Pamirs – and his wife adopted a young Pamiri girl, Gulbegim Barakat, who returned with them to Finland at the end of their tour of duty.

In 1896, scientific expeditions (botany, glaciology) were organised by Vladimir Ippolitovich Lipsky (1863–1937)[51] and Sergey Ivanovich Kordjinsky (1861–1900).[52] Lipsky returned in 1897 and 1899 and, as we have seen, Olga Alexandrovna Fedchenko and her son Boris Alexeyevich undertook research on the flora of the Pamirs from 1900 to 1904, exploring several 'new' passes, including the Shtam pass.[53] Between 1903 and 1928, Nikolai Leopoldovich Korjenevsky (1879–1958), an autodidact, made major contributions to geological and geographical knowledge of the Pamirs and, in 1904, was the first to explore the Muksu valley from end to end.[54]

D.I. Golovnin and Mrs. Yu. D Golovnina, with M.M. Voskoboyinikov and N.P. Bartenjewa in 1898 and Nicolas de Poggenpohl in 1907 visited the Pamirs as perhaps the first Russian 'tourists'.[55] The first archaeological and ethnographic surveys were undertaken by A.A. Bobrinsky in 1898.[56]

The Russian presence in the Pamirs was now firmly established; all the valleys and several of the main passes had been comprehensively surveyed and mapped: the age of the pioneers was past. The region settled down and the Russians introduced many innovations, including medical posts (with trained medical personnel – 'feldschers'), infrastructure improvements, vocational training and the first cabbages and potatoes. In 1905 the post of deputy (Beg) of the Emir of Bukhara in Shughnan was abolished, and administrative authority over the whole of the Pamirs passed to the Russian head of the Pamir detachment.

Kivekes was replaced successively by Andrei Yevgenevich Snessarev (from 1902 to 1908), Grigori Andreevich Shpilko (1908 to 1914) and Ivan Dionisievich Yagello (1914 to 1917). Snessarev wrote several books and articles on the ethnography and history of the Pamirs[57] and Shpilko left a substantial collection of photographs, several of which are now in the Khorog museum.[58] The famous British archaeologist, Aurel Stein (see below) had a fortuitous encounter in the Alai with Colonel Yagello in 1915, and described him as 'an oriental scholar deeply interested in the geography and ethnography of the Oxus regions, and anxious to aid whatever investigations could throw fresh light on their past.'[59]

In 1907, a Captain of Russian Joint Staff, A.K. Razgonov, undertook a thorough survey of the inhabited areas of the Pamirs and in his report, published by the

Kivekes and his adopted Pamiri daughter

Turkestan military district in 1910, in addition to cultural and religious information, estimated the local population at 25,000 Tajiks in the valleys leading to the Panj and 2,000 Kyrgyz on the high plateau.[60]

Several Russian scientific expeditions to the Pamirs were subsequently organised, of which the most important were:[61]

1915–1932: I. Nalivkin (geological research);

1916: N. Vavilov (botanist) visited Shughnan and Rushan districts and discovered many wild species of grains in the Pamirs;[62]

1923: first Soviet expedition led by Korjenevsky (topography, glaciers, geology, flora and fauna of the remote regions of the Pamirs). N. Raikova participated in this expedition and continued her work in the Pamirs for more than five years;

1928: Soviet-German joint expedition led by Nicolai Petrovich Gorbunov and Willi Rickmer Rickmers (eleven Russian and eleven German participants). The expedition surveyed and mapped most of the glaciers in the NW Pamirs – including Fedchenko – and made geophysical, botanical, zoological and ethnographic studies (the results published by the German team are described in the separate section on Rickmer Rickmers in the next chapter);

1932–1935: Tajik-Pamirs expeditions led by Gorbunov and Pavel Nicolaevich Luknitzsky.

The results of the multi-disciplinary expeditions undertaken from 1928 to 1935 were published by the Academy of Sciences in Moscow. The abstracts and bibliography alone, published in 1936,[63] comprise 249 pages and they effectively filled in the last blank spots on the map of the Pamirs.

British and other Adventurers and Explorers

After the 'pundits', the most extensive British exploration of the Pamirs was carried out by Ney Elias, who crossed from Western China to Rangkul in September 1885 and travelled throughout the Pamirs, surveying parts of Afghan Badakhshan, the Shakhdara, Ghunt, Alichur and Bartang valleys, as well as the Panj from Ishkashim as far as Voznavd. From the Bartang, he assessed several passes across to the Yazgulem valley and concluded that these were not suitable for any Russian military movements. By taking measurements at Vomar, Elias was able to conclude definitively that the Panj – and not the Aksu-Murghab-Bartang – was the main stream of the Oxus. He estimated the population on the right bank of the river at about 4,000 in Shughnan and 3,000 in Rushan, and the Kyrgyz population of the Eastern Pamirs at about 5,000.[1]

In the same year that Elias was travelling in the Pamirs, a British mission under Colonel W. Lockhart, including Colonel Woodthorpe, Captain Barrow and Dr. Giles, was sent to survey Chitral: in 1886, they were briefly in the Wakhan.[2]

The first complete north-south crossing of the Pamirs to India by Europeans was undertaken in 1887 by three French adventurers, Pierre Gabriel Édouard Bonvalot (1853–1933), Guillaume Capus and Albert Pépin.[3]

In 1888–9, a number of other 'tourists' visited the Pamirs for hunting and/or adventure, including: Major Charles Sperling Cumberland (1847–1922), Lieutenant H. Bower, the Vicomte de Breteuil, L. Richard, H. Dauvergne (a French trader), Raymond Casal and two Americans, H. Ridgeway and Arthur O'Connor, followed in 1891 by H. Lennard, R. Beech and Lieutenant J.M. Stewart, who were in the southern Pamirs.[4]

Francis Younghusband (1863–1942), whom we have already met in the context of the travels of Grombchevsky and Ionov, was in Sarikol and the Tagdumbash Pamir in 1889 on the way to Hunza (having travelled all the way from Beijing); in 1890, he travelled extensively in the Great and Alichur Pamirs, accompanied by George Macartney (British representative in Kashgar), visiting Yashil Kul, Rang Kul and Kara Kul. In 1891, he and Lieutenant Davison left Kashgar for a further exploration of the Pamirs that was to lead to the famous 'Pamir incident' referred to above. They returned together through the Pamir-i Wakhan to Gilgit.[5]

In 1890, St George R. Littledale hunted at Kara Kul and in 1892 crossed from Osh to India with Mrs. Theresa Littledale, who was the first non-indigenous woman in the Pamirs. They returned in 1895 and travelled through Irkeshtam to Kashgar and Peking.[6]

In 1892, Charles Adolphus Murray, Earl of Dunmore (1841–1907), accompanied by Major Roche, undertook a twelve-month journey from Ladakh through the Taghdumbash, Great and Alichur Pamirs, to Osh.[7]

By this time, the age of the pioneer explorers was past and the stream of visitors was steadily increasing. In 1893, the French explorer Vicomte Edmond de Poncins crossed the Pamirs from north to south,[8] and an Italian, Felix de Rocca, travelled from Daroot-Kurgan to Gharm, Kala-i Khum and Vanch,[9] followed the next year by a Dutchman, Comte de Bylandt and a future Viceroy of India, the Hon. George Nathaniel Curzon, who was accompanied by H. Lennard.[10] It was on this expedition that Curzon effectively put an end to the burning controversy over the exact source of the Oxus. From the Taghdumbash Pamir, Curzon crossed the Wakhjir Pass (4,927m) to the watershed of the west-flowing stream, the Wakhjir.

> From far above, the main glacier can be seen winding round from the north or left hand to the head of the gorge, in which, however, its point of discharge is not visible. Descending to the shingle-bed, which varies from 100 to 350 yards in width, the channel being divided into several branches of from 6 to 18 inches deep, I rode up it to the source. There the river issues from two ice-caverns in a rushing stream. The cavern on the right has a low overhanging roof, from which the water gushes tumultuously out. The cavern on the left was sufficiently high to admit of my looking into the interior, and within for some distance I could follow the river, which was blocked with great slabs of ice, while there was a ceaseless noise of grinding, crunching, and falling in. Above the ice-caves is the precipitous front wall or broken snout of the glacier, from 60 to 80 feet in height, composed of moraine ice, covered with stones and black dust. I clambered up this to the level of the top of the moraine, and from there could see the big glacier, with its jagged ice-towers and pinnacles and crevasses coming down from a valley on the left. A lofty mountain crowned with snow blocked up the end of the main valley, and from a nullah on the right of this, another ice-field contributed its volume to the main glacier, whose terminal moraine was jammed up and contracted in the narrow outlet of the two valleys. The source of the river is, therefore, not in three great glaciers, but in one great glacier, to which smaller glaciers contribute.

Curzon went on to demolish the arguments in favour of the other 'candidates': as far as the Pamir river (flowing from Zorkul or 'Wood's lake') was concerned:

> Neither in length, volume, nor any of the requisite characteristics, can it base any claim to be really accounted the parent stream, and we may therefore dismiss it from consideration.

As far as the other hypotheses were concerned, Trotter had discovered in 1874 that the outflow from the Chakmaktynkul was not in a westerly direction but east to the Aksu; and the current in the Aksu-Murghab-Bartang river had been shown by Elias in 1885 to be stronger than the Panj at their confluence only at the height of summer, and less deep throughout the year.

Sven Hedin, one of the best-known explorers of the 19th century, was in the Pamirs in 1894–95 and was the first foreign visitor to the Pamirsky Post, meeting up briefly with the Boundary Commission in the Wakhan.[11]

In 1897–98, Ralph Patteson Cobbold travelled extensively in the Western Pamirs and was the first European to travel all the way down the Bartang to Vomar; his account[12] was accompanied by photographs taken by a British couple, Mr. and Mrs. Leslie Renton, who had recently crossed the Pamirs from north to south but left no other record of their travels.

Rickmer Rickmers Expedition [1898]

Ole Olufsen, a lieutenant in the Danish army, led a Danish expedition to Alichur, Wakhan, Khorog, Yazgulem, Vanch and Gharm in 1896–7 and a second in 1898–9 when they established winter quarters in Khorog and returned to Osh in deep snow in early 1899.[13] Later that year, George Saint Yves, a French geographer and archaeologist, was in the eastern Transalai[14] and, in 1900, the first German traveller 'discovered' the Pamirs: Wilhelm Filchner (1877–1957) rode on horseback from Osh to Kashgar via the Taghdumbash Pamir, where he ran into the famous archaeologist Aurel Stein.[15]

Stein was one of the most indefatigable explorers of the modern era and his third expedition in 1915 – a journey of three months – brought him back to the Pamirs. Starting from Kashgar, his route took him down the Alai, across the Ters Agar pass to Kara Kul, and then down the Tanimas and Ghudara rivers to the newly formed lake in Sarez, of which he left a photographic record. From there, he travelled across the Langar pass to Yashil Kul, over the Bashgumbez pass to Zorkul and the Wakhan and from there down the Panj, stopping in Khorog and making excursions into the Bartang, Yazgulem and Vanch valleys and the Karategin, reaching the latter by crossing the high passes rather than following the Panj to Kala-i Khum.[16]

In 1903, an American geologist, Raphael Pumpelly (1837–1923), travelled as far as Kara Kul and a member of his expedition, Ellsworth Huntington, explored the northern slopes of the Trans-Alai.[17] In 1905, 1909 and 1911–12, another German, Arved von Schultz, travelled extensively in the Pamirs and took the first photograph of the Sarez lake.[18]

In 1913, the Austrian and German Alpine associations organised a joint expedition to the Pamirs, led by Willi Rickmer Rickmers – who participated later as the joint leader of the Soviet-German expedition in 1928.[19]

The 1911 Encyclopaedia Britannica commented – perhaps with a touch of irony – that "since 1875 the Pamirs have probably been the best explored region in High Asia.

Gabriel Bonvalot (1887)

In February 1886, three Frenchmen, Gabriel Bonvalot, Guillaume Capus and Albert Pépin, embarked in Marseilles for a voyage to Central Asia that was to last eighteen months and that very nearly cost them their lives.[1] Even though the members of the group were relatively wealthy, their expedition was financed by the French government. Indeed, during this golden age of exploration, public money was freely available and within the French Ministry of Education there was even a departmental committee that reviewed proposals for the funding of expeditions overseas. They also received substantial assistance en route from the Russian military in Central Asia – and, something they themselves probably never envisaged, from the government of India. Bonvalot, an accomplished explorer although only 24 at the time, was the leader of the expedition and in charge of historical and ethnographic information; Capus, a medical doctor, was to collect data on natural history; and Pépin was to take photographs and make sketches.

In 1880–1882, Bonvalot and Capus had been on the lower Oxus between Khiva and Mazar-i Sharif, and had travelled from there to Siberia[2]; the aim of the present journey was to explore the upper Oxus and attempt to reach Kafiristan (present-day Nuristan in Eastern Afghanistan). Although Bonvalot and his group are probably best remembered as being the first Europeans to cross the Pamirs to India, this route was not what they had originally planned and was forced on them by the unrest in Afghanistan at the time. Shortly after crossing the Amu Darya near Termez in the autumn of 1886, they were arrested by the Afghans and held for nearly a month – their release, Bonvalot remarks sardonically, was "above all due to the fact that they took us for Russians."

Returning to Samarqand, they met with General Karalkoff (who had been their host some months earlier), and explained to him their difficulties in pursuing their expedition and their desire to travel to India. Karalkoff suggested they should travel via Kashgar, but – having also discussed with the Russians in Samarqand the most recent Russian expeditions in the Pamirs (see above) – they decided to attempt to reach India over the Pamirs and across the Wakhan. Despite the extensive exploration by Putyata, Bendersky and Ivanov, no Russian had yet crossed the Wakhan[3], although it would not be long before Grombchevsky's ride to Hunza and the famous meeting between Ionov and Younghusband in Boza-i Gumbaz.

Helped in their preparations in Osh by Grombchevsky, they set off on 6 March 1887. Winter lasts six months in the high Pamirs and they could expect severe weather conditions en route. Bonvalot and his companions decided not to wait for better weather: they had heard reports that there was little snow on the Kyzyl Art pass and that the upper valleys were open all year round; the Kyrgyz herders and the Afghan and Chinese frontier guards would have left for winter quarters and would not interfere with their progress; moreover, the lakes and rivers would be frozen and could be crossed easily or used as roads. It was a decision taken with only partial knowledge of the risks involved and, in the aftermath, Bonvalot admitted that it was "imprudent."

> *Nous avions à traverser un désert à la température du pôle, souvent plus haut que la cime du Mont-Blanc, où n'avions ni combustible, ni fourrage, rien, rien que la neige et de fréquentes tempêtes en perspective, qu'on disait être épouvantables. Il fallait s'armer contre ces difficultés et contre les quelques bandes de brigands kirghis, rebut des tribus de la plaine, que les vendettas qui les menacent obligent à se réfugier dans les vallées les mieux abritées, ainsi que font les bêtes méchantes chassées de partout.* (We were obliged to cross a desert at a temperature one finds at the North pole, often at an altitude above the summit of Mont-Blanc – we had no fuel, fodder, nothing, nothing but the snow and frequent storms ahead of us, storms that were reputed to be terrible. We had to be prepared for these difficulties and for the gangs of Kyrgyz brigands, outcasts from the tribes on the plain, forced by the vendettas against them to seek refuge in those valleys offering the best protection, hunted everywhere like wild animals.)

For heating, they carried petrol, alcohol, tinder and wood, as well as a large metal plate on which their fire could be set up in the snow. They bought medicines and ointments (for frozen extremities), ready-cooked millet and dried apricots against altitude sickness, spades, picks, axes, horseshoes, nails, iron tentpegs and local rope – made with horse hair and easier to handle at low temperatures with numb fingers. Having doubled the best estimates of the volume of provisions required for eight men for two months (the expected length of their journey to India), they stocked up with sugar, tea, large quantities of biscuit, mutton fat, oil, salted meat, flour, barley and smoked mutton and fish. They agreed that, if ever they had to escape from an attack, each would stuff his fur coat with his notes and as much smoked fish as he could carry and that their only luggage on the run would be a rifle and a plentiful supply of cartridges.

For clothing, they had boots of thick felt, with leather soles, long felt socks, thick cotton underwear, wide trousers into which was tucked a close-fitting sheepskin jacket, and, covering all, a heavy fur coat with long wide sleeves, narrow at the wrist. Their headgear was a sheepskin bonnet, covering the ears, on top of which was placed a large hood reaching to the shoulder that could be drawn across to cover the mouth and nose in extreme cold. Finally, the eyes were protected by thick blue goggles. Bonvalot aptly described their appearance as resembling a pre-historic monster.

They already knew on leaving that it was snowing heavily in the Alai, that the Terek pass was impracticable and that they would have to go over the Taldyk pass, which no European explorer had yet attempted at that time of year. At the foot of the pass a strong wind was blowing, it was snowing heavily and the temperature had already gone down below -10°C.

It was only due to the extraordinary efforts of a team of 200 Kyrgyz workmen recruited for them by the Russian military that they were able to get across in three days, after which they fully expected the remainder of their journey to be easier.

On 17 March they reached the edge of the Alai to find it covered in thick snow, three metres deep in places. Thirty horses were sent on ahead with provisions to await their arrival at the foot of the Kyzyl Art pass, but no precautions were taken to ensure that there would be no pilfering – this would prove to be a costly error.

Je regarde, tout est blanc, éblouissant, on a la sensation d'être dans un autre monde, d'être tombé dans une planète désolée. J'aperçois les collines de la vallée de l'Alai enchevêtrées comme des boucliers blancs de guerriers, faisant la tortue aux pied des cônes immenses et impassibles du TransAlai, ce second rempart du Pamir. De quelque côté que l'oeil se dirige, tout est blanc, un linceul immaculé est développé sur cette nature sans vie, au calme cadavérique; on dirait une terre abandonnée de ses habitants partis pour

Nöth and Finsterwalder, Russo-German Expedition [1928]

un monde meilleur. (I look out, everything is white, dazzling, and I have the impression I am in another world, that I have fallen on a desolate planet. I perceive the hills of the Alai valley, entangled like white warriors' shields, in tortoise formation at the foot of the immense impassable peaks of the Transalai, the second rampart of the Pamirs. All is white, as far as the eye can see – an immaculate shroud now covers this lifeless nature and there is a corpse-like calm; one might think its inhabitants had left this land for a better world.)

In the Alai, the snow was so deep that their progress fell to a crawl – 10 to 20 metres a minute, and the firmness of the snow ahead had to be tested carefully with a long stick. After several days of this, the Kyrgyz porters threatened to return and Bonvalot had to promise a full day of rest and extra rations of mutton to persuade them to continue. On the other side of the valley they picked up the provisions sent on ahead – but four hundred kilos of barley and wood were missing. Finally, on 24 March, they were within sight of Kara Kul, where there was much less snow. With the exception of one guide and four chosen bearers, the Kyrgyz refused to continue. In the night, a few fled with several sacks of barley and the party was reduced to eight with eighteen horses, half the reserves of food and only 300kg of fodder for the horses. As we have seen, Fedchenko, Kostenko, Oshanin, Severtsov and others, aware of the dangers, did indeed turn back when faced with similar difficulties – but Bonvalot and his group pressed on.

The snow was still deep beyond Kara Kul in the Akbaital valley and they decided to leave it. They went up to the Uzbel pass and crossed to Rangkul, where they found a few Kyrgyz herders and rested the horses for two days.

Afraid that the Kyrgyz would pass word of their presence to the Chinese authorities, Bonvalot and his companions kidnapped the leaders and stole their horses. On 1 April, they continued their route up the Aksu to Aktash, using similar forcible means to acquire provisions and transport.[4]

On 9 April, their guide disappeared with the best horse. The snow remained deep and treacherous and the passes to the Taghdumbash Pamir were inaccessible – the weather worsened with day-long snow flurries. In Aktash there were too many Kyrgyz for them to use force to obtain provisions, and they continued to the Andaman pass where they 'requisitioned' horses from a Kyrgyz camp there. With the exception of their two servants Sadik and Aldurasul, the Kyrgyz had already returned and the Wakhis recruited to replace them had run away after only three days. Finally, in the

Wakhan, there was less snow and – reaching Sarhad on 7 May – they found pasture for the horses.

Hearing that Afghan troops were on their way from Kala-i-Bar Panj to arrest them, they sent Sadik and Aldurasul back to Ferghana – because of the force used against the Kyrgyz, they were by now wanted men and would in any case not be safe in Chitral – and set off on 10 May, with only eight horses, a little mutton fat and some flour. On 24 May, Bonvalot sent Capus and Pépin ahead with a letter to the British authorities and to get help from the ruler of Chitral, Aman ul-Mulk. Finally, having satisfied himself that they were not Russians, the Viceroy, Lord Dufferin, sent money and passports and they were able to continue through Punyal and Yasin to Kashmir, where they arrived on 14 August and were debriefed by the British.

Bonvalot's expedition was certainly an adventure, but it is difficult to define a clear scientific purpose for it. The group was badly prepared (they left without some basic scientific instruments such as a thermometer or hydrometer) and greatly underestimated the risks they were taking at the end of the Pamir winter. Their use of force and theft from the local population to compensate for their poor planning and lack of vigilance leaves a bad taste. It is not enough to claim, as Bonvalot does, that the Kyrgyz they met en route were grasping, scheming and venal: subsequent travellers such as Littledale, Cobbold and Filchner, as well as the many Russians travelling in small groups in the Pamirs at this time, make no such complaints and – through financial incentives and persuasion – almost always obtained the collaboration they needed from the local population.

Capus had written articles on his botanical discoveries on his first expedition with Bonvalot in 1880–1882 and Bonvalot's subsequent expedition to Tibet and China with Prince Henri d'Orléans resulted in the collection of many zoological specimens[5] – but from their expedition to the Pamirs nothing of scientific interest was brought back. After his return Capus did indeed write a number of articles on subjects relating to the Pamirs[6] but they are largely derivative and do not add much to the sum of knowledge already collected more systematically by the Russians. As far as their geography is concerned, Curzon commented with some understatement that "their descriptions and nomenclature are … confused and inexact."

Curzon also complained of their lack of gratitude for the substantial help provided by the Indian government to get them out of difficulty[7] and Bonvalot's character can perhaps best be judged from the bombast of his closing words to the *Société de Géographie* on 14 January 1888:

Un mot pour finir. A Simla nous nous sommes trouvés en société d'officiers et de hauts fonctionnaires des Indes, qui s'intéressent fort à notre voyage. L'un d'eux nous dit avant de nous quitter "Je suis assuré que vos compatriotes seront fiers et qu'ils vous couvriront d'honneurs." – "Je ne sais pas ce qui adviendra," lui répondis-je, "ni si l'on sera très fier de nous. Quoi qu'il en soit, je puis assurer que nous avons agi de notre mieux en pensant à faire, autant que possible, honneur à notre pays." (Just a word in conclusion : in Simla, we found ourselves in the company of officers and important officials of India, who were very interested in our journey. One of them said to us before we left: "I am certain your compatriots will be so proud of you that you will be covered in honours." – "I do not know what awaits us," I replied, "nor if people will be very proud of us. But whatever happens, I can assure you that we did our best in the hope, as far as possible, of bringing honour to our country.")

Bonvalot went on to a successful career in French politics.

Mr & Mrs St George R. Littledale (1890 & 1892)

On 11 April 1890, two of the most indefatigable and engaging travellers of the nineteenth century left their home at Wick Hill House in Bracknell, England, for Odessa, Batumi and adventure in Central Asia. Mr. and Mrs. St. George Littledale were about to start on the first of their two joint journeys to the Pamirs, with the aim of reaching Kashgar through Badakhshan and Chitral (in the previous year, not accompanied by his wife, Littledale had got as far as Kara Kul and had brought back some hunting trophies). Theirs was only the second expedition by European explorers to cross the Pamirs from north to south (Bonvalot, Capus and Pépin were the first in 1887). Mrs. Littledale has the additional distinction of being the first non-indigenous woman in the Pamirs[1] and, from Littledale's accounts of their travels together, she must be counted one of the most intrepid women explorers of all time.

Apart from the reports submitted by Littledale to the Royal Geographical Society[2], they did not, unlike several other explorers of the period, publish any more comprehensive account of their travels. Littledale became a friend of President Theodore Roosevelt,[3] another big game hunter, and worked with him on the introduction of elk to New Zealand in 1905. He made a gift of one of his trophies to King Edward VII and, on his death in 1921, bequeathed his taxidermic specimens to the Natural History Museum in London.[4] A sub-species of the Marco Polo sheep, the *Ovis ammon littledalei* from the Tien Shan, is named after him.[5]

Of Mrs. Littledale we only know that she was born Theresa Newcomen Julia Eveleigh Harris on 12 August 1839 at Eldon House, London, Ontario, Canada, that Littledale was her second husband and that she died, childless, in 1928 in Hertfordshire, England.[6] From an early photograph, showing a rather conventional young lady with a girlish air about her, only the set of the mouth and head gives any hint of the strength of will that carried her through some of the most difficult mountain terrain then known to man. Although she fell seriously ill on the second of her trips to Central Asia,[7] there is, as we shall see, only one record of any complaint on her part about the rigours of travel there.

Armed with official permits from St. Petersburg and letters from the Russian Ambassador in Britain, the Littledales landed in Batumi on the Black Sea on 19 April and began confronting the first of many obstacles put in the way of their pioneering journey with a sense of humour that never deserted them until they finally arrived in Srinagar five months later. Littledale's guns had been carried as freight and the importation of arms was strictly forbidden unless as personal baggage – the Russian Ambassador's letter carried no weight with the Batumi customs officials. Frantic telegrams from the British Consul to St. Petersburg finally freed the guns under seal until his next stop, Usun-Ada, on the Eastern Caspian, at the head of the Trans-Caspian railway, where they were to be unsealed and inspected by the officials there before he was allowed to proceed.

The Customs chief at Usun-Ada was away and his deputy was unwilling to take any risks until he received confirmation from Batumi of the instructions in the letter carried by Littledale. The next steamer, however, was not due for two days and, in his reaction to this apparent setback we get a first glimpse of Littledale's ingenuity and resourcefulness as a traveller; indeed, throughout the narrative the reader is struck by how well the Littledales had prepared for all eventualities, including the alternative itineraries on their route, which were scarcely common knowledge at that time:

> One learns not only to be patient, but also wily when travelling in the East, so, with the aid of an obliging officer of the Russian Guards, with whom we had made friends in a quiet way, we thoroughly scared the official who refused to take off the

seals, and then set to work to interview every likely and unlikely functionary. At last we unearthed one, who, after a brief consultation with our friend, tore off the seals, and we were free.

They finally started on the rail journey to Samarqand on 29 April.

The Russians had laid on every comfort for them: a special rail carriage, good food, the hospitality of the Governor of Ferghana in Marghilan, General Korolkoff, and of the commander in Osh, Colonel Deubner, as well as the practical assistance of the latter in putting together their caravan.

In Osh they collected a total of twenty-five horses, baked two thousand biscuits as rations for the men accompanying them and bought clothing appropriate for the expedition on which they were about to embark.

> I invested in a coat reaching down to my heels, cloth outside, sheepskin within, and a cap with a kind of curtain all round which made a cape over my shoulders, also of sheepskin. Mrs. Littledale had brought lots of wraps, but we had an extra lining of Khotan lambskin put into a cape of Harris cloth, which had already a thick wadding; it was heavy, but she only wore it riding; it completely covered her and the saddle. She found it delightfully warm.

In Tbilisi they had "bought every dried ox tongue we could lay our hands upon," since they "are very portable and made a delightful change from the inevitable mutton we had to live upon later on." Great attention was also paid to proper personal comfort.

> I attribute the good health we have always enjoyed on our expeditions mainly to the fact that no matter how cold or wet the weather may have been, we have always had warm and dry beds at night. Our tent was ten feet square, American drill, with a dark-blue lining, and an outer fly with a porch. It weighed, without poles, 80 lb. Edgington made it to our own design seven years ago. We have used it every year since then, and it looks good for another seven years. If a tent is properly made in the first instance, and is never kept folded up for any length of time when wet, it will last for years .... Our camp beds were very strong and serviceable, and most comfortable, weighing about 20 lb. apiece, made after the plan of the Indian charpoi, but lighter; a very thin tarpaulin ground sheet, which is lighter, more durable, and far cheaper than mackintosh, kept everything dry below. We had also a most ingenious folding stove, made in Canada, and recommended to me by a great sportsman, Mr. Otho Shaw. A folding chair, table and stool, and a small light

carpet, completed the furniture. With tent, bedding, trunks, rifles, ammunition, tent poles, pegs, chair, and table, we had just three pony-loads between us.

On 22 May they left Osh and travelled to Gulcha and up the valley of the river of the same name.

There they were faced with three options to get to the Alai plain: the Terek Pass (3,855 m), east of Sopu Korgon; the Shart Pass (3,900 m), south-east of Ak-Bosogo; or the longer way across the Taldyk pass (3,535 m) and down to what is now Sary Tash; all three passes are closed by snow during the winter months, although today the road that goes over the latter is kept open by snow ploughs to the extent possible.

After listening to many travellers' tales en route – Littledale notes wryly that "one of the difficulties of travelling in this part of the country is the almost impossibility of getting reliable information" – they finally decided to attempt the Taldyk pass and reached the Alai valley without incident.

From there they forded the Kyzylsu and crossed the Alai plain.

> The Great Alai Mountains looked grand, appearing like one long wall of snow-clad peaks, running up to 22,000 or 23,000 feet. Seen across the twelve or fourteen miles of plateau, the air was so clear, they looked much nearer, and they stretched east and west as far as the eye could reach. There seemed to be such masses of snow as to preclude all chance of our being able to cross them for a long time to come. In the Kirghiz tongue Alai means paradise, but that is hardly an accurate description of the plain, for from the end of August till the middle of June, or nine months and a half, owing to the severity of its climate it is quite uninhabited, and as we saw it on 3rd of June it looked very desolate; the ground was quite brown, the snow having only just melted, and, except marmots and some great bustard, not a living thing was in sight.

There was, however, no snow on the Kyzyl Art pass and on the way there they met Major Cumberland, going in the opposite direction, as though it was by now the most normal thing imaginable to cross the path of a fellow countryman in the middle of nowhere.[8] They were able to hand over to him some travel documentation they no longer needed, to help him on the rest of his journey home.

Just below the pass, they camped to wait for a consignment of fodder that they had ordered to follow them from Osh and took time to admire the scenery.

> … there were some magnificent snow-peaks, considerably over 20,000 feet; close to the lake was very weird scenery, and some of the side valleys were choked with

glaciers. This Central Asian scenery has a type of its own, quite different from the Swiss or Caucasian mountain scenes, where your eye when tired wanders from grand ice-fields above to a pleasant change of green pastures and then forests of pine below. Here, though the mountains are higher, the glaciers, owing to the small snow fall, are much more puny, while below there is a picture of utter desolation that would be hard to match in any other part of the world. The all but complete absence of vegetation gives a weird and uncanny character to the scenery of the valley in which we camped, which is called by the Kirghiz the Black Valley.

At the beginning of June they reached Kara Kul and continued their journey along the eastern shore.

From the top of the hill the lake looked beautiful, the water the bluest of the blue, and completely surrounded by snow mountains. Two peninsulas jut out, one from the north and the other from the south, and almost cut the lake in half.

Their route to what is now Murghab took them on almost exactly the same itinerary as the road built by the Russians a few years later (1897): over the Akbaital pass and down the river of the same name to its junction with the Murghab river.

Although it was June, they were caught first in a heavy snow storm and then by a strong gale that almost carried away their yurt. When the storm subsided they were able to enjoy spectacular views of Mustagh Ata.

The headman of a Kyrgyz encampment came to see them.

I asked if he could read Chinese. He said no; so it was a fine opportunity! I produced my Chinese passport, and enlarged to him the fearful pains and penalties he would incur if he failed to get me a reliable guide. He was apparently much impressed, and he left and returned with the smallest, thinnest, and most woe-begone lamb either of us ever set eyes on, some koumis and cream, and in return we gave him a musical-box, needlebook, and some tea.

Musicians at Sary Mogol

Finding he was not satisfied, I added an extra fur-cap I had brought – as, although our presents were two or three times the value of his, we thought it prudent to get a character for liberality, otherwise the guide might not be forthcoming.

Cumberland had advised them not to attempt to go via Chitral because "the fords in Chitral were deep and dangerous at this time of year, and that they ran a good chance of losing their luggage,"[9] and they appear to have decided as a result not to travel to Badakhshan but to the Wakhan, and from there across the Baroghil and Darkot passes to Gilgit.

There are several routes to the Wakhan from Murghab: up the Ak Su river to Shaimak (Aktash) and over to the Little Pamir; across the Alichur plain and then either over the Bashgumbez pass – about halfway across the plain – or along the Alichur river to Yashil Kul and over the Khargush pass. All are spectacularly beautiful.

The Littledales, having first started in the direction of Bashgumbez, were discouraged by reports from local Kyrgyz that the pass was blocked by snow and

Lower Western Pshart valley, Murghab

decided to take the Khargush route. On 17 June they forded the Murghab river and went up towards the Alichur valley. Recurring problems with their Kyrgyz horsemen delayed them, but Littledale's resourcefulness and firm response rapidly found a solution.

> The head of the Kirghiz told me he could not find us a guide, so I said I was very sorry, but until he got me a man he could not possibly leave us; that put a new complexion on affairs, and a man appeared in a couple of hours. ... The horses were missing again this morning; it turns out that all the horses we have hired belong to two men, with the exception of one solitary animal which belongs to the third, all the wages which he gets being the hire of this horse. This man being poor the others bully him, and expect him to watch the horses all night alone, while they are curled up in their sheepskins. It is of course impossible that one man can walk all day and watch horses all night, consequently he goes to sleep and the beasts wander; being close to the frontier the chances of robbery are much greater, and if our horses were stolen we should be in a most serious condition. The men returned to camp to get some food, having found about fifteen of the thirty odd, and started again on a fresh hunt, when I found that, contrary to my express order, they had left their own horses in camp and had ridden out on our horses to look for the runaways. I was very angry and had all their horses saddled and sent every one of them out with Kirghiz on them to look for the runaways. They were all collected at last; the caravan people were very angry at their horses being used, and said they would return home, and absolutely refused to pack the horses. I stood some distance apart and beckoned the head of the caravan to come; he took no notice of me till I walked straight for him, when he saw I was not going to be trifled with, and he came. At first he was defiant and said they were all going back, so I told him that he was welcome to go but I had engaged their horses for as long as I liked, and I meant to keep them, and if they attempted to take them I would shoot every horse they had. I pointed out that if they returned to Turkistan and broke their contract they would certainly be put in prison; on the other hand, if they did their duty they would not only get their wages but a present as well. The storm died out as quickly as it had arisen, and anybody who had seen them in the evening feasting on a sheep I thought it politic to discover I did not want, would have never imagined they were the same people who were so infuriated in the morning. They were just like children, but firmness at first, and then conciliation, got over all our difficulties.

They passed close to Yashil Kul and then south across the Khargush pass to the Pamir river. Their Kyrgyz companions, who might have been expected to be well-adjusted to it, suffered severely from the altitude – the pass is at 4,344 m – but the Littledales were not affected: such are the vagaries of this debilitating and unpredictable affliction. Following the Pamir river, they made a detour to Zorkul (Wood's Lake – Lake Victoria), camping there on 27 June.

> The view from our camp over the lake was very grand, but on ascending the slopes of the hills on the north side, the lake was very disappointing; it looked so narrow, like a canal, but the mountains came triumphantly out of the ordeal.

A look at the mountains to the south, however, "knocked on the head any idea I had of finding a path across them direct to the foot of the Baroghil." Their new guide advised that the route up the Wakhan was almost impossible because the river was in flood at that time of year[10] and they decided to look for a pass that would bring them into the Little Pamir rather than continue down the Pamir river to Kala-i Panj. Passing the Kokjigit lake – "named, so the Chinese guide said, after a celebrated brigand, who flourished, robbed and murdered here many years before" – they found the Andamin pass (now known as the Bendersky[11]) and crossed without incident on 7 July to the Little Pamir lake, Chakmaktynkul. A fishing net improvised by Littledale gave them a welcome change from their previous fare[12] and they continued down to Boza-i Gumbaz (site of the 1892 'Pamir incident' between Younghusband and Ionov – see pages 315 and 425–6) and then up towards the Wakhjir pass.

At this point, so close to British India, their plans were very nearly frustrated. News of their arrival in what was now legally Afghan territory had reached the local Afghan potentate and they were prevented by his troops from proceeding. Mrs. Littledale, confirming the courage that had brought her this far, joined her husband in an attempt to parley.

> We explained that we wanted to cross the Hindu Kush into Chitral and did not want to stay in their territory at all. I produced the passport, and pointed to Lord Salisbury's signature, saying he was the greatest friend the Queen had, and the Persian interpreter enlarged on the dreadful things that might happen if we were kept waiting.

This had no effect whatsoever on the Afghans, who forced them to go back down the Wakhan to Sarhad to seek permission to continue their journey to the Baroghil pass, only some 10km away.

On the fourth day we heard shouting, and a number of men arrived; it was the Governor of Wakhan, Gholam Russul Khan, a good-looking young man; he stated that he had nearly reached Faizabad when he heard we were here, and he had come to see that we were comfortable. He said "Our Queen was their Queen, their country our country." I had to reply, "Yes indeed, we were brothers," but I could not help wishing all the same that our new relatives would cut their hair, and be generally a little cleaner. He wore a smart turban, with the name "I. Greaves and Co., Manchester," stamped conspicuously upon it.

Finally, on the evening of 21 July, a messenger arrived with a letter and later they were allowed to leave. The next morning, making presents all round in the hope of securing the Afghans' good will, they reduced the caravan to the strict minimum, said farewell to the remainder and set off with an Afghan escort to the Baroghil, camping on the other side, already in Chitral but still not secure.

Our fifteen men were reduced to seven. Three of them and a yak started ostensibly to get food and never returned, the others were going off and I forcibly stopped them, and at last made them confess that they had all been told to desert us. I talked to them and promised them high pay; they wanted an advance. One of them, by good luck, happened to have owned a sheep, which the Afghan Governor had presented to us, and which when we had afterwards discovered its owner, we had paid well for, and he said that people who would do that could not be thieves, and they would stay. We took however the precaution of putting them to sleep in the tent and watching them all night.

An extremely difficult and dangerous descent from the Baroghil and Darkot passes brought them finally to Yasin.

We paid a visit to the Governor of Yasin. He came out to meet us, and led me by the hand into his tower. We gave him some presents and a sheepskin coat. The old reprobate said he was obliged for the presents, but he would like some money too. I told Joseph to talk civilly to him, but we paid a hurried adieu; for we felt if we stayed longer we did not know what fresh demand might be sprung upon us, so we fled.

Regretfully leaving behind the Tajiks from Wakhan, they were obliged to take local people from Yasin for the continuation of their journey:

… a more lazy, worthless set I have never had the luck to come across. We had two men for each horse, but only two or three out of the whole lot were of any use whatever.

The journey to Gilgit necessitated numerous river crossings, one of which was by a locally constructed bridge.

> These bridges are formed by three ropes made of willow twigs; you walk on one, and the other two you hold on by your hands; it starts high above the water from the rocks, and sags down in the middle. Mrs. Littledale had always announced that she was ready to go anywhere or do anything except cross a rope bridge, and how I was to get her over in the morning I did not know. We selected a strong man, and she got on his back, and they started off across the bridge. ... She had got one-third of the way across ... but she had opened her eyes, and the height, the rushing water underneath, and the swaying of the bridge had frightened her, and she was telling them to take her back. The interpreter unfortunately was not there, but I shouted to them in Hindustani, in Russian, and in Kirghiz, to go on quickly and take no notice, but they did not understand me, and thought I was telling them to return, and back they came. Mrs. Littledale said she was ready to try again if we would tie her on, so that if she fainted she would not fall, but it could not be arranged. We had to think what was to be done. The men said if I would go away out of hearing they would carry her across whether she liked it or not. Women are little thought of in those parts. I suggested a raft; they said at first it was too dangerous, but, since there was no other course, we tied inflated sheep-skins to a camp bed, and sent it on a trial trip with five men swimming alongside, each man having his own skin. It was so buoyant that Mrs. Littledale said she was willing to cross in it. They made her lie down, tied her fast and started. The river flowed over great boulders, and though the raft was often lost sight of in the spray, it got across safely, having been taken by the current a quarter of a mile down stream. We took some dry things over the bridge for Mrs. Littledale, who had been lying half under water when the

"A locally constructed bridge", Ghunt Valley

raft was stationary, and when she arrived on the other side a more draggled specimen of humanity was never seen. Our horses had to swim across and three or four of them were nearly drowned.

They were then confronted with the famous 'hanging passages' we have already encountered.

It was a rough scramble over rocks and round corners on logs jammed into crevasses of the rocks, and then down a perpendicular crack in the rock by ladders formed of single poles with notches cut for steps. One man went in front to hold Mrs. Littledale's feet in the notches, while another held on to her dress above.

On 7 August, they reached Gilgit, where they enjoyed the hospitality of the acting British political agent, Manners Smith, and ended their journey in Srinagar on 4 September. En route, Mrs. Littledale, having shown extraordinary courage on the journey so far,[13] "established a great reputation of another kind; a sick man had come to her to be healed, and she thinking that certain widely advertised pills would please the man, and at the same time could do him no possible harm, gave him a couple; the effect was marvellous, and the fame of the cure spread through the country; our tent was besieged by poor creatures..."

Littledale's account, read to the Royal Geographical Society on 23 November 1891 by its Secretary, gave rise to a lively debate that illustrated major differences of opinion on geographical exploration between the Society and the British government and also between British and Russian officialdom.

At the outset, the RGS Secretary criticised the British government's paranoia about a possible Russian invasion of India across the Pamirs (see Chapter 4 on the Great Game):

... the tales of summer pastures of extraordinary richness told to Marco Polo and repeated to Mr. Littledale refer, so far as they are true at all, only to isolated oases, and the fertile tracts described at the end of Mr. Littledale's paper lie in valleys outside the Pamir region. The country in question cannot feed the caravans that cross it; far less could it sustain the baggage animals of an army on the march. No one in his senses could consider that in itself the Pamir is a desirable acquisition. Any value it may have is in relation to adjoining lands. From the north there is comparatively easy access to it from Russian Turkistan. From the east the Chinese and their subjects climb up the long ascent from the Khanates, and pass through gaps in the encircling horseshoe of mountains on to the portions of the tableland they claim. From the south-east M. Grombchevsky found a pass a waggon might cross into Hunza. From the south a route, which seems from Mr. Littledale's experience to be anything but a military route, leads over glacier passes, and through well-nigh impassable gorges into Yasin and Gilgit, and so to Kashmir. To the south-west easier routes, little known or little described as yet, lead into the wild regions of Kaffiristan and Afghanistan.

He also asked and answered a series of rhetorical questions:

Why, undeterred by the experiences of which that entertaining traveller and Anglophobe, M. Bonvalot, had lately given so alarming a picture, should an Englishman and his wife cross this desert? Mr. and Mrs. Littledale are eager in the pursuit of rare game. They were old travellers; they had sojourned in the forest wildernesses of the Western Caucasus; they had on a previous occasion penetrated Central Asia. A pair of horns were to them what a bit of rock from a maiden peak is to others.

And lastly, why did Mr. and Mrs. Littledale go from north to south? Why did they, being English, make Russian territory their starting point? Thereby hangs a tale. – Because our Anglo-Indian Government prohibits all independent travel in its trans-frontier lands. Something may be said for this course, but it does not stop there. It also gags its own official explorers. It carries yearly farther and farther the policy deprecated by Sir H. Rawlinson in this Hall, when he said, "Russia deserves all honour for her services to geographical science in Asia. I only wish I could say as much for ourselves as regards our own frontiers."

No one, least of all the Council of this Society, would ask for the publication of any tactical information our military authorities desired to withhold. But the military authorities go along with us in asking for an intelligent censorship in place of a wholesale system of suppression of the mass of knowledge, general and scientific, acquired by the servants of the State in our frontier and trans-frontier lands. We believe, and the Council have represented to H.M. Government, that the present practice is not in accordance with the existing official rules, that it was intended and has been ordered that expurgated copies of all official reports of public interest should be given to the public. They hope that the departments concerned will before long be instructed to give practical effect henceforth to any such instructions that may exist, and thus that the forward march of English power may once more, in Asia as elsewhere, be accompanied by a general advance of scientific knowledge.

Finally, in concluding the discussion, the President, Sir Grant Duff, expressed an opinion confirmed by several travellers' accounts.

> It is extremely agreeable to me, knowing that there are present two gentlemen from the Russian Embassy, to acknowledge – and it is by no means the first time that a President of the Geographical Society has had to acknowledge – the extreme courtesy shown by the Russian Government to an English traveller.

This contrasts sharply with the negative attitude taken by the British government at this time towards exploration of the regions under its own authority, on which, similarly, several explorers had occasion to comment.

Three years later, the Littledales were again in the Pamirs, but only en route to Kashgar, crossing this time by the Terek pass to Irkeshtam. This journey – the declared purpose of which was to collect specimens of wild camels and ending in Peking – is beyond the scope of the present narrative, but certainly rivals their crossing of the Pamirs in terms of risk and adventure[14]. Littledale's narrative, however, is equally entertaining and contains further illustrations of the couple's courage and resourcefulness, as well as many examples of Littledale's irrepressible dry humour.

Just beyond Lop Nor, they found their first camels.

> The men said that one of the camels was thirty-five or forty years old; Mrs. Littledale, who tried to eat some of it, saw no reason to doubt that statement.

Confronted with threatening tribesmen,

I gave them a practical explanation of the repeating rifle, omitting to inform them, however, that after firing five shots it was necessary to reload, and they left under the impression that it went on shooting indefinitely. … The repeating rifle was expounded with such marked effect that when Rozahun [their Ladhaki guide] proposed to explain the beauties of the revolver, they begged him to put it by. Whatever their original intentions may have been, they were far too great cowards to face us when they saw we were prepared, and they rode away, looking with their long lances very wild and picturesque.

In Kwei-hwa-cheng

We were most hospitably received by Dr. Stewart, a medical missionary. In describing the difficulties of the Chinese language to beginners, he told me, among other things, that the words for chicken and wife closely resembled each other. Once when prescribing for a sick Chinaman he found he had told him to cut his wife's throat and make broth of her. Another missionary ordered his servant to go to the bazaar and buy a chicken; the man was gone nearly all day, and returned saying that good-looking women were awfully scarce just then …

Transalai Mountains   *Camels near Daroot Qurghan in the lower Alai valley*

The Earl of Dunmore (1892–93)

On Christmas day 1891, Charles Adolphus Murray, eighth Earl of Dunmore, left England for Karachi, where he disembarked in February 1892 at the start of a journey that was to take him over 2,200 miles through Central Asia, crossing sixty-nine rivers and forty-one mountain passes, some among the highest in the world.

His account of this journey, *The Pamirs; being a Narrative of a Year's Expedition on Horseback and Foot through Kashmir, Western Tibet, Chinese Tartary and Russian Central Asia*, was published in London in 1893. It reveals a man of considerable strength, erudition, good humour and courtesy. While the first was a requirement and the second not unusual for all the early explorers of the Pamirs, the latter two qualities were more exceptional. Dunmore was also an accomplished linguist, amateur botanist, poet, painter and musician, with a fine sense for natural beauty.

> On the Pamirs I have often seen evening tints in the sky, the colours of which I do not believe that any landscape painter in the world could give a name to, and the after-glows, which would almost answer to our twilights in Europe, are so exquisite in their refinement, that it were absolutely impossible to attempt to describe them.

His qualities stand out even more in comparison with some of the dry accounts published by contemporary travellers on the Pamirs. Major Charles Sperling Cumberland, for example, travelled in almost the same areas as Dunmore three years previously and met Grombchevsky, Dauvergne and a team from Nikolai Mikhailovich Prjevalsky's last expedition to Tibet en route, but his book *Sport on the Pamir and Turkistan Steppes*, published in 1895, contains hardly a single interesting or amusing story: it comprises essentially a series of excruciatingly detailed hunting reports. Where Dunmore frequently expresses concern for the welfare of his native companions, Cumberland is less put out at the death of one of his native guides than at the loss of one of his ponies.

Of course, many of these trips – whatever their real purpose – were indeed described by those participating as 'sport'. Dunmore – aged 51, remember – on the way up the Taghdumbash Pamir, at an altitude of nearly 5,000m, in temperatures of about minus 15°C, spent several days and nights stalking Marco Polo sheep, sleeping out on the snow and, on one occasion, sliding headlong down a glacier into a crevasse. He notes, with imperceptible irony, that "there is no doubt that we have come here at the wrong season of the year." On meeting a bear, he comments sardonically that he held his fire until the bear was dangerously close because he could only see his head and to aim at it "would have shattered his skull, which was the only part of him I wanted to keep."

Nothing should surprise today's reader about the explorers of an age where there were considered to be no limits to knowledge or to human endeavour and improvement. General Sir Charles MacGregor had described the ideal cogently in 1882 in his *Wanderings in Balochistan*.

> The sight of a map with blank spaces on it produces in me a feeling of mingled shame and restlessness. Of course it is not any particular fault of mine that maps have blank spaces on them, but I always feel the glaring whiteness of the blanks looking reproachfully at me. Judging from my own feelings, I think it would be a good plan if the Geographical Society were to have all unexplored tracts painted on their maps some conspicuous colour, say scarlet, as the sight of these burning spots, thus prominently brought to their notice, would, I feel sure, rouse much of the latent energy of young Britons, and perhaps divert a good deal of it from mooning about the Row to more useful wanderings to unknown regions.

A broken rib sustained in a riding accident in Rawalpindi led to a short delay in setting off but gave Dunmore time to review his plans and extend his planned itinerary from the Pamirs to other parts of Russian Central Asia. The fitting out of the expedition included procurement of not only tents, stores and sporting guns, but also scientific instruments for making observations en route.

> Baggage includes eight tents, thirty beddings, camp-furniture, stores, carpenters' tools, medicine chest; navvies' tools, horse-shoeing tools, 3000 nails and 420

The Earl of Dunmore [1892]

horseshoes, guns, rifles, ammunition, spare saddlery, our own kit and that of thirty men; kitchen utensils, scientific instruments, photographic apparatus, etc. ... fifty-one men and 130 live animals [74 yaks and 56 ponies].

Dunmore was joined at Leh in Ladak by Major Roche of the Indian dragoons, who stayed with him until they reached Kashgar six months later and, on 23 June, their party set off for the Chinese frontier, crossing the Karakoram pass on 9 July. They reached Yarkand on 4 August and, two weeks later, headed west towards the Pamirs, reaching Tashkurgan and Sarikol at the end of August. Dunmore notes that the population of Sarikol "numbers about 6,000 souls and is purely Aryan.... They all look upon His Highness Agha, Sahib of Bombay, as their spiritual leader, who in virtue of his being the offspring of the prophet and himself a pious man, has alone the power of absolving his followers from their sins. Some of the Sariq-qolis who are his most ardent disciples go so far on the road towards Buddhism, as to believe that Ali takes birth in every successive Agha."

Dunmore notes that the Ismailis of Sarikol were respectful of their women who "are not treated as mere machines, as they are in other Mahameddan countries, but are looked up to with respect by their husbands and children and are entrusted with the entire household arrangements ... they are free to come and go as they please, without any restriction; and the use of the veil is practically unknown to them."

On 1 September they reached the foot of the Taghdumbash Pamir – their ranks increased by this time to thirty men and sixty horses (having had an undignified fall from a yak, Dunmore seems to have abandoned the idea of using these animals). There they were welcomed by an unseasonable snowstorm: "Roche and I sat huddled up together, trying to imagine we were getting shelter from a juniper bush three feet high. The ground was wet, and so were we, and bitterly cold into the bargain ... As we were ravenously hungry, we thought to pass the time by ordering imaginary dinners – Roche at the Naval and Military, I at the Guards' Club." Their privations, however, were mitigated by the arrival of a parcel from Younghusband, for this was a time when it was a matter of course to send runners from Hunza to a mountain pass in the Pamirs just to deliver tobacco and newspapers for the sahibs.

The incompetence and corruption of the local Chinese officials encountered by Dunmore – together with the legendary hospitality of the Kyrgyz – goes far to explain the warm welcome they received from the local nomadic herders and the rapid spread of rumours that they were official envoys of the British government, come to take

possession of the Pamirs. The Kyrgyz of the Little Pamir preferred the British to the Russians, since the latter had told them that they would be liable to military service if found on what the Russians claimed as their territory in the Little Pamir.

> Some of the Kirghiz head-men from Aktash, wishing to cross over into Hunza to buy grain, came and asked me to give them a pass to Captain Younghusband, as they are afraid of being turned back at Misgah by his Kunjuti outposts as none but dâk [official communications] carriers are allowed to pass. Ahmed Din wrote them a sort of passport in Persian to show at the outpost, and I signed it. … I hope these men will get through. They wish to become British subjects and emigrate over into Hunza as a body, as they say the Chinese will not do anything for them, but allowed them to be turned out of their homes by the Russians.

The Chinese were, indeed, concerned that any mission by Englishmen in the frontier region at that time was for more than just hunting Marco Polo sheep. Dunmore recounts that shortly after the British had subdued Hunza in December 1891, the Chinese had prepared a boundary stone, with appropriate ancient-looking inscriptions asserting that it marked the Chinese frontier, and had buried it with an image of Buddha at the top of the Minteke pass leading into Hunza, where – if there were ever a boundary dispute – it could conveniently be 'discovered'.

Kyrgyz man on a yak, Eastern Pamir

On 27 October, Dunmore and Roche received an official visit from a representative of the government in Urumchi, to check on what they were doing.

> He had the same drawling hesitation in his speech that I have already noticed, especially in the case of the Amban of Kargalik, who used to remain on the drawl on one particular note, say B flat, and then jerk his voice up to F natural, and come out with his sentence. This Amban, when hesitating in his speech, lacked the musical (?) drawl of the other one, and simply said 'jigga, jigga, jigga, jigga' with the utmost rapidity, which resembled much more the going off of an alarum than the articulation of a human being, and he continued jigga jigga-ing until he got the word he wanted.

A few days later, the party left to find a way through the Little Pamir to Zorkul (known to the British then as Lake Victoria). This was not the route taken either by Wood or by Trotter, who was the next European to arrive there in 1874, and the way had to be sought among the many small side valleys. The indefatigable Littledales had been there in 1888 and had gone over the Andamin (Benderski) pass above Chakmaktynkul, but Dunmore did not have their travel report with him and had to improvise. In the previous year, Younghusband had intended to try to cross this way but had been stopped by the Russians at Boza-i Gumbaz in the Wakhan.

A further problem was that, naturally enough, none of the local people recognised the name Victoria. More confusion was caused by the different, often similar names used by local people for various natural phenomena – a glance at the map of the region reveals a multitude of names combining *ak* (white), *kara* (black), *kyzyl* (red), *tash* (stone), *su* (river), *kul* (lake), *qurghan* (tower), *kum* (sand), *gumbez* (dome) etc. Dunmore notes that in the Pamirs there are "two Tashkurgans, two Serez, two Neza Tash passes, three Gaz-Kul lakes" and that the lake in the little Pamir which is the source of the Aksu river bears several different names: Chakmaktyn, Oikul, Kul-i-Pamir Khurd (Little Pamir lake), Barkut Yassin, Challap and Gazkul. Zor Kul also appeared on British maps as Serikol or Sir-i Kol, which invites confusion with Sarikol.

In addition to problems of terminology, Dunmore's guides turned out not really to know the terrain well or to have any sense of time or distance[1] and he occasionally gives vent to an unusual display of frustration: "… if our different Chinese and Kyrgyz guides could understand the Queen's English, they would hear many remarks unflattering to themselves. They also seem to have a passion for crossing rivers unnecessarily."

By now it was -22°C inside their tent and Dunmore's narrative could only be continued by periodically getting the cook to unfreeze the ink bottles, until finally he had to resort to pencils. A further catastrophe was the discovery that their stock of tea was almost exhausted and they had to resort to the shocking expedient of actually boiling the leaves in the water in order to make it go further. Anyone who has enjoyed the abundant hospitality of the Kyrgyz in the Pamirs will sympathise also with his complaint that "we have now been eating mutton twice a day for 179 consecutive days."

On 4 November, they crossed the Little Pamir over the Andamin pass and followed the river of the same name down to the Great Pamir plain.

It was now even colder and Dunmore admits, for the second time, with fine British understatement, that "Roche and I have finally come to the conclusion that the winter is not exactly the season to choose either for purposes of sport or of exploration on the Pamirs."

The next day they camped on the frozen shores of Lake Kokjigit, and, in the morning, rode the three miles to the eastern end of Zorkul, noting the presence of seagulls and an abundance of sea shells. They stayed close to the lake for a further two days and then headed along the Pamir river as far as Khargush, with "the thermometer last night only registering 40° of frost or 8° below zero (-22°C)."

> Although this temperature is nothing really abnormal, still we seem to feel the cold very severely, Personally I feel it ten times worse than I ever have before, either in the Arctic regions of Spitzbergen, or in Canada, where I have frequently marched with troops, with the thermometer ranging from 30° to 40° below zero [-34° to -40°C]. It is just the difference between an absolutely still cold and a cold with wind like we have here. In the morning the men cannot use their hands either to strike the tents or load the ponies ...

On 9 November, "as this was the Prince of Wales' birthday, we drank His Royal Highness's health, and although the toast was drunk in tea, I venture to think that the wishes for his health and prosperity were quite as hearty as if the toast had been drunk in champagne." They then struck north towards the Alichur Pamir rather than south along the Pamir river since, as Dunmore admits in an unusual moment of candour, "our object was to find a new pass between the Karghoshi and the Besh-Gombez."

Once on the Alichur plain, they passed Sasik Kul (the "stinking lake", although quite why it has deserved this name is a mystery, as there is no apparent smell from or near the lake) and Tuz Kul ("salt lake"), noting the saltpetre deposits on the shore which can be seen today exactly as then. Arriving in Bulunkul on 10 November, their party was astonished at the large quantity of fish in the lake. The fish are there in similar quantities today and have led to the establishment of a sizeable community of fishermen and their families from Shughnan, an island of non-Kyrgyz in what is today the largely Kyrgyz district of Murghab, offering a welcome respite for today's traveller from the local diet of mutton about which Dunmore had complained earlier.

Next day they pushed on round the eastern end of Yashil Kul to Sumantash (Dunmore calls it Surmatash), where two military campaigns in the Pamirs had been decisively concluded. The most recent had taken place four months before Dunmore's arrival (see page 427) between Cossacks of the first Russian 'flying' detachment under Colonel Ionov and a group of Afghan soldiers.

The earlier campaign concluded in Sumantash in 1759 with the rout by the Chinese of the Khoja (Muslim) rulers of Kashgar. It is commemorated by a stone now in Khorog, capital of Gorno-Badakhshan.

The two Muslim leaders reached Badakhshan but were subsequently killed by Sultan Shah, the ruler there. A legend arose that, in their death throes, they laid a curse on Badakhshan and prayed that it might be three times depopulated. As Sir Henry Yule points out in his account of the incident, "in fact, since then it has been at least three times ravaged; first, a few years after the outrage by Ahmed Shah Durani of Kabul, when the treacherous Sultan Shah was put to death; in the beginning of this [19th] century by Kokan Beg of Kunduz; and again in 1829 by his successor Murad Beg, who swept away the bulk of the remaining inhabitants, and set them down to die in the marshy plains of Kunduz."

Some years before Dunmore was in Sumantash, another explorer, T.E. Gordon, reported that the fleeing Muslims "are said to have driven their women and children, mounted on camels and horses, into the lake, to meet their death by drowning rather than that they should fall into the hands of the enemy. The Kirghiz have a legend that the sounds of lamentation, and of people and animals in terror of death, are often heard near the lake."[2]

Sumantash Stone, Khorog Museum of Regional History

Until the conclusion of the final border agreement with China in 2002, it was feared in Tajikistan that this stone – indeed of less doubtful authenticity than the one placed on the Minteke pass above Hunza (see page 463) – might be used by the Chinese at some time to reassert sovereignty over the Alichur Pamir.[3]

On 15 November, Dunmore's party had crossed the Alichur plain, past the enormous Chatyr Tash, rising from its centre and resembling, in Dunmore's words, "the Sphinx of the pyramids of Egypt, without its head" and was in sight of Murghab.

The Russians were expecting them and sent an escort with three officers (the interim commander Savonov – Ionov was absent – and Captains Reiffeld and Brjesickis) to welcome Dunmore, one of whom proudly informed him that he had been present at the famous occasion when Younghusband had been threatened with arrest in 1891 at Boza-i Gumbaz (in the Wakhan); another had, in the same year, "had the pleasure of meeting Davison at Yashil Kul" – a euphemism for his being packed off to the Russian base at Marghilan as a prisoner: both were incidents of some discomfort for the British as they were statements of the extent of the authority claimed by Russia in the Pamirs.

The Russians had prepared yurts for their distinguished British guests and, within the limits of the supplies of the Murghab garrison, everything was done to make their stay comfortable. Dunmore was able to reciprocate by introducing them to the game of Ludo.

On 19 November, accompanied by Savonov, Brjesickis and an escort of Cossacks, they left Murghab up the Akbaital valley. Shortly before the turn east to Rang Kul, Savonov left them and returned to Murghab: "it was with genuine regret, I hope on both sides, on ours at any rate, that we bade each other adieu; we felt indeed that it was impossible for us to express to him our gratitude for the many kindnesses he showed us during our sojourn in his hospitable camp."

Chatyr Tash

The party continued past Shor Kul to Rang Kul, noting on the way the so-called 'Lamp Rock' ('Chiragh Tash') at the top of a cliff, the luminous properties of which Dunmore ascribes to a cave pierced through the rock (see page 617). The local Kyrgyz today ascribe to the light to the presence of phosphorescent matter and it is still visible today, despite the fact that the rock was used as target practice by the Russian border guards in the 1990s. Dunmore notes that Rang Kul is the smaller of the two; this is no longer the case, although these are "intermittent" lakes, the size of which varies according to the seasons and from year to year.

A specially prepared yurt was awaiting them again in the Rang Kul fort and the next day, well-rested but cold at -23°C, Dunmore and the Russians "had recourse to various expedients to keep warm." After Russian peasant and cossack dances, he taught the officers the intricacies of Scottish dancing to the sound of a Russian accordion: "the first Highland reel ever danced on the Pamirs."[4]

The next day, it was so cold the pin of the thermometer was frozen fast to the glass at the lowest temperature registered by it: -20°F (-29°C). Dunmore estimates that in reality it must have been about -34°C. The group, with Brjesickis and the cossack escort, rode up towards the Chinese frontier enjoying splendid views from the Kok Beless pass (4,246m) of the high mountains in Shughnan and Rushan to the west and Kongur and Mustagh Ata to the east, and spent a last night on Russian territory, again in a yurt prepared for them by the Russians, at the foot of the Ak-Bhirdi mountain.

Despite the yurt, in the morning "our blankets were white with small icicles, where our breath had touched them, and my beard was the same" and he spares a thought for the men who had "suffered a good deal" sleeping outside. They parted company with the Russians and set off up the mountain. Brjesickis, displaying excellent knowledge of the British sense of proprieties, "did not attempt to embrace us" although one of his officers did and caused great indignation on the part of Roche "at being kissed by a great hairy man, while I, who did know their ways, submitted like a lamb."

Their route took them north over the Ak-Bhirdi mountain, for the "so-called Ak-Bhirdi pass is, in reality, no pass at all ... it being the actual summit of a mountain, 17,330 feet above sea-level." Although Brjesickis informed them that no Europeans had ever been this way before, Dunmore subsequently found out that Captain H. Bower of the 17th Bengal Cavalry had been across it in 1891.[5]

The descent down the Chinese side was very precipitous and the "frozen snow and

sheets of ice we met with were so slippery … that in one very steep place I had to crawl down on my hands and knees backwards, so as to face my horse, and thus be able to avoid his slipping down on the top of me." They had spent five and a half hours on the mountain and stopped at an encampment, where again they were offered a yurt for the night and a gift of sheep by the hospitable local Kyrgyz.

On 24 November, they were met by an emissary of Macartney from Kashgar who brought food, fodder and newspapers. Dunmore disgustedly compares "the trash which is served up for the public to digest" with the reality that he has encountered en route. For example

Newspaper paragraphs

"Colonel Younoff reports that from several towns in the Pamirs, the natives have come to him to pay their respects and to ask to be united with Russia."

"The Chinese had arrived in the Pamir territory 500 strong and fixed their head-quarters at Shindi. Hearing the Russians were advancing on the Chinese Pamirs, they advanced eastward 250 strong, against the Akbaital pass, and when they advanced against the village of Aktash, the party of Chinese from Shindi opposed them. A fight ensued, which ended in the signal defeat of the Chinese. Meanwhile the Russians fortified their position at Aktash."

Building a yurt, Altyn Mazar [1928]

"Pamir is a country infested by wild tribes."

Comments on same

There is not a single house nor village, much less a town, on the Pamirs."

There has not been a single Chinese soldier on the Pamirs during the year 1892, except a non-commissioned officer and eleven men at Aktash. Shindi is a village in Sariq-qol, about seventy miles east from the Pamirs, with a high mountain range between them, and if the Chinese had advanced eastward, they would have gone towards Yarkand, and in the contrary direction to the Pamirs. The Akbaital pass is 120 miles from Shindi, with six mountain ranges between them. The Tash-korum pass is 130 miles from Aktash, with eight mountain ranges between them. No fight has ever taken place between the Russians and Chinese on the Pamirs. Aktash is not a village. It is a large white rock on the plain of the Ak-su river, and there is not a house within many a hundred mile of it. So far from fortifying themselves at Aktash, the Russians pulled the Chinese fort down and then retired unassailed on Murghabi.

The Pamirs are not infested by wild tribes, but are the summer grazings of a quiet, peaceable, nomad tribe called Kirghiz.

Reporting of the Tajik civil war in 1992–1993 in the European press was marginally more accurate but not much, although there was conceivably less interest by the outside world in these reports than in those quoted by Dunmore.

After being detained temporarily by Chinese frontier guards, they reached Kashgar on 1 December and were welcomed by Macartney, who had organised a few protocol visits for Dunmore, the only problem being that he had no suitable clothes.

On Tuesday, Mr. Macartney had made arrangements that I should visit the Taotai [local head of civil and military affairs] Li-Tsung-Pin (I make use of the first personal pronoun, because I could never persuade Roche to visit anybody), and as we had already received an ample apology from the Chinese Government for our detention at the Frontier, with an assurance that the culprit, "Ching-Wang," should be severely punished, there was every reason I should go and visit the chief official of Kashgar. Had the apology not been tendered, I should not of course have visited the Taotai, and the matter would have then been placed on another, and more serious footing, as Mr. Macartney would have referred it to the Government of India. Things, however, having been satisfactorily arranged, I made my preparations to pay the Taotai a visit of ceremony.

No clothes that I could produce, amongst the small stock which constituted my wardrobe, would please Macartney, who said that a Chinaman judged a European by his outward appearance entirely, and he regretted very much, that I had not brought some uniform with me!

Fancy taking a uniform over the Karakoram and into the Pamirs!

At last, to please him, I consented to array my person in an old uniform great-coat of Younghusband's, with a political officer's brass buttons and an imposing cape on it.

It being two sizes too small for me, it was therefore very tight and uncomfortable; but I thought of the old lines, *Dulce et decorum est pro patria mori*, and bore the discomfort with Christian resignation, being told it was for my country's good; so the whole of this original and grotesque costume being supplemented by a Tartar fur cap, I was pronounced at last as "fit to be seen," and, mounting our horses, we rode through the bazaars, preceded by Macartney's chuprassie, Jaffar Ali, clothed in a bright scarlet *halat*, and followed by an admiring rabble of the youth of Kashgar. Being market day, the streets and bazaars were crowded, and locomotion was difficult, but we eventually arrived in safety at the Taotai's Yamên [office and residence] ....

Passing through the inner chamber of a sort of pagoda, reserved only as a passage-way for guests of the highest distinction, we reached a large hall in which stood the Taotai himself got up in his very best, waiting to receive us.

He is an oldish man – in fact, for a Chinaman, a very old man – portly and with a jolly sort of look about him, as if he was in the habit of "doing himself pretty well." He advanced to meet us and shook hands most cordially, Chinese fashion,

Aktash, Eastern Pamir

and then conducted us to an inner chamber and seated us on a raised dais, covered with red cloth, with a table in the middle of it, on which he placed with his own hands, most reverently, two cups of tea, much in the same way as a priest places a holy vessel on to an altar, and then seating himself on our right, the conversation commenced by his putting to me the usual Chinese query, as an opening to a dialogue, of "How old are you?" After having put him in possession of this piece of valuable information, he commenced by making profuse apologies for the manner in which "my excellency" had been treated by a Chinese official at the Frontier, etc., etc.

Undoubtedly, Macartney was right, and Younghusband's great-coat was working wonders, as I saw the Taotai's eye wandering with unfeigned admiration up and down the two rows of brass buttons.

After the usual interchange of remarks about the weather, which I find that as a topic of conversation, when every other one fails, holds its own in Central Asia equally with Europe, the Taotai conducted us to another spacious hall, where eight Chinese servants stood round a table laid for three. On seating myself, I found opposite to me a small saucer, two chopsticks, a diminutive soup-ladle, and a small china cigarette ashtray, which turned out to be a wine-glass.

The rest in Kashgar had obviously revived Dunmore's spirits as well as his sense of humour. On 13 December, he left Kashgar, having divided the caravan: half continuing with him, the other half returning with Roche to Kashmir via Maralbashi on the Tarim river. Dunmore's group reached the last Chinese settlement at Ulukchatt, where he was held up by an official who was finishing his dinner and requested that Dunmore wait until he had finished.

This I flatly refused to do, and told the messenger to inform the Amban that if he did not choose to look at my passes *at once*, I should proceed without further delay, and report him to the Taotai at Kashgar, for keeping me waiting. The arrogance of these small Chinese officials is as well known as is the courtesy of those holding higher positions, and I had been long enough in the country to know that the only way to deal with this class of gentry was to pay them back in their own coin, only with interest …[6]

After a day spent hawking in the company of a group of Kyrgyz, met by chance on the road, Dunmore reached the Russian frontier at Irkeshtam on the evening of 20 December and was warmly received by the commander and his wife. He left the next day, accompanied by the commander and an escort of 30 Cossacks, who sang their way through to evening, when they returned to the fort and left Dunmore to camp and continue the next day towards the Terek pass, Gulcha and Osh.

It is perhaps surprising, with our knowledge of the route to Irkeshstam (and to the Pamirs) over the Taldyk pass chosen later by the Russians for construction of a road, that until well into the 20th century the apparently much more difficult route via the Terek pass was the route of choice. Dunmore describes the Kok bel pass as "a very difficult pull"; a little way up the Kok-su river he was confronted with "another precipitous ascent", the Borak pass, and he describes the descent from the top of Terek-davan to Sufi-Kurghan (Sopu Korgon on today's maps) in the Gulcha valley as "awful". Ralph Cobbold, who travelled in the Pamirs a few years later than Dunmore (refer pages 480–496) commented that "passes such as the Therek-dawan, or even the Alai, are not to be taken for roads; there is not, in most places, even an attempt at a road; horses make their own path in the snow according to the conditions of the weather and season. This caravan road is open all year round, and when in summer time the melting snow makes the Therek-dawan impracticable the caravans make the circuit over the Alai, which is two or three days longer but not so steep."[7] Lady Macartney, a few years later, explained that "at midsummer the Terek pass is closed on account of avalanches, and caravans must go by the Taldik, which, for about a month, is free from snow, and has a wide easy road over it; but it is a considerably longer way."[8] Once motor transport was available, the Taldyk became the obvious choice – moreover, as a result of climate change, the Taldyk pass is now snow-free for at least four months.

On Christmas Eve, the coldest night on the journey, when the temperature dropped to -40°C, Dunmore camped in the snow at the foot of the pass and next day crossed to Sufi-Kurghan, where he was met by an emissary of Colonel Grombchevsky and taken yet again to a specially prepared yurt. The emissary, Hassan Beg, turned out to be from Badakhshan and they conversed in Persian. It being Christmas day, Dunmore, with typical good humour, decided to have a Christmas Pudding for dinner.

> … calling in Ramzan, I commenced by explaining to him as best I could in the Urdu tongue that this day was the great festival of the Christian's year, and one on which all right-minded Franghis were wont to spend the first half of the day at their Mosques, the inside walls of which were decorated with green branches and made as much as possible to resemble a jungle, and the other half of the day and most of

the night in over-eating themselves with the most unwholesome food their Khansamas could procure in the *bazaars*, and, therefore, as I did not wish to be behind-hand in following the example of my brother Franghis, but wished – in the absence of my mosque – to keep the day as near as possible in accordance with the articles of my faith, I called upon him as a good Mussulman, to come to my assistance in the manufacture of the most unwholesome edible compound the united ingenuity of our inventive brains could devise.

So after a long discussion and close inspection of our resources, we built up between us, using the Beg's doster-khan [literally table-cloth, here a gift of food for guests], a Christmas Pudding, which turned out so successful that I cannot refrain from giving a minute description of its architecture.

First of all we took some dark-coloured Kirghiz flour and some baking-powder and the frozen yolks of six Kashgar eggs, which we scraped with a knife into a yellow powder, and after being well kneaded, this compound was rolled out, my telescope making a grand rolling-pin. We then stewed in a small Degchi [cooking pot] all the Beg's apricots and raisins with some of my own honey. Another corner of the fire was occupied by a frying-pan, in which I fried the kernels of the pistachio nuts, in the only butter I could get, which I very carefully took out of a fresh tin of *Sardines au Beurre*. When the paste looked as like the beginning of a roly-poly pudding as we could make it, we poured the apricot, raisin and honey stew into the middle of it, then rolled it up and stuck the outside of it full of the fried kernels of the pistachio nuts, until the result looked like a new-born porcupine. We then proceeded to bake the whole thing as best we could, and I venture to say that no cook in Europe, on the 25th December, 1892, could have been as proud of his Christmas Pudding as I was of mine.

Although its manufacture was not the least interesting part of it, still the eating of it was more pleasurable than most enforced duties are usually, notwithstanding the slight suspicion of a flavour of sardines about it, which at any rate was a new departure in Christmas Puddings, and possessed the one great advantage and charm of novelty.

En route to Gulcha, Dunmore encountered the Austrian archaeologist Dr. Troll, on his way to Peking, and, at the end of his trip, met the Littledales in Trebizond, on their way back to China through Turkestan and handed over to them his faithful caravan leader Ramzan. Decidedly, travel in the region was becoming a little common-place.

After a pleasant stay in Marghilan, where he was entertained by the Russian commander, General Karalkoff, and treated to an excellent performance in the latter's residence of classical music by a Captain Bourkowsky on a "very good full-sized grand piano, of German manufacture", Dunmore's account ends with his arrival in Istanbul (then Constantinople) on 15 February 1893. With typical courtesy, he expresses his gratitude not only to the Russians ("Of the civility we received from the Russians of all ranks, I cannot speak too highly") but also the Kyrgyz ("undoubtedly the most hospitable people in the world") and compliments his caravan leader and the "excellent and hard-working" Ladakis who had travelled with him all the way.

Dunmore was, no doubt surprised to find a concert grand piano in Marghilan. He would have been even more surprised, had he returned to the Pamirs a few years later, to find a piano in Khorog. In 1914, Grigori Andreevich Shpilko, the Russian Commander in Khorog arranged the transport of a piano made in 1875 by J. Becker of St. Petersburg, from Osh more than seven hundred kilometres away. It was brought by cart as far as Murghab, and then the remaining 300 km by some twenty bearers. It was placed in the chapel of the military base where in the evenings officers and their wives would gather. It now has pride of place in the Khorog museum.[9]

What was the real purpose of Dunmore's trip? There is, indeed, something odd about it. Dunmore recounts receiving a confidential despatch from the Viceroy

The first piano in the Pamirs [c. 1915]

containing "the views of the Foreign Office regarding my attempting to cross either the Chinese or Russian Central Asian frontiers," the content of which he coyly declines to share with the reader. Since however, all the stops were pulled out by the British government to facilitate his journey and he was received as a VIP wherever he went, there must have been a serious political purpose behind his projected travel plans that met with full official approval.

That he spent five weeks in the inhospitable Taghdumbash Pamir and that Macartney, British representative in Kashgar (NB not Consul, only Russia had consular status)[10] joined him in this location, would seem to confirm that his "sporting" trip was indeed officially sanctioned and had the purpose of assessing potential threats to British India from the Pamirs. As noted above, Younghusband had been stopped in the Wakhan by the Russians in 1891 before being able to explore the route to Zorkul (Lake Victoria) through the Little Pamir. His failure may explain why the British government gave such encouragement to Dunmore's itinerary.

Roche's role too is a mystery. The party carried a compass, thermometer and aneroid barometer but no surveying equipment, although we learn that he took many photographs (most of which, regrettably for him and for us, were lost in a snowstorm on the Boujil pass on his way back to Kashmir). He does not appear to have been stimulating company for Dunmore, since scarcely any of Dunmore's anecdotes directly involve him, nor does he appear to have been a talented hunter – although, according to Dunmore, he used to whistle popular tunes, he appears to have been rather dour, and was "very much averse to visiting or receiving visits from any Oriental;" indeed, as already noted, Dunmore "could never persuade him to visit anybody." We may fairly assume that Roche was part of British intelligence, that this was known to the Russians and was the reason why he was not permitted by them to accompany Dunmore on the second leg of his journey from Kashgar to Alai and other parts of Russian Turkestan. They politely but firmly turned down his application for a special passport: Petrovsky, the Russian consul in Kashgar, informed him, pointedly and with irrefutable logic, that "to obtain permission to visit Russian Turkestan is almost as difficult as to obtain a permit to cross the frontier of the Hindu Kush."

The much later release of Foreign Office papers reveals that, in addition to his travel notes, Dunmore was indeed sending confidential reports back to his sponsors in Simla and that their main cause of concern at the time was Chinese weakness in policing the territories they claimed in Central Asia. This weakness left a vacuum that the Russians were rapidly in process of filling. While the British felt they had little to fear from the Chinese, who were unlikely to have strategic designs on British India, the Russians were expanding and must be contained before they came too close to the Hindu Kush. Dunmore's long stay in the Taghdumbash Pamirs, close to the entrance to Hunza, and his highly critical remarks about the failure of the Chinese to occupy and defend the forward positions on their western frontiers all relate to this nagging British preoccupation and gave urgency to the need to envisage negotiations with the Russians on defining frontiers in the Pamirs.

In one of these confidential reports, Dunmore states confidently the official position that

> There is no doubt but that China and Afghanistan meet on the Alichur Pamir. The Chinese Mandarin, in charge of the Pamir frontier, told me that his Government claim from Uz-Bel north of the Kizil-Jik pass to Sarez west of longitude 73° on the Murghab river, then in a line south taking in the whole of Yashil Kul Lake. The Afghans claim the whole of Roshan, Shignan and Wakhan, including Yashil Kul and Surmatash as far east as Chadir Tash on the Alichur Pamir.[11]

More realistically, he recognises that

> The Chinese by way of asserting their rights to the Alichur Pamir placed posts on different points in 1879 after the defeat of Amir Yakub Beg and their recovery of the province of Kashgaria, but these posts were subsequently removed and at this date *the Chinese have no posts on any part of the Pamirs*. [Dunmore's emphasis] The Wakhan district of the Pamir extends as far east as Aktash. The Chinese claim Victoria Lake and east of Aktash. To sum up, it may be said that the Afghans claim everything the Chinese claim, and Russia claims the whole. I am in possession of the Chinese official map of the Pamirs 1892 (manuscript) on which is shown over 20 forts on different parts of the Pamirs, whereas they have none.[12] ... I consider it a grievous error on the part of our Imperial Government to allow [the Russians] to advance any further south or to allow them to take possession of Shignan and Roshan west. Once the Russians have the two latter districts, then the Badakhshan, which is at the moment ripe for revolt against the Amir of Kabul, would assuredly fall into their hands, and as a Russian possession, would be of infinitely more danger to us than if the whole of the Pamirs were Russian.

Dunmore was badly mistaken in his scornful dismissal of the British newspaper reports he received on arrival in Kashgar that the inhabitants of the Pamirs had requested assistance from the Russians: these were, indeed, substantially correct and, in his comment that "there is not a single *house* nor *village*, much less a *town*, on the Pamirs," he showed that he was totally unaware of the situation of the western Pamirs.

In 1883, contrary to understandings reached between the British and Russians in 1873, and unchecked by the British, the Afghan Amir, Abdur Rahman Khan, claimed the territories of Shughnan and Rushan, on the right bank of the Oxus, and invaded them. Ney Elias had warned much earlier that "the Afghan rule in Shignan and Badakhshan was detested, and that the inhabitants would probably welcome the advent of Russians."[13] Major E.G. Barrow, of Indian Intelligence, had also recorded in an official report in 1888 that "Afghan tyranny has sown the seeds of rebellion and there is not a Tajik from Badakhshan to the Great Pamir who would raise a finger to resist Russian aggression."[14] In 1889, even Francis Younghusband – not otherwise inclined to give any support to Russian claims – noted on his visit to Tashkurgan that "this year many fugitives from Shighnan had been driven here by the Afghans."

The brutal treatment of the local population at the hands of the Afghan invaders was such that they did indeed seek Russian help against the Afghans, even requesting (as some of their leaders did again at the height of the civil war in 1992) direct annexation by Russia.[15] Ralph Cobbold, writing to the Foreign Office in 1898 after his trip to the Western Pamirs, reported that

> Owing, however, to the 'zulm' [wrong-doing] and extortion practised by the officials of the Amir, the Tajiks of Roshan and Shighnan invited the Russians to take these valleys under their protection … [They] showed them the only possible roads in this most difficult country, and helped them with transport and supplies, [and] forced the Afghans to cross the Panja after the fight at Somatash, and later on a skirmish at Yaims [Yemts], above Kala-i-Wamar.[16]

The Russians were somewhat reluctant to oblige until they knew exactly how the cards were stacked but, as far as Dunmore's travel was concerned, they obviously joined in the sport, since they had nothing to hide: they were already firmly in control of Kokand and, *de facto*, in possession of the Pamirs: they could only gain by showing this to Dunmore. Indeed, such was the official British concern at Dunmore's eyewitness reports, that, as we have seen (pages 320 and 432), it did not take long from Dunmore's return before final agreement was reached with the Russians in

1895–1896 to fix the Pamir borders that obtain today. Both Empires saw an interest in creating a buffer zone in the Wakhan Corridor; the Afghans were presented with a *fait accompli* and the Chinese hardly consulted.

The Russians had achieved their objectives: with the exception of some last paroxysms in Tibet (well described in Meyer and Brysac's *Tournament of Shadows*), the Great Game was over. One may legitimately wonder if, indeed, there was ever a real 'game' or – as suggested in Chapter 4 – whether it was all a figment of the over-excited imagination of a few jingoist politicians, journalists and officers on both sides.

Certainly, the competition for influence and resources in Central Asia continues today – with different players and different stakes. However, anyone who has seen the incessant convoys of trucks travelling full from China to the former Soviet republics of Central Asia – and travelling back empty, or with, at best, a cargo of scrap metal – must be aware that this 21st century extension of the 'game' is also almost over – the Chinese are in no hurry.

Yashil Kul, site of the Chinese stone

Captain Ralph Patteson Cobbold (1897–1898)

In August 1897, somewhat to his surprise, Ralph P. Cobbold, Captain in the 60th Rifles Regiment and scion of a prominent Suffolk banking and brewing family, received permission from the Indian government to travel through Gilgit and Hunza for a sporting expedition to the Pamirs. Although he submitted a private report to the Foreign Office from Srinagar after his return, in October 1898, it would appear to have been unsolicited and we can probably take him at his word when he professes to have had no official mission or status and that his aim was, indeed, adventure. As we shall see, he found it.

His account of his journey, *Innermost Asia – Travel and Sport* in the Pamirs, published in London in 1900, reveals an intrepid and quick-witted traveller, with a gift for precise observation and an ability to get on with almost everybody he met. Like Dunmore, Cobbold tells his tale with humour and intelligence; however, unlike Dunmore, he does not shrink from criticism of his government and compatriots. He accompanies his narrative with a choice of very apposite – if somewhat conventional – 19th century romantic poetry of which Lord Byron (1788–1824) is one of his favourites:

Are not the mountains, plains and skies a part
Of me and of my soul, as I of them?
Is not the love of these deep in my heart
With a pure passion?

(From *The Siege of Corinth* –
Cobbold has substituted 'plains' for Byron's 'waves' in the first line)

When he wrote it, he had just returned alive from a highly dangerous journey in almost uncharted territory. Before him, only two other Europeans had followed the route he took: the Englishman Ney Elias, who, as we have seen, by his humility and personal warmth left a strong impression on the local population wherever he went in the Pamirs; and the Russian Captain Vannovsky in 1893, a member of Ionov's Pamir detachment.[1] The poem captures well his sense of fatigue at the end of this physically trying experience and the difficulty he had in settling down again after his return to 'civilisation' – probably shared by many others who have been through similar adventures. It is not therefore surprising that, only two years afterwards, he was

off again on a special mission to the
Emperor of Abyssinia, marching with
the latter's army during the Somaliland
campaign in 1901 and then
participating in a joint Abyssinian,
Italian and British expedition sent to
put down the Islamist revolt in
Somaliland led by Sayid Maxamad
Cabdulle Xasan[2].

His book includes some of the first
photographs of the Pamirs, several of
which were provided by Mr. and Mrs.
Leslie Renton who had "recently
concluded a most adventurous journey
by traversing the Pamirs from Osh to
the British frontier." They do not,
however, appear to have provided a
written account of their travels, which
is a pity, since Mrs. Renton shares
with Olga Fedchenko, Mrs. Skersky,
Mrs. Kivekes and Mrs. Littledale the
remarkable distinction of being the
first European women to travel in the Pamirs.

On 13 September, Cobbold left Srinagar for the dâk (post) house near the summit
of the Tragbal pass, where he was joined the next day by Captain H.H.P. Deasy,
another intrepid traveller and surveyor – subsequently to make motoring history by
driving a car up a mountain track railway near Montreux in Switzerland, among other
feats. They travelled together through the Taghdumbash and Sarikol Pamirs, where
Deasy left to do some surveying in Yarkand. Cobbold pressed on to Tashkurgan and
Kashgar.

In Kashgar he established a warm relationship with the Russian Consul-General
Petrovsky, for whose professionalism and competence he had the greatest admiration
and noticed friction between the latter and Younghusband.

Captain Ralph Cobbold [1897–8]

Exploration map

Non-Russian explorers

——————	Forsyth Expedition 1873-74
– – – – –	N. Elias 1885
··········	G. Capus + G. Bonvalot 1887
——————	Mr. + Mrs. Littledale 1891
– – – – –	S. Hedin 1895
··········	O. Olufsen 1896-97, 98-99
——————	R. Cobbold 1898
– – – – –	A. Stein 1915

I then bade farewell with much regret to the Consul-General, who had been most civil and hospitable to me during my stay. I am at a loss to this day to account for the misunderstanding between Petrovsky and Captain Younghusband which the latter chronicles in his admirable volume [*The Heart of a Continent*, p. 284]. Petrovsky, as I gauge him, is certainly not the man to quarrel with an acquaintance on the score of an unintentional breach of etiquette, and the explanation given by the Consul-General, that the reason he had taken offence was because his visitor had paid a formal call in the afternoon instead of the morning, must be regarded as a pretext for concealing the real cause of the ill-feeling whatever it may have been.

Petrovsky, however, had not been impressed by Younghusband and was fully aware of his amateurish efforts to stir up the Chinese against the Russians (see page 317).

Of Captain Younghusband's mission a few years previously the Consul-General had much to say, and he ridiculed the policy of the Indian Government in sending an explorer 'ignorant of the Chinese language and unacquainted with the duplicity of the Chinese character,' to conduct a political mission as delicate as that involved in a settlement of the Pamirs question. And he told me that all the while that Captain Younghusband was interviewing the Taotai [head of the Chinese administration in Kashgar] and urging him to despatch troops to the Pamirs to complete an effective occupation in anticipation of a Russian advance, the Taotai was keeping Petrovsky daily informed of the purport of Younghusband's proposals, acting on which the Russian agent took steps to render the Russian occupation effective before the Chinese troops were half-way to the Pamirs. Petrovsky related this fact with evident relish, and he expressed himself as being greatly amused at the fact that the Indian Government had decorated the explorer in recognition of his political services.

As we have seen, Younghusband was somewhat full of his own self-importance and was even a little racist, announcing publicly his view that "no European can mix with non-Christian races without feeling his moral superiority over them."[3] Perhaps with Younghusband in mind, Petrovsky had shared with Cobbold his criticism of the British attitude to "the natives":

I was especially interested in his criticisms on our methods of dealing with the natives under our rule, and was struck by the insistent manner in which he refused to believe that they felt any affection for their rulers. He pointed out that we English are too cold and haughty, and hold ourselves too far aloof from our inferiors to gain their good will. He also ridiculed the freedom with which the Indian Government permitted irresponsible globe-trotting M.P.s to spend the cold weather in India haranguing native audiences, and asking them if they were happy under British rule. Such a question, he affirmed, put to a Russian native subject in Turkestan would mean a serious risk of the interrogator being sent to Siberia for life.

A visit to the 'sous-prefect' of the Akbashih district near Kashgar, Sozonstov, leads Cobbold to comment favourably on Russian dealings with the local population:

> Mr. Sozontoff was shortly going to Kashgar to arrange with the Russian Consul-General there for the construction of a postal road from Akbashih. He told me that the undertaking would not cost his Government anything. The Kirghiz would all subscribe according to their means, as a good road would enable them to get about in the mountains, and take their sheep and beasts to the Kashgar market with greater ease than at present. One is struck by this example of the use Russians make of the inhabitants of countries that come under their rule, and it seems a pity that the Indian Government does not take a leaf out of their book, and endeavour to open out communication on our frontier in similar conditions. The Russian method of dealing with the native population of their dominions has been arrived at by the Russian dislike of the policy of sending expeditions to burn villages and levy fines and then run away. Where the Russians go they stay, and this is a proper method of dealing with Asiatic tribes. Since Russia has taken over the vast tracts of Turkestan, Ferghana and Bukhara, they have never had any trouble whatever with the people, and consequently they are able to devote their time and attention to the opening of roads and the construction of railways in all directions.[4]

Cobbold had intended to travel from Kashgar to Marghilan, via Ferghana, and return through the Alai to the Pamirs. Petrovsky advised him – probably in good faith – that Vrewsky, the Russian Governor-General in Tashkent, had been replaced and that Cobbold's passport, issued by the former *régime*, might no longer be valid. He decided therefore to travel directly to Kara Kul through the Kontemis (Chon Rangsu) valley and over the Kara Art pass.

Coming down towards Kara Kul, Cobbold noted the military road running between Osh and Murghab – opened in 1897 – that enabled mail carts to travel the distance in ten days. Although it was the end of April, everything was still covered in snow. From Kara Kul he made his way through Kokjar and down the Tanimas / Ghudara river to Pasor and the junction with the Murghab river near Tashkurgan (today Savnob), where the Bartang begins. He noted that the inhabitants of the Western Pamirs had different physical features from the Kyrgyz whom he had

encountered until then on his route in the eastern
Pamirs: in Vomar, for example, "fair hair was not
at all uncommon, and I noticed red hair once or
twice."

> The Tajiks have long heads with high brow,
> expressive eyes shaded by dark eyebrows,
> finely chiselled nose, florid complexion, and
> full brown hair and beard. They form the
> intellectual aristocracy of Turkestan; but
> beneath their exterior culture they inherit
> many social vices, notably avarice, rapacity, a love of gambling, and licentiousness.

> The Gulchas are the agricultural highlanders who inhabit the Western slopes of
> the Pamirs in Darwaz, Roshan, Shighan, Wakhan and Badakhshan, and are also
> Iranian stock, but of a purer type. The chiefs claim descent from Alexander. They
> have broad heads, delicate features, and firm lips. De Ujfalvy chronicles having met
> some closely resembling the Celtic peasantry of Savoy. They compare favourably
> with the Sarts and Tajiks on account of their simple habits and upright character;
> hospitality is a sacred duty for them, and every village contains a house reserved for
> strangers; no slavery is tolerated among them, and polygamy, though authorised, is
> rare. Traces of an old world fire-worship exist among this people. Lights must not
> be blown out, torches are kept burning round the cradle of the newly born and the
> couch of the dying, and towers are still to be found standing along the banks of the
> Panja which are attributed to fire-worshippers. ... The women are fairly good-
> looking, but fade while still young.

After resting in Roshorv, situated on a plateau above the river, and engaging
bearers, he began the most difficult part of the descent of the Bartang, along the steep
and narrow gorges leading to Basid and further on to Bhagoo. His route combined
'rickety ladders' fixed along the face of the cliff, 'hanging passages' (identical to those
described by the Chinese traveller Yu Huan in Hunza sixteen hundred years
previously), swaying bridges made of birch twigs and logs placed across precipices. He
was forced to divide his baggage into smaller parcels and the ponies had to be held
on ropes as they swam around jutting rocks.

Contrasting Pamiri faces, Vanj district (above)

Shrine 'Hozirbosht' ('Be ready') in Savnob village, Bartang valley (left)

His account of this hair-raising experience is prefaced by an apposite quotation from Percy Bysshe Shelley (1792–1822) *Revolt of Islam*:

> I stood upon a point of shattered stone,
> And heard loose rocks rushing tumultuously
> With splash and shock into the deep

The path by the right bank being the shorter, the men carrying the baggage crossed the bridge while I kept on to left with the ponies, and found that the path improved, there being few difficult places until we reached a point some miles below the bridge, where the mountain side descends sheer into the river, and a path, composed of birch twigs tied together and suspended by binders from rocks above, afforded the only means of progression. Shingle and earth had been laid over the twigs, and the path thus provided was good enough in itself. The weight of a dozen ponies traversing it, however, proved too much for some of the binders holding it up, which did not appear as though they had been renewed for years. I had stayed behind to pick some flowers, and seeing that the ponies had crossed in safety had no thought of danger as I hurried on after them. I had gone just halfway across when to my consternation I heard the binder above me snap and instantly felt the path giving way beneath my feet. I clutched desperately at some roots growing in the side of the rock as the path fell into the water below with a sickening thud. The noise of the torrent as it tore along below me was so great that I feared that there was little chance of my being heard, but I shouted for help with all my might. Luckily one of my men and two Tajiks were behind me, and immediately they perceived the danger of my situation they scaled the cliffs above me like cats and taking off their turbans threw the ends down to me. I seized the ends firmly and having wound them well round my wrists I trusted to the men above and swung off into midair. It was a distinctly perilous position, one of the nastiest I remember. We had still twenty yards to go and I feared that it was practically impossible for the men above me to find a firm foothold and support my weight of ten stone. I looked below me and made up my mind to try and gain a footing on a projecting rock some distance down if the worst came and they let me fall; but they didn't. They held on like grim death and occasionally as they worked their way along I eased the tension by thrusting my fingers and toes into crevices in the rock and thus we gradually reached the path again in safety. The whole incident had not occupied more than five minutes, but it seemed to me an age, and when the acute tension was over I felt that all my strength had deserted me and that I was too weak to move. But I soon pulled myself together and we all sat down, the men and I, and I formally thanked

them for saving my life at the peril of their own, which the brave fellows acknowledged by seizing my hands and laying them on their foreheads, vowing that I was their lord and master and that their lives were at my disposal.

The ponies had to swim the river several times, and I nearly met with an accident which would have effectually brought my travels to an end. We came to a deep rift in the face of a precipice, over which a single log had been laid, this being held firm in its place between large stones. Several coolies had crossed in safety, and when it came to my turn I straddled the log and had got half way over when the large stone holding it in its place on the further side began to oscillate and finally rolled down the precipice, while the beam with its rounded ends began to turn and roll towards the edge. Fortunately the cries of the men behind me attracted the attention of a coolie, who ran to the log and held it secure till I had crossed. Probably I should in any case have managed to scramble over in time, but the feeling of being seated on a rolling log some hundreds of feet above a raging torrent is not calculated to soothe the nerves of the coolest.

The Russian explorer, Fedchenko, wrote of an even more hair-raising method of crossing sheer cliffs:

The direct road between Kila Khumb and Shighnan presents many obstacles; during certain months it is impracticable, and then the only means of

Cliff passage in Darvaz [1915]

communication between the two countries is by means of baskets (corbeilles). I had often heard of this kind of carriage at Samarkand, on my voyage to Khokand, and at first I did not believe the accounts, but I finished with being convinced that there was some truth in it. In impracticable defiles where some large river flows, they can only get along, I was told, by imbedding iron pins in the rocks, and suspending from them baskets attached to cords at intervals of about seven feet. The traveller places himself in the first basket, swings himself along, passes into the second basket, and so on to the end.[5]

Although the Tajik side of the Panj now has an asphalt road, built into the rock with explosives during the Soviet period, traces of the kind of perilous cliff route described by Fedchenko can be seen today on the Afghan side – albeit without the baskets!

Cobbold's arrival in the Bartang had been reported to the Bukharan representative in Vomar, and, on arrival in Bhagoo, he was met by an envoy who offered him his full assistance while in Bukharan territory, "which he told me extended up to the Panjah as far as Langar Kisht, opposite the Afghan fort of Kala Panj." As we shall see, this offer was not in fact honoured, since the Russians were suspicious of his real intentions.

The Bartang widens out at this point, and he was able to continue his journey to Vomar by raft. He stopped at Yemts, where the village leader offered him "a kind of sweet cake made from white mulberries dried and beaten into flour and then mixed with butter", a delicacy called 'Pikht' that is still offered to visitors to the Western Pamirs today.

Cobbold arrived not long after the Afghans had been finally expelled by the Russians from the right bank of the Oxus (see pages 466 and 608–609). Cobbold reports on the last stand of the Afghans in Yemts in 1893 and notes that they were detested by the local population for their brutal methods

> …they made the most of their time in getting all they could out of the Tajiks, who state that when the Afghans eventually left the valley for good, the natives had been reduced to severe straits for the necessaries of life by the extortions practised on them, whilst there was not a chaste woman to found among their daughters.

In Vomar, one of the senior Bukharan representatives confirmed to Cobbold that "the Bukhariots detested the Afghans and their ruler, and that the Tajiks along the Oxus had been ruined by the extortion practised by Abdurrahman's agents, from

which they would take some years to recover. He also told me that the Amir had recently issued an order prohibiting the export of grain and horses from Badakhshan and that trade was at a standstill owing to the exorbitant duties imposed along the Afghan frontier, which practically killed commerce." The failure of the crops in 1897 had made matters worse.

In Vomar, he was held a virtual prisoner and received confirmation that, as Petrovsky had warned him, his previous permission to travel in the Pamirs had indeed been cancelled, perhaps because of Russian concerns at the possibility of British meddling in the Muslim revolt in Andijan, that had just broken out. Cossacks from Murghab had received orders to detain him while he was still in the upper Bartang but had been unable to follow his adventurous progress down river. The Russian Commander in Khorog, Edward Karlovich Kivekes – visited him in Vomar to explain the situation and, embarrassed by it, permitted him to return with him to Khorog, where he put him up in his own residence.

Bidding farewell to the Bukharan representatives, "who had been extremely kind to me", he set off with the Russian officers. They crossed the Bartang on rafts and followed the right bank of the Panj down to Khorog. He was surprised to see the

Bridge in upper Yagnob valley

frugal conditions in which Russian officers travelled: "a single fly tent, in bad repair, sufficed for their covering, camp furniture was practically non-existent, and they both slept on the ground in valises."

In Khorog, he received a hearty welcome from the Russian officers and the Cossacks took a great interest in his arrival:

> At the time of our arrival the garrison was in straits for supplies, as the annual caravan from Osh, on which they relied, had been delayed somewhere, and they were out of vodka and brandy, which they found inconvenient. I spent several pleasant days here, and found my hosts a most genial set of men, who appeared unaffectedly glad to meet an Englishman, and discussed politics with me daily. They were particularly anxious to know if I thought there would soon be war, and if I knew whether the Afghans were going to construct a fort at Ishkashim, as they had heard rumoured? When did I think the Amir would die? I was especially struck at the excellent information they possessed respecting frontier questions, and was astonished at their knowledge of Indian politics. This I put down as being due to the extensive system of espionage which is encouraged by the Russian Government along the Indian frontier. The measures taken with a view to keeping themselves posted as to events in Afghanistan are very thorough. Trusty men in disguise are constantly coming and going between the Russian frontier, Kabul and Chitral, and these are encouraged to gain all the information possible compatible with their own safety. This policy is of course directly opposed to that favoured by the British Government, and it is curious that while Russia does all she can to encourage individual enterprise in the form of travel and exploration among her military men, and awards honours for the results of their efforts, our Government do all in their power to discourage the efforts of its officers to add to our store of knowledge, and put all possible difficulties in the way of travellers and sportsmen who desire to visit the countries about the frontier.

The Russian officers were looking forward to war with Britain in the near future:

> They have of course nothing to lose and everything to gain. Their pay is insignificant, they are most of them deeply in debt, and their prospect of advancement in time of peace is *nil*. In the event of war advancement comes within the reach of all employed.

He stayed for "a restful holiday" of three weeks in Khorog, during which Kivekes even permitted him to cross the river to visit the commander of the Afghan fort in

Kala-i Bar Panj, just downstream from Khorog. Finally Kivekes informed him that although he had received no instructions from the Russian headquarters in Marghilan, "he had so satisfied himself as to my *bona fides*, that he felt justified in permitting me to return to the Chinese frontier *via* the Bartang valley". Cobbold leapt at the offer, but, since he now had no money left, was forced to sell all the possessions he could spare, receiving a total of fifty roubles.

> I parted from Kevekiss with the greatest regret, which was, I believe, mutual. It had been a great pleasure to make the acquaintance of so charming a man in such an out-of-the-way corner of the earth, and I was greatly indebted to him for many acts of kindness which tended to make my stay at Charog a pleasant one.[6]

The friendship was indeed mutual and Cobbold and Kivekes subsequently corresponded with one another.

Accompanied by a Cossack escort provided by Kivekes for his safety, Cobbold returned up the Bartang, "one of the vilest roads in Asia", and reached the Kara Art pass on 7 July 1898. He found en route that the local people, Tajiks and Kyrgyz alike, had been punished by the garrison in Murghab for the assistance provided to him on his outward journey and provisions and bearers for the return were only secured with the help of the Cossacks' whips.

> The Cossacks had been very useful to me during the journey, and I rewarded them to the extent of my means. I had been greatly impressed by the conduct of these men, who appeared cheerful and contented under the greatest trials, and endured all sorts of hardships without complaining. They had no tent and no flour, and eked out their existence on what they could get. They were in no sense well-cared for, and as often as not half-starved; yet they always seemed fit and sound, and appeared to be thoroughly hardy and able to stand any rough work they might be called upon to do.

It was with a sense of relief that Cobbold crossed into Chinese territory, for Kivekes had warned him that instructions for his arrest might be on their way from Marghilan. He continued to Tashkurgan and the Taghdumbash Pamir and crossed the Wakhjir Pass and finally the Minteke into Hunza. He was inexplicably delayed for a week by the British authorities, and again in Gilgit, until permission was received from the Indian Government for him to proceed to Kashmir and gives vent to his anger at the incompetence of British 'politicals' in India:

When in India just before starting for the Pamirs the previous year I had been utterly astonished at the ignorance displayed by officials whose business it was to be thoroughly acquainted with frontier matters. A certain official, a very big man high up in the service, whose name I will for the present withhold, to whom I went for assistance and information respecting the regions I proposed to visit, exhibited the haziest idea respecting Central Asia, and was evidently unaware that the spheres of influence beyond the Hindu Kush had been definitely determined. He warned me that the country was one of great danger and difficulty, where political complications might result with Russia or with China if British travellers were encouraged. He showed the utmost ignorance respecting the literature of the subject, was entirely unacquainted with the standard works of Curzon and Younghusband, and yet held a post which required his having every atom of information regarding the trans-frontier regions at his fingers' ends.

This contrasted with what he had experienced among the Russians:

The fact which struck me more than any other in relation to the Russian occupation of innermost Asia was the extraordinary intelligence and amount of accurate information on military and political matters possessed alike by the civil and military officials. I found that the officers in the furthest corners of the Pamirs were thoroughly well posted not only in matters relating to their command and surroundings, but on subjects connected with regions far away, and I was greatly

Tank of the Civil War, upper Khingob valley

impressed by the fact that these men, situated hundreds of miles from civilisation and surrounded by ranges of snow-clad mountains, which often effectually shut them off from communication with the outer world, were well posted not only in the latest news but also in the most recent literature, and I have not the slightest doubt that within a few weeks of its publication this volume will find its way to the library of the general staff at Marghelan, and thence in due course will be forwarded for the perusal of my friends at Charog. … Possessed of the most perfect underground system in the world, the Russians know that there is no secret so closely guarded as to be impenetrable, and appreciating this fact, and ignoring the density of the so-called "intelligence" departments of our own public offices, they make no pretence of concealing any information which may be of general value. Thus the Russian maps, the general staff maps especially, are not only far in advance of our own in point of detail and up-to-date information, but they are published at an absurdly low cost, and can he obtained by anybody so inclined either at St. Petersburg or at Moscow. Nor in the case of information is there any mystery made. I have no doubt but that the Russian War Department is richly stocked with confidential reports which have not been and are not likely to be published, but it is amusing to remark that reports which are pigeon-holed at our Foreign Office, and which, being regarded as confidential, are not published, are well known to Russian officers, and their purport, if not their whole contents, freely discussed.

He reached Srinagar in August and very soon addressed a report to the British Foreign Office, expressing many of the views cited above. By this time, however, he had been perhaps too free with his criticism of the shortcomings of British officials and he must have become a thorn in their flesh. The Foreign Office appears not to have taken any notice of what he had to say, and it very likely became one of the "pigeon-holed reports" to which he had referred sarcastically earlier.

Ralph Cobbold received no recognition of his extraordinary travels either from the British government or from the Royal Geographical Society. Captain Henry Deasy, however, with whom Cobbold had started his journey, received the Founder's Medal of the RGS in 1900 for the work he did in Yarkand after parting company with him in the Taghdumbash Pamir.[7] Cobbold was not alone in this: Ney Elias had also been snubbed by British officialdom and although he had received the RGS Founder's medal for his surveying of the Yellow River, his exploits in the Pamirs went equally unrewarded.

Of his arrival in Kashmir, he writes, however, better than any of the other explorers of the Pamirs and it is a pity that his book is out of print.

> Throughout my wanderings I was often conscious of how much I missed; and when from the lonely land of innermost Asia, where it seemed almost in the fitness of things that one *should* be solitary, I came down into the glorious sunny valley, a world of smiles and freshness, I felt more than ever the want of one kindred spirit, without which happiness is only a broken arc.
>
> It was a beautiful world which I was in now. The flowers, the cool shades, the great trees murmuring with gentle breezes, all rested and delighted my eyes, long accustomed to snow and ice and cold monotony. Certainly the soft influences of this land of fruits and flowers should teach one a more sunshiny creed than belongs to those whose work is in sterner climes or among the tares of fallen humanity. I shall never forget the first evening on the Wular.
>
> 'Twas when the hour of evening came
> Upon the Lake, serene and cool,
> When Day had hid his sultry flame
> Behind the palms of Baramoule   [*Lalla Rookh,* Thomas Moore, 1779–1852]
>
> that I felt that to the valley of Kashmir nothing needs to be added. It is a "lodge in some vast wilderness" for which one often sighs when in the midst of a bustle at once sordid and trivial. The scenery satisfies the soul: it is magnificent, and the air is lifegiving.
>
> From my boat I watched the sunset that evening. Haramuk, the Tragbal, and the mountains towards the east, stood out in a medium of quiet, deep violet against the amber light in the sky, their grey, bleached summits peaked, turreted and snow-slashed, piled above the dark forests, gleamed with glory. The Wular lay "one burnished sheet of living gold," every ripple made by our boat reflected the deep violet mountains. To the west was a carnival of colour – indescribable. Every instant it changed, deepened, reddened, melted, growing more and more wonderful till at last it faded even off the highest jewelled peaks, and they became wan as the face of death.
>
> A sunset breathes a tonic sadness, always brave, never hysterical. Upon the crowded, noisy life of the world the evening gradually falls, and the lights are extinguished. The inevitable end draws near, and is welcome. To read a sunset well is to anticipate experience, and when the hours of the long shadows fall for us in reality we may hope to face them with a mind as quiet.

Lieutenant Wilhelm Filchner (1900)

Sven Hedin's accounts of his adventures in Central Asia were standard reading for young Germans well into the second half of the twentieth century and, for one young army officer in the Royal Bavarian Infantry, reading Hedin's *Durch Asiens Wüsten (Through Asia)* just after its first publication in 1899 awakened in him an urge to follow in Hedin's footsteps. Lieutenant Wilhelm Filchner, at the age of 21, had spent seven weeks touring Russia in 1898 and had just read the recently published work by the Prussian General, Count Yorck von Wartenburg,[1] on Russian advances in Asia *(Vordringen der Russischen Macht in Asien)*. He decided to see for himself the situation in the region where Russian and British interests collided.[2]

On 24 May 1900, with a minimum of baggage – but including scientific instruments and a revolver – he started on a four-week train journey from Munich to Andijan, made possible by the extension of the Transcaspian railway from the ports of Krasnovodsk and Usu-Nada on the Caspian to Tashkent (since 1889) and Andijan (extension completed in January 1899) with the aim of travelling on horseback across the Pamirs to Wakhan and then across the Baroghil pass to British India, returning home some three months later by boat from Bombay.

Filchner's journey would certainly not have been possible without the cordial hospitality and invaluable logistical support he received from the Russian military in Tashkent, Marghilan, Osh and the Pamirs. In Tashkent he stayed a week with General Ivanov, deputising for the Governor-General, Duschovskoi, absent on sick leav, was well received by other senior officers with whom he exchanged opinions about Munich breweries, went drinking with the military pastor and was impressed with the range of languages spoken by his Russian hosts, including French, German and English. He was briefed at the Russian staff headquarters and provided with the latest 1:1,700,000 map of Turkestan by officers who were familiar with the Pamirs, including Captain Snessarev, later to become commander in Khorog, and was introduced to the German wife of the commander of the Russian garrison at Pamirsky Post (present day Murghab). He also came across Count Borghese and his Swiss mountain guide, who were at the start of a trip across the Altai mountains to Lake Baikal and Beijing – this was truly the golden age of adventure.

Armed with official letters of recommendation from Tashkent, he arrived by rail on 20 June in Marghilan, where he and Count Borghese were received at dinner by the Governor of Ferghana, General Tchaikovsky, whose territory included the Pamirs. The next day, with additional letters from Tchaikovsky to the commander in Osh, he continued by rail to Andijan, and then five hours by a rudimentary postal coach to Osh.

The post house in Osh was primitive and Filchner, who was carrying three hundred gold Marks for his travel expenses, on hearing suspicious noises from the other side of the wooden partition in his room, prepared for an attempt at robbery, cocked his revolver and set up a barricade of furniture against the door.[3] A little while later, the door burst open and, instead of robbers, an embarrassed Russian gendarme entered asking for his papers; the noise from the other side of the wall turned out to be animals moving in the night. The apologetic gendarme accompanied Filchner the next morning to the headquarters of the Russian commander in Osh, Zaitsev, who gave him final permission to cross the Pamirs.

With the help of the gendarme, he acquired two hardy horses of Central Asian race for his journey and, finding that a Kyrgyz rider *(jigit)* was about to depart for the Russian detachment at Pamirsky Post, he prepared to leave Osh the next day. His strange baggage was quickly assembled: revolver with 40 cartridges, compass, aneroid sextant, thermometer, telescope, camera (Kodak No. 2) with 300 exposures, supply

Istyk river in the Great Pamir, looking north

of basic medicines, two watches, 'Loden' jacket, woollen trousers with leather gaiters, half-boots, brown felt Kyrgyz hat, oats for the horses, two bottles of sherry, five tins of Riga sausage and sauerkraut, one tin of caviar, some chocolate, a loaf of bread, a bottle of schnapps, four pounds of sugar, small cooking stove and a leather bag for liquids. Once on the road, his tinned food was quickly consumed and his staple diet became mare's milk, chocolate and sugar for the rest of his journey.

The first part of his ride took him to Gulcha, the Taldyk pass and Kara Kul, where he arrived on 27 June, and he recalls affectionately his first encounters with the nomadic Kyrgyz of the Pamirs, who were then travelling to their summer pastures *(jailoo)*.

He remarked that the eldest daughter of the family would ride separately on a camel, wearing the richly decorated Kyrgyz traditional headdress.

Filchner is a pleasant and entertaining narrator, with a good eye for detail. Agreeably for the reader, he lightens his narrative with personal feelings, not least his interest in female beauty. After passing Kara Kul he had the first of several encounters with handsome Kyrgyz women, and, in an isolated yurt, was offered food by a mother who continued suckling her child in his presence.

> I must comment on the many positive sides of the Kyrgyz, a simple people close to nature. I was above all astonished at their honest hospitality and highly developed sense of justice. I am aware that not everyone has had the same opportunity as I to get to know these qualities with such intensity, since most travellers will prefer to arrive with greater pomp, which is bound to awaken greed among them.

Such scenes of unaffected kindness to strangers persist to this day in the Pamirs.

At this point, Filchner suffered a fairly severe attack of altitude sickness, the symptoms of which he describes as 'headaches and palpitations' accompanied by

Young Kyrgyz woman with headdress

'profound apathy', as well as vomiting similar to sea-sickness: the altitude at Kyzyl Art is 4,336 m, and remains above 4,000 m almost all the way to Murghab (3,630 m). Sven Hedin had described the scenery in this part of the Pamirs as a 'moonscape' and Filchner could only agree.

Finally adjusting to the altitude, he reached Pamirsky Post on the morning of 28 June, where he was welcomed with some surprise by the Russian troops and immediately invited by their commander, Anosov, to share breakfast with the officers. His hosts were impressed that his ride from Osh of some 450 km had taken him only five days; he noted, however, that transport of artillery would be difficult and that large troop movements would be hampered by the problem of securing supplies and fodder, despite the eight staging posts set up by the Russians for storage of supplies between Osh and Pamirsky Post, in which simple accommodation was available for travellers.

> It was an uplifting feeling to be the guest of the Russian army in this important outpost at the end of the world. Captain Anosov of the General Staff, whose courageous wife had accompanied him to this isolated spot, drafted a telegram in French to the German Minister of War, von Gössler, with the following content: "The officers' corps of the Pamirs congratulates His Excellency the Minister of War on the first visit of a German officer to the Pamirs, and takes the opportunity to request H.E. to convey to the German army the warmest greetings from their Russian comrades. Signed: "Chef du détachement le capitaine d'Etat Major Anosov, le lieutenant capitaine M. Trubtschaninov, lieutenant Trubtschaninov, le lieutenant M. Naslidov, B.Stankewitsch."

The telegram was sent with a rider to the telegraph office in Gulcha and the health of the German Kaiser was drunk in vodka.

The Russians were about to set off on an expedition towards Zorkul and Wakhan to investigate reports of aggressive moves by the Afghans; Anosov advised Filchner that travel in that direction would be too dangerous and that he should rethink his planned itinerary. Leaving the fort the next day, Filchner rode with the Russians as far as the Yaman river and then, accompanied by a Kyrgyz rider provided by Anosov for his safety, cut south-east towards the military outpost in what is today Cheshtepe on the Istyk river, where he again enjoyed Russian hospitality, noting that the inside of the yurt placed at his disposal was covered with pictures from a Russian women's fashion magazine – pinups are far from a modern invention.

Reaching Kizylrabot the next day, he spent the night in the yurt of Kyrgyz herders and on 2 July, crossed the Beik pass (4,662 m) into the Taghdumbash Pamir. Here his Kyrgyz companion, terrified of the Afghans, abandoned him to find his way alone to the Minteke pass where Afghan, Chinese and British territory converged. He rode down the rock-strewn valley of the Khadariash (Beik) river to its junction with the Karachukursu, where his attempt to cross the swollen river nearly ended in disaster. After an exhausting struggle to save his horses and his life, he was finally noticed by helpful Kyrgyz at the Chinese frontier post on the other side of the river, who showed him the only practicable fording point.

The next day, making his way to the Minteke pass, he ran into the famous British/Hungarian explorer Aurel Stein, at the start of his first Central Asian expedition, who was travelling in the other direction through the Taghdumbash Pamir to Tashkurgan. Stein informed him that he would not be able to cross into British India without special permission from Gilgit but that, while waiting for it, he was welcome to stay with his caravan. At dinner that evening, Stein informed him that the Boxer rebellion had just broken out, that the German Minister in Peking had been murdered (on 20 June) and that China had declared war on Germany and the other colonial powers.

Filchner, already concerned that, since he was coming from Russian territory, there might be difficulties in obtaining permission from the British to travel to India, decided to travel with Stein to Tashkurgan and then go on to Kashgar, where he would seek the assistance of the Russian consulate in joining any Russian detachment moving east for military action against the Boxers: Count Yorck von Wartenburg, the author of the book he had just finished reading, had been placed in command of a joint German, Austrian and Italian expedition to try to put down the rebellion. He travelled with Stein for another day and then, finding the pace of Stein's caravan too slow, set off for Tashkurgan alone. Stein gave him a letter of introduction to the British agent there, Sher Mohammed, with whose help he was able to obtain a Chinese passport from the Chinese post in Tashkurgan – most of the troops in which appeared to be under the influence of opium.

With the help and hospitality of Kyrgyz herders, including another beautiful young Kyrgyz woman, whose horse-riding skills evoked his admiration, Filchner found a route round the Mustagh Ata massif to the south-east and passed through the difficult Tengitar gorge, arriving in Kashgar on 13 July, where he stayed with the

manager of the Russo-Chinese Trading Bank, Hammerbeck. He also enjoyed the hospitality of the Russian Consul-General, Petrovsky, and confirms other travellers' high opinions of him.[4] An international expedition had just returned to Kashgar and was on its way home through Osh, having been prevented by the disturbances from continuing eastwards and Filchner recognised reluctantly that his plan to travel east would not be possible. Resting himself and his horses for a few days, he followed the expedition towards Irkeshtam, crossed the Terek pass and caught up with them in Sopu Korgon, arriving in Osh on 24 July, just two months after starting out from there for the Pamirs.

Still determined to seek military action in China, he sent a telegram to Munich requesting assignment to any German forces being sent in that direction, and, on arriving in Istanbul, received confirmation that his request had been accepted. He was never to get there, however, since, on boarding ship in Istanbul for Europe on 12 August, he was struck down with a virulent attack of malaria – probably contracted in Kashgar (there are few mosquitoes in the Pamirs).

It took Filchner eight months to recover – but his illness gave him the time to write up his copious notes and polish his account of a unique ride across the Pamirs.

Ice and snow, Koitezek Pass

If somewhat lacking in humour compared with some contemporary English explorers, he shows considerable learning for a junior military officer and genuine interest in the history and culture of the places he visited: no less an authority than the oriental scholar Dr. Friedrich Hirth advised him, for example, on the history of Kashgar. His uncomplicated and warm personality gained him many friends on his journey and may even have saved his life on more than one occasion.

Filchner's Pamir ride made his reputation as an intrepid and resourceful explorer. By 1903, he was well enough to lead an expedition to Tibet and, in 1905, was put in charge of the second German expedition to the Antarctic.[5] Despite his early military ambitions, exploration became his passion; although he was one of the first recipients of the German National Prize in 1938 (created by Hitler in emulation of the Nobel Prize, that Germans were not allowed to accept), he was opposed to the Nazi regime and avoided involvement in the second World War by settling in India, only returning to Europe in 1948 where he made his home not in Germany but in Switzerland. In all, he wrote 27 books on exploration and popular science and died at the age of 79 in Zurich. A major part of his archives are kept at the Bavarian Academy of Sciences in Munich.

His 'Pamir ride' also made him some enemies, however. His compatriot, Willi Rickmer Rickmers (1873–1965), one of the most accomplished Pamir explorers and joint leader of the joint German-Soviet expedition to the Pamirs in 1928, complained bitterly in 1907 that Filchner's detailed account of Russian military dispositions in the Pamirs had led to the closure of the area to other explorers.

> It was a very plucky journey, very sporting, but in his book he spoke freely about the military importance or non-importance – I forget which – of the Pamirs, of the roads, etc. These are no secrets, but the Russian Ministry of War rightly thought that this was indiscreet. Naturally someone said to the officials, who had given the permission, 'You allowed a spy to come in.' The officials, annoyed, promptly turned the key. I was not allowed to visit the Pamirs simply because my friend and countryman could not keep his very unimportant revelations to himself. I call that spoiling the game for others.[6]

Filchner's lone ride across the Pamirs was unrivalled by any subsequent traveller and Sven Hedin, in the preface to Filchner's account, pays him the ultimate tribute: "Crossing the Pamirs is not a bed of roses – I know this from my own experience."

Willi Rickmer Rickmers (1913 and 1928)

Willi Rickmer Rickmers was the last great non-Russian explorer of the Pamirs. The expedition of the Austrian and German Alpine associations that he led in 1913, and the Soviet-German expedition in 1928, of which he was joint leader, uncovered some of the last remaining secrets of the remotest corners of the Pamirs.[1]

He was born in Bremerhaven in 1873 into a German family of ship-owners and ship-builders.[2] Although Bremen is far from any mountains, he developed an interest in climbing from a very young age and, as a student in the Faculty of Natural Sciences in Vienna, joined the academic section of the Austrian Alpine Association and did much climbing in the Alps. In 1894, he climbed Mount Ararat in Armenia and, prior to the 1913 Pamirs expedition, had already made eight scientific expeditions to mountainous regions of the Caucasus and the Khanate of Bukhara, of which the territory of present-day Tajikistan was a part. He made his first acquaintance with Turkestan on his travels to Samarqand and Bukhara in 1894 and 1895. On his 3rd and 4th journey in 1896 and 1898 he went deeper into the mountains of Eastern Bukhara and, travelling through Dushanbe, Baljovan and Khovaling, he reached the

Russian and German members of the 1928 expedition

upper Yakhsu valley, where he started commercial gold mining until he was stopped by an edict of the Tsar forbidding foreigners to dig for gold. His journey of 1906, together with his intrepid British wife Mabel, *née* Duff (his marriage to her was the "most brilliant idea of my life"), brought him deep into the Fan mountains and on to the Zarafshan glacier, where he made important contributions to glacier research. The journey also brought him to Kala-i Khum – the closest he had yet been to his long-standing objective: the Pamirs.

In his autobiography, he wrote:

I was impressed above all by things massive and superlative. In this way I became a mountaineer. I was searching for the untouched, for the unsung. And so I became an explorer. Mountains are the most monumental of sculptures, and their counterpart was the desert, the most monumental etching. And so I became attached to Turkestan, where mountains and deserts are inseparably linked.[3]

By the end of the 19th century almost all the valleys and rivers of the Pamirs had been fully mapped and surveyed. In a paper presented to the Royal Geographical Society in April 1929, Rickmer Rickmers commented, with his usual dry humour:

The old Russian survey of 10 versts to the inch (1:420,000) has served as the foundation or framework for every subsequent map of the Pamirs. As time went on more or less sketchy

Rickmers in the dress of a Lama

Rickmers in the 1930s

Syr Darya

Khudjand

Jizak

R u s s i a n   T u r k e s

Ora Tappa

SY

Ko

Samarqand

Penjikent

Zarafshan

Zarafshan

Macha Pass

Pakshif
Pass

Kitab

Yagnob

Iskander
Kul

Gharm

Surkhob

Mura
Pass

Karatag

Dushanbe

Kafirnihan

Ob-i Garm

Tavildara

Khingob

Kh
Pas

Dehnau

Hissar

Norak

Vakhsh

Yakhsu

Kala-i
Khum

Baisun

Khovaling

Baljuvon

E m i r a t e   o f   B u k h a r a

Surkhan Darya

Kafirnihan

Muminabad

Oxus

Qurghan Tappa

Kulob

Kabodion

Vakhsh

Urta
Tugai

Termez

Panj

A f g h a n i s t a n

Exploration map
The Germans

——— W. R.Rickmers 1898

- - - W. R.Rickmers 1906

········· W. R.Rickmers 1913
Expedition of the German and
Austrian Alpine Association

━━━ W. R.Rickmers 1928
German-Russian Alai-Pamir Expedition
Other German members

– – – W. Filchner 1900

——— A.v. Schultz 1905, 1909, 1911-12

© Airphoto International Ltd

improvements were added in irregular patches. Without exception this new topography had to do with inaccessible mountains, inaccessible that is to say from the military surveyor's point of view, for he had to work with a certain rapidity in order to finish the map of Russia's newly acquired possessions in Turkistan. Eating his way through the cake he struck hard objects in the shape of clusters or chains of peaks, glaciers, and gorges. Even had he been a member of the Alpine Club he could not have wasted time on these lumps of last resistance, for army and administration wanted to know as quickly as possible about all the places where war could be waged and taxes levied. By a process of natural elimination the glacier districts were left over for the mountain explorer.

… the old surveyor was possessed by a horror of the void. His aesthetic sense apparently revolted against white patches. These he peopled with contorted caterpillars created partly from hearsay, partly from his inner consciousness. A few larger areas, however, he tinged a lighter yellow, notably around the headwaters of the Bartang, Yazgulem, Vanch, and Khingab, on both sides of the Muk Su, and in Qarategin north of the Surkhab. These then are the big "white patches" of the Alai-Pamirs.

…After my first visit to Bukhara in 1894 I gradually moved eastward, attracted by the cream-coloured patches of Eastern Bukhara and the Western Pamirs mentioned above.[4]

In 1913, the German and Austrian Alpine associations put together a joint expedition with the aim of filling in some of these blank spots. The expedition left Vienna on 2 May and returned on 13 December 1913 at a total cost of £1,350.

Besides myself the official staff consisted of the late Dr. W. Deimler (topographer) and Dr. (now Professor) R. v. Klebelsberg (geologist). The latter had then already begun to specialize in glacier work. Five members came at their own expense: Dr. H. v. Ficker, now head of the Prussian Meteorological Service; Dr. A. Kaltenbach as physician and zoologist; Frau Kaltenbach, Mrs. Rickmers, and Herr E. Kuhlmann [engineer]. …[5]

They explored the mountains and passes on the southern slopes of the Gharm valley, the upper Khingob valley, the Garmo glacier and the mountain passes leading to Vanch and the Muksu and took the first photograph of what is now known as Peak Ismoil Somoni.[6] They ascended about thirty peaks, the highest of which was at 5,700 m. Rickmer Rickmers commented:

As we climbed for topographical and geological purposes only, we had no time to waste on the highest and most difficult mountains.[7]

Deimler produced a photogrammetric survey of part of the Rasht valley (Karategin) and the Peter the Great range, and a map in a scale 1:50,000 which, after 100 years, is still the best map available of the Tupchok glaciers; Klebelsberg wrote *Beiträge zur Geologie Westturkestans (Contributions to the Geology of West Turkestan)*, Innsbruck, 1922; and the Vienna Academy of Science published Ficker's *Untersuchungen über die Meteorologischen Verhältnisse der Pamirgebiete (Research into meteorological conditions in the Pamirs)*, Vienna, 1919. Rickmer Rickmers considered that Klebelsberg's most brilliant discovery was that of the great 'Vakhsh fault' marked by hot springs (Ob-i Garm, 40°C) and frequent earthquakes (destruction of Karatag in 1907).

The 1928 joint Soviet-German expedition was a much larger one, with some thirty members, and also an unusual example of international collaboration by the Soviet regime at a time of incipient paranoia under Stalin. In addition to the members, the expedition included forty servants, a hundred and eighty horses and seventy camels; the combined baggage weighed eight thousand kilos. The sponsors were the 'Notgemeinschaft der Deutschen Wissenschaft' ('German Society in Aid of Science') in Berlin and the U.S.S.R. Academy of Sciences in Leningrad, with support from the German and Austrian Alpine Association; the team comprised eleven specialists each from Germany/Austria and the Soviet Union. The costs were shared by both sides and the expedition lasted six and a half months.

> The official name of the expedition is now the Alai-Pamir Expedition. During its inception it had however been decided to camouflage it as the Alai Expedition. Its main objective, the Sel Tau [an old name for the unmapped heart of the Pamirs, the mysterious area of glaciers and mountains of which the Fedchenko is the centre], was ruled out as being too little known. We did not like to mention the Pamirs, fearing to arouse suspicion, for the Pamirs are like three mighty hands clasped in a grip of steel, each holding on for dear life, yet each hoping that the others might let go. Now that all is over, one realizes that the schemers of dark plots would not have taken a dozen foreigners into their confidence, least of all map-makers. All the same the governor of Kashgar concentrated troops on the border, and many Qirghiz fled into Chinese territory when they heard of our coming.[8]

The main task was to draw up a map of as large an area of the Sel Tau as possible (Finsterwalder, Byelyaev, Dorofeev, Issakov, Biersack) overlaid by geological (Nöth) and meteorological (Zimmermann) observations. Around this solid centre was to be grouped the work of the linguist (Lentz), zoologists (Reichardt, Sokolov, Reinig), botanist (Gorbunov), and many other specialists in highly technical branches (geomagnetism, radiology, etc.). Professor Korjenevsky, to our great regret, had to turn back in the Alai valley owing to a weak heart. The well-known company Mejrabpomruss was represented by Messrs. Shneiderov and Tolchan, who produced a very fine film.[9] Herr Wien took charge of the radio for time-signals.[10]

The craving for a few special plums of adventurous discovery was to be satisfied by the crossing of mysterious passes and the ascent of the highest peak. The biggest discovery however, that of the inordinate length of the Fedchenko glacier, came as a complete surprise. The leader, the topographers, and the geologist were necessarily mountaineers. They were supported by a force of crack climbers (Borchers, Allwein, Wien, Kohlhaupt, Schneider) for reconnoitring.[11]

Altyn Mazar looking towards Fedchenko Glacier (above)
Fedchenko Glacier with Ismoil Somoni Peak (right)

Rickmer Rickmers, as the main organiser, was very much aware that this was a different expedition from any previous one.

> There simply had to be no adventures if our task was to be done thoroughly and in time. Formerly discoverers went out in search of adventure, for they opened up new ways across oceans and continents, and an unknown road always means adventure. Now adventure has been driven from the highroads to the lanes and by-paths. For the modern leader any adventure worth talking about means an engineering accident or a flaw in the organization. If thus he foregoes the full measure of popularity which is the reward of mighty deeds, he should remember that it was the heroism of his countless predecessors which made a science of travel possible.
>
> A sympathetic public will have to change its mental attitude towards explorers, if in future it wishes to do them justice, for the adventure of accidents is gradually being transformed into the adventure of organization, almost of high finance. Instead of the sensational fight with unexpected obstacles there is the noiseless war with detail, with equipment, tactics, and accounts. Only the final result of the undertaking becomes visible. For ever invisible remain the sensations surging in the breast of the leader.[12]

He complained later of his essentially passive role as a 'manager'.

> The zoologist and the linguist remained invisible for months, preferring regions where bees buzz and humans hum. Porters came trickling in at irregular intervals, trickling out again to look after their miserable barley crops. I never had more than fifteen strong men, and sometimes only a few cripples. What with supplying the

higher camps, and what with three parties ever on the move with instruments or sleeping kit, I often found it difficult to make both ends meet.

But all hands worked with a will, and gradually the topography began to clear up. Two of the 'die-hards' found and crossed the Kashal-ayak, the only easy pass over the main range. It connects the Fedchenko Glacier with the Vanch valley. One can go down the Fedchenko to Altin-masar or over the Tanimas to the Pamirs. A party of Russian mountaineers discovered and crossed the pass from the Yazgulem valley. In future times the best base will be at Altin-masar where food, fodder, and men are easily obtainable. From there the Fedchenko Glacier forms an ideal highroad.[13]

The German team published the voluminous results of the expedition in the following articles and books:

Petermanns Geographische Mitteilungen 1928, p. 40;

Willi Rickmer Rickmers, 'Die Alai-Pamir-Expedition 1928' in *Zeitschrift des Deutschen und Österreichischen Alpenvereins*, Innsbruck 1929;

Heinrich von Ficker (Ed.), 'Pamir Expedition 1928'. Vorläufige Berichte der deutschen Teilnehmer ('Pamir Expedition 1928. Preliminary Reports by the German Participants'), in *Schriftenreihe Deutsche Forschung*, Vol. 10, Berlin, 1929;

Dr. Philipp Borchers, 'Bergfahrten im Pamir' ('Mountain Journeys in the Pamirs'), in *Zeitschrift des Deutschen und Österreichischen Alpenvereins*, Innsbruck 1929;

Richard Finsterwalder, 'Das Expeditionsgebiet im Pamir' ('The Expedition Area in the Pamirs'), in *Zeitschrift des Deutschen und Österreichischen Alpenvereins*, Innsbruck 1929;

Willi Rickmer Rickmers, *ALAI! ALAI! Arbeiten und Ergebnisse der Deutsch-Russischen Alai-Pamir-Expedition.(ALAI! ALAI! The Work and Results of the German-Russian Alai-Pamir Expedition)*, Leipzig 1930;

Dr. Philipp Borchers (Ed.), *Berge und Gletscher im Pamir (Mountains and Glaciers in the Pamirs)*, Stuttgart 1931 (Contributions by Eugen Allwein, Richard Finsterwalder, Wolfgang Lentz, Erwin Schneider und Karl Wien);

Dr. Wolfgang Lentz: *Auf dem Dach Der Welt. Mit Phonograph und Kamera bei vergessenen Völkern des Pamir (On the Roof of the World. With a recorder and camera among forgotten peoples of the Pamirs)*, Berlin 1931;[14]

Heinrich von Ficker (Ed.), *Wissenschaftliche Ergebnisse der Alai-Pamir-Expedition 1928 (Scientific Results of the Alai-Pamir Expedition 1928)*, Berlin 1932. (Part I: Richard Finsterwalder: Geodesic, topographic und glaciological results. Part II: Ludwig Nöth: Geological research in the north-west Pamirs und central Transalai. Part III: W. Reinig: Contributions on fauna of the Pamirs).

Willi Rickmer Rickmers was one of the pioneers of skiing in Europe: he contributed to the development of Kitzbühel and Cortina as resorts for winter sports and was an honorary member of the Ski Club of Great Britain. In 1901, he donated his collection of more than 5,000 books on mountains and mountaineering to the German Alpine association in Munich, enabling it to open its first library. The collection was almost totally destroyed by bombs in 1943 and he helped to re-constitute what is today, with some 70,000 books and maps, one of the most important alpine libraries in the world. In 1902 he donated his ethnographic collection to the Ethnographic Museum in Berlin (Dahlem).

In 1930 the Alpine University in Innsbruck awarded him an honorary doctorate for his work in Central Asia. He was elected a Life Fellow of the Royal Geographical Society in London in 1895 and had lectured there; his membership was rescinded "with regret" during the First World War, but restored shortly thereafter and in 1935 he received the RGS gold medal "For long-continued travels in the Caucasus, culminating in his leadership of the Alai-Pamir Russo-German Expedition in 1928." The expedition also holds a modest mountaineering record: until the ascent of Pik Kaufmann by team members Allwein, Schneider and Wien in 1928 (7,134m), the highest mountain yet climbed was Trisul in the Himalayas (7,120m). In recording their achievement, Rickmer Rickmers commented with his usual sense of humour:

> Anyway, I have learnt something new on this trip. I shall take a secretary. She will do the writing, and I shall do at least some climbing and not only hear about the climbs that the others have done. Fortunately there is still a lot to be accomplished in and around the Pamirs.[15]

In his later years he said about himself that he was in reality a philosopher manqué – and was the anonymous author of a highly philosophical book. Willi Rickmer Rickmers died in 1965 at the age of 92 in Munich, where he had lived since 1930. With a final touch of humour he wrote his own epitaph for publication on his death:

> "He sends you all best wishes – the funeral has already taken place."

Tanimas Valley at 3,100 m (following page)

Travel in the Pamirs

The Pamirs, from which several of Asia's highest mountain ranges radiate, including the Karakoram, Himalayas, Hindu Kush and Tien Shan, were known to early Persian geographers as *Bam-i Dunya*, or 'roof of the world'. They are the most interesting tourist destination in Tajikistan, but also the most physically (and mentally) challenging. Air connections to Khorog, capital of Gorno-Badakhshan – although regularly scheduled – are frequently irregular because planes from Dushanbe only leave if visibility is near perfect and there are enough passengers. Roads are pot-holed and dusty and the distances that need to be travelled both to get there and to enjoy the main attractions can be daunting. Accommodation and sanitation leave much to be desired for the fastidious traveller. Finally, altitude sickness – as well as stomach upsets – can unexpectedly bring down even the most hardened travellers. The 'tourist season' is short: the ideal time to visit is between May and October – at other times of year travel can be hampered by snow and extreme cold.

Having said this, however, the rewards far outweigh the risks and inconveniences. The unspoilt scenery is spectacular, Pamiri hospitality is legendary, the local people are unlike any other people on earth and they are more than generous in sharing their love of music and dancing, religious and secular, even with the most casual of visitors. As a virtually undiscovered tourist destination, the Pamirs offer a freshness no longer found in other locations that share similar natural advantages.

The Pamiri people are fervent Muslims and have one of the lowest per capita incomes in the world. A visit to the Pamirs, however, gives the visitor a new perception of the meaning of some common-place terms such as 'happiness', 'poverty', 'joy', 'hope', 'faith', 'Islamic fundamentalism'. Tajikistan belonged to the former Soviet Union, a statue of Lenin stands in front of the government building, the main street in Khorog is still called Lenin Street and portraits of Lenin hang in many public offices. A visit to the Pamirs, where there is almost 100% literacy and good – if declining – health services, also offers a chance to get some current political and economic terminology in better perspective: 'capitalism', 'communism', 'free enterprise', 'progress', 'development'.

For most travellers, a visit to the Pamirs is likely to be different from any previous travel experience and the rewards for the unhurried and open-minded traveller include, in addition to the above reflections and a wealth of new visual impressions:

- tangible traces of human settlement and civilisation going back to the Bronze Age
- an understanding of the strategic importance of this region (from the time of the Silk Road and the 'Great Game' to contemporary geopolitics)
- and, perhaps, time for self-discovery.

• • • • •

The Gorno-Badakhshan Autonomous Oblast ('province') – abbreviation GBAO – is in the far eastern part of Tajikistan. It borders Afghanistan in the south and west, China in the east and Kyrgyzstan in the north. The southern and eastern boundaries are determined by the Pamir and Panj rivers. The Panj becomes the Amu Darya after being joined by the river Vakhsh, before continuing along the Uzbek border on the way to what is left of the Aral Sea – the Panj/Amu Darya was generally known until the twentieth century by its ancient name of Oxus

Gorno-Badakhshan offers:

- the warm hospitality and vitality of its people;
- a tolerant interpretation of Islam – with links to the Sufi tradition and marked in particular by respect for women;
- some of the highest mountains in the world: Peak Ismoil Somoni – formerly Peak Communism (7,495 m), Peak Lenin (in 2006 renamed 'Independence Peak', 7,134 m), Peak Karl Marx (6,723 m) and Peak Engels (6,510 m) as well as the Fedchenko Glacier – the longest mountain glacier in the world (77 km); from Murghab there are views of Mustaghata – 'Father of Ice' (7,546 m) just across the border in China;
- spectacular unspoilt lakes, rivers and landscapes;
- traces of the Silk road and other archaeological sites, including over 10,000 rock paintings and petroglyphs going back more than 10,000 years, castles and fortresses going back more than 2,000 years and ancient shrines to Muslim saints, witnessing the fervour of the local religion;
- one of the most successful development programmes ever implemented.

The archaeological wealth of the region was fairly comprehensively explored during the Soviet period, but very little of this research has been reported in Western languages. The present guidebook is the first to deal extensively with the history of the Pamirs, drawing on this work. Gorno-Badakhshan is therefore almost 'virgin territory' for eco-cultural tourism.

What is a Pamir?

Nineteenth century explorers of the Pamirs concluded that the term 'Pamir' was used in Central Asia to describe any high mountain area of valleys and plateaux. Francis Younghusband, one of the most intrepid Great Game players, noted that the Kanjutis of Hunza used the term for "a nearly level plain or very shallow and wide trough between high mountains on either side." He also gave a useful and succinct explanation of their geological origin:

> The other Pamirs which we visited differed but very slightly, so that a detailed description of this one [the Little Pamir] will suffice. We have, then, a level plain bounded by ranges of mountains of varying height on either side; and perhaps the best idea of what this is like will be gathered from an account of how it is formed. We must therefore look back some hundreds of thousands of years, to the time when these mountains were first upheaved. Whether that upheaval was sudden, … or gradual, …, there would in either case be clefts and hollows between the unevenness which formed the various ranges of the mountain chain. Snow would fall in the upper parts, collect in masses in the hollows, and gradually form into glaciers. Then these glaciers, each with its burden of *débris* of rocks and stone from the mountain-sides, would come creeping down and gradually fill up the bottoms of the valleys parting the various ranges. In former times, in these Pamirs, glaciers descended much lower than they do now, and in all parts of them the moraines of old glaciers may be seen down in the valley bottoms to which no glaciers now descend. All these Pamirs were therefore in former times filled with vast glaciers, and as the ice of them melted away the stony detritus remained and formed the plains which are seen to this present day. If the rainfall were more abundant, this detritus would of course be washed out by the river flowing through the valley; but in these lofty regions, where the very lowest part of the valleys is over twelve thousand feet above sea-level, the rivers are frozen for the greater part of the year, they are unable to do the work that is required of them, and the valleys remain choked up with the old glacier-borne *débris* of bygone ages. Lower down, however, in the states of Wakhan, Shighnan and Roshan, where the rivers have reached a level low enough to remain unfrozen for a time sufficiently long to carry out their duties properly, the valleys have been cleared out, the Pamir country has disappeared, and in place of the broad flat valley bottom, we see deep-cut gorges and narrow defiles.[1]

Ralph Cobbold, who, in 1898, was one of the first Europeans in the Western Pamirs, defined a 'Pamir' as follows:

The main characteristics of a Pamir are the bordering presence of snow-crowned mountain peaks, a valley of varying width in parts consisting of sandstone-covered wastes, in others covered with stunted grass broken with swampy patches, the whole intersected by waterways, which in places unite and expand into lakes of considerable size. A Pamir is, in plain fact, a mountain valley of glacial formation, differing from ordinary mountain valleys only by reason of its superior altitude and the degree to which it has been filled up with alluvium, until it has obtained almost the appearance of a plain. The leading visible features of the Pamirs are the scarcity of trees, the abundance of pasturage and the severity of the climate.[2]

St. George Littledale, who travelled with his wife (the first non-indigenous woman to cross the Pamirs) in 1892, noted that the combination of high valleys of glacial formation and wide plateau areas is specific to the Pamirs, and has no real counterpart in other high mountain regions such as Tibet.[3]

Willi Rickmer Rickmers, the famous 20th century German explorer of the Pamirs, linked the distinctive nature of the Pamirs to their glacial formation.

The glaciers of the Pamirs have certain distinctive features. We owe to the climate the wonderful preservation of those elementary geomorphological shapes and signs of glaciation which, in the Alps, are scoured by the rain and overgrown with vegetation. In the Pamirs, rivers have sawn sharp-edged canyons into sediments without carrying away the walls. There are many instances of rocky projections from the valley flanks, cut through because they were embedded in sediment like microtomic specimens embedded in paraffin. The remnants of valley floors attached to the mountain side make platforms dotted with tarns. Bluffs and terraces abound, and the traveller finds himself in a veritable geological museum. No self-respecting glacier is without its black tail of ice moraine, or dead ice – half rock and half ice. Anything between a mile or 10 miles up stream, this ice moraine abuts on to the end of the white, or live glacier; comparatively sudden starvation has forced the glacier to sacrifice part of its living body. It is, however, possible that the connection has not been severed entirely, so that the upper end of the ice moraine still receives a modicum of supply, and therefore does not melt as fast as the lower end. This ice moraine owes its preservation to the mantle of rubbish that partly shelters it from the sun, partly offers openings through which hot air gnaws at its vitals. The nearer its end, the more the ice moraine presents a welter of hummocks, ridges, chasms and deep funnels with a lake at the bottom.

The most likely explanation of this formation is the very fast retreat of the glacier, processes in the Pamirs being subject to what may be termed the law of

Bears Glacier with Peak Garmo (far left), upper Vanch

extremes – which is the law of the desert. The Pamirs occupy a place in the line of transformations between desert and luxuriant jungle. They are sensitive and react quickly, whereas the Alpine glaciers are sluggish, and their tongues have longer in which to melt. Without the glaciers on the Roof of the World, there would not have been empires in Turkestan. By the way, I do not like the new fashion of calling the Himalaya 'the Roof of the World'; the Pamirs can justly claim priority to this legendary and poetical title.[4]

The etymology and precise meaning of the name 'Pamir' are problematic. The name is encountered for the first time in Xuanzang's account of his travels as "the valley of Po-mi-lo" (see page 276)[5] which corresponds to no known expression in modern Chinese and must have been Xuanzang's attempt to transliterate the name then used by the local inhabitants. This designation was confirmed six hundred years later by Marco Polo, who recorded the name as 'Pamier'.

There are many theories of its etymology:[6]

Sanskrit:
'upa-mery' – the country behind the bank of the river;
'upa-meru' – the country above Mount Meru (legendary holy mountain of Hindu mythology, abode of the gods and centre of the universe)

Old Persian:
'pa-i mehr' – the land at the foot of the sun;
'pa-i-mikhr' – pedestal of Mitra, the sun god;
'bom-ir' – land of the Aryans;
'pa-i mir' – foot of the mountain peaks;
'pa-i mir' – foot of the Mir (Hazrat Ali);
'fan-mir' (or 'famir') – the lake country of the Fani, who according to Strabo founded Balkh – here 'mir' is etymologically identical with Indo-European words for sea or lake, as in the name 'Kashmir' and modern German 'Meer'.

Turkic:
a desert; or a plateau

Most of what is today known as 'The Pamirs' is located in Gorno-Badakhshan in the Republic of Tajikistan. Cobbold defined eight different 'Pamirs':

1. Taghdumbash Pamir, situated immediately to the north of the Kilik pass. This stretches from the upper Wakhan to the Chinese town of Tashkurgan on the north-east.

2. Great Pamir, comprising Zor Kul (Wood's Lake) and a number of smaller lakes.

3. Little Pamir, with Lake Chakmaktyn Kul as far as Aktash (Shaimak).

4. Alichur Pamir, which stretches to the borders of Shughnan, and contains Yashil Kul and Sasik Kul.

5. Sarez Pamir, which includes part of the upper Murghab river and the town of Murghab.

6. Khargosh Pamir, including Kara Kul.

7. Rang Kul Pamir, in the area of the lake of that name, in today's Murghab district.

8. Pamir-i Wakhan, the smallest, comprising the extreme upper reaches of the Panj.

Some would add a) the 'Sarikol Pamir', the mountainous area north of the Taghdumbash Pamir, south of the Rangkul Pamir and east of the Little Pamir and b) the 'Tagharma Pamir'[7] to the north of it and to the west of the peaks Muztaghata and Kongur. Today, moreover, 'Western Pamirs' is used conveniently to describe those regions east of the Panj and adjacent to the other Pamirs (in the districts of Ishkashim, Shughnan, Rushan, Roshtkala, Vanch and Darvaz), together with the eastern mountainous part of what is today Badakhshan in Afghanistan and belonged to the historical territories of Wakhan, Shughnan, Rushan and Darvaz.

The local Tajiks, together with the Russians, French and Germans, however, use Pamir in the singular to describe the whole area. Colonel B.L. Grombchevsky, one of the first Russian explorers in the Pamirs, explained with typical Russian pragmatism that "I term the whole of the table-land 'Pamir', in view of the resemblance of the valleys to each other."[8] Willi Rickmer Rickmers commented with some humour in 1929:

> The term Alai-Pamirs covers the mountainous regions between the Amu Darya, the Sir Darya and the Chinese border. Hence it applies to the Pamir block and its westerly fringes. In accordance with political frontiers one might also speak of the Russian Pamirs. Besides having acquired a definite morphological meaning (a pamir = a valley of the Pamir type), the Pamir has become very elastic in a topographical sense, not to speak of the plural which appears to be of English origin. Khargush Pamir, Alichur Pamir are divisions of the whole (that part of the Pamir called Hare Pamir) like West London or South London. The Londons would therefore correspond to the Pamirs. We observe a transition from place-name to general term. It reminds me of a Russian peasant who once asked me: "Is your Volga as big as ours?"[9]

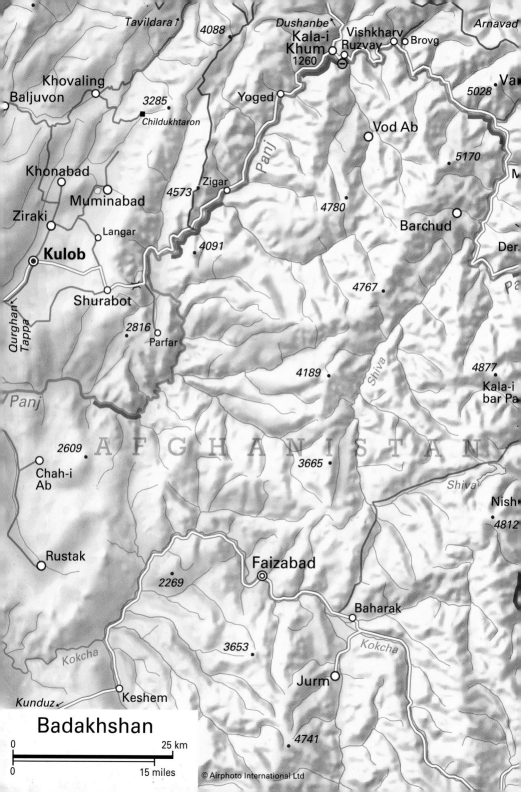

Badakhshan

0   25 km

0   15 miles

© Airphoto International Ltd

As in the case of 'Pamir', the name 'Badakhshan' occurs first in the narrative of the travels of the Chinese Buddhist traveller Xuanzang in about 630 CE,[10] as the kingdom of *Po-to-chang-na*, located by him in the Upper Oxus; it is also mentioned in the 'Book of Kings' by the Persian poet Firdousi (*Shahnameh*, i, 24) composed in the tenth century. Much earlier, however, Greek and Roman historians and geographers wrote about the lands beyond the Oxus (Amu Darya) and Jaxartes (Syr Daria) and the people who inhabited them; their maps record contemporary 'knowledge' of the Pamirs. The southern extensions of the 'Silk Road' passed through the Pamirs and, from the second century BC to the seventh century AD, traders and Buddhist pilgrims brought back accounts of the lands near the western frontiers of China. Following the Arab conquest of Bactria in the eighth century AD, Arab travellers and geographers also contributed records of the region.

Badakhshan was famous in antiquity for its rubies and *lapis lazuli* and was the only known source of the latter. The 'balas' ruby (in gemmology, a spinel) takes its name from 'Balascian', the medieval name of Badakhshan. Probably the most famous spinels are the 170-carat 'Black Prince's ruby' worn by Henry V on his battle helmet and now in the Imperial State Crown of Great Britain, and the 352-carat 'Timur Ruby', part of the UK Royal Collection, on the face of which are engraved the names of some of the Mughal emperors who previously owned it. The account of Marco Polo's travels in the 13th century mentions ruby mining in Shughnan and the *Lale Badakhshan*, as it is known in Shughni and Tajik, is still mined today in the Pamirs.

> No sapphire in Inde, no Rubie rich of price,
> There lacked than, nor Emeraud so grene,
> Balès, Turkès, ne thing to my device.
> (Chaucer, *Court of Love*)

> *L'altra letizia, che m'era già nota*
> *per cara cosa, mi si fece in vista*
> *qual fin balasso in che lo sol percuota.*

(The other joy, a precious thing that I had seen, now seemed to me like a fine balas ruby, lit by the sun.)
(Dante, *Paradiso*, ix. 67)

Mentions of 'sapphire' in ancient texts in all probability refer to *lapis lazuli*: Pliny refers to 'sapphirus' as "a stone sprinkled with specks of gold" and the Book of Job refers to sapphires that contain "dust of gold" (xxviii, 6). Wherever *lapis* is found in antiquity, therefore, there is *prima facie* evidence of trade with Badakhshan. Egyptian records, for example, show that lapis lazuli was being imported in the late predynastic period (fourth millennium BC) and much lapis lazuli was found in the Sumerian tombs at Ur (Mesopotamia) and the royal palace in ancient Ebla (Syria), which date to the third millennium BC. The most famous ancient object incorporating lapis is probably the funeral mask of Tutenkhamun (second millenium BC). Written records of the Pamir region are not, however, found until much later.

Getting There

There are two main ways of getting to Gorno-Badakhshan and the Pamirs: through Dushanbe, the capital of Tajikistan, and through Osh in southern Kyrgyzstan. There are now bridges at Khorog, Ruzvay (Darvaz district) and Ishkashim giving access from Afghan Badakhshan, but it is prudent to verify with the Tajik and Afghan consulates whether this mode of access is available before starting out in this direction.

1) *via* Dushanbe

Once in Dushanbe, unless they have been able to obtain a mention of Gorno-Badakhshan on their visa, travellers must obtain a special permit authorising them to travel there. (See the section on Permits for help in obtaining this.)

From Dushanbe, travel to Gorno-Badakhshan is either by air to Khorog or by road. Subject to the provisos listed below, there are one or more flights every day to and from Khorog. Although the flight from Dushanbe to Khorog is obviously less physically tiring, it is worth considering the road journey: it offers splendid scenery and will give you a better idea of the isolation of Gorno-Badakhshan. The road journey can, of course, be continued along the Pamir Highway to Osh.

BY AIR

Flights to Khorog are in a small plane that must cross a high mountain range (the 'Rushan gate') before swooping down to follow the narrow Panj valley to Khorog – sometimes, it seems, almost within touching distance of the valley walls.

Outward flights only leave Dushanbe if there is no cloud cover on the mountains on the way into Khorog and if Tajik Air determines that there are sufficient passengers to make the flight economical. All flights originate in Dushanbe, which means that there is only a flight Khorog-Dushanbe if the flight Dushanbe-Khorog has taken place. In the absence of flights, arrangements must be made for travel by private car or bus.

BY ROAD

The alternative to the flight is one of the two road routes from Dushanbe into the Pamirs, both in very bad repair for much of the distance.

a) through Kulob, to the southeast of Dushanbe and then from Shurabad along the river Panj to Zigar (the first village in Darvaz district) and Kala-i-Khum (Kulob route); or

b) along the valley of the Surkhob to the east as far as the junction with the Khingob (Obikhingou) river and then along the course of the Khingob as far as the bridge at Dasht-i Sher (the territory of Gorno-Badakhshan lies on the other side of the river); then from Kala-i Husein across the Khaburabot pass to Kala-i Khum (Saghirdasht-Tavildara route).

Dushanbe-Khorog by both routes takes some 16 hours in a modern 4x4, considerably more in a minibus (called locally 'marshroutka'). A seat in a Russian jeep for the 530 km from Dushanbe to Khorog will cost at least 150 Somoni (US$ 44) – and probably slightly more in winter, when you should allow 2 days), though if you are a group it may be better and more comfortable to hire the whole vehicle for about US$ 300. A ticket in an overcrowded minibus ('marshroutka') will cost at least 80 to 100 Somoni (US$ 23–29), and probably more than US$ 250 for the hire of the whole vehicle (about ten seats). Cars, jeeps and minibuses depart Dushanbe early in the morning from Avtobaza 2929, Ahmadi Donish Street, just before the airport – you would be advised to organise this the day before you wish to travel.

Kulob route: The route through Kulob is open throughout the year, except when some of the northern tributaries of the Panj are in flood and cannot be forded – this can happen occasionally if there has been a heavy snow fall in winter and a sudden and sustained rise in temperature in April or May. At these times of year, it is therefore advisable to try to get up-to-date information on the state of the road before leaving.

From its junction with the Panj, this road follows the river all the way to Khorog. While for most of the distance it clings to the rock face of the cliff, sometimes with only the width of a single vehicle and at some height above the river, there is an unreal stretch of nearly 40km of perfectly paved two-lane highway between Zigar and Shkev, with curb stones and insets for bus stops. This 'mirage' does not last long, however, and any talk of a highway from Dushanbe to Xinjiang in China is premature.

The section of the Kulob route along the Panj (from Shurabad and then from Kala-i Khum) offers magnificent views of the villages and mountains on the Afghan side.

Saghirdasht-Tavildara route: The second route travels east from Dushanbe through Kafirnihan and follows the Surkhob river and, from the entrance to the Rasht valley (also known as Karategin or Gharm), the Khingob (N.B. 'ob' is Tajik for 'water' or 'river'). It then crosses the Khingob into Gorno-Badakhshan at Dasht-i Sher and goes over the Khaburobot pass (also called Saghirdasht) – closed approximately December to April – to the Panj at Kala-i Khum – offering superb views en route – where it joins the Kulob route described above.

Although life on the Afghan side has improved somewhat over the past ten years as a result of the work of international development agencies – especially the Aga Khan Development Network – there is somehow a feeling of timewarp between the Soviet-funded infrastructure on the Tajik side – asphalt roads and power and telephone lines, albeit rapidly deteriorating – and the total lack of infrastructure on the Afghan side.

Mazar of Hazrat-i Burkh, upper Khingob Valley

2) *via* Osh in Kyrgyzstan

Osh, the second largest city in Kyrgyzstan, is situated in the south of the country. A paved road runs south from Osh to the Kyrgyz checkpoint at Bordoba, south of the last Kyrgyz settlement Sary Tash, (about 200km, 4 hours by private vehicle). From there a partially paved road leads across the Pamir plateau to Khorog (530km, 12 hours – several passes at altitudes higher than 4,000m). The various checkposts may not allow travellers to pass unless their Tajik visas mention specifically the destination of Gorno-Badakhshan or they are in possession of the special GBAO permit listing their intended destinations.

There is no public transport available between Osh and Khorog. Travellers must try to make their own arrangements either with private vehicles or with one of the trucking companies operating out of Osh.

With the exception of a small settlement at lake Kara Kul, the road from Osh in Kyrgyzstan is uninhabited between the last Kyrgyz town of Sary Tash and Murghab (230km, altitude 3,640m). A good way to break the journey is by a short side trip west from Sary Tash to the village of Sary Mogol where, if the weather is clear, you will have breathtaking views of Pik Lenin and the snow-covered Transalai range. For about fifty years, this village was a Tajik enclave inhabited by people originally from Murghab, and the land was leased from Kyrgyzstan for the purpose of growing fodder for cattle in Murghab; they have recently been given Kyrgyz nationality but retain their Tajik traditions of hospitality. The excellent Kyrgyz Community Based Tourism Association (CBT, 58 Gorkiy St., 720031 Bishkek, tel. +996 312 44 33 31, mobile +996 502 570 67, e-mail reservation@cbtkyrgyzstan.kg) has a homestay in Sary Mogol – otherwise contact the village chairman, Kutmakam Kenjebaev.

On the way to Murghab, the Pamir Highway from Sary Tash lies close to the no-mans-land between Tajikistan and China (it follows about 200km of boundary fence) and goes over some very high passes, of which the highest is Ak Baital at 4,655m: if you have no problems at Ak Baital, you will probably not suffer from altitude sickness in the Pamirs. On the other hand, if you do, then the first thing to do is to reduce all physical activity to a minimum and increase blood sugar by eating dried apricots, glucose tablets or sugar – aspirin also helps relieve the accompanying headache.

There is much to see in Murghab district (see page 606) and simple accommodation – including yurts – is available through the Murghab Ecotourism Association META (meta@acted.org – tel. +992 3554 21 453). META is located in a large yurt-like building on the Pamir Highway on the outskirts of Murghab, in the direction of Osh.

The Mountain Societies Development Support Programme (MSDSP) has a guesthouse in Murghab town and there is also a privately run guesthouse, where travellers are assured of a warm welcome and there is plenty of room: on arrival in Murghab ask for Suhrob Garibmamadov.

At the start or end of your trip along the Pamir Highway, you will find several hotels and bed-and-breakfast places in Osh: one of the best is the Guest House of Zhukov, 40 Frunze Street (actually at the back of Alymbekova St.), 714018 Osh, Kyrgyz Republic; e-mail ladaosh@mail.ru, tel. +996 3222 2 75 76, mobile +996 503 24 73 54. The owner, Lada Khasanova, also offers tours of Osh and the surrounding area.

Travel in Gorno-Badakhshan

From Khorog, there are now cheap minibus ('marshroutka') services along the main valleys – down the Panj as far as the district centres of Rushan, Vanch and Kala-i Khum, and upstream to Langar, the furthest Tajik village in the Wakhan in Ishkashim district. Bus services also operate to Jelondy, the furthest village on the Ghunt in Shughnan district, and Sezhd, three-quarters of the way up the Shakhdara valley (Roshtkala district). For an additional fee, bus drivers may be willing to take you further up the valley than their normal final destination. Minibuses leave from the bus station near the Khorog bazaar on the main road on the way to the airport. It is advisable to check early in the morning when buses are expected to leave: you may have to wait some time, since the bus will not leave until the driver thinks he has enough passengers, but by getting there early you will at least get a window seat.

To travel up the Bartang (Rushan district) and Vanch valleys and through Murghab district you will need to hire a car or jeep in the bazaar in Khorog (or other district centre). There is also an increasing amount of private traffic (cars and trucks) along all the main roads in GBAO, and you will have very little trouble in getting a vehicle to stop for you, at least when one finally comes along. Travel in the back of a 20-year old Russian truck is slow, cold and uncomfortable, but – for the true adventurer – infinitely superior to the confines of a bus or comfort of a Toyota Landcruiser.

The Aga Khan Foundation and its local NGO the Mountain Societies Development Support Programme (MSDSP) have just supported the establishment of a Pamirs Eco-Cultural Tourism Association (PECTA) that is the central point for marketing and information on local tourist service providers (travel agencies, homestays, drivers, guides etc.). During the course of the next few years PECTA will be establishing quality criteria and training programmes for the improvement of these

services. Up to date information on the PECTA list of local service providers can be found on www.pamirs.org (in section 'Help for Tourists') or directly from PECTA:

Pamirs Eco-Cultural Tourism Association (PECTA)
736000 Khorog Central Park, Elchibek Street 10,
Gorno-Badakhshan Autonomous Oblast, Tajikistan
Tel: +992 919 262 965; E-mail: pecta@pamirs.org

Where to Stay

At the time of writing there were only a few hotels of acceptable standard in GBAO: the Serena in Tem, just outside Khorog, run by the Aga Khan Development Network; the Parinen in Khorog, 69/50 Lenin Street (in the centre of town, near the bus station and main market); the Pamir Lodge, at Kuchai Gagarin 46, UPD Microrayon; and the Bizmitch Hotel, Karamshoeva Street 17/4, Khorog. This situation is rapidly changing, however, and a number of new bed-and-breakfast places are being opened. Again, up-to-date information can be obtained from PECTA or the website www.pamirs.org.

The Serena offers the high quality associated with the Serena group (see http://www.akdn.org/agency/akfed_8b.html) and is recommended for those seeking the best comfort available in the Pamirs. The 2008 basic room rate for tourists is USD 80 for a single and USD 100 for a double room - including breakfast, but not tax - with substantial discounts for groups of three or more and for stays longer than a week. The Serena also offers four-bed tent accommodation for USD 120, including breakfast. Reservations can be made at the following address:

Serena Inn, Khorog
Tel (local line): +992 35222 3228; Satellite Tel/Fax : +882 1689 802184
Mobile : +992 93 511 4474; E-mail: khorogserenainn@akdn.org.

At the Parinen, 2007 room rates were USD 35 for a single and USD 50 for a double room. Reservations can be made by e-mail: parinen_hotel@mail.ru; or by tel: +992 35222 5499. The Pamir Lodge is a bed and breakfast, run by a married couple who know western tastes well; he is from the UK and she is from Khorog. Reservations can be made by tel: +992 35222 6545, mobile: +992 93 592 1004, e-mail: pamirlodge@hotmail.com. Their website is http://www.geocities.com/

Woman in shepherd's camp, upper Vanch

pamirlodge/. 2007 room rates at the Bizmitch were USD 25 for a single and USD 50 for a double including breakfast (tel: +992 35222 6492 or mobile: + 992 93 581 4696, e-mail: bizmich.gh@mail.ru).

Subject to availability, the Pamirs Eco-Cultural Tourism Association (see page 531) can arrange reservations in Khorog hotels and some homestays. As already noted, the Murghab Ecotourism Association has a similar programme in Murghab district.

The adventurous traveller will find that there is a welcome for foreigners in every village in Gorno-Badakhshan and accommodation will certainly be found at short notice. Please, however, do not abuse this simple, traditional hospitality and insist on leaving some money with your hosts - US$5–10 per night would be appropriate in rural areas.

Tour Operators

There are not many tour operators offering packages to and in the Pamirs and the offer is not constant. It is best to search the Internet when planning your trip to see what is on offer: for general information begin with the search terms Tajikistan and tours – refine your search with one or more specific locations, e.g. Pamir, Somoni, Pik Lenin, Sarez, Bartang, Zorkul. For tour operators located in the Pamirs, contact the Pamirs Eco-Cultural Tourism Association (contact details page 531).

Three Swiss agencies, *Horizons Nouveaux* in Verbier, *Globotrek* in Bern and *Indo Orient Tours* in Zurich have organised tours to the Pamirs in recent years. See

http://www.horizonsnouveaux.com/esprits/central/asiecentrale.htm

http://www.globotrek.ch and

http://www.indoorient.ch/programme/Tadschikistan-Jeep-Tour.html

Two other agencies – *Oriensce Voyages* in France and *Nomad Reisen* in Germany – added the Pamirs to their programmes: see

http://www.oriensce.fr/tadjikis.html and

http://www.nomad-reisen.de/seit_reis/asien/Tadjikistan/tad574ein.html

For trekking, contact PECTA (see page 531) for a list of trained guides. Surat Toimastov in Dushanbe also knows the Pamirs very well: e-mail pamirad@gmail.com or info@pamir-adventure.com; tel: +992 372 235424, mobile +992 95 151 7567 (See also his website http://www.pamir-adventure.com). See section on Trekking page 540).

If you are a hunter, or want to see Marco Polo sheep – or just want to visit one of the most remote corners of the Pamirs and stay in a hunting camp with a hot spring (*Jarty Gumbez* in the Great Pamir) – get in touch with:

Murghab +992 355421 333   Khorog +992 35222 2982
Dushanbe +992 37 223 34 00   Moscow +7495 362 0830 / +7495 361 4284
E-mail: murgabhunt@mail.ru.
or
Tolibek Gulbekov, 66 Lenin Street, Murghab. Tel: +992 355421 639
Also in Dushanbe: Dekhoti Street 21/3, Apartment 33. Tel: +992 37 234 0620

Permits
For details of the permits required for travel to GBAO and the Pamirs, please see page 28.

Maps For details of relevant maps, please see page 36.

Other Services
New tourist services in the Pamirs are developing rapidly. At the time of writing, mountain bikes are available for rent in Murghab for USD 6 per day from Marbet and Kanibek Saparov, 62 'Seventy years street' ('Ulitsa Semdesyat let'), above the market. META also organises rafting.

Health Care

VACCINATIONS: There are no compulsory vaccinations required for entry to Tajikistan.

MALARIA: Malaria prophylactics are recommended by the UN and the WHO website states: 'Malaria risk—predominantly due to *P. vivax* – exists from June through October, particularly in southern border areas (Khatlon Region), and in some central (Dushanbe), western (Gorno-Badakhshan), and northern (Leninabad Region) areas. Chloroquine and sulfadoxine-pyrimethamine resistant *P. falciparum* reported in the southern part of the country. Recommended prevention in risk areas: III.'

This text has been included in *toto* from the WHO website. However, the inclusion of Gorno-Badakhshan in this list at recommended prevention level III is

very surprising since malaria is almost unheard of in the Pamirs, apart from a few cases in the 1990s that were almost certainly the result of infection in other areas of Tajikistan. Moreover, Gorno-Badakhshan is definitely not a 'western' area!

ALTITUDE SICKNESS: Travellers in Gorno-Badakhshan may have trouble with altitude sickness, which can be totally debilitating. Consult your doctor for advice and medication. N.B. The Mirza, one of the British 'pundits', who travelled on foot in the Pamirs in 1869, recommended eating a little dried fruit and sugar. I can confirm this from personal experience: an aspirin is helpful too, combined with plentiful tea or water. Local drivers on the Pamir Highway also eat 'kurut', a hard ball of cheese that can be found in most Central Asian markets. The only effective remedy is to descend as soon as possible to a lower altitude.

STOMACH UPSETS: Beware also of stomach upsets and diarrhoea – take appropriate medication with you. Be prepared also for food heavy in fat.

SANITARY CONDITIONS: Sanitary conditions are basic. Be prepared – especially if staying in private homes in villages for the absence of hot and running water and primitive (squat) pit toilets.

Woman in market, Sary Mogol

Tajik trader selling kurut – dried yoghurt balls at the market in Istaravshan

HEALTH FACILITIES: During the Soviet period, Gorno-Badakhshan had an extensive system of hospitals and medical centres. With the collapse of the Soviet Union, there was an immediate decline in health services and the availability of medicines. A number of development agencies (Aga Khan Foundation, Médecins Sans Frontières, Pharmaciens sans Frontières, International Federation of Red Cross/Red Crescent Societies and others) began funding projects to arrest this decline. There are now basic facilities and trained personnel in all districts of GBAO; the Aga Khan Health Services have rehabilitated the Oblast Hospital in Khorog, and provided some basic equipment and training for staff; the Rotkreuzspital Lindenhof in Bern, Switzerland has also provided equipment and training.

There are other hospitals in various stages of rehabilitation in Kala-i Khum, Vanch, Vomar (Rushan), Roshtkala, Ishkashim and Murghab. If you need special medicines, take them with you: they may not be available locally. Be aware that medical emergency evacuation will be dependent on the availability of flights from Khorog (see Travel section); the distances between the districts and Khorog must also be borne in mind when assessing risk.

Musicians at Sary Mogol

CLOTHING: Almost all locations in Gorno-Badakhshan are above 2,000m (in Murghab above 3,500m); take appropriate dress for high mountain climate – warm during the day in summer and autumn but cool in the evenings (early/late summer and autumn); from late October to early April it can be extremely cold. MSDSP guest houses are adequately equipped with blankets, as are most private homes recommended by PECTA. Nevertheless, sleeping bags, while not essential, can be useful during this period.

USEFUL ITEMS: Most personal toiletry items can now be found in markets in Gorno-Badakhshan, but may be of inferior quality. The following is a non-exhaustive list of items that may be useful (for trekking equipment, see Trekking section):

- Personal soap/shampoo.
- Toilet paper.
- Personal medicines, especially against diarrhoea (and altitude sickness and car sickness if you are susceptible to either – most of the passes on the road Osh-Khorog are above 4,000m and much of the rest of the terrain between Osh and Khorog is high plateau above 3,000 m).
- High protection suncream in summer (especially for arms when riding in the front of a jeep).
- Sunglasses.
- Sun hat.
- US dollars (NB not earlier than 1990 issues – for the $100 bill preference is given to the 1996 series with enlarged portrait of Benjamin Franklin) – adequate number of small bills. N.B. You may have difficulty in using credit cards and travellers' cheques in Central Asia, although they will be accepted in the main hotels in Dushanbe, Almaty, Bishkek and Tashkent. Almost all transactions in the Pamirs will be in cash.
- Torch/flashlight.
- Gifts (for hospitality in private homes – soap, tea and children's toys are always welcome – for gifts from women to women, cosmetics or tights; chocolate is also popular but will melt in your luggage in the hot summer months).
- Camera/video camera and adequate supply of film and spare batteries – you will be surprised how many pictures you will take, almost everyone runs out of film. If you use a digital camera, remember that there are some places in the Pamirs where there is only limited electricity, and even in others there are occasional power cuts; take at least one extra battery pack and remember to recharge whenever you can.

- Strong shoes (warm boots in autumn, winter and spring).
- Warm clothes for visit and/or overnight in Murghab (all seasons).
- Plastic bottle for water/water purification tablets.
- Adaptor (or voltage reducer) for electrical appliances (European two-pin – 220v).

Do's and Don'ts

In addition to the advice given on page 21 about courtesy and etiquette, the following should also be borne in mind for the Pamirs.

RESPONSIBLE TOURISM:

Bear in mind at all times that you are privileged to be experiencing an exceptionally pristine natural environment with a population largely untouched by the negative aspects of the Western development model. Respect the purity of both. The archaeological sites you will see today are unprotected: help preserve them for future generations.

HOSPITALITY:

- always bear in mind that the Pamiri people are among the poorest in the world; they will, however, share their last crust with you and go into debt to offer hospitality. Be sure to bring gifts and pay for accommodation and meals even if your hosts do not ask for money;
- alcohol may be offered – it is expensive and you should only accept if it is clear that your hosts want to drink; you should only drink vodka during a toast.

MANNERS:

- in Murghab you may be offered a sheep's head – it is acceptable to cut a small piece of the ear and eat it, and then pass the head to the most important local guest present; if you can bring yourself to eat an eye, you will gain the respect of your hosts;
- in a traditional Pamiri house, the place next to the pillar closest to the entrance of the living area is reserved for the *Khalifa* (community religious leader) – if you are asked to sit there, leave a little space next to you for the *Khalifa*, even if he is not expected;
- greeting a man can be done by handshake, while placing your left hand on your heart and bowing slightly; if a handshake is not appropriate (e.g. for a younger single woman), place your right hand on your heart and bow slightly;

- show respect to an old person by taking his/her hand in both of yours; as a sign of special respect you may also raise his/her hand to your lips, while bowing slightly;
- whether or not alcohol is served, you will be expected to propose a toast at some point after your host and any VIPs have proposed theirs; at larger gatherings there may be a 'master of ceremonies' (*Tamadan*) who will ask you for a toast when it is your turn.

MUSIC AND DANCE:

- as a courtesy to your hosts, you will certainly be expected to dance and your prowess (and bravado) will be much appreciated and loudly applauded;
- never refuse an invitation to dance offered by a woman – if you are embarrassed, take a few symbolic steps and thank your partner before sitting down again;
- Pamiri dancing is highly rhythmic but there is no physical contact between dancers, although eye contact is essential; it is perfectly acceptable for people of the same sex to dance together.

Bread sellers at Qurghan Tappa (above)
Dancers in Past-Khuf, Rushan district, GBAO (below)

Bread:

- there is a saying in Tajik 'Bread is life': never throw away a piece of bread or give it to an animal and never turn your back towards the bread on the table;
- bread should always be broken, never cut and the pieces should never be placed on the table upside down.

Tea rituals:

- before serving tea it is first poured into a cup and poured back into the pot three times (this is called 'marrying the tea');
- the cup will be passed to you with the right hand while your host's left hand will be placed on his heart; take the cup and repeat this gesture while looking him in the eyes;
- the teacup is never filled to the brim, and is normally served only half full;
- in rural villages you may be offered shirchai – milk tea with salt.

Violin player, Siponj (above)
Musicians, Khejez (below)

Trekking

PETER BURGESS

"Why would one wish to travel on foot in this uninhabited mountain region with its hazards of sudden blizzards, avalanches, rockfalls, crevasses, accidents, sunburn, frostbite and all forms of high-altitude illness?" The question was asked rhetorically by the Russian academic and mountaineer Vladimir Ratzek in 1980. Ratzek himself certainly knew the answers, which quickly become apparent to anybody who ventures out into the mountain fastness of the Pamirs.

The Pamir mountains of Tajikistan are, without doubt, the least visited mountain range in the world, yet one which offers some of the most magnificent landscapes, picturesque rural scenes, exhilarating trekking and genuine hospitality to be found anywhere on the planet. Summers, and thus the standard trekking season, are short, winters long; locally available supplies, transport and maps are limited; a lack of even the most elementary Russian or Tajik languages can leave the visitor floundering in frustration; the internal security regulations of the Vazorati Amniyat (the Ministry of Security, the Tajik successor to the Russian KGB), or the Tajik Border Guards (who patrol the external i.e. Tajik-Afghan and Tajik-Chinese borders) can prove to be the final insurmountable obstacle; but the rewards outstrip the time and energy invested in organising a trip on the Roof of the World.

Interest in the Pamirs is growing today and, of course, they have played host to a series of illustrious travellers and explorers, whose adventures are described earlier in this book. The real heroes, the true pioneers, are of course the Tajiks and Kyrgyz who settled the valleys and high pastures of the Pamirs and withstood the winters year in, year out, for centuries, irrigating the land with thread-like channels running many kilometres across rocky mountain slopes, subsisting off meagre grain harvests and their livestock, building their own houses and making their own clothes, occasionally trading with distant markets in Afghanistan, Kashgar, and Bukhara. These were communities that were truly isolated and dependent on their own ingenuity for their survival.

When to go

Generalisations about seasonal climatic variation in the Pamirs are difficult; elevations increase dramatically from west to east and thus while the middle of the summer is the best season on the high-altitude Murghab plateau (3,800 m) in the east, the

The Aylaq

Aylaq/ayloq is the Tajik word for the high pasture shepherd camp, occupied in the summer on a transhumance basis. While the mountains appear barren and desolate from a distance, in the upper valleys, beyond the final village and road-head, you will come across dazzling pastures, to which the shepherds head with their flocks of sheep and goats and herds of cattle and yak. Most families in the rural areas of the Pamirs own at least one or two head of livestock, and within any village, certain families (usually the poorest) have assumed the role of collective shepherd. The seasonal migration begins in early June; the shepherds drive the livestock along well-worn paths, taking with them bedding, supplies of wheat, cooking utensils and the paraphernalia for converting milk into other dairy products. From village to aylaq may take up to three days; once at the aylaq, the shepherds usually remain in the same place for the whole of the summer, driving the livestock to different pastures on different days. Sheep, goats and milking yaks are grazed and milked on a daily basis; the male yaks, far more independent and virtually immune to predation by wolf or snow leopard, are left on their own in the furthest pastures for weeks at a time. Having crossed a high pass and picked your way down interminable glacier and moraine, your first sighting of grazing herds on the hillslopes below is a welcome sight – you know that the warm hospitality of an aylaq is not far away.

The shepherding season is short; by September the shepherds are heading back down to their village for the winter. Shepherd families travel and live as a unit; the men and boys spend the days on the hillslopes with the livestock, the women and girls are responsible for the daily milking of the animals and the processing of the milk into less perishable dairy products. Most common are butter and yoghurt, both of which are consumed in vast amounts by the shepherds during their time at the aylaq. Kurut is a hard, pungent cheese made from sun-dried whey, with a liberal component of dust and hair; for foreigners it is an acquired taste, but once acquired it is a welcome seasoning compliment to what are likely to be your otherwise meagre rations (and, according to local people, a preventive medicine for altitude sickness).

The shepherds' camps consist of low, gloomy, dry-stone huts. The huts are extremely basic; each winter they partially collapse under the weight of accumulated snow, and in May men will already be repairing them to allow a minimum of shelter. The aylaq will usually consist of a cluster of two or three small huts adjacent to a livestock corral, surrounded by bare, trampled and dung-covered earth. The inside

of each hut will contain a small hearth (occasionally shepherds also carry with them portable enclosed metal stoves) and a low platform on which everybody sleeps. A recess at the back is used for storage and processing of dairy products. Fuel for cooking and heating is dried animal dung and, when available, brush-wood. When occupied, you will usually smell these aylaqs (smoke and animal dung) before you see them. Almost certainly you will be invited for tea and yoghurt, and – if it is past noon – to stay the night. While the huts provide welcome shelter and hospitality, be prepared for a cramped, stuffy, smoky night; be prepared too for ticks and fleas. When not occupied, especially before the winter deterioration, you can still use them as shelter.

The pastures also provide small ecological niches for wild flowers, bees and butterflies.

Parnassius charltonius deckerty (female); elevation: 4,100m (right)

Tajik girls by a Kyrgyz yurt, Shurali valley (above)

trekker is liable to be plagued by high humidity, hazy skies and raging flood waters in the sub-tropical valleys of Darvaz (1,200 m) in the west. Similarly, variations in precipitation dictate that around the Peak Somoni massif in the central Pamirs, the glacier line is at around 2,800 m, while on the arid wind-swept Murghab plateau it is at around 5,000 m.

However, the most comfortable season for wilderness trekking in the Pamirs is July-September. Deep snow prevents the crossing of even the lowest mountain passes until late June, while after September serious winter equipment is needed and the Tajik and Kyrgyz shepherds, a glimpse into whose rugged lives is one of the highlights of any trip, have started to retreat from the high pastures. In these summer months, diurnal temperature ranges can be dramatic with daytime temperatures of over 30 degrees, and frost registered every night above 4,000 m. The mountains, always barren beyond the irrigated fields of the villages, can appear at their most desolate; yet in the upper valleys, beyond the final village and road-head, you will come across dazzling Alpine pastures, to which the shepherds head with their flocks of sheep and goats and herds of cattle and yak. Their camps comprise dry-stone *aylaqs* (huts) in the case of the Tajiks, yurts in the case of the Kyrgyz (in Murghab district).

Beyond the final shepherds you will soon be into glacial moonscapes, where the river crossings are treacherous, and eventually the glaciers themselves. At this time of the year you can readily cross the high passes, most of which lie from 4,600 to 5,000 m, from one major valley to the next.

Autumn, running from late September to late November, affords the most picturesque landscapes as the skies are clearer, the rivers are running lower and turquoise blue, while the fields and orchards of the villages are a blaze of colour and harvest activity. Lower night-time temperatures must be contended with and the shepherds are leaving, but on the other hand the high passes are even freer of snow. Lower altitude trekking, village to village, is truly sublime at this time of year.

Kyrgyz girl with yaks

The first of the heavy snow fall usually hits Khorog in late December, but the higher villages in all the river valleys will be under snow one month before then. While the winter-wonderland scenery is truly majestic, winter trekking in the Pamirs is a serious business, with all but the lowest passes impossible. In 2001, Bulunkul meteorological station in Murghab district recorded -58°C, and if you are not adequately prepared you can expect frostbite. High-altitude sunshine is fierce, and the winds correspondingly so. Running water is hard to come by and you will need a stove not only for cooking food but also for melting snow. Perhaps the greatest impediment is not the cold temperatures, which can be mitigated, but the shortness of the days and the corresponding long nights. You will need to be in your 4-season sleeping bag from when the sun goes down at 5pm to when it hits your tent at 9am, and after several nights of this you will be all-too-familiar with the personal habits and histories of your companions.

Spring, running from late March to June, is the least rewarding time for high-altitude trekking in the Pamirs. High valleys and passes are still clogged with snow, the mountains are frequently cloud-covered, and the risk of avalanches and rockfalls is at its highest. Trekking at lower altitudes is enhanced as the village fruit orchards are in full blossom and the winter wheat is emerald green in the fields.

Safety & Organisation

IMPORTANT NOTICE: Large tracts of the Pamirs are uninhabited and, as in any mountain environment, weather and temperature are subject to sudden changes. This can result in avalanches, mudslides, flash floods, and damage to, or destruction or blockage of, pathways and bridges. Trekkers should act prudently at all times and ensure that they have adequate equipment, supplies and warm clothing. This section is intended as a general guide to trekking possibilities in the Pamirs and offers no guarantee of the safety of any particular route at any particular time. The publishers and authors of this book decline all responsibility for accidents.

Supplies

Wherever you plan to go, remember that you are in one of the remotest, most poorly supplied regions of the world, and you need to be absolutely independent. There is no formal accommodation in the villages of GBAO, apart from basic MSDSP guesthouses in the district centres. In villages you can expect to be invited to stay at private houses (see the note on hospitality below), but most of the treks described below are higher than the villages. This means carrying tent, sleeping bag, stove (essential in winter, preferable at other times) and all your own food. You can get the basic foods – bread, rice, lentils, tinned fish and meat, sausage, biscuits, chocolate, dried fruit, tea, coffee, sugar, milk powder – in Khorog bazaar, but you cannot depend on the other district centre bazaars. Quality dehydrated foods need to be brought in from outside. You will find ample pure spring water along the way (apart from in the frozen winter).

All other equipment – stoves, ropes, camera films and batteries, need to be brought in from outside. Bear in mind that there are still villages without a regular supply of electricity for recharging batteries. Low quality petrol and diesel can be bought in all district centres, but you need to bring in other fuels. In the summer, a tent is a matter of personal choice – the alternative is to sleep out (in which case you should probably still carry a bivvy bag) and in shepherds' camps – but in the winter it is vital. Your clothing, sleeping bag and tent need to be the best that you can afford, 4–5 season and totally waterproof. If you are intending to go through the high passes or onto the glaciers you will need crampons, ropes, ice axes and trekking poles. Sun-block and good sunglasses are also vital and can make the difference between exhilaration and total misery.

Maps
The best maps for trekking – giving the most detail of the terrain – are the Russian military maps (1:100,000) although they are very difficult to find today. The next best is Markus Hauser's *The Pamirs – a tourist map of Gorno-Badakhshan, Tajikistan, and background information on the region* (see section on Maps on page 36).

Porters
The concept of porters is unknown in the Tajik Pamirs, though you can hire donkeys and horses in the villages and shepherds' camps. These are not cheap and you may be asked for US$20 per animal per day, plus something for the donkey-man/horseman.

Guides
The University of Central Asia, an Aga Khan institution with campuses in Kyrgyzstan, Kazakhstan and Tajikistan (Khorog), is beginning a series of courses for

local people in tourism service, including in particular, guiding. But for the moment, be prepared for bemusement if you ask for a guide. Everyone will enthusiastically point the way and tell you of friends and relatives crossing the passes – to find someone who has actually done it is a far different proposition. While it is certainly the case that most of the passes provided routeways in former generations, the construction of roads in Soviet times, linking the valleys at their lower ends, meant the abandonment of such routes, and the loss of knowledge of their passage. Occasional tumbledown cairns on passes indicate that someone came through here once upon a time, but for the most part you will feel like you are the first.

I would personally recommend Surat Toimastov, a Tajik biologist in Dushanbe, who would be able and willing to assist in obtaining authorisations, transportation and supplies, and to accompany a trek as a guide. Surat has recently started his own tour company: e-mail pamirad@gmail.com or info@pamir-adventure.com; tel +992 372 2235424, mobile +992 935 087019. See also his website http://www.pamir-adventure.com. If you are looking to get into the high peaks and glaciers, Surat Toimastov is the man to get you there.

Trekkers at glacier wall, Tanimas

Pamiri Hospitality

Pamiri hospitality is legendary, and you will undoubtedly meet with it along the way, whether in villages or shepherds' camps. Interaction with local communities is always one of the most rewarding and memorable experiences of a visit to any foreign culture, and you will doubtless be entertained by raw musical performances in the cultural treasure troves that are Pamiri houses or Kyrgyz yurts. However, it is easy for such hospitality, especially in the economic conditions of Tajikistan, to be abused. You will be offered the same food to eat as that eaten by the poverty-stricken people of the settlements in which you are staying – that means bread, salt-tea, dairy products, meat which unless freshly slaughtered is likely to be somewhat dubious, and, either fresh or dried fruits (apricots, mulberry). If you accept the hospitality, you will be obliged to eat the food. If you produce your own food, you should be prepared to share it around, and it won't go very far in a household of over 10 people. If you are more than two people it is in any case unfair to accept the hospitality of food-deficit families. Gifts, preferably cash, will be refused at first but accepted eventually, and you should persevere. The amount is up to you, you soon learn to gauge it, but I would suggest US$5–10 per night. If you supplement this by taking photographs of the family, and honouring your promise to forward the prints, the host family will be delighted. Remember that you may not be near a settlement at night. Furthermore, the limited space and means of shepherds' camps, and the eye-stinging smoke of the aylaq, may mean you have to (or prefer to) sleep outside anyway.

Trekking suggestions

Trekking in the Tajik Pamirs is about as difficult as it gets. You need to be well-equipped and fully independent in terms of supplies. The terrain is tough, and there are no tea-shops or lodges along the way. Once you are above the shepherds' camps you are on your own, and paths are often non-existent. Note the permissions required, as described on page 27.

Sunburn and snow blindness can be a danger

On the other hand, all the treks outlined below offer stunning scenery, are highly enjoyable and manageable with a minimum of technical equipment and expertise. They have been graded 1–5 in terms of physical (non-technical) difficulty. They are those that the author knows well and are, of course, only a selection from all the treks available; Markus Hauser's Pamirs map shows many others.

Eastern Pamir

The Eastern Pamir, the true Pamir – the Bam-i Dunya (Roof of the World) – comprises Murghab district and the upper reaches of the Pamir River in Ishkashim district. The lowest point of this area (3,000m) is where the Pamir River begins its steep descent to its confluence with the Wakhan at Langar, but the lowest point of Murghab district itself is over 3,500m on the Murghab River downstream (west) of Murghab town. The Khorog-Osh Pamir Highway crosses three passes above 4,000m in Murghab district – the Koitezek (4,273m), the Ak Baital (4,655m) and the Kyzylart (4,336m). Landscapes are wide-open and awesome but barren, almost lunar, the only vegetation being the summer pastures that stretch ribbon-like along the main rivers – Aksu/Murghab, Alichur, and Pamir – and higher streams, and isolated patches of tersken that provide fuel for the Kyrgyz inhabitants of the plateau. It is in the distant reaches of the Murghab valleys that you are likely to see Marco Polo sheep, ibex, and if you are truly fortunate, snow leopard.

Trekking in Murghab district is not to be undertaken lightly due to the high altitudes, waterless expanses, deceptive distances and the very real possibility of getting lost. Wind and cold, sun and snow glare, are pervasive while altitude sickness can be debilitating; writing of British Indian agents in the (Afghan) Pamir in 1869, Captain Montgomery of the Great Trigonometrical Survey wrote "... the intenseness of the cold was extreme whenever the wind blew, and they then felt as if they were going to lose their extremities, the glare from the snow was very trying to the eyes, all suffering from snow-blindness; their breath froze on their moustaches, and everyone moreover had to walk in order to keep some warmth in the body...".

Nowadays, however, you don't need to start walking at any of the main roads – your jeep can go cross-country for many miles at almost any point in Murghab; the jeep tracks you follow will invariably lead you to a Kyrgyz shepherds' camp. Indeed many of the routes outlined below can be travelled without even leaving your jeep. Note that while Tajik shepherds generally visit the same aylaq year in, year out (and even if they do not, their stone dwellings remain in place and can be used as shelter) the Kyrgyz are more nomadic, and move their yurt encampments more frequently.

1. The Alichur Valley

The Alichur Valley is the jewel of Murghab district, dotted with yurt encampments throughout the summer. The valley runs in an east-west direction for approximately 65 kms and is bounded at its western end by Yashil Kul Lake. The Pamir Highway runs through the valley, entering it at Alichur village. At its widest the valley is approximately eight km. Numerous side-valleys run north and south from the main valley, and most of these are jeepable for the first several km. Of particular interest is Bash-Gumbez, the road to which is 28 km east of Alichur village. From Bash-Gumbez village you can walk east, south or west into the Southern Alichur range; the route south-east will bring you to Uchkul Lake (one day, grade 2), while the route south will lead you over the Bash-Gumbez pass (4,720 m) to Zorkul Lake (two days, grade 3) at the head of the Pamir River, the Afghan border. Note that Zorkul lies within the restricted border zone, and to visit it you must gain prior permission from the Tajik Border Guards in Khorog (see Section on Permits).

11 km east of Alichur village you can head north up the Bazardara valley, and drive almost to the foot of a pass at 4,664 m. In certain years you may even be able to drive over the pass and continue on down the other side. From the foot of the pass on the far side you can climb Peak Alichur (5,803 m) in one very long day (grade 5). Otherwise, continue down, following the broken road to the confluence with another stream (14 km) coming in from the left (also confusingly called Bazardara) – about 5 km up this valley you will find the ruins of the ancient stone settlement of Bazardara (grade 1). From the confluence you can continue downstream (north) on paths to the confluence with the Murghab River (grade 3, see Murghab/Aksu Valley below).

From Alichur village you can walk down the Alichur River, off-road (the road here swings away south to the Koitezek Pass) 26 km to the eastern shore of Lake Yashil Kul (3,720 m, grade 2). The Alichur river here meanders stunningly through its valley. Just before Yashil Kul, on the right side of the river, there is a hot spring and some very broken Chinese tombs. At this point you can cross the Alichur River and head south to the dust-blown village of Bulunkul (10 km, grade 2) and thence a further 18 km down a road to the Pamir Highway. Alternatively, you can continue walking along the north shore of Yashil Kul, following a clear trail, across the Big and Small Marjenai valleys to the downstream end of the lake, over a pass at 3,920 m and on downstream (now the Ghunt, the main river of upper Shughnan district) to the confluence with the Langar River at the Langar aylaq (two relaxed days, grade 2). At this point you can turn north and take up one of the treks to Lake Sarez (see Central Pamir, below), or continue down to the village of Bachor and on to the Pamir Highway (two days, grade 3).

2. MURGHAB/AKSU VALLEY

Murghab town bestrides the Murghab River at an altitude of 3,650 m. Younghusband visited it in 1890 and wrote "It is a dreary, desolate spot … with a certain amount of grassy pasture and a few scrubby bushes by the river, but surrounded by barren hills, and bitterly cold. How these Russian soldiers can support existence there is a marvel … shut up in dreary quarters, with nothing whatever to do – week after week, month after month passing by in dull monotony…" Over a century later, nothing much has changed.

Downstream, the Murghab River flows west, meandering delightfully, as the main feeder of Lake Sarez – you can drive the dirt road 37 km to the final semi-permanent settlements of Madian, beyond which you can walk (two days, involving crossing the Murghab River) to the confluence with the Bazardara stream and south to Bazardara, grade 4. 30 km downstream from Murghab you can cross a bridge and head 4 km up the tributary Elisu River to the hot springs at Issyk-Bulok (means 'hot spring' in Kyrgyz). From Issyk-Bulok you can continue to trek south for a full day into the head of the valley.

Upstream from Murghab, the river is known as Aksu, and passes through one of the widest, flattest sections of the plateau. The only way to travel through here is by

Murghab River below Madian   *Yurts in the snow, Murghab*

jeep. On a clear morning in Murghab town you can see Muztaghata, (7,546m) in China, but it is 110 km away in a direct line. The road up the Aksu valley, however, is dramatic, passing through the settlement of Tokhtamish to Shaimak (106 km) at 3,840 m. The main road continues for a few more km to a hot spring. This is High Asia at its most exhilarating – you have the tip of the Wakhan Corridor in front of you to the south, China to the east.

From Tokhtamish a road heads south-west 40 km to the tiny isolated shepherds' settlement of Chechtepe, but you will need a guide, even if you are driving. From Chechtepe you can continue south-west to the hunters' camp and hot spring at Jarty-Gumbez (30 km), again, visited by Younghusband in 1890, past Kokjigit Lake to the eastern shore of Zorkul Lake (another 34 km), but again you will need a guide and, for Zorkul, permission from the Tajik Border Guards in Khorog.

3. ZORKUL LAKE

In 1837–1838, Lieutenant Wood of the British India Navy explored the Panj and Pamir rivers as far as the latter's source in Zorkul (the true source is actually the glaciers at the head of the Kara-Jilgasu River in the mountains to the south of Zorkul. To visit Zorkul you must get prior permission from the Tajik Border Guards in Khorog. From Ishkashim, you can drive up the northern side of the Wakhan Corridor to the final village, Langar (105 km), then continue up the Pamir River a further 46 km to the Tajik Border Guards check-post at Khargush. Once through here, it is a further 40 km to the Tajik aylaq of Bash-Gumbez, and a further 4 km to the western shore of Zorkul (4,130 m). If you cannot pass through the Khargush checkpost you must turn north and drive 32 km over the Khargush Pass (4,344 m) to the Pamir Highway just south of Bulunkul.

The north side of Zorkul is full of Tajik shepherds in the summer; from the aylaq at Bash-Gumbez you can trek north (2 days) to the Bash-Gumbez in Alichur valley (see Alichur Valley above). Zorkul itself is 20 km long – the road runs along its northern shore and you can continue to Jarty-Gumbez, Chechtepe and Murghab (see Murghab/Aksu Valley above).

4. KOITEZEK PASS

The Koitezek Pass is long and wide, with its highest point at 4,271 m on the Pamir Highway, 144 km from Khorog. Days can be spent exploring the side valleys and lakes to the north and south of the main road, and you will come across several Tajik *aylaqs* (grades 2–4). Peak Kyzyldong (5,704 m), standing proud to the south of the main road, is a steep climb for which you will need crampons. Allow 2 days (grade 5).

Central Pamir

The Central Pamir comprises the whole of Shughnan, Roshtkala and Rushan districts – including the Bartang valley – and Ishkashim district downstream of the confluence of the Pamir and Wakhan Rivers. (N.B. this is my designation, for convenience of grouping the treks.) Roads allow access along all the main valleys, and to an extent up many of the tributary side valleys. There are numerous side valleys in these districts, many of which have challenging, but manageable, passes at their heads. You have a good chance of seeing ibex around these high passes. The delight of trekking in these districts is in crossing from one main valley to the next, as this involves being off-road and away from the highest villages. The upper side valleys are studded with rich pastures and glacial lakes, and dominated by ice-peaks at their heads. You will pass Tajik *aylaqs* on both side of the passes, passes which themselves will frequently be ice-clad.

1. ROSHTKALA DISTRICT TO ISHKASHIM DISTRICT

Roshtkala district encompasses the whole of the Shakhdara Valley which flows predominantly south-west to its confluence with the Ghunt at Khorog. Shakhdara is one of the prettiest, more intimate valleys of GBAO, with almost constant settlement and cultivation on both sides of the road for the first 60 km. The treks outlined below involve crossing the Wakhan Range.

From Khidorjiv (12 km from Khorog) you can trek south over a 4,380 m pass and down to Nishusp on the Panj River, 27 km from Khorog (grade 2). Allow 2 days, overnighting on the Shakhdara side. From the pass you can see Lake Shiva, 18 km away in Afghanistan. You can do a similar trek from Tusion (16 km from Khorog), following the valley upstream before climbing the western slopes beyond the first of the major *aylaqs* that you come to.

From Vezdara (40 km from Khorog) you can trek south-west and west over a glacier and snow-covered pass at 4,870 m and steeply down into the upper Garm Chashma valley of Ishkashim district (grade 4). Allow 2–3 days for the walk all the way to Garm Chashma where you are rewarded with a hot spring. From Garm Chashma it is 6 km down a road to Andarob on the Panj River, and a further 37 km downstream to Khorog.

From Badomdara (43 km from Khorog) you can trek south-west, again into the upper reaches of Garm Chashma valley (grade 4). From the Badomdara turn-off it is about 13 km to the semi-permanent hamlet of Badomdara. Another 3 km brings you to the Darmaidovan stream coming in from the west – follow this to its glacial head, and over the steep slopes (avoiding the ice) to Garm Chasmadara. Allow 3 days for the full walk to Garm Chashma. This walk is actually easier from the Garm Chashma side.

Alternatively, you can continue straight south up Badomdara almost to the head of the valley, up to the obvious looking pass at 4,940 m, and pick your way carefully down to the upper reaches of Darshaidara (Ishkashim district). This is a difficult trek (grade 5). From Badomdara to Darshaidara allow at least 2 days. Down at the Darshaidara River you can head upstream an hour or so to the wide open pastures of Budum and Tung, full of shepherds in the summer, and the approaches to Peak Mayakovskiy (6,095m) – you could spend 3 or 4 days exploring the valleys and glaciers up here. From Budum it is 2 days down a clear path to the village of Darshai on the Panj River, 36 km upstream from Ishkashim town. If you don't fancy the Darshaidara pass, you could hike the Darshaidara from the village of Darshai to the pastures and *aylaqs* of Budum and Tung, and return the same way (grade 3).

From the village of Rubot (98 km from Khorog) you can trek south up the Vrang valley, over the ice-bound Vrang Pass at 5,070 m and down the long steep Vnukut valley to Vrang on the Panj River, 77 km upstream from Ishkashim town (grade 5). Allow at least 3 days for this walk. You emerge on to a magnificent stretch of the Wakhan corridor – look out for the Buddhist (Zoroastrian?) temple on the descent into Vrang village. 9 km downstream from Vrang, at the village of Torkh-Goz, you can climb back up the slopes one steep hour past the village of Yamchun, to a fortress with commanding views up and down Wakhan, and the exquisite Bibi-Fatima hot spring.

Jawshangoz, at 3,580 m, is the final village in Roshtkala district, 110 km from Khorog. The upper Shakhdara valley here is flat and wide, approaching the high Pamirs slightly further to the east. From Jawshangoz the road continues straight east for 11 km, affording magnificent views up side valleys to the south, of Peaks Marx (6,723 m) and Engels (6,507 m).

All the valleys to the south of Jawshangoz can be explored (grades 2–4); if you want to get through to Ishkashim district, the best way is to proceed from Jawshangoz to the head of the valley and at the point where the road swings north towards Djelondy head south instead, then east, over the 4,432 m Mats Pass, and follow the good trail down to the Pamir River and the road, 121 km upstream from Ishkashim town (grade 4). From Jawshangoz to the Pamir River you should allow at least 2 days.

2. ROSHTKALA DISTRICT TO SHUGHNAN DISTRICT
The treks outlined below involve crossing the Shughnan range.

A couple of km past the village of Shihirizm (63 km from Khorog), leave the main valley and head north up the tributary Chandin-dara (means 'many valleys') - you can drive approximately 9km, then pick up an excellent trail further up the valley. Trek about 7 km north, then head 12 km northwest up the tributary Khtsumetsdara past a series of dazzling blue lakes (the trail fizzles out after the first one but you can make out where to go) to the Chandin Pass (4,500 m). From here, follow the stream down past Chandin Lake, then a series of other lakes, again following your own route, until you pick up the Bogev-dara, and follow it all the way down to the Ghunt River at

Bogev (about 28 km from Chandin Pass, 15 km from Khorog). An alternative from Chandin Lake is to head straight north to the Bogev Pass (2 km, 4,630 m), then again down past a series of lakes, and so to the Bogev-dara. Either way, allow about 4–5 days for trek which is probably more comfortably done coming the other way (grade 3).

At the Khtsumetsdara, the alternative is to continue north up the Chandin-dara, another 6 km to

Women shepherds above Langar

another lake, stocked with fish, and then another 11 km before turning west in the tributary Khodjarot-dara; climb moraine and glacier (5 km) to the obvious looking pass (there are two, go for the one to the right; 4,650 m), then descend glacier and moraine to the head of the Shorip-dara. Follow this all the way down to the village of Kolkhozabad on the Ghunt River (about 20 km from the pass, 23 km from Khorog). Allow 4–5 days for this trek (grade 4).

From the village of Nimos (89 km from Khorog) trek north 25 km to the head of the valley, over the ridge-pass at 4,860 m, and down the glacier into the upper Rivakdara valley. This is a tough pass (grade 5); the long walk out past Rivak Lake brings you eventually to Rivak village on the Ghunt River, 30 km upstream from Khorog. Allow 3–4 days for this trek.

101 km from Khorog, the Shakhdara road makes a large detour north to cross the Soktosh stream before resuming its eastward course towards Jawshangoz. At the Soktosh stream you can continue north and east along a side road that after 24 km brings you to the western shore of Lake Turumtaikul (4,200 m). From Turumtaikul you can trek back south in less than one day to Jawshangoz (grade 2), or continue

Buddhist stupa in Vrang, Wakhan

along the southern shore of the lake 12 km to the Jawshangoz-Djelondy road at the Mysara Pass (grade 2). 15 km up the Soktash road, at the big turn east towards Turumtaikul, you can head steeply north 4 km up a side stream over the 4,400 m Duzakhdara pass and continue on 19 km downstream to the village of Duzakh on the Ghunt river, 100 km upstream from Khorog (grade 4). At the first major confluence downstream from the pass, detour upstream 3 km to the picturesque Kulin lakes with views north to Peak Skalitskiy (5,707 m). Allow 2–3 days for this trek, which is more comfortably done coming the other way.

At the head of the Shakhdara Valley beyond Jawshangoz the road swings north and over the Mysara Pass (4,230 m) to Jelondy (45 km from Jawshangoz) on the Pamir Highway. At the Mysara Pass you can detour left a few km to view Lake Turumtaikul.

3. Shughnan district to Bartang Valley (Rushan district)

The treks outlined below involve crossing the Rushan range, from the Ghunt Valley to the Bartang. The best routes to Lake Sarez are through here, passing lakes, *aylaqs* and glaciers, with a choice of passes, traversing some of the most magnificent scenery in the Pamirs.

From the village of Shitam (62 km from Khorog), the route climbs steeply uphill to the Shitam Pass at 4,859 m. From the precipitous pass it is a steep drop down ice and snow to the glaciers at the head of the Shuvdara valley. Once off the pass it is a long walk out (15 km) to the confluence with the Ravmeddara valley, and another 9 km downstream to the village of Khijez in the Bartang valley. Allow 3 days for this trek (grade 5). From the confluence of the Shuvdara and Ravmeddara valleys you can detour up the Ravmeddara, 6 km to the village of Ravmed, and 17 km more to the ampitheatre of glaciers at the head of the valley. From Khijez, it is 27 km to the Panj in Rushan district and a further 55 km upstream to Khorog.

At the village of Shazud (94 km from Khorog), the Pamir Highway leaves the Ghunt valley and begins the climb to Jelondy. At this point, a side road crosses the Ghunt to the true right bank and progresses upstream 22 km to the village of Bachor. The treks to Sarez begin at Bachor. 4 km upstream from Bachor you come to the confluence of the Ghunt and the Andaravaj rivers, the latter flowing down from Zarushkul Lake. Trek north along the Andaravaj River to the pass at 4,587 m, from which you look down and across to Zarushkul Lake with its magnificent backdrop of ice peaks. You then descend past a string of ribbon lakes to Vykhinch, an aylaq settlement one full day's walk above Lake Sarez. Allow 3 days from Bachor to Vykhinch (grade 4). As an alternative (grade 4), from Bachor you can pass Andaravajdara and proceed further up the Ghunt to the aylaq at Langar, just below the Yashil Kul dam. This puts an extra 12 km on to the trek. At Langar, turn north into the Langar valley, and follow an alternative route to Vykhinch. The main route crosses the Langar-Kutal pass at 4,629 m after 20 km, and then descends to Vykhinch via the three lakes of Uchkul/Kulin. As an alternative to the Langar-Kutal pass, follow the Chapdara valley past the sublime Chapdara Lake, rejoining the main route above Uchkul/Kulin. Yet another alternative is to descend the Ghunt from Yashil Kul, and pick up the route at Langar (see Alichur Valley above). From the pastures above Uchkul/Kulin it is possible to detour north-east over a low pass and down to the Ramayiv lakes.

From Vykhinch, it is a long day (grade 3) down the left side of the river to Irkht on Lake Sarez (3,255 m), where there is an old and barely-functioning meteorological-hydrological-seismological station. From Irkht, you can arrange for a boat to take you round to the natural dam at Usoi; it is possible to walk to Usoi around the lake and over the Marjenai Pass (one day, grade 4), but this path is badly degraded and, with its precipitous drops into the lake below, not for the faint-hearted. From Usoi, it is another full day (grade 3) across the massive dam and down the Murghab River to the stunning village of Barchadev. From Barchadev it is 120 km to the Panj in Rushan district and a further 55 km upstream to Khorog.

The alternative (shorter) trek to Lake Sarez is to begin at Barchadev, walk up to the lake (one long day) and back again the next day (grade 3).

Western Pamir

The Western Pamir comprises Vanch and Darvaz districts (my designation), and can be said to extend northwards into the Khingob and Karategin (Rasht) valleys. The heads of the Vanch and Khingob valleys culminate in the Peak Somoni (formerly Peak Communism) massif (7,495 m). While the valleys are lower than those of the Central and Eastern Pamir, the passes are as high and the trekking, if anything, more arduous. The Western Pamir is wetter than the mountains further east, and as a result the glacier line is considerably lower, reaching down to 2,800 m. There is considerably more vegetation than at equivalent altitudes further east, and while you may still see the occasional ibex in the passes, you are just as likely to see bears lower down. Most of the treks in this region encompass technical glacial traverses, and this section therefore describes only one, which is manageable with a minimum of technical expertise and equipment.

VANCH VALLEY TO YAZGULEM VALLEY

Note that this trek should only be attempted in the autumn when the water levels are at their lowest in the Yazgulem River (grade 5 because of the river crossing, otherwise grade 4). The trek starts at the village of Langar in the Vanch Valley, 35 km above the district centre of Vanch, which is in turn 170 km from Khorog. From Langar a disused and broken mining road leads up the Langardara valley to the southeast. This road actually continues half-way up the Langar glacier to a disused quartz mine on the glacier's true right side. From the glacier you can look back across the

head of the Vanch valley for one of the few views you can get anywhere in the Pamirs of Peak Somoni (7,495 m). An easy ascent up the true left side of the glacier gets you to the Langar Pass at 4,418 m from where you drop down into the Gujovasi valley, and on to its confluence with the Yazgulem. From Langar allow 3–4 days to this point. Head downstream the Yazgulem River looking for a suitable crossing point to the true left bank – this is the most dangerous part of the trek and you'll need a rope. Be prepared to get wet. Ahead you'll see the fields of the hamlet of Ubaghn on the left bank.

From Ubaghn there is a clear trail 24 km down the valley to Zhamag, the road-head. From Zhamag it is 20 km down the pretty Yazgulem valley to its confluence with the Panj, and from there a further 134 km upstream to Khorog.

Peter Burgess lived in Tajikistan from 1995 to 2002, working for the Aga Khan Foundation in Khorog and subsequently for the European Commission in Dunshanbe. During this time he travelled and trekked extensively in the Pamirs. Since 2003 he has continued to work for the EC in Afghanistan and India, and is currently in Nicaragua.

Girls with lamb

Tanimas, five glaciers coming from the south (top)
Glacier No. 3, Upper Tanimas Valley (middle right)
Overlooking the wild Grum Grshimailo glacier to Black Horn peak (middle left)
The Usoi dam formed the 56 km long Sarez Lake (bottom)

Mountaineering in the Pamirs   RICK ALLEN

Topography

The sweep of the great mountain ranges of Asia, west and north along the fringes of the Tibetan plateau and Chinese Xinjiang culminate in the Pamirs, a great trapezoid of high land covering over 250 km^2 in the Gorno-Badakhshan Autonomous Oblast (GBAO), in Eastern Tajikistan, much of which is over 3,000 m high. To the south-east lie the Karakoram, to the south, the Hindu Kush, to the east, the Kun Lun and to the north-east, the Tien Shan.

With the exception of the Markansu (that flows east and ends in the Tarim basin), all drainage from the TransAlai flows into the Kyzylsu, that in turn drains into the Panj. The Southern flanks drain directly into the Panj and thence into the other great central Asian river, the Amu Darya. Within the region lie 3 peaks over 7,000 m in height, the farthest west and some of the most northerly in Asia.

The Pamirs comprise a number of discrete sub-ranges or ridges of mountains. Along the Northern fringes lie the Trans-Alai ranges, including Peak Lenin, at 7,134 m the second highest in the Pamir and third in the former Soviet Union. From Peak Lenin the Zulumart ridge goes south with just three principal summits.

The great Academy of Sciences range also runs north-south. Here lies the highest peak of the region, Ismoil Somoni Peak previously known at various stages as Peak Communism and Peak Stalin. At 77 km in length, the Fedchenko glacier flows northwards along the eastern flanks of the Academy of Sciences range and is one of the longest bodies of ice outside the polar regions.

From the Academy of Sciences range a number of subsidiary ridges extend westwards, separated by deep river gorges that cut down to the Panj. South of the Bartang river lies the Rushan range which forms the northern skyline of the valley of the Ghunt River. Further south again lies the Shughnan range and, forming a right angle above the steep bend in the Panj River along the border with Afghanistan, are the Ishkashim and Shakhdara ranges. An isolated knot of rounded peaks in Murghab district to the north-east forms the Muzkol range in a high, arid environment in stark contrast to the ridges and valleys to the west where most precipitation is trapped. Other ranges are mentioned below in the section on Mountaineering Opportunities.

Access

The Pamir highway skirts the mountains on 3 sides so that they may be approached either from the Tajik capital Dushanbe to the west or from Osh across the border to the north in Kyrgyzstan. The high mountain camp on the glacier below Ismoil Somoni Peak may be accessed either by helicopter or on foot from the Muksu River in a very tough 4-day approach. An interesting alternative is to approach the main massif of Ismoil Somoni from the Khingob valley. This was the side chosen by the British-Soviet Pamir Expedition in 1962, when two of the British members, Wilfrid Noyce and Robin Smith died when descending after a successful climb from Pik Garmo. Both are buried close to the junction of the Kyrgyzob and Gharm valleys.

Mountaineering History
Peak Lenin 7,134 m

First seen and referenced by A.P. Fedchenko in 1871, this mountain was thought at the time to be the highest peak in the range and was named after K.P. von Kaufmann, first Governor General of Turkestan. In 1928 a joint Soviet-German expedition under the joint leadership of N.P. Gorbunov and W.R. Rickmers explored the head of the

Peak Garmo from Abdulkhagor Valley, Upper Vanch

Fedchenko glacier from the direction of the Tanimas valley and then descended the glacier to the Muksu River and the place known as Altyn Mazar. From there a group of three German climbers, Allwein, Schneider and Wien, moved east up the Saukdara valley, attained a pass later named after N.V. Krylenko and reached the summit of Pik Kaufmann via the east ridge. In 1929, the Peak was renamed Pik Lenin. This ascent was not acknowledged by the Soviet authorities for 20 years. The first successful Soviet ascent was made in 1934 when V. Abalakov, Chernuka and Lukin climbed what is now called the Lipkin spur to reach the mountain from the north-east. This is one of the classic routes commonly climbed on the mountain today, along with the north-west ridge. Both are rated Russian 5, although that is primarily based on altitude and not technical difficulty. They would be graded PD+ or AD in the European Alps.

PEAK ISMOIL SOMONI (PEAK COMMUNISM) 7,495 M

Gorbunov and Krylenko (of the eponymous pass mentioned above) continued to lead expeditions into the Pamir and, during the 1928 expedition, a peak higher than Peak Lenin was identified in the Academy of Sciences range. This was referred to in some publications as Peak Garmo, a name also applied to a neighbouring peak. The Soviet cartographers faced a tricky problem: what should one call a peak higher than Peak Lenin? In the prevailing political climate, the answer was soon obvious and the mountain became Peak Stalin.

The Tajik Pamir expedition of 1933 was conceived as a grand scientific, sporting and propaganda endeavour to map the resources of the newly created Tajik Soviet Socialist Republic. Forty separate teams were charged with a variety of surveying functions and the 29th team was assigned the task of surveying and climbing Peak Stalin.

The expedition, led personally by Gorbunov, established its base camp at the snout of the Fedchenko glacier and approached the mountain via the Bivouac glacier. Four camps were established over a month and the lives of a climber and a local guide were lost as the team tackled the gendarmes of the East face. Finally, on the 3 September, Yevgeniy Abalakov, brother of the first Soviet climber to conquer Peak Lenin, reached the summit climbing solo in poor weather after his leader and climbing companion Gorbunov dropped back with altitude problems. Within 5 years of receiving acclaim for this ascent, the expedition leaders, Gorbunov and Krylenko, both prominent Bolsheviks, were to die, victims of Stalin's purges in the late 1930s. A second ascent of Stalin Peak was made in 1937.

In 1955 a Georgian party approached the peak from the Garmo glacier and, coming from the Belaev glacier, were able to reach the Academy of Sciences range below Peak Pravda. Turning this on the East, they ascended the south ridge of Peak Stalin to the summit. Two years later a Moscow team climbed the west ridge from the Garmo Glacier over Peak Kubyshev. In 1962 the Peak was renamed Peak Communism as the cult of Stalin's personality was swept away by Krushchev. In the same year the first British ascent was made by Joe Brown, Ian McNaught Davis and Malcolm Slesser. A number of other alternative routes were taken in the 1960s but it was not until 1968 that Borodkin climbed from the Valter glacier on to the Pamir ice plateau and thence onto the west ridge, now the standard route of ascent – rated Russian 5a, European D/D+. The first winter ascent of the Borodkin route was made in 1986.

Peak Yevgeniya Korzhenevskaya 7,150 m

The Russian Geographer N.L. Korzhenevskiy named this peak in the Academy of Sciences range after his wife Yevgenia. It is located just to the north of Peak Somoni. A pre-war attempt failed to reach the main summit and it was not until 1953 that a team led by Ugarov approached the peak from the Fortambek glacier. They passed the gorge of the Korzhenevskiy Glacier to gain the summit by the north ridge. The south ridge was climbed in 1961 from the Moskvin glacier and in 1966 a large team made four separate new routes on the mountain including the south ridge buttress, the south-east face and the east ridge.

Both Peak Somoni and Peak Korzhenevskaya are commonly climbed today from the established base camp at the junction between the Valter and Moskvin glaciers. The base operates each summer from mid July to late August providing basic food (and a sauna).

Peak Revolution 6,948 m

At the head of the Fedchenko glacier in the Yazgulem range lies Peak Revolution. The first attempt to climb it was made during the 1928 expedition but failed below the top because of danger of avalanches. It was not until 1954 that again Ugarov succeeded in climbing the now classic north-east ridge.

Further south in the Shakhdara range lie the twin peaks of Karl Marx and Engels. The west ridge of Karl Marx was climbed in 1946 and the south ridge by a Georgian party in 1954. In the same year a couloir on the south face of Engels provided the line of its first ascent and in 1964 a team from Leningrad led by Budanov made the first

ascent of the north face of Engels and a traverse of both Marx and Engels. The north-east wall of Engels has provided fruitful territory for a number of difficult mixed routes, notably that of S. Efimov's team in 1982 which won the Soviet mountaineering prize for that year.

Current Mountaineering Opportunities

Exploratory opportunities abound it the remote Pamir region. Most mountaineering expeditions have concentrated on the big peaks of the central Pamir where a mountain base has been established and helicopter access has enabled hundreds of climbers to approach the peaks. The majority of peaks have only one route on them, some two. Many will only have been climbed once.

There is no recent tradition of human porterage in the Pamir. Pack animals with their minders can be arranged at most villages but advance notice is wise if lengthy delays are to be avoided. However, pack animals have their limitations and journeys

Peaks Karl Marx, 6,723m (right) and Engels 6,510m (left) (above)

that involve steep, snowbound passes or glacier travel will oblige the mountaineer to say farewell to the animals and shoulder all his or her own equipment.

Some 7 or 8 mountain ranges extend Westwards from the central Pamir knot.

To the north, the Transalai range (Peak Lenin) extends westwards from the border with China towards Jirgatal above the Muksu river. 5,000 m peaks accessible 15 km, 2 days, from the ends of tracks.

The Peter the First range runs west from the central Pamir knot, including 6,785 m Peak Moskva, 30 km, 4 days from the closest track and many 5,000 m peaks, the nearest of which are 15 km, 2 days from tracks.

Moving south, the Mazor range of 5,000 m peaks involves access of 30 km, 4 days. Both the Peter the First and Mazor ranges are accessible from the Khingob valley

The road along the Vanch river runs north-east into the mountains and facilitates easier access to the Darvaz range including Peak Arnavad, 5,992 m.

South of the Vanch river is the Vanch range itself, mainly 4,000 m peaks. A base to strike at these peaks could be reached in one day from the road.

Moving south again, the Yazgulem range, culminating in Peak Vudor 6,132 m, involves 3-day approaches from Zhamag, the last village on the track which leads east from the main road on the Panj river up the Yazgulem tributary.

The main road heading east from Khorog along the Ghunt river, the Pamir Highway passes within a couple of days walk of bases to approach the south side of the long Rushan range. The highest peak, Peak Patkhor, 6,083 m, could be approached from either the Ghunt or the Bartang valley.

Peak Lenin panorama

South of the Pamir Highway is the Shughnan range, culminating in Peak Skalisty, 5,707 m, to be approached in 2–3 days from the road. Further east, and lying just one or two days walk to the north of the Pamir Highway is the more compact Banchigir group of peaks, topped by Banchigir itself at 5,809 m. Due south on the other side of the highway is the southern Alichur range of 5,000 m peaks including Kyzyldong with 5,704 m, just south of the Koitezek Pass.

As the Pamir Highway turns north towards Murghab, it skirts the northern Alichur range but approaches to the base of the un-named 5,624 m highest point would entail at least 4 days. The highway curves around the remote Muzkol range including the Soviet Officers peak 6,233 m. The map intriguingly classifies a track approaching the southern flanks of this group as permitting motor transport at up to 20 km/hour. Access to bases for 5,000 m peaks here would require 3 days.

North from Murghab the Pamir Highway skirts the huge Kara Kul lake. East of the road and forming the border with China is the Sarikol range including numerous 5,000 m peaks. Although they appear to be within Tajikistan, a substantial border fence topped with barbed wire runs along the eastern side of this road and these peaks must be considered out of bounds.

In the extreme south of the Pamirs and stretching eastwards into the Wakhan lies the Shakhdara range, including the prominent 6,723 m Karl Marx peak and nearby peak Engels, 6,507 m. The Pamir River runs south of the range until it meets the Wakhan river and becomes the Panj river. The border and a road run along the Pamir and Panj rivers and a two day approach to the southern side of the range is feasible. Tracks leading into the northern side of the range originate along the Mats and Shakhdara rivers. The track along the former is accessible from the border road at the eastern end of the Pamir section of the range or from Vrang and over the 5,000 m Vrang pass but the total distance to the base of the peaks is around 50 km, say 5 days. Mayakovskiy Peak, 6,095 m, is accessible from Darshai in the lower Wakhan, a 3-day trek leads to the base camp.

Rick Allen has been mountaineering in the greater ranges of Asia for over 25 years. He has made a number of difficult first ascents and led clients to the summit of Everest in 2000. He first visited Tajikistan in 1992 and now lives with his wife Zuhra in Dushanbe from where he continues mountain exploration and guiding.

Regional Travel Details

Darvaz, Vanch and Yazgulem

'Darvaz' means gate in the Persian languages, and the district of Darvaz in Badakhshan (on both sides of the river Panj) was indeed the gate from the Western Pamirs to ancient Bactria and Khorezm (and to the later Emirate of Bukhara).

Access from Dushanbe is discussed in the Travel Section. Both options (through Kulob or Saghirdasht/Tavildara) are attractive, although long (approx. 16 hours to Khorog). The Kulob route is being improved, as the all-weather route of choice to and from the Kulma pass at the Chinese border (see section on Murghab), and offers dizzying views of the Panj from the high cliff sides along which the road passes. The Saghirdasht route – only open in the late spring, summer and autumn (check before leaving if you plan to take this route) and not well-maintained – is more peaceful and offers excellent views at Kala-i Husein and the Khaburabot pass, and a pleasant descent down the pretty Khumbob (Obikhumbo) river into Kala-i Khum.

The territory of Darvaz (population approx. 24,000) and Vanch (28,000) lying on the Panj is the lowest in Gorno-Badakhshan and the climate is milder than elsewhere in the Pamirs. Figs and black mulberries grow there, and turkeys and chickens run free; oranges are cultivated near Zigar.

On the Kulob route (some 30km before Kala-i Khum) lies the lovely village of Yoged, with four shrines: *Ostoni Khoja Khizr, Ostoni Shoh Owliyo, Ostoni Khoja Chiltan* and *Ostoni Khoja Nazar.* There are fine walks above Yoged – a good place for breaking the journey from Dushanbe to Khorog (homestays next to a tumbling stream or use of the nearby guesthouse can be arranged through PECTA). The villagers of Yoged, on their own initiative, have set up a small museum to house the various ancient objects found in the vicinity, as well as some traditional tools and old kitchen utensils.

The fortress that gave its name to Kala-i Khum ('kala' means fortress, 'khum' means jar), located on the left bank of the Khumbob river just above the confluence with the Panj, no longer stands.

Albert Regel, son of the director and founder of the St. Petersburg botanical garden, travelled here in 1882 and described his impressions for the German-language newspaper of St.Petersburg.

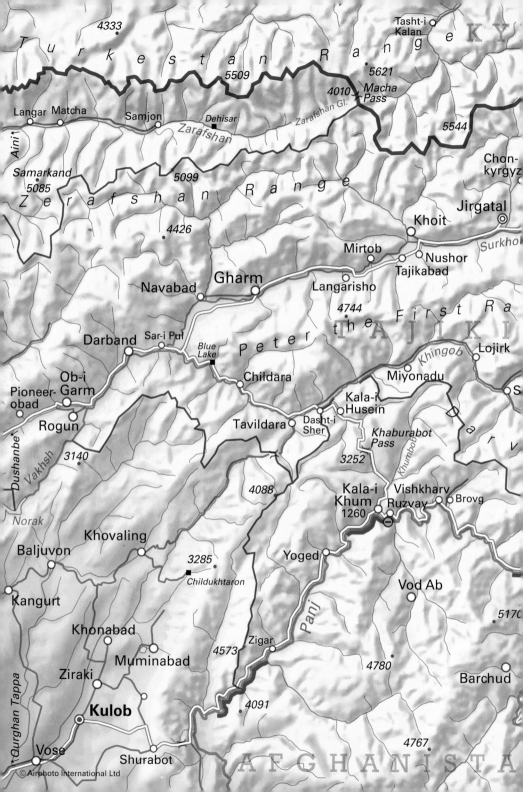

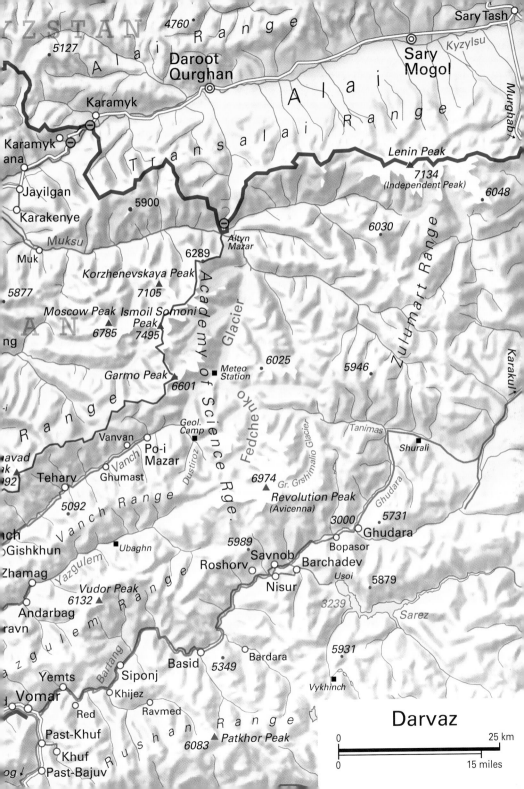

Darvaz

Whoever sits in this garden with the green stone throne that belonged to the magician Ka-Kai, or looks with wonder at the two huge stone bowls, that are called 'khumb' and have given their name to the town and the river that flows into it, cannot fail to think of the ghosts of Iranian heroes and of Alexander the Great. For a long time Darvaz was the most important of the kingdoms along the Amudaria, whose rulers claimed that their descendants were Macedonians. When the king refused to follow the king of Karategin to Bukhara, Khudai-Nazar invaded in the winter of 1878 over the snow-covered mountains and defeated two relatives of the king on the Khumbob and put them to death – he then took over the fortress and sent the king into captivity. This conquest was followed by an insurrection of the remaining descendants of the ruling clan. A brave champion invaded from the Afghan side and reached Khuf on the lower reaches of the Panj, but was repulsed by a Bukharan force and pursued as far as Rakh in Badakhshan. The Afghans were forced by the English to extradite the fugitive. The king's son, left to his fate, shot and killed some fifty Afghans but was nevertheless captured, extradited and immediately executed by the furious Afghans and his head was displayed on the battlements of the fortress in Kala-i-Khumb. ...

No soft meadow, no green tree tops hide the bareness of the broken shapes of the mountains and there are only sparse pomegranate bushes clinging to the narrow hill terraces that reach down to the river walls. Then there appeared Eden-like groves in the bends of the river and mighty plane trees and the wide foliage of date palms gave shade to the tumbling streams; thick-trunked fig trees basked in the sun at the foot of the hot cliffs. Surrounded by the rich foliage of the mulberry trees, the gabled houses of the inhabitants of Darvaz greeted us with laughter and, on the cliff edge high above, we could see their towers and airy verandas – so close that we could make out at a distance the childish red drawings of trees and animals on the white walls. Their storehouses were built on isolated stone blocks, from which they fetched provisions for their clay bread ovens with ladders. Here there were men tilling a small cotton plantation, surrounded by stones, and a field of sunflowers; there, we could see women and girls at the spinning wheel, their blond and dark hair woven into tresses with coloured ribbons falling over their round shoulders. The people of Darvaz differ from other Tajiks only in their moderate approach to Islam and their free choice of bride. Such were the different impressions of our first days.[1]

Willi Rickmer Rickmers, one of the greatest 20th century explorers of the Pamirs, visited Kala-i Khum a few years later in 1913 and recorded his impressions in his unpublished diary:

Here again we found nothing larger than a big hamlet, picturesquely enough situated on the banks of the Panj and frowned upon from the opposite shore by the gloomy, barren hills of Badakshan. The Bazaar is meager in size and scarcely deserves the name. It is the favorite lounge of the native soldier who looks quite imposing in his Russian boots, red knickerbockers, white blouse and fur cap while the officers are tricked out in white Russian coats, probably obtained second hand.

We had an opportunity here of seeing native attempts at gardening, for each mud hovel had its little patch of ground gay with orange colored zimas and purple asters and filled with melons and cucumbers. A noticeable feature of Kalai Khumb were the stones which the villagers had removed from the fields. These are piled up as dikes and cairns and give a dreary appearance to the scene, though their cold grey is sometimes relieved by the beautiful mulberry trees everywhere abounding and by the scarlet patches made by the peppercorns which the inhabitants hang up and heap together to dry.

While at Kalai Khumb we were again to taste the charm of Russian intercourse. This time it was the Consul Baron Cherkasoff whose kindly hospitality did so much to enliven the next few days of our travel. We found him at Kalai Khumb on our arrival there, he himself having just returned from a ten months sojourn in Shughnan. And here, without indulging in fulsome flattery I should like to say that if Russia employs many officials of the type of character of Baron Cherkasoff her rule in Central Asia is assured. An accomplished linguist – he speaks Arabic, Turkish, Persian and Tajik fluently – his manner with the natives showed that happy mixture of urbanity and dignity which none appreciates better than the Oriental. Nothing could exceed the courtesy of his bearing with the native members of his suite and as far as we could judge the "Consul" as he was called was a general favorite.[2]

There is a fine teahouse almost exactly where the Khumbob flows into the Panj. A homestay in the summer, sleeping outdoors under a huge plane tree in the garden of a house next to the tumbling Khumbob, is an unforgettable experience.

Some 8km further up the Panj, on a rocky promontory behind the village of Ruzvay, there are the ruins of a small fortress. Further upstream, just past the village of Vishkharv, there is a side valley to Brovg, offering pleasant walks at the top.

87km south of Kala-i Khum the river Vanch joins the Panj. The gorge of the Panj is narrower and steeper between Kala-i Khum and the Vanch valley and passes within view of a number of Afghan villages and of the precipitous paths clinging to the cliff face on the Afghan side (known locally as *ovrings*).

As you drive along in your jeep or minibus, note the difference between the asphalt road (albeit rapidly deteriorating), telephone poles, power lines and occasional schools and medical centres on the Tajik side and the almost total absence of signs of development on the Afghan side and pause to reflect on the real achievements of the Soviet Union in this far-flung outpost (including 99% literacy, male and female).

Of the fortress that was once in the district centre (Vanch town) almost nothing remains. Some five kilometres before the town centre, on the left bank, there is an ancient burial site *(Dashtirogh)*; other burial mounds can be found on the right bank just outside Vanch town *(Gishkhun)*. According to local legend, each has its own name: *Shafar-Kheddin, Akbarsho, Davlatbek, Sher, Ghioss, Makhkam, Mullonur* and *Muhammed*. The ruins of a small fortress can be found near the village of Ghijovast, some 40km upstream from Vanch town on the left bank. There is a small museum in the town centre.

The Vanch valley is much broader and more fertile than the other valleys feeding the Panj, and – if less dramatic – offers pleasant scenery, especially at the top. In 1882, Albert Regel was in Vanch too and described the valley in poetic prose:

In the morning the tumbling Vanch river was visible beneath the shutters and from the fortress garden on its bank there rose a fragrance from late-ripening peaches. Golden fields of wheat and leafy hamlets lay spread across the valley floor, surrounded at its edges by the prominent mountain ranges; a huge snow colossus with three sharp peaks, approaching in height the most famous mountains of the Asian continent, seemed to dominate the sky in the light of the rising sun. In order to avoid difficulties, we had to limit our stay to two days. The inhabitants approached us peacefully, their necks disfigured with goitre … Destiny has not been kind to them: their small fields do not always bear a good harvest and in winter they often have to depend on flour from mulberries for a bread that is sweet and sticky.[3]

Some things have changed. Goitre in Gorno-Badakhshan – a typical ailment of impoverished mountain communities, caused by lack of iodine in

Woman in shepherd's camp, upper Vanch

the soil – was virtually eradicated during the Soviet period. Although there was some recurrence in the early 1990s, it is no longer a major health issue as a result of improved health services and a targeted programme for iodine supplements promoted by the Aga Khan Health Services. Vanch is today one of the most productive valleys in the Pamirs and the development programmes that brought self-sufficiency in grain production from 16% to around 75% in Gorno-Badakhshan between 1993 and 2006, have enabled Vanch to produce a wheat surplus that brings cash in the markets. There is a local saying: 'Wanji manu ganji man', meaning 'my Vanch and my treasure', reflecting the relative wealth of the valley.

In the last village at the head of the valley, Po-i Mazor, there are two shrines (*Sardi Saïd and Sardy Bard*) and what is, according to local legend, the tomb of Ali. On the left bank, shortly below Poi-Mazar, in a hamlet called Garm Chashma, there is, appropriately, a warm spring ('*garm*' means 'warm/hot' and '*chashma*', 'spring'). At the end of the road on the right bank, in the village of Vanvan, there is a shrine (*Khojai Sabz Push*). 'Sabz Push' means literally 'green mantle' and is an allusion to *Hazrat Khizr* ('green' in Arabic) who is famous in Islamic legend (see section on Shrines).

Khingob Valley beyond Tavildara

Beyond Po-i Mazor there are splendid views back down the valley and east to the Academy of Science Range beyond, at the top of which lies the great Fedchenko Glacier. It is reported that a path leads east 17km beyond Po-i Mazor to a shrine, *Abdulkakhori Sarmast*, although recent travellers were unable to find it.

If you take the road up the valley you pass first the glacier of the Russian Geographical Society, cross a bridge and, heading south into the Abdulkhagor valley, reach the Bears glacier, one of the best studied 'surge' glaciers in the world. Before reaching the snout of the glacier you will find the remains of a Soviet geological camp. The people from Vanch removed most things of value and took them further down the valley, including a 200MW diesel generator. The name of the glacier comes from a night encounter with a bear experienced by two members of the Russian-German Pamir Expedition in 1928 as they came down the glacier. There are still brown bears in the Dustiroz valley opposite the glacier. Experienced mountaineers may cross or pass the Bears glacier, where they may still find remains of Soviet installations. The area was well known for quartz, and was mined during the Soviet period for use in rockets.

From Gishkhun, on the opposite side of the valley to Vanch town, a trekking route leads across the Gishkhun pass (4,336m) to Zhamag in the Yazgulem valley (see below) and, through Ubaghn by a difficult route, to Roshorv in the Bartang valley (see section on Rushan and the Bartang Valley); another trekking route leads from Ghumast (Langar) further up the valley past old mining settlements to Roshorv, or back through Ubaghn to Zhamag (N.B. this route involves fording the Yazgulem river, which can be hazardous).

About 20km south of the point where the Vanch joins the Panj, a charming side valley leads up the Yazgulem river. The fortresses in Motravn and Andarbag no longer exist, but the ruins of a fortress can be seen in Zhamag. There are shrines in Motravn and Zhamag. In Zhamag there are also some petroglyphs close to the shrine. Further up the valley, beyond Ubaghn, there is a shrine known locally as the 'tomb of Alexander'.

A trekking route goes from Motravn across the Yodudi pass (4,208m) to Vomar (Rushan) – just south of Motravn, the route passes a very beautiful waterfall. From Andarbag another route leads across high passes to Siponj in the Bartang valley.

Rushan and the Bartang Valley

The population of Rushan district is approximately 24,000. Vomar, the district centre (also known as Rushan), lies just below the confluence of the Bartang with the Panj. Part of the fortress occupied by the representatives of the Emirate of Bukhara until they were ousted by the Russians in 1905 still remains. The name 'Rushan' means 'luminous' or 'bright'.

There is an important shrine in Vomar (section Langar), above the confluence of the Vomardara, *Shoh-Tolib*, that is distinguished by its old and beautiful plane trees, and another nearby on the other side of the Vomardara, *Ostoni Sayyid Jalol*. According to local legend, Shoh Tolib Sarmast and Sayyid Jalol Bukhori spread the Ismaili religion in the Pamirs after Nasr Khusraw. It is believed that Shoh Tolib is buried in the shrine bearing his name. Sayyid Jalol is supposedly buried in the shrine bearing his name in Tavdem (see section on Roshtkala and Shakhdara).

Vomar also has a small museum. Above the town, high in the cliffs, you can see a horizontal line of vegetation marking the path of an irrigation channel that takes the water high up in the valley and leads it in channels several kilometers down the valley to fields and villages on the upper slopes. Many other such channels exist in the Pamirs; in Switzerland they are known as *bisses* and have existed since the early middle ages (the agricultural development of the canton of Valais – one of the most productive areas of the country today – was made possible by this type of irrigation). The repair and extension of these channels in Gorno-Badakhshan by the Mountain Societies Development Support Programme (a project of the Aga Khan Foundation) was a major factor in overcoming local food shortages during the Tajik civil war.

A little further south of Vomar on the road to Khorog, is the village of Past-Khuf, where there is a shrine *Bobo Alisho*. Other shrines to *Bobo Alisho* can be found in Siponj (see below) and Derzud, some 5km beyond Vomar in the direction of Vanch.

Above Past-Khuf is Khuf, where there is another shrine, *Mustansiri Billoh*, and the ruins of a 19th century fortress. The road up to Khuf has good views of the Panj valley and passes a disused goldmine. The valley above Khuf is a good area for a short walk. About ten kilometres further up the Panj from Past-Khuf towards Khorog, there is the village of Past-bajuv, offering a delightful walk (or a high drive) to the village of Bajuv above. You can also do a high walk between Bajuv and Khuf and from Khuf to Ridde in the Bartang valley. In the local Shughni (and Roshani) language 'past' means 'below' and is frequently encountered in local place names, suggesting that the original settlements in Gorno-Badakhshan were usually high above the river.

The Bartang is part of the longest river system in Gorno-Badakhshan: starting as the Aksu in south-east Murghab district, it becomes the Murghab after joining with the Ak Baital river north of Murghab town, and then the Bartang after passing through lake Sarez and joining with the Ghudara river near Savnob.

If not as spectacular as the Wakhan with its breathtaking views of the Hindu Kush, the Bartang is a very beautiful valley with narrow and steep sides ('Bartang' means 'narrow passage') and varied scenery at each bend in the river. Until well into the 20th century, passage along the Bartang required the use of a complex and vertiginous system of ladders, wooden platforms and even swinging baskets attached precariously to the rock face (known locally as 'ovrints' or 'ovrings').

Aurel Stein came down the Bartang in 1915 on his way back from Turfan, and described his impressions of the valley:

> The two days' journey which thence carried us down to Kala-i-Wamar sufficed to impress me with the exceptional difficulties offered to traffic by the tortuous gorges in which the Bartang river has cut its way down to the Oxus. I now understood why Roshan has always remained the least accessible of all the valleys descending from the Pamirs, and why in the stock of its people and in its traditional ways it has retained most of its early inheritance.

Barchadev village on the Murghab river below the Sarez lake

The line of progress lay everywhere through narrow, deep-cut gorges, between towering mountain masses wildly serrated above and exceedingly steep at their foot. After crossing from Khaizhez [Khijez] to the right bank of the river on a raft of goatskins, there followed a succession of trying climbs up and down precipitous rock faces where the track led along narrow ledges or was represented only by footholds a few inches wide. Glad enough I felt that it was possible for a few of us to avoid some of the worst of these awrinz by taking a small goatskin raft where the absence of dangerous cataracts allowed of its employment. Guided from behind by dexterous swimmers, it let us glide down the tossing river in scenery of impressive wildness. Boldly serrated snowy peaks showed again and again above the high frowning rock walls which, as we rapidly passed them, ever seemed to close in upon us like the jaws of an underworld. Meanwhile the baggage was being carried in safety by sure-footed Roshanis past sheer precipices; seen from the river, the men looked like big spiders.[1]

The Bartangis are among the most hospitable people in the Pamir, and have a lively tradition of music and dancing.

Yemts, the second village up the Bartang, has an important shrine, *Mushkilkusho*, and the ruins of a small fortress. From Yemts the road clings tightly to the river bank through the pretty village of Bhagoo, before reaching Khijez, a little further upstream

on the left bank. From Khijez, a trekking route goes up the right bank of Ravmeddara to the village of Ravmed (where there is also a shrine) and to the foot of the Patkhor Peak (6,083m).

Yemts and Bhagoo were the scene of one of the last skirmishes between the Russians and Afghans at the end of the 19th century, when a small Russian reconnaissance party was forced to flee over the mountains to the Yazgulem valley and await reinforcements. Boris Leonidovich Tageyev was an ensign in the Russian detachment in the Bartang and described the incident in his memoirs:

> We received information that the Afghans had established themselves in Kala-i-Vomar and that they had put an advance guard of ten soldiers in a narrow defile at Yangi-Aryka to the east of the village of Shujand, with orders not to allow the Russians to pass. The Afghans were reported as saying that "If we have to face the Russians in a wider part of the valley we shall all perish." Our informants also learned that fresh forces were being brought to Kala-i-Vomar from Kala-i-Bar-Panj: by 3 September, about 70 had arrived, and 100 were expected.
>
> The Tajiks also told us that the population of Shughnan was angry with the Afghans and was awaiting with impatience the arrival of the Russian detachment to rise up against Afghanistan, and that the Afghans had removed the population of Kala-i-Vomar and neighbouring settlements to Kala-i-Bar-Panj. ...
>
> Having left the post in Bhagoo under command of second lieutenant Rukin, Vannovksy set off north, intending to cross the mountains directly over to Yazgulem and from there to Darvaz. We had heard that there was a pass there but it was not certain that pack animals could cross – the Tajiks did not even know the name of the pass. Nevertheless, Vannovsky resolved to take this route and, with great hardship, succeeded.
>
> In places our men used tools to cut footholds in the ice walls, going up the ice-covered mountain step by step; with great difficulty they dragged our packs and led the horses over a slippery ice track. This pass is now marked on the map and was named after Vannovsky in honour of this courageous officer who ventured with pack horses on a route that even the skilled Tajiks crossed only with great caution and without animals. They were amazed at the courageous decision of the Russian officer.[2]

Just beyond Yemts, there is a footbridge leading to the unspoilt scenery of the Geisev valley, where a pilot ecotourism project was started by the Mountain Societies Development Support Programme in 2006, offering homestays and trekking.

In the next village on the left bank, Visav, there are the ruins of a 19th century fortress. Just beyond Visav, on the right bank, is the sub-district centre, Siponj (sometimes referred as 'Bartang'), where there is a tomb close to the village school known as *Bobo Alisho*, which is, according to local legend, the tomb of Ali. There are similar legends in Khuf and Derzud in Rushan district, and in Poi Mazar in the Vanch valley.

There are several caves above Siponj village, that served in the 19th century and earlier as refuge from slave hunters from Afghanistan – at that time, the local ruler of Shughnan was also notorious for selling his own people into slavery. They are known locally as the *Mobegim bayen* ('Mobegim caves') since, according to legend, a local woman called Mobegim, renowned for her beauty, was hidden there to escape the marauders.

There are two shrines in Basid, *Hazrati Khodjai Nuruddin* and *Safdaron*. The former is perched on a rock high above the village.

Just beyond Basid, on the right bank of the Bartang, is the pretty village of Chadud. In summer, if you are lucky, you can see children riding the current on inflated animal skins – much the same technique as used by Alexander the Great to cross the Oxus in 329 BC.

The German explorer Arved von Schultz, from the 'Kolonial Institut' in Hamburg, who travelled extensively in the Pamirs in 1909 and again in 1911–12, was in the Bartang on both journeys.[3] In an article published in 1910, he described the use of animal skins to cross the Bartang.

> Throughout the western Pamirs, the Tajiks generally use a single inflated goatskin to cross rivers; the nomads in the central Pamirs, on the other hand, are able to ford the rivers on their horses. The 'Burdyuk', a goatskin (not a sheepskin, as in the descriptions from the Near East) is sewn up carefully and inflated, and has a simple

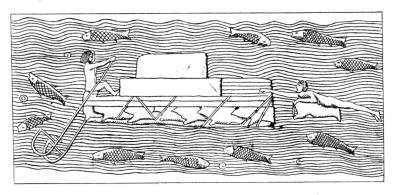

Drawing of a raft and inflated skin from an ancient Assyrian relief.[4]

opening on one of the legs to let the air in and out. The swimmer rides the skin on his stomach, holding on with a ring fixed to its neck, and paddles with his legs and free arm. It requires some skill to stay on the round slippery Burdyuk and the Tajik children learn the art very early. In summer, all the boys in the larger villages gather to practice under the supervision of adults. Accidents are rare and are mainly caused because the rider slips under the Burdyuk.

This primitive means of transport is of very great importance in the Bartang. The difficulty of travelling upstream in this narrow gorge cannot be exaggerated: in summer, at least, it is possible to travel downstream without too many problems in relative – if risky – comfort on a 'Turssuk' [local name for a raft built above several goatskins strapped together]. Along the 150km course of the lower Bartang there are three paths, one above the other, that must be taken in turn, dependent on the nature of the terrain. One of these follows the river bank and its use is limited mainly to the autumn when the water level is low; at any moment this route may require that the Burdyuk be used to swim to the other side in order to pass the frequently vertical cliffs. Horses can – at some risk – be led along. The second path is the shortest and is only for pedestrian traffic: it is the one used most by the local people. It follows the cliff face across the 'Ovrings' – simple steps and ladders that

the Tajiks make from trunks of poplar. It requires some practice to follow one's guides and porters along these swaying perches, often at a dizzying height above the water. Pack animals can only be taken on the third and highest path that winds its way through the mountain ridges, with enormous detours, almost always leading to loss of time and animals.[5]

A few kilometres upstream from Chadud is a side valley on the left bank that leads to the lovely village of Bardara, tucked away above a

Boys with inflated animals skins for use as rafts, Shadud, Bartang valley (above)
Girls, Bartang valley (below)

narrow valley with splendid views of the mountains beyond. In Bardara there is a shrine, *Farmon*, located at the foot of an old juniper tree, named after the 'farmon' (firman) sent by the late Aga Khan Sultan Mohamed Shah (Aga Khan III) to confirm receipt of offerings from Bardara – a document still kept in the village.

The ceremonial building next to the shrine contains some of the finest examples of woodcarving in the Pamirs.

There are very few juniper trees in the Pamirs and the tree at the *Farmon* shrine is perfectly aligned with two others, in a NNE-SSW direction and at a distance of exactly 508m on each side. On the windswept plain above the village of Roshorv in the Bartang valley there were until fairly recently three juniper trees – only one exists today – sharing an identical alignment. The presence of these perfectly aligned trees is somewhat of a mystery, particularly above Roshorv where there are no trees of any kind anywhere in the vicinity. According to one legend, they were planted by Ali to mark the route he took through the Pamirs. According to another, they were planted by Nasr Khusraw for the same reason.

A trekking route from Bardara to the Ghunt valley, Langar Pass and Yashil Kul follows the path up the Bardara river used by local shepherds to bring their sheep over a 5,000m glacier pass to summer pasture in the area of Vykhinch.

Ghudara, Upper Bartang

The Bartang valley is prone to flooding in summer (especially with a combination of heavy snow in winter, a cold spring and a rapid rise in temperature in early summer) and the road can be impassable beyond Basid due to rock falls and stone slides – check whether the road is open before planning a trip further upstream. The best time to visit Bartang is in the late spring, when the apricot trees are in blossom and the roads are open.

The ruins of a 19th century fortress can be seen in Roshorv, one of the largest villages in Gorno-Badakhshan, from which there are splendid views of Peak Lapnazar (5,990m), recently renamed 'Peak Azalsho Olimov' in honour of the wrestling champion of the Soviet Union from the 1950s, who came from Roshorv. 'Lap Nazar' means 'many eyes', or 'many rays' and in the evening the rays from the setting sun behind the mountain explain the origin of the old name.

Roshorv has a very strong musical tradition and was the home of the late Mamadyor Khujamyorov, one of the most famous singers of religious *(madoh)* and popular songs. Many well-known contemporary Tajik singers came from Bartang and Rushan, including Daler Nazarov, Nobowar Chinorov, Mojon Nazardodova, Gurminj Zawkibekov (who created a museum of Pamiri musical instruments in Dushanbe) and the late Muboraksho (Misha), as well as the dancers Mahingul and Zaragul. A popular saying well captures the joyful nature and talent of the people of Rushan: *'Rawshandiloni Rushon oyinai safoyand, Zang az dili gharibon sayqal zada zudoyand'* ('The bright people of Rushan are like a crystal mirror. They remove the rust from the hearts of the traveller').

There are four shrines in Roshorv: *Borkhatsidj, Sho-Tolib, Sho-Husein* and *Andrim*. Below Roshorv is the pretty village of Yapshorv, where there is a shrine, *Khoja-i Shayuz* ('King of the leopards').

Further up the Bartang, at Nisur, a road leads off to the east to the beautiful village of Barchadev on the Murghab river, from which a path goes up to the Sarez lake – for which a special permission is required (see sections on Permits and Trekking). There are three shrines in Nisur, *Sho Husein, Pir Nosir,* and *Hazrat-i Daoud*; and an unusual apple tree that gives fruit twice a year. In Barchadev a small guesthouse is being built at the time of writing and a homestay is available at Nisur.

Lake Sarez (3,265m), probably the most spectacularly beautiful lake in Gorno-Badakhshan, emerged as a result of a powerful earthquake in 1911 (6.5–7.0 on the Richter Scale) at Sarez village just above the junction of the Murghab and Ghudara rivers. The earthquake caused a huge landslide of 2.2 million cubic meters, that blocked the outlet. This natural dam, known as Usoi after the village buried under the rockfall, led to the flooding of the whole valley over the next few years and created a lake that is now 60 km long and 500 m deep at its deepest point, and that covers 80km^2 and contains 17 million cubic metres of water. It was not until April 1914 that the water found a way through the dam and refilled the bed of the Murghab river below. By 1920 the surface of water had reached the level of today. The dam itself, with a height of over 550m and a length of over 3 km, is the tallest natural dam in the world.

The news spread round the world and on 8 November 1922 a report on the disaster was given to the Geological Society of London:

> The earthquake took place on the night of the 5th–6th February, 1911 (O.S.), the time, as locally determined, varying from 11.15 p.m. to 1.20 a.m. The central region lay close to the junction of the Tanimas with the Murghab, or Bartang, river, in about lat. 38° 15' N., long. 72° 38' E., and here the destruction, not only of villages but of roads, bridges, and all means of communication, was so complete that nearly six weeks had passed before news could reach either the military headquarters at the Pamir Post [Russian military base at Murghab], or the civil headquarters at Khorog. Two attempts to reach the devastated region were made: Capt. Zaimkin was despatched down the Murghab valley, and at Sarez found further progress impossible; while, from the Oxus valley, the official despatched by the Governor of Roshan found his progress towards Oroshor [today Roshorv], the headquarters of the district, stopped by complete destruction of the roadway, at some place unspecified, before he could reach his destination. According to Col. Spilko's account, written two years later, the total loss of life amounted to 302 men, women, and children; details are given of separate villages and settlements, some of which I have been unable to find on any map; but the easternmost of those that I have been able to identify is Sarez, which escaped rather lightly with a loss of some houses and no deaths, and the westernmost Basid, which was almost completely destroyed. The distance between these two places is about 35 miles in a direct line; but the region over which the earthquake reached a destructive degree of violence evidently exceeded this limit, for it is recorded that the first news of the disaster that reached the Oxus valley was brought by a plucky Tajik, a resident of Basid, who descended the Bartang in a native boat (probably an inflated skin), and from this account it is evident that the destruction of the roadway and interruption of all land communication extended for some distance westwards, or downstream, from Basid. In this region, besides the destruction of buildings, of bridges, and of the galleries

by which the roads were carried round the faces of cliffs, caused by the direction of the earthquake, there were numerous landslips.[6]

In the winter of 1911/1912, as we have seen, less than a year after the catastrophe, the German explorer Arved von Schultz was in the Bartang and took the first photograph of the Sarez lake, showing that the village had not yet disappeared under the water. In 1915, the Anglo-Hungarian explorer, Aurel Stein was the second non-Russian traveller to visit the newly formed lake.

> The fall of a whole mountain, completely blocking the river, had since February 1911 converted the so-called 'Sarez Pamir' into a fine alpine lake, which already in 1913 was over 17 miles long and had since been spreading up the valley. Enormous masses of rock and detritus had been shaken down from the range on the north and had been pushed by the impetus of the landslips up the steep spur flanking the mouth of the Shedau valley. The gigantic dam thus formed seemed even then, four years after the great landslide, to rise more than 1,200 feet above the level of the new lake. Stone avalanches were still descending from the scarred mountain side above the barrage ...

Irkht, Sarez lake

At the very foot of the spur above mentioned, in a dismal mud-filled depression, I had the good fortune to find a small Russian party under Professor J. Preobrazhenski just arrived in camp from the side of the Alichur Pamir for a systematic survey of the great barrage. A detailed record of the results of this has since been published by him in the Russian Geological Committee's Matériaux pour la géologie, & c. (Fasc. 14, Petrograd, 1920). The Russian scientists had arrived by skin raft from the southern extension of the lake, which they had reached across the Langar pass. In the course of their very kindly welcome they expressed their belief that my intended passage with baggage along the precipitous slopes above that inlet would prove impracticable. As, however, the plucky Roshani headmen with us were quite prepared to make the attempt, the spur was ascended to a height of about 13,200 feet and camp pitched beyond near a small spring some 600 feet lower.

When next morning a steep descent of some 2,000 feet had brought us down to the dazzling green waters of the Yerkh fiord, we realized readily enough the difficulties of farther progress along the precipitous rock slopes thrown down by the earthquake and over dangerous debris shoots in many places still liable to move. Fortunately the men collected from the uppermost hamlets of Roshan were all excellent cragsmen and quite expert in building rafaks or ledges of brushwood and stones along otherwise impassable precipices. It was fully five hours before a tolerably safe track had been made higher up and we had crossed the worst of those treacherous scarps; yet the direct distance was scarcely more than a mile. At last we reached the head of the inlet, lined with half-submerged thickets of birch-trees and juniper. Ascending the valley amidst fine groves of trees for a couple of miles and then crossing what looked like an old terminal moraine, we arrived at a widening stretch where cultivation had been resumed, since the earthquake, by six Roshani families. Their smiling fields of barley and oats lay at an elevation of about 11,000 feet and some 500 feet above the level of the lake as it stood then. Yet even here dread was felt of the continued rise of its waters.

During a day's halt at this pleasant spot our hillmen succeeded in improving the track above the Yerkh inlet sufficiently to bring, somehow or other, their sure-footed ponies across. Accordingly on August 19th we moved up the valley to the south, which contains at its bottom a succession of small lakes formed by glacier action between old moraines. Small hanging glaciers showed at the heads of the side valleys on either side. The route had never been surveyed and had come into use only since that across the Marjanai pass between Sarez and the Alichur Pamir had been blocked by the newly formed lake. As our route led continuously over old moraines and boulder-strewn fans, progress was troublesome. But fortunately on arrival at Ushinch, about 11 miles farther up, where the valley bottom widens in view of an amphitheatre of ice-crowned peaks to the south, we were met by fresh Kirghiz transport kindly sent by the Commandant of Pamirski Post. This opportune help made it possible to push up the valley, which now turned to SE. and widened into a Pamir-like expanse. After passing three more small lakes we camped at an elevation of about 14,400 feet.

Next morning, ascending first to SE. and then turning east, we reached after a march of 5 miles the Langar pass, forming an almost level talus-covered saddle at about 15,400 feet. A large hanging glacier to the NW. of the pass sends its drainage partly to the small lake of Emin-köl, which we had come to before reaching the pass, and partly to the Langar-köl on the other side. The descent into the Langar valley was easy and brought us mostly over gentle grassy slopes to the stone huts known as Langar. There we camped at an elevation of about 12,300 feet, after a total march of 20 miles.[7]

Gorno-Badakhshan is a zone of high earthquake risk and in scientific circles Lake Sarez is widely referred to as a 'time-bomb', particularly since 1968 when a powerful landslide of 20 million cubic meters close to the principal dam caused waves two metres high.

In October 1997, a 'Regional Scientific Conference on Lake Sarez' was held in Dushanbe and concluded that the dam was very unstable and that another powerful earthquake might cause it to collapse. In 2004, however, the World Bank completed a 'Lake Sarez risk mitigation project' that concluded that the dam is stable and not in danger of imminent collapse. One result of the project was the installation of satellite monitoring and an early warning system. FOCUS Humanitarian Assistance (part of the Aga Khan Development Network) is also working with the local population on early warning procedures in the Bartang valley, with support from the Swiss and US governments. Currently the principal source of danger is the right bank of the lake, where a strong localised earthquake could cause a partially detached body of earth and rock with a mass of roughly 3 km³, to fall into the lake. This might then produce an enormous wave which would wash over the natural dam and destroy the upper part.

None of this should however discourage the traveller who wants to see one of the most beautiful sites in the Pamirs. The section on 'Trekking' describes the routes to the Sarez Lake.

The fortress at Nisur was almost totally destroyed by an earthquake in 1911, but in Savnob, the first village up the Ghudara river, the ruins of a fortress still stand. In the 19th century Savnob was known as Tashqurghan ('stone tower' in the Turkic languages) because of the fortress located there. Although the fortress dates only from this period, a local legend recounts that in the middle ages a skilful builder called Hasan built a very strong castle somewhere in Khorasan. The king of Khorasan cut off Hasan's right hand so that he could not build the same castle in any other part of the country. Hasan travelled round the world and ended up in Savnob, where he decided to build a new castle with his left hand from local stones and clay, that lasted until today. The ruins offer splendid views of the river below.

There are four shrines in Savnob: *Hazrat-i Daoud* (containing blacksmith's equipment, as the prophet David is supposed to have been able to melt iron), *Mahfil Oston, Khuja-i Khizr* and *Hozir Bosht*. The last of these – the name of which means 'be prepared' – is located close to a network of caves in the hillside above that served as protection for women and children from Kyrgyz marauders. Just above the village there is a solar calendar.

In Rukhch, just beyond Savnob, the fortress no longer exists but in both villages there are caves that provided refuge to the local population from the Kyrgyz. In Bopasor, the next village (and home of Sahib Nazar, a legendary Kyrgyz robber), there is a shrine *Khoja Aliamdor*.

From Pasor a trekking route goes up over a pass to the lower Grum-Grshimailo Glacier and from Ghudara, the last village in the valley, a track leads up the Tanimas river, and then up the Kokuibel river valley (passing en route a geoglyph in Shurali) to the Pamir Highway near Lake Kara Kul (N.B. the road is used rarely and may only be passable with difficulty by jeep – local enquiries should be made before starting on this route). There are three shrines in Ghudara: *Shoh Husayn, Shoh Tolib* and *Hazrat-i Daoud*.

From Kok-Jar the route leads up the Tanimas valley, passing several large glaciers coming from south, to the Fedchenko glacier. In 1928, this route was taken by Gorbunov and Rickmers, joint leaders of the Russian-German Pamir Expedition – an expedition that mapped most of the last undiscovered corners of the Pamirs.

Interestingly several villages in the upper Bartang had Turkic names until about 1917: as noted, Savnob was Tashqurghan; in addition Rukhch was Kara-Qurghan, Pasor was Agach-Qurghan and Ghudara was Yangi-Qurghan ('new tower').

Khorog and the Ghunt Valley (Shughnan)

Khorog, the capital of the Gorno-Badakhshan Autonomous Oblast (GBAO), is a quiet little town of some 28,000 inhabitants, situated on what used to be called the Khorog or Suchan river, stretching from the confluence of the Ghunt and Shakhdara rivers to the point where the Ghunt flows into the Panj. Until the establishment of the Russian base in Khorog in 1896, Khorog was a very small settlement: the capital of Badakhshan was then Kala-i Bar Panj, on the other side of the Panj in Afghanistan, a little further downstream. Today there is a bridge in Khorog to the Afghan side that is open for tourists who have a valid Afghan visa (obtainable at the Afghan consulate in Khorog). The total population of Shughnan (not including Khorog) is approx. 36,000.

Khorog is the site of the GBAO offices of the Aga Khan Development Network (AKDN) and the Mountain Societies Development Support Programme (MSDSP) and hosts the Tajikistan campus of the University of Central Asia. It is one of the few places in GBAO where there are restaurants and internet cafés. There are a number of hotels in Khorog now and new bed and breakfast places and homestays are available (see Travel section).

The Khorog Museum is in Lenin Street (very close to the MSDSP offices) and contains archaeological and historical exhibits, including the piano that was carried in 1914 by twenty bearers from Osh in Kyrgyzstan, over seven hundred kilometres away, for the daughter of the Russian commander Shpilko. Khorog also boasts the second highest Botanical garden in the world, offering a fine view of the town (the highest is the Lijiang Alpine Botanical Garden in Yunnan Province in southern China). Just outside Khorog, in the village of Tem, there is a shrine to Imam Zainulabiddin (the shrine is also known as *Shotimur*), next to which there is what is believed to be the footprint of Ali's horse, Sumbi Duldul.

In the first years after the break-up of the Soviet Union, the market in Khorog had hardly any goods for sale – today one can find almost everything in the market, which is situated next to the bus station at the western end of Lenin street (the main road through Khorog). Buses from

Bogev, Pre-Zoroastrian fire temple

here travel at least once a day to all districts of GBAO. (N.B. In many cases, for an extra fee, the bus driver can be persuaded to continue some distance beyond his normal final destination.) Khorog airport is located on the Panj, just outside the town, on the road to Vomar.

From the east of Khorog, the Pamir Highway follows the Ghunt valley upstream as far as Sardem, where it then follows the course of the Toguzbulak ('nine springs' in Kyrgyz) to the Koitezek ('sheep dung' in Kyrgyz) Pass and crosses the high Pamir plateau to Murghab and Osh (see section on Murghab). From Sardem, a road goes to the village of Bachor, a starting point for treks to Lake Sarez and Lake Yashil Kul. The Ghunt carries little glacial residue and is almost always a pure turquoise colour.

Some ten kilometres from Khorog, on the Pamir Highway, is the village of Bogev, where there are traces of what are believed to be ancient Aryan (pre-Zoroastrian) fire temples located on a cliff above the road, and of a medieval fortress known as *Kafirkala*. Not far from this site there is a shrine known as *Mushkilkisho*. According to legend, Ali prayed here on a rock that now bears the imprint of the palms of his hands, his knees and his forehead. No far from there is a stone on which there is reputed to be the footprint of Ali's horse.

View of Khorog from the Botanical Gardens

Other historical and cultural sites on the Pamir Highway can be found in or near: Vibist (petroglyphs dating back some 10,000 years), Sizhd (*Shoh Malang* shrine), Ver (*Sumbi Duldul* shrine) and Charthem (petroglyphs and the shrine of *Malika*). One of the prominent Shughni men of the 19th century, Qazi Nizokatsho, lived in Chartem. His grave is still there.

There is a legend that a princess called Malika used to live in Chartem. She requested local people to bury her in a place that could not be reached by insects. They did as she requested and buried her on top of a rock. In the morning when they came to visit the grave a big snake crept out.

There is another story among the people of Shughnan that in the ancient times Charthem used to be a flourishing place and a rich and cruel man used to live there. Once during the harvest, using magic force, he stopped the movement of the sun and people had to work for him for three days and nights without rest. After gathering the crops he let the sun go, but by now it was midnight. The next morning when people got up instead of the harvest there were stones and instead of the fields rocks had appeared. The Ghunt valley is one of the areas where you can still see enormous piles of stones in the fields. The removal of stones was neglected during the late Soviet period, but when the Aga Khan Foundation succeeded in getting the local government to privatize the land and disband the state farms, private farmers again started extensive stone removal – leading to higher productivity and an increase in the area of arable land.

Some 20km beyond Chartem is the sub-district centre, Vankala. A hamlet close by is called 'Imom', after the shrine there (*Imom Muhammed Bokir*, also reputed to have a footprint of Ali's horse). The present building was put there in the 19th century by the local representative of the Emir of Bukhara and there is a poem written on a stone about the history of its restoration. There are stones at the entrance of the shrine that legend says were once watermelons, melons and boots that turned into stones. According to legend, Imam Muhammed Bokir came and converted the local people. After completing his mission he entered a cave from which spring water emerges at present. Before disappearing into the cave, he told the local people to come for help, if faced by the hardships. But some people called on him even when not faced by hardships. Immediately, he came out of the cave in anger and said: *"Goh ghunt u*[1] *goh parishon"* (sometimes together and some times dispersed). It is said that since then the Ghunt valley was sometimes full of people and at other times for different reasons people disappeared and it became empty. The *Imom Muhammed Bokir* shrine is one of the holiest places in the Ghunt valley and is also visited by people from Kyrgyzstan. The area was turned into a school during the Soviet period and the shrine was destroyed. After the collapse of the Soviet Union the local people restored it and now, at festivals, it is always full.

In Jelondy (the name means 'snake'), the last village before the Koitezek pass (about 110km from Khorog), there is a public hot spring bath and guesthouse on the left-hand side of the road, just before the entrance to the village. There is an old Kyrgyz graveyard just beyond the Koitezek pass to the left of the road at Tagarkaki. From the Koitezek pass there are splendid views of Kyzyldong (5,704m).

Going north from Khorog along the Panj towards Vomar, there is the lovely village of Porshnev some 10km from Khorog, where there are several shrines and holy places.

The shrine *Pir-i Shoh Nosir* (in the part of Porschnev known as 'Midenshor') is dedicated to Nasir Khusraw and has a teahouse and holy spring. Local tradition holds that Nasir Khusraw was passing and heard that the village had no water: he turned his face to Mecca, hit the ground with his stick and a spring emerged. He planted his stick and it grew into the willow-trees that are there today. Another version is that Nasir Khusraw was thirsty and asked a girl for water from a jug she was carrying. She refused and he struck the ground in anger. There is now a teahouse *(choikhona)* at the spot; a stone beside the spring bears, it is believed, words inscribed by Nasir Khusraw himself.

The other shrines in Porshinev are: *Mir Sayyid Ali Hamadoni* (Kushk); *Sumbi Duldul* (Barchiddara); and *Gumbaz-i Pir Sayyid Farukhshoh* (Saroi Bakhor). At the latter site there is some remarkable calligraphy on the ceiling of the shrine, and also a stone bearing the panjtan (5 fingers of the hand) symbolising the holy family Mohamed, Fatima, Ali, Hasan and Husayn.

Further north there are shrines in Yomj *(Oston-i Shoh Tolib)* and Sokhcharv *(Pir-i Dukman)*.

The intrepid British traveller, Ralph Cobbold, took this road as he went under escort to Khorog, after having been detained in Kala-i Vomar by the representatives of the Emir of Bukhara after his descent of the Bartang.

> About four miles above the junction [of the Bartang and Panj rivers] the river narrows and flows between high banks. The natives call the place Darband, and

here there is a fine old tower perched on a lofty rock, with precipitous sides, which overhangs the Panja. Darband was formerly the frontier between Roshan and Shignan. Continuing, the path crossed the entrance to several small nullahs, from which easily fordable streams issue on their way to join the Panja. The bridle path is for the most part easy going, passing through several small villages, surrounded by waving cornfields and prolific orchards of mulberry, apricot and walnut trees. We met a fair number of Tajiks on the way, who respectfully saluted the Russians as they passed. Most of them seemed very poor, and they all wore small tight-fitting skull caps.

We stopped at Sacharb [Sokhcharv] and had some food in the middle of the day, resting afterwards under a fine apricot tree, on which the fruit was already formed. At this point the Panja passes through a fine gorge, and the current runs in great waves over some rocks, whose tops protrude. The path then ascends a

barren spur by zigzags. At a small village called Peshnev [Porshnev], four miles beyond Sacharb, the valley of the Oxus widens out as the hills on the Afghan side retreat. Numerous villages are dotted about the plain thus formed, and in the distance can be seen the fort, Bar Panj, standing high on some whitish-coloured rocks, with a village nestling below amidst the fruit trees and gardens. We continued along the river bank, passing opposite the Afghan fortress, and two miles further on reached the Russian fort of Charog, thirty-five miles from Kala-i-Wamar. I received a hearty welcome from the Russian officers of the fort, and the Cossacks appeared to take a great interest in my arrival. The post lies a short distance below the junction of the Suchan [Ghunt] with the Panja,

(above) Girl dancing at Bhagoo
(below) Shrine bearing the hand (panjah) of Ali

and stands about a mile from the latter's bank. It is strongly built of clay, wood and stones, and the earthworks are of great thickness.[2]

In addition to the treks to Yashil Kul and Sarez (mentioned above) there are challenging trekking routes from Rivak on the Pamir Highway across the Shughnan range to Nimos (on the Shakhdara), from Duzhak ('forked branch' – near Miyonakuh) on the Pamir Highway to the Kulin Lakes, and from Duzhak or Jelondy past Turumtaikul Lake to Jawshangoz at the top of the Shakhdara (not recommended in winter).

Roshtkala District and the Shakhdara

The Shakhdara flows into the Ghunt at the eastern end of Khorog, a short distance before the Ghunt joins the Panj. Roshtkala district (population approx. 24,000) covers the Shakhdara valley between the Shughnan and Ishkashim ranges, together with the high plateau between the Shakhdara and Shughnan ranges.

Not far from Khorog there are shrines in: Hichih (left bank – *Sho Burhon* – see below); Khidorjev (left bank – *Khoja Zur*) with a spring that reputedly has healing properties; Bodom (right bank – *Khoja Nur*, sister of Khoja Zur, and *Sumbi Duldul*, Ali's horse); Shuvjev (left bank – *Khoja-i Sabz Push*[1]); and in Barwoz (above Bodom) there is a shrine to *Pir Fokhmamad*, who, according to legend, is the *pir* (saint) of all hot springs in Pamirs, including the most famous of these, Garm Chashma in Ishkashim district. He is revered at several other shrines, e.g. in Bidiz further up the Shakhdara valley and in Darshay in Ishkashim district.

In Tusion (left bank) there is a shrine to *Shoh Burhoni Vali*, the leader of a major Sufi order. According to legend, four Sufi brothers from Tus in Iran came here in the 16th century and named the village after this ancient Iranian city (birthplace of the famous poet Abdulkasim Firdousi, who is believed to have been an Ismaili).

The four were called Said Muhammad Isfahani (also known as Said Shahi Koshon), Abdurrahman (also known as Said Shah Khomush), Shoh Malang and Shoh Burhon. There are other shrines in Gorno-Badakhshan dedicated to the latter two. It is believed that they first settled on the other side of the Panj, in (Afghan) Badakhshan, but after the invasion of Badakhshan by the Bukharan ruler Abdurakhmon Shaiboni in the 16th century, Shias were persecuted and many fled to Shughnan, including the four brothers. That they were given refuge there is taken as

evidence of the courage of the Shughnan people of the time in asserting their Shia faith. The shrine to *Shoh Burhon* in Tusion was destroyed during the Soviet period, but was rebuilt by the local people in the 1990s. Some of the descendants of Shoh Malang currently serve as Khalifas in the village of Porshnev in Shughnan.

In Tavdem, on the right bank, there is an important shrine to *Sayyid Jalol Bukhori* the grandson of *Shoh Burhon*. In the 1990s, local people renovated the shrine and built a new protective structure over it. Despite his name, a family genealogy extant in Tavdem does not support the idea that *Sayyid Jalol* came from Bukhara.

Tusion lies on a narrow winding road high above the river valley; from the plain at the top there are splendid views of the surrounding mountains. There is a trekking route from Tusion to Nishusp on the Panj. An alternative trekking route to Nishusp can be taken from the village of Khidorjev closer to Khorog. Beyond Tusion there are shrines in: Midensharv (left bank – *Sho Abdul*); and Baroj (right bank – *Sho Burhon*).

In Roshtkala, the district centre, there was – until quite late in the Soviet period – a fortress, but now only stones remain, mostly used for cattle sheds on the site, which nevertheless offers good views of the valley below and the rugged mountains behind. The original fortress was built in the 9th–10th century AD and was mentioned by the Persian scholar al-Biruni, from Khorezm, as being then the capital

Roshtkala Castle

of Shughnan. Roshtkala means 'red fortress' and, according to legend, when the king of Shughnan was conquered by a rival from Afghanistan, the blood flowed so freely that it was given this name.

In the garden close to the fortress ruins there are remains of a shrine to *Pir Yakhsuz*, that was destroyed in the 1930s by the Uzbek commissar in Roshtkala and has not yet been restored. According to local legend, Pir Yakhsuz freed the Roshtkala valley from glacier ice ('Yakhsuz' means 'ice-flame' in Tajik and Shughni). There is another shrine in the town, dedicated to *Bobomafil* who was reputed to be able to melt snow and ice with his prayers. A little further upstream, in the village of Ambav, there is another shrine, *Chiltan-i Pok*. Trekking routes lead from Vezdara and from Bodomdara to Garm-Chasma in Ishkashim district.

In Bidiz, there is a shrine to *Pir Fokhmamad*, built next to a willow tree reputed to be a thousand years old. Just beyond Bidiz, the Shakhdara flows through a deep gorge, where there is one of the only remaining forest areas in Gorno-Badakhshan.

The road follows the right bank, passing what was once a fortress in Sindev on the opposite side (known as *Kafirkala*, suggesting pre-Islamic origins), the stones from which were used to build the nearby residence of the descendants of the last *Mingbashi* (ruler) of Shakhdara, Azizkhan, executed by the king of Shughnan in the mid-19th century. In 1894, after the flight of the Afghans before the Russian occupying forces, Azizkhan's nephew, Azizkhan Abodillokhon, was appointed Russia's representative in Shakhdara at the request of the local people and remained in this position until 1918.

Azizkhan Abodollokhon, born in 1849, had been a herdsman until he was delegated by the people of Shughnan and Roshtkala to take a petition to the Russians in Tashkent asking for Russian help against the exactions of the Bukharans (*Mangit* dynasty) and the Afghans. He travelled twice to Tashkent, the second time with Sayid Usufalishoh of Shughnan and, in 1894, took a delegation to the Russian command at Pamirsky

Girl at Roshtkala

Post (Murghab) that included Khudoyor from Tinkhan and Sayidmakhsum Sayidkudus from Porshinev with letters from the people offering support to the Russians in their incursion into the Western Pamirs. After the Bolshevik Revolution, Azizkhan took no further part in politics but in 1939 he was imprisoned for participation in a religious ceremony and never returned to the Pamirs. He died in 1940. In 1990, at the instigation of his grandson, Shahbozkhon Buttaev, and with wide popular support, he was rehabilitated.[2]

A few kilometres further on, just beyond the village of Shoh Khirizm, there is a narrow road to the left leading up a pretty side valley to Chandindara ('many valleys'). In Shoh Khirizm there is a shrine to the saint of this name.

There are trekking routes from Chandindara to Bogev and to Kolkhozabad on the Ghunt in Shughnan. In the village of Sezhd further up the main road there are three shrines. The name of the first, *Vordjbid*, means 'hoof prints' (it also known as *Mazor Bobo Abdul*). Legend says that Hazrat-i Ali on his horse Duldul jumped over a small river here and left the hoof print of his horse on the stone. The other shrines are: *Shoh-i Wiloyat*, also connected to the name of Ali; and *Qadamgoh*. According to popular belief, there is a big cave under the stone at the latter shrine, that extends to Shughnan, and it is said that in ancient times a horseman travelled through the cave from the Ghunt valley and came out here.

In the next village, Vrang, the Shakhdara passes through a narrow gorge with attractive rapids and a small waterfall. To the left of the road, near Vrang, a path leads up to the beautiful lake of Durumkul.

Some 20 kilometres beyond Vrang is the village of Nimos, the starting point for a long and difficult trek across the Shughnan range to Rivak on the Ghunt. In Nimos there is a shrine *(Shoh Abdol)* consisting of two caves, where, according to legend, *Imom Muhammad Bokir* is supposed to have found refuge. The road then goes past a small early mediaeval fortress in Shoshbuvad. From Rubot, just beyond Shoshbuvad, there is a tough trekking route over the Vrang pass to the Wakhan.

The road then climbs to the Jawshangoz plain, offering the first glimpses of Peak Karl Marx (6,723m) and Peak Engels (6,510m).

A Russian reconnaissance detachment was here in July 1894. One of the officers, Lt. Col. Adrian Georgievich Serebrennikov, who designed the Russian base in Murghab – and subsequently the one in Khorog – described their trek across from Bulunkul, close to what is now the Pamir Highway.[3]

We started at 6.50 a.m. in fine weather. At 9.10 a.m. we reached the top of Mount Koi-Tezek (14,000 feet) which marks the frontier line of Shughnan. During six months of the year this mountain is covered with snow, and it is then quite impassable; in the summer, however, there is no difficulty. On the very summit the road forks, the right-hand branch leading to the valley of the Toguz-bulak river, a tributary of the Gund, and the left-hand one to the Shakh-Dara valley. Here we halted, and after dividing up our baggage train our party split up, I myself being with the division which pursued the Shakh-Dara route.

We reached the Kok-bai plateau, which is surrounded by snow-capped mountains. We were now at a great altitude, many of our party suffering from incipient head¬ache, and all were glad when the road, after turning to the left, descended along the banks of the stream Kok-bai-Chat, source of the river Shakh-Dara. Here we camped for the night, starting again at 7.15 a.m. As we proceeded, the character of the country gradually changed, and the scenery began to get more diversified.

… But although the scenery was now more cheering to the eye, this was an advantage only purchased at the expense of weary limbs, for the roads went from bad to worse. We stumbled on, however, encouraged by the sight of wild-rose bushes and the warmer-tinted vegetation which bordered our route. A wild rose is perhaps not much, in an ordinary way, to make a fuss about, but to any poor wanderer, like ourselves, whose eyes were tired and aching from the monotony of a Pamir landscape, it will appear, as it did to us, as a sign from God in the midst of the wilderness. But we still had to go through some wearisome plodding, for the road hereabouts is most precipitous. My heart knocked apprehensively against my ribs several times when my horse stumbled on the edge of some chasm or slipped in some deep rut on a breakneck descent. The best thing for a man to do in such cases is to trust implicitly to his horse; and not to attempt to control or guide it in any way, for the horse's instinct will be a surer and safer guide out of the danger than the judgment of its rider. Many a life has been lost, of horse and man, through humanity's insufferable conceit in its own prowess, and through its often ignorant contempt for the powers of that noble servant of man, the horse.

Alter a rough up-and-down scramble, a steep descent brought us to the confluence of the Kok-bai-Chat and the Mats. From this spot we had a truly splendid view of the distant snow-capped Wakhan mountains and the green valley of the Jaushankoz river, the latter being one of the sources of the Shakh-Dara. Of the Wakhan mountain range, two peaks tower pre-eminent, one rising to a height

of 23,000 feet, and the other, the Tsaritsa Maria, to 20,000 feet above sea-level [now called Pik Engels; the other mountain referred to by Serebrennikov, then called the Pik Tsar Mirotvortz ('peacemaker Tsar'), is today Pik Karl Marx]. These two majestic mountains stand adjacent and tower above all the others in their impressive majesty and might.

We soon came out into the valley of the Jaushankoz river, and thence to a place called by the Kirghiz Depchi-utun, "the trough-like." The path then became very steep and broken but afterwards improved greatly.

At the entrance to the plain in Deruj there is an imposing ruined fortress, dating originally from the 2nd–3rd century AD (late Kushan empire); the remaining towers were probably built in the early middle ages. Very close to the fortress in an area known as Yuzhbokh there are ancient graves from the bronze age and later. From Deruj, there is a trekking route across the Duzakhdara pass to the Ghunt at Miyonakuh, a route the famous Anglo-Hungarian traveller Aurel Stein took in 1915 on his way back home from China to Europe.

In the 18th and 19th centuries, Jawshangoz was also the scene of clashes between nomadic Kyrgyz and the settled Tajik population. Caves above the village were used for refuge and mass Kyrgyz graves have been found. A mountain track leads from Jawshangoz to the Koitezek pass. Just beyond Jawshangoz there are breathtaking views of Karl Marx and Engels Peaks (see page 564). A few kilometres further on there is a turn off for a detour to the beautiful Turumtaikul lake.

A trekking route leads southeast across the Mats pass to the Pamir river and the Wakhan.

Side valley, Shakhdara   *Deruj Castle, Upper Shakhdara*

Ishkashim District and the Wakhan

Ishkashim district (population approx. 26,000) is undoubtedly the most attractive destination in Gorno-Badakhshan for its wealth of archaeological sites (castles, petroglyphs and more than sixty shrines and holy places) and spectacular scenery, with views across the Wakhan to the snow-covered Hindu Kush in Pakistan.

The road from Khorog to Ishkashim town follows the Panj south and at Anderob ('two rivers'), about 30km from Khorog, there is a road leading up a side valley to the hot spring of Garm Chashma (literally 'hot spring'), first described by the Danish explorer Ole Olufsen in 1897.

In Garm Chashma there is a shrine to Ali, who is believed to have opened the hot spring with a stroke of his sword *Zulficar* while he was fighting the dragon. There is a wooden 'panja' (hand symbol) and a place for sacrifice with candleholders and a wooden frame. From Garm Chashma a trekking route goes to the Shakhdara valley (Vezdara, Badomdara). Another more difficult route goes over to the Wakhan (Darshay), with views of Peak Mayakovsky (6,095m).

South of Andarob the main road passes the ruby mine *Kuh-i Lal* ('ruby mountain'). The mine was famous in antiquity and was mentioned by Marco Polo. The *Lale-Badakhshan* or 'Balas' ruby – in gemmology 'spinel' – is still mined there today. In the nearby village of Sist is a shrine *Masar Khuja-i Lal*. According to legend, King Solomon lived here and forced the devil to mine rubies for him.

In the village of Shanbedeh there is a shrine, *Oston-i Shohburhon*. A little further on, in Kosideh, a road leads up a side valley to Bagush, where there are petroglyphs and a large graveyard dating back to the 13th century AD. Beyond the graveyard, the valley widens and offers beautiful scenery. Further south, in the village of Oudj, near Yakhshvol, there is a sanatorium with a hot spring bath.

At the town of Ishkashim, the Panj takes a right-angle bend. After flowing east-west from its source it turns south-north (as far as Kala-i Khum, where it again turns at a right-angle east-west. The Panj valley to the east of Ishkashim is known as the Wakhan. The Chinese Buddhist traveller Xuanzang probably travelled back to Kashgar up the Wakhan in the 7th century AD and described it as follows (modern travellers will recognise the reference to constant winds – moreover, harvesting of grain is difficult even today in the upper Wakhan):

> On the north-east of the frontier of the country [Shang-mi], skirting the mountains and crossing the valleys, advancing along a dangerous and precipitous road, after going 700 li[1] or so, we come to the valley of Po-mi-lo. It stretches 1000 li or so east

and west, and 100 li or so from north to south; in the narrowest part it is not more than 10 li. It is situated among the Snowy mountains. On this account the climate is cold, and the winds blow constantly. The snow falls both in summer and spring-time. Night and day the wind rages violently. The soil is impregnated with salt, and covered with quantities of gravel and sand. The grain which is sown does not ripen; shrubs and trees are rare; there is but a succession of deserts without any inhabitants.[2]

Marco Polo mentions the Wakhan and may also have travelled up it:

At the end of those twelve days you come to a province of no great size, extending indeed no more than three days' journey in any direction, and this is called VOKHAN. The people worship Mahommet, and they have a peculiar language.

The 'peculiar language' may well have been Wakhi, an Iranian language very dissimilar to the other Iranian dialects spoken in the Pamirs and found only in the Wakhan and adjacent areas such as Northern Hunza in present-day Pakistan. In 1995 a German ethnologist was directed with great excitement to a village in the Wakhan where he was told there were 'Nemetsky' (Russian for Germans). When he arrived he found only that the villagers spoke a version of Wakhi that their neighbours did not understand. The etymology of the word *Nemets* (Немец) in Russian is linked to the concept of inability to speak (неметь) and it turned out that the people of the neighbouring village simply spoke a dialect not understood in the rest of the district, and had no connection with Germans.

In Ishkashim town there is a small museum *(Ibrohim Ismoilov)* and just outside the town, in a place called Nut, there are the ruins of a caravanserai dating from the 6th–7th century. In Ryn, just beyond the district centre, there is a shrine *Ostoni Zanjiri Kaba* and a stone sun calendar. Some ten kilometres further east, near the village of Namadgut, are the ruins of a vast fortress known as *Kakhkaha*, the oldest parts of which date probably from the second century BC (Kushan Empire). *Kakhkaha* is believed to have been the leader of a fire-worshipping tribe, the *Siah-Posh* (black-robed), that ruled in the Wakhan and was defeated around the time of the conversion of the region to Islam. The descendants of the *Siah-Posh* now live in present-day Nuristan in Afghanistan. The fortress is occupied by the Tajik border guards and it is advisable to seek permission before exploring the interior of the ruins. At this point the Panj is very narrow and, according to archaeological evidence, there was once a bridge here to what is now the Afghan side.

On the other side of the road from the fortress is the shrine *Oston-i Shohi Mardon* ('Holy site of the King of Men', one of the names attributed to Ali). According to legend, it was Ali who defeated the *Siah-Posh*. There are petroglyphs in Namadgut. The name 'Namadgut' is thought to be related to the Sanskrit word 'namatgata' ('holy place'). The outer gate to the mazor itself is covered in calligraphy and the door to the mazor is a good example of early wood carving.

In Darshai – some twenty kilometres beyond Namadgut – there are the ruins of a fortress (6th–9th century AD), the shrine *Oston-i Pir-i Fokhmamad* and some petroglyphs.

Up the side valley here (Darshaydara), close to the ruins of a watchtower ('Topkhona') there are a number of rocks with Arabic inscriptions (and one in the ancient Kharoshti script – also known as the Gandhari script – dated 4th–3rd century BC according to the Soviet scholar A.N. Bernshtam). A very good trekking route leads up the valley to Peak Mayakovsky (6,095m) – count on two days to the foot of the mountain. One of the last remaining 'ovrings' or 'hanging passages' (paths clinging to the rock face) on the Tajik side can be seen on the way there. The path on the Afghan side of the Panj in, for example, Vanch district, has many examples of precipitous 'ovrings'.

In Shitkharv, ten kilometres beyond Darshai, is the shrine *Oston-i Bobo Khoki*. Legend tells that the holy man Bobo Khoki was born after the death of his mother and emerged from her grave: his name means 'Grandfather from the Ashes'.

In Zumudg, the next village, there is a roadside shrine and a solar stone used for determining the spring solstice *(Navruz)* by alignment with the sun shining through

Zamr-i-atish-parast (Fortress of fire worshippers) *in Yamchun overlooking the Wakhan*

a gap between two higher rocks in the distance.

In Ptup, some 5km from Zumudg, there is a shrine to *Shoh Isomuddin* (also known as *Shoh Samiddi* or *Shoh Hasan Medina*) with a fine garden filled with old twisted sacred trees. Shoh Hasan Medina is believed to be one of the first Ismaili envoys who preached to and converted the local people. During religious festivals, the

villagers gather here to offer food, light candles and recite verses *(ayah)* from the Qur'an.

Probably the most spectacular site in the Wakhan is the area above the village of Yamchun, a few kilometres beyond Ptup, with the imposing 'Zamr-i atish parast' ('Fortress of fire worshippers') complex and nearby hot spring *Oston-i Bibi Fotima-i Zahro* ('holy site of the sleeves of Bibi Fatima'). Parts of this fortress date to the Graeco-Bactrian and Kushan periods (3rd to 1st centuries BCE) – other parts are from the early mediaeval period. On the lower eastern side of the site on an isolated rock there is a smaller fortress known as *Zulkhomor*. According to legend *Zulkhomor* was the sister of *Kakhkaha*, who built the fortress for her – it is thought by Tajik archaeologists to be more recent than the main fortress, probably 7th–8th century CE. The ruins of a fortress supposedly built by *Kakhkaha* for another sister,

Sun calendar at Yamg (above)

Zulhasham, can be seen on the Afghan side of the Wakhan between Namadgut and Ptup. The *Bibi Fotima* hot spring in Yamchun is believed to improve female fertility.

A few kilometres beyond Ptup, in the village of Yamg, is a museum in the residence of the astronomer and scholar *Sufi Muboraki Vakhoni* (1839–1930). The museum houses his manuscripts and exhibits a collection of traditional tools, musical instruments and clothes and is a very fine example of a traditional Pamiri house with superb carved pillars and beams. Just outside the museum is the solar calendar used by Sufi Muboraki for determining the start of the *Navruz* festival.

In Vnukut, the next village, there is a roadside shrine, *Chehel Murid* ('the forty faithful').

A little further along the Wakhan, in the village of Vrang, there is a Buddhist stupa, surrounded by caves that served as cells for the monks (and, much later, as refuge for the local people from marauding Afghans). At top of the stupa there is a stone with an incised footprint that, according to legend, is that of the Buddha. In the early 7th century AD, the famous Chinese traveller, Xuanzang, noted the existence of Buddhist monasteries in the Wakhan.

Below the stupa is a shrine and museum, *Osorkhona-i Abdullo Ansori*, dedicated to the famous mystic and Sufi poet *Abdullo Ansori* (Ansari of Herat), who lived in the 11th century AD. Above Vrang are the ruins of an old fortress. A trekking route goes from Vrang to Rubot in the Shakhdara valley. Another goes from Langar along the Pamir river and across the Mats pass to Jawshangoz (see section on Shakhdara).

In Zugvand, the next village, there is a shrine *Ostoni Panjai Shoh* and, a little further on, in Zong, there are the following shrines and holy places: *Mazor-i Shasti Murtuzo Ali, Osorkhona-i Pir Saidkaramalishoh* (museum), *Mazor-i Pir Saidkaramalishoh, Mazor-i Khoja Behzod, Oston-i Khona-i Khudo, Oston-i Murodgokhi Murodoson* and *Oston-i Gesuyi Balogardon* (literally 'Gesuy, who prevents harm'). According to legend, in ancient times worship at this holy place prevented the spread of cholera in the upper part of the Wakhan valley, and it therefore acquired this name.

Just above the village of Zong is the imposing site of *Vishimkala* (it means 'Silk Fortress' in the Wakhi language and is also known by its corresponding Tajik name of *Abreshimkala*) dating from the medieval period.

Opposite Zugvand, the ruins of the *Kala-i Panj* fortress can be seen on the Afghan side. This fortress, dating back also to the *Siah-Posh*, once controlled the passage down the Wakhan from the east.

In Hisor, the next village, there is a shrine *Oston-i Nuri Muhammad* and the ruins of a fortress *(Zangibar)*.

In Langar there is an important shrine, *Mazor-i Shoh Kambar-i Oftob*, meaning literally 'Master of the Sun', which would suggest that, like many other holy places in the Wakhan, it was revered already in pre-Islamic times – its location is known as Khriz (from the ancient Iranian 'khvar' – 'place of worshipping the Sun'). The garden also has old sacred trees. Opposite the shrine, there is a guesthouse containing a small museum and with intricately carved pillars and beams, one of the finest examples of a Pamiri house in Gorno-Badakhshan). It also functions as a guesthouse. There are a large number of petroglyphs near Langar, many from the bronze age.

From Langar, the road leaves the Wakhan to follow the Pamir river to Zorkul and the Pamir Highway (see separate section on Murghab district). There is a fortress in Ratm, above Langar, overlooking a deep gorge down to the Pamir river, and offering superb views of the Wakhan. The name is thought to come from the old Persian *fratam*, meaning 'first', since this fortress would have been the first line of defence against invaders of the Wakhan from the east. The original fortress was built by the Kushans in the 2nd or 3rd century BC, and was probably used by the Korean-Chinese General Kao Hsien-chih in 747 AD as one of his bases for attacking the Tibetans in the Wakhan and ousting them from the Pamirs (see historical section).

In the 1930s the Soviet frontier with Afghanistan was closed, and until 2003, there were only two bridges from the Tajik side of the Panj to Afghanistan – at Ishkashim and Langar – both of which were constructed to facilitate the passage of Soviet troops. The Langar bridge – recently re-opened, although not for tourist traffic – is at the foot of the mountain on which the Ratm fortress stands, at the junction of the Pamir and Wakhan rivers. The immense investment in 1930–34 by the Russians in the road from Osh to Khorog (728km across some of the highest passes in the world), was, of course, undertaken also for military purposes and it was improved at the time of the 1979 invasion. In 2003, communications with Afghan Badakhshan were re-established through construction of new bridges on the Panj (Oxus) with funding from the Aga Khan Development Network.

The route along the Pamir river from Langar to Khargush ('hare' in Tajik) is very beautiful. Just as the river leaves its deep gorge, there is a small domed caravanserai on the Afghan side that is thought to have been there since Buddhist times – we may speculate that perhaps Marco Polo stayed there on his way across the Pamirs. Khargush is the turn-off point for travel to lake Zorkul (for which special permission must be obtained from the Tajik Border Guards in Khorog – see section on Permits).

Murghab District and the Great Pamir

Murghab district (population approx. 15,000) comprises more than half of the land area of Gorno-Badakhshan. The name means 'river of birds' in Persian.

The majority of the population of Murghab is Kyrgyz. Until fairly late in the Soviet period, the population was mainly nomadic. Guillaume Capus, the French adventurer, noted in 1890:

> These Pamiris, as they should properly be called, are Kyrgyz and thus of Turko-Mongol origin. They belong to the large ethnic group of Kara-Kyrgyz or 'black Kyrgyz', also known as Buruts; some physical traits differentiate them from the Kyrgyz of the three hordes of the plain, but the main difference is in their habitat. The former call themselves Kyrgyz, while the latter have taken the name 'Kazaks' or 'Kaïzaks'. The Kara-Kyrgyz are nomadic tribes inhabiting the mountains of the Talas and Chatkal valleys, the Tien-Shan foothills, the Issyk-Kul lake, the Alai and the Pamirs. According to Ivanov, the Pamir Kyrgyz belong to four tribes: the Teitts, Hadirchas, Naïmans and Kipchaks. In summer they number several thousand in the Pamirs, but in winter only a few hundred remain, spread widely among the best protected valleys of the huge mountain mass. One meets them in groups of two to twenty tents (ois) in the corners of the valley near Rangkul, in the Charput and Kochagil valleys, on the Murghab near Ak Baital, on the Aksu near Istyk, at Aktash, on the Little Pamir at Kyzylgorum, Mulkale and Andaman and on the Alichur. Ivanov and Putyata met them spending the winter in up to twenty tents in the valleys of the northern and southern Gez river and in the Kokuibel and Ghudara valleys. There are also Kyrgyz from these tribes on the upper Tagharma. Almost all

of them pay tribute to the Chinese in Kashgar, and … others pay tribute to no one and collect tribute themselves. According to Ivanov and Putyata, the Teitts and the Hadirchas occupy mainly territories in the west and south-west, while the two other tribes share the north-eastern area of the Kashgar Pamirs. The Teitts seem to be the most numerous, and most of those we met on the Pamir in winter belong to this tribe, which is related to the tribes of the Alai.[1]

During the Soviet period permanent settlements were constructed for the Kyrgyz of Murghab and only a few now set up their yurts in the high pastures (*jailoos*) and on the Alichur plain in the summer months.

Most of Murghab district is semi-desert high plateau and is traversed by the Pamir Highway from the Koitezek pass (4,271m, on the way from Khorog) to the Kyzylart pass (4,336m, on the way to Sary Tash – 'yellow stone' – the first settlement in Kyrgyzstan, and Osh).

Murghab contains the longest mountain glacier in the world, the Fedchenko (more than 70km); two of the highest mountains in the Pamirs: Peak Ismoil Somoni (formerly known as Pik Communism – 7,495m) and Peak Lenin (now Peak Independence – 7,134m). The highest mountains in the Pamirs, Muztaghata ('father of the ice' – 7,546m) and Kongur (7,719m), are just across the frontier in China (Muztaghata can be seen from Murghab town).

An amusing – probably apocryphal – anecdote explains the origin of the name 'Muztaghata. 'Muz' means 'ice' in Kyrgyz, 'tagh' means 'mountain' and 'Ata' means 'father', a term of respect for older people. One of the first travellers to see Muztaghata asked a local Kyrgyz the name of the mountain and received the answer: "it's a mountain of ice, sir."

Murghab also contains the four biggest lakes in the Pamirs: Kara Kul, Sarez (the western part is in Rushan district), Yashil Kul and Zorkul.

The Fedchenko glacier and Peak Somoni are only accessible for mountaineers (or by helicopter), whereas excellent views of Peak Lenin can be seen from the village of Sary Mogol in the Alai valley, about 30km west of Sary Tash.

Murghab can be reached from Khorog or Osh (Pamir Highway) or Ishkashim (Wakhan route – see Ishkashim section). The latter offers the more interesting scenery, as the road follows the majestic Wakhan corridor and, from Langar, the peaceful meandering of the Pamir river north to the Khargush pass (4,344m) before joining the Pamir Highway 126km south of Murghab town (3,630m).

As long as the destination 'Ishkashim' is marked on the GBAO permit, no further authorisation is required to travel on this route. However, special permission is required from the Tajik border guards for the detour east from the Khargush checkpoint to Zorkul and the Great Pamir. Your papers will be checked at the Khargush check-point before you are allowed to make the turn-off.

There are no roads in the Great Pamir and if you are travelling by jeep it is essential to have drivers who know the area. The terrain in the Great Pamir can be treacherous in the early summer as floods caused by rapidly melting snow leave a deep layer of sticky clay under a thin sun-baked hard surface – vehicles easily break through the surface and become trapped in the clay: in addition to experienced drivers, take more than one vehicle so that a trapped vehicle can be pulled free. If your driver knows the way, he can take you to the hunting camp and hot spring at Jarty Gumbez.

A track just west of the junction between the Pamir Highway and the road from Khargush leads to the village of Bulunkul (and the lake of that name) and the vast expanse of Yashil Kul (3,719m – 'yashil' means 'green' in the Turkic languages and the lake lives up to its name). Yashil Kul was formed like Sarez – although much earlier – by a natural dam created by a landslide.

On the north shore of Yashil Kul, close to the mouth of the Great Marjonai river, there are pre-historic stone circles and several Saka (Scythian) burial sites a little further up the valley. Traces of ancient mining settlements (probably from the 11th century AD) can be found in the area. At the eastern end of the lake are the remains of a caravanserai (or tombs) and a hot spring at Sumantash (Bekbulat).

Sumantash is the site of two brief – but important – military skirmishes in the past: the first, in 1759, ended with the rout by the Chinese of the Khoja (Muslim) rulers of Kashgar, who fled to Afghan Badakhshan. The Chinese commemorated this by a stone now in storage at the museum in Khorog. This stone has a long slit on the top that is believed to have served as a primitive letterbox and – according to the British adventurer Lord Dunmore who saw it in 1892 – it originally carried a panel in Chinese with the following text (Dunmore's translation): "On the crest of the mountains 10,000 men laid down their arms. The Chinese soldiers, coming from the four points of the compass, then went unopposed as if penetrating into an uninhabited country. The two ringleaders, therefore, seeing that further efforts would be in vain, took to flight, whilst our soldiers in pursuit resembled tigers and leopards, chasing hares and foxes. Before our soldiers had advanced far after them, and when they were still crossing the mountains, our men were in good fighting order."

The second skirmish took place between Russian and Afghan soldiers on 12 July 1892, and effectively ended Afghan (and Chinese) presence in the eastern Pamirs. It was followed in the summer of 1893 by the construction of the Russian base 'Pamirsky Post' on the Murghab river (site of present-day Murghab town). In 1896, the Russian base in Khorog was built and became the Russian headquarters in the Pamirs in the following year.

Lord Dunmore writes that he saw the inscription in a museum in Tashkent and it must have been separated from the stone by the Russian 'Flying Pamir Detachment' under Colonel Mikhail Ionov and taken there after the campaign (the stone itself being too heavy to transport easily).[2] The stone itself is reliably reported by local inhabitants to have remained in Sumantash until the early 1960s, when it was removed to Khorog and placed in front of the local museum in Lenin Street. Until the conclusion of the final border agreement with China in 2002, it was feared in Tajikistan that this stone might be used by the Chinese at some time as evidence of earlier Chinese sovereignty over the Alichur Pamir. In 1969 – at a time of border tension with the Chinese – it was replaced by a bust of Lenin and buried next to the pedestal. In 2004, when the main road in Khorog was widened, this important historical monument of the Pamirs was dug up and is awaiting a final resting place.

In 1886, the British explorer, Ney Elias, expressed the view that the Chinese had very little claim to sovereignty.

> The circumstance that a Chinese party once crossed the Pamirs as far as the border of Shighnan territory, has been exaggerated, by some writers, into an assertion that Badakhshan was conquered by the Chinese and was in fact, at one time a Chinese possession. What really happened was, I believe, as follows. When the Chinese occupied Kashgar in 1759, and turned out the Kalmak dynasty, the two Khojas,

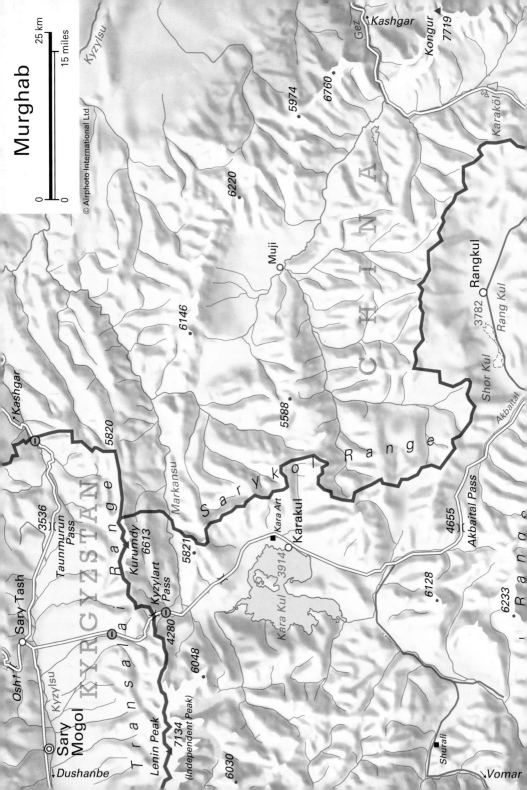

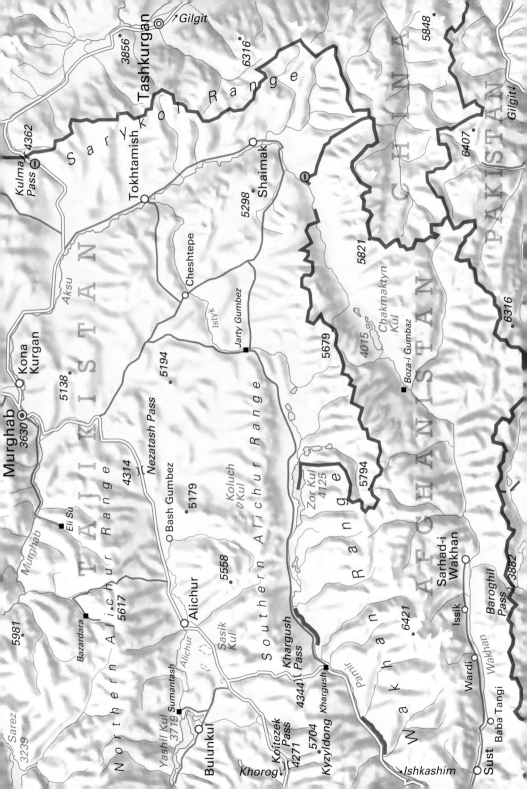

with a large party of Kalmak followers and a certain amount of treasure, fled from Kashgar, by the Gaz route, intending to take refuge in Balkh. A Chinese party, under a certain Ku Ta jen, usually known in these parts as the Sakal Amban, or "bearded Amban," was sent in pursuit, and followed the fugitives as far as Yeshil Kul, at the western end of the Alichur Pamir. Here he is said to have cut some characters on a rock like those at Kara Kul, and then to have returned to Kashgar. The Khojas and their party passed unmolested through Shighnan and had reached Argu, below Faizabad, when they were attacked by Sultan Shah, the Mir of Badakhshan, and taken prisoners. Sultan Shah plundered the whole party, beheaded the Khojas, and kept the Kalmaks as slaves, his motive being plunder and not the fear of the Chinese, who had never even ventured into the inhabited parts of Shighnan, and who had, moreover, returned to Kashgar long before the Khojas had arrived at Argu. On the news of the death of their enemies being received at Kashgar, the Chinese were so pleased at the action of Sultan Shah that they consented to extend to him the privilege they had just previously granted to the Khan of Khokand, of appointing an Aksakal in Kashgar, who was empowered to levy taxes on his nationals residing there, and remit them to the Mir of his own country. Thus so far from Badakhshan ever having been subject to, or even tributary to China, it would appear, rather, that the Badakhshis obtained an important concession from the Chinese, which they continued to hold, up to the expulsion of the latter from their Turkistan provinces in 1865.[3]

An easy trekking route follows the north shore of Yashil Kul – N.B. crossing the Alichur river at the entrance to the lake can be difficult in spring and early summer when the water level is high. A jeep track follows the southern shore; it is also difficult to ford the outflow river at the western end of the lake (look out for the pulley cable, which may or may not be functional) – moreover, work is currently being undertaken here on a new dam for the Pamir-1 hydropower station in Tang near Khorog and it may not be possible to continue by jeep as far as the left bank outflow. Along the left bank, from the western end of the lake, the trail continues down to Bachor and the Ghunt valley, or north via more difficult trekking routes via the Langar pass (4,629 m) or Chapdar lake (4,529 m) to Lake Sarez. From the eastern end of Yashil Kul it is possible to walk upstream to Alichur – on your way you will pass a small geyser.

To the east of the Bulunkul turnoff, the Pamir Highway goes past Tuz Kul ('salt lake') and Sasik Kul ('stinking lake').

Further along the Pamir Highway in the direction of Murghab town is the village of Alichur (3,863 m) – the name means 'Ali's curse' and is reputed to have been spoken by the prophet's son-in-law Ali on a journey through the area, on account of the harsh climate and penetrating winds there. From this point on, the scenery increasingly resembles a moonscape, the rock colours alternating between red, yellow, brown and green. The mountain tops on both sides are rounded and smooth; this plateau area was once on the sea floor – indeed, the coral so frequently used in old Pamiri jewellery was once collected here in the side valleys of the Alichur plain.

Some 10km beyond Alichur in the direction of Murghab a side valley leads across the Bazardara pass (4,664 m) to the 11th century silver mining settlement of Bazardara. You might be able to drive this as some new road construction has been undertaken with a view to reopening the workings, but don't count on it. In Ak Jilga, close to Bazardara, there are interesting petroglyphs representing, among other things, chariots (see section on Petroglyphs). From Bazardara, the route continues down the Bazardara and up the Murghab rivers to Madian (this section has to be on foot, and involves a crossing of the Murghab River) and Murghab. Near Madian there are petroglyphs and, in a side valley, a hot spring *(Eli Su)* that can be reached by jeep from Murghab (about 10 km).

Some 10 km from Alichur towards the town of Murghab there is a beautiful clear pool with fish, revered as a holy place by the local Kyrgyz and known as *Ak Balik* ('white fish' in Kyrgyz): no fishing is permitted.

Twenty kilometres further on there is a huge rock in the middle of the Alichur plain – known as 'Chatyr Tash' ('house rock') on top of which there are graves. Near here a track goes off to the south to the village of Bash Gumbez, from where a trekking route leads to the southern Alichur range past Koluchkul lake.

Half-way between Chatyr Tash and Murghab town, a track leads to Shakhty, where there is a cave with bronze age pictographs. This site is protected by the Murghab Eco-Tourism Association META (see below) and visitors should seek permission from META to go there.

Just beyond Chatyr Tash another track leads to Jarty Gumbez hunting camp, with its own hot spring; excursions can be made from the camp to the Great Pamir and Zorkul (with the necessary permissions). Near the camp, on the Istyk river, are Saka tombs and old Kyrgyz graves. Tracks also lead from Jarty Gumbez to the Aksu ('white water') river at Tokhtamish and Kyzylrabot/Shaimak (see below) – N.B. these tracks are difficult to find and you will need an experienced driver: at one point the track disappears into a seemingly impenetrable rock face, through which there is a narrow passage, just wide enough for a jeep, to the other side. The hunting camp can also be reached from the Khargush checkpoint (with permission).

In Murghab, tours (trekking, safari, wildlife watching, historical sites, camel tours) and guides can be organised with the help of the Murghab Ecotourism Association (META – set up by the French NGO ACTED), including stays in private homes, yurts and on the high summer pastures (*jailoo* in Kyrgyz). META can also assist in obtaining the special permissions to visit local restricted sites (meta@acted.org – tel. +992 3554 21 453). META and its handicrafts shop, the Yak House, is located in a large yurt-like building on the Pamir Highway on the outskirts of Murghab, in the direction of Osh.

To the west of Murghab town, a track leads down the Murghab river to the hot spring in Madian, as noted above. To the north of Murghab town, a difficult jeep track follows the Pshart valley to the ruins of the 9th century mining settlement of Sasyk – passing Saka petroglyphs on the right hand side of the valley and on down to the Murghab river to a beautiful spot called Chot-Tokaï. META can help organizing a 5-day trekking tour starting with a car from Murghab.

At the time of writing, META does not offer yurt stays on the supremely peaceful Alichur plain. This is a good place to break your journey and Dr. Kurbanbay Kydyrov offers hospitality in his beautifully decorated yurt just off the Pamir Highway 8 km east of Alichur town: you will find him an intelligent and humorous host and you can watch yaks being milked and cheese (*kurut*) being made.

From Murghab town, at the junction of the Ak Baital and Aksu rivers – where the river becomes the Murghab – a road branches off the Pamir Highway to the east, leading past the village of Kona Qurghan with its interesting graveyard, along the Aksu valley and then further east, incongruously on a paved road, to the Kulma pass – open for commercial truck traffic but not for individual tourists at the time of writing.

The road continues further up the Aksu valley to Tokhtamish, Shaimak (3,852m) and the Little Pamir. In the late spring and summer, there are several fine 'intermittent' lakes between Tokhtamish and Shaimak, including Kyzylgorum and a 'dragon lake' (Ajdarkel).

Ajdarkel may be the 'dragon lake' described by the Chinese Buddhist pilgrim Xuanzang in the 7th century AD.

> In the middle of the Pamir valley is a great Dragon Lake (Nâgahrada); from east to west it is 300 *li* or so, from north to south 50 *li*. It is situated in the midst of the great Tsung-ling mountains, and in the central point of Jambudvipa.[4] The land is very high. The water is pure and clear as a mirror; it cannot be fathomed. The colour of the lake is a dark blue, the taste of the water sweet and soft.[5]

Shaimak is the present-day name of the place formerly known as Aktash ('white rock'), a landmark known to earlier travellers, and, indeed, sits at the foot of a huge whitish/yellow cliff.

In Shaimak there is a hot spring and a surprisingly beautiful mosque. Just outside Shaimak to the south, at a place called Ak-Beit, there are Saka graves. Shaimak is 126km from Murghab.

Ajdarkel Lake (left)   *Murghab town (above)*

At the time of writing, META does not offer homestays in Shaimak but excellent hospitality (and a hot spring) are available from Alipbek Akjolbekov in his house next to the mosque.

Some 19km north of Murghab town on the Pamir Highway, a road leads east to the beautiful iridescent lakes of Shor Kul and Rang Kul. Ney Elias was here in 1885:

> The region of Rang Kul having been thoroughly explored and reported on by the Russian expedition of 1883, I need hardly give any detailed description of it here. Its feeders were all dry at the time of my visit, and, indeed, they only flow during the summer. There are, in reality, two lakes connected by a narrow strait, as shown by the Russian survey; and the upper lake is considered to be fresh, while the lower or western basin is called salt, though, on tasting the water, I was scarcely able to perceive any trace of salt. No outlet is to be seen – though the Kirghiz affirm that the water flows underground to the Ak Baital, a distance of some nine miles. The Ak Baital, however, runs dry about the end of September, and does not flow again till late in spring; the water of the lake, moreover, has no appearance of being absorbed by sands or loose soil, for the banks of the lower basin are hard and stony. It is difficult, therefore, to account for an underground outlet; while the fact that the Ak Baital flows only in summer, is fully accounted for by the melting of the neighbouring snows at that season only. The upper lake is, to a great extent, a series of swamps at this season, like the upper end of the Little Kara Kul, and the banks and islands are covered with efflorescent and incrusted salts. Here the wildfowl swarm – geese, duck, and teal – till towards the end of October, when they go southward (probably to India) and return again about May. The lower basin is a fine blue sheet, set in brown and yellow hills like the great lakes of Ladak, but the scenery has none of the impressive grandeur of Little Kara Kul, where the peaks, mentioned above, tower over its valley on two sides to a height of 25,000 feet, and an opening to the north affords a panorama of some of the loftiest summits of the Kizil Art ranges. The Kirghiz of Rang Kul were beginning to leave the valley of the lake to take up winter quarters in the neighbouring ravines, where better shelter and more pasture are to be found during the winter months than on the open plains. The geese were becoming uneasy, and could be heard at night rising from the lake, at intervals, to escape being frozen in; while each successive squall that swept up the valley from the west left a lower line of snow upon the hill-sides. In short, winter was approaching fast, and I had, reluctantly, to give up a projected visit to the Russian frontier at the Kizil Art pass – some four marches distant – and to continue

my journey on the 14th October towards Shighnan. The absence of water in the Ak Baital (the "white mare" river) and its tributaries, compelled us to make the journey from the upper end of Rang Kul to the Murghabi in one day. In following the track down the south shore of the lake, a rock, or cliff, is passed, standing about 100 yards from the water's edge and presenting a sheer front of about 100 feet in height towards the lake. This is called the Chiragh Tash or "lamp rock," famous over these regions, for a light which always burns in a cave near the top of the cliff, and is the object of a great deal of superstitious awe on the part of all Kirghiz, Shighnis, and others who know the locality. To all appearance, a steady white flame burns within the cave, but even with a powerful field-glass I could make out nothing more. My impression was that there must be some phosphorescent substance far back in the cave, but this, I was assured, was quite an erroneous view, the real fact being that vast treasures are stored in it, which are guarded by a dragon with a large diamond set in his forehead, and it is this diamond that shines by day and night. The cliff did not appear difficult to scale, but no native of these parts would ever venture to pry so closely into the secret of the light, as to attempt to enter the cave.[6]

In 1891 Francis Younghusband, another player in the Great Game, climbed the 'lamp rock' to seek the explanation for the mystery of the light, and concluded that it came from a hole at the back of the cave. The cave was also explored in the late 1930s by the Ukrainian mountaineer, A.V. Bleschunov, who brought back some treasures supposedly left there by Chinese travellers: they can be seen in the Bleschunov museum in Odessa. (N.B. Bleschunov said nothing about a hole in the back of the cave. Judge for yourself: perhaps there is a dragon there – legends have their charm. I was there in September 2007 and was unable to see any opening on the other side of the rock: moreover, according to local people, the light shines also at night, which would support Elias's hypothesis.)

From Rangkul village a track leads south along the border zone between Tajikistan and China. Travel here requires special permission from the Tajik border guards, but it is worth trying to obtain permission for the sake of the spectacular views of Muztaghata and the huge sand dunes on this route, which ultimately joins the asphalt road from Murghab town to Kulma.

The road north from Murghab crosses the Ak Baital pass – at 4,655m the highest pass on the Pamir Highway. Some 40km from the pass a turn-off leads west along a track to the Muzkol valley, then southwest down the Kokuibel valley, and west to the

geoglyphs at Shurali, before finally turning south down the Tanimas river to the uppermost village in the Bartang, Ghudara. (N.B. This route is marked clearly on Markus Hauser's map but the track is not maintained and may not be jeepable to Ghudara and the Bartang.) There are spectacular trekking routes up the Tanimas, over to the Kokuibel and Belandkiik rivers in unspoilt and virgin territory (see Trekking page 540).

Ralph Cobbold, the English adventurer, was here in 1898:

> Two miles beyond we came to another nullah called Kokjar, where I found a Kirghiz camp, in which we took shelter while it came on to snow. One of the Kirghiz seemed to be a man of some importance, and he told me that quantities of alum and sulphur were found in the neighbouring valleys, and that his tribe carried on a considerable trade in these products with the Alai.
>
> ... Our position was a very romantic one. We were surrounded by mountains of great height, whose precipitous side rose sheer from the valley on all side. Through the cliffs on my right I noticed a narrow defile intersecting the rocky mountain side, which I learnt afforded a passage by the Yangi-Dawan Pass to the Alai. In our front the valley seemed closed by a huge conglomerate of dazzling snow and ice, from which issued the stream of limpid water which we learnt was called Thanwas [Tanimas].[7]

Cobbold was followed in 1909 by Arved von Schultz, who commented:

Geoglyphs in Shurali, unique to the Pamirs   *Shaimak Mosque*

The upper reaches of the Tanimas valley are an unexplored area. The gold deposits in the valley have attracted some speculators, but these explorations have so far not gone beyond the lower reaches of the river. There is no point in the Pamirs that is more difficult to reach as this area and yet it is the only one that could be of economic importance for the Pamirs.[8]

Beyond the Muzkol turnoff, the Pamir Highway leads along the eastern shore of the spectacular lake Kara Kul, that can already be seen from a distance at about this point. Kara Kul means 'black lake', but in spring, summer and autumn the waters are almost always turquoise blue. At the northern end of the lake, near the rest-house at Kara-Art, a track turns off west to geoglyphs and Saka graves, located about 500m from the turnoff.

There is an important archaeological site in the Markansu valley ('Markansu' means 'death valley' in the Turkic languages), north-west of Kara Kul, dating from the late Mesolithic period (approx. 8,000 BC).

The Pamir Highway finally leaves Gorno-Badakhshan at the Kyzyl Art pass (the checkpost on the Kyrgyz side is at Bordoba) and continues down into the Alai valley (known as the *Alaika*) and on to Sary Tash and Osh in Kyrgyzstan.

LANGUAGE IN THE PAMIRS   Robert Middleton

Article 2 of the 1994 Constitution of the Republic of Tajikistan states that: "The state language of Tajikistan is Tajik. Russian is a language of communication between the nationalities." In Gorno-Badakhshan many other languages are spoken. The lingua franca during the Soviet period was Russian – today it is Tajik. Many people in the Western Pamirs speak Tajik and Russian, as well as their local Pamiri language. In Ishkashim, Roshtkala, Rushan and Shughnan districts and in the Yazgulem valley of Vanch district several distinct old Iranian languages are widely spoken. Vanchi, spoken formerly in the Vanch valley, is now extinct and Tajik is the language spoken there today (with the exception of the Yazgulem valley where Yazgulami is also used) as well as in Darvaz district.

The native language in the Eastern Pamirs (Murghab district) is Kyrgyz, although many people also speak at least some Russian. Some ethnic Tajiks (i.e. Tajik-speakers) ethnic Tajiks live in Murghab district. Very few Kyrgyz live in the Western Pamirs.

The official medium of education in the Western Pamirs is Tajik; in Murghab the medium is Kyrgyz, although there are a few Tajik-medium schools in Murghab town catering to the ethnic Tajik population there. Government business in the Western Pamirs is conducted in Tajik and Russian, although Tajik is increasingly coming into the ascendant compared with the immediate post-Soviet period. Many young people in Khorog now speak English (some very well) as this is perceived as the passport to good careers, and, for the Ismailis, has the additional incentive of being the language spoken by their Imam. Quite a few teachers were trained in German during the Soviet period and some older people still speak it. In Murghab, government business is mainly conducted in Kyrgyz.

The different local languages of the Western Pamirs are sub-divided largely by the valleys in which they are spoken (a situation somewhat similar to that of the Swiss-German dialects): Wakhi, Ishkashimi, Shughni, Rushani, Yazgulami. Within some groups there are also separate sub-groups or dialects. For example, scholars recognise variants of Shughni related to the localities Bajuv, Khuf, Rushan, Bartang, Roshorv and Sarikol. All are unwritten, oral languages, and frequently not mutually comprehensible between valleys or even within the same general area. In Gorno-Badakhshan, Sarikoli is mainly spoken in the south-eastern part of Murghab district by immigrants from the Tashkurgan Tajik Autonomous County in China.

Outside the Pamirs, languages belonging to the Pamiri group are also spoken in: Afghan Badakhshan (Wakhi, Ishkashimi, Shughni, Rushani); Tashkurgan in Xinjiang, China (Sarikoli); and Hunza in Pakistan (Wakhi). Yaghnobi, spoken by the Yaghnob people, from the Sughd region of Tajikistan, is also related to the Pamiri language group. The Munji language, which belongs to the Pamiri group, is spoken in Afghan Badakhshan but not in Tajikistan.

The first explorers of the Pamirs and Yaghnob areas called these and their inhabitants *Ghalchah* or *Galcha*, possibly linked to the Iranian word *gar* ('mountain'). Research into the Pamir languages began in the late 19th century[1] and was more thoroughly investigated during the Soviet period. In a study published in 1948, the Russian scholar W. Ivanow[2] (formerly Assistant Keeper at the Asiatic Museum of the Russian Academy of Sciences in St. Petersburg) suggested that the growth of local languages in the Pamirs may have taken place over a long period:

> Nasir [Khusraw] had a very unflattering opinion of the local inhibitants, most probably the peoples of local Shina or Darda stock of whom possibly no trace remains now. It would appear that the area generally was very sparsely populated, the people were very primitive, and missionary work amongst them hardly satisfied

Yagnob people [1896]

an ambitious man like Nasir. Personally I would not in the least trust the local tradition of Badakhshani Ismailis which regard Nasir as the person who converted them to Ismailism. However paradoxical that may be, I venture to express an opinion that the present Shughnis, Wakhis and others were not yet settled there in Nasir's time. They came to that locality much later on.

Being much interested in the study of Persian dialects still spoken in various corners of the country, I often found many proofs of the theory that wherever there is a 'nest' of villages speaking different dialects, we have to deal with a case of comparatively recent migrations, produced by peaceful or other causes. The fact that in such an arid, rocky and inaccessible locality as the valley of the Upper Wakhsh [Panj] there are numerous hamlets the population of which speak various dialects, sometimes considerably differing one from the other, may indicate that such composite populations are due to a complex set of migrations. The existence of the Soghdian-speaking enclave of Yaghnob, South of Samarqand, may point to the direction in which our search for explanation should go. It is not beyond the limits of possibility to suppose that the 'hill Tajiks' who inhabit the hamlets of the Upper Wakhsh [Panj], and speak such a large set of profoundly varying dialects, are early immigrants from the Soghdian plains who shifted there under the pressure of repeated waves of invaders, such as the Turks, later on the Mongols, and then again the Turks. As such migrations certainly were unorganized, the original inhabitants

Irrigation workers, Rushan

of one and the same locality could have been split and settled in many corners, and there, in different milieu, under varying influences, their original languages could have evolutionized in diverse ways, in the course of centuries deviating very considerably from their sister-dialects. If we also assume that the immigrants were sometimes compelled to migrate owing to religious persecutions, and that especially the Shi'ites found themselves persecuted, it would be easy to understand why the population of Badakhshan (in a broad sense) professed Ismailism, perhaps since an early period, and remained faithful to Shah Sayyid Nasir, creating the legend of their having been converted by him.[3]

In 1967 a Department of Pamir Languages was established in the Dushanbe Institute for Language and Literature. However, despite the extensive research on Pamiri languages and folklore during the Soviet period, these languages were never promoted or taught in school at that time, and the only alphabet developed for the Shughni language was also prohibited in 1939 and remained unpublished. In the early years of the period of *Perestroika* and *Glasnost* there was a revival in teaching and occasional writing in these languages in regional and district newspapers; a special newspaper *Farhangi Badakhshon* published stories and poems by authors in Pamiri languages and some local television and radio programmes were made in the local idiom. The Dushanbe Department of Pamir languages was transferred to Khorog in early 1990s as a special Institute of Humanities focusing on research into various aspects of society in Gorno-Badakhshan, especially into the languages and folklore of the Pamiri people. Under the aegis of this institute the late Professor Karamshoev, a native Pamiri linguist, published the first Shughni alphabet using Cyrillic characters. Since then, however, there has been a drop in interest and enthusiasm for promoting knowledge of these languages – partly, no doubt, because of the spread of Tajik as the official and national language.

Woman and young boy, Tavdem

RELIGION   Robert Middleton

The territory of present-day Tajikistan was part of the Iranian Empire, the religion of which – at least from the Achaemenid period (559–338 BC) – was Zoroastrianism. When the Iranian Sassanids were defeated by the Muslim Arab armies in 636 AD, Islam was gradually spread throughout the Central Asian region.

The religion of the vast majority of Tajikistan's population today is Sunni Islam. In the Pamirs, however, a majority of the people profess the Ismaili faith, a branch of Shia Islam that considers Ismail, the eldest son of the Shia Imam Jafar al-Sadiq – d. 765 – as his successor; the spiritual leader of the Ismaili community is the Aga Khan, the 49th Imam of the community since the time of Ali. Until the 19th century, when the Emir of Bukhara imposed forcible conversions on the population of Darvaz and the Vanch and Yazgulem valleys, most of what is now Gorno-Badakhshan professed the Ismaili faith and there were also substantial Ismaili communities in what is now Khatlon district. Ney Elias, the British explorer, reported in the diary of his journey in the Pamirs in 1885 that

> The people of Darmorakht, Gharan etc. are murids of Mizrab Shah, the Shah i Munjan who is himself a disciple of Agha Khan. The people of Zebak are disciples of Shah Abdur Rahim, also a disciple of Agha Khan. … In Ghunt, murids of Mirza Sharaf of Suchan, disc. of Agha Khan. In Roshan, Bartang and many in Shighnan, as well as in Darvaz, are murids of Shah Zada Hassan of Deh Roshan, disc. of Agha Khan.[1]

According to local tradition, the Pamiris were converted to Ismailism in the 11th century by the Persian poet, traveller and philosopher Nasir Khusraw. The historical reality, however, is more complex. There is now evidence that the Ismaili faith was already extant in Badakhshan before Nasir Khusraw's arrival, which made it possible for him to take refuge there after fleeing Seljuk persecution in Balkh.

From the time of Nasir Khusraw, the Ismailis in Central Asia were subject to persecution by their external rulers. Sarfaroz Niyozov, an Ismaili scholar from Gorno-Badakhshan, explains that

> [t]he development of the post-Mongol history of Central Asia coincides with the creation of ethno-religious states (e.g., Shi'ite Safawid in Iran, and Sunni Timurid and Shaibanid in Central Asia). Numerous assaults of Mongols and Turkic rulers in the name of Islam subjected those whose faith did not fit within the 'canonical'

interpretation of religion to barbaric genocides. The history of this brutality continued during the pre-modern times with the creation of Afghanistan, which together with the Bokhara Emirate competed in enslaving and repressing the region's Ismailis. All this considerably reduced the Ismaili influence in Central Asia. Throughout the post-Mongol period and after, Ismailism survived largely due to the geographical remoteness and the institute of pirship [religious leaders appointed by the Ismaili Imam of the time] whose structures, in the physical absence of the ever-present Imam due to adversities of time, resembled Sufi Tariqahs.[2]

Sadruddin Aini, a prominent Tajik writer and scholar, describes in his book *Ghulomon* ('Slaves') more recent persecution of the Ismaili population of Badakhshan and, only a generation ago, the atrocities against them were certainly within living memory (see Chapter 6, parts 1 and 2 for eyewitness reports by some of the first Russian officers in the Pamirs and by Ralph Cobbold, the British adventurer who travelled down the Bartang in 1898). People would flee into the mountains (some even fled to Western China and now compose the Sarikol Tajik community) to escape their oppressors who took their livestock and carried men and women into slavery. These stories help to explain the fact that the inhabitants of the Western Pamirs welcomed the arrival of the Russians at the end of the 19th century and assisted them

Pilgrims praying on the way to Hazret-i Burkh

in occupying the Western Pamir in the closing phases of the 'Great Game'.[3] Gorno-Badakhshan had, of course, great strategic importance for the Soviet Union, but there was also another factor:

> ... the Soviets, considered Badakhshan ... as an example of socialist revolution in the Muslim East and invested heavily in its modernization. In the Soviet period (i.e., 1917–1991), the region was renamed the Mountainous Badakhshan Autonomous Province and incorporated into the Soviet Socialist Republic of Tajikistan. The Tajik Ismailis played a vital role in the creation and development of Tajik statehood. The Soviets subsequently built modern schools, hospitals, cultural centers, power stations, roads, and airports in all major areas of the province. Free education was provided from kindergarten to doctoral studies. The literacy rate increased from less than 2% in 1913 to more than 99% in 1984. Badakhshan stood amongst the first in the whole of the Soviet Union in terms of the number of holders of higher education degrees. It produced a great number of highly educated professionals who made valuable contributions to Tajik society. The improved health, education, social welfare and security resulted in rapid demographic change and greater mobility. Many Ismailis migrated to Tajikistan's lowlands and other parts of the Soviet Union.[4]

Despite persecution and the imposition of atheism under the Soviet regime, the Ismaili faith was able to survive in Central Asia partly due to a degree of Soviet tolerance of diversity in this isolated and strategically important frontier region (especially after the death of Stalin), but certainly also to the strength imparted by the Ismailis' devotion to a living Imam, to the greater importance in their tradition of private prayer as opposed to organised worship,[5] and to the well-tried and necessary Ismaili response to persecution of dissembling their religion *(taqiya)*.

A Tajik Ismaili now living in the West informed me that when she was in school one of her fellow pupils reported her to the teacher of atheism for having confided that she thought perhaps God really existed. The teacher, also an Ismaili, disciplined her, saying "You and I both know that there is a God, but I forbid you ever to talk about it in school." She subsequently obtained the school prize for atheism and, irony of ironies, now performs an important religious function in one of the communities of the European diaspora.

Another factor in the religious identity of the Pamiri people is the survival of pre-Islamic rites in their worship, giving them a confidence in the continuity of their religious tradition. Niyosov points out that

> Tajik Ismailis as one of the oldest Ismaili communities have creatively incorporated some of the famous pre-Islamic Mithraist, Zoroastrian and other rites. These traditions have become Ismaili in content to the degree that many scholars claim that these rituals have always been Islamic. One of these traditions is charoghrawshan (tsirow-pithid in Shugnani). Tsirow-pithid begins with the gathering in the deceased's house on the third day after the death, which is accompanied by the singing of Madohs (devotional poetry from classical poets such as Rumi, Hafiz, Nasir Khusraw, Attar, Sanoi, etc.). Close to the ceremony's end, a candle, created from the fat and wool of a freshly-slaughtered sheep, is lit, accompanied by the continuous recitation of special prayers. It is believed that the soul of the deceased will thus be purified by the recitation of the special prayers, light, and devotional poetry, and leave the house and find rest in eternity.
>
> Another factor is the peculiar structure of the Pamiri house (cheed, chod in local languages). ... [See page 637] The Ismailis of Badakhshan also celebrate Nawruz as a broad cultural celebration marked throughout Tajikistan. Since 1995, i.e. after His Highness [the Aga Khan]'s historic visit to Badakhshan, the local Ismailis started to celebrate Ruz-i Nur (the Day of Light) on the 25th of May. This day is a celebration where religious and cultural aspects are brought together. Lastly, the Tajik Ismailis have also incorporated a number of Sufi traditions such as paying tributes to the shrines and ostons (mazars), which have served them to maintain their identity and connection with God throughout Soviet antireligious campaigns.[6]

Apart from delegations that travelled to Bombay on foot in the early 20th century to deliver *zakat* (tithing), the Ismailis of Central Asia had no direct contact with their Imam until the visit of the Aga Khan to Tajikistan in 1995. During the humanitarian crisis in Gorno-Badakhshan that followed the break-up of the Soviet Union, Sunni communities in the region commented how fortunate their Ismaili neighbours were to have a living Imam and some even began celebrating the Aga Khan's birthday as a sign of gratitude for the non-sectarian work of the Aga Khan Foundation in Gorno-Badakhshan.

THE SHRINES OF THE PAMIRS[7]   Robert Middleton

Another reason for the continuity of religious tradition in the Pamirs is the wealth of local shrines ('Mazar', pronounced locally 'Mazor') and sacred places ('Oston') dedicated to holy men. The majority of these are venerated by the Ismaili community, but there are also shrines in a few remote Sunni villages, such as Poi-Mazar at the upper end of the Vanch valley where there is, according to legend, the grave of Ali.

The shrines of Gorno-Badakhshan are characterised by the presence of sacred stones and the horns of ibex and Marco Polo sheep (Ovis Poli), symbols of purity under Aryan and Zoroastrian religious traditions, long before the introduction of Islam; they also show evidence of regular use for fire rituals, in which aromatic herbs ('strachm' or 'yob') and animal fat ('roghan') are burnt. The local traditions and legends attached to some shrines also pre-date the introduction of Islam in the Pamirs.

This section has been put together with the kind assistance of Professor Jo-Ann Gross, of the College of New Jersey, who is currently preparing a scholarly study of Tajik shrines. A non-exhaustive list of shrines in Gorno-Badakhshan follows, the more interesting of which are shown in bold. N.B. The name of the village is followed by the name of the shrine(s) there.

Zumudg roadside shrine

Professor Gross subdivides the shrines of Badakhshan in the following categories:

– sacred places associated with nature, including hot and/or mineral springs, large or unusual trees, caves, and rock formations;

– shrines where eminent religious figures are buried (Ismaili pirs, khalifas, or Sufis);

– shrines in places where eminent religious figures are believed to have visited in the past (including figures from early Islamic history such as 'Ali or Muhammed Baqir);

– sacred places where animals carrying early Islamic figures passed or are believed to have left footprints in the ground or rock.

Prominent at most shrine sites are collections of animal horns and special stones, which also have sacred properties. In general, rituals associated with sacred places are reserved for special holidays such as Navruz or Eid-i Qurbon, rather than the previous practice of weekly Friday village gatherings.

Graveyard Po-i Mazar, with hand of Ali visible at the top of the pole

DARVAZ DISTRICT

Yoged:	Oston-i Khoja Khizr, Oston-i Shoh Awliyo, Oston-i Khoja Chiltan, Oston-i Khoja Nazar

VANCH DISTRICT

Po-i Mazar:	Sardi Saïd, Sardy Bard, Abdulkakhori Sarmast
Vanvan:	Khoja-i Sabz Push
Ubaghn:	'Alexander's tomb'

SHUGHNAN DISTRICT

Porshinev:	Mir Sayyid Ali Hamadoni (Kushk), Sumbi Duldul (Barchiddara), **Gumbaz-i Pir Sayyid Farukhshoh (Saroi Bakhor), Pir-i Shoh Nosir (Midenshor)**
Tem:	Imom Zaynulobidin
Sokhcharv:	Pir-i Dukman
Suchon:	Shoh-i Viloyat
Sijd:	Shoh Malang
Ver:	Sumbi Duldul
Vankala:	Imom Muhammad Boqir
Charthem:	Malika

ROSHTKALA DISTRICT

Hichih:	Shoh Burhon
Parshed:	Khoja-i Zur
Bodom:	Khoja-i Nur (sister of Khoja Zur), Sumbi Duldul
Barwoz:	Oston-i Pir-i Foqhmamad
Tavdem:	**Sayyid Jalol Bukhari**
Tusyon:	Shoh Burhoni Vali
Midensharv:	Shoh Abdul
Shuvjev:	Khoja-i Sabz Push
Baroj:	Shoh Burhon
Roshtkala:	Pir Yakhsuz, Bobo Mafil
Ambav:	Chiltani Pok
Bidiz:	Pir-i Foqhmamad
Sezhd:	Vorjbid, Shah-i Wiloyat, and Qadamgoh
Nimos:	Shoh Abdol (Imom Boqir)

RUSHAN DISTRICT

Vomar:	**Oston-i Sayyid Jalol, Shoh Tolibi Sarmast**
Yemts:	Mushkil-kusho

Siponj:	Bobo Alisho
Bassid:	**Hazrat-i Khoja-i Nuruddin**, Safdaron
Bardara:	**Farmon**
Roshorv:	Borkhatsij, Shoh Tolib, Shoh Husein, Andrim
Savnob:	Hozirbosht, Khoja-i Hizr, Mahfil Oston, Hazrat-i Daoud
Yapshorv:	Khoja-i Shayuz
Nisur:	Shoh Husein, Pir Nosir, Hazrat-i Daoud
Bopasor:	Khoja Aliamdor
Ghudara:	Shoh Husayn, Shoh Tolib, Hazrat-i Daoud
Pastkhuf:	Bobo Alisho
Khuf:	Mustansiri Billoh
Yomj:	Oston-i Shoh Tolib

ISHKASHIM DISTRICT

Garmchashma:	Pir-i Foqhmamad
Sist:	Masor Khoja-i Lal
Shambedeh:	Oston-i Shoh Burhon
Ryn:	Oston-i Zanjiri Kaba
Namadgut:	**Oston-i Shoh-i Mardon**
Darshay:	Oston-i Pir-i Foqhmamad
Ptup:	**Mazor-i Shoh Isomiddin**
Shitkharv:	Oston-i Bobo Khoki
Vrang:	**Osorkhona-i Abdullo Ansori and museum**
Zong:	Mazor-i Shast-i Murtuzo Ali, Osorkhona-i Pir Said Karamalishoh (museum), **Mazor-i Pir Said Karamalishoh**, Mazor-i Khoja Behzod, Oston-i Khona-i Khudo, Oston-i Murodgokh-i Murodoson, Oston-i Gesuyi
Zugvand:	Oston-i Panja-i Shoh
Langar:	**Mazor-i Shoh Qambar-i Oftob**
Hisor:	Oston-i Nuri Muhammad

In addition there are a number of small roadside shrines, especially in the Wakhan, for example in Zumudg and Vnukut ('Chil Murid' – 'forty faithful').

The glossary below may be helpful in understanding the religious and legendary significance of some of the shrines. The reader wishing to study further some of the concepts and beliefs of Ismailism will find a useful glossary on the website of the Institute of Ismaili Studies in London,

http://www.iis.ac.uk/glossary_list.asp?f=a&t=c&l=en.

Alexander (locally Sikander/Sikandar): In Gorno-Badakhshan there are many legends about Alexander the Great, including the claim that he was actually in the Pamirs. The kings of Shughnan and Roshtkala claimed to be his descendants.

Ali Hamadoni: A 14th century Sufi teacher from Hamadan in Iran, whose mausoleum is in Kulob – famous also in Kashmir.

Alisho: Refers to Ali, son-in-law of the Prophet. There are many sites in Gorno-Badakhshan where Ali is supposedly buried.

Awliyo/Awliya: Plural of Arabic *waliyy* ('saint', 'protector'), someone who has attained wilayat (q.v.).

Bobo: Means 'grandfather'.

Burhon: One of four Sufi brothers who promulgated the Ismaili faith in the Pamirs in the 16th century. The others were Said Muhammad Isfahani (also known as Said Shahi Koshon), Abdurrahman (also known as Said Shoh Khomush) and Shoh Malang.

Cheheltan (Chiltan): A holy group of forty spirits who protect and assist the faithful ('chehel' means forty). The Cheheltan have magic powers, similar to those of *Khizr (q.v.)*.

Dowud/Daoud: The prophet and king David.

Mazar, Wakhan. The passing woman puts her hand in the niche in the wall to receive a blessing

Firman/Farmon: An instruction or communication from the Ismaili Imam to his followers (Persian *farmân* meaning 'decree' or 'order').

Fokhmamad/Foqmamad: An Ismaili Pir *(q.v.)* in ancient times who is the patron saint of hot springs in the Pamirs.

Farrukhsho: An Ismaili Pir *(q.v.)* from the village of Porshinev.

Gumbaz/Gumbez: Grave or tomb.

Hazrat: Honorific Islamic title used to honour the spiritual status of a person. The literal translation of *Hazrat* means 'Great Presence'.

Imam: In general usage, a leader of prayers or religious leader. The Shia restrict the term to their spiritual leaders descended from Ali and the Prophet's daughter, Fatima.

Jalol: Sayyid Jalol Bukhari was the grandson of Shoh Burhon *(q.v.)*, and is also revered for having spread the Ismaili faith in the Pamirs.

Khalifa: A religious leader in Pamiri villages – who also has important functions as a revered village elder, confidant and family adviser. Khalifas were appointed by *Pirs (q.v.)* and today the position is normally hereditary.

Khizr/Khidr: One of the four prophets recognised by Islamic tradition as being 'alive' or 'immortal' *Hazrat Khizr* is famous in Islamic story as a wise and mystical person or angel who helped the prophet and Ali. Islam inherited his story from earlier mythology, and he is associated with, for example, Moses (he corresponds to Elijah/Elisha) and Alexander the Great. In the middle ages he came to represent a form of esoteric mystical knowledge. Although not mentioned by name in the Qur'an, it is generally accepted that verses 60–82 of chapter 18 refer to him. *Khizr* or *Khidr* means 'green' in Arabic, the colour of Mohamed's banner, symbolising Islam. See also 'Muskil-kusho' and 'Sabz Push'.

Khuja/Khoja: A Persian word literally

Pilgrims on the way to Hazret-i Burkh

meaning 'lord' or 'master' – was used in Central Asia as a title of the descendants of the famous Central Asian Naqshbandi Sufi teacher, Ahmad Kashani (1461– 1542). In the contemporary Ismaili context, the Khojas are one of the Ismaili communities originating from the Indian subcontinent and now living in many countries of the world.

Khudo: 'God'.

Malang: See 'Burhon'.

Mahfil: A saint who reputedly freed parts of the Pamirs from ice and snow.

Mardon: People, men. **Shohi Mardon** is a title of Ali.

Muhammad Boqir/Muhammad al-Baqir: The fourth Ismaili Imam.

Murid: Murid is a Sufi term meaning 'committed one' or 'one who seeks'; in the Ismaili context it means 'believer' or 'follower'.

Mushkil-kusho/Mushkil Gusha: Means 'remover of difficulties' and is an allusion to Ali and to the Ismaili Imam of the time. Also linked to the mythical 'Khizr'.

Mustansiri Billoh/Mustansir bil-Lah: The 18th Ismaili Imam.

Nosir/Nasr/Nasir: Nasir Khusrow, 11th century poet and philosopher, credited by the Ismailis of Badakhshan with introducing the Ismaili religion to the region.

Pir: The word 'Pir' in Persian literally means an old person; in the Ismaili context it refers to a religious leader appointed by the Imam of the time.

Qadamgoh/Ghadamgah: Means literally "place of the step" – place where a saint stayed. Also a town in Khorasan, Iran.

Sabz Push: Means literally 'green mantle' and is an allusion to *Hazrat Khizr (q.v.)*.

Saïd/Sayyid: A descendant of the prophet Mohamed through his grandsons Hasan and Husayn.

Shoh/Shah: A title of respect meaning 'king' or 'leader'.

Sumbi Duldul: The name of Ali's horse.

Tolib: Shoh Tolib Sarmast is revered for spreading the Ismaili faith in the Pamirs. Sar Mast is a town in Iran near the west coast of the Caspian.

Wiloyat/Wilayat: In Shia theology, *wilayat* is the authority invested in the Prophet and his family as representatives of God on earth. In Shia Islam, it refers to the authority that the Imam has over his believers.

Vorjbid: Means 'footprint' (of Ali's horse).

Zaynulobidin/Zain al-Abidin: The third Ismaili Imam.

PETROGLYPHS AND PICTOGRAPHS   Robert Middleton

Gorno-Badakhshan has more than 10,000 images engraved on rock (petroglyphs) and rock paintings (pictographs), several more than 10,000 years old. Most are (fortunately for their preservation) some distance from the main roads and many villagers are unaware of their presence.

Rock paintings are concentrated in Murghab district in what is known as the Shakhty cave. In 1958, the distinguished and much-regretted archaeologist V.A. Ranov,[1] one of the last Tajik scholars of the Soviet period, discovered a series of rock paintings that he dated, on the basis of comparisons with European cave paintings in Europe, Africa and Asia, as belonging to the Mesolithic or early Neolithic period (approx. 12,000–8,000 BC). He catalogued seven, of which four separate groups were in good condition, depicting, in red mineral paint, a bear, bulls, wild boar, ostriches (and a hunter disguised as an ostrich) and arrows. Shakhty, at 4,200m, is the highest known location of pre-historic cave paintings and the representation of a bear and ostriches is most unusual.[2]

The Shakhty cave site is protected by the Murghab Ecotourism Association (META) and visitors must seek permission from the META/ACTED office in Murghab to see the paintings (meta@acted.org – tel: +992 355 421453 or satphone +882 165 060 15 13).

PETROGLYPHS

Although there are petroglyphs in more than 50 locations throughout Gorno-Badakhshan, the two most interesting sites are in Akjilga in Murghab district (at 3,800m) and Langar in the Wakhan (Ishkashim district). There are other important groups in the valley above Vibist and near Chartem in Shughnan (approx. 40km and 70km respectively from Khorog on the Pamir Highway); and in Namadgut in the Wakhan.

V.A. Ranov dated the petroglyphs at the Akjilga site from the end of the second millennium BC to the beginning of the first millennium BC (Scythian-Sarmatian).[3] The most complex depict chariots with human figures, horses and yaks; others show archers (see reproduction of a petroglyph at Akjilga to right).[4]

The Akjilga site in Murghab district was discovered by the geologist V.P. Bulin in 1971 near Bazardara, a silver mine worked in the early middle ages. There is also an old mining site at Akjilga, dating from the Iron Age (2nd millennium BC). The old workings in Bazardara have recently been reopened for possible future mining activity and measures have been taken by META/ACTED to protect the whole site.

In the area around the village of Langar at the junction of the Pamir and Wakhan rivers at the upper end of the Tajik Wakhan there are some 6,000 petroglyphs. The most frequent subject is the ibex *(Capra sibirica)*. It is very difficult to date the ibex petroglyphs, since the style of the Stone Age examples has been copied in subsequent representations. Other petroglyphs represent riders on horseback, hunters with bows (sometimes with what appear to be guns) and running men. A much later group depicts Islamic motifs or religious texts or poems in Arabic/Farsi script – clearly post 8th century when Islam was introduced in the region.[5]

Normally the 'patina' method is used to date petroglyphs, by which the surface of the engraved lines is examined for iron and manganese traces, although these can also be affected by the location of the petroglyph and the angle of its exposure to the sun. The oldest are those where the colour of the lines is almost identical to that of the rock. The tradition is continuous and man has made engraved figures on rocks in the Pamirs probably until the beginning of the 20th century. Today, unfortunately, graffiti prevail.

Petroglyph, hands of Ali (above)
Stone Age pictograph of a boar, Shakhty (below)

Petroglyph of rider at Langar

SYMBOLISM IN THE PAMIRI HOUSE

Robert Middleton

One of the most important repositories of the culture of the Pamirs is the traditional Pamiri house, locally known as 'Chid' in the Shughni language. What to the untrained eye looks like a very basic – even primitive – structure, is, for the people who live in it, rich in religious and philosophical meaning. Tajik writers consider that it embodies elements of ancient Aryan and possibly Buddhist philosophy – some of which have since been assimilated into Pamiri traditions. The symbolism of specific structural features of the Pamiri house goes back over two and a half thousand years and its distinctive architectural elements are found in buildings in several other areas close to the Pamirs.

The Anglo-Hungarian explorer Aurel Stein noted these similarities on his journey through the Western Pamirs on his way back from Kashgar in 1915.

> The hamlets nestling here and there at the mouth of ravines and half-hidden amidst fine fruit trees relieved in pleasant contrast the uniform grimness of these forbidding defiles. The dwellings at the places where we broke our journey looked from outside unpretending rubble-built hovels.

Exterior of house, Basid

But in the interior, smoke-begrimed as it was, there could be seen arrangements indicative of rude comfort and interesting as obviously derived from antiquity. Thus the living hall, in its ground plan and in the arrangement of the skylight ceiling and sitting platforms, invariably showed the closest resemblance to the internal architecture of residences excavated at ancient sites in the Taklamakan and of others still occupied by the living in Hindukush valleys to the south. This small corner of Asia, in its alpine seclusion, seemed indeed as if untouched by the change of ages. I felt inclined to wonder whether it could have presented a very different picture to some Bactrian Greek or Indo-Scythian visitor in the centuries before Christ.[1]

The house itself is the symbol of the universe and also the place of private prayer and worship for Pamiri Ismailis – the Ismailis have as yet no mosques in Gorno-Badakhshan. The Pamiri house is normally built of stones and plaster, with a flat roof on which hay, apricots, mulberries or dung for fuel can be dried. The layout of the house is as described below, although some houses have a mirror-image of what is described.

Inside, most houses comprise a small internal lobby – frequently used for sleeping or eating in the summer months – and a large square room, entered through a door in the lobby. Beyond this door is the main room, entered through a small corridor (with space to the left and right for washing and storage); the corridor leads into an open area comprising the following standard elements:

a) Three living areas ('Sang', or 'Sandj'), symbolising the three kingdoms of nature: animal, mineral and vegetable: the floor ('Chalak'), normally of earth, where the fire (or more frequently today, a cast-iron oven) burns, corresponds to the inanimate world; the first raised dais ('Loshnukh') corresponds to the vegetative soul; and the third floor level ('Barnekh') to the cognitive soul.

b) Five supporting pillars, symbolising the five members of Ali's family: Mohamed, his son-in-law Ali, Mohamed's daughter Bibi Fatima (Ali's wife), and their sons Hasan and Husayn – the pillars are thought to correspond in Zoroastrian symbolism to the major gods/goddesses ('Yazata' or 'Eyzads'): Surush, Mehr, Anahita, Zamyod and Ozar. The number five also reflects the five principles of Islam.

1. The pillar symbolising the prophet Muhammed ('Khasitan-Shokhsutun'), to the left of the entrance, was traditionally made of juniper – a sacred tree and symbol of purity, the smoke of which has healing and disinfectant properties; today, there are

no longer enough junipers of adequate size for making this pillar in newly constructed houses. The child's cradle will normally be put close to this pillar.

2. The pillar symbolising Ali ('Vouznek-sitan') is situated diagonally left from the entrance. In Zoroastrian tradition, this pillar corresponded to the angel of love ('Mehr'). At weddings, the bridal couple will be seated at this pillar, in the hope of being blessed with good fortune and happiness ('Barakat'). Tradition requires that – in addition to her own father and father-in-law – the bride must have a third father, the person who, at this pillar, ritually uncovers her face from seven veils during the ceremony.

3. Diagonally right from the entrance is the pillar symbolising Bibi Fatima ('Kitsor-sitan'). It is the place of honour for the bride at the engagement ceremony and her engagement dress corresponds to the traditional perception of Fatima (and the goddess Anahita): red dress, bracelets, rings, ear-rings. In Zoroastrian tradition, this column corresponded to the angel who guarded the fire. The stove or family fire is closest to this pillar and it serves also for fire-related rituals.

4/5. The fourth (Hasan) and fifth (Husayn) pillars are joined to show the closeness of the relationship between the two brothers. The crossbar is carved with Aryan symbols, frequently including a central depiction of the sun, and is sometimes decorated with the horns of a Marco Polo sheep (Ovis poli).

Rasht valley [1928]

Skylight   *'Hasan' and 'Husayn' pillars*

The 'Hasan' pillar ('Poiga-sitan') is the place of family and private prayer and is considered the place of honour for the religious leader ('Khalifa') or a chief guest. The chief guest will normally leave a small symbolic space next to him/her against the pillar showing that it is reserved for the Khalifa. It is believed that, in Zoroastrian tradition, this pillar personified 'Zamyod'.

Mourning ceremonies – with a ritual lamp or candle lit for three days – are carried out close to the 'Husayn' pillar ('Barnekh-sitan'). In Zoroastrian tradition this pillar may have been associated with 'Ozar'.

c) Two main transversal supporting beams – one across the 'Mohamed' and 'Ali' pillars, one across the 'Fatima' and 'Hasan/Husayn' pillars. For Pamiri Ismailis, the first symbolises universal

'Ali pillar' showing Zoroastrian sun symbols   *Fireplace*

Aerial shot of house

reason ('Akli kul'), and the second the universal soul ('Nafsi kul'). The two beams are thought to have corresponded to the material and spiritual worlds in Zoroastrianism.

d) Several groups of beams. The total number varies according to the size of the house and local interpretation of Pamiri tradition. There are several different theories concerning their number. For some the total must be the number of Ismaili Imams (49), for others they are equal to the number of Ali's Army, when they were killed in Dashti Karbalo (72). In most cases, there are thirteen intermediary beams: six – over the fireplace – representing Adam, Noah, Abraham, Moses, Jesus and Mohamed, the six prophets revered in Islam (in Zoroastrianism East, West, North, South, Upper, Lower); and seven representing the first seven Imams.

In the Zoroastrian religion, the number seven is of symbolic importance. God created seven heavenly bodies: Sun, Moon, Saturn, Jupiter, Mars, Venus and Mercury and there are seven principal Amesha Spentas or 'Holy Immortals'. The Ismailis are 'sevener' Muslims: for them Ismail was the seventh Imam.

Other beams on the ceiling may include groups of eighteen or seventeen beams corresponding to elements of Ismaili cosmogony.

e) A raised platform (approx. 50cm) around the inside walls of the house. Underneath the platform is a storage area, but – prior to the widespread introduction

Design of a skylight from the report of a German expedition [1904–1907]

of metal stoves, which now stand in the open floor area – it would have incorporated the family hearth, as in the photo on page 640.

f) A skylight, the design of which incorporates four concentric square box-type layers, called 'chorkhona' ('four houses') in the Shughni language, that represent, respectively, the four elements earth, water, air and fire, the latter being the highest, touched first by the sun's rays. The opening is called 'rauzan'.

The illustration on page 641 is taken from the report on the second and third German expeditions to Turfan 1904–1907 by Albert Grünwedel, head of the Indian Department of the ethnographic museum in Berlin and shows that the design of the skylight in Pamiri houses is very ancient and may combine Aryan and Buddhist symbolism.[2]

Other decorative elements in a Pamiri house – in addition to the carved Aryan/Zoroastrian symbols – frequently include a combination of red and white, symbolising respectively (in both Zoroastrianism and local Ismaili belief):

• Red: the sun, blood (the source and essence of life) and fire and flame (the first thing created by God);

• White: light, milk (the source of human well-being).

At the Persian New Year ('Navruz'), a willow wreath (in the form of a circle containing a cross) is dipped in flour and used to draw designs on the walls and columns of the main room. Stripped willow twigs are bound together (to resemble a vegetable stalk) and placed between the beams as a token of abundant crops in the new year.

For the people of the Pamirs, willow is the symbol of new life, because in spring it is the first tree that 'wakes up' after a long sleep. It plays a role in wedding ceremonies, when a willow twig is used to lift the bride's veil and when an arrow made of willow is shot through the skylight. In old times when a husband wanted to divorce his wife, he took a stick of willow and broke it above her head.

At burials, a willow stick is used to measure the length of the body and determine the size of the grave to be dug.

MUSIC AND DANCING   Robert Middleton

Ole Olufsen, leader of the Second Danish Pamir Expedition, 1898–99, was one of the first modern travellers to write about the songs, music and dancing of the Pamirs. In his report published in London in 1904 he commented:

> These people are earnest and severe, a consequence of their hard struggle for very existence; they are rarely heard to laugh or sing, yet they are not devoid of taste both for vocal and instrumental music. They never sing in the open air during the summer; but in winter, at their parties and feasts, they exhibit their musical talents in the house.

Olufsen was not a musicologist and seems not to have grasped the central importance of music in Pamiri daily life, which is surprising for someone who demonstrated in other parts of his report a greater degree of cultural sensitivity. The second Danish expedition, about which he was writing, took place in the winter, and perhaps he had little opportunity to see some of the more joyful manifestations of Pamiri music. It is of course true that in 1898 the population had only recently been freed from Afghan depredations and Russian agricultural improvements (potatoes, cabbages and other vegetables) had not yet raised living conditions: the people may have had little occasion to be joyful. In 1908, the head of the Russian military administration in Khorog from 1902 to 1908, Andrei Yevgenevich Snessarev, a more sympathetic observer, was able to report that "the Tajiks are a gifted, energetic and active people, full of initiative and capable of developed forms of social life and high culture …" and was touched by Pamiri music.

> We listen to the song that echoes towards us; the monotonous oriental scale, which you can hear to excess again and again in the Caucasus, in Persia, and in Russian Turkestan, changes here to what we might call a European scale, mostly in a minor key. There are, however, not many such songs – they thereby gain in interest. If you hear them, you will instinctively say you have heard them before: in their legends and folktales you will recognize familiar scenes from sagas and epic poems. The same heroes, the same heroic deeds and miracles. The same lively and inquisitive imagination created them – perhaps they even have the same common origin as our own European tales.[1]

In the early 1990s, again at a time of extreme food shortages, when the first western visitors came to the Pamirs they were welcomed in every village by music and dancing – and laughter.

Pamiri music is recognised today as belonging to a very ancient folk tradition, and is studied by musicologists from all over the world. Pamiri musical groups appear now in western concert halls and on television and recordings of their music are readily available.

The Aga Khan Development Network (AKDN) sponsors a 'Music Initiative in Central Asia' and their website provides a wide range of information on Central Asian music, including the musical traditions of the Pamirs, with a survey of the instruments and musical genres: many documents in pdf format can be downloaded. (See http://www.akdn.org/Music/Musicin.htm.) The website of the Institute of Ismaili Studies (IIS) in London (part of AKDN) offers samples of Pamiri music (http://www.iis.ac.uk/view_article.asp?ContentID=106046).

For Pamiris, music and dance are intimately linked; many Pamiri songs also contain both popular and religious elements, frequently referring to the Ismaili Imam. The pre-eminent vocal and instrumental genre of devotional music in the Pamirs is known as *madoh*, devotional songs of praise that can embody the spiritual power known as *baraka*. They serve several cultural functions and are also used with prayer and in the context of traditional healing.[2]

Other Pamiri music includes: *falak* (song of fate), *dargilik* (song of separation – *dargilik* means 'melancholy'), *lala'ik* (lullaby), *khalqi* (traditional popular songs), *ghazal* (love songs, but can also be devotional), *hikayat* (versified stories) and *munajat* (supplicatory religious song). *Dargiliks* are normally sung in private settings, not at weddings or ritual ceremonies such as funerals. Many traditional songs are in a minor key.

Man playing a tanbur (top)   *Girl dancing in traditional dress, Shpad village (bottom)*

The main instruments used in Pamiri music are the following:

Tavlak: a drum-type percussion instrument. The wooden or ceramic glass-shape box is covered with leather. The leather is heated before use and different parts of the surface produce different sounds. The tavlak is local to the mountainous regions of Tajikistan. It is used to accompany vocal pieces and folk music orchestras.

Daf: a drum-type wooden percussion instrument similar to a large tambourine. The daf is popular in all regions of Tajikistan. It usually accompanies other instruments in an orchestra or small group. In Pamiri musical heritage, the daf plays a very important role and is played during the most joyous of wedding music as well as to accompany songs of deep nostalgia. There is a daf in each Pamiri house and groups of women play complex rhythmic patterns to welcome guests.

Afghan Rubob: an ancient stringed pizzicato lute. The Rubob is popular in the musical cultures of Afghanistan, Pakistan and Central Asia It has many playing and resonance strings, 4–5 fixed frets and additional frets on the finger board. It consists of two sounding boards, one wooden and one leather. Fish skin is best for covering the board. The Rubob is used as a solo instrument and in folk orchestras. Very

Pamiri instruments: l. to r. tanbur, Afghan rubob, Pamiri rubob, tor, setor [above], gejak [in front], Pamiri rubob lying on a daf [drum] (top)
Musicians at a 'didor' (religious ceremony with the Aga Khan), Roshtkala (bottom)

often it is played in pairs with the nay (flute) or the sitar. Musicians prefer the Rubob to be from apricot or mulberry trees.

Ghijak: a stringed bow instrument, which can have 2–4 strings. The ghijak consists of a spherical or rectangular box (made of metal or wood), sometimes covered with horse leather, sometimes only the original metal box. The bow is made of horse hair. It is used as solo instrument, as well as in string orchestras. In Badakhshan, it is mostly used for the dance melodies known as 'Rapo' and 'Kish-Kish'.

Nay: a longitudinal whistle flute, which is 30–35cm and has six holes. Apricot tree roots are preferred for making the nay. The Tajiks call the nay a 'Spring melody' instrument, because it is regularly played on spring mornings. It has two active pitches, which give it a very mild and pleasant sound. The nay is used in folk orchestras and is the most popular instrument among shepherds.

Tanbur: a long-necked lute with an oval lower soundboard covered with skin. Seven gut strings are attached to the peg-box and tuned with wooden pegs. The strings are plucked with a wooden plectrum.

Tar (or **tor**): A stringed instrument similar to the *Rubob*, with a soundboard shaped like the figure 8.

Pamir Rubob: an ancient stringed short-necked lute. The box is covered with goat or cow leather. The strings are venous. The Rubob has a deep but very mild sound. The Pamir Rubob is very important for playing *madoh*.

Sitar (or **sitor**): a stringed pizzicato instrument, which can have from 5 to 14 strings. The sitar is popular in Badakhshan, India, Pakistan, and Afghanistan and is used as a solo instrument as well as in the traditional Badakhshan string orchestras. The box is of mulberry wood.

In addition to these typical Pamiri instruments, modern instruments such as the accordion are frequently used in popular singing and the *ghijak* is sometimes replaced by the violin.

The most important means of musical expression in the Pamirs remains the human voice, used with a characteristic throaty and sometimes nasal sound. *Madoh* are usually accompanied by Rubobs (or *tanbur*) and *daf*.

There is a saying in Tajikistan that the people from Leninabad (Sughd) govern, those from Kulob fight, in Garm they pray – and the Pamiris dance. Certainly it is difficult to imagine life in Gorno-Badakhshan without the perpetual accompaniment of music and dancing. Every village has excellent musicians, young and old as well as expert dancers.

Men and women dance together, although there is no contact. Women perform as solo singers and occasionally as accordion players.

In the eastern Pamirs (Murghab district) musical traditions are very different. The main instrument is the *komuz*, with three wire strings plucked by the finger or by a plectrum. It produces a clear, penetrating sound.

The Murghab Kyrgyz are less fond of dancing than their Tajik compatriots in the Western Pamirs, but maintain a lively musical tradition.

HANDICRAFTS   Robert Middleton

The handicrafts of Gorno-Badakhshan are being revived today by projects sponsored by the Murghab Ecotourism Association (META), a project of the French NGO ACTED, in the Eastern Pamirs (for Kyrgyz crafts) and by the Mountain Societies Development Support Programme (MSDSP), a project of the Aga Khan Foundation, in the Western Pamirs (mainly for crafts of the Western Pamirs). Funding for these projects has been provided by several far-sighted donor agencies, including Aid to Artisans, The Christensen Fund, the Open Society Institute, UNESCO, the Canadian, Japanese, Swiss and US governments and the Dutch development agency *novib*. The projects aim to create additional sources of income for artisans and promote and protect local culture.

In 2001, the Murghab Ecotourism Association opened *The Yak House* in Murghab for training and sales; outlets now exist in Khorog, Dushanbe *(Bactria Cultural Centre)* and Bishkek. The skills supported by *The Yak House* are weaving and embroidery (carpets, wall hangings, table runners, cushion covers, handbags, purses) using traditional techniques and designs.

In the Western Pamirs, a local organisation, *De Pamiri Handicrafts* was created in 2004 and is training its partner artisans to increase the quality of their products and to sell them through the *De Pamiri* shop in Khorog and partner shops in Dushanbe.

De Pamiri sponsored handicrafts include: felt crafts (carpets, toys, slippers);

knitted crafts (socks, skull caps, scarves and other items); embroidery (wall hanging, skull caps, purses); woven carpets (from sheep wool and goat or yak hair); traditional musical instruments; wood carvings; woven baskets; hats; and toys.

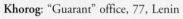

Outlets for *De Pamiri* handicrafts:

Khorog: "Guarant" office, 77, Lenin street. Tel: 00992-35220-3796, 00992-35220-5804, 00992-35220-4475
E-mail: yorali@rambler.ru

Dushanbe: Silk road shop, 32, Shotimur Street; Bactria Cultural Center, 22 Mirzo Rizo. Tel: 227 02 57 / 227 03 69 / 951 31 42 05

Antiques are hard to find in the Pamirs. Until a few years ago it was still possible to find old coral and silver jewellery from the Western Pamirs and embroidered head-dresses with silver decorations, for ceremonial occasions, from the Eastern Pamirs.

Pamiri skullcap, with traditional design of Yoged village, Darwaz (top)
Old Pamiri necklace with coral beads and beaten silver work (bottom, left)
Traditional Pamiri knitted socks (Jurab) ((bottom, right)

GLACIERS: FROZEN TREASURES OF THE PAMIRS

Wilfried Hagg

The Pamir mountains are one of the most heavily glaciated mountain systems in the mid latitudes. Glaciers generally occur where snow that falls in the winter is not dissipated completely by melt during the summer. Such climatic conditions occur in extensive parts of the Pamirs with its highest peaks reaching almost 7,500 m. Glaciers grow principally from the accumulation of snow and its conversion to ice. Under the influence of gravity they move to lower reaches where melting overbalances snowfall. Like great rivers of ice, glaciers have sculpted mountains and carved out valleys. They are not only beautiful elements of high mountain landscapes, but also active creators of this scenery. Moreover, glaciers are known to be key indicators for climate change. Since former glacier extents remain visible for long time periods in the form of deposits and moraines, they also help us to reconstruct and understand the climate of the past. Last but not least, glaciers are important water reservoirs, especially where mountains are surrounded by arid lowlands as in central Asia.

The exploration of glaciers in the region began with the Pamir expedition of the German and Austrian Alpine Club in 1913 and was continued by the German Alai-Pamir expedition led by Rickmer Rickmers in 1928. These two ventures gave the first insight into a part of the world that was almost completely unknown before. During the second expedition, Professor Finsterwalder surveyed and mapped the Fedchenko glacier, which is now recognised as the world's largest glacier outside the polar regions. Fedchenko is a dendritic glacier system with more than 100 smaller glaciers feeding the main stream. From the uppermost firn basins to the tongue, the glacier has a length of more than 70 km and covers an area of 800 km². At the confluence of two streams with debris along the sides, medial moraines emerge and form a fine set that is typical for this gorgeous glacier.

In the 1970s, about 4,400 glaciers with a total area of 5,600 km² existed. They play a major role in the regime of the mountain rivers, because they store huge masses of water in the form of snow and ice and release it during the growing season, when it is needed most urgently for irrigation and food production in the lowlands. This fact was recognized by Rickmer Rickmers, who wrote in 1929: "There is no culture without glaciers. Since it never rains in summer, the fields completely depend on artificial irrigation and the water in the streams is exclusively glacier melt. Without the mountains, where the winter snow is stored and compressed to ice, the lowlands would be a desert". The dying of the Aral Sea (of whose drainage basin the Tajik glaciers are a part), one of the major ecological crises at present time, is not linked to changes in glaciation or the water cycle in the mountains, but due to an increased demand for water in the lowlands. The expansion of irrigated land and the use of old and inefficient irrigation systems built during the Soviet Union are the main causes of excessive water consumption, especially in downstream riparian countries.

In the last 150 years, a worldwide retreat of mountain glaciers has been observed. This is the response to the global warming trend, which is at least partly a result of human activities. In the highly continental climate of the Pamirs, the glacier wastage was less dramatic than in more maritime mountain ranges. Analysis of airborne imagery showed that from the 1950s to the 1980s only 30% of the observed glaciers were retreating, another 30% were stable and 40% even showed an advance. Nevertheless, the overall change has been a reduction of glacier area by 10% in this 30 year period. In the northern Tien Shan mountains, as a comparison, the retreat rate was double during the same time span.

Why do Pamir glaciers react less than others? There are several possible reasons, but the complete picture is not yet totally understood, because there are relatively few scientific investigations in this remote region. One cause may be that these large glaciers need more time to react to climate changes, which means that we must still wait to see the full answer. The Fedchenko glacier retreated 700m from 1928 to 1979, which is not much in relation to its total length. But this may have been only the answer to climate changes that already took place in the 19th century. The main reason for the slow retreat probably is the fact that these glaciers are simply not that much affected by global warming, because they are located in such high altitudes above the snow line, where a warmer atmosphere also means more snowfall and this effect may partly compensate enhanced melt rates. However, visiting the Pamirs now gives you the chance to see glaciers that are still in a more or less healthy condition, compared to other high mountain environments on the globe.

If global warming continues with the speed that is projected by scenarios of the Intergovernmental Panel on Climate Change, glacier degradation will also be accelerated in the Pamirs. This will have great impact on the water cycle. In a first step, streamflow will be increased due to enhanced melt rates, leading to more floods especially in summer. After the majority of the water storage is wasted, there will be a different picture. In the dry summers, a distinct shortage of water will raise major problems for agriculture and the supply of drinking water. Without glaciers, the rivers are fed only by summer rainfall and this is very scarce in the region. It will therefore be essential to develop adaptation strategies and water resource planning together with the neighbouring countries such as Uzbekistan and Turkmenistan who also are in the need of this precious resource. Bilateral decisions and treaties are essential to avoid conflicts that can easily arise along trans-boundary rivers in arid regions.

Wilfried Hagg studied Physical Geography and works at the Commission for Glaciology of the Bavarian Academy of Sciences and Humanities in Munich, Germany. In 2002, he visited the Fedchenko region as a member of a Tajik-German exploratory expedition. His research focuses on Central Asian mountain systems.

Mushketov glacier, Hissar range [Lipsky, 1896]

BIRDS AND MAMMALS IN THE EASTERN PAMIRS

Dr George Schaller

East of lakes Sarez and Yashil Kul, the rugged peaks, glaciers, and gorges give way to wide flat valleys bordered by high rolling hills seldom more than 5,200m in elevation. This part of the Pamirs is a high-altitude desert, an alpine steppe with a sparse cover of grasses and dwarf shrubs such as sage. Only in the upper mountain valleys where melting snows provide moisture and along rivulets and streams are patches of meadow which in summer are intense green and specled with bright flowers, blue gentian, mint, iris, yellow potentilla, primula, and others. This is the home of the magnificent Marco Polo sheep, the icon of these uplands. When Marco Polo traveled across the Pamirs to China in 1273 he saw the horns "of sheep of huge size." By the late 1800s the Marco Polo sheep had become one of the most coveted prizes of trophy hunters, and it still retains that almost mythical aura today. Hunters will pay US$25,000 to kill an animal. This money could benefit conservation and local communities if it were allocated for that purpose.

The casual visitor is unlikely to encounter Marco Polo sheep except in winter when heavy snows drive the animals down from the high summer pastures in search of forage along the base of hills. The December rut brings rams and ewes together, but by spring the sexes segregate again, often in different valleys. However, even a fleeting glimpse of this grandest of all wild sheep is worth a climb into remote hills. Rams may weigh 150kg and have horns 160cm long, measured over the curve (the record is 191cm). No adequate census of sheep numbers has been done, but everyone agrees that there has been a decline in recent decades because of uncontrolled hunting for meat and market by the Kyrgyz herders, officials and the military. Estimates for the whole of Tajikistan range from 3,000 to 14,500 animals, and the actual number is probably somewhere between these figures.

Marco Polo sheep

The only other widespread wild hoofed animal within the realm of Marco Polo sheep is the Asiatic ibex, a wild goat partial to steep terrain. Where ibex are fairly abundant the snow leopard also stalks the crags. To encounter one of these elusive cats is a matter of luck, but its spoor can be found along the base of cliffs and on mountain passes – scats, tracks, and scrapes made with hindpaws in soft soil. (See special topic on Snow Leopards.) Brown bears are rare, but sometimes one finds an excavation where a bear tried to dig a marmot out of its burrow. The marmot is the most abundant of the larger mammals, and, sitting bolt upright in its golden coat, it gives loud chirrs of alarm at one's approach. When marmots hibernate between October and April the hills seem empty. Red foxes roam the slopes hunting among colonies of grey hamster and Pamir vole and are also alert for any large meal such as Tolai hare. Wolves travel widely alone or in small packs. They are much detested by herders because they occasionally kill livestock, especially in winter. The wolf's summer diet consists mostly of marmot (55%), Marco Polo sheep (41%), birds (3%), and grass (1%), as determined from an analysis of scats. A naturalist in the Pamirs must look at such artifacts of an animal's passing because actual sightings of most mammals are so infrequent. Because the Marco Polo sheep readily cross into neighbouring countries, Tajikistan, Pakistan, Afghanistan and China have agreed to cooperate in the establishment of a Pamir trans-frontier or peace park.

But birds offer constant pleasure. A summer list may include at least 40 species. Along rivers and creeks are common merganser, dipper, white-winged and black redstarts, and redshank. Common terns and brown-headed gulls wheel over lakes, and along the margins are ruddy shelduck and occasionally some bar-headed geese. Blue hill pigeons are common, as are both red-billed and yellow-billed choughs. Golden eagles and Himalayan griffon ride the updrafts, and an occasional bearded vulture glides along slopes in search of a carcass. A saker falcon may perch motionless on a boulder. Horned larks and Brandt's mountain finch abound on alpine slopes where white-winged snowfinch, desert wheatear, great rosy finch, brown accentor, and flocks of twite are also seen. Both Tibetan and Himalayan snowcock are high on ridges, stripping grass seeds, but their melodious call is heard more often than the birds are seen, usually scurrying away. Around villages are citrine and pied wagtails and Spanish sparrows. Many of these species leave when winter grips the heights and when in a day's walk only a raven or two may be sighted.

Dr. George Schaller is a field biologist with the Wildlife Conservation Society in New York. He has worked widely on conservation issues in Central Asia.

THE SNOW LEOPARD:

PHANTOM OF THE HIGH MOUNTAINS   Rodney Jackson

Snow leopards (*Panthera uncia*) primarily occur in the western portions of Gorno Badakhshan, in such valleys as the Bartang, Yazgulem and Vanch, east to the Muzkol Range, and in isolated spots along the Wakhan Corridor and Eastern Pamir. There is no reliable population estimate, but Tajikistan is reported to have 120–300 cats.

Standing 60cm at the shoulder and with a body-tail length of 1.8–2.3m (almost half being tail), the snow leopard is well adapted for life in its cold, high mountain habitat. Large paws and a long, thick tail give the cat its renowned agility for negotiating steep terrain or jumping along the narrow cliff ledges. It has an exquisite smoky-grey pelage, tinged with yellow and patterned with dark grey, open rosettes and black spots. Adaptations for cold include an enlarged nasal cavity, long body hair with a dense, woolly underfur (belly fur up to 12cm in length), and a thick tail that can be wrapped around the body. Males average 45–55kg in body weight compared to 35–40kg for females.

The ibex is the snow leopard's primary prey in this region, along with marmots (*Marmota caudata*) after they emerge from months of hibernation in spring to feed on forbs and grass near their burrows. The Pamir hare *(Lepus tolai)* is taken year-round, along with the occasional Marco Polo sheep *(Ovis ammon polii)* and game birds like the Tibetan snowcock *(Tetraogallus tibetanus)* and Chukor partridge *(Alectoris chukor)*.

Snow leopards are rare and seldom seen. Look for them along high ridgelines and rocky outcrops, especially in rugged gorges at elevations of 3,000m or above. The best season for spotting these elusive cats is during late winter and early spring, during its mating season when it marks most prolifically – leaving scrapes, scent-sprays and faeces along its travel routes. This marking behaviour is intended to inform other cats of their presence. Snow leopards are usually more active in the early morning and late afternoon or evening, an activity pattern termed crepuscular by scientists. Beside the valleys mentioned above, look for these cats around Bachor, Roshtkala and Sarez Lake, and in Istyk River in the eastern Pamir.

There is a favorite Kyrgyz folklore story relating the snow leopard's unique way of hunting its favorite prey, the wily ibex that has excellent senses.

Early in the morning the snow leopard creeps up the mountain ridge, getting above the ibex, which are having their morning meal below the cliffs and rocky areas

Snow leopard

where there is more forage. The cat makes sure it is up-wind of the ibex, and then rolls a round teresken bush down the steep slope. The frightened ibex look up, prepared to run away, but see that it is only a bush. So they go back to feeding. After a few minutes the snow leopard rolls another bush down, and again the ibex jump up. But quickly resume feeding when they realize it is only another plant.

Now the snow leopard curls itself into a tight ball, tail wrapped around face and rolls down the hill toward its unsuspecting victims. Thinking it is another bush, the ibex barely lift their heads. The next second the snow leopard rushes forward and kills the nearest ibex!

Snow leopards were ruthlessly hunted up until 1968, although poaching still continues as Tajikistan's nature protection measures have not been enforced for lack of funding and staff, and limited awareness among pastoralists who occasionally lose livestock to the superbly camouflaged feline. Such events primarily occur in winter when deep snow forces the cat closer to human settlements, when they are most vulnerable to poaching. They may result in a household losing its entire capital or "bank account," fueling anti-predator sentiment.

With support from the Christensen Fund (TCF), The Snow Leopard Conservancy (SLC) is working with local organizations like META (Murghab Ecotourism Association) to promote community-based stewardship of this species by developing innovative participatory approaches to linking community based nature conservation with strengthening cultural identities and sustainable livelihoods. The goal is to make snow leopards worth more alive than dead, bringing benefit to people while serving as symbols of an intact ecosystem.

Rodney Jackson is considered the world's leading snow leopard expert, having devoted his life to working with local communities to conserve the cats. He founded the Conservancy in 2000. For more information visit www.snowleopardconservancy.org.

Tajik Vocabulary and Phrases

General phrases:

Hello	*Salom aleikum*	Goodbye	*khair*
Good morning	*subh bakheir*	How are you?	*chi heli?*
Good, thank you	*khubam naghz*	Excuse me	*bebakhshid*
Please	*iltimos*	Thank you	*tashakur*
Yes	*bale, ha*	No	*ne*
My name is…	*Nom-i man … ast*	I am English	*Man Inglisi am*
I am from America	*Man az Amriko am*	I am a tourist	*Man turist am*
Do you have…?	*Shumo … dorid?*	I have…	*Man … doram*
What is that	*On chist?*	Where is/are…?	*… kujo ast?*
Wait!	*Sabr konid!*	Don't look!	*Negoh nakonid!*

Do you understand English? — *Shumo Inglisi mifahmid?*
I do not speak Tajik — *Man zabon-i Tojik namifahmam*
I don't understand you — *Man shumoro namifahmam*
How much is…? — *… che qadar ast?*
Where are the toilets? — *Khojatkhona kujo ast?*
Where is the American Embassy? — *Saforatkhona-i Amriko kujo ast?*
One is not allowed (to do…) — *kas … imkon nadorad*

At the airport:

Airport *forudgoh* — Customs *gumruk*

Sir, do you have your passport and visa? — *Ako, pasport va viza-i shumo dorid?*
How long will you stay in Tajikistan? — *che qadar vaqt shumo dar Tojikiston mi-istid?*
For what reason have you come to Tajikistan? — *Baro-i che be Tojikiston omadid?*
For tourism/business — *bo sababho-i jahongardi/tijorati*
Are these your suitcases? — *Oyo in jomandonho mol-i shumo hastand?*
Yes, these are my suitcases? — *Bale, in jomandonho mol-i man ast*
Please open this suitcase — *iltimos in jomandonro kushoyid*
Everything is in order — *Hama be tartib*

Panjshanbe market, Khudjand

At the hotel:

Hotel	*mehmonkhona*
I would like a room	*Be man khona lozem ast*
For how many people?	*Baro-i chand kas?*
For myself/two people	*Baro-i khodam/du kas*
For how many nights?	*Baro-i chand shabonaruz?*
For three nights	*baro-i se shabonaruz*
I don't have a room	*man khona nadoram*
How much is this room for one night?	*in khona baro-i yak shabonaruz che qadar ast?*

Food and restaurants:

Food	*khurok*	Restaurant	*restoran*
Waiter	*pishkhidmat*	Fork	*changol*
Knife	*kord*	Spoon	*qashoq*
Glass	*stakon*	Water	*ob*
Cup	*piyola*	Coffee	*qahve*
Tea	*choi*	Milk	*shir*
Beer	*pivo/ob-i jav*	Wine	*sherob*
With sugar	*bo shekor*	Bread	*non*
Meat	*gusht*	Beef	*gusht-i gav*
Chicken	*gusht-i murgh*	Mutton	*gusht-i gusfand*
Lamb	*gusht-i barra*	Fish	*mohi*
Egg	*tukhum*	Vegetables	*sabzavot*
Rice	*berenj*	Fruit	*miva*
Apple	*sib*	Grape	*angur*
Apricot	*zadrolu*	Peach	*shaftolu*
Plum	*olu*		

A cup of coffee	*yak payola gahve*
A glass of red/white wine	*yek stakon sherob-i surkh/safed*
What would you like?	*Che mikhohid?*
I would like...	*man ... mikhoham*
I'd like a table for four people	*man miz baro-i chor kas mikhoham*

Transport within Tajikistan:

Bus	*otobus*	Train	*pozid, qator*
Taxi	*taksi*	Ticket	*bilet*
Train Station	*vokzal-i roh-i ohan*	Railway	*roh-i ohan*
Bus Station	*istgoh-i otobus*		

When does the train leave? *Pozid kei miravad?*

When does the bus from Hissar arrive? *otobus az Hissar kei mioyad?*

How can I get to Hissar? *be Hissar che hel beravam mitavonam?*

By bus or by train *bo otobus yo bo qator*

What route does the bus take to Istaravshan? *otobus be Istaravshan bo kadom roh miravad?*

Shopping:

Market	*bozor*	Open	*kushoda*
Closed	*baste*	Money	*pul*
Expensive	*qimat*	Cheap	*arzon*
Big	*bozorg*	Small	*kuchek*

Around town:

Bank	*bank*	Tea-house	*choikhona*
Castle	*qala*	City-centre	*markaz-i shahr*
Guide	*rohbar*	Town hall	*hukumat-i shahr*
Museum	*muze*	Square	*maidon*
Shop	*maghoza*	Mosque	*masjed*
Church	*keliso*	River	*rud*
Police station	*poliskhona*	Bridge	*pol*

Health:

Doctor	*tabib*	Ill	*kasal*
Hospital	*kasalkhona*	Pharmacy	*dorukhona*
Medication	*doru*	Dentist	*dandonsoz*
Cold	*zukom*	Flu	*grip*
Fever	*varaja*	Ankle	*bujulak-i po*
Arm	*dast*	Right arm	*dast-i rost*

Left arm	*dasi-i chap*	Hand	*panja*
Eye	*chashm*	Foot	*po*
Knee	*zonu*	Shoulder	*kift*
Finger	*angusht*	Head	*sar*
Tooth	*dandon*		

My tooth hurts	*dandonam dard mikunad*
I have a headache	*dard-i sam doram*
I have a stomach ache	*dard-i me'da doram*

Numbers:

One	*yak*	Eleven	*yazdah*
Two	*du*	Twelve	*davazdah*
Three	*se*	Thirteen	*senzdah*
Four	*chor*	Fourteen	*chordah*
Five	*panj*	Fifteen	*punzdah*
Six	*shash*	Sixteen	*shonzdah*
Seven	*haft*	Seventeen	*hifdah*
Eight	*hasht*	Eighteen	*hizdah*
Nine	*nuh*	Nineteen	*nuhzdah*
Ten	*dah*	Twenty	*bist*
Twenty-one	*bist o yek*	Twenty-two	*bist o du*
Thirty	*si*	Forty	*chil*
Fifty	*panjoh*	Sixty	*shast*
Seventy	*haftad*	Eighty	*hashtad*
Ninety	*navad*	One hundred	*sad*
Two hundred	*devist*	Three hundred	*se sad*
Four hundred and thirty-two	*chor sad o si o du*		
One thousand	*hezar*		

Time and Date:

What time is it?	*Soat chand shud?*
One o'clock	*yak soat*
Ten o'clock in the morning	*dah soat dar subh*
Five o'clock in the afternoon	*panj soat baad-i nesf-i ruz*

Centre of Dushanbe from the air [1935]

Six-thirty	*hash soat o nim*
Minute	*daqiqe*
Ten minutes past seven	*dah daqiqe az haft*
Five minutes to eight	*panj daqiqe kam hasht*

Day	*ruz*	Night	*shab*
Week	*haft*	Month	*moh*
Year	*sol*	Today	*emruz*
Yesterday	*diruz*	Tomorrow	*fardo*

RECOMMENDED READING

ALEXANDER THE GREAT

In the Footsteps of Alexander the Great by Michael Wood. BBC Books, 2007. A perceptive and entertaining study of the story of Alexander. Michael Wood mixes the account of his own adventures as he followed in Alexander's footsteps.

Alexander the Great by Robin Lane Fox. Penguin Books, 2004. A scholarly and well written account of the story of Alexander.

ARCHITECTURE

Monuments of Central Asia: A Guide to the Archaeology, Art and Architecture of Turkestan by Edgar Knobloch. I.B. Travis, 2001. An excellent overview of the architectural heritage of Central Asia.

The Road to Oxiana by Robert Byron. Oxford University Press, 2007. A poetic and scholarly account of Robert Byron's journey in the 1930s in search of the origins of Islamic architecture.

RECENT HISTORY

Beyond the Oxus – the Central Asians by Monica Whitlock. John Murray, 2003. An intimate and lucid account of the dramatic events in Central Asia over three generations, brought to life using eye witness accounts, unpublished letters and first hand reporting. It brings together the complex threads of the civil war in Tajikistan with great clarity and insight.

Extreme Continental: Blowing Hot and Cold through Central Asia by Giles Whittell. Trafalgar Square, 1996. One of the seminal books on the recent history of Central Asia.

Goodnight Mister Lenin: Journey Through the End of the Soviet Empire by Tiziano Terzani. Picador, 1993. An eye-witness account by a great journalist of the fall of the Soviet Union as it unfolded in Central Asia.

The Birth of Tajikistan, by Paul Bergne. I.B. Travis, 2007. A seminal work on the appearance and evolution of the Tajik Republic by a brilliant former diplomat and academic.

The Lost Heart of Asia by Colin Thubron. Vintage, 2004. An eloquent piece of travel writing about Central Asia just after the fall of the Soviet Union. Rather down-beat.

THE GREAT GAME

The Great Game: On Secret Service in High Asia by Peter Hopkirk. Oxford University Press, 2001. A thrilling account of the exploits of British and Russian officers who played out the secret war between the two empires in the nineteenth century for control of Central Asia.

Setting the East Ablaze: Lenin's Dream of an Empire in Asia by Peter Hopkirk. Kodansha International, 1997. An equally thrilling account of the continuation of the Great Game by the Bolsheviks, who attempted to set the east ablaze, with Lenin's eyes on British India.

THE SILK ROAD

Aurel Stein on the Silk Road by Susan Whitfield. Serindia, 2004. An evocatively illustrated account of the intrepid adventures and amazing discoveries of the great explorer and archaeologist Sir Aurel Stein.

Life Along the Silk Road by Susan Whitfield. University of California Press, 2001. Really brings alive the Silk Road at its heyday, with entertaining accounts of the lives of ten of its inhabitants. Very readable and hides meticulous scholarship in crafting the stories.

Silk Road: Monks, Warriors and Merchants on the Silk Road by Luce Boulnois. Odyssey Books & Guides, 2007. The English version of the best selling French classic account of the history of the Silk Road.

Silk Road: Xi'an to Kashgar by Judy Bonavia. Odyssey Books & Guides, 2008. An authoritative and beautifully illustrated guide to travel along the Chinese section of the Silk Road, covering the many interweaving routes that began in Xi'an and wound their way towards Central Asia.

The Silk Road: Two Thousand Years in the Heart of Asia by Frances Wood. University of California Press, 2003. An excellent and clear account of the history of the Silk Road and its place in the context of world history of the period.

TRAVELLERS

Nasir Khusraw – The Ruby of Badakhshan: A Portrait of the Persian Poet, Traveller and Philosopher by Alice C.Hunsberger. I.B. Travis, 2003. A very readable study of one of the foremost poets of the Persian language, and a major Ismaili thinker. Nasir Khushraw (born 1004 in what is now Tajikistan) undertook and described a journey from Central Asia to Mecca and back to Badakhshan.

THE NOMADIC EMPIRES
Genghis Khan – Life, Death and Resurrection by John Man. St Martins Griffin, 2007. A lively and readable account of the life and legacy of one of the great conquerors. *Tamerlane: Sword of Islam, Conqueror of the World* by Justin Marozzi. Harper Collins, 2005. An engaging mixture of history, travelogue and contemporary portraiture of a complex man. *The Empire of the Steppes – A History of Central Asia* by Rene Grousset. Marboro, 1988. The great classic masterpiece account of the nomad empires of Attila, Ghenghis Khan and Tamerlane.

FOOTNOTES

BSG – Bulletin de la Société de Géographie, Paris

RGS – Royal Geographical Society, London

GJ – Geographical Journal (of the RGS)

JRGS – Journal of the RGS

PRGS – Proceedings of the RGS

IOLR – India Office Library and Records, London

IRGS – Imperial Russian Geographical Society

IIRGS – 'Izvestia' ('Bulletin') of the IRGS

Introduction
[1] Guillaume Capus, *Le Toit du Monde*, Paris 1890, p. vi. See Chapter 6, part 2.

Chapter 1 – The First Inhabitants of the Pamirs and Early Trade Routes
[1] See Louis Dupree, "Prehistoric Research in Afghanistan (1959–1966)", *Transactions of the American Philosophical Society*, New Series Volume 62, Part 4, Philadelphia 1972.

[2] V. Ranov and M. Bubnova, 'Uncovering the History of the Roof of the World', *American Journal of Archaeology*, Vol. 65, No. 4 (Oct. 1961) pp. 396–397.

[3] 'On the Afghan Frontier: A Reconnaissance in Shughan', *GJ*, Vol. XVI No.6, December 1900, p. 679.

[4] Herodotus, *The Histories*, Penguin Classics, 2003, pp. 258–264 and passim.

[5] *History of the Civilizations of Central Asia*, Vol. II, UNESCO Paris 1994, p. 315.

[6] P.B. Golden, "Al-Sakaliba", *Encyclopedia of Islam*, 2nd edition, vol. viii, 1995, 876–887.

[7] 'Barba e capelli rossi' in the original – translation by Sir Henry Yule, *Cathay and the Way Thither – Being a collection of Medieval Notices of China*, Hakluyt Society London 1916, Vol IV, p. 210 (Reprint by Munshiram Manoharlal, New Delhi, 1998).

[8] T.E. Gordon, *The Roof of the World*, London 1876, p. 135; and Ralph T. Cobbold, *Innermost Asia*, London 1900, p. 192.

[9] *BSG*, 1879, 6e Série, Tome 17e, p. 252.

[10] T.A. Joyce, "Notes on the physical anthropology of Chinese Turkestan and the Pamirs" in *Journal of the Royal Anthropological Institute*, vol. xlii, London, July–Dec. 1912: reprinted in Stein, *Serindia: detailed report of explorations in Central Asia and westernmost China*, Vol. 3, Oxford 1921, pp. 1352–89. See http://dsr.nii.ac.jp/toyobunko/VIII-5-B2-9/V-3/page/0329.html.en.

[11] Sir Aurel Stein, *Ruins of Desert Cathay*, London 1912, vol. I. p.89 (quoted in Yule, *Cathay and the Way Thither*).

[12] K.M. Baipakov, T.V. Savalieva and K. Chang, Средневековые города и поселения северо-восточного жетысу *(Medieval towns and settlements in north-east Semirechye)*, Ministry of Education, Almaty 2005, pp. 181–187.

[13] 'Markansu' means 'valley of death'.

[14] Interview with Mira Alexeyevna Bubnova, Dushanbe, July 2005, who referred to recent work by Zadniprovsky and herself, updating earlier research by Bernshtam and Litvinsky.

[15] Xian (called Changan in the Han and Tang dynasties) is located in the central area of the Northwest of China, and is now the capital of Shaanxi Province.

[16] About 200km?

[17] Histories, chapter 12: quoted by Sir Henry Yule in *Cathay and the way thither : being a collection of medieval notices of China*, Vol. 1, London 1866, p. cxlix.

[18] Smith's *Dictionary of Greek and Roman Geography*, 1873.

[19] Quoted by Dr. Nicolas Severtzow in "Les anciens itinéraires à travers le Pamir", *Bulletin de la Société de Géographie (BSG)*, Paris, 3e trimestre 1890, pp.426–7.

[20] Stein, *Innermost Asia. Detailed report of explorations in Central Asia, Kan-su and Eastern Iran*. (Oxford: Clarendon Press 1928; Vol. II, p. 848).

[21] Xuanzang referred to the city as Che-shih. Other Chinese chronicles mention a possession called Shi or Chzheshi with a capital with the same name since the 5th century CE.

[22] Prof. J-B. Pacquier considered that this was the route taken by Marco Polo: "Je n'hésite pas à croire que Marco Polo se trouvait là dans le voisinage de cette grande voie de commerce, qui par la *Vallis Comedarum* aboutissait au pied de l'Imaüs. Il n'a pas dû s'aventurer à la légère, l'espace de cinquante journées de marche, dans un pays complètement inconnu. Arrivé au haut de la vallée de Chihgnan, il trouva sans doute un chemin tout tracé qui conduisait dans la petite Boukharie. C'était là la route la plus suivie dans l'antiquité pour se rendre de la Bactriane dans la Sérique; et Ptolémée nous en a, pour ainsi dire, posé les jalons, d'après Marin de Tyr, par la *Vallis Comedarum* (vallée du Chihgnan actuel); la *Turris Lapidea* et la *Statio Mercatorum* (aux environs de Tashkurgan, la capitale de la province actuelle du Sar-i-Kol)." (I have no hesitation in believing that Marco Polo was in the neighbourhood of that great commercial road, which by the 'Vallis Comedarum' reached the foot of the Imaues. He probably did not venture on a journey of fifty marches in an unknown country. At the top of the Shihgnan Valley, he doubtless found a road marked out to Little Bukharia. This was the road followed in ancient times from Bactrian to Serica; and Ptolemy has, so to speak, given us its landmarks after Marinus of Tyre, by the 'Vallis Comedarum' (Valley of actual Shihgnan); the 'Turris Lapidea' and the 'Statio Mercatorum', neighbourhood of Tashkurgan, capital of the present province of Sar-i-kol.) (*Bulletin de la Société de Géographie*, 6e Série, Vol. XII., Paris 1876, p. 126 – translation by Henri Cordier.)

Chapter 2 – Chinese Travellers in the Pamirs

[1] Jaxartes (Syr-Daria), Oxus (Amu-Darya), Indus and Tarim rivers? See, for example, *Genesis* 2: 10 "…and a river went out of Eden to water the garden and from thence it was parted and became into four heads." Similar accounts can be found in the Avesta and other Zoroastrian texts.

[2] Trans. A.C. Graham, *The Book of Lieh-tzu: A Taoist Classic* (New York: Columbia University Press, 1990), pp. 102–103.

[3] The book no longer exists but is referenced in *Shan Hai Zin, Leizi: Mu Wang Zhuan*, and *Shiji* (see below).

[4] Friedrich Hirth, *China and the Roman Orient: Researches into their Ancient and Mediaeval Relations as Represented in Old Chinese Records* (Shanghai & Hong Kong, 1885). See East Asian History Sourcebook: *Chinese Accounts of Rome, Byzantium and the Middle East*, c. 91 BCE–1643 CE on http://www.fordham.edu/halsall/eastasia/romchin1.html

[5] The Yuezhi were probably identical with the Kushans who, from the second century BCE, established an empire that included much of the territory of present-day Afghanistan, Tajikistan, Pakistan and Western China.

[6] The *Shiji* were begun by Sima Tan, the father of Sima Qian (d. ca. 110 BCE), and continued by the son. See the translation by Burton Watson in *Records of the Grand Historian of China* 2 vols. (Columbia Univ., 1961) – reprinted in Alfred J. Andrea and James H. Overfield, *The Human Record: Sources of Global History*, 3rd ed., Vol. I: To 1700, (Boston; Houghton Mifflin, 1998) pp. 164–167. Available on http://campus.northpark.edu/history/Classes/Sources/ZhangQian.PS.html.

[7] http://en.wikipedia.org/wiki/Image:ZhangQianTravels.jpg.

[8] Almost identical language was used 2,000 years later by the Russian Consul in Kashgar in response to a request to allow a British officer to travel through Russian Turkestan (see Chapter 6).

[9] "The Ta-Yuan were probably the descendants of the Greek colonies that were established by Alexander the Great in Ferghana in 329 BCE, and prospered within the Hellenistic realm of the Seleucids and Greco-Bactrians, until they were isolated by the migrations of the Yueh-Chih around 160 BCE. It has also been suggested that the name 'Yuan' was simply a transliteration of the words 'Yona', or 'Yavana', used throughout antiquity in Asia to designate Greeks ('Ionians'), so that Ta-Yuan (lit. 'Great Yuan') would mean 'Great Ionians'. The interaction between the Ta-Yuan and the Chinese is historically crucial, since it represents the first major contact between an urbanized Indo-European culture and the Chinese civilization, opening the way to the formation of the Silk Road that was to link the East and the West in material and cultural exchange from the 1st century BCE to the 15th century." (http://www.reference.com/browse/wiki/Ta-Yuan.)

[10] Watson, *Records of the Grand Historian of China*.

[11] "Hence it came to pass that the Arimaspi drove the Issedonians from their country, while the Issedonians dispossessed the Scyths; and the Scyths, pressing upon the Cimmerians, who dwelt on the shores of the Southern Sea, forced them to leave their land." Herodotus, *Histories* Book IV

[12] *Han Shu*, as translated by A. Wylie in the *Journal of the Anthropological Institute of Great Britain and Ireland*, Vols. III (1874), pp. 401–452, V (1876), pp. 41–80, and X (1881), pp. 20–73, and XI (1882), pp. 83–115, accessible on http://depts.washington.edu/uwch/silkroad/texts/hantxt1.html#yueshi

[13] *The Peoples of the West from the Weilue by Yu Huan: A Third Century Chinese Account Composed between 239 and 265 CE; Quoted in zhuan 30 of the Sanguozhi, Published in 429 CE*, draft English translation by John E. Hill, September, 2004, on http://depts.washington.edu/uwch/silkroad/texts/weilue/weilue.html

[14] The text was discovered by Heinrich Julius Klaproth in 1816 and published in a French translation by Jean Pierre Abel Remusat in 1836, in which Klaproth collaborated. An English translation (*The Travels of Fah-Hian*) was made by Samuel Beal and published in London in 1869 (and, in a revised version, in 1884) – included in *Buddhist Records of the Western World*, Munshiram Manoharlal Publishers, New Delhi 2004.

[15] *The Mission of Sung-Yun and Hwei-Sang to obtain Buddhist books in the West (518 AD)*. Translated by Samuel Beal, London 1884 – also included in *Buddhist Records of the Western World*, Munshiram Manoharlal Publishers, New Delhi 2004.

[16] The *li* corresponds to 415.8 metres (see the note on measurements in John Hill's translation of the *Weilue* on http://depts.washington.edu/uwch/silkroad/texts/weilue/weilue.html).

[17] See http://www.ncbi.nlm.nih.gov/entrez/query.fcgi?CMD=Display&DB=pubmed and http://www.shef.ac.uk/~capra/4/treasures.html)

[18] Less common romanisations of Xuanzang include Hsüan-tsang, San-tsang, Yuanzang Hhuen Kwan, Hiouen Thsang, Hiuen Tsiang, Hsien-tsang, Hsuan Chwang, Hwen Thsang, Xuan Cang, Xuan Zang, Shuen Shang, Yuan Chang and Yuen Chwang; he is also known as Chen Yi, or Mokshadeva, or Muchatipo.
See http://www.britannica.com/eb/topic?idxStructId=274015&typeId=13 and http://xuanzang.iqnaut.net.

[19] *Ta-t'ang-si-yu-ki*: translated by Samuel Beal in *Buddhist Records of the Western World* (London: Trubner & Co. Ltd., 1884), available on the Silk Road Seattle website: http://depts.washington.edu/uwch/silkroad/texts/xuanzang.html

[20] For a lively account of the conflicting theories, see Curzon *The Pamirs and the Source of the Oxus*.

[21] Tukhara in Sanskrit, Tokharistan in Arabic: Scythian Bactria. Elsewhere, Xuanzang writes: "This country, from north to south, is about 1000 *li* or so in extent, from east to west 3000 *li* or so. On the east it is bounded by the T'sung-ling mountains, in the west it touches on Po-li-sse (Persia), on the south are the great Snowy Mountains, on the north the Iron Gates. The great river Oxus flows through the midst of this country in a westerly direction."

[22] *History of the Civilizations of Central Asia*, Vol. III, UNESCO Paris 1996, p. 362. The authors (Mu Shun-ying and Wang Yao) also note that, according to some records "the Tibetans may also have invaded India in search of relics of the Buddha in Magadha and set up an iron column on the Ganges."

[23] *A Chinese Expedition Across the Pamirs and Hindukush*, AD 747, Indian Antiquary, 1923, accessible on http://ccbs.ntu.edu.tw/FULLTEXT/JR-ENG/aurel.htm.

[24] Edouard Chavannes in *Documents sur les Turcs Occidentaux* St. Petersburg 1903. The Western Turks, also known as the 'Oghuz', were among the indigenous Turks of Central Asia who from the 9th to the 12th centuries CE migrated towards western Asia and eastern Europe via Transoxiana. They were the founders and rulers of several important Turkic kingdoms and empires, the most notable of them being the Seljuks, and the Ottomans.

[25] At its height, the rule of the Tang dynasty extended to Kabul ('Tohuolu') in Afghanistan, and as far west as the Aral Sea and the Caspian Sea

[26] China's first mosque was established at Xian, the capital city of the Han dynasty, and still stands today.

Chapter 3 – From the Arab Invasion to the 19th Century

[1] The dates given in this section are approximate as there is no firm evidence.

[2] According to the Scottish orientalist, H.A.R. Gibb, Qutaiba-ibn-Muslim certainly never penetrated as far as Kashgar and even Arab raids on the city may be the stuff of legend rather than fact. Islam was not introduced to Kashgar until the 10th century. See 'The Arab Invasion of Kashgar' in *Bulletin of the School of Oriental Studies*, University of London, Vol. 2 No. 3 (1922), pp. 467–474.

[3] Arabic, having no letter 'p', often changes the Persian 'p' to 'f' or 'b' (e.g. Yakut Al-Hamawi writes of 'Banjshir' in Afghanistan).

[4] Nicolas Severtzow, *Les Anciens Itinéraires à travers le Pamir, Société de Géographie*, Paris, 3e trimestre 1890. The river that bears the name Vakhsh today is one of the major tributaries of the Panj/Amu-Darya and it, in turn, is fed by the Kyzyl Su (as it is known in Kyrgyz in the Alai) and Surkhob (in Tajik, as its continuation in the Karategin/Rasht is known) – in English 'red river', from the red alluvial sand it carries throughout its course.

[5] V.V. Barthold, *Turkestan*.

[6] A.E. Snessareff, "Religion und Gebräuche der Bergvölker des westlichen Pamir," in *Keleti Szemle*, Band IX, Budapest 1908: reproduced by Markus Hauser, *Pamir Archive*.

[7] See *The Rubies and Spinels of Afghanistan – A brief history*, by Richard W. Hughes on http://www.ruby-sapphire.com/afghanistan-ruby-spinel.htm; http://www.bgd.gea.uni-sofia.bg/materiali04/Kostov.pdf and http://members.tripod.com/~wzzz/MASUDI.html

[8] Sarfaroz Niyozov, "Shia Ismaili Tradition in Central Asia: Evolution, Continuities and Changes. in Central Asia and Caucasus." *Journal of Social and Political Studies* No. 6 (24). pp. 39–47.

[9] In Persian, *Khorasan* means "whence the sun comes" and the name was given to the eastern province of Persia during the Sasanid empire.

[10] "Poetic form developed in pre-Islamic Arabia and perpetuated throughout Islamic literary history into the present. It is a laudatory, elegiac, or satiric poem that is found in Arabic, Persian, and many related Asian literatures. The classic *qasida* is an elaborately structured ode of 60 to 100 lines, maintaining a single end rhyme that runs through the entire piece." (Encyclopaedia Britannica)

[11] Alice C. Hunsberger, *Nasir Khusraw – The Ruby of Badakhshan*, I.B. Tauris, London, 2000; in association with the Institute of Ismaili Studies.

[12] Nasir Khusraw, *Diwan* (edited by Said Husein Taqizoda), Tehran: Simoi Donish Publishing House, 1378 (hijri), pp. 320–321.

[13] Venus is 'Zuhra' in Tajik. "As part of the Abrahamic tradition, Nasir refers to the common concepts for the three religions. He also uses ideas from Greek and Persian literature. As Parvez Moruwedge points out in his introduction to *Knowledge and Liberation* ('Kushoish wa Rahoish', edited by F. M Hunzai, 1998), he is one of the global thinkers of his time." (Note by Sarfaroz Niyozov)

[14] Nasir Khusraw, *Diwan*, p. 344.

[15] Nasir Khusraw, *Diwan*, p. 462.

[16] Nasir Khusraw, *Diwan*, p. 299.

[17] V. Ivanow, *Nasir-i Khusraw and Ismailism*, Series B No. 5, Section 5; edited for the 'Ismaili Society', Bombay; accessible on http://www.ismaili.net/Source/khusraw/nk2/nasir_kusraw2.html.

[18] Yule, *The Travels of Marco Polo*, Introductory Notice 19

[19] In the nineteenth century, the name Bolor gave rise to much scholarly speculation about ancient kingdoms and regions, well summarised by Henry Yule in *JRGS*, Vol 42 (1872), pp.473–480. George Nathaniel Curzon concluded that there was no kingdom of Bolor, but that the name was applied "throughout the Middle Ages to the elongated belt of mountain country south of the main range of the Hindu Kush, including the valleys of Kafiristan, Upper Chitral, Yasin, Gilgit, and Hunza-Nagar (and in the pages of some writers having an even wider application)." (*The Pamirs and the Source of the Oxus, GJ*, Vol. 8, No. 3, 1896) The name may even have arisen from a misunderstanding: the pundit Faiz Buksh (see Chapter 5) suggests a link with the Turkic word 'Bilur' (crystal), or 'Bulut' (cloud).

[20] See, for example, Prof. J-B. Paquier, 'Itinéraire de Marco Polo à travers la région du Pamir au XIII e siècle' (Marco Polo's itinerary across the Pamirs in the 13th century), *Bulletin de la Société Géographique*, 6e Série, Paris August 1876, pp.113–128.

[21] *Ancient Khotan : detailed report of archaeological explorations in Chinese Turkestan* – Vol. 1 1907, p. 24. See http://dsr.nii.ac.jp/toyobunko/VIII-5-B2-7/V-1/page/0056.html.en.

[22] The 3rd century Chinese traveller, Yu Huan, described three routes to the West: the southern one went "through the Congling [the Pamirs], and through the Xuandu [the 'Hanging Passages'] to enter (the territory of) the Da Yuezhi [Kushans]."

[23] See, for example, Frances Wood, *Did Marco Polo go to China*, Westview Press, 1998. The famous explorer and naturalist Alexander von Humboldt (1769–1859) was also an early sceptic: "How is it that he does not say that he himself had seen how the flames disperse and leap about, as I myself have so often experienced at similar altitudes in the Cordilleras of the Andes, especially when investigating the boiling-point of water?" (*Asie Centrale*, Vol 1., 1843, p. 588) – quoted by Henri Cordier in his notes to the Badakhshan chapter of *The Book of Ser Marco Polo the Venetian concerning the Kingdoms and Marvels of the East*, trans. and ed. by Henry Yule, 3rd ed. revised by Henri Cordier, London: John Murray, 1903).

[24] Ian Blanchard, "The Middle Ages – A Concept too Many?", Inaugural Lecture (Edinburgh, 1996) – accessible on www.esh.ed.ac.uk/CEU/paper1.pdf .

[25] From the middle of the 12th to the end of the 13th century it was widely believed in Europe that a wealthy and powerful Christian potentate called Prester John, ruled over vast territories in the far East. An account of Prester John was also given by other medieval travellers to China, including the Franciscan monk Odoric of Pordenone.

[26] Account by P. du Jarric, quoted by Sir Henry Yule, *Cathay and the Way Thither – Being a collection of Medieval Notices of China*, Hakluyt Society London 1916, Vol IV, pp. 174–175 (Reprint by Munshiram Manoharlal, New Delhi, 1998).

[27] Yule, *Cathay and the Way Thither*, pp. 213–214.

[28] *Cathay and the Way Thither*, p.179.

[29] C. Wessels, *Early Jesuit Travellers in Central Asia (1603–1721).*, First published in 1924, The Hague (Reprint: Asian Educational Services AES, New Delhi 1992); and *An Account of Tibet – The Travels of Ippolito Desideri of Pistoia S.J., 1712–1727*, London

Chapter 4 – The Great Game – Myth or Reality?

[1] Political officers – many of whom were Army officers on secondment – were responsible for the civil administration of frontier districts in India.

[2] Rawlinson was at that time facing a Persian army in Kandahar and its Russian 'advisers'.

[3] *The Making of a Frontier*, Algernon Durand, London 1899, p. 88.

[4] Bernard Pares, *A History of Russia*, London 1965, p.428.

[5] In 1800, three months before his death, Tsar Paul had ordered the conquest of India.

[6] Hopkirk, p.204.

[7] As we shall see later in Chapter 5, Ney Elias was a notable exception to this practice and his career probably suffered as a result.

[8] Wilhelm Filchner, *Ein Ritt über den Pamir*, Berlin 1903, p. 33.

[9] Murghab is still a meteorological station and, surprising as it may seem, it is possible, by consulting CNN and other websites giving international weather, to find the weather forecast for the high Pamir plateau.

[10] *The Quarterly Review*, October 1865 (reprinted in *England and Russia in the East*, London 1875, p. 145).

[11] *PRGS*, Vol 15 No. 3 (1870–1871), pp 198–199.

[12] Although Dost Mohammed may have hoped to strengthen his negotiating hand with the British, it is difficult to see how he could have refused to see the Russian envoy.

[13] Gerald Morgan, *Anglo-Russian Rivalry in Central Asia 1810–1895*, London 1981, p. 36.

[14] The Tripartite Treaty concluded between Auckland, Ranjit Singh, and Shah Shuja in June 1838 provided that the Lahore Government would maintain an auxiliary force of not fewer than 5,000 men to provide support to Shah Shuja'.

[15] *Tournament of Shadows*, p. 63.

[16] Hopkirk, p. 302.

[17] Suhash Chakravarty, *Afghanistan and the Great Game*, Delhi, 2002, p. 14 and Hopkirk, p. 304.

[18] Pares, p. 429.

[19] Morgan, p. 8 – in 1801, Tsar Paul had proposed to Napoleon an alliance against England.

[20] An article by Professor Nigel Allen of the University of California at Davis, in the journal *Post-Soviet Geography and Economics*, 2001, 42, No. 8, pp. 545–560 elucidates this issue by referring to the 'magisterial' Routes in Asia by General Frederick S. Roberts (1878) of the British Army in India, in which Section 2, "*Routes in Afghanistan*" is a reprint of Captain H. Garbett's 1840 report. Prof. Allen points out that "Roberts' compendium, with accompanying maps at different scales, has never been cited by any scholar in the 20th century, yet it remains a pivotal source of information on why the British in India never advanced beyond the crest of the Hindukush as a military force."

[21] The Minute is given in full in Appendix 2 of Morgan, *Anglo-Russian Rivalry*.

[22] *Russian Advances in Asia*, War Office, 1873. Quoted in Chakravarty, p.17.

[23] Quoted in Hopkirk, p. 362.

[24] *Russia in Central Asia*, pp. 120–121.

[25] Hopkirk, pp. 433–34.

[26] *Russia in Central Asia*, p. 297.

[27] Durand, p. 41.

[28] Meeting of the Royal Geographical Society on 23 November 1891 (*Proceedings RGS*, Jan. 7, 1892).

[29] Cobbold, p. 301.

[30] "Statement regarding the recent political States of Maimena, the Petty Chiefs between Balkh and Oxus and Badakhshan", 1872, quoted in Chakravarty, p. 123.

[31] Quoted in A.V. Postnikov, Схватка на «Крыше Мире» – Политики, разведчики и географы в борьбе за Памир в XIX веке (Struggle on the "Roof of the World": Politicians, spies and geographers in the contest for the Pamir in the 19th century), Moscow 2001, p. 120.

[32] Letter from Prince Gorchakov to Lord Granville, quoted in *Indian Frontier Policy*, General Sir John Adye, London 1897.

[33] D.P. Singhal, India and Afghanistan – A Study in Diplomatic Relations, University of Queensland Press, 1963, p. 11. (Reprint by South Asian Publishers, New Delhi, 1982). The author of this excellent but little known book analyses meticulously (and quotes extensively from) the contemporary diplomatic correspondence of the period. His judgements are sound and well-backed.

[34] An expression 'borrowed from Sir James Macintosh by J. Wyllie, an official in the Government of India's Foreign Department' (Morgan, p. 77).

[35] Quoted in Singhal, p. 16.

[36] *Tournament of Shadows*, p. 184.

[37] *Russia in Central Asia*, p. 328, footnote

[38] In 1877, Lytton had already stretched the bounds of propriety by circulating a pamphlet recommending an alliance with Germany against Russia – a breach of protocol that almost led to his immediate recall.

[39] Singhal, p.40.

[40] Morgan, p. 189.

[41] Singhal, p.40.

[42] Mike Davis, *Late Victorian Holocausts – El Niño Famines and the Making of the Third World*, London 2001, p. 34.

[43] Singhal, p.46.

[44] *Russia in Central Asia*, p. 321.

[45] The record of the boundary commission's extraordinarily rapid work can be found in *Northern Afghanistan, or Letters from the Afghan Boundary Commission, with Route Maps*: Bk. 3 C.E. Yate, Rudolf Abraham (Editor), Cambridge 2002, together with all the material and maps from the original 1888 edition, including the plan of Balkh.

[46] Handwritten report by Lieutenant-Colonel Grombchevsky dated 14 March 1891 (cf. http://militera.lib.ru/research/grombchevsky/index.html). See also *PRGS*, Vol. 11, No. 3, pp. 171–4.

[47] Hopkirk, p. 470.

[48] IOLR, MSS Eur / F197 / 142.

[49] Quoted in Postnikov, p. 251.

[50] Postnikov, p. 248.

[51] The words chosen by the distinguished Central Asian scholar Paul Bergne.

[52] Postnikov, p. 232.

[53] "*Note On the Question of Delimitation on the Upper Oxus Territories*" IOLR , Curzon Collection, MSS Eur F111 / 113, paras 7–8.

[54] Postnikov, p. 239.

[55] Postnikov, p. 252.

[56] Singhal, p.147.

[57] Reproduced in Gooch and Temperley, eds. British documents on the origins of the war, 1898–1914, London HMSO, 1927–29, pp. 306–7. See
http://victoria.tc.ca/history/etext/afghan.anglo.russian.html.

[58] Chakravarty, pp. 69–70.

[59] Curzon, *Russia in Central Asia*, p. 45. Curzon also suggests that "the employment of the natives in the construction of the line, and the security they thereby enjoyed of fair and regular pay, has had a great deal to do with the rapid pacification of the country" (p. 50). The extension to Andijan was completed in 1899.

[60] Article on Grombchevsky's travels in *The Asiatic Quarterly Review*, January–April 1892.

[61] Wilhelm Filchner, *Ein Ritt über den Pamir*, Berlin 1903, pp. 75–78

[62] *Russia in Central Asia*, pp. 388–389.

[63] Hopkirk, p. 285 and 501.

[64] Hopkirk, p. 422–3.

[65] Ralph P. Cobbold, *Innermost Asia*, London 1900, pp. 66–67.

[66] The inconsistency of this conclusion, in the light of the similar distance between London and Delhi, seems to have escaped Ripon.

[67] Quoted in Singhal, p. 95.

[68] Chakravarty, p. 221.

[69] Hopkirk, p.307.

[70] Quoted by Curzon, *Russia in Central Asia*, pp. 85–86.

[71] *Russia's March Towards India*, by 'An Indian Officer', London, Sampson Low, Maeston & Company (Limited), 1894, Part II, Chapter 12.

[72] Chakravarty, p. 231.

[73] Cobbold, pp. 67–68.

[74] *Russia in Central Asia*, p. 356.

[75] See the splendid summary of their adventures in Fitzroy MacLean, *A Person from England and Other Travellers*, London 1958.

[76] A similar conclusion is suggested by Meyer and Brysac in *Tournament of Shadows* in relation to Tibet (e.g. pp. 423 and 447).

Chapter 5 – Scientific Exploration in the 19th Century

[1] *Quarterly Review*, London April, 1873, p. 548.

[2] *JRGS*, Vol. 48 (1878), p.198.

[3] *Russia in Central Asia*, p. 144.

[4] Ralph P. Cobbold, *Innermost Asia – Travel and Sport in the Pamirs*, London 1900, p. 193.

[5] *JRGS*, Vol. 42 (1872), pp. 478–480

[6] *PRGS*, Vol. 17, No. 2 (1872–1873), pp. 110–112.

[7] *PRGS*, Vol. 10, No. 6 (1865–1866), pp. 301–317.

[8] After reviewing in detail all the evidence, he comments wryly that "it will be a brave man who undertakes to re-examine them."

[9] Others would include Burnes, Bellew and Yate. We have already noted Curzon's racist remarks, which are matched by those of Francis Younghusband who stated publicly in his travelogue *The Heart of a Continent* that "no European can mix with non-Christian races without feeling his moral superiority over them."

[10] Faizabad was, however, rebuilt a few years later after the death of Murad Beg, when Mir Yar Beg, a descendant of the exiled former ruler, returned. The official report on the Havildar's second journey to Badakhshan noted that "from that time until the present it has been fairly prosperous," although the oppression of the population continued.

[11] Sir Aurel Stein (*Ancient Khotan : detailed report of archaeological explorations in Chinese Turkestan* – Vol. 1 1907) pointed out "the same uncertainty of spelling in the case of one of the several alternative native names for Wood's Lake on the Great Pamir." (p.23)." The mountain range to the east of the Great Pamir is, of course, known as the Sarikol Pamir and this designation may well have been used also by the local Kyrgyz in relation to the lake. Stein comments that "this spelling reproduces the pronunciation of the name as generally heard by me during my passage through the district, from both its Tajik (Iranian) and its Kirghiz inhabitants. I am unable to decide how far this modern pronunciation conforms to the etymology of the name; for the derivation is not quite certain. If Mirza Haidar, whose mention is the oldest I can at present trace (*Tarikh-i-Rashidi*, ed. Elias, pages 297, 312), is justified in writing Sarigh-kul, the name would be Turki, meaning 'Yellow-Lake': As kol is a common variation of kul through all dialects of Eastern Turki, and as i for igh would easily be accounted for by the well-known phonetic processes of assimilation and subsequent 'supplementary lengthening', the modern form of the name could be readily explained on the basis of this etymology. But the form Sirikol (Sirikul) is also met with in Oriental records, and has found acceptance among numerous European geographers, perhaps on account of its supposed semi-Persian etymology (Sir-i-kul, 'head of the lake')." See http://dsr.nii.ac.jp/toyobunko/VIII-5-B2-7/V-1/page/0055.html.en.

[12] See *Embajada a Tamerlan*, Miraguano Ediciones, Madrid 1984.

[13] Sidi Ali actually got as far as Taloqan, from where he crossed the Oxus to Kulob. His account of his travels can be accessed on http://www.columbia.edu/itc/mealac/pritchett/00generallinks /sidialireis (*Mirat ul-Memalik*, translated by A. Vambéry and published in London in 1899).

[14] Jenkinson was the main agent of the Muscovy Company, the first major joint-stock English trading company, formed in 1555 by the navigator and explorer Sebastian Cabot and various London merchants.

[15] C. Wessels, *Early Jesuit Travellers in Central Asia* (1603–1721). First published in 1924, The Hague (Reprint: Asian Educational Services AES, New Delhi 1992); and *An Account of Tibet – The Travels of Ippolito Desideri of Pistoia S.J.*, 1712–1727, London 1937 (Reprint: AES, 2005).

[16] Born in 1829, Adolph Schlagintweit was the second son of a family of distinguished scholars and explorers. In 1854, on the recommendation of Alexander von Humboldt, three of the Schlagintweit brothers (Robert, Hermann and Adolph) were chosen by the East India Company to map parts of India and the Himalayas. (*See Results of a Scientific Mission to India and High Asia*, Leipzig, 1860–1866 and http://www.schlagintweit.de/engl/easien.htm – the exquisite illustrations by Herrmann Schlagintweit can be found on this site and are also accessible, together with the maps on http://dsr.nii.ac.jp/toyobunko/XII-4-2.) Adolph was the first European to visit Kashgar since Marco Polo, but, suspected of being a Chinese spy, was put to death by Vali Khan, ruler of Kashgar. His head was later recovered and brought by a Persian traveller to the British authorities in India, inspiring the closing scene in Rudyard Kipling's story *The Man Who Would Be King*.

[17] Derek Waller, *The Pundits – British Exploration of Tibet and Central Asia*, University Press of Kentucky, 1990, p. 22. I am especially grateful to Professor Waller for his generosity in sharing with me some of the source material for his book.

[18] *PRGS*, Vol 15 No. 3 (1870–1871), p. 203.

[19] 'Pundit' is the Hindi word for an educated person; the equivalent in Arabic (used for Muslim Indians) is 'Munshee', 'Moonshee' or 'Munshi'.

[20] T.G. Montgomerie, '*On the Geographical Position of Yarkund and Other Places in Central Asia*', Proceedings of the Royal Geographical Society (PRGS) Vol. 10, No. 4, 1865–1866, pp. 162–165.

[21] *Proceedings of the Government of India*, Foreign Department Political, 1861, P/204/55, pp. 91–101; and 'Report of a Journey to Kokan' in *Records of the Government of India*, Foreign Department, No. 39, Calcutta 1863. (India Office Library and Records, ref. IOR V/23/7).

[22] See 'Route from Jellalabad to Yarkand Through Chitral, Badakhshan and Pamir Steppe, Given by Mohamed Amin of Yarkand, with Remarks by G.S.W. Hayward,' *PRGS*, Vol. 13, No. 2, (1868–1869), pp. 122–130.

[23] Both were married to daughters of Nazir Khyroola, a merchant of Bukhara, who had interceded on behalf of Stoddart and Conolly after they were arrested by the Emir of Bukhara and was thus in favour with the British.

[24] 'Report of a Journey to Kokan', section 15.

[25] Postnikov, p. 74.

[26] 'Report of the Mirza's Exploration of the Route from Caubul to Kashgar'; PRGS Vol. 15 No. 3, (1870–1871), pp. 181–204; Major T. Montgomerie, *Report on the Trans-Himalayan Explorations in Connection with the Great Trigonometrical Survey of India during 1869*, Cambridge University Library, Mayo Papers, MS Add. 7490/48/14; and *JRGS* 41, 1871, pp. 132-93. Another pundit, Munphool, was in Badakhshan in 1867, but his report (*JRGS*, Vol. 42, 1872, pp. 440–448) dealt mainly with the physical resources of the region, and gives general information on its history, geography and political situation but nothing about his route or the circumstances of his travel: since he does not appear to have been trained in surveying, the primary purpose of his journey was probably private.

[27] Another local remedy for altitude sickness, used frequently by drivers on the Pamir Highway, is 'kurut', a hard ball of cheese, available in most Central Asian markets.

[28] For the Mirza's report, see Major T. Montgomerie, *Report on the Trans-Himalayan Explorations in Connection with the Great Trigonometrical Survey of India during 1869*, Cambridge University Library, Mayo Papers, Add 7490 p. liii – also JRGS 41, 1871, 132–93.

[29] See 'Journey from Peshawar to Kashgar and Yarkand in Eastern Turkestan, or Little Bokhara, through Afghanistan, Balkh, Badakhshan, Wakhan, Pamir and Sarkol', *JRGS*, 42 (1872) 448–73. Another pundit, Ibrahim Khan, also joined the mission, travelling from Srinagar through Gilgit and Yasin to the Little Pamir, and from there to Tashkurgan, but his report is also somewhat uninformative. ('Route of Ibrahim Khan from Kashmir Through Yassin to Yarkand in 1870', PRGS, Vol. 15, No. 5 (1870–71) pp. 387–392.)

[30] 'A Havildar's Journey through Chitral to Faizabad in 1870', *JRGS*, Vol. 42 (1872), pp. 184–185.

[31] *JRGS*, Vol. 42 (1872), p. 190.

[32] For the Havildar's second trip to Badakhshan, see: Captain Henry Trotter, 'The Havildar's Journey from Badakhshan to Kolab, Darwaz, and Kubodian' in *Report on Trans-Himalayan Exploration by Employees of the GTS of India during 1873–74–75*, Calcutta 1886, pp. 4–20; also Trotter's note in *GJ*, Vol. 48 no. 3, 1916, p. 229.

[33] Derek Waller, *The Pundits – British Exploration of Tibet & Central Asia*, University Press of Kentucky, 1990, p. 92.

[34] 'On the Geographical Results of the Mission to Kashgar, under Sir T. Douglas Forsyth in 1873–74', *JRGS*, Vol. 48 (1878), pp. 210–217.

[35] Waller, p. 158.

[36] 'Narrative of Munshi Abdul Subhan's Journey from Panjeh to Shighnan and Roshan with a short account of his return to India via Kabul' in *Political and Secret Letters and Enclosures received from India*, Vol. 4, filed with no. 22 (India, 21 June 1875), 393–422, India Office Library and Records, ref. L/P+S/7/4.

[37] Today, the fortress in Yamchun is in a better state of repair, Kahkaha having been occupied by the Russian borderguards for several years.

[38] See Chapter 1, p. 267 where it is suggested that this is the route described by Maës Titianus and reported by Ptolemy.

[39] The Munshi reported that the local inhabitants drink "very freely of a strong red wine somewhat like curaçoa [sic], large quantities of which are manufactured in the country from cherries." Trotter adds that "fondness for wine is a failing very prevalent among the Shia or unorthodox Mahometans of Central Asia."

[40] Identified by Trotter as the *Sir*, by Moulvi Imama Afzul Khorassani.

[41] *Reports of Trans-Himalayan Explorations in Badakhshan* (1883), India Office Room 0011, C.2c. Survey General's Office, Library General Number 7372.

[42] It would have been virtually impossible to retrace the footsteps of Mukhtar Shar (and the other pundits) without the superb new map of the Pamirs by Markus Hauser (http://www.geckomaps.com).

[43] The landslide that created the Sarez lake occurred in 1911 and, at the time of Mukhtar Shah's survey, the village of Sarez still existed.

[44] *JRGS*, Vol. 48 (1878), p. 205.

[45] Quoted in *Tournament of Shadows*, p. 407.

[46] 'Sher/shir' is Farsi (and Urdu) for 'lion and 'babur/babbar' for 'tiger'.

[47] Reports of Trans-Himalayan Explorations in Badakhshan, p. 7 and p. 22.

[48] Dix Années de Voyages dans l'Asie Centrale et l'Afrique Equatoriale, Paris 1885.

[49] Gerald Morgan, *Ney Elias – Explorer and envoy extraordinary in High Asia*, London 1971.

[50] Ney Elias: 'Notes of a Journey to the New Course of the Yellow River in 1868', *JRGS*, 1870; and 'A Journey through Western Mongolia', *JRGS*, 1873.

[51] See Section 'What to See: Khorog and the Ghunt Valley (Shughnan)', page 589.

[52] *Report of a Mission to Chinese Turkestan and Badakhshan in 1885–86*, by Ney Elias. Political Agent on special duty ', British Library (IOLR F111/378) and 'Pamir Journey 1885–6', RGS Archive (Ney Elias Special Collection NE33).

[53] 'Pamir Journey', p.57. See, however, Ivanov's report below.

[54] Cobbold, pp. 176–180.

[55] Cobbold, p. 158.

Chapter 6 Part 1 – The Russian Expeditions

[1] "The Pamirs and the Source of the Oxus", *GJ*, Vol. 8, No. 3, September 1896, p. 256.

[2] A comprehensive list of materials collected and reports produced by Soviet expeditions to the Pamirs in the period 1928–1935 was published by the Academy of Sciences in Moscow in 1936: the list alone ran to 200 pages! (Памир – Таджикистан – Средняя Азия: Обзор Трудов и Материалов Экспедиций 1932–1935 и 1928–1932 гг. – *'Pamir – Tajikistan – Central Asia : List of Works and Materials from the Expeditions of 1932–1935 and 1928–1932'*).

[3] The Russian "verst" is equivalent to 1,066 metres.

[4] This and subsequent quotations from Fedchenko's reports are from Памир (The Pamirs), Moscow, 1987 (available on http://www.chakhma.narod.com/pamir/pamir.htm).

[5] *Mittheilungen des Vereins für Erdkunde zu Leipzig*, 1872, pp. 7–8. The territory known by the ancient geographers as "Wachia" is still known locally as "Wachio".

[6] Summarised by de Khanikoff for the French Société de Géographie (*BSG*, 1872, pp. 60–64).

[7] This and subsequent quotations from Kostenko's report are from *JRGS*, Vol. 47 (1877), pp. 17–47. A summary – based on the *Russische Revue* No. 12, 1876, was also published by the SdG in 1877.

[8] "Памир и Алай" (Pamir and Alai), Живописная Россия (Picturesque Russia), T.10, Русская Средняя Азия (Russian Central Asia), St. Petersburg-Moscow, 1885, pp. 299–322.

[9] See *BSG*, Paris, 1879, pp. 527–9.

[10] Curzon, *The Pamirs and the Source of the Oxus*, p. 80.

[11] See also *PRGS* 1882, Vol. IV, pp. 412–417.

[12] In 1884, reports on Regel's 1883 travels were published in the *Izvestia* (Proceedings) of the IRGS (Vol. XX, pp. 268–273: "Путешествие в Шугнан" – "Travel to Shughnan") and in *Petermann's Geographische Mittheilungen* (pp. 86–89 and 332–334). See also: *RGS* 1886, ref. mr Tajikistan S.9 – 542758I (map of 1882 itinerary); and *Izvestia* 1883, Vol. XIX p.332 (provisional report of Shughnan itinerary with map).

[13] *IIRGS*, 1884, summarised by Curzon, *The Pamirs and the Source of the Oxus*.

[14] Памир (The Pamirs), Planeta, Moscow, 1987 (extracts on http://www.chakhma.narod.com/pamir/pamir.htm).

[15] Also published by the RGS in 1884: *The Pamir – Illustrating the Russian Explorations in 1883. From a map compiled by M. Bolsheff – translated for the Royal Geographical Society by J.F. Beddeley.* (RGS ref. mr Asia S/S.50).

[16] *IIRGS*, Vol. XX, 1885, p. 230.

[17] Ivanov had given his notes on the Shughnan language to the IRGS. They attracted the attention of one of the leading philological scholars of the time, Karl Germanovich Zaleman, a Baltic German and member of the St. Petersburg Academy of Sciences. In 1890 he succeeded V.V. Radlov as director of the Asiatic Museum in St. Petersburg and became responsible for its rich collection of manuscripts; in the same year he also assumed responsibility for part of the library of the Academy. In 1895, Zaleman published the *Shughnan Glossary of D.L. Ivanov* with his own analyses and commentaries (Восточные заметки [Eastern Notes], St. Petersburg, 1895, pp.269–320).

[18] Handwritten report by Lieutenant-Colonel Grombchevsky dated 14 March 1891 (cf. http://militera.lib.ru/research/grombchevsky/index.html). As we have seen, a year later Petrovsky also prevented Grumm-Grshimailo's party from going into the Wakhan. His motives may have been genuine concern for their safety, but more likely a desire not to exacerbate the already tense relations with the British about the status of the Wakhan.

[19] Ibid.

[20] Letter from Grombchevsky to Veniukoff of 22.10.1889, cited in *Bulletin de la Société de Géographie (BSG)*, 1890, No. 1, pp. 6–7. See also *BSG*, 7e Série, Tome 12e, 1891, p. 417; and *BSG*, 1892, 7e Série, Tome 13e, p. 406–7.

[21] Handwritten report, 14.3.91 – see note 11.

[22] Francis Younghusband, *The Heart of a Continent*, pp. 234–5.

[23] Hopkirk, pp. 457–8.

[24] Article and interview by W. Barnes Steveni in *Asiatic Quarterly Review*, New Series Vol. II, July–October 1891, p. 257–8.

[25] Ibid. pp. 257.

[26] *BSG*, 1890, Nos. 16–17, "Communication de M. Veniukoff", pp. 566–7; BSG 1891, 7e Série, Tome 12e, pp. 416–7; and *BSG*, 1892, 7e Série, Tome 13e, p. 406.

[27] Postnikov, p. 231.

[28] *Asiatic Quarterly Review*, New Series Vol. III, January–April 1892, p. 32.

[29] Grabczewski, Bronislaw: Kaszgaria: Kraj i ludzie, 1924; Przez Pamiry i Hindukusz do ´zródel rzeki Indus, 1925; W pustyniach Raskemu i Tibetu, 1925; Na sluzbie rosyjskiej, 1926. See http://www.routledge-ny.com/ref/travellit/azentriesg2.html.

[30] Памир (The Pamirs), p. 85.

[31] Younghusband, pp. 289–290.

[32] Нива (Field), 1893 No. 47, pp. 1074–75 (see http://zerrspiegel.orientphil.uni-halle.de/t892.html#2).

[33] It will be recalled from Chapter 4 (p. 295) that Younghusband had indeed attempted to raise the Afghans against the Russians.

[34] Нива, 1893 No. 50, pp. 1146–1147 (see http://zerrspiegel.orientphil.uni-halle.de/t893.html).

[35] "Cast off uniforms of all sorts were imported from India by way of Peshawar and used by the Afghan army. One might see Afghan soldiers dressed as railway porters, or even as admirals." (Note by Bijan Omrani.)

[36] Нива, 1895, No. 10, pp. 225–229 (see http://zerrspiegel.orientphil.uni-halle.de/t995.html).

[37] B.L. Tageyev, Русские над Индией. Очерки и рассказы из боевой жизни на Памире (Russians above India. Reports and stories of military life in the Pamirs), St. Petersburg, 1900 – accessible on http://militera.lib.ru/memo/russian/tageev_bl.

[38] *Through Asia*. New York/London: Harper, 1899. Wilhelm Filchner, a German officer whom we shall meet later, was one of the next to describe his impressions.

[39] Памир (The Pamirs), p. 92.

[40] Памир (The Pamirs), pp. 89–90

[41] See: Tageyev memoirs, p. 307–24; N.N. Pokotilo, "Travels in Central and Western Bukhara in 1886," *Proceedings IRGS*, Vol. XXV, No. 5, 1889; Postnikov p. 165; A. Serebrennikov, "Sketch of the Pamir", Военный Сборник (*Military Collection*) St. Petersburg: No. 6, June 1899, p. 443 and Nos. 11–12, November 1899, p. 230; and S.E. Grigoriev and G.S. Kharatishvili, Россия и Афганистан (Russia and Afghanistan) – on http://www.frinc.ru/snp/books/russia_orient/afgan.html.

[42] Сборник Географических, Топографических и Статистических Материалов по Азии. (*Collection of Geographical, Topographical and Statistical Materials throughout Asia*). Volume lvi. Military Scientific Committee of the Russian General Staff, 1894.

[43] Extracts were published in *GJ*, Vol. XVI No.6, December 1900, pp. 666–679. The date in the *GJ* extract is given erroneously as 1892.

[44] Tageyev memoirs, op. cit., Chapter 21.

[45] A. Serebrennikov, "Sketch of Shughnan", Военный Сборник (*Military Collection*) St. Petersburg: Vol. CCXXV, Nos. 11–12, November 1895, p. 175. His numerous articles in this periodical summarise all the then available knowledge of Shughnan, Shakhdara and Wakhan and record in much detail the life of the inhabitants of the Western Pamirs.

[46] *GJ*, Vol. 7, No. 1, January 1896, pp. 92.

[47] A brief summary was published "The Monthly Record" of the *GJ*, Vol. 7, No. 1, January 1896, pp. 91–93. More detail appeared in: "The Proceedings of the Pamir Boundary Commission", *GJ*, Vol. 13, No. 1, January 1899, pp. 50–56; and a letter from Trotter in *GJ*, Vol. 13, No. 4, April 1899, pp. 442–8.

[48] The British were more pessimistic than the Russians about the chances of concluding the work before winter!

[49] *Report on the Proceedings of the Pamir Boundary Commission*, Calcutta 1897. IOLR Mss Eur F111/657.

[50] Памир (The Pamirs), pp. 93–94.

[51] Vladimir Ippolitovich Lipsky, Горная Бухара – результаты трехлетних путешествий в Среднюю Азию в 1896, 1897 и 1899 гг (*Mountain Bukhara – results of journeys over three years in Central Asia in 1896, 1897 and 1899*), St. Petersburg, 1902.

[52] Sergey Ivanovich Kordjinsky, Очерки растительности Туркестана (*Sketches of vegetation of Turkestan*), 1896.

[53] Olga Alexandrovna and Boris Alexeyevich Fedchenko, Флора Памира (*The Flora of the Pamirs*), St. Petersburg, 1901, 1905 and 1906; Материал для флоры Памира и Алайского хребта (*Materials for the Flora of the Pamirs and the Alai Range*) and Материал для флоры Шугнана (*Materials for the Flora of Shughnan*), Botanical Museum of the Academy of Sciences, St. Petersburg.

[54] http://www.alpklubspb.ru/ass/49.htm, http://dipkurier.narod.ru/dip03-2/rusturkestan5.htm and http://vivovoco.rsl.ru/vv/papers/bio/peters.htm.

[55] Памир (Pamirs), p. 81. Yu. D. Golovnina, На Памирах - Записки русской путешественницы. (In the Pamirs – Notes by a Russian Traveller), Moscow 1902. Nicolas de Poggenpohl, "Aux sources du Mouksou par la région montagneuse du Pamir occidental", *La Montagne*, Club Alpin Français, 5e Année, No. 8, 20 August 1909, pp. 461–486.

[56] A. A. Bobrinsky, Горцы Верховьев Пянджа (*Mountain people of the Upper Panj*), Moscow 1908.

[57] http://www.zharov.com/snesarev/index.html and http://george-orden.nm.ru/Port/snesarev.html.

[58] D. Karamshoev and I. Kharkavchuk, Пограничники и Жители Памира, (Borderguards and the People of the Pamirs), Dushanbe 1995.

[59] *GJ*, Vol 48, No. 3, (Sep. 1916), p. 212.

[60] See A.K. Razgonov, По Восточной Бухаре и Памиру (*Across East Bukhara and Pamir*). Tashkent, 1910; and Salavat Iskhakov, Население Памира глазами российских военных (*Pamiri peoples through the eyes of Russian soldiers*), on http://www.kyrgyz.ru/forum/index.php?s=4e9061796ffff9d1ae386054471210f1&showtopic=304

[61] http://enrin.grida.no/htmls/tadjik/soe2/eng/htm/research.htm. This list does not include expeditions of which the main aim was climbing. For information on these adventures, see http://www.alpklubspb.ru and http://www.mountain.ru.

[62] http://www.ipgri.cgiar.org/pgrnewsletter/article_es.asp?id_article=6&id_issue=124 and http://www.vir.nw.ru/history/vavilov.htm.

[63] Памир – Таджикистан – Средняя Азия: Обзор Трудов и Материалов Экспедиций 1932–1935 и 1928–1932 гг. (*Pamir-Tajikistan: Summary of works and materials of the expeditions 1932–1935 and 1928–1932*), Academy of Sciences, Moscow 1936. See also http://www.asia-travel.uz/expedition.html; http://www.alpklubspb.ru/persona/gorbunov.htm;

http://enrin.grida.no/htmls/tadjik/soe2/eng/htm/research.htm and
http://www.alpklubspb.ru/persona/luknickiy.htm and *Pamirs: the north Pamirs and the Fedchenko Glacier*,
Tajik-Pamir Expedition, Leningrad.

Chapter 6 Part 2 – British and other Adventurers and Explorers

[1] *Report of a Mission to Chinese Turkestan and Badakhshan in 1885–86; By Ney Elias, Political Agent on special duty*, Calcutta 1886, IOLR F111/378; Ney Elias, Journal "Pamir Journey 1885–6", *RGS* Archive, ref. NE 33. Gerald Morgan, *Ney Elias. Explorer and Envoy Extraordinary*, London, 1971.

[2] Curzon, p. 77.

[3] Gabriel Bonvalot, "Voyage dans l'Asie Centrale et au Pamir", *BSG*, Paris, 4e trimestre 1890, pp. 469–498; "Aux Indes par terre et à travers le Pamir", Extrait de la *Revue des Deux Mondes*, 1 octobre 1888, pp. 600–631; *Du Caucase aux Indes à travers le Pamir*, Paris 1889; *De Paris au Tonkin à Travers le Tibet Inconnu*, Paris 1891. Guillaume Capus, *Le Toit du Monde* (Pamir), Hachette, Paris 1890.

[4] C.S. Cumberland, *Sport on the Pamir and Turkistan Steppes*, William Blackwood and Sons, Edinburgh and London 1895; GJ, 1896 Vol. v, p. 240. Curzon, pp.78–79. Raymond Casal, *Deux Voyages aux Pamirs*, Paris 1910.

[5] Francis Younghusband, *The heart of a Continent: a narrative of Travels in Manchuria, across the Gobi Desert, through the Himalayas, The Pamirs and Chitral, 1884–94*. London 1896; 'Journeys in the Pamirs and Adjacent Countries.' *PRGS*, xiv (1892), pp. 205–234. Patrick French, *Younghusband – The Last Great Imperial Adventurer*, Harper Collins, London 1994.

[6] St George R. Littledale: 'A Journey Across the Pamir from North to South'. *PRGS*, Vol. XIV. (1892), pp. 1–35; "A Journey across Central Asia", *GJ*, Vol. III, (1894), p. 446; and 'A Journey Across Tibet, From North to South and West to Ladak', *GJ*, 7/5 (1896).

[7] The Earl of Dunmore, *The Pamirs; being a Narrative of a Year's Expedition on Horseback and Foot through Kashmir, Western Tibet, Chinese Tartary and Russian Central Asia*, John Murray, London 1893; and *GJ*, Vol. 2, No. 5 (Nov. 1893), pp. 385–398.

[8] *BSG*, séance du 1.2.1895, 4e trimestre 1895.

[9] Felix de Rocca, *De l'Alaï à l'Amou-Daria*, Paris 1896.

[10] Curzon p. 79; *BSG*, Paris, 1er trimestre 1895.

[11] Sven Hedin, *Through Asia*, 2 vols., London 1898; *My Life as an Explorer*, New York 1926 (reprint by Asian Educational Services, New Delhi, 1998); *Scientific Results of a Journey in Central Asia*, Stockholm, 1905–1906; *Central Asia and Tibet*, London, 1903; and http://www.travelhistory.org/exploration/InUnexploredAsia/InUnexploredAsia01.html.

[12] R.P. Cobbold, *Innermost Asia – Travel and Sport in the Pamirs*, William Heinemann, London 1900.

[13] O. Olufsen, *Through The Unknown Pamirs – The Second Danish Pamir Expedition, 1898–99*, on http://www.iras.ucalgary.ca/~volk/sylvia/Pamir1.htm; O. Olufsen, *The Emir of Bokhara and his country*, London 1911; O. Olufsen, 'Über die dänische Pamir-Expedition im Jahre 1896', *Verhandlungen der Gesellschaft für Erdkunde zu Berlin*, Band XXIV, 1897; O. Olufsen, 'Die zweite dänische Pamir-Expedition', *Verhandlungen der Gesellschaft für Erdkunde zu Berlin*, Band XXVII, 1900; O. Olufsen, *Gennem Pamir*, Kopenhavn 1905; numerous articles in the *Geografisk Tidskrift* of the Royal Danish Geographical Society between 1897 and 1905; see also *Nomads of the Pamir Plateau*, Esther Fihl, London, Thames and Hudson, June 2000; Esther Fihl, *Exploring Central Asia. Collecting Objects and Writing*

Cultures from the steppes to the high Pamirs 1896–1899, Thames & Hudson and Rhodos International, København 2002; also http://www2.adm.ku.dk/kub/kub_www4.puf_inst_liste_aar?p_stedid=4321&p_aar=2002 and http://www.rhodos.com/htmlforlag/mainesther.html.

[14] *BSG*, 1er Semestre 1900, pp. 58–60; Jules Chavanon et Georges Saint-Yves, *Contes cruels des steppes*, Paris 1905.

[15] Wilhelm Filchner, *Ein Ritt über den Pamir*, Berlin 1903; and
http://www.swr.de/swr2/pamir/hintergrund/filchner.html.

[16] *GJ*, Vol 48, No. 3, (Sep. 1916), pp. 193–225; Aurel M. Stein, *Innermost Asia: Detailed report of explorations in Central Asia, Kan-su and Eastern Iran*, 5 vols. Oxford 1928 (Reprint: New Delhi. Cosmo Publications,1981), Chapters XXV and XXVI; and *On Ancient Central-Asian Tracks – Brief Narrative of Three Expeditions in Innermost Asia and North-West China*, London 1933 (reprinted 1964 by Pantheon Books, New York). For Stein's other travels, see *GJ* Vol. 34, No.1 (Jul. 1909), pp. 5-36; Vol. 46, No. 4, (Oct. 1915), pp. 269–276; Vol 47, No.5 (May 1916), pp. 358–364; and *Serindia – Detailed Report Of Explorations In Central Asia And Westernmost China Carried Out And Described Under The Orders Of H.M. Indian Government By Aurel Stein, K.C.I.E.* Oxford 1921 (on http://dsr.nii.ac.jp/toyobunko/VIII-5-B2-9/V-2/page/0007.html.en).

[17] R. Pumpelly (Ed.) Explorations in Turkestan with an account of the basin of eastern Persia and Sistan – Expedition of 1903, under the direction of Raphael Pumpelly, Washington D.C., 1905; and Adventures of Raphael Pumpelly, 1920. See also http://www.lngplants.com/Pumpelly.htm.

[18] Arved von Schultz, *Die Pamirtadschik*, 1914; and *Länderkundliche Forschungen im Pamir*. Hamburg 1916. Von Schultz also produced a map of the Pamirs (1: 750.000) based on the Russian 10 verst map of 1895 (approx. 1:420.000). See also: PGM 1912 and *Abhandlungen des Hamburgischen Kolonial-Instituts*, Band XXXIII.

[19] Willi Rickmer Rickmers, Vorläufiger Bericht über die Pamir-Expedition des Deutschen und Österreichischen Alpenvereins 1913', in *Zeitschrift des Deutschen und Österreichischen Alpenvereins*, Innsbruck 1914. Raimund von Klebelsberg, *Beiträge zur Geologie Westturkestans: Ergebnisse der Expedition des Deutschen und Oesterreichischen Alpenvereins im Jahre 1913*, Innsbruck 1922; and Das Gebirge Peter des Grossen, Utrecht 1929 (http://webapp.uibk.ac.at/alo/cat/collection.jsp?id=5012352

Gabriel Bonvalot 1887

[1] Bonvalot gave a brief account of the expedition to the *Société de Géographie* in Paris on 14 January 1888 ("Voyage dans l'Asie Centrale et au Pamir", published in the *Bulletin de la Société de Géographie*, 4e trimestre 1890, pp. 469-498 – accessible on http://gallica.bnf.fr) and a more substantial account in *Du Caucase aux Indes à travers le Pamir*, Paris 1889, with illustrations by Pépin. Capus' book *Le Toit du Monde* was published in 1890 (also accessible on http://gallica.bnf.fr).

[2] *La Nature*, 1882, p. 92 (accessible on http://cnum.cnam.fr).

[3] In 1883 Putyata had intended to cross the Wakhan to Chitral but had been prevented by the military activities of the Afghans that led to the annexation of the territories of Shughnan and Wakhan.

[4] Capus seems to have had some qualms about this use of force and does not mention it in his account.

[5] See, for example, *La Nature*, 1882, 1883, 1884 and 1891 (accessible on http://cum.cnam.fr).

[6] For example: *Association française pour l'Avancement des Sciences* 1890 "Les Kirghizes du Pamir"; *Asiatic Quarterly Review* 1892 "The agriculture of the aryan tribes in the sub-pamirian region"; BdlSdG 1890

"Pamir et Tchitral"; BdlSdG 1892 "Observations et notes météorologiques sur l'Asie Centrale et notamment les Pamirs"; CIdSG 1889(1) "Le Kafiristane et les Kafirs-Siahpouches"; RdG 1890 "Remarques sur les sources de l'Oxus"; RdG 1891 "Du groupement ethnique des peuplades dans la région prepamirienne"; RS 1888 "Les effets de l'altitude sur les hauts plateaux du Thibet"; RS 1889 "Le Kafiristan et les Kafirs-Siahpouches".

[7] *The Pamirs and the Source of the Oxus*, p. 78.

Mr. & Mrs. St. George R. Littledale – 1890 and 1892

[1] Mrs. S.G. Skerskaya, wife of the Russian commander in Murghab, was the second in 1894.

[2] *PRGS*, Vol 14, No. 1, pp. 1–35. The pictures accompanying this section were taken at about the same time of year (albeit a century later) as that during which the Littledales made their pioneering journey and give a fairly accurate impression of what they would have witnessed. However, comparison of the pictures with Littledale's account would seem to confirm significant climate change in the intervening period.

[3] Theodore Roosevelt, *An Autobiography*, 1913. (see http://bartleby.school.aol.com/55/2.html)

[4] See http://www.berkshirehistory.com/villages/warfield_ham.html

[5] See http://www.trophyhunt.ru/eng/hunting-tours/Littledale-Argali.php

[6] See http://www.geocities.com/lis716harris/main.html – photo J.J. Talman Regional Collection, University of Western Ontario, London, ON. Harris Family Fonds, Box 4182–4186, 5109, P178–190, P620–634. Harris and Magee Law Firm, Box 4060–4062.

[7] *GJ*, Vol. 7, no.2, p. 198.

[8] In an interesting parallel, it was usual in the early 1990s, when travelling in a Toyota on the Osh-Khorog "Pamir Highway" to stop and greet other similar vehicles travelling in the opposite direction. Now that there is much more traffic on the highway, this is no longer done.

[9] Major C.S. Cumberland, *Sport on the Pamirs and Turkistan Steppes*, William Blackwood and Sons, London and Edinburgh, 1895, pp. 261–262.

[10] It is certainly in part for this reason that several of the travellers we have so far encountered decided to travel in the Wakhan in winter.

[11] Named after a Russian officer, member of the 1895 Pamirs boundary commission (see Section 6.1).

[12] It is a remarkable indictment of the apathy induced by the Soviet policy of wholesale subsidisation in the Pamirs that the abundant resources of fish have never been exploited and that fish forms no part of the regular diet of the Pamiris.

[13] "We were much amused at hearing that one man had stated that he did not leave Kashmir until he had seen the lady who walked from Europe."

[14] *GJ*, Vol. 3, No. 6, pp. 445–472.

The Earl of Dunmore 1892–93

[1] This is still the case. After more than ten years' travelling in Central Asia I have come to the conclusion that the Tajik word "nazdik" (nearby) can mean anything from 100m to 20km and that "hozzer" (shortly) can mean anything from 5 minutes to five days.

[2] T.E. Gordon, *The Roof of the World*, London 1876, p. 158.

[3] Dunmore says that he saw the inscription in a museum in Tashkent and it must have been separated from the stone by Ionov's troops and taken there after the campaign (the stone itself being too heavy to

transport easily). The stone is reliably reported by local inhabitants to have remained in Sumantash until the early 1960s, when it was removed to Khorog and placed in front of the local museum in Lenin Street. In 1969 – at a time of border tension with the Chinese – it was replaced by a bust of Lenin and buried next to the pedestal. In 2004, when the main road in Khorog was widened, this important historical monument of the Pamirs was dug up and is awaiting a final resting place.

[4] Just over 100 years after Dunmore's dance in Rangkul, I had the privilege of dancing the Gay Gordons at the confluence of the Yazgulem river and the Oxus with Barbara Hay, the British Ambassador, not to keep warm but to show the local people, in response to their hospitality, that we too could dance – perhaps the second time Scottish music ever sounded in the Pamirs.

[5] It is possible that Ney Elias, too, had taken this route in October 1885.

[6] Dunmore's technique still works in Central Asia.

[7] Cobbold, p. 293.

[8] Lady Macartney, *An English Lady in Chinese Turkestan*, Oxford 1985, p. 104.

[9] Some years earlier, Catherine Macartney – wife of the British representative and later Consul-General in Kashgar from 1890–1918 – had brought a piano from England that had to be carried in a similar way over the passes to their home in Kashgar. (Lady Macartney, *An English Lady in Chinese Turkestan*, Oxford, 1985.)

[10] After the Chinese overthrow of Yakub Beg in 1877, Russia rapidly recognised Chinese sovereignty over Xinjiang and was rewarded accordingly. The British were "punished" for the official overtures made to Yakub Beg by the trader Robert Shaw and the explorer George Hayward in 1869 and the Chinese did not agree to the opening of a British consulate in Kashgar until 1908. (Lady Macartney, p. 62.)

[11] Quoted by A.V. Postnikov in Схватка на «Крыше Мире» – Политики, разведчики и географы в борьбе за Памир в XIX веке (Struggle on the "Roof of the World": Politicians, spies and geographers in the contest for the Pamir in the XIX century), Moscow 2001, ISBN 5-88451-100-0, page 285.

[12] This Chinese map was based on the information provided to them by Grombchevsky two years previously – see Chapter 5.

[13] Postnikov, p.232.

[14] Postnikov, p.211.

[15] B.L. Grombchevsky, unpublished notes from a military report, New Marghilan, 1891, quoted in Памир (Pamir), M.S. Asimov (editor), Moscow 1987; and B.I. Iskandarov, Восточная Бухара и Памир во второй половине XIX века, (Eastern Bukhara and the Pamirs in the second half of the 19th century) Dushanbe 1962.

[16] *Report by Mr. Cobbold on his journeys on the Pamirs and in Chinese Turkestan*, National Archives, Kew (ref. PRO FO 881 7079X), p. 2.

Captain Ralph Patteson Cobbold 1897–1898

[1] Cobbold notes that Ionov himself had been forced to abandon the attempt to bring a larger group down the Bartang after the loss of all his horses down the sheer cliffs of the valley. Another Russian officer, Captain Bedryag, made a reconnaissance of the upper Bartang in 1893 Сборник Географических, Топографических и Статистических Материалов по Азии. (*Collection of Geographical, Topographical and Statistical Materials throughout Asia*), vol. lvi, Military Scientific Committee of the Russian General Staff, 1894.

[2] Cobbold's papers from this campaign are held by Yale University – see
http://mssa.library.yale.edu/findaids/stream.php?xmlfile=mssa.ms.1663.xml
[3] *The Heart of a Continent*, p. 320.
[4] This was, of course, an exaggeration: from time to time there were uprisings by the local population against Russian rule, such as the one that served as a pretext for Cobbold's subsequent arrest in Vomar, as well as the riots in Tashkent in 1892 during a cholera epidemic and, in 1898, another Muslim uprising in the Ferghana valley (in Andijan). Typically, however, they were put down with extreme force.
[5] Quoted by Henry Trotter in *Report of the Trans-Himalayan Explorations – 1873–74–75*, p. 15 footnote.
[6] Such are friendships established in the Pamirs: Stanley Escudero, the US Ambassador in Dushanbe 1992–1995 – with whom I had the pleasure of a similar relationship – held that "the Pamirs are not the end of the world: but you can see it from there."
[7] Born in Dublin in 1866, Deasy joined the army in 1888 and retired in 1897. He became a pioneer of the British motor industry, and in 1903 helped promote the Rochet Schneider Company by driving a car from London to Glasgow non-stop. He went on to found the Deasy Motor Car Manufacturing Company in 1906. (See http://www.motorsnippets.com/cars/siddeley/index1.htm.)

Lieutenant Wilhelm Filchner 1900
[1] His son was executed in 1944 for his involvement in the attempt on Hitler's life.
[2] Wilhelm Filchner, *Ein Ritt über den Pamir*, Berlin 1903.
[3] Filchner recommends to the reader intending to follow in his footsteps to use the network of the Russo-Chinese bank rather than carry large amounts of cash. A hundred years later, the banking system in the former Soviet Union had collapsed and again travellers to the Pamirs – including the author – were obliged to carry sums of $100,000 and more in cash for emergency and development programmes.
[4] An article in the *New York Times* of 11 February 2007 reports that the former Russian consulate in Kashgar has been converted to the Seman Hotel.
[5] See http://www.south-pole.com/p0000103.htm .
[6] W. Rickmer Rickmers, *Proceedings of the Central Asian Society*, "Impressions Of The Duab (Russian Turkestan)," Central Asian Society, London, 1907.

Willi Rickmer Rickmers 1913 and 1928
[1] For the results of the 1913 expedition, see:
Willi Rickmer Rickmers, "Vorläufiger Bericht über die Pamir-Expedition des Deutschen und Österreichischen Alpenvereins 1913", in *Zeitschrift des Deutschen und Österreichischen Alpenvereins*, Innsbruck 1914; Raimund von Klebelsberg, *Beiträge zur Geologie Westturkestans: Ergebnisse der Expedition des Deutschen und Oesterreichischen Alpenvereins im Jahre 1913*, Innsbruck 1922; and *Das Gebirge Peter des Grossen*, Utrecht 1929.
[2] A 'windjammer' bearing the family name can be visited today as a floating museum in Hamburg – see http://www.Rickmer rickmers.info/82.html.
[3] Quoted in obituary by Prof. Hans Kinzl, *Nachrichtenblatt der Universität Innsbruck*, 1965–66, p. 88.
[4] "The Alai-Pamirs in 1913 and 1928", *The Geographical Journal*, Vol LXXIV No 3, September 1929.
[5] "The Alai-Pamirs in 1913 and 1928", *op.cit.*

[6] At this time, Pik Kaufmann (shortly after renamed 'Lenin') was still considered to be the highest mountain in the Pamirs. The peak photographed by Rickmer Rickmers was identified by him as Pik Garmo but was shown on Klebelsberg's 1914 map as Pik Sandal. Sandal is actually the highest peak seen from Ters-Agar and the two were thought to be identical. When the error was discovered by the 1932 Soviet expedition and the true positions and heights were determined, the higher of the two was renamed Pik Stalin. In 1962 Pik Stalin became Pik Communism and in 1998 Pik Ismoil Somoni. It was climbed for the first time in 1933 by Yevgeny Abalakov – see http://lexikon.freenet.de/Pik_Ismail_Samani. (With thanks to Markus Hauser for clarifying this complex situation.)

[7] "The Alai-Pamirs in 1913 and 1928", *op.cit.*

[8] "The Alai-Pamirs in 1913 and 1928", *op.cit.*

[9] The film was shown in Germany in the late 1920s and early 1930s under the title 'Pamir' and was reportedly a great success.

[10] "The Alai-Pamirs in 1913 and 1928", *op.cit.*

[11] "The Alai-Pamirs in 1913 and 1928", *op.cit.*

[12] "The Alai-Pamirs in 1913 and 1928", *op.cit.*

[13] "On the Fringe of the Pamirs", *The Alpine Journal*, Vol. 41, Nos. 238–239, London 1929, p. 159.

[14] Lentz spent several weeks in Roshorv in the Bartang for his ethnographic research and was "surprised by the wealth of oral literature in verse and prose which he found in the miserable villages of the Bartang." (Rickmers, "The Alai-Pamirs in 1913 and 1928", op.cit.). He also made wax-roll recordings in the Yazgulem, Vanch, Panj, Khingob and lower Alai valleys. They are stored at the Ethnographic Museum in Berlin.

[15] "On the Fringe of the Pamirs", *op.cit.*, p. 160.

What is a Pamir?

[1] Francis Younghusband, *The Heart of a Continent – a narrative of travels in Manchuria, across the Gobi desert, through the Himalayas, the Pamirs and Hunza 1884–1894*, London 1904, p. 231 and pp. 259–260.

[2] Ralph P. Cobbold, *Innermost Asia*, William Heinemann, London 1900, pp. 32–33.

[3] 1911 edition of the Encyclopaedia Britannica, entry 'Pamirs'.

[4] "The Pamir Glaciers," *Geographical Journal*, Vol. 131, No. 2 (Jun., 1965), p. 219.

[5] *Ta-T'ang-Si-Yu-Ki:* translated by Samuel Beal in *Buddhist Records of the Western World* (London: Trubner & Co. Ltd., 1884), p. 291. (Reprint by Munshiram Manoharlal, New Delhi, 2004.) Part also available on the Silk Road Seattle website: http://depts.washington.edu/uwch/silkroad/texts/xuanzang.html.

[6] See, for example, Shokhumorov Abusaïd, *Pamir – the land of Aryans*, Dushanbe 1997, pp. 31–32; B.I. Iskandarov, История Памира (*History of the Pamirs*) Khorog 1996, p. 11; George Nathaniel Curzon, "The Pamirs and the Source of the Oxus", in *The Geographical Journal*, Vol. 8, No. 1, 1896, pp. 29–30; and *Proceedings of the Royal Geographical Society (PRGS)* Vol 14, No. 1, 1892, p.34.

[7] Younghusband, p. 241

[8] *Asiatic Quarterly Review*, quoted by Dr. G.W. Leitner in *Proceedings of the Royal Geographical Society (PRGS)* Vol 14, No. 1, 1892, p.34.

[9] "The Alai-Pamirs in 1913 And 1928", *The Geographical Journal*, Vol LXXIV No 3, September 1929.

[10] *Buddhist Records of the Western World*, p. 297.

Trekking
[1] Suggestion by Rick Allen.

Darwaz, Vanch and Yazgulem
[1] 'Albert Regels Reisen nach den Amudarialändern' (Albert Regel's journeys to the regions on the Amudarya) in Supplement to the *Allgemeine Zeitung*, Munich, 17 July 1884. Translation from the original German by Robert Middleton.
[2] Manuscript in the German Alpine Museum.
[3] Supplement to the *Allgemeine Zeitung*, Munich, 17 July 1884.

Rushan and the Bartang Valley
[1] *On Ancient Central-Asian Tracks*, 1964 new edition, pp. 279–280.
[2] Tageyev, Русские над Индией. Очерки и рассказы из боевой жизни на Памире (*Russians above India. Reports and stories from military life in the Pamirs*), St. Petersburg, 1900, pp. 321–322 (translation Robert Middleton). Tageyev, born in 1871 in Saint Petersburg, was one of the most famous military writers of the beginning of the 20th century. Many of his writings were published under the pseudonym Rustam-Bek. He was arrested by the People's Commissariat of Internal Affairs (NKVD) in 1937 and executed in January, 1938.
[3] Arved von Schultz, *Die Pamirtadschik*, 1914; and *Länderkundliche Forschungen im Pamir*. Hamburg 1916. Von Schultz also produced a map of the Pamirs (1: 750.000) based on the Russian 10 verst map of 1895 (approx. 1:420.000). See also: *PGM* 1912 and *Abhandlungen des Hamburgischen Kolonial-Instituts*, Band XXXIII.
[4] Reproduced in the article by von Schultz – from Austen Henry Layard, *Discoveries in the Ruins of Nineveh and Babylon; With Travels in Armenia, Kurdistan, and the Desert*, London 1853. The Assyrian word 'Kellek' may be related to the Gaelic word 'curach' (boat).
See http://rsnz.natlib.govt.nz/volume/rsnz_21/rsnz_21_00_003790.html.
[5] Arved v. Schultz, 'Der *Turssuk*, Verkehrsgeographische Betrachtungen aus dem westlichen Pamir' (The '*Turssuk*' – reflections on transport in the western Pamirs), *Globus – Illustrierte Zeitschrift für Länder- und Völkerkunde*, Brunswick 1910, pp. 107–108. Translation from the original German by Robert Middleton.
[6] Richard Dixon Oldham, 'The Pamir Earthquake of 18th February, 1911', in *The Quarterly Journal Of The Geological Society Of London*, Vol. 79, 1923, pp. 237–245.
[7] Aurel Stein, Innermost Asia : detailed report of explorations in Central Asia, Kan-su and Eastern Iran, Vol. 2, London 1928, pp. 855–856. (See http://dsr.nii.ac.jp/toyobunko/T-VIII-5-A-a-3/V-2/page/0007)

Khorog and the Ghunt Valley (Shughnan)
[1] This may be the origin of the name 'Ghunt'.
[2] Ralph P. Cobbold, *Innermost Asia*, William Heinemann, London 1900, pp.198–199.

Roshtkala District and the Shokhdara
[1] For explanation of 'Sabz Push', see section on Darwaz, Vanch and Yazgulem.
[2] Information from manuscripts in the possession of Azizkhan's great-grandson in Sindev.
[3] A. Serebrennikov 'On the Afghan Frontier: A Reconnaissance in Shughnan', *GJ*, Vol. 1 No. 6, December 1900, pp. 669–671.

Ishkashim District and the Wakhan
[1] The *li* corresponds to 415.8 metres.
[2] *Si-yu-ki: Buddhist Records of the Western World*, translated by Samuel Beal (London: Trubner & Co. Ltd., 1884), p. 297.

Murghab District and the Great Pamir
[1] Guillaume Capus, 'Les Kirghizes du Pamir', in *Association française pour l'Avancement des Sciences – Compte rendus de la 19e session*, Paris-Limoges 1890, p. 534. Translation from the French by Robert Middleton.
[2] This is confirmed by Aurel Stein (*On Ancient Central-Asian Tracks*, p.266).
[3] Report of a Mission to Chinese Turkestan and Badakhshan in 1885–86. By Ney Elias, Political Agent on special duty, Calcutta 1886 (British Library, IOLR F111/378), pp. 22–23.
[4] Jambudvipa ('Rose Apple Island') is the innermost of the seven continents in ancient Sanskrit literary tradition.
[5] *Si-yu-ki: Buddhist Records of the Western World*, translated by Samuel Beal (London: Trubner & Co. Ltd., 1884), p. 297. The li corresponds to 415.8 metres.
[6] Report of a Mission to Chinese Turkestan and Badakhshan in 1885–86. By Ney Elias, Political Agent on special duty, Calcutta 1886 (British Library, IOLR F111/378), pp. 26–28.
[7] Ralph Patteson Cobbold, *Innermost Asia – Travel and Sport in the Pamirs*, London 1900.
[8] Arved von Schultz, *Landeskundliche Forschungen im Pamir*, Hamburg 1916.

Language in the Pamirs
[1] In 1876, for example, Robert Shaw, an English adventurer and amateur ethnographer, published a book entitled *Ghalchah Languages*.
[2] It is said that Aga Khan III, Sultan Mohamed Shah, once gathered all his scholars and told them that Ivanow knew more about Ismailism than all of them together.
[3] V. Ivanow, Nasir-i Khusraw and Ismailism, Series B No. 5, Section 5; edited for the 'Ismaili Society', Bombay; accessible on
http://www.ismaili.net/Source/khusraw/nk2/nasir_kusraw2.html

Religion
[1] Ney Elias, manuscript *Pamir Journey 1885-6*, RGS Archive – Ney Elias Special Collection NE33, entry for 30.11.1885.
[2] Sarfaroz Niyozov, 'Shi'a Ismaili Tradition in Central Asia: Evolution, Continuities and Changes', *Central Asia and the Caucasus*, Journal of Social and Political Studies, No. 6 (24), Harvard University 2003.
[3] See, for example: A. Bobrinski, Секта Исмаилия (The Ismailis), Saint-Petersburg 1902; and B.I. Iskandarov, Восточная Бухара и Памир во второй половине XIX века, (Eastern Bukhara and the Pamirs in the second half of the 19th century), Dushanbe 1962.
[4] Niyozov, 'Shi'a Ismaili Tradition in Central Asia', op. cit.
[5] There are no Ismaili mosques in Gorno-Badakhshan, although one is being built in Dushanbe.
[6] Niyozov, 'Shi'a Ismaili Tradition in Central Asia', op. cit.

The Shrines of the Pamirs

[1] This section has been put together with the kind assistance of Professor Jo-Ann Gross, of the College of New Jersey, who is currently preparing a scholarly study of Tajik shrines.

Petroglyphs and Pictographs

[1] V.A. Ranov died in 2006. The only surviving scholar from the Soviet period still active is Mira Alexeyevna Bubnova, who continues to publish archaeological works at a remarkable rate.

[2] V.A. Ranov, 'Рисунки Каменново Века в Гроте Шахты' (Paintings from the Stone Age in the Shakhty Cave) in Советская Этнография (*Soviet Ethnography*), Academy of Sciences, Moscow 1961, Vol. 6, pp. 70-81.

[3] V.A. Zhukov and V.A. Ranov, Археологические Открытия 1971 Года (*Archaeological Discoveries in 1971*), Academy of Sciences, Moscow 1972, pp. 540–541.

[4] Reproduced in V.A. Zhukov and V.A. Ranov, Археологические Открытия 1971 Года (*Archaeological Discoveries in 1971*), Academy of Sciences, Moscow 1972, pp. 540–541.

[5] See 'Alte Felszeichungen von Ljangar (Westpamir) – Ancient petroglyphs in Langar (Western Pamirs), in *Das Altertum*, Vol. 3, Berlin 1973, pp. 161–170.

The Symbolism of the Pamiri House

[1] Sir Aurel Stein, *On Ancient Central-Asian Tracks*, New York 1964, p. 280.

[2] *Altbuddhistische Kultstätten in Chinesisch-Turkistan*, Berlin 1912.

Music and dancing

[1] A. Snessareff, 'Religion und Gebräuche der Bergvölker des westlichen Pamir' (Religion and Customs of the mountain people of the western Pamirs), in *Keleti Szemle (Revue Orientale)*, Budapest 1908, pp. 180-205. Translation from the German by Robert Middleton.

[2] A recent doctoral thesis by David Koen for the University of Ohio demonstrated that the ritual performance of *madoh* is used in the Pamirs "as a preventive practice for health maintenance, as an adjunctive medical treatment, and as a curative ceremony." See *Devotional Music And Healing In Badakhshan, Tajikistan: Preventive And Curative Practices*, Dissertation Presented in Partial Fulfillment of the Requirements for the Degree Doctor of Philosophy in the Graduate School of The Ohio State University By Benjamin David Koen, M.A.; The Ohio State University 2003.

INDEX

Compiled by Don Brech,
Records Management International Limited

Aerial view of mountain range, north of Khovaling (right)

Hamsafar
Travel
—your travelling companion

The Hamsafar Travel Company specialises in taking small groups on adventurous holidays to Tajikistan.

Our team includes Rick Allen, mountain leader, who has been climbing in the greater ranges of Asia for over 25 years and has followed in the footsteps of early explorers in the Pamir region. The principal tour guide is Ruslan Nuriloev who is steeped in the history and culture of Tajikistan and has led tours for 7 years.

Hamsafar offers expeditions and treks throughout the Pamir and the Fann mountains, 4WD jeep tours along the ancient silk routes of Central Asia, cultural tours, horse trekking photo-safaris in a nature reserve on the edge of the Pamir, guest house accommodation in Dushanbe and visa support for travellers.

We operate a small fleet of modern Toyota or equivalent vehicles that are maintained to a high standard and we also offer vehicle rental and logistical services at competitive rates to commercial organisations. Contact us to discuss your interests and we can arrange a trip to meet your needs. Our team includes English, Russian, French, Tajik, Uzbek, Farsi and Arabic speakers.

Address: Hamsafar Travel, Proletarskaya 5/11, Vodonasos, Dushanbe
Website: www.hamsafartravel.com
Email: ruslan@hamsafartravel.com; rick@hamsafartravel.com; hamsafarinfo@yahoo.com
Phone: +992 228 0093 daytime, +992 93 501 4593, +992 93 501 5431